3

THE MERCHANT CLASS
of MEDIEVAL LONDON

[1300-1500]

By *SYLVIA L. THRUPP*

ANN ARBOR PAPERBACKS
THE UNIVERSITY OF MICHIGAN PRESS

Sharon McKee

TO THE MEMORY OF
EILEEN POWER

Third printing 1977
First edition as an Ann Arbor Paperback 1962
Copyright © by The University of Michigan 1948;
renewed 1976 by Sylvia L. Thrupp
All rights reserved
ISBN 0-472-06072-4
Published in the United States of America by
The University of Michigan Press and simultaneously
in Rexdale, Canada, by John Wiley & Sons Canada, Limited
Manufactured in the United States of America

Contents

List of Abbreviations

Add. MSS	Additional Manuscripts, British Museum
Add. MSS, Guildhall	Additional Manuscripts, Guildhall Library
Archdeaconry, London	Register of wills proved in the court of the archdeacon of London
B.H. Deeds	Bridge House Deeds (city of London archives)
B.M. Cat. Seals	*British Museum Catalogue of Seals*
Beaven	A. B. Beaven, *The Aldermen of the City of London* (2 vols., 1908–13)
Blomefield	Francis Blomefield, *An Essay towards a Topographical History of the County of Norfolk* (1805–10)
Bridges	John Bridges, *History and Antiquities of Northamptonshire*, ed. P. Whalley (2 vols., 1791)
C	Chancery
C.W.C.H.	*Calendar of Wills Proved and Enrolled in the Court of Hustings*, ed. R. R. Sharpe (2 vols., 1889–90)
Cal. C.R.	*Calendar of Close Rolls*
Cal. Ch. R.	*Calendar of Charter Rolls*
Cal. E.M.C.R.	*Calendar of Early Mayor's Court Rolls*
Cal. L. Bk.	*Calendar of Letter Books*
Cal. P. & M. Rolls	*Calendar of Plea and Memoranda Rolls*, ed. A. H. Thomas (4 vols., 1926–43)
Cal. P.R.	*Calendar of Patent Rolls*
Cal. Proc. C.	*Calendar of Proceedings in Chancery*
Cal. Rolls A.N.D.	Manuscript Calendar of Rolls of Assize of Novel Disseisin (city of London archives)
Cat. Anc. Deeds	*Catalogue of Ancient Deeds*
Chart. St. Thomas	*Chartulary of the Hospital of St. Thomas the Martyr, Southwark, 1213–1525* (privately printed, 1932)
Clode	C. M. Clode, *Memorials of the Guild of Merchant Taylors* (privately printed, 1875)
Comm. Lon.	Registers of wills proved in the court of the commissary of the bishop of London
Cussans	J. E. Cussans, *The History of Hertfordshire* (3 vols., 1870–81)
D. & C. St. Paul's	Dean and Chapter of St. Paul's Cathedral
D.K.P.R.	Deputy Keeper of the Public Records
Dugdale	Dugdale's *Monasticon Anglicanum*, ed. J. Caley, H. Ellis, B. Bandinel (6 vols., 1830)
E	Exchequer
E.C.P.	Early Chancery Proceedings

E.E.T.S.	Early English Text Society
EHR	*English Historical Review*
Ec. H.R.	*Economic History Review*
Gough	R. Gough, *Sepulchral Monuments in Great Britain* (1786–96)
Grocers of London	S. L. Thrupp, "The Grocers of London, a Study of Distributive Trade," *Studies in English Trade in the Fifteenth Century*, ed. Eileen Power and M. M. Postan (1933), pp. 247–92
H.M.C.	Historical Manuscripts Commission
Haines	H. Haines, *A Manual of Monumental Brasses* (1861)
Hartshorne	A. Hartshorne, *Portraiture in Recumbent Effigies and Ancient Schools of Monumental Sculpture in England Illustrated by Examples in Northamptonshire* (1899)
Herbert	W. Herbert, *The History of the Twelve Great Livery Companies* (2 vols., 1836–37)
Hist. Parl. B.	Josiah Wedgewood, *History of Parliament, 1439–1509, Biographies* (1936)
Hist. Parl. Register	Josiah Wedgewood, *History of Parliament, 1439–1509, Register* (1936)
Hust. R.C.P.	Hustings Rolls of Common Pleas
Hust. R.P.L.	Hustings Rolls of Pleas of Land
Hust. R.W.D.	Hustings Rolls of Wills and Deeds
Inq. p.m.	Inquisitions post mortem
Journals	Journals of the Court of Common Council (city of London archives)
K.B.	King's Bench
Kingdon	J. A. Kingdon, *Facsimile of the First Volume of the MS. Archives of the Worshipful Company of Grocers of the City of London, A.D. 1345–1463* (2 vols., 1883–86)
L. Bk.	Letter Books of the City of London (city of London archives)
Leland	J. Leland, *Itineraries*, ed. L. T. Smith (1908)
Lib. Alb.	*Munimenta Gildhallae Londoniensis*, Vol. I
Lib. Cust.	*Munimenta Gildhallae Londoniensis*, Vol. II
Lysons	S. Lysons, *The Environs of London* (4 vols., 1792–96)
Middlesex Fines	*A Calendar of the Feet of Fines for London and Middlesex*, ed. W. J. Hardy and W. Page (2 vols., 1892–93)
Mercers' Acts	*Acts of Court of the Mercers' Company, 1453–1527*, ed. L. Lyell (1937)
Mill Stephenson	Mill Stephenson, *A List of Monumental Brasses in the British Isles* (1926)
Newcourt	R. Newcourt, *Repertorium ecclesiasticum parochiale Londinense* (2 vols., 1708–10)
Palgrave	F. Palgrave, *The Parliamentary Writs and Writs of Military Summons* (2 vols., 1827–34)
Prideaux	W. S. Prideaux, *Memorials of the Goldsmiths' Company* (2 vols.; privately printed, 1896–97)
P.C.C.	Prerogative Court of Canterbury
P.R.O.	Public Record Office

R.S.	Rolls Series
Riley, *Chronicles*	*Chronicles of the Mayors and Sheriffs of London*, ed. H. T. Riley (1863)
Riley, *Memorials*	*Memorials of London and London Life in the XIIIth, XIVth and XVth Centuries, A.D., 1276–1419*, ed. H. T. Riley (1868)
Rot. parl.	*Rotuli parliamentorum*
Stothard	C. A. Stothard, *The Monumental Effigies of Great Britain* (1876)
Stow	John Stow, *A Survey of London*, ed. C. L. Kingsford (2 vols., 1908)
Unwin	G. Unwin, *The Gilds and Companies of London* (1908)
V.C.H.	*Victoria County History*
W.A.M.	Westminster Abbey Muniments
Waller	J. G. and L. A. B. Waller, *A Series of Monumental Brasses from the Thirteenth to the Sixteenth Century* (1864)
Weever	J. Weever, *Ancient Funeral Monuments* (1767 ed.)

Acknowledgments

A WRITER in the field of medieval economic and social history cannot know the sum of his obligations, for his work is essentially a social enterprise. In its technical aspect it draws upon centuries of scholarship and of care in the preservation of records, and in the formulation of the questions it should ask it draws inevitably upon the social thought of the present day. My chief indebtedness is to Professor Eileen Power and to Professor M. M. Postan, in whose lively seminar at the Institute of Historical Research I first began work in this field, and to Dr. A. H. Thomas, who as deputy keeper of the records of the Corporation of London gave me invaluable guidance in the city archives and later graciously read and criticized part of my manuscript. For special privileges in the use of indispensable material I am under great obligations to the Librarian of St. Paul's Cathedral, the Keeper of the Muniments of Westminster Abbey, the authorities of the College of Arms, and the clerks of a number of the city companies, in particular, of the mercers, the grocers, the goldsmiths, the skinners, and the merchant tailors. I am grateful also to the librarians of Lambeth Palace and of the Society of Antiquaries and to the Archivist of the City of Bristol for giving me access to special items and to officials and members of staff at the Public Record Office, the British Museum, the Guildhall Library, and the Probate Division of Somerset House. I owe much to the encouragement of Professor Harold Innis of the University of Toronto in the long intervals when I have been out of touch with the sources and have had little time for writing. I wish to thank Professor Postan for his kindness in giving me acute and careful criticism of most of the final draft. Thanks are due also to the editorial staff of the University of Chicago Press.

SYLVIA L. THRUPP

April 1948

Introduction

THIS book is in no sense a general economic or institutional history of medieval London. Its intention is simply to explore the social context in which the activities of London merchants took place. These men were the dominant class in the city and had interests that made them of national importance. Their decisions, arising out of the nature of their incentives and their conservatism, affected vital sectors of English economic development. The incentives and the conservatism in turn grew out of the background in which their personal lives were set. Admittedly, through this distance of time, one has to be content with fragmentary knowledge of the personal; London merchants were obscure people, and in each of the two centuries covered their numbers ran into thousands. Only the main contours of life appear, forming a general pattern of common or similar experience. This does not explain cases of exceptional initiative. But it enables one roughly to plot normal family cycles in the accumulation and dispersal of wealth and to recognize the chief social influences, as distinct from political events and policies that affected economic affairs, to which these were subject.

The most obvious of the common conditions affecting merchants' life-activities was their class status. To be a merchant, in the particular occupational sense in which that term was used, was to be known, wherever one went, as belonging to a group with a distinctive economic position, referring to the conduct of wholesale trade, and with a distinctive political position, that of controlling municipal government. The merchants of each town formed a class there, locally, and these local classes may be regarded as linked together to form a more or less uniform segment of the nation. The merchant's status had two aspects. In the nation as a whole he belonged merely to one of several social strata that were of middling status. Locally, in his own community, he stood much higher. In both aspects, locally and in other relationships, what was shared in common was only one element in personal status. A merchant and all members of his family had a certain basic minimum importance, as it were, by virtue of his occupation. Beyond this, his status depended partly on his success in filling the various roles that the community expected him to play and partly on the achievement of wealth or power above the average.

The typical career was well rooted in the relationships of family life. Although broken by apprenticeship, early childhood associations were not forgotten. Apprenticeship was passed in a family atmosphere, and marriage followed soon after. Other relationships sprang up within the fraternal organization of the company, all adding to and testing the young merchant's ambition and sense of responsibility. The reputation he built himself depended further on the part he played in parish life and city politics. Sometimes there was a tie with a patron outside the city community, which widened the merchant's social horizon as well as assured him of special business connections and of a measure of assistance in legal difficulties. The purchase of land might also involve new social relationships in the country.

For the purpose in hand it is not enough to describe these situations on the plane of active behavior alone; it is necessary to probe also into attitudes and ideas. In each of the social roles that filled the typical career and formed the cultural pattern of the class one is dealing with a complex of action, thought, and feeling. This makes it desirable to use as wide a variety of sources as possible.

In sheer quantity, the relevant sources of the period are very formidable. The small separate decisions by which business was conducted and property secured were recorded in innumerable types of document, most of which are still extant in representative series. Acknowledgments of indebtedness and clues to its varying consequences are sown thick among recognizances and inventories and other miscellaneous files and rolls of chancery and exchequer. Endless files of original deeds illustrate the accumulation and dispersal of landed property. The city husting court enrolled copies both of deeds and of such portions of citizens' wills as affected titles to London property, and ecclesiastical registers contain copies of hundreds of other London wills. Political action is outlined in the minutes of aldermanic and common council deliberations, in the legislation and judicial decisions that followed, in official correspondence, and in stray comments by chroniclers. Crosslight on all forms of activity, from family quarrels to conspiracy against the king, can be found in the records of litigation. These, however, are so overwhelming in bulk that, apart from the long and lively set of proceedings in chancery, it has not been possible to do more than sample them.

Much of the emotion that accompanied the activity is also on record, if less openly. Some of it lurked behind conventional attitudes, as in the flattery and self-depreciation that lard petitions and in the mingled pride and humility of mottoes and epitaphs. Again, there is the evidence of symbols, not only those that marked religious and secular loyalties, but the devices that were set on signet rings, on coats-of-arms and merchant marks, and other objects of aesthetic taste. To recover the special private signification that pictorial symbols may have had for those who so employed them is neither necessary nor possible. Yet, viewed in relation to the whole body of imaginative art of the age, they can be a guide to the more common emotional needs in merchant culture. Direct expression of purely personal emotion is rare but is not entirely lost. It breaks through sometimes in court pleadings and, in more restrained form, in the last wishes and exhortations in wills.

In a modern retrospective view the distinctive mark of medieval merchant culture is usually found in the promotion of rational calculation as a means to the advancement of interest. Rational calculation was certainly the heart of the formal education that was given to boys and is stamped on all the London merchants' public activity, on their business, on their angling for patronage and political appointments, and also on their guidance of government and judicial processes in their city. But in the larger sense in which it could have played a directive role within configurations of action and feeling the place of rational thought in the culture of the class is very hard to assess. It is difficult even to identify the concepts with which it may have operated. Neither the concepts nor the direction of thought can be read by literal interpretation of declared aims of action, which might have been cast in conventional common form or might have been framed with some devious intent to deceive. There is better evidence in business and political policy, in patterns of expenditure and of provision for spiritual welfare; yet rational consistency could here merge into an irrational adherence to custom. All that is known with certainty is the contemporary fund of lore and learning on which a London merchant, being able to read and being in the habit of listening to sermons, could potentially draw. What he selected from this fund—what a merchant thought, in the abstract, about such problems as the just price, the salvation of the soul, obligations to authority, or his own place in the social order—remains obstinately hidden.

Another limitation inherent in the sources accounts for the lack of a chapter on merchant biographies by which a reader might check the writer's interpretation of what constituted a typical career. The rounded and connective detail that one requires for biographical narrative is extraordinarily elusive. Separate items, again and again, will show promise of uncovering some unusual character, someone who, instead of following the well-trodden ways of custom, should have been capable of a good deal of innovation. But as likely as not each episode will refer to a different person, and all else one will know of him will be that he ate dinners at his company hall, was sued for debt, and died. Except for a few men who were very prominent in politics and finance, the only biographical reconstruction that is feasible is in the form of type biography, a silhouette portrait that is a composite of many profiles and coincides with none.

It is inconvenient, too, that much of the evidence bearing upon personal reactions in typical situations tends to be chronologically scattered and too unevenly to allow one to sketch trends with any confidence. To piece it together without regard to chronology makes a picture that is artificially static, and the alternative is to offer only partial or tentative conclusions. It may be that the book does insufficient justice to elements of change; but at least it avoids the assumption that there was no change.

The major findings refer to the question of social mobility. The London merchant class was a stable unit through the period; its size did not vary much, and there was no essential change in the basis of power by which it was distinguished. The families composing it, however, did not show the same stability. There was a constant current of movement out of the class; and, since many families died out in the male line while they were in trade, a considerable inflow was required in order to maintain numbers. Evidence of the movement is definite, yet, because of the scarcity of comparable material dealing with conditions of mobility in other places and periods, it is awkward to interpret. Even present-day currents of social circulation are not very well measured or understood, and there is no general historical perspective in the matter. A reader may therefore be likely to compare these London figures with some private impression of what would represent a high or a low degree of mobility.

On a number of other points conclusions can as yet amount to little more than a statement of problems that require a great deal more research. London merchant families were linked by ties of blood with many groups in the middle strata of the nation of which there is no detailed account for any part of these two centuries. How close were the cultural affinities between them? Where were the quickest avenues to the accumulation of wealth, and what other satisfactions were valued? Without answers to these and allied questions one cannot fully judge the nature of incentives in the merchant class.

Chapter I

THE ECONOMIC AND SOCIAL POSITION OF LONDON MERCHANTS IN THEIR OWN COMMUNITY

I. THE GROUPING OF THE POPULATION BY CRAFTS AND OCCUPATIONS

LONDON in 1300 was already a metropolis, bearing far more resemblance to the great cities of northern Continental Europe than to any other English town. The poll tax returns of 1377 point to a resident population of between thirty thousand and forty thousand, more than three times that of York or Bristol, which were the largest of the provincial centers, almost five times that of Coventry, and six times that of Norwich.[1] Londoners delighted both in the city's size and in its political importance. Fitz Stephen, in the twelfth century, had written of it as the seat of the monarchy, remarking that it was joined to Westminster by a suburb; and it was spoken of as the king's chamber, as a mirror to all England, the capital city, and the watchtower of the realm.[2] "I Richard Chalkhill Citezen and Taylor of the noble Cite of London bequeth my soule to God . . . ." runs the confident beginning of one local patriot's will, as though London citizenship would be a valid and helpful passport on his journey from this world to the next.

The city's population was heterogeneous, drawn together by the diverse interests of trade and industry, government, the law, and the church. In numbers it fluctuated quite widely, all of these interests being affected by more or less regular seasonal changes. There was a permanent element of government servants, who

1. For poll tax returns see *Archaeologia*, VII (1783), 337; C. Oman, *The Great Revolt of 1381* (1906), pp. 163–64; C. Creighton, "The Population of Old London," *Blackwood's Magazine*, CLIX (1891), 482–86.
2. *Cal. P. & M. Rolls*, I, 15, 77; Riley, *Memorials*, p. 492.

could not all be accommodated in Westminster, and another large permanent element in the service of the church that included legal and administrative officials under the archbishop of Canterbury and the bishop of London, inmates of religious houses, cathedral and parish clergy, and chantry priests. Some of the provincial bishops and abbots maintained houses in London for occasional use, and the nobility were beginning to find it convenient and pleasant to do the same.[3] Lawyers, law students, and litigants flocked in and out as the law terms came and ended, and waves of suitors and hangers-on at court followed the movements of the king and his ministers. Sessions of parliament and convocation swelled the population still more. Noblemen and their retinues could overflow into the capacious premises of some of the great religious houses; other visitors had to be crammed into the commercial inns. In order to carry these peak loads of business the catering and service industries in general no doubt drew upon versatile and mobile labor from the suburbs and surrounding countryside. Other industries and trade had, in comparison, only minor fluctuations. Country dealers came to and fro for wholesale buying, and foreign trade brought transient groups of French, Italian, Flemish, and German merchants. Not least conspicuous in the floating population were itinerant entertainers and beggars and discharged soldiers and sailors.

At all times the bulk of the population was contained in the permanently resident industrial and commercial community, and this, rather than any of the interpenetrating contexts in which the clergy, the officials, and the gentry in the city moved, is the London to be described. The members of the community were in the habit of classifying themselves in two ways, first, by legal status, and, second, by either craft membership or occupation. Although the distinctions drawn were common to most medieval cities, their meaning is not clear apart from some picture of the organization of economic life in the locality. The first division was into those who were enfranchised and those who were not. Only the former, who had sworn loyalty to the city government and undertaken to bear their share of taxation and public duty, could style

---

3. On this point see A. H. Thomas, "Some Recent Contributions to the Early History of London," *History*, IX, 101-2. On the residential population in general see T. F. Tout, "The Beginnings of a Modern Capital," *Collected Papers*, III, 267-72.

themselves citizens or freemen and claim the various privileges that were guaranteed to the community by royal charter; they alone, for example, could exercise the local political rights, and they alone were legally entitled to buy in the city with the intention of reselling and to keep shops for selling at retail.

The unenfranchised were regarded, technically, as outsiders. All of them who were English-born, including even those who had been born in London itself, were referred to as foreigners, or "foreigns." They are not to be confused with those born overseas, who, unless they could obtain naturalization, were always described as aliens. Many of the foreigns were poor, being employed in some inferior capacity, as porters, water-carriers, hucksters, or casual laborers, or else in making articles in their rooms, on the putting-out system, for sale by citizens. But some managed to do their own selling, from market stalls, and some prospered well enough to be able to rent shops that opened on the street and could thus attract customers at any hour. The prohibition against their doing so could not be rigidly enforced. As a compromise, there was an attempt to put them at a disadvantage in advertising their wares by forbidding them to follow the general custom of working outside the shop, in the street; and in 1463 the city authorities attempted to segregate the foreign shopkeepers, ordering them all to stay in, or move into, the district near Mark Lane known as Blancheappleton.[4] Certain trades, such as basket-weaving, tended to fall entirely into their hands. In short, although the foreigns were all under the same legal and political disabilities, they were not otherwise a homogeneous group. Nor, from an economic point of view, does any clear distinction arise between them and the citizens. The foreigns were either employed as wageworkers on various systems of payment or were independent artisans and shopkeepers, and all these types were numerous among the citizens.

In the early years of the fourteenth century it became the custom to take up citizenship through one of the formally organized trades. At that time the organizations went under the name of "crafts" or "misteries"; later they were more commonly called "companies" or "fellowships." It was important to be able to identify a man with the group that had sponsored his admission to the freedom; consequently, in all legal and quasi-legal docu-

4. Journals, 5, fol. 220b; Cal. L. Bk., L, p. 37.

ments it was usual, after mentioning a man's status as citizen, to add the name of the craft to which he belonged. The classification by crafts was of more significance politically than economically. A craft took its name from some one commodity or class of commodities or some skill with which its members were associated, but so bare a nomenclature gave no indication of the separate types of economic activity that might be involved or of the differing ways in which these activities might be combined. For example, a man who was described as a citizen and goldsmith might have been a wageworker, an independent craftsman with his own small shop, or a great merchant and financier with his fingers in many lines of business besides that of manufacturing articles of precious metal. In many trades the grouping constantly altered, as internal dissension split large crafts, as small ones decided to amalgamate, or as new ones obtained recognition. Yet in general there was a fairly simple pattern of correspondence between craft membership and economic position.

In some crafts all members carried on the same kind of economic activity. The tilers, for instance, were all wage-laborers, the fusters were pieceworkers for the saddlers, and felmongers and woodmongers were examples of small traders in raw materials. An industry would remain in the hands of small independent men who could organize together harmoniously, if three conditions coincided, namely, if the raw materials were in open and abundant supply, if the process of manufacture was simple and could be carried out in one stage, and if the product could be sold locally, direct to the consumer. These conditions held for bakers, cooks, turners, and in most of the metal trades. Still other crafts were formed of men who were primarily dealers, selling articles that were manufactured locally by subordinate groups of workers; the saddlers, the leather-sellers, and the hatters were crafts of this mercantile type.

Differentiation of function within the same craft could occur in several ways. It developed in the construction trades because of the need of contractors who could take charge of an entire operation. A majority of the masons and carpenters worked either independently on small jobs or as assistants hired by a minority who were essentially contractors. Differentiation tended to develop in any industrial craft in which members began to diversify a luxury product or to reach outside London for customers. For a time they might all work on a similar and roughly equal basis, feeding country demand with occasional packloads of goods taken off their hands by peddlers. But a cumulative advantage would fall to those who had the enterprise to acquire a wider circle of customers, whether by transporting goods to provincial fairs or by cultivating local demand for goods of special quality. It then became convenient for those members to put manufacturing work out, especially in finishing processes, either among foreigns who had the requisite skill or among those poorer members of the craft who had fewer customers of their own. In the latter case a poorer section of the craft might gradually fall into dependence on' the most enterprising section. This situation existed in a number of companies in the fifteenth century. A statement made by some of the girdlers in 1435 referred to "many fremen of þe same craft which have but small quantitee of goodes of their owen and were wont to live by the work þat þei made oþer men of þe same craft"; and regulations of the fullers, hurers, curriers, cutlers, coopers, and pouchmakers, which were registered later in the century but may have been of long standing, show that they too were in the habit of putting out work in finishing processes both to foreigns and to enfranchised members.[5]

Men who thus took the lead in the industrial crafts often went in for mixed enterprise, including trade. Contractors among the masons and carpenters dealt in building materials, and fullers and other textile craftsmen edged their way into the cloth trade. Such men were inclined to deal also in other staple commodities as occasion might offer. The custom of London affirmed the right of every citizen to buy and sell wholesale what commodities he pleased; and in the case of wool, cloth, and fish, which were supplied from numerous sources, and of wine, which was in universal demand, wholesale trade was actually wide open; anyone whose credit was good might take a plunge.[6] One can find instances of a surgeon trading in wool, of a weaver selling six hundred quarters of wheat to a draper, of a barber buying a quantity of fur from a skinner, of a painter, who painted banners for the duke of Lancaster, intrust-

5. Cal. L. Bk., K, p. 200; L, pp. 224, 242, 263–64; J. F. Firth, Historical Memorials of the Coopers' Company, pp. 17–23; Riley, Memorials, pp. 360–61 (date, 1371).
6. On the fourteenth-century dispute over this right and for sources of evidence of the actual situation see Grocers of London, pp. 261–72.

ing money to a mercer to be invested in trade. Very exceptionally, men of the industrial crafts had interests in coastal or overseas trade or participated in it in person. There are fifteenth-century examples of a brazier who invested the sum of 50 marks in the fourth share of a ship, of a pewterer who took £300 of cloth to Antwerp, and of a glover who bequeathed a chest "that I brought from beyonde the see at my last being there." In crafts in which there was no real differentiation of industrial function some men might yet obtain an advantage over their fellows by enterprise in trade, either in the materials of the craft or in other staple commodities. The wealthier butchers ran a stock business, and bakers would sell fodder for horses.

A third form of differentiation within a craft was between men who were primarily wholesalers and those who were primarily retailers or artisans. In the fourteenth century this could be seen among the mercers, grocers, drapers, fishmongers, goldsmiths, skinners, tailors, and vintners; in the next century the ironmongers, salters, and haberdashers were added to the list.[7] On account of their wealth and the political preponderance that they came to exercise these will be referred to as the "greater companies." They will also be called the "merchant companies," because practically all the citizen merchants were enrolled in their ranks. In late medieval usage the term "merchant" was usually reserved for a specific type. The merchant was a man of mixed enterprise, who primarily represented wholesale trade but combined with it one or more of a number of other interests. It is true that the word may technically be applied to anyone who buys and sells and that in the early middle ages it was applied to mere retail shopkeepers and to peddlers. Here, however, it will be used exclusively in the late medieval sense.[8]

Each of the London merchant companies had certain privileges in the trade from which it took its name, making it profitable for members to concentrate to some extent on that particular line. In two cases they were able for some time to attain a virtual monop-

7. This statement is based on thorough checking of London names in customs accounts with city and craft records identifying craft affiliations. Evidence of wholesale trade by fourteenth-century skinners, ironmongers, and salters is less than for the other companies named but is not lacking.

8. See discussion of the type by N. S. B. Gras, *Business and Capitalism* (1939), pp. 67–92.

oly, the mercers in fine textiles, the grocers in spice. Most merchants had preferential interests either in the special trade with which their company was connected or else in some one of the great staple commodities, such as wool or cloth; at the same time they were ready to deal wholesale in any other merchandise that came their way, from iron to eels. In addition they had either a direct or an indirect interest in retailing the special commodity of their company. Merchant mercers no doubt derived considerable profit from retail business in their luxury fabrics. One man's shop in 1332 displayed four kinds of imported coverchiefs, "de lumbard," "dalemaign," and of Worms and Valenciennes manufacture, along with lace and cloth from Lucca and from Venice, Cyprus gold thread, and curtain material from Cologne; the stock also included good English products—Cornish blanket cloth, London silk, Bury napery, coverchiefs from Lewes and of Norfolk make, stained cloth from Aylesham, and fine linen and towels from Wilton and Elmham. The grocers retailed miscellaneous small wares as well as spice and medicines, and the haberdashers' shops had by the end of the period absorbed all the best grades of ornamental trifles that were on the market. The drapers and probably the tailors too sold cloth retail as well as wholesale. Vintners arranged for the retailing of their wine through tied taverns, and some merchants of other companies who dealt regularly in wine did the same. Fishmongers retailed directly in the city market places and indirectly through hucksters. Goldsmiths and probably also skinners retailed articles that were made by subordinate members of their companies.[9]

The merchants helped to foster at least a dozen different industries, either participating in them directly or else financing the production of goods which they subsequently sold. Direct participation was perhaps most common in the goldsmiths' company, whose merchant members, although concentrating on salesmanship, retained sufficient technical knowledge to be able to supervise the execution of special orders in workshops of their own. They also put material out among subordinate artificers, who worked in small chambers. Some of these were enfranchised mem-

9. Inventories of shops in Grocers of London, pp. 280–84; Cal. P. & M. Rolls, III, 167–68; Riley, Memorials, pp. 422, 455. Example from stock of Richard de Elsing (E, 154/1/18a).

bers of the company, and some were members of a group of alien craftsmen that was subject to the company's control. The best known of the merchant goldsmiths were in frequent demand at court to take orders for crown jewels and other ornaments and tableware, and they made excellent use of contacts there and in official circles to obtain large commissions. Roger de Frowyk, an alderman, had a valuable share in the business of supplying Edward I and Edward II; a single order, obtained while he held the office of controller of the king's exchange, was to convert silver worth £100, the metal being provided, into vessels for the king's use.[10] On a humbler scale, the artificers sought customers of their own, both by offering to work up materials and by selling ready-made goods. They may quite well have found a good deal of independent business, for the use of personal jewelry and of silver cups was widespread, but it was one of their grievances that the merchants interfered with their freedom in selling ready-made articles. According to a petition that the artificers put before the parliament of 1377, the merchant goldsmiths forbade them to sell to anyone but themselves except at treble the prices that were current within the company.[11] One would infer that the merchants did not directly finance all production in the industry. Yet they aimed at complete control over it by the expedient of canalizing all sales through their own hands.

Merchants provided both equipment and materials in several other industries. The most popular activity of which there is any early evidence was that of supplying the people's drink, beer; this was always a safe and profitable side line. A report of a brawl at a brewhouse in 1325 shows that it was owned by a wealthy stock-fishmonger and was adjacent to his house; it was in charge of a brewer in his service, whose duties included the retailing of beer to be drunk on the premises.[12] Brewers employed in this way could have belonged to the brewers' company, which had a large complement of servant members. In the fifteenth century there were some connections with the metal trades, the instances few in number but important. The metal-workers were well organized, so that it was necessary to obtain their good will before setting up in production. The largest pewter workshop in the city was run by a

10. *Cal. C.R., 1313–18*, pp. 47, 524.
11. Unwin, p. 80.   12. *Cal. Coroners' Rolls*, p. 115.

mercer, Thomas Dounton, who took out a second company membership with the pewterers. In 1456 he was employing a staff of eighteen in his pewter business, eleven apprentices and seven hired servants. This is the largest staff to be mentioned in any of the medieval London craft records. One other pewterer had twelve workers, but the majority of the masters had only one or two assistants apiece. The scale of employment at this date ran as in Table I.[13] Ten other men are mentioned without any note of their status in the company; possibly they were masters working alone. The situation in the founders' company may have been somewhat

TABLE 1

Masters	Apprentices per Master	Servants per Master	Total Employees per Master
1	11	7	18
1	8	4	12
1	6	3	9
1	5	2	7
1	4	1	5
3	3	1	4
4	3	0	3
1	1	2	3
15	2	0	2
6	1	1	2
6	1	0	1
3	0	1	1
43	98	31	. . . .

similar, a fifteenth-century family of fishmongers and a wool merchant in the skinners' company operating bellfoundries.[14] A merchant obtained a life appointment as master of the ordnance in 1456 with an immediate commission to produce sixty serpentine guns and twenty tons of gunpowder.[15] The making of gunpowder,

13. C. Welch, *History of the Pewterers' Company* (1903), pp. 21–25. The records of this company, being stored at the National Safe Deposit, were not accessible to me, but they were very fully abstracted by Mr. Welch. Dounton had been made free in the mercers' company by apprenticeship in 1422.

14. On Giles Jordan, described on his brass at Loughborough, Leicestershire, *ca.* 1439, as "late fischmonger of London fundour," and Henry Jorden, fishmonger, who left alms for "xx of the poire housholders wtin the Crafte of Founders" and had tried to take a bellmaker's servant away from him, see J. C. L. Stahlschmidt, *Surrey Bells and London Bell-founders*, pp. 57–70; and A. D. Tyssen, "Sussex Church Bells," *Sussex Archaeological Collections*, LVII, 27–28, 94–95. In a pardon of 1472 William Chester, skinner, wool merchant, is given the alias of "belfounder" (*Cal. P.R., 1467–1476*, p. 347).

15. John Judde, *Excerpta historica*, ed. S. Bentley (1831), p. 10.

which was stimulated at first solely by government demand, was a likely field for merchant enterprise, always in touch with government needs. One of the first manufacturers of it in London may have been John Nicholl, a grocer who supplied the master of ordnance under Edward IV with considerable quantities and could have had it mixed in a mysterious "Workynghous" that stood in his garden.[16] The only commodity for industrial use that merchants seem to have been interested in producing was the coarse black soap that was used in clothmaking. The grocers controlled the sale of this in the city, selling it by the barrel, and the few instances of its manufacture, all in the late fifteenth century, refer to grocers. It was made on a small scale, one man's will mentioning three servants who were employed at his soaphouse.[17] There was some interest in the manufacture of tiles, for which there would have been a safe market in city needs for building repairs. Sir William Heryot, a draper, mentioned possession of a tile kiln in Essex in his will; and Peter Pemberton, a vintner, had a tile business. In his case the evidence is in a charge against him in chancery of having resorted to "a man that loked in a glasse by the Crafte of Nigromancie" in an effort to induce a country tilemaker to enter his service.[18] Although he denied the charge with indignation, the incident indicates that manufacturers had to compete with each other for skilled labor. Scarcity of skilled labor helps to account for the small number of merchant-owned workshops and for their small size.

Merchants were also interested in industries that did not require fixed equipment, all that was needed being to bring labor and materials together. Such industries naturally lent themselves to organization under the putting-out system, but it is not certain how

16. Between July and October, 1461, he received £61 odd for deliveries of gunpowder and the following June, £56, mostly for saltpeter (E, Issue Rolls, 822, *m.* 3, 824; *mm.* 4, 5, 825; *m.* 5, 8). (I owe these references to the kindness of Margery Bassett.) In 1467 he was assigned certain revenues toward payment of £559 owing him for gunpowder (*Cal. P.R., 1467–1477*, p. 25). He died in 1477, leaving lands at Keston, Hunts., and at Islip, Northants. (P.C.C., Wattys, 36).

17. John Payntour; he left them 20*s.* each (P.C.C., Adeane, 17 [1506]). He had bought the soaphouse, which was apparently beside a dwelling-house, from Thomas Clarell, grocer (see Clarell's will, P.C.C., Vox, 7). William Potter, grocer, had left 20*d.* each "to all who are in the soap-house" (will entered in Grocers' Register, fol. 14 [1457]). Goods of John Chelmsford, grocer, bankrupt in 1398, included 1 soap kettle, 18 vats of wood ashes and lye, worth £4 1*s.* 4*d.*, and black soap valued at £8 7*s.* 11*d.* The company set 2 cwt. as the standard content of barrels of black soap (Records, Vol. 300, fol. 43).

18. E.C.P., 46/425.

widely the medieval Londoners adopted this plan; some of the merchants may have been content to run small workshops in the outhouses of their courtyards. An example in point is the manufacture of rope. In the fourteenth century this was at least partially under the control of a group of merchants who lived near a district known as the Ropery; they called themselves corders and belonged to the grocers' company. In 1399 one of them left small legacies to his "operariis servientibus"; the term refers to manual workers but is otherwise ambiguous, suggesting that they may have been merely the staff of a small workshop attached to the merchant's house. About forty years later a fishmonger provided by will that, if they could not repay, servants of his called "ropiers" were to be pardoned the debts they owed him; this sounds as though he had been advancing them raw materials.[19] The making of hose was probably arranged in the same way. A concern of the drapers, it came under company regulation to the extent that members who were hosiers were supposed to "set on work" citizens in preference to foreigns; there is an instance of a draper calling himself alternatively draper and hosier as early as 1367.[20] One of the wealthiest of the haberdashers, Sir Robert Billesdon, who at his death in 1492 was worth several thousand pounds, left £5 in alms among "the spinners of wool and knitters of caps" who had served him. Work of this kind must undoubtedly have been put out, some of it perhaps in the country. A few of the mercers specialized in the making of ecclesiastical vestments. Like secular embroidery, this required a central workshop, where sections of the design, that might have been put out separately, were sewed together on the vestment. Mercers who were in the business relied largely on apprenticed labor, the company allowing them to enrol apprentices for this purpose at the age of twelve, younger than was permitted if they were to learn trade, for a term of fourteen years.[21]

Still other industries may have felt the stimulus of London mer-

19. Wills of Adam de Carlile, grocer (Comm. Lon., Courtney, 458), and John Welles (P.C.C., Rous, 17).

20. Drapers' Wardens' Accounts, fol. 57, note of penalty imposed on a member for breaking the rule, 1493; date of the rule not given. Drapers and hosiers, Liber Dunthorne, fol. 392; C. Misc., 114/49; *Cal. P.R., 1436–1441*, p. 377.

21. *Mercers' Acts*, pp. 105, 236, 546; W. D. Selby, *The Charters, Ordinances and Byelaws of the Mercers' Company* (1881), ordinance No. 50; ordinances of broiderers, *Cal. L. Bk., L*, pp. 306–8.

chant enterprise. One more example in the city may have been the preparation of skins and fur. The records of the company show that some skinners had only a chamber and no shop; it is therefore likely that they worked up material for the merchant members to sell.[22] Further examples of enterprise reaching out into the country could be found, but these may be neglected here as having no direct effect on social grouping within the city. The position of the fishmongers, however, might be noted as exceptional. The strong hold they acquired on the coastal fishing industry and consequently on the transportation of an essential part of the London food supply made them an extremely powerful group. To some extent they financed both the fishing industry and the salting of fish. Debts owed them by fishermen tell the story. One fifteenth-century fishmonger's will pardoned all debts that were owing to him by "anny Rypiers that have been outher myn hoosts or servaunts of whate contrey soevur they be the which have borowed any money of me for seefissh and staunden in my boke"; the same man was owner of a "saltehous" at Winchelsea.[23]

Merchants did not limit themselves to these branches of trade and industry. Their interests fanned out widely in many other directions, into investment in real estate of all kinds, into finance, shipping, and government service. Wherever there was gain to be had, there were merchants to bid for it or intrigue for it. They bought and sold prisoners of war who were being held for ransom and pursued the political influence that would bring them opportunities to buy the wardships and marriages of young tenants-in-chief. They did not necessarily combine many of these interests simultaneously. The majority of the London men may have concentrated on their trade or turned from one concern to another; but the wealthier kept their eggs in at least two or three different baskets.

By the fifteenth century the merchant companies were in the habit of dividing their membership into those who were entitled to wear an official "clothing," or livery, in company colors and those who were not. The liverymen were the economically dominant group. In respect of economic position the group that was excluded from the livery was very mixed in character. In the mer-

22. Skinners' Book of the Fraternity of Our Lady's Assumption, ordinances.
23. Laurence Fyncham, P.C.C., Logge, 3 (1480).

chant companies it contained men who had never succeeded in launching themselves in wholesale trade but had continued to depend on retail shopkeeping for their living. Among the tailors, the skinners, and the goldsmiths, the retail trade would normally have been combined with the work of an independent artisan; skinners and goldsmiths, it has been noticed, might not even have a shop of their own, being obliged to work for the more successful shopkeepers or for merchants, either as pieceworkers or as hired servants. In all the merchant companies there was also a select group of young men with capital and influence who were preparing to enter the livery. For a few years, in their mid-twenties, they served under the older men, to gain experience. They then set up in business independently, and, if successful as wholesalers, they would be admitted to the livery at about the age of thirty or soon after.[24] Finally, there were former liverymen, business failures, men who had been compelled to resign from the livery through inability to pay their dues. By convention it was usual to refer to these composite sections of the merchant companies, made up of men of all ages, as the yeomanry, or the bachelors.

In the course of the fifteenth century a number of the lesser companies followed the example of the greater in distinguishing a section of the membership by a livery. The dividing lines were drawn by ability to pay dues and fell along the lines of differentiation of economic function that were traced above. The liverymen of the lesser companies were those who could give out work to others, who traded in the raw materials of their craft and sometimes dabbled in general wholesale trade. They had some interests in common with the liveried merchants.

These were the most obvious of the dividing lines that were recognized within the industrial and commercial community. The division between the citizens, who formed the self-governing chartered body, and the foreigns and aliens outside it was primarily legal. The division of the citizens by craft affiliation was economic, having to do with specialization in the production or sale of different commodities. The internal divisions within the crafts referred to differing combinations of function in the processes of production and exchange by which the community lived. All the dis-

24. Based on 23 cases in the grocers' company, mid-fifteenth century, in which, on the average, nine years elapsed between admission to the freedom and admission to the livery.

tinctions that were drawn had some social and political significance, and there were efforts to keep them literally visible. Foreigns who could open shops, that is, all foreigns who were not already conspicuous by their poverty, were supposed to be segregated in a single district. The crafts were distinguished by an extensive symbolism that pictured tools, articles of trade, and patron saints, and the contrasts that craft liveries produced were the life-color of civic pageantry.

2. THE RECOGNITION OF INEQUALITY

The kind of grouping that has been outlined was universal in medieval town life and formed the basic pattern in which differences of economic and political power were grounded. The main variations in the economic lines of the pattern have long been familiar. The simpler the town's economic life, that is to say, the more it approximated to a mere market town serving a small district, the more the independent artisan and shopkeeper predominated. In proportion as a town took part in interregional trade and especially as it developed industries that were dependent on distant markets for their supply or outlet the merchant came into ascendancy and tended to control the governmental structure. Where this condition persisted for any length of time, social distinctions hardened into the lines of a definite class structure, and political and economic crises were likely to generate class conflict.

In England, where the roots of urban culture were relatively shallow, the extreme condition of open class conflict in the towns was rare. Yet inequalities were general and were very explicitly recognized in language that included many of the terms in use for the same purpose in Continental towns. This language shows something of the spirit in which differences of economic and political power were accepted as leading to a personal, social inequality.

Official civic documents in London made use of a standard set of formal attributes, which indicated how citizens were conventionally rated. Whether in French, Latin, or English, the same attributes occur from the thirteenth century through the fifteenth. Precepts to the aldermen to summon their wardmotes use the comparative form of the adjectives, referring to those citizens who were expected to take the lead in ward politics. They were the more sufficient (*pluis sufficeauntz*), the abler or more powerful (*poten-*

tiores, pluis vaillantz). The ability or power in question was the same thing as the sufficiency, a matter of wealth, the ability to contribute to public charges. The more sufficient and more able were at the same time the better people. The moral epithet was not intended to imply that the rich had all the Christian virtues. Its connotation, as alternative attributes suggest, was more specifically political, with a flavor of respectability added. The better people were the more honest, the wiser, the more prudent, and the more discreet. All these qualities were assumed to be present in maximum strength in the richest of the citizens, the best, the most sufficient, and to be at a low ebb among the poorer citizens. On occasions of political disturbance the latter were sometimes called the plebs or the lower people (*de plebeis, inferiores*).[25]

These official phrases were not a mere empty traditional formula but represented a conscious blending of moral, economic, and political considerations. Before any man could attain the legal status of an enfranchised citizen, he had to show proof of some positive qualification on each of these scores. He had to give assurance of his political soundness by taking an oath of loyalty to the king and to the government of the city, and he had to produce evidence that he was both of good reputation and capable of earning his livelihood in some trade. If he had been apprenticed to a citizen, his master's sponsorship was adequate; if he was seeking the freedom by redemption, that is, by purchase, he was supposed to find six citizen sureties.[26] In recognition of having passed these tests, all citizens were by courtesy styled good folk (*bons gens*) and were to be regarded as men of probity (*probi homines*). When the poorer citizens and the unenfranchised were spoken of in a derogatory way, it was with implied or specific reference to their inability to pay taxes, to their general ignorance, and to their inexperience in public affairs. The writer of a partisan thirteenth-century chronicle had looked on an opposition movement as supported by the *populo minuto*, remarking that many of these people had been born without the city, "of divers mothers."[27] This was at a time when the line between citizen and foreign was not drawn very

25. L. Bk., *passim*.

26. *Cal. L. Bk., E*, p. 13; *G*, p. 211; *Lib. Cust.*, I, 268–73.

27. Riley, *Chronicles*, p. 38; *De antiquis legibus liber*, Camden Society, No. 34 (old ser., 1846), pp. 86, 99.

strictly, so that a great many shopkeepers and artisans neglected to take up the citizenship, with its stamp of respectability. More than a century later, however, the same term was being used, in English; it occurs in an unsympathetic account of John Northampton's mayoralty, which accused him of drawing his support from "mochel smale poeple that konne non skyl of governaunce ne of gode conseyl."[28]

The records of company affairs echo the same ideas. The leather-sellers elected their wardens "des meillours et pluis sufficeantz"; the skinners made up a court of assistants to the wardens from "the moste wise and discrete," later defined as sixteen "of the worshipfull"; other terms describing those who were chosen to preside were "the reputable," "the worthy and notable." The adjective "simple" was current, in the fifteenth century, as synonymous with small, in the sense of a negative capacity in goods or understanding. An ordinance of the cutlers that was approved in 1485 deplores the fact that "many simple people" in the craft had been taking more apprentices than they could afford to keep and subsequently selling the boys' terms of service to "other simple people of the same Crafte of none habilete or Connyng to teche and enforme theim."[29]

The central psychological prop of the economic and political inequalities that developed was in the individual's inescapable respect for authority. Attitudes to authority oscillated between extremes and, whether subservient or resentful, were likely to be extraordinarily emotional. The obligation to obey seems to have been regarded less as a rational obligation than as a purely personal matter, deep-grounded. The tendency to resent and repudiate it was held in check by recognized irrational sanctions. To disobey a parent, a lord, a master, or to be disrespectful to a magistrate was to commit sin.

The bourgeois context did nothing to free the individual from this kind of pressure but seems rather to have intensified it. Since everyone knew that the preservation of the local civic liberties hung upon the continuance of orderly behavior, all emotional resources were drawn upon to secure this end. The merchant con-

28. *A Book of London English*, ed. R. W. Chambers and M. Daunt (1931), p. 29.
29. L. Bk., *L*, fol. 210*a*.

trolled his staff of apprentices and servants by the help of some of the overtones that were to be found in the ideas of lordship and paternity. A man's authority over his apprentices was always semipaternal in nature; he could also be spoken of as their "seigneur," and the will of one alderman's servant refers to his master as his lord.[30] Unruly apprentices were punished in some way that would dramatize the duty of deference. The arbiters in a dispute between a mercer and his nephew, apprenticed to him, awarded that the young man should help to buy his uncle a horse and should hold the stirrup for him when he mounted, in token of respect and obedience.[31] The same dramatic note recurs in a fishmonger's expression of gratitude to an alderman who had defended the privileges of his company; all the fishmongers in the city, he said, owed it to this man to put their hands under his feet.[32] Implicit in emotion of this kind was the habit of thinking of a man in high authority as backed by some element of supernatural sanction. This was particularly true of those who held judicial office, and it contributed greatly to their personal status.

As supreme authorities in the city, the mayor and the aldermen were in formal documents styled sovereign lords, variants using the words "gracious," "wise," and "worshipful"; one petitioner addressed them as "your high wisdams."[33] In records of the early fourteenth century the names of some of the aldermen are prefixed by *dominus* or *sire*, a style that was later dropped, except for the mayor, and in the fifteenth century a few of them were eulogized as "noble" or "reverend."[34] The dignity of their judicial status was symbolized by scarlet robes of office on ceremonial occasions and by a distinctive cut of hood that identified them on the

---

30. *Lib. Cust.*, I, 81 (case of 1308); *C.W.C.H.*, I, 487 (a servant of Pultney).

31. *Cal. P. & M. Rolls*, I, 268.

32. Unwin, p. 147.

33. L. Bk., *passim*; *Cal. L. Bk.*, *K*, p. 254; Harl. MSS, 3988.

34. *Cal. L. Bk.*, *A*, p. 156; *B*, pp. 137, 237; *C*, p. 147; *D*, p. 182. *Cal. E.M.C.R.*, p. 123 (1263–1310). In the grocers' books Andrew Aubrey and John Grantham, mayors, are styled "Sire" (Kingdon, I, 2, 31 [1345–46]). Richard Whittington, "desu noble merchant," in an acquittance under seal of the mayoralty to his executors (L. Bk., *K*, fol. 54). Robert Chichele, "vir nobilis et prudens" (Brewers' Records, fol. 65); cf. his epitaph, ".... corpore procerus .... et arte grocerus" (Weever, p. 195). Simon Eyre, "nobilis et potens vir" (Stow, I, 153). John Wells, "the nobylle aldyrman" (*Collections of a London Citizen in the Fifteenth Century*, Camden Society [1876], p. 184). A woolpacker, apologizing for slander of an alderman, referred to him as "this worshipfull estat" (Riley, *Memorials*, p. 633 [1416]).

street.[35] Rude or damaging remarks made to them or about them were always held to involve disrespect to the king and were clearly thought of as sin rather than as misdemeanor. A woman who called an alderman a thief when he complained of untidiness outside her house was imprisoned; another, found guilty of slandering William Walworth, was sentenced to pay him £40 in damages and to stand in the pillory, although on her promise of good behavior the sentence was remitted. A butcher who grumbled that aldermen rode over the pavements and taunted one with being unable to afford the price of his meat was made to walk barefooted and bareheaded like a religious penitent, carrying a lighted wax torch, from Newgate prison to the Guildhall chapel. Penance of walking bareheaded through Cheap was imposed on a mercer for nicknaming a recent mayor the "witless"; and a younger mercer in the service of an alderman who swore at his master in public and prayed that hell would devour him was sent to prison and escaped the pillory only at his master's intercession.[36]

The prestige attached to judicial office was reflected on a magistrate's family, no matter how short a time he had served. A widow whose husband had served only as sheriff, for one year, was at pains to remind the chancellor in a deposition that she had been "a Welthy Woman a fore tyme Shryves of London and in Worship."[37] Although their husbands used no personal title, the wives of aldermen seized upon the title of Lady, which was used by the wives of knights and esquires, and clung to it to the end of their lives, even when widowed and remarried to men who held no office.[38] When fear of the expenses of the mayoralty made men reluctant to join the circle of aldermen and sheriffs, from whose number the mayor was chosen, wives spurred them on. If the

35. Mayor, aldermen, and sheriffs wore a furred livery when the mayor took his oath of office at Westminster and another, lined with silk, at Whitsuntide. They were forbidden to give these away (*Lib. Alb.*, I, 35).

36. *Cal. P. & M. Rolls*, II, 6; Riley, *Memorials*, pp. 433–34, 502–3, 663, 592–93. Other inflictions of penance and an apology, *ibid.*, pp. 490–94, 500–502, 630–34. Merchants who offended were likely to be merely bound over (*ibid.*, pp. 78–79, 592–93).

37. Widow of Simon Smyth, grocer (E.C.P., 87/61).

38. See Richard Hill's description of his former master's widow as "my lady dame Agnes Wyngar" (Roman Dyboski [ed.], *Songs, Carols*, etc. [E.E.T.S., No. 101 (extra ser., 1907)], p. xiv). In spoken usage "ma dame" was already in broader use. See Chaucer's quip on the wives of craftsmen belonging to a religious fraternity: "It is ful fair to been y-clept '*ma dame*,'/And goon to vigilyes al bifore,/And have a mantel royalliche y-bore."

sneers that flew in one family quarrel rang true, at least one mercer's wife procured her husband's election as sheriff.[39]

Election to office as master or warden in any of the city companies was also an honor, its importance varying with the size,
wealth, and influence of the company. By the middle of the fourteenth century these officials wielded a formidable complex of authority. In matters concerning supervision of their particular
branch of manufacture or retail trade in the public interest they
were agents in the city's system of economic administration. After
election they were supposed to take an oath before the mayor and
aldermen, binding them to be loyal to the king and the city, to be
honest and impartial, and to administer all approved craft ordinances "and noon other."[40] A city ordinance of 1364 prescribed
penalties for all whom the wardens should find "rebelle, con-
trariount ou distourbant," ranging from a 10s. fine with ten days
imprisonment on the first offense to 40s. and forty days on the
fourth; and the mayor's serjeants, for a fee, were ready to assist
in searching shops and confiscating condemned goods.[41]

In addition to the trade regulations governing their organization
as a company, craft, or mistery, it was customary for the wardens
to administer another set of rules by which it was constituted as a
fraternity or fellowship. A fraternity was at the same time a
benevolent and religious society and a social club with its rules
covering various provisions for mutual aid, the arbitration of disputes, and the procuring of spiritual benefits. It was not considered
necessary to have these ratified at the Guildhall, but sometimes
they were registered, and trade rules also, in a spiritual court. If
the members were bound by an oath, the rules would in any event
have the sanction of the spiritual courts, regardless of whether
they were registered or whether they would have been considered
by the mayor and aldermen as in the public interest. Unwin's

39. Thomas Shelley "in grete derysion & skorne Japed & Mokked his said brother of his
Shirrifhode / callyng hym boy Shirrif / and said he was unable & unworthy to occupie
thoffice of Shirrifaltie and also said that by mean of my lady he was made Shirryff" (Mercers' Acts, p. 86 [1475]). John Shelley, warden of his company in 1463, was sheriff in 1471;
he died in 1486 without having held any further office. See Richard Cely's pleasure that his
father had been named as a possible shrieval candidate (Cely Papers, p. 74).

40. The English, the later, version of the oath is more emphatic on this point than the
French (Cal. L. Bk., D, p. 3; Lib. Alb., I, 258).

41. L. Bk., G, fol. 135b. The grocers paid the serjeants a shilling and their assistants
8d. for each search.

classic study of the London gilds showed how this connection with the church lent the fraternities their peculiar power, and showed also how in consequence it involved them in political disfavor. The circumstances leading up the the governmental inquiry of 1389 into the affairs of all gilds are well known. Jealousy of the church was rife, nervous government officials saw in every society a potentially criminal or revolutionary organization whose members might be sworn "to live or die together,"[42] it was believed that conspiracies to raise prices and wages were spreading, and it was known that some of the lesser crafts in London had made use of oaths for these purposes. The inquiry made it plain that the government regarded these ends as illegal and, further, made it necessary for fraternities to obtain the king's license before they could legally hold property.

This meant that the wardens of the misteries were now encouraged to acquire what was in effect, since they did not forgo the sanction of the church for their club activities, a third source of authority. Several of them already possessed royal charters sanctioning or extending their rights of search. As the mayor could give the citizens little protection against the competition of country workers who sent their products into the city for sale and since he had no very clear jurisdiction over the outlying suburbs, it had been natural for some of the manufacturing crafts to look to the king for help. With the object of establishing uniform standards of measurement and quality, Edward III had granted the skinners and the girdlers rights of search throughout the whole realm; he had also confirmed the rights of search of the goldsmiths and the tailors within the city.[43] New charters, granted after 1390, con-

42. Prohibited by proclamation in 1383, also in 1312 (Riley, *Memorials*, p. 480; *Cal. L. Bk., D*, p. 295).

43. In 1327 the goldsmiths, although not granted general rights of search, were intrusted with the responsibility of giving the touch to representatives of the trade in all other cities and towns (Herbert, II, 174, 289, 309–10, 520–21; L. Bk., *E*, fol. 183*b*; *F*, fol. 88*b*; Riley, *Memorials*, pp. 153–56). The mayor and aldermen in 1344 authorized the tapicers to sue out writs in chancery forbidding the sale of blankets made of pig's wool in any city or borough; in 1356 the tapicers obtained royal recognition of their right to elect officers to remedy abuses (*Cal. P. & M. Rolls*, I, 208; *Cal. L. Bk., G*, p. 200). Conflicts of jurisdiction between the girdlers and the saddlers in 1356 and between the goldsmiths and the cutlers in 1404 came before parliament, but the latter was referred back to the mayor (*ibid.*, pp. 66, 67, 70; Herbert, I, 104). A complaint by alien cobblers of oppression by the cordwainers in 1395 was referred by the king to the mayor; an attempted settlement by the king was later set aside by the mayor and aldermen as unsuitable (Riley, *Memorials*, pp. 539–41, 571–74; *Cal. L. Bk., I*, pp. 73–74, 96, 187, 194).

tinued to authorize rights of search within the city and immediate suburbs, seemingly overriding, or derogating from, the authority of the mayor and aldermen in these matters. Others merely incorporated the mistery, permitting the annual election of officers and the acquisition of property. In either case the king implicitly sanctioned some power of making ordinances. Furthermore, as Unwin emphasized, the mere fact of incorporation, insuring a continuous and permanent existence, enhanced the prestige of the organization and thus indirectly endowed it with more political influence.

Finally, fraternities possessed a residual power that was not derived from any outside source but was born simply of their own members' spirit of solidarity. Such public opinion as was represented in parliament and in the pulpit dreaded this power, for it was known to be exercised for selfish purposes.[44] The mercers' court, solely on its own authority, forbade members of the company to transport goods to other towns for sale or to peddle in the countryside. Fines up to 10 marks were collected from offenders; one man, fined £10, was pardoned all but 20s. but only on condition that he swore "on a book" never to trespass again.[45] The grocers forbade members to reveal any "secretis" that had been discussed in meetings, on pain of expulsion from the company. Punishments for breach of price agreements took the form of fines running up to £10 and sometimes of a temporary boycott.[46] It was also usual to forbid members to sue each other at law without first submitting their quarrel to arbitration by the wardens. The mercers went so far as to urge members not to engage in suits with any other citizens but, unless they stood to gain some greater advantage by law than by arbitration, to bring all disputes before their wardens; and the merchant tailors believed that the calling-in of all gild ordinances for inspection by the chancellor, under act of

44. See Grocers of London, pp. 259–60; Unwin, pp. 161–62.

45. Mercers' Accounts, fols. 102v, 103, 120 (1428–35).

46. The forms of oath preserved, of the time of Edward IV, bind everyone to secrecy: the apprentices were to keep "the secretis of ths seid felishippe," the freemen "all leefull councels of the felishipe"; and the liverymen ("the Sociatte") took a further oath to "kepe secrete alle soche maters as ye shall be here comoned be the wardens and the felishipp associatte." An ordinance providing for expulsion from the company on betrayal of counsel was passed in 1443 and confirmed in 1463. A committee of 14 men set prices in 1455 (Grocers' Records, Vol. 300, fols. 1, 3, 34; Vol. 400, fol. 30). On the whole policy and its failure to secure a permanent spice monopoly see Grocers of London, pp. 270–72. On the drapers' secrecy in regard to prices paid for cloth see Herbert, I, 426.

parliament in 1508, was due to the enmity of the legal profession, jealous of the companies' success "in pacifying matters that were debateful."[47]

In all these directions the powers of company wardens were supported by the sanction of the individual's inner fear to displease established authority and by additional persuasion from the secular arm of the law. Merely for disrespect, for having criticized the wardens' severity in expelling a member, one fifteenth-century goldsmith was driven to do penance, abasing himself on his knees before the entire company. Another was subjected to the same humiliation for having appealed to the bishop of Winchester to approve a piece of workmanship that the wardens had condemned as faulty. For refusal to pay the full amount of a certain levy assessed by the wardens, a third was brought before the mayor, who committed him to prison. Chief Justice Sir John Fortescue upheld both the wardens' action and the mayor's and obliged the man to ask the wardens' forgiveness. When they numbered aldermen among their wardens, as was frequently the case, the merchant companies were in a position to exercise an iron discipline over their members because they were able to combine the authority of the two offices. A rebel could be threatened with imprisonment and actually could be committed to prison without the formality of being brought before the mayor. The threat of summary imprisonment was used as an indirect support of price agreements. An alderman who was a warden of the mercers sent a fellow-member of the company to prison for failure to observe a boycott that had been imposed on another member for breach of a price agreement, and a resolution once passed by the grocers, setting a penalty of 40s. for breach of a boycott, provided that if an offender could not pay the fine, he should "lye in prison" at the command of the aldermen holding office in the company, "ther to be corrected bi ther discretions." A merchant tailor, himself a former warden of his company, was sent to prison for being rude to his successor in office and remained there until he agreed to apologize.[48]

Company affairs were conducted as democratically as the leisure

47. *Mercers' Acts*, pp. 43–44 (1457); Clode, pp. 199–200.
48. Herbert, II, 161, 193–95; Mercers' Wardens' Accounts, fol. 91 (1426–27); Grocers' Records, Vol. 300, fol. 48; Merchant Tailors' Minutes, 1488–93, fols. 45–46.

and interest of the members would permit, with the result that most citizens were schooled in responsible discussion and voting and came to value discreet and capable leadership. The duties of company officers were fairly exacting. They had charge of the search of shops, the purchase of cloth for liveries, the distribution of alms and the advance of loans, the arbitration of disputes, and the discipline of refractory members. In the richer companies they had the responsibility of numerous trusteeships in connection with chantries and charitable foundations, and they were sometimes expected to augment the common funds by trade. Although ordinarily the work was lightened by division among four wardens and by the employment of a clerk, only men who were well established in business could afford to hold the senior offices, and even they often hesitated. In the greater companies it was not the policy to allow such men to serve continuously for more than a year or two at a time, but after an interval they would be brought back.[49]

In the circumstances the wealthier and more successful men of each company tended to have an option upon office. This contributed greatly to their status, for it meant that they were potentially vested with authority and could accordingly command a ceremonious respect from the poorer members. The shipwrights insisted on as much, by formal ordinance:

If there by any man of the Crafte that meeteth with any man that beareth charge or hath borne charge in the said Crafte, or with any honest man likelie to beare charge in tyme to come, that hee doe hym reverence and worshipp as other craftsmen doe their soveraigns uppon pain of twelve pence.

The rule was one of a set of ordinances copied out into a new book in 1496 but may have been of earlier date. Throughout the century repeated terms of office had tended to raise a man's status. In merchant companies it became the custom to address veteran wardens as Master not only while they were presiding but for life. The title was still a genuine distinction, no other citizens enjoying it except a few in special occupations, such as doctors and lawyers and the chief masons and carpenters. Wives of veteran merchant wardens were not slow to assume the equivalent prefix of mistress or, better still, of my Lady, which set them apart from the wives of

49. Between 1390 and 1460 the four wardenships of the mercers were held by 158 different men, of whom 102 served once only, 23 twice, 16 three times, 12 four times, 20 five times, and 1 six times. Among the grocers the influence of the wealthier men, especially of those who were aldermen, became more marked as the fifteenth century wore on.

other merchants. Wives of wardens in the lesser companies seem to have been content to be called "goodwife."[50]

The system of punishments adopted by the city courts accentuated the dependence of personal worth and dignity upon money and position. For certain classes of offenses the poor were subjected to the public humiliation of the pillory. This served to relieve the strain on prison accommodation and worked less economic hardship than imprisonment, with its interruption of employment and the burden of jailers' fees. Some of the offenses in question occurred only among the poorer people or in the city's underworld. Such were the practice of magic, the passing of counterfeit money, the use of loaded dice, perjury, scolding, thieving, pimping and procuring, deceit in begging, spreading false rumors, and extortion by the sale of false pardons.[51] Others, notably commercial fraud, forestalling of food supplies on their way to market, slander, breach of an oath, and rudeness to magistrates, occurred in almost all circles; yet money and position could nearly always protect an offender's personal dignity. Bakers, who were by law liable to the pillory for selling loaves of poor quality or short weight, could escape it by paying fines.[52] Commercial fraud among merchants rarely came before the city courts because their own companies were supposed to deal with the problem, and cases that received public notice were not severely punished. A mercer who was about to sell two dozen barrels of rotten eels suffered no penalty save their confiscation and burial, and fishmongers caught with baskets below standard size ordinarily suffered only confiscation of the measures and their contents.[53] There are two exceptions to this leniency on record. Hamo de Chigwell, himself a fishmonger, while he was mayor deprived a man of his company of the freedom for using short measures, and John Northampton, waging a cam-

---

50. At the end of the fifteenth century the merchant tailors began to style their head warden the venerable master or the Right Worshipful (Clode, pp. 74 ff.). On wives' titles of distinction see Kingdon, II, 216; Ironmongers' Records, fols. 48, 49*b* (1504), Leather-sellers, Liber Curtes, fol. 43*b* (1488).

51. L. Bk., *passim;* some of the proceedings are translated in Riley, *Memorials, passim.* See also *The Great Chronicle,* pp. 253, 258, 262, 264, 281, 289; *Cal. P. & M. Rolls,* I, 232, 251, 256; II, 97, 199.

52. Before 1297 bakers had been liable to the still more degrading penalty of the hurdle, but some had always been allowed to make fine, and the later fifteenth-century Journals show that they were rarely pilloried.

53. Riley, *Memorials,* pp. 516–18; *Cal. L. Bk., E,* pp. 42–43, 46.

paign for cheaper food, sent one fishmonger to the pillory with some of the fish that he had been selling too dear dangling from his neck.[54] But the fishwife who tried to sell a few bad sole, the countrywoman who brought "corrupt" butter to market, the country coal vendor whose sacks were too small, the cook, the butcher, and the poulterer who stocked unwholesome meat or birds or were guilty of forestalling, the cornmonger who concealed moldy oats under good or bid up the price of wheat, the chapman who passed off base metal as gold or silver, were all familiar figures in the pillory, the cause of their punishment hung about their neck or burning under their nose. Passers-by were once exhorted by proclamation not to throw "any maner thyng" at the victims but to let them "stand there in peas."[55]

The offense of forgery, however, was considered so heinous that it brought several people to the pillory who were well above the rank of those ordinarily convicted of petty fraud. Two scriveners, an Italian merchant, and an esquire were sentenced and two young merchants who were not yet in the livery. One of them, a skinner who had arranged the forging of a deed to enable him to cheat his stepchildren of their property, was forbidden entrance to the livery of any company in the city or to any civic office; he was to be "held and reputed for the future as one defamed, false and infamous."[56]

The same values that crystallized in the documentary record of public civic life and in the semipublic activity of the crafts also permeated the more intimate life of the neighborhood. This had its larger focus in the parish churches, of which the city contained over a hundred, some serving very small districts. The business affairs of a parish were in the hands of four churchwardens, who were named by election in a parish meeting every year or two. They were chosen, naturally enough, from among the merchants and other "more sufficient" citizens. Trustees of chantries were by preference appointed from the same kind of people. One merchant's will left the appointment of a chantry priest who was to sing for the souls of his family to the parson and four "of the

54. Northampton sentenced a second fishmonger for bringing in a shipload of bad fish for sale, but he had to be excused the pillory on account of holding an appointment under the king (*Cal. L. Bk., H*, pp. 202-3; Riley, *Memorials*, pp. 471–72).

55. Journals, 6, fol. 104.

56. Riley, *Memorials*, pp. 333–35, 404–5, 412–14, 527–29; L. Bk., *K*, fol. 308*b*.

worthyest and myghtyest" of his fellow-parishioners. Local reputation in general, apart from such appointments, depended upon a
combination of wealth, trustworthiness of character, and public
spirit, and it rose and fell with business success. One reads of a
cutler who "had been a worshipfull man" in his parish but "was
fallen in decaye" and of a brewer boasting that he had formerly
been "of metely substance."[57]

People seem constantly to have thought in terms of a series of
ranks in which one could ascend or fall. Charitable funds might be
left for disposal either among poor householders or among neighbors of middling rank, "de medio statu."[58] To be certain of a place
near the top, one had to be certain of a large income, and this was a
subject, in merchants' less dignified moments, of boastful quarreling. A quarrel along these lines is reported in full in the minutes
of the merchant tailors' court for 1490. A former master of the
company became enraged when the court gave judgment against
him in a dispute over an apprentice who had left him, and he had
to be reminded that he must submit. "Sir," said the presiding
master, "I most be your Juge this yere," to which the other replied
in heat:

> Sir ye take to moche upon you for I have sitten in the Rome [the master's
> seat] as well as ye now do and was as able therto for I may expende xxx li by
> yere as long as I lyve and ye take upon you more than ye nede and so wole
> xx moo sey as well as I.[59]

On the whole question of rank it is admittedly the voice of the
wealthier people that speaks through most of the evidence that is
extant, and it is more than likely that resentful and dissenting
views could have been heard among the poorer Londoners, especially in the revolutionary years of the late fourteenth century.
Yet no alternative system of valuation gained currency. The cult
of secular equality implicit in the slogans of the peasants' revolt
may have had its sympathizers in the city, but it found no prophets
there. The only grounds on which the poorer citizens claimed
equality with the rich was in their legal rights as citizens or
"commoners." As Unwin pointed out, it was historically most

57. H. Littlehales (ed.), *Medieval Records of a City Church*, E.E.T.S. (1904), I,
6; E.C.P., 63/120, 163/58.

58. Will of John Abbot (P.C.C., Luffenham, 34 [1444]).

59. Merchant Tailors' Minutes, 1488–93, fols. 45–46.

significant that they were able to do so, to feel that as members of the incorporated city they had some equal rights with the rich and could protest against abuses. Whether they questioned the idea that the rich should lead and dominate, however, is doubtful. The poorer goldsmiths, petitioning in parliament in 1377 against oppression by the merchants in the matter of prices, called themselves "les poueres Co'es de la Mistier d'Orfeverye," complaining of the practices of a group of "grantz and riches Orfeveres," which included one of the senior aldermen. There is another parliamentary reference to "aucuns Grantz" among the London merchants a few years later.[60] Might not acceptance of the current terms in which the high status of the rich was expressed indicate a certain degree of acquiescence in the prevailing scale of values, the language itself having some persuasive effect? Petitions to the mayor and aldermen in which poorer citizens referred to their own condition show a corresponding acquiescence in conventional attitudes and valuations. The hurers allowed the clerk who drafted a petition for them in 1376 to describe them as "men of low degree and simple," the horners began a petition on a similar note, "mekely shewen . . . . the pour men of the little craft of horneris," and the journeymen bakers pleaded for permission to continue a fraternity that was under suspicion as "youre symple pouere servitors."[61]

3. THE DELIMITATION OF THE MERCHANT CLASS

Inequalities and allied cultural differences between people in different types of occupation were a pervasive and dividing influence in the Londoners' social life. Perhaps only because more evidence survives about people who had property, it seems as though division was sharpest near the top of the occupational scale. Certainly the members of merchant families held together, as forming the citizens' upper class.

The division is apparent in circles of intimate friendship. A merchant's close personal friends, the men whom he would trust to administer his estate or act as guardians of his children, the men to whom he would leave substantial legacies or personal gifts of

60. *Rot. parl.*, III, 9, 292.
61. Riley, *Memorials*, p. 402; H. G. Rosedale, *Some Notes on the Old Book of the Worshipful Company of Horners*, p. 6; L. Bk., *K*, fol. 198b.

jewelry and clothing, were almost invariably merchants. Frequently they were members of his own company, friendship having arisen out of association in business or in company affairs, but they might belong to the livery of any one of the greater companies. In this respect the situation did not change from one part of the period to another. The wills of any date tell the same story. To illustrate from the first decade of the fifteenth century, from which 218 merchants' wills are extant, only 6 men in a hundred named members of any of the lesser companies among their friends or executors, and only 10 per cent of 208 members of lesser companies whose wills were proved in that decade named merchants as friends or executors.

Marriages tended to be restricted in the same way. It was the custom to arrange them with an eye to avoiding social disparagement, a conventional idea which called for a nice balancing of considerations of birth, occupation, wealth, and prospects. A deficiency in one point might be overlooked if other points were advantageous. The mayor and aldermen, who together with the city chamberlain formed a court of orphanage and were concerned to prevent guardians from arranging marriages without regard to their wards' interests, laid official stress upon the idea. As applied to merchants' daughters, they interpreted it as meaning that marriage should be into merchant families. They steered 53 out of 63 merchants' daughters who were in their charge after 1360 into marrying merchants, that is, 84 per cent; of the other 10 girls, 5 were married to gentlemen and 5 to citizens of lesser companies.[62] In second marriages a still higher proportion of merchants' widows chose to remain in their own sphere. In 37 cases in the fifteenth century 2 married knights, 1 a scrivener, and the rest took merchant husbands again, 22 of them from the same company as their first husbands. This was a practical choice on their part, since the second husband could then carry on the first one's business; suspicion of the betrayal of trade secrets made it difficult to transfer from another company for this purpose.[63]

Merchants and their sons married into lesser citizen families more often than their daughters did. In a hundred fifteenth-century cases, taken from deeds referring to the ownership of city property, only 67 of the wives were daughters or widows of mer-

62. L. Bk., *passim*.   63. See *Mercers' Acts*, pp. 209, 228, 229.

chants, 6 were daughters or widows of gentlemen, and 27 were daughters or widows of members of one or the other of the lesser companies. If the latter had brought their husbands comfortable dowries, it is unlikely that any idea of disparagement of rank had arisen. Marriage was recognized as one of the best means of obtaining capital for a merchant's business, and the need of capital was very great. To marry a rich woman of one's own rank or better was considered a great personal triumph, assuring a young merchant's advancement. When one of the mercer's yeomen announced his engagement to a wealthy vintner's widow, the court felt that the whole company was honored, "whiche is a worship to the felyshipp a yonge man owet of the lyverey to be preferred to such a riche mariage," and he was immediately promoted to the livery.[64]

The drawing-apart of the merchants as a superior social class was nowhere more conspicuous than in the life that centered in their companies. The liverymen controlled all their company affairs, discussing them in quarterly meetings which the yeomanry did not attend. The young merchants in service or waiting to enter the livery were subordinated along with the poorer shopkeepers and artisan members, but it was emphasized that this was simply on account of their youth. The division between merchants and yeomanry became more conspicuous in the fifteenth century, when the companies acquired their pleasant and commodious halls. These were large enough to serve as club premises as well as for administrative headquarters. The liverymen, who in each company already constituted a club, gave themselves special privileges in the use of the premises. Dining apart from the yeomanry at the quarterly dinners which in all the companies were a regular institution, they lavished expensive entertainment on friends and patrons whose favor they hoped to cultivate, noblemen, government officials, and lawyers. In short, the liveried merchant was a man of dignity. The grocers made all apprentices in the company swear to be obedient not only to the wardens but to "alle the clothinge of the felishipe in dew Reverence."[65]

The social separation between merchants in livery and the yeomanry could occur in despite of common organization in a fraternity with religious dedication. The goldsmiths had a single fraternity, all members contributing to a single alms fund for the relief of artisans suffering from blindness and other disabilities of which their occupation put them in danger. The tailors had a single fraternity, dedicated to St. John the Baptist, whose funds were devoted to the accumulation of spiritual benefits. Separate clubs formed within each of these. By 1415 the yeomen tailors had adopted the custom of honoring the fraternity's patron saint by attending church together on the feast of his decollation instead of on the feast of his nativity, which was the day the livery celebrated.[66]

In other companies liveried merchants and yeomanry drew apart in separate fraternities. The drapers in livery contributed to a fraternity alms box that was for their own exclusive benefit.[67] The merchant fishmongers were divided among several liveried fraternities, in different parts of the city, until late in the fifteenth century, and the yeomen had at least two, one in Bridge Street and one in Old Fish Street.[68] The grocers' yeomanry, or bachelors, were well organized. They had an annual "revell" of their own at Shrovetide, and both they and the mercers' bachelors had their own barge in mayoral processions.[69]

In two of the merchant companies the fraternities acquired a prestige and popularity through their religious dedications and activity that made them the principal religious fraternities in the city. The skinners' liverymen organized a solemn procession on the feast of Corpus Christi, to which their fraternity was dedicated. The mayor and aldermen and a great many of the clergy took part in the procession; it was a major event in the year's round of pageantry. The yeomen had a separate fraternity, also with a popular dedication, to Our Lady's Assumption. The tailors added to the appeal of their trade patron, St. John the Baptist, by spending much more money than was usual on spiritual benefits. They employed several priests, and by the end of the period had two chapels of their own, in which special indulgences were offered to regular worshipers. They had also accumulated shares in the spir-

66. Clode, pp. 23, 24, 49 n., 236, 514–17, 520.
67. Herbert, I, 428.
68. See bequests in wills of Thomas Goldwell (P.C.C., Logge, 16); Laurence Fyncham (Logge, 3, Milles, 24).
69. Kingdon, II, 219, 230, 253; Grocers' Records, Vol. 400, *passim*; *Mercers' Acts*, pp. x, xi, 219, 274.

itual profit accruing from the prayers and pious works of eight religious houses, and members could claim remission of a seventh part of all penances that might be imposed on them.[70] These attractions induced people who had no connection with the company's trade to seek admission on the grounds of piety. To join in this way, they did not have to be citizens. They would subscribe to the fraternity funds in return for sharing in its spiritual benefits, they could attend the annual religious service and perhaps, by invitation, the annual banquet, but they would have no right to attend meetings on company business.

The character of the outside membership of the two skinners' fraternities was plainly affected by the difference in social standing between liverymen and yeomanry. Beginning with the admission of Edward III as a brother, the former enjoyed royal patronage continuously. Between 1327 and 1500 the Corpus Christi roll lists, in all, 26 entries of royalty or nobility and 13 knights and gentlemen. Two provincial merchants were admitted and 30 liveried merchants of other London companies but only 6 citizens from the lesser companies. In addition there were priests and clerks, and many members joined with their wives. The fraternity of Our Lady's Assumption was much easier of entry, between 1397 and 1482 enrolling nearly 500 members from outside the company. The majority came from the more prosperous of the lesser companies. Brewers, chandlers, bakers, shearmen, and pewterers were heavily represented, and there were a few people from poorer trades, such as tilers and patten-makers, a woman burnisher, and a goldwire-drawer. There was also a country membership of village artisans and people described as yeomen or husbandmen from several neighboring counties. A minority, of about one in five, was made up of citizens in the livery of a merchant company, with a few country merchants and country gentlemen. Until the reign of Edward IV, when members of two noble families entered their names, there was no aristocratic patronage. The tailors' fraternity being a single organization, the list of outside members admitted from outside the trade does not distinguish between those who entered as patrons and friends of the merchants and those who entered as friends of the yeomen. Both were included. Following the example set by royal patronage, scores of noblemen, officials,

70. Clode, pp. 49–52; *Cal. Papal Registers*, XI, 240–41 (1455).

and gentlemen joined, many with their wives, with over 200 merchants from other companies and a few from the provinces. Along with these came representatives from about 50 of the lesser companies.[71]

Whether any of the London groups below the rank of merchant was clearly delimited as a class, with a definite class status attached to all its members, a characteristic outlook on public affairs or life in general, and a consciousness of cultural difference affecting marriages, friendship, and daily social intercourse, it is at this distance difficult to say. The faces of the very poor escape us or appear only in the unfriendly bias of criminal records. Above them were strata of obscure respectability, visible only as supplying labor for industry and transport, as receiving the occasional charity of the rich in bread and coals to tide them over winter hardships, as making up the rank and file of trade and religious organizations, generation after generation. Unless they were arrested or headed some licensed organization or acquired and registered a title to property, individuals left not even their names behind them. Those who retained some economic independence were acknowledged to be of middling rank. There is an early fourteenth-century reference, in the civic records, to the *mediocres;* they included craftsmen who were anxious to sell their wares in market places, that is to say, men who were too poor to rent shops in the better districts but were still struggling to retain their independence against the wealthier shopkeepers and the great merchants.[72]

This broad middle group breaks roughly into two, for the more prosperous of the men who led the lesser companies, the trading elements therein, were far above craftsmen who had to carry their wares to a market place in basketloads. Some of them enjoyed economic power and authority in company offices in a greater degree than the less successful merchants; some were as large employers of labor. William Woodward, a founder who cast a multi-barreled cannon for Richard II, at his death in 1421 had 13 men in his workshop, and he was able to leave £67 among them in lega-

71. Skinners' Book of the Fraternity of Our Lady's Assumption, *passim;* extracts are printed in J. J. Lambert (ed.), *Records of the Skinners of London* (1933); Merchant Tailors' Records, Lists of Freemen.

72. *Cal. P. & M. Rolls,* I, 1; cf. references to *mediocres, menes genz,* "middle people," in W. Hudson and J. C. Tingey (eds.), *Records of the City of Norwich* (2 vols., 1906–10), *passim.*

cies.[73] A leather-seller who died in 1440 left 8 apprentices. On account of labor shortage in the city, craft rules restricted the number of workers that any master might employ, and in 1474 the mayor and aldermen imposed a fine of £10 on a man who had tried to avoid penalty by joining two companies, the girdlers and the leather-sellers, and combining the quotas of labor allowed by each. Fullers and shearmen were not supposed to employ more than 6 apprentices and servants, but they were allowed to put work out. The founders, who required all their labor in their workshop, had a sliding scale of restriction according to rank, wardens and former wardens of the company being allowed to take 4 apprentices, other members in livery 3, and masters not in livery only 2.[74] Employment on work for the king, such as Woodward the gunfounder obtained, and Henry Yevele the architect, king's mason, brought a man exceptional rewards in prestige as well as in profit. The broiderers and painters who could execute first-class heraldic work had similar opportunities. One embroiderer, Giles Davynell, sold over £700 worth of work to the Black Prince.[75] Such men were frequently friends of merchants, married into their families, and apprenticed their sons in merchant companies.

All these circumstances were constant through the period. Politically, as the next chapter will show, the situation altered. Throughout the fourteenth century leading members of the lesser companies were intermittently able to play a challenging role in city politics. Later they were of less political importance. To compensate for ground lost in this direction, there came an increase in economic power, as royal charters extended company control of standards in industry over suburban areas. The prestige of the office of warden rose with this and also as companies accumulated wealth and, like the merchant companies, settled their headquarters in halls of rambling spaciousness. These halls, several of which had once belonged to nobility, had an air that was symbolic of aristocratic ease and authority. Ceremonial observances, such as the wearing of expensive livery, grew correspondingly, always emphasizing the social separation of the more prosperous members.

73. P.C.C., Marche, 52; on Woodward see T. F. Tout, "Firearms in England in the Fourteenth Century," *Collected Papers*, II, 249–57.

74. Will of John Osyn (P.C.C., Rous, 16 [1440]); Journals, 8, fol. 55; *Cal. L. Bk.*, *L*, pp. 205, 261, 272.

75. *Cal. of Black Prince's Register*, IV, 476.

The question arises whether these men who led the lesser companies should not be thought of as forming a separate entrepreneur class, a kind of secondary merchant class, satellite to the merchant class proper. They were not so described in their own day, however, and it would be confusing in the extreme to adopt too complicated a way of describing a group that was so local in its character. They were looked on simply as the upper layer of the city *mediocres*, as the more substantial citizens of middle rank, and the same description will serve well enough here.

The record of parish life gives another view of the grouping within the community. During the fourteenth century the inhabitants of most of the city parishes developed sufficient initiative to found and keep alive at least one fraternity organization that had no direct connection with a trade. Some would die from lack of interest, but from time to time new ones were founded. They were suspected of screening political activity behind a front of piety, but no evidence of this was unearthed, and nothing is apparent now but the official aims that they avowed and the general nature of their membership.

Some had for their main purpose the accumulation of property that would produce a permanent income to be dedicated to the upkeep and beautification of a church. These drew together all the wealthier parishioners, both merchants and men in lesser companies. The fraternity of St. Katherine at St. Mary Colechurch in Cheap was supported by ironmongers, drapers, and other merchants and by armorers, the high entrance fee of 1 mark excluding all but the well-to-do. Its founders built a chapel to their patron saint; later members endowed a perpetual chantry at her altar and arranged for "more worthy services with music" in the church.[76] Two fraternities in the parish of St. Magnus joined forces in 1344 under the joint dedication of *Salve Regina* to repair and enlarge the church and to provide for the singing of anthems in honor of St. Mary and St. Thomas. The parish was a center for fishmongers, and they figured prominently in the fraternity but did not keep it to themselves. Master Henry Yevele, king's mason, a vintner, a fletcher, and several chandlers were among the wardens, and the

---

76. C, 47/41/199; *Cal. P.R., 1399–1401*, p. 284; *C.W.C.H.*, II, 556; Unwin, p. 114. On the location and number of gilds see C. L. Kingsford, *Prejudice and Promise in Fifteenth Century England* (1925), p. 141.

benefactors included a prosperous glover, a girdler, and a purser.[77] The gild of St. Mary and St. Giles, which helped to enlarge the church of St. Giles Cripplegate and to keep it in repair, was, on the contrary, supported mainly by people of upper middle rank, such as painters, poulterers, and brewers. This was natural, since they predominated in the parish. In 1424 all four wardens were of this type, a brewer, a currier, a painter, and a smith. But gentlemen and merchants were also among its supporters. Trustees of its property in the parish, which in the 1440's was worth 9 marks yearly, were a gentleman city official, a poulterer, a brewer, and a waxchandler. Its reputation was high in the city at large, at least three people who were parishioners of other churches, a vintner, a mason's widow, and a horner, naming the wardens as ultimate or alternative trustees of property with which they wished to perpetuate chantries and obit services.[78]

In many parishes the generosity of individual merchants sufficed to produce church building funds as they were needed. Here gilds arose primarily as mutual aid societies, offering the secular benefit of alms and loans and the assurance of a respectable funeral and the spiritual benefit of a co-operative chantry. Since it was desirable that members should have confidence in each other's character and ability to keep up subscriptions, there was usually some provision for social meetings as well as for religious services. Brethren were urged not to go to law with each other, and on their admission both men and women might have to give all the old members a symbolic kiss "in tokening of love and charite and pees."[79] Membership might be conditional on keeping a reputation for private and business morality, as, for example, in the twentieth rule of the gild of St. Peter at the church of St. Peter Cornhill:

> Also, it is ordeyned that if it may be preved that ony of the same fraternite be ony commune contectour, hasardour, lechour, chider, fals usurour, or use ony other shrewed tacches, and thanne ther of be resonabilly warned and reprevid onys twyis thriys by the wardeyns of the same fraternite withe vii or viii the more discrete and wele consciencyd mene of the same fraternite, and he thus warnyd and reprevyd wille noght be correctyd, thanne he . . . . be put owte of the fraternite for evermore.

77. C, 47/42/208a; *Cal. P. & M. Rolls*, III, 238–39; *C.W.C.H.*, I, 642, II, 114; Hust. R.W.D., 170/50; Unwin, p. 115.

78. *Cal. P. & M. Rolls*, IV, 172; *Cal. P.R., 1441–46*, p. 140; *C.W.C.H.*, II, 162–63, 217, 302, 318–20, 333, 350, 358, 385, 435, 455, 513, 565.

79. H. F. Westlake, *The Parish Gilds of Medieval England* (1919), p. 68.

The gild of St. Peter was traditionally associated with the wealthy fishmongers of the parish, and its constitution provided that two of the four wardens should always be fishmongers. It was able to employ two chaplains and had a large loan fund from which members could borrow as much as 5 marks for a period of three months. The entrance fee was set at the fairly high level of half a mark. Citizens of upper middle rank, a tallow-chandler, a hosteler, and a horner, were among its benefactors. The membership must therefore have been mixed, with fishmongers and other merchants heightening their influence in the parish by controlling the disposal of its loans.[80] Another gild with a strong element of merchant membership had a dedication to Corpus Christi and was attached to a chapel in Conyhoop Lane. The grocers, whose hall was near by, in 1471 paid 10 marks to have 20 of their liverymen admitted to it in a body.[81] A new fraternity that was licensed about this time, dedicated to St. Mary, in the church of St. Bride Fleet Street, had a mixed membership; the men who applied for its license were headed by the bishop of Salisbury and Lord Ferrers and included vintners and pewterers, a bowyer, and a currier.[82]

The only complete membership list extant is for the unusually popular gild of Holy Trinity at the church of St. Botolph's Aldersgate, founded in 1369 and rededicated in 1374, which drew members from parishes all over the city with some from Westminster and some from Kent. The gildbook lists the names of 530 men who joined between 1374 and 1415 and 1443–45 and 274 women. Headed in 1374 by a capper and a weaver, they were predominantly of middle citizen rank or lower, with a few gentlemen, one noble patron, the lord Roos, and a few liveried merchants. The women were mostly wives of craftsmen, entering with their husbands; among the few who entered alone were a marbler's wife, a huckster, and a single woman named Juliana Ful of Love, occupation undesignated. The occupations of the men, so far as they are given or can be ascertained, were as follows: 65 clergy, 22 gentry and officials, 22 citizens of merchant companies, some of them liverymen, 12 brewers, 4 maltmen, 4 dyers, 3 weavers, 3 armorers, 3 car-

80. The rules are printed in H.M.C., *6th Report*, *Appendix*, pp. 412–18, and summarized in Westlake, *op. cit.*, pp. 79–84; *C.W.C.H.*, II, 494; and will of John Waleys, poulterer (Comm. Lon., Broun, 170).

81. Grocers' Records, Vol. 401, fol. 220.   82. *Cal. P.R., 1467–77*, p. 553.

penters, 3 cooks, 3 smiths, 2 chandlers, 2 cappers, 2 masons, 2 butchers, 2 saddlers, with 1 representative of each of the following: barber, bladesmith, chapman, cooper, cordwainer, currier, drover, glazier, gold-beater, herald, leech, painter, spurrier, surgeon, taverner, tiler, waterman, and Kentish husbandman. The remainder must have been of similar trades and humble rank, for their names are not identifiable. A decline in popularity in the middle of the fifteenth century led to amalgamation with another gild at the same church, dedicated to St. Fabian and St. Sebastian. Thereafter the merchants and gentlemen took more of a hand in its affairs, although they did not displace the other type of member. The wardens in 1459 included a merchant of the staple; in 1500 they were a squire, a gentleman, and a brewer, and among the new lay members of that year were Lord Willoughby and his wife, a squire and his wife, and two goldsmiths.[83]

On the whole the parish gilds were much more popular with the citizens of middle rank than with the merchants. Only 7 of the 218 merchants' wills of the first decade of the fifteenth century contain bequests to a fraternity not connected with a company, whereas the 208 wills of other citizens, of the same date, contain 26 bequests to 19 different parish gilds. One reason for the merchants' relative lack of interest lay in the fact that they provided for themselves so well in the fraternities of their companies. All of these employed priests to pray for the souls of members and their families, living and dead, and all took pains to meet the craving that was felt for ceremonial funerals by obliging members to attend the body of a deceased brother to the place of burial wearing their livery. If he died at home in London, a merchant was therefore assured of a first-class funeral procession, dignified by his company colors, and in some companies by a richly embroidered funeral pall. Lesser citizens, envying this observance of ceremony, paid their parish fraternities to brighten their funerals. A baker's will contains a bequest of half a mark to his parish fraternity on condition that his body might lie under its pall of cloth of gold. Many of the parish fraternities were much more emphatic in the stress that they laid upon the "amending of lives" and on the virtues of diligence and temperance than were the merchant fraternities.

83. Add. MSS, 37,664. Extracts from this gildbook are printed in W. Hone, *Ancient Mysteries* (1825), pp. 77–85, and in Westlake, *op. cit.*, pp. 68–72.

The gild of St. Anne in the parish of St. Lawrence Jewry expressly threatened to expel forever any member who lay in bed too long, who haunted taverns, or who ran about to wrestling matches when he should have been at work procuring a livelihood for his family.[84] Such concern reflects the spirit of people who have not long attained security, who have much to lose by laziness and much to gain by sobriety and hard work; they join together partly to encourage one another in these virtues. So much is clear of the common cultural milieu of the citizens of middle rank.

Of the milieu in which the poorer inhabitants of the city lived, little survives but the contemporary impression of their poverty. They formed a few religious gilds of their own; these saved money and attracted bequests. Two were dedicated to the Conception of the Blessed Virgin Mary, one at the church of the Carmelite Friars and one at the church of St. Sepulchre, outside the city walls; this one had by 1361 acquired a tenement. Unable to afford permanent chantries, these poorer gilds contented themselves with keeping up sacred lights, hiring a priest only on their annual festival and at funerals, and in place of the 14d. or 16d. weekly relief that more flourishing ones offered to members in temporary distress, they could offer only 6d. or 7d. The brotherhood of Jesus at St. Botolph's Aldgate, to which a glover bequeathed three of his funeral torches "to bery the pore pepull wt all and they to pay no thynge therefore" may have been one of these poor men's gilds. The "penny brotherhood" of St. Ursula, at the church of St. Lawrence Jewry, mentioned in the will of a pewterer, has also a modest ring. There were several fraternities of aliens.[85]

It would be misleading to suggest that the Londoners were perpetually preoccupied by considerations of rank and class. The emotion that was evoked by religious teaching and festivals and neighborhood loyalties, growing up around the parish churches, did much to keep friendships open between families that otherwise moved in different social spheres. At their christening, children were sponsored by godparents of both higher and lower rank than their parents.[86] Poor neighbors, as well as wealthy people whom

84. Toulmin Smith (ed.), *English Gilds*, E.E.T.S., No. 40 (original ser., 1870), p. xl.
85. C, 47/41/189, 201; *C.W.C.H.*, II, 45; will of Sage (Comm. Lon., Lichfield, fol. 11 [1483]).
86. See notes on family of Richard Hill, grocer, in Dyboski, *op. cit.*, pp. xiii–xiv.

the family wished to honor, were invited to the funeral suppers of well-to-do citizens. Stow tells us that it was the medieval custom, at all saints' festivals falling in June and July, for the wealthy citizens to light bonfires in the streets and set tables loaded with food and drink beside them, "whereunto they would invite their neighbours and passengers also to sit, and bee merrie with them in great familiaritie, praysing God for his benefites bestowed on them."

Nevertheless the fact could not be ignored that all the more coveted prizes of this life that fell within the community fell to merchants. No one could make any conspicuous fortune except by the business of a merchant, and wealth was a prerequisite for holding high judicial office. Out of a total of over 260 aldermen elected in the fourteenth century, only 9 were citizens of lesser companies; one of these, a cornmonger, was shortly after his election obliged to resign for lack of means. The others were a dyer, a butcher, a cornmonger, a leather merchant, a fuller, a waxchandler, an armorer, and a broiderer, all men of upper middle rank, who had held office in their companies. Nicholas Crane, the butcher, supplied meat to the king's household and was described alternatively as a merchant. He made enough money to buy from another alderman one of the grander houses in the city, "La rouge sale." The other men may also have been moving into the business of merchant. The list of fourteenth-century sheriffs includes not more than two other citizens of lesser companies. In the fifteenth century no one held office either as sheriff or as alderman who was not in the livery of a merchant company.[87]

In the early years of the fourteenth century, family influence carried more weight in city politics than later. Possibly this was due to some lingering tradition of respect for birth, inherited from the previous century. At all events, families tended to cling to judicial office. Between 1300 and 1350 three brothers of the Gisors family sat in the court of aldermen, three Rokesles, and two members each of nine other families: Abyndons, Blunds, Chigwells, Combemartyns, Caustons, Conduits, Lambyns, Leyres, Refhams. In addition the court saw two generations each of Betoynes, Nortones, and Selys, and three generations of Costantyns. Two Dolselys, grocers, were in office together in the 1350's, and two Bammes,

87. Beaven, *passim;* on Crane's business and property, *Cal. C.R., 1337–39,* pp. 124, 342; Hust. R.W.D., 79/8; cf. chap. ii, n. 109.

goldsmiths, in the 1380's. One other alderman, in this half of the century, was the son of an alderman, and three others were probably nephews or cousins of previous members of the court. Later there was almost no recurrence of family names in office. Position went to the wealthy, regardless of birth.

An aspect of the merchant's occupation that struck imagination in the fifteenth century was the fact that a man's name and the marks that he stamped upon the bales of merchandise he sold could become known in distant lands. The hero of a moral interlude that had been adapted from either French or Italian sources, a merchant named Sir Arystory, was made to introduce himself as

> A merchante myghty of a royall araye;
> Ful wyde in þis worlde spryngeth my fame . . . .
> In all maner of landis, without ony naye,
> My merchandyse runneth, þe sothe for to tell. . . . .[88]

When in 1502 they decided to call themselves merchant tailors, the London tailors and linen-armorers adopted the same tone of hyperbole, professing that their connections had always been worldwide, that their members, "or at least the sounder part of them have from time whereof the memory of man is not to the contrary and daily do use occupy and exercise in all quarters and kingdoms of this world all and every kinds of merchandises."[89]

It was immaterial that only a minority of the tailors were actually exporters. The glamour of connection with distant countries could hang about the whole company. In the same way it did not matter that most merchants did not make a great fortune or hold judicial office. It was common knowledge that the opportunity to make a fortune and the possibility of holding offices of high dignity were restricted to the merchant class. These circumstances were sufficient to give the class a collective status in which all members shared and which had a bearing upon all their chances in life. The basic status that a young merchant enjoyed by virtue of his occupation gave him a chance of marrying into a family that would provide a dowry useful for his business. His personal status in the community might vary considerably from one period of his

---

88. O. Waterhouse (ed.), *Non-cycle Mystery Plays*, E.E.T.S., No. 104 (extra ser., 1909), p. 57. On sources of the play see C. Cutts, "The Croxton Play: An Anti-Lollard Piece," *Modern Language Quarterly*, V (1944), 45–60.

89. Charter of 1502 (Latin) printed with translation in Herbert, II, 525–26.

life to another according as he took an active part in public affairs
or not and according as he prospered in his business. Yet no re-
versal of fortune could entirely deprive him of his class status.

4. NUMERICAL ESTIMATES OF THE POPULATION

The medieval city authorities never took a census of the population under their charge. Indeed, few official enumerations of any
groups of the population survive except of citizens who were summoned to mayoral elections, were elected to common councils, or
made voluntary contributions to public funds. Most of the chamberlain's records, among which tallage lists would have been kept,
and notes of the receipt of all payments for admission to the freedom are lost. To give exact figures for the size of the merchant
class or of other groups of the city population at any particular
date or to state exactly how these numbers varied from one part
of the period to another is therefore not possible. The relative size
of the groups, however, has so important a bearing on their social
and political relations that it is worth while to give the picture at
least some approximate numerical dimensions.

For this purpose company records are invaluable. Containing accounts of quarterly fees, subscription lists, dining lists, notes of the
admission of new freemen and apprentices, and stray complete
membership lists, they offer a valid basis for computing the numbers of male citizen householders in various trades and for classifying them by their economic and social status. Unfortunately, the
notices of fourteenth-century date are very scanty, allowing only
the general impression that the greater companies had usually a
hundred or more merchant members. The only note of the number
of mercers is of 107 who paid dues in 1347. The grocers had varying
numbers through the century, up to 135, some of whom later fell
back into the yeomanry. The goldsmiths had 150 members sworn
to obey ordinances in 1369 and 140 riding with the queen in 1381.
It is unlikely that these were all merchants. The skinners had 170
members, counting livery and yeomen together, in 1397. The fishmongers have no records for this century; it is known only that in
1290 no less than 89 of them had been fined for illicit transactions.
The tailors and drapers were also numerous. In 1413 the latter
had 127 men riding in a civic procession, and the tailors raised a
fund in 1406 from 228 subscribers, made up of both merchants and

yeomen. There is no clue to the number of merchants among the vintners, ironmongers, salters, or haberdashers at these dates.[90]

Notices of the size of the lesser companies in the fourteenth century are still scantier. A chronicler guessed the number of taverners in the city in the year 1309 to be 354 and the number of brewers as 1,334.[91] He did not distinguish between proprietors and servants or apprentices, and in the case of the brewers he must have been attempting to guess not only the number of servants employed but also the number of people who engaged in the business as a side line, through wife or servants. In 1418 the brewers' company had 234 paid-up members; two years later a city census of the trade counted 269, including 20 women.[92] Three other fourteenth-century figures give 27 masters in the armorers' company in 1322 and 54 fullers in 1376 and in twenty of the wards in 1384 a total of 197 innkeepers.[93]

Toward the end of the next century the picture fills out. The city records contain a list of the number of citizens in the livery of 47 companies in the year 1501–2, together with the names of 22 others in which there was no livery division.[94] This may be compared with a second list preserved among the miscellaneous documents of the exchequer of the year 1537–38 giving the names of the liverymen in 8 of the companies and the names of all the freemen in 31 more.[95] Both lists may in turn be checked against company records. As a result, we have the basis for computation of the size of the merchant class shown in Table 2. It will be noticed that the companies' own figures tend to exceed the others. Yet, being de-

90. Mercers' Wardens' Accounts, fols. 2–4; Grocers of London, p. 254; Goldsmiths' Wardens' Accounts, Book A; Skinners' Book of the Fraternity of Our Lady's Assumption, fol. 1; note on fishmongers, Unwin, p. 39; A. H. Johnson, *History of the Worshipful Company of Drapers*, I (1914), 105; Merchant Tailors' Transcripts of Accounts, Vol. I, fols. 63–65.

91. *Chronicles of Edward I and Edward II*, cited by R. R. Sharpe (ed.); *Cal. L. Bk.*, D, p. xix.

92. Brewers' Records, 1418–40, fols. 5–9; *Cal. L. Bk.*, I, pp. 233–35.

93. Riley, *Memorials*, p. 145; *Cal. L. Bk.*, H, p. 37; *Cal. P. & M. Rolls*, III, 79.

94. Journals, 10, fol. 373*b* (printed in E. B. Jupp and W. Pocock, *An Historical Account of the Worshipful Company of Carpenters* [1887], pp. 290–91).

95. "The severall companyes of all the mysteryes craftes and occupaciones within the Cytie of London wt the names of every free-man beyng householder wtin the same" (E, 66/93 [T.R. Misc., Chapter House Books, Vol. 94], printed in *Middlesex and Hertfordshire Notes and Queries*, Vol. III). This list has been used by Herbert and other company historians, without a check against company records for that year, on the unwarranted assumption that it gives complete lists of membership in all cases.

rived from lists of paid-up membership, they cannot possibly be overstatements and may on the contrary be in some instances too low.[96] It would therefore be safe to set the number of liveried merchants in 1501–2 at 700.

In addition to the liverymen, the merchant class included an indeterminate number of young men who had prospects of entering the livery; there were also the wives and children. The young mer-

TABLE 2

	NUMBERS IN LIVERY, 1501 LIST	NEAREST CHECK FROM COMPANY RECORDS		NUMBERS IN 1537–38 LIST	NEAREST CHECK FROM COMPANY RECORDS	
		Livery	Total Membership		Livery	Total Member-ship
Mercers........	66	....	ca. 273	55	....	ca. 263
Grocers........	84	ca. 75	ca. 177	59	71	191
Drapers........	80	125	248	76	....	....
Fishmongers....	76	....	....	109	....	....
Goldsmiths.....	51	59	168	52	....	....
Skinners........	54	....	....	151 (prob-ably total membership)	....	....
Merchant tailors.	84	....	230	96	....	....
Haberdashers...	41	....	....	120 (prob-ably total membership)	....	....
Salters........	30	50	....	40	....	....
Ironmongers....	25	Over 44 (1454)	....	40	ca. 27	93
Vintners........	26	....	....	33	....	....
Totals......	617	....	....	831	....	....

96. There are no complete lists of the mercers' membership. But in 1475 there were at least 102 worth 100 marks or more (see below, p. 45). The figures given are arrived at by adding the admissions to the freedom for the previous twenty years. Figures for the grocers are from quarterage lists of 1470 and 1539–40 (Grocers of London, p. 254; Wardens' Accounts [date, 1534–55]). The drapers recorded their complete membership in 1493 (Johnson, op. cit., I, 364). In 1463 the goldsmiths had 62 liverymen, 49 freemen, and 31 "dowchemen" subscribing to the expenses of their charter; in 1477 there were 198 paying quarterage, including 41 aliens (Wardens' Accounts, Book A). The figures given are from 1492 (Herbert, II, 167). The skinners admitted 39 new members to the livery between 1488–98; at that rate the livery might have numbered about 80. The ironmongers assessed 44 members in 1454 toward purchase and repair of a hall; in 1437 they had 27 liverymen and 11 yeomen furnishing armed men for the midsummer watch. Their yeomanry book of that year lists 66 "names of brethren and yeomanry" (Register [dates, 1454, 1537]; Yeomanry Book [1532–45]). The tailors' freemen for the 1490's are listed in a minute-book, Book 37. The salters were 50 strong at a dinner in 1506 (T. Gillespy, Some Account of the Worshipful Company of Salters [1867], p. 14).

chants, both those who were hired servants and factors and those who were in business for themselves, may have been almost as numerous as the liverymen. If they made up half the yeomanry, there would have been about 500 of them, bringing the number of merchant freemen to 1,200. Again, each liveryman had at least 1 or 2 apprentices who by reason of family connections, the payment of premiums, and their own abilities and ambition were assured of a career as a merchant. Many of these had to continue in apprenticeship until they were past twenty-one years of age. The number of adult men in the class may thus have been in the neighborhood of 1,900. Practically all liverymen and some of the younger merchants were married. It would be reasonable to set the number of family households at approximately 1,000. The average number of children in a merchant family may be estimated with confidence at not more than 2. Carl Bücher found the average number of children in burgher families in Nuremberg in 1449 to be only 1.81. Pirenne reckoned the average number in a certain quarter of Ypres in 1506 as only 2, and there is no reason to suppose that fertility was any higher in London than in Continental cities.[97] To an estimated 2,000 children in the merchants' own families there must then be added the junior apprentices who were being assimilated into the class. Very few of these, as will be shown later, were sons of London merchants; most of them were from the country. Some boys were soon unhappy in the city and went home, and many died before their terms were up. It is probable that there were at least twice as many apprentices under the age of twenty-one as over it. The number under age who should be counted as belonging to the merchant class would on this basis be 1,400. One more group remains, namely, the merchants' unmarried daughters over the age of twenty-one. There were a few of these, helping to manage households or working in the silk industry, but they were so few that they may be left out of account. The other figures run as shown in Table 3, pointing to a total class size, in 1501, of 6,300.

The same sources, the list of 1501–2 supplemented by other figures from company and civic records and by the names listed in 1537 as a check, give information as to the number of citizens who

---

97. C. Bücher, *Die Bevölkerung von Frankfurt-am-Main im XIV und XV Jahrhundert* (1886), p. 42; H. Pirenne, *Les Dénombrements de la population d'Ypres au XVᵉ siècle* (1903), p. 16.

wore livery issued by the lesser companies. These were the people who felt that they were above the general run of the _mediocres_, who although they were not merchants, as that term was understood, carried on enough trade to acquire the reputation of being substantial citizens, people of upper middle rank. The sources give the figures in Table 4.

The total of 784 is too low bcause the separate items, as given in the civic list of 1501-2, are slightly below the figures that are indicated by the companies' own records and because the list of companies is not complete. Among those omitted are the broiderers, the clothworkers, the glovers, the hatter merchants, the latteners, the scriveners, the shipwrights, the upholders (upholsterers), and the woodmongers, all of which, with the possible ex-

TABLE 3

Merchants in livery	_ca._	700
Younger merchants, enfranchised	_ca._	500
Apprentices over twenty-one	_ca._	700
Apprentices under twenty-one	_ca._	1,400
Wives		1,000
Merchants' children		2,000
		6,300

ception of the latteners and the upholders, had members who were substantial citizens. In 1537 the broiderers and the clothworkers had 33 and 69 members, respectively; a liveried fraternity of glovers had in the 1440's 29 members; and the latteners, in 1421, had 10 men in a fraternity.[98] In all, the 9 companies could probably have brought the number of the more substantial middling citizens up to about 1,000. It is likely that some of the yeomen of the greater companies should be added to this number. Men who were able to keep mercers' shops or high-class tailoring or skinners' shops were above the ordinary run of retailers and artisans. If one allows for an addition of 200 of these, the number of citizen masters of upper middle rank rises almost to equal the number of citizen merchants. It is a question whether many of their servants or apprentices were counted as of the same social rank; yet if there was only one in each household of assured rank and prospects, the number of adult men in this sphere would have come to 2,400, as

98. Coote, _op. cit._, p. 37; Anc. Deeds, B 8003.

TABLE 4*

	Numbers in Livery 1501 List	Nearest Check by Company Records		Numbers in 1537–38 List	Nearest Check by Company Records	
		Livery	Total Membership		Livery	Total Membership
Armorers.......	20			48		
Bakers.........	16			65		ca. 60
Barber-surgeons.	38			185		
Blacksmiths.....	16	ca. 31 (1509)	67 (1434)	25	ca. 25	
Bladesmiths.....	12					
Bowyers........	10			19		
Brewers........	65	73	ca. 185 (1501)	89	51	
Butchers.......	26	102 (1544)				
Carpenters......	30	ca. 40 (1477)				
Coopers........	17		76 (1502)	63	26 (1536)	92
Cordwainers....	26			56		
Curriers........	16	ca. 20 (1496)		38		
Cutlers.........	24	22	43 (1462)	65		
Dyers..........	19					
Felmongers.....	2					
Fletchers.......	11			44		
Founders.......	22	30	94 (1497)	65		85 (1522)
Fullers.........	34					
Girdlers........	21					
Innholders......	16			43		
Joiners.........	14			52		
Leather-sellers ..	33	42	127 (1495)	116		
Masons.........	11			37		
Painter-stainers..	23			53		
Pewterers.......	25		84 (1456)			
Plumbers.......	12			25		
Poulterers......	10					
Saddlers........	33			60		
Shearmen.......	51		60 (1452)			
Spurriers.......	6			20		
Tallow-chandlers	36			99		
Tilers..........	22			90		
Waxchandlers...	17			44		
Weavers........	30		70 (1456)	30		ca. 43 (1536)
Wiresellers......	12					
Woolmen.......	8					
Total......	784					

* See S. L. Thrupp, *A Short History of the Worshipful Company of Bakers of London* (1933), p. 100. The blacksmiths' names and those of their servants are printed in H. C. Coote, *Ordinances of Some Secular Guilds of London* (1871). The 31 of 1509 were all nominated for warden (Blacksmiths' Account Book, 1500–50, Guildhall MSS, No. 2883). The total of 190 brewers does not include 27 servants or 82 new apprentices engaged in 1501 (Wardens' Accounts, 1502–47). The carpenters' paid-up subscription list for their charter of 1477 has 42 names (B. Marsh, *The Records of the Worshipful Company of Carpenters*, II [1914], 53). The coopers in 1452 had 25 in livery, 61 out, and 12 "Duche Cowpers howsholders." In 1432 the marks of 47 coopers had been registered; at the end of the century there were only 30 marks. In 1536 they listed only 12 journeymen not free (Records, *18 Henry VI to 1525; Account Book, 1529–71; Cal. L. Bk., K*, p. 134; *L*, p. 1). In 1501 there were 139 brewers paying the maximum quarterage, 4s.; in 1536 only 116 were fully paid up (Accounts). On curriers see *Cal. L. Bk.*, *L*, p. 314. Only 25 new cutlers were admitted to the freedom of the company between 1475–96. The 1462 figures are from paid-up quarterage accounts (C. Welch, *History of the Cutlers' Company of London*, I, 371 ff.). Founders' figures from quarterage accounts and 1522 list of members (W. N. Hibbert, *History of the Worshipful Company of Founders* [1925], pp. 17, 292). Quarterage accounts of leather-sellers (Liber Curtes). Numbers of the shearmen given on registration of their fraternity rules in the consistory court of the bishop of London, printed in Coote, *op. cit.*, p. 47. *Facsimile of the Ancient Book of the Weavers' Company* gives names of woolen and linen weavers (cf. F. Consitt, *The London Weavers' Company* [1933], I, 124–25). Paid-up membership from 1536 quarterage accounts (*ibid.*, pp. 123, 159).

against an estimated 2,000 in the merchant class. Marriage was as common as among the merchants, the evidence of wills indicating only that families may have been smaller. If all the 1,200 masters were married and had only 1 child apiece, however, and 1 apprentice from the country of equivalent rank, the group would have numbered at least 6,000. A few hundred more children would have made the group exceed the merchant class in numbers. *mediocre*

The number of citizens below this rank is more difficult to calculate. It included about 300 of the poorer yeomanry of the merchant companies. A second group to be counted consisted of freemen of the companies named in Table 4 who were not in livery. Assuming, where there is no other indication, that the numbers in livery and out of it were equal, one reaches a total here of a little over 1,000. A third group was in the 9 companies mentioned as being omitted from Table 4. A conservative estimate would allow these on the average 20 members each, not in livery. This raises the total above 1,200. There were also the members of 28 other companies known to have been in existence in 1501. Nineteen of these—the cheesemongers, coppersmiths, corsours, "ferrours" [probably farriers], fruiterers, fusters, glaziers, graytawyers, linen drapers, lorimers, marblers, netters, pastelers, paviors, pouchmakers, stationers, tapicers, turners, and wheelwrights—are on the list of 1501 as companies having no livery. By 1537 the pastelers had 47 members and the fruiterers 39; as of 1501 the 19 companies could reasonably be assigned an average of 30 members. Mention of 7 other companies occurs both in fifteenth-century records and in a list of 70 crafts said to have been in existence in 1533[99]—the beadmakers, coffer-makers, horners (amalgamated with the bottle-makers), hurers, organ-makers, plasterers, and stringers. Except for the plasterers, these were probably smaller groups. Finally there were the cobblers, who by an order of 1476, confirmed in 1499, were limited to 44 masters, and the minstrels, of whom 6 were licensed as "waits" in 1476 and were recognized as forming a fellowship in 1499.[100] This makes a total of about 2,000 citizens below the upper middle level.

The majority of these, probably at least 1,200 of them, were economically independent masters. If each master was married

99. Harl. MSS, 5111.
100. *Cal. L. Bk., K*, p. 146, Journals, 10, fol. 113; 8, fol. 112; and 11, fol. 320.

and had on the average, in 1501, 1 child in his family and 1 apprentice, the group would have numbered only 4,800 persons; single women in business and those working as responsible domestic servants in merchant households would have brought the number to 5,000 or above.

The remainder of the citizens, the 800 assumed to have been in service with the independent masters or living by piecework, would have had fewer apprentices, and the marriage rate may not have been so high among them as among other citizens. Many of those in service, however, were married and had some kind of home of their own. The bakers' free servants stated in 1441 that most of their number were "weddid men"; it was one of their grievances that they could spend so little time at home with their wives.[101] The group of 800 citizens may therefore be reckoned as accounting for over 2,000 people.

There is no exact means of estimating the extent to which the numbers either of the independent masters or of the dependent masters were swelled by foreigns. At different dates throughout the period fourteen sets of craft ordinances tolerated the existence of independent unfree masters in the trade and sixteen banned them. The glovers and the painters complained of an "influx of foreigns" in the latter part of the fifteenth century; the only men to give an estimate of how many unfree masters were operating in their trade were the glaziers, who stated in 1474 that there were more than 28 unfree masters competing with them in the city and suburbs, some of whom were aliens.[102] If there was so appreciable a degree of competition of foreigns with citizens in all the 30 trades in which they are mentioned as masters, they would have contributed very considerably, with their families, to the size of the independent-master group, bringing it well beyond the numbers in the two groups that were above it in the economic and social scale. Without counting aliens, the group may well have numbered over 6,000.

The number of foreigns who worked for wages in general services or in industry or who took industrial piecework escapes direct calculation altogether. In many of their occupations the age composition would have varied from the normal, and the proportion of

101. *Cal. L. Bk.*, *K*, p. 266.
102. *Ibid.*, *L*, p. 119.

married women and of children would have been low. In others, child labor may have been used extensively.

An indirect means of reaching a rough estimate of the proportion of foreigns to citizens is by comparison of the figures that are available for the rest of the industrial and commercial community at the date of our survey, 1501, with the figure that is contained in the poll tax return of 1377. Over much of the intervening period the city's population had remained stationary or may even have declined, but by 1501 it had recovered and was probably larger than in 1377. A total of 23,314 persons had paid the poll tax. The figure was exclusive of aliens, clergy, and children under the age of fourteen. It was made up of citizens, foreigns, women, children old enough to be apprenticed, and lawyers and officials. It is unlikely that more than a few hundred of the latter paid tax as resident in London. The other elements may therefore be regarded as adding up to the round number of 23,000. Detailed returns from other centers, showing the collection both of this tax and the heavier poll tax of 1381, which was widely evaded, suggest that collectors were inclined to overlook boys and young girls living at home, as well as apprentices and the more poorly paid women workers. Only two fragmentary schedules dealing with the collection of the tax of 1377 in London have come to light. One, listing names of persons liable to the tax in ten parishes, credits 305 married couples with only 4 sons and 3 daughters over the age of fourteen, only 78 of the couples are represented as employing servants—67 men and 60 women—and, although there are 54 other single men on the list, it names only 17 other single women.[103] This shows plainly where the tendencies to evasion lay. Apprentices were not counted at all, and many women must have been spared. Analyses of medieval town populations on the Continent invariably reveal an excess of women over men. The schedule is indeed so faulty that it cannot represent anything but a preliminary survey; if the collectors had proceeded on this basis, they would have touched barely half their final total. Another fragmentary schedule, giving a few

103. E, 179/144/6. The schedule is headed as referring to the wards of Candlewick, Walbrook, Queenhithe, and Bishopsgate but incorrectly so, as one of the parishes covered, St. Alban's, is in Cripplegate Ward. Only three other parishes named are identifiable, St. Clement's, in Candlewick; St. Helen's, in Bishopsgate; and St. Swithin's, in Walbrook. The others named are St. Martin's, St. Michael's, St. Nicholas', St. Peter's, St. Andrew's, and All Saints'—all dedications that were duplicated. Over 300 of the people are listed in columns without any parish address heading.

dozen names for Tower Hill, Shoreditch, St. John Street, and Holborn Bar, includes proportionately more servants, up to 5 for a householder.[104]

For the purpose of comparison with estimates based only on company membership, it does not matter if the poll tax return was in the end still short of honest inclusion of apprentices and other young people. The object of the comparison is simply to discover whether the unenfranchised made up a large or a small proportion of the population. In short, how many of the 23,000 taxpayers of the industrial and commercial community may be accounted for by citizen households? Company membership indicates that in 1501 there were about 4,400 citizens. If in 1377 there had been about 4,000 citizens, each of them obliged to pay the poll tax and each having a wife and on the average 1 child over fourteen and 1 servant or apprentice, all equally unable to evade payment, then citizen households would have accounted for only 16,000 of the taxpayers. The foreigns—men, women, and children over fourteen—would then have amounted to some 7,000. This would have been exclusive of the population of Southwark, which was largely unenfranchised. According to the poll tax return of 1381, probably very defective as a census, Southwark then had 1,059 inhabitants over fourteen, among whom were 314 married couples.[105]

Between 1377 and 1501 there was no added pressure to make foreigns take up the citizenship and no other obvious circumstance that would either have increased or reduced their numbers in proportion to the citizen population. If in 1501 there were still as many as before, that is, 10,000 or more, counting their younger children and those who lived in Southwark, they would have balanced off the city's social structure symmetrically, broadening the group of independent masters, and filling out the group of dependent workers.

The alien population further broadened the lower sections of the structure. An alien subsidy roll of the year 1485 lists 15 merchants, 8 holders of beerhouses, 435 householders, and 1,138 servants, that is, in all, 1,596 men. Servants in the brewhouses were exempt and also all Venetians, Genoese, Lucchese, and Florentines.[106] An earlier schedule from the reign of Henry VI, giving the names of

104. E, 179/141/35.   105. E, 179/184/30.   106. E, 179/242/25, 269/34.

some of the poorer alien workers, a Flemish and German group, in such trades as goldsmith, capper, water-bearer, shows a low incidence of family life, only 48 men out of 134 being listed as married.[107] This may have been the normal condition among the poorer English workers also. The alien population in 1501 must nevertheless have been at least 3,000 strong.

The various items that have been collected may now be arranged as in Table 5. The most definite figures are those for the citizens, for the total number of persons in the merchant class, and for the alien group. Uncertainty as to the numbers of children and

TABLE 5

LONDON POPULATION, 1501-2

	Citizens		Estimates of Total Persons
Merchants...............	1,200	With wives, children, apprentices.	6,300
Other citizens in company livery.................	1,200	With wives, children, apprentices. Alien elements of superior rank...	6,000-7,200 500
Small masters and workers..	2,000	With wives, single women, children, apprentices	7,000
		Foreigns, small masters, and workers, with families, including suburban population.............	10,000
		Aliens, small masters, and workers, with families, including suburban population	2,500

apprentices that should be counted makes the number of persons to be reckoned as of substantial, upper middle rank, less definite. The two figures given are reckoned according as families might have had only one child on the average, at the time of the survey, or two, like the merchants. For the smaller masters and workers it has been assumed that, on the whole, marriage was less common and that there were fewer children and servants or apprentices to be included. The figures in the right-hand column of Table 5 are all conjectural, but it is likely that they all err on the side of understatement rather than the reverse.

From these calculations one would judge that the resident industrial and commercial community, exclusive of the ecclesiastical,

107. E, 179/144/73.

official, and floating population of the city, numbered roughly 33,000. This is a conservative figure, possibly underestimating the numbers both of children and of the unenfranchised. In its picture of the structure of the community, Table 5 is also deficient, failing to note the exact distribution of the children among the various groups and lacking any measure of the proportions in which the large lower group was made up of small independent masters and of dependent workers. But correction for these items would not materially alter the general outline of the picture. From the fact that the merchants and the other substantial citizens in company liveries were about equal in number and from the probability that with their families and following the two groups of men made up about a third of the community, it is obvious that there was no very steep social pyramid. Although the more successful merchants constituted a peak of wealth and power, the merchant class, regarded as a whole, was broadly based.

Chapter II

CONTROL OF THE CITY GOVERNMENT

I. MERCHANT EXPERIENCE IN THE ROYAL SERVICE

THE London merchants' political horizon was not bounded by their city walls but extended wherever government service or business might lead them. Their greatest opportunities to play a part on the national stage came in the first half of the fourteenth century. Edward I had brought the country's wool merchants into the limelight by consulting them on the question of supply, and his successors, who like him were forced to rely upon the wool trade for the financing of war, followed his example. The climax of the merchants' power coincided with the outbreak of the Hundred Years' War. As Eileen Power showed in her Ford lectures, this nurtured a succession of adventurous financiers who were able to use political influence in manipulating the trade, to their own advantage, through small closed syndicates. Unfortunately for them, these privileges could be enjoyed only on condition that they constantly advance the king loans that ran into four and five figures, and in the course of two decades the ensuing risks proved to be ruinous. The profits of the wool trade and the risks of financing the government were thereafter more evenly divided among a larger body of men, organized as the Merchants of the Staple.[1]

The Londoners did not control the wool trade and so did not dominate these arrangements. In the deliberative merchant assemblies, which were summoned on a regional basis, they formed only a small minority. It is likely, however, that they always had more chance of government employment than merchants of other ports or interior regions. In the early years of the fourteenth cen-

1. Eileen Power, *The Wool Trade in English Medieval History* (1941), pp. 67-70, 82–85, 90–94, 97–100, 116–18; cf. B. Wilkinson, *Studies in the Constitutional History of the Thirteenth and Fourteenth Centuries* (1937), pp. 55–81, and G. Unwin (ed.), *Finance and Trade under Edward III* (1918), *passim*.

tury a number of aldermen and other leading men held appointments at the king's exchange, in the customs service, and as king's butler.[2] Two men resigned from aldermanries in the year 1322, one owing to pressure of work as a collector of customs, the other because he was occupied with business for the king in the north.[3] Walter Crepyn, son of a city official, was several times employed in the county of Middlesex as assessor, collector of scutage, and commissioner of array, and he also held the important office of king's escheator; Geoffrey de Hertpool was a surveyor of measures in Kent, Surrey, and Sussex, and Henry Gisors a tax-collector in Kent.[4] Some of these men may have been officials first and merchants second; others were primarily merchants who accepted official appointments with an eye to the business connections they might bring.[5] When war broke out with France, it is probable that a number of the greater London merchants were very favorably placed for receiving army contracts. Many of the key men in the privileged wool-exporting syndicates of 1337–50 and their partners were Londoners; some flourished, several suffered heavy losses and terms of imprisonment.[6]

Politically and as financiers the merchants of the next century and a half were lesser men. No comparable combination of speculative business and political influence recurred, and ambition for power was tempered by a justifiable distrust of the royal favor. In Edward III's last years, it is true, and under Richard II events conspired to bring several London magnates into nation-wide

2. Butlers: Adam de Rokesle, 1299–1301; William Trente, 1301–7; Benedict de Fulsham, 1325 (Beaven, I, 377, 380, 383; *Cal. L. Bk., C*, p. 116). Richard de la Pole was king's butler when he took up residence in London in 1331 (H. R. Fox Bourne, *English Merchants* [1886], pp. 37–39). Roger de Frowyk was controller of the exchange (*Cal. C.R., 1313–18*, p. 47). William de Hedersete and William Servat were customs collectors (Beaven, I, 380, 382). All these men served as aldermen.

3. Hedersete and Nasard (*Cal. L. Bk., E*, p. 172).

4. Palgrave, II, Part III, 735; *Cal. P.R., 1321–24*, pp. 124, 225; *Cal. L. Bk., C*, pp. 98, 154; *D*, pp. 229, 236; *E*, p. 76; *Cal. C.R., 1339–41*, p. 177. See H. M. Chew, "The Office of Escheator in the City of London during the Middle Ages," *EHR*, LVIII (1943), 322–23, on this office and on Walter of Gloucester's tenure of it. On his identification with Walter Crepyn, alderman, see Appen. A.

5. As, e.g., Roger de Frowyk and William Servat (*Cal. C.R., 1313–18*, pp. 124, 524; *Cal. P.R., 1307–13*, p. 461). Many of the offices were without salary. On the whole problem of the status, influence, and remuneration of amateur officials at this time see W. A. Morris and J. R. Strayer (eds.), *The English Government at Work, 1327–1336*, II (1947), esp. 17–35, 156–67, 175–77.

6. Power, *op. cit.*, pp. 115–19. John Malewayn, one of those who suffered most severely, was a London alderman.

fame: William Walworth, through the firmness of his conduct in opposing the rebels of 1381; John Philpot, through his generous contributions to national defense; and Richard Lyons and Nicholas Brembre, as two of the most hated and unfortunate of the royal supporters.[7] These and other leading citizens acquired influence in official circles through coming to the government's assistance with loans.[8] Yet during this reign and the next three no one merchant, either in London or elsewhere, lent the government more than £2,000 or £3,000 at a time, a modest fraction of William de la Pole's maximum advance of £18,000.[9] It was only during periods of relatively weak government that men were called upon individually for loans; at other times adequate corporate loans could be raised.[10] It may be inferred that the political influence and prospects of wealthy merchants were in inverse ratio to the strength of the government and that they suffered a marked decline toward the end of the century.

The merchant did not aspire to a political career. The tangible favors for which he looked were in the shape of business for the royal household, military victualing contracts, and minor offices of profit. While still a young man, Richard Whittington was supplying the Great Wardrobe with quantities of cloth of gold, embroidered velvet, and other valuable mercery, running to well over £1,000 in a year.[11] William Estfeld, another London mercer, who on account of many financial services rose high in the favor of Henry VI, had the opportunity of selling the king the great jewel known as "the George."[12] Two other mercers and aldermen, Hugh Wyche and John Lok, engaged in a great deal of business for Henry VI's household; and during the same reign Thomas Walsingham, a vintner, resigned his aldermanry on account of the pressure of royal business.[13] Throughout the Hundred Years' War numbers of men from the chief London companies went to France to organize supplies at vital centers of defense, and others were

7. Most histories of the period list chroniclers' references to these men.

8. See *Cal. C.R., 1377–81*, p. 31; *Cal. L. Bk., H*, pp. 79–81, 87, 88; *I*, p. 28.

9. Power, *op. cit.*, pp. 119–20.

10. A. Steele, "The Receipt of the Exchequer, 1413–32," *Cambridge Historical Journal*, VI, 46–47.

11. E, 101/402/13, *mm.* 3–5.

12. The sum of 1,000 marks was set aside for this purchase (F. Devon, *Issues of the Exchequer* [1837], p. 437).

13. *Cal. P.R., 1452–61*, p. 511; *Hist. Parl. B.*, pp. 548–49; *Cal. L. Bk., K*, p. 109.

posted to Guernsey, to Ireland, and to Berwick on similar business.[14] Some sought office at the mint or in the customs service or
contrived to use royal influence in winning an appointment as one
of the public weighers or measurers in the city; some were rewarded with a minor court office that carried a title of rank, as
yeoman or serjeant or king's esquire, but did not require actual attendance at court. One of Henry VI's financial agents, Richard
Joynour, a grocer who was active in trade and money-lending, held
temporary appointments both in the customs service and at the
mint and was given the rank of king's esquire. Richard Hakedy,
another grocer, combined the posts of apothecary to the king,
serjeant of the chandlery, and garbler of spices in London, Southampton, and Sandwich; he also obtained a life pension fourteen
years before his death of 40 marks a year and held the rank of
king's esquire.[15]

The king often employed merchants in diplomatic negotiations
abroad concerning trade, and in such cases it was usual to include
one or two of the leading London men. These missions represented
perhaps the most important political service that merchants had
an opportunity of performing, but they carried little or no reward
save the honor of being associated with the king's close advisers.[16]
Again, wealthy Londoners were sometimes called upon to lend
their services on various commissions, not only in London but in
neighboring counties also. Estfeld was a justice of the peace in
Hertfordshire for the last twelve years of his life and was on several commissions in that county and in Kent.[17] Most merchants

14. Pultney, Henry Darcy, John de Oxenford, and other Londoners were among the
first contractors in the opening phase of the war (*Cal. C.R., 1337-39*, p. 458). The patent
rolls and French rolls contain numerous references to victualing contracts, but it would be
difficult to compile a list of the contractors, since many men alleged that they were going
abroad as victualers merely in order to obtain writs of protection, which would prevent
creditors from suing them.

15. On Hakedy see *Cal. P.R., 1436-41*, p. 525; Kingdon, II, 291; *Rot. parl.*, V, 191b; cf.
Grocers of London, p. 259. He was succeeded as king's apothecary and garbler by another
grocer with the rank of yeoman of the chamber (*Cal. P.R., 1452-61*, p. 334). The next
garbler was also a grocer, appointed by influence of the treasurer of the king's household
(L. Bk., *L*, fol. 5b). Henry Barton, skinner, possibly the alderman of that name, was pur-
veyer of furs and pelts for over twenty years, with the rank of king's serjeant, salary of a
shilling a day, and livery of a serjeant of the wardrobe (*Cal. C.R., 1401-15*, p. 408; *Cal. P.R.,
1429-36*, p. 287). On Joynour see *Cal. P.R., 1445-52, passim*.

16. Diplomatic agents were not necessarily men of high station; king's yeomen could
be used, and king's clerks were prominent in embassies (H. S. Lucas, in *The English Government at Work, 1327-36*, ed. W. A. Morris, I [1940], 310-14).

17. *Hist. Parl. B.*, p. 304.

would probably have welcomed appointments of this kind in which they served side by side with the county gentry, but they shrank from the unpopular work of collecting taxes outside the city, some going so far as to buy grants of exemption.[18]

Finally, it was the merchants who exercised the privilege of representing the city in parliament. Foremost among the qualifications desired in members was a good knowledge of civic affairs. More than half the men elected for London during the fourteenth century were already members of the court of aldermen, and all the city's fifteenth-century representatives were either aldermen or city recorders or merchant members of the common council.[19] It was almost equally important for them to have an understanding of the wool trade, on which the national finances so largely depended. Men who had both sets of qualifications would be sent to several parliaments. Forty-five per cent of the fourteenth-century members served once only, but 27 per cent attended from three to seven parliaments.[20] The latter group, with few exceptions, consisted of great wool merchants, firmly seated in the court of aldermen. Some, like Anketin Gisors, were of old-established London families; one, Robert de Kelesey, had legal experience as common pleader for the city; and others, such as John Hadley, who had the distinction of being elected four times in succession, were among the chief creditors of the crown. Some had also been singled out, either by individual royal summons or by election, to attend the special assemblies that met at intervals during this century to discuss trade and taxation. These, therefore, were men of considerable political experience and training. The men who represented London in the next century were on the whole less experienced. Not only did they lack the opportunities that the special merchant

18. For examples, including exemptions from being put on assizes and juries and from being made constable, mayor, collector, or any other officer, see *Cal. P.R.*, *1408-13*, p. 287; *1436-41*, p. 468; *1494-1509*, p. 130. Geoffrey Feldying, mercer, bought a blanket exemption from serving on grand assizes, as customer, as knight of a shire or citizen in parliament, as mayor, and from compulsion to take up knighthood (*ibid.*, *1441-46*, p. 331). Yet he became both a member of parliament and mayor after this date. By charter of 1462 aldermen of London who had been mayor were exempt for life, and other aldermen during their term of office, from serving outside the city on assizes, juries, inquisitions, etc., and from offices outside the city in connection with taxation (*Cal. Ch. R.*, VI, 189).

19. See lists in Beaven, I, 263, 273.

20. Based on elections to forty-one parliaments between 1305 and 1351 and on Miss M. McKisack's calculations for the latter part of the century, in *The Parliamentary Representation of the English Boroughs* (1932), pp. 40-41. Total members counted, 139; number elected three times or more, 38.

assemblies had offered, but 60 per cent of them were elected to one parliament only; nearly 23 per cent, however, attended from three to six sessions.[21]

There is no reason to suppose that the Londoners were indifferent to parliament or reluctant to take part in it. As early as 1328 the mayor and aldermen are found advising the king that a parliament ought to be held to consider the affairs of the kingdom and should be held at Westminster.[22] They were concerned not merely because the sessions brought business to the city but also because they provided a valuable medium both for protesting against infringement of the city's franchise and for pushing various private interests.[23] The men who were elected to represent the city were evidently anxious to make as dignified an appearance as possible and were encouraged to do so. By 1388 they were accustomed to outfit themselves and their servants with new clothes for the occasion at the city's expense; and when parliament met in the provinces, they were voted further liberal allowances to cover the costs of traveling and hostelry. The four who attended the parliament held at Cambridge in 1388 rented and furnished a house there, hired a staff of household servants, and bought so much wine that they should have been able to entertain handsomely.[24] In the negotiation of city business, members sometimes had the assistance of citizen committees, and money might be subscribed through the companies to help in overcoming the opposition of officials. During the session of 1429–30 the diplomacy and influence of William Estfeld, then mayor, and a fund subscribed in part by the mercers enabled the members to win the city's legal exemption from restrictions that a recent statute had placed on apprenticeship.[25]

21. Based on 220 elections between 1403 and 1497, in which 123 men were chosen, 28 of them three times or more (see Beaven, I, 270–73; cf. McKisack, *op. cit.*, pp. 64–65).

22. *Cal. P. & M. Rolls*, I, 69.

23. The attitude of burgesses to parliament is fully discussed in McKisack, *op. cit.*, esp. pp. 22, 42–43, 133–45.

24. *Ibid.*, pp. 82–86. They spent £112 7s., not including the cost of pewter ware bought for them by the chamberlain.

25. On committees of 1460 and 1472 see *Hist. Parl. B.*, p. 153 (Cantelowe), p. 590 (Middleton); McKisack, *op. cit.*, p. 137. On lobbying by the grocers, mercers, and merchant adventurers see Grocers of London, p. 257, *Mercers' Acts*, pp. 50, 117–18, 198. The interests of these groups kept them also in close touch with exchequer officials; small presents passed, such as a gift of three pounds of pepper and a loaf of sugar to the remembrancer (Kingdon, II, 307, 346, 348; cf. C. H. Haskins and M. D. George, "Verses on the Exchequer in the Fifteenth Century," *EHR*, XXXVI, 58–62).

Except in regard to local affairs, the London members do not appear to have been very active in parliament. Neither, for that matter, were other burgess members; the landed knights and gentry were in the habit of taking the lead.[26] Only one Londoner was elected as speaker; this was a lawyer, Sir Thomas FitzWilliam, city recorder; and at the time, in 1489, he was representing not London but Lincolnshire.[27] Nevertheless, two of the London members in the Good Parliament, Walworth and Pyel, had shown themselves capable of taking a firm stand.[28]

Election to parliament must from the very first have been useful and gratifying to men who wished to become better known and to attract the patronage of powerful lords. The exertion of strenuous efforts to climb the ladder of noble and official favor may help to explain the fact that several Londoners were elected to fourteenth-century parliaments for other constituencies. Walter Crepyn sat twice for Middlesex, and Nicholas Exton, later in the century, four times; Sadlingstanes, city recorder, and Fastolf, a fishmonger, sat for Northumberland and Yarmouth, respectively, where each had close personal connections; Richard de la Pole for Hull and for Derbyshire, Richard Lyons for Essex, and John Northampton for Southwark.[29] The stormy partisanship of the next century measurably enhanced the value of a parliamentary seat, both governments and their enemies being anxious to pack the commons with supporters. Careerist lawyers and officials took over the representation of many of the smaller boroughs, with the result that burgesses sitting for their native towns, who had formerly made up the majority of the commons members, dwindled into a minority.[30] At the same time, a number of merchants joined the ranks of the careerists. Between 1445 and 1491 at least twenty-six London merchants were elected to represent other boroughs, chiefly in the south and west. At least ten of these men, and a

26. McKisack, *op. cit.*, p. 120.

27. Beaven, I, 288.

28. T. F. Tout, "Parliament and Public Opinion, 1376–88," in *Collected Papers*, II, 179.

29. See Beaven, I, 298. Beaven's other identifications are less certain.

30. Of the 194 borough members returned in 1442 only 116 were resident burgesses, constituting 43 per cent of the total membership of the commons in that year; there were in addition a few merchants representing shires (*Hist. Parl. Register*, pp. 32–43). In the parliaments of 1472–75 and 1478 only half the borough members were genuine burgesses (McKisack, *op. cit.*, pp. 106–12).

number of others who sat for London only, held offices or grants of some kind under the crown.[31]

Indirectly, through contributing materially to build up their prestige, these connections with the machinery of royal government made it easier for the merchants to retain a firm hold on the municipal government. The net effect on their political outlook probably varied widely at different periods and with different individuals. But parliamentary sessions, lasting as they sometimes did only a few days, at most only a few weeks, were too brief to mature men's political education or produce a truly national point of view. It was only in exceptionally dynamic sessions, as in 1311 and 1376, that any stir of political thinking seems to have been communicated to London. Otherwise, as all observers have noted, a stolid absorption in business interests and local problems persisted. This narrowness had the countervailing advantage of blanketing the majority of the citizens in indifference to the dynastic factions of the fifteenth century.

2. PROBLEMS INHERITED FROM THE THIRTEENTH CENTURY

Before considering the merchants' conduct of municipal affairs in the two centuries under review, one must in fairness recall that they had inherited power from their predecessors under difficult circumstances. Although systematic progress had been made in the differentiation of the work of the courts of justice,[32] as late as the mid-thirteenth century the constitutional framework within which these functioned was little better than a confused accumulation of ambiguous precedent and privilege. The citizens had long been recognized as forming a body corporate, with the right to appoint their own mayor and sheriffs, but the charters granting these rights neglected either to define the meaning of citizenship or to prescribe the methods of appointment.[33] The resulting freedom of

31. *Hist. Parl. Register*, pp. 134, 136, 141, 168, 171, 173, 234, 286, 309, 329, 331, 362, 409, 412, 417, 420, 422, 433, 437, 446, 464, 473, 489, 553, 556, 559, 562, 579, 609. The number includes some, such as John Payn, elected for Southampton, who had property and citizenship in the constituency. During the same period at least 20 London lawyers sat for other constituencies.

32. For an account of the evolution of the court of husting, the sheriff's court, and the mayor's court at this period see A. H. Thomas, *Cal. E.M.C.R.*, Introd.

33. Henry I had granted the right to farm the sheriffwicks of London and Middlesex; this was confirmed by John, whose last charter, in 1216, specified that a mayor should be elected annually (see *Lib. Alb.*, I, 128–29, 133–34).

development and growth of custom suffered, in the latter years of the reign of Henry III, a rough check. Then and throughout the next two reigns royal supervision became close and exacting, so that the magistrates in office had continually to be on the defensive against interference with traditional liberties. The king's hand was always beside them in the person of the coroner and tended to intervene more and more in the person of the escheator.[34] For two prolonged periods, from 1265 to 1270 and from 1285 to 1298, the mayoral elections were arbitrarily suspended and a royal warden placed in charge of the city. During the interval of free government the king's control was adroitly extended by the device of compelling the mayor and sheriffs to shoulder more responsibility for keeping peace and order.[35]

While the officials in power were thus harassed by the central government, they had also to face trouble within London itself. The successive attempts that were made by Henry III and the party of De Montfort to win genuinely popular support in the city gave new heart to all who were discontented. One of the chief objects of resentment was the secretive control that the ruling oligarchy maintained over the mayoral elections. Whereas both Henry I and John had granted the appointment of sheriffs to the citizens at large, the right of choosing the mayor had been assigned to "the barons" of the city. It is not clear whether this term had any precise meaning, but there is reason to believe that mayoral elections had been managed from the beginning by an exclusive group.[36] The fact that in the thirteenth century the citizen body was not well defined would have made this all the easier. The privileges of which citizens were assured by royal charter were of interest mainly to merchants; hence, until there were fur-

34. The office of coroner was exercised in the city by the king's chamberlain, who was also the king's butler (R. Sharpe, *Cal. L. Bk., B,* p. vii; *E,* pp. iv, v, n. 1; G. Norton, *The City of London* [3d ed., 1869], p. 318; see Chew, "The Office of Escheator," *op. cit.,* pp. 320–24).

35. For an account of the steps taken, which constituted an important move toward the development of the system of justices of the peace, see Thomas, *Cal. E.M.C.R.,* pp. x–xxi.

36. W. Page, *London, Its Origin and Early Development* (1923), p. 224. A. H. Thomas (in his *Cal. P. & M. Rolls,* II, xxi–xxiii), disagreeing with Page (*op. cit.,* pp. 120, 122, 219–21, 224–29), urges that there was no distinction between the terms "baron" and "citizen." J. Tait (in *The Medieval English Borough* [1936], pp. 256–62) argues from analogy with the Cinque Ports that "the barons of London were those who held land in the city and contributed to all the city's expenses."

ther tangible advantages in taking up the freedom of the city, it is probable that few of the ordinary craftsmen troubled to apply. In any case their political status might have remained doubtful, because there was no systematic method of recording admissions to the freedom.[37] But, during the crucial years between 1261 and 1265 and again in the next decade, the dramatic leadership of Thomas FitzThomas and Walter Hervey roused a formidable political consciousness in hitherto apathetic sections of the population. Whether or not their followers were all actually citizens, they demanded voting power as their right. At the re-election of FitzThomas as mayor in 1263 it is noted, as though it were a revolutionary innovation, that the choice was made by the people, with scant regard for the wishes of the aldermen and the principal men; at the attempted re-election of Hervey, in 1272, the aldermen fought back with the claim that the choice of mayor ought to lie solely with them, in their capacity as heads and judges.[38] Further dissension arose from the belief that the administration was corrupt. Henry III had played into the hands of the popular leaders by causing six of the aldermen to be removed, in 1257, on charges of irregularity in the assessment of tallage, and the issue dragged on drearily.[39]

Unwin believed the true nature of the forces with which the aldermen were opposed to be concealed in the fact that both these popularly elected mayors favored the formation of crafts.[40] This process had formerly been held in check, and after Hervey's fall it was again repressed. The new political ferment may well have centered in groups of retailers and craftsmen anxious to maintain prices by restricting production. Such people, naturally including the more prosperous craftsmen, would have been among those most resentful of dishonesty in the handling of taxation. In this they would have had the alliance of merchants outside the aldermanic circle. In respect to other grievances they had also the enthusiastic support of the poorer inhabitants of the city. Fitz-Thomas gave free rein to hatred of the landlord and the usurer by his energy in challenging the right of the rich to block public lanes and build tenements on public lands, and he permitted the mob,

37. See Thomas, *Cal. P. & M. Rolls*, II, xxviii.
38. *De antiquis legibus liber*, Camden Society, No. 34 (old ser., 1846), fol. 132*b*.
39. *Ibid.*, fols. 72*b*–75*b*, 163.
40. Unwin, pp. 63–65.

or so his enemies declared, to break into the houses of Caorsin merchants and wealthy citizens.[41]

Toward the end of the century these tensions subsided, although the underlying antagonisms were not entirely resolved. It is true that opposition to the spread of crafts gradually weakened. The aldermen no longer felt the same concern for keeping down prices in the interest of the consumer and the alien merchant buyer, because they had been increasing their own stake in general trade.[42] The leadership of the craft movement had remained with the relatively prosperous trading manufacturers and retailers of victuals, with whose interests the great fishmongers and cloth merchants were able to sympathize. The cloth merchants, moreover, were coming to depend less on town workers and to deal more with country clothworkers;[43] for this reason they may have felt more willing to tolerate the growth of organization among town workers. Thus the edge was wearing off some of the old hostilities.

Edward I's influence in the city was exerted chiefly on the behalf of alien merchants and toward combating violence and crime. From 1281 the mayor was given broad powers of summary jurisdiction in breaches of the peace.[44] While the mayoralty was suspended, the wardens tightened up the customary arrangements for setting guards at the city gates and for patrolling the streets at night, and they sought to introduce a kind of police registration system, to be worked out by employers in each trade. The employers were to indict all workers on their lists who might be under suspicion of disloyalty and to present them in their wardmote, after which they were to be arrested by the alderman of the ward.[45] The picking-up and presentment in the wardmotes of suspicious and disorderly characters had never been so highly organized before but had been left to the action of neighborhood opinion. Nor had it been so directed against hired workers. The new scheme was probably unpopular, for the mayor and aldermen, as a judicial court, were most reluctant to take action under it.[46] Much to the

41. *De antiquis legibus liber*, fol. 85*b*.

42. Unwin, pp. 58–59, 67–68.

43. On this change see E. M. Carus Wilson, "An Industrial Revolution of the Thirteenth Century," *Ec. H.R.*, XI (1941), 39–60.

44. See Thomas, *Cal. P. & M. Rolls*, I, xv–xxiii.

45. Riley, *Memorials*, p. 35; *Cal. L. Bk.*, *B*, pp. 240–41.

46. Thomas, *Cal. P. & M. Rolls*, I, xx–xxiii.

indignation of the king's justices, they were also unwilling to set
a watch over felons who had taken sanctuary, although it was
notorious that the latter frequently escaped.[47]

Royal intervention may have helped to raise standards of
honesty and efficiency in the conduct of city business,[48] but it
failed to advance the solution of any of the constitutional problems that were coming to a head in the latter part of the thirteenth century. One of the most pressing of these concerned the
mode of election of mayor and sheriff. In 1285 and for several years
thereafter the citizens' right to choose their own sheriffs was arbitrarily suspended, appointments being made by the exchequer
officials; later the warden allowed them to be elected in special
citizen assemblies convened from the wards for that purpose.[49] On
the restoration of the mayoralty in 1298, the new mayor was elected in a similar assembly consisting of twelve citizens from each
ward.[50] In neither case were any rules laid down to govern future
procedure in nomination or voting. The way therefore remained
wide open for the steering of elections by interested aldermen. The
mode of election of the aldermen was a still more delicate problem. They were supposed to be chosen by the men of the wards,
but no details of the procedure are on record. It is clear only that
the wards had no means of getting rid of aldermen who became unpopular and did not wish to resign. The mayor could remove an
alderman, but he rarely did so except under the orders or advice
of the king.[51] In 1293 the warden took the novel step of ordering a
general aldermanic election. This may temporarily have cleared
the air, but it was a mere gesture that cautiously avoided the

47. Sharpe, *Cal. L. Bk., B*, pp. xiii–xiv, 215.

48. E.g., in 1273, in insisting upon fining a corrupt sheriff whom the mayor had merely
removed from office (*De antiquis legibus liber*, fol. 138a). In 1303 a citizen was accused of
remarking, in disrespect to the ruling mayor, that he wished to God the royal warden was
still in charge of the city, because under him business was dealt with speedily (*Cal.
E.M.C.R.*, pp. 147–48).

49. *Cal. L. Bk., A*, pp. 197–98. In 1244 the leading citizens had elected one of the
sheriffs; and the lesser citizens, with the assent of the mayor, the other (*De antiquis legibus
liber*, fol. 66a). In 1278 both had been elected by the mayor and aldermen and "the reputable men" of the city (*Cal. L. Bk., A*, p. 196).

50. *Cal. L. Bk., B*, p. 213.

51. The mayor acted on his own responsibility in FitzMary's case, in 1249; in Hervey's
case he first consulted the king; in 1257 the king acted (*De antiquis legibus liber*, fols. 67b,
75a, 141a). Carpenter held that aldermen were formerly not removable unless they committed some offense grave enough to warrant their forfeiture of the freedom of the city (*Lib.
Alb.*, I, 36).

roots of future difficulty. The elections were made in a single assembly in which there was room only for "the wealthier and wiser men" of each ward, and practically all the men in office were re-elected.[52]

A third problem arose out of the desirability of sounding public opinion and obtaining some measure of popular approval for legislative and administrative policy. There was a long-standing precedent for summoning selected panels of citizens to assist the mayor and aldermen on important matters,[53] and this the royal wardens were scrupulously careful to maintain. In 1285, 40 "reputable men" were under oath to consult with the aldermen on common affairs of the city.[54] They were selected so as to represent all the wards and were well-to-do men. More than half of them can be readily identified as merchants, 4 of whom later became aldermen. But they were not exclusively merchants: 1 was a surgeon and 1 a metal-working contractor.[55] During a single month in 1297 as many as 128 different citizens, merchants and others, were called on to take part in public business, 52 at a meeting held to abolish a peddler's market, and 88, three weeks later, for the imposition of a tax.[56] Yet no move was made to convert these panels into a regular council or assembly that should meet under clearly defined rules.

At the opening of the fourteenth century, then, London was governed by a highly privileged oligarchy of twenty-four aldermen. Neither individually nor collectively were these men responsible to the citizens, nor was there any effective popular control over the filling of vacancies in their number. Sheriffs might be chosen from outside their ranks, but the mayor had always to be a senior alderman. In fact, the only existing curb on their power, beyond their own sense of discretion and responsibility, lay in that of the king. Nevertheless, for the time being they appeared to enjoy the confidence both of the king and of the citizens. There was

52. *Cal. L. Bk., C*, pp. 11–12; Beaven, I, 22, 99, 106.
53. For its early history and speculation as to its derivation see Tait, *op. cit.*, pp. 304–6. A. H. Thomas holds that the councils go back to the eleventh century ("Some Recent Contributions to the Early History of London," *History*, IX, 97).
54. *Cal. L. Bk., A*, pp. 209–10.
55. John le Poter, contracting to build a 33-foot washtub at Ramsey Abbey (*ibid.* p. 172). Another member of the panel, Laurence le Potter, may have been of the same trade.
56. *Ibid., B*, pp. 236–39.

no serious dispute with the royal officials and no open democratic agitation. The same mayor, John le Blund, a draper, was re-elected seven times and in 1306 was honored by inclusion among the courtiers and young noblemen who were knighted with the Prince of Wales.

3. FOURTEENTH-CENTURY EXPERIMENTS IN REFORM

The atmosphere of calm did not long survive Edward II's accession to the throne. A spirit of partisanship soon began to place the aldermen in an awkward position. In 1309 Edward made a bid for London support for his friend Gaveston by requesting the office of common serjeant of the city for one of the latter's servants. He was refused, the post having been hastily filled by promotion of a city servant who had the backing of the earl of Lincoln.[57] During the next two years twenty king's men, royal servants and nominees of royal officials, succeeded in gaining admission to the citizenship either at reduced fees or free.[58] Among the men who as mayor or alderman granted these favors there may have been the nucleus of a king's party in the city; yet during 1311 and 1312 some of the same men, notably Richer de Refham, John Wengrave, and John Gisors, were responsible for conceding similar favors to five candidates put forward by the Lancastrian leaders.[59]

Pressure to choose between the barons' side or the king's did not embarrass the aldermen so much as the rising tide of discontent with their own government. This was in part derived from the same currents of irritation over the increasing efficiency and cost of justice and over the powers of permanent officials, as the Lords Ordainers were seeking to mobilize against the national government. The third and fourth of twenty articles of civic reform that were finally approved by the king in 1319 limited each sheriff's staff of clerks and serjeants to four and sought to restrict the activity of the mayor's court.[60] The latter enabled the sheriffs to prosecute citizens who resisted them in carrying out such duties as

57. Riley, *Memorials*, pp. 69–71.

58. *Cal. L. Bk.*, *D*, pp. 35, 39, 44, 45, 48, 49, 54, 55, 59, 60, 63, 68, 73, 77, 78. Half of them were merchants and craftsmen.

59. *Ibid.*, pp. 53, 60, 83, 90, 95. The new citizens included valets of the earl of Gloucester and of Sir John Sandale and a Frenchman named by the earl of Hereford and a draper by the earl of Pembroke.

60. *Lib. Alb.*, I, 142.

the confiscation of goods distrained for debt or the detection of attempts to smuggle goods up the river without payment of customs.[61] Antibureaucratic feeling was the more easily inflamed by reason of the existence of petty corruption. The officials of the London courts were not abnormally venal for their time. The lengthy inquiry held by the royal justices in 1321 failed to discover any very serious abuses.[62] But there was a universal habit of offering gifts to win the favor of officials that made it extremely difficult for any of them to preserve a reputation for impartiality or for their superiors to enforce fixed scales of fees. Every medieval advance in the organization of authority was hindered by the suspicion and resentment that this practice invited.

The unrest among the citizens, however, was no mere chorus of unconstructive grumbling but gave rise to practical demands for constitutional reform. The Lords Ordainers, faced by an urgent need to insure adequate policing of the city while the parliament of 1311 was in session at Blackfriars, were induced to lend their patronage to the movement. In August of that year they came in person to an assembly convened at the Guildhall by Mayor Richer de Refham. Twelve citizens from each ward had been summoned, and fourteen aldermen were in attendance. This meeting proceeded to lay down the principle that aldermen were individually responsible to the men of their wards. Should they neglect to consult with them or to assemble the regular wardmotes, it was officially ordained that they be removed from office.[63] Seven months later a meeting of "good men of the Commonalty" at which John Gisors, then mayor, and eight of the aldermen presided, laid down the further principle that the mayor and aldermen were collectively responsible to the citizens at large. For the first time it was ordained that they must obtain the unanimous consent of a citizen assembly before setting the common seal on any document of importance; the seal, for safety, was to be kept under six locks, the keys being distributed among three aldermen and three other citizens.[64]

The reformers stopped short of hammering out a constitution

61. On the history and functions of the mayor's court see Thomas, *Cal. E.M.C.R.*, Introd., esp. pp. xxi–xxiv.

62. *Ibid.*, pp. xliv–xlv. 63. *Cal. L. Bk., D*, p. 286.

64. This ordinance was later approved by another meeting of the mayor and 14 aldermen (*ibid.*, pp. 283, 284).

for the citizen council. How it was to be chosen, how often it should meet, and how large an attendance should be required for the transaction of different types of business—elections, administrative business, legislation—were left as matters for experiment. In the past the numbers called had varied with the nature of the affairs in hand. A committee of seven, chosen "on behalf of the commonalty," had in 1299 sufficed to authorize the dispatch of a mission to the king; whereas for the election of members of parliament an assembly of twelve men from each ward was considered proper.[65] Often the clerk on duty did not trouble to count the exact number in attendance, contenting himself with noting vaguely that "good men of the commonalty" had appeared. Sometimes he stated that the whole commonalty was present in the Guildhall. Since the idea of representation was in mind, this probably meant that representatives had come from all the wards.

The only radical change to be attempted was the experiment of shifting the basis of representation for one of the councils that met in December, 1312, from the wards to the crafts.[66] The main object at the time may have been to lessen aldermanic control over the choice of members, an aim which would have appealed to the more extreme reformers on general principles but would not have appealed to those who had vested interests in any existing forms of corruption.[67] Whether from this cause or not, election by craft failed to establish itself. Ten years later another change was authorized to the effect that the councils, at least for legislative work, should be cut to a standing panel of forty-eight members, two to be elected in each ward. Although expressly designed "to save the commonalty trouble," this plan, too, was a failure, varying numbers of citizens continuing to be summoned as before. The reference to election of members in the wards has been read as though this right were a new grant, dating from 1322, but the evidence for this interpretation is not conclusive.[68] In any event, there are no detailed records of elections to show whether they were conducted in such a way as would have insured freedom from aldermanic control.

65. *Ibid.*, *B*, p. 74. See election of members of parliament in 1312 (*ibid.*, *D*, p. 289).

66. *Ibid.*, *E*, pp. 12–14. Six or 4 good men from every craft in the city were said to have been present. The total attendance or number of crafts represented is not known.

67. See below, n. 70 and p. 70.

68. *Cal. L. Bk.*, *E*, p. 174; cf. Tait, *op. cit.*, p. 308.

Apparently no plan was put forward for enlarging the basis of popular assent in the elections of mayor and sheriffs. The revolutionary tradition of the days of Hervey, which assumed that any citizen had a right to take part, remained at odds with the conservative custom of allowing no one to attend except on individual summons. Instead of attempting to work out a compromise, the reformers relied on last-minute packing of election meetings with their own supporters. In retaliation their opponents in 1315 obtained a royal writ indorsing the conservative custom.[69]

Nor were any concerted efforts made to standardize the mode of election of aldermen by improving the organization of the wards. This would, it is true, have been a formidable task. The ward was the traditional unit of local government, cumbered with responsibilities for police, defense, sanitation, and general civic administration. Its routine work devolved upon a staff of permanent officials, consisting of a beadle, and as many serjeants, constables, and scavengers as were considered necessary. The mayor exercised a general supervision, but salaries were in each ward paid through assessment on the inhabitants, a system that would have tended to breed a certain amount of petty corruption. The aldermen ordinarily confined themselves to heading arrangements for defense on occasions of emergency and to presiding, once or twice a year or as need arose, over wardmotes called for the purpose of making current civic regulations known and of holding inquests for the discovery of local offenders. All male residents over fifteen except knights and clerks were by ancient custom supposed to attend,[70] but there is some reason to doubt whether they did so regularly. The meeting place was the principal church of the ward,[71] which might not in all cases have been able to contain all the male inhabitants. In the circumstances one cannot be certain that there was any large popular attendance at the meetings at which aldermen were elected.[72]

69. *Cal. L. Bk.*, *D*, pp. 24–26. The election was to be "par les aldermans & par les plus suffiseauntz & plus discretz communeys."

70. On the history and machinery of the wards see Thomas, *Cal. P. & M. Rolls*, IV, xxiv–xli. Grouped juries of 20, representing several wards, presented the names of offenders requiring correction to the mayor, sheriffs, and coroner (*ibid.*, I, 124, n. 1).

71. A wardmote for Farringdon Without was held in 1339 in the church of St. Sepulchre, and special meetings for police and military purposes were held in churches (*ibid.*, p. 109; *Cal. L. Bk.*, *D*, p. 278; Riley, *Memorials*, pp. 143, 500).

72. At the period the elections were probably held in the husting court; in Carpenter's time they were held in the wards. While annual elections were held, from 1376 to 1394,

The two reform platforms of 1312 both stressed the need of greater strictness in admissions to the citizenship. By the first it was ruled that strangers should no longer be admitted by the permission of aldermanic committees but only in a citizen assembly or in the court of husting, and the second added the requirement that strangers have the approval of citizens of the trade that they professed.[73] These demands were obviously prompted by the economic interests embodied in the organized crafts. Citizenship, formerly of little value save to the greater merchants, was becoming a passport to economic privilege in the lesser trades. Almost three hundred new citizens were being sworn in each year at this time, many of them old inhabitants of the city who had not found it necessary to take the step before. Over 70 per cent, not having been properly apprenticed, had to pay charges that in the case of merchants ran up to £5 and in the case of artisans and retailers, who made up about four-fifths of the redemptioners, were often 10s. or more.[74] The fact that aldermanic committees allowed a number of craftsmen to enter for smaller sums or free, in order to please noble patrons or royal officials to whom the men referred them, could therefore have loomed as a serious grievance.

It is likely that the crafts were for the time being acting as political clubs and that the whole agitation for reform generated among their leaders. The most helpful of the aldermen was John Gisors, head of one of the older merchant families in the city, who presided over two of the reform assemblies.[75] Later he discredited himself by imprisoning a number of people who had ac-

---

the ward was probably livelier. In 1388 a citizen was imprisoned for refusing to attend a special meeting of the reputable men of Walbrook (Riley, *Memorials*, pp. 500–502). In the early fifteenth century there must have been some revenue from the fines for nonattendance at the wardmotes, for they were earmarked in turn for a public building fund and for providing fire-fighting equipment (*ibid.*, p. 591; Journals, 3, fol. 55b). The sessions cannot have been very interesting, for identical nuisances and offenders were presented with monotonous regularity for up to sixteen years in succession, nothing being done about them (*Cal. P. & M. Rolls*, IV, 118, 120–21, 125, 130, 133, 136, 138, 152, 157).

73. *Cal. L. Bk.*, *D*, p. 283; *E*, p. 13.

74. Admissions of 1309–12 are listed in *ibid.*, *D*, pp. 35–179. For statistical analysis see Thomas, *Cal. P. & M. Rolls*, II, xxxii. It would look as though a majority of the master-bakers were included, 44 entering by redemption; whereas in 1304 there were only 53 reported in the city (Mayor's Court Roll, *F*, *m.* 4b). Groups of 38 brewers, 35 cooks, 26 cooks, and 23 butchers, 9 of them by apprenticeship, also entered. Over a hundred other occupations were represented.

75. All the lay aldermen were present at one or other of these three reform meetings, but only John Gisors, John de Wyndesore, and John Wengrave attended all three.

cused him of favoring a fraudulent baker.[76] His successor, Stephen de Abyndon, began negotiations for a royal charter to sanction some of the desired reforms. As finally granted[77] in 1319 this made no direct reference to assemblies; it declared that the aldermen were to share the custody of the common seal with elected commoners and that the chief salaried officials were to be elected by the commonalty, but it did not specify the mode of election. It sanctioned craft exclusiveness by providing that strangers were to be admitted to the freedom only in the husting court and must obtain six citizen sureties in any trade they might wish to follow. It also prescribed the startling innovation of annual aldermanic elections; these were to be made a reality by forbidding men to stand for election twice in succession. This radical reform, however, was destined to remain a dead letter for nearly sixty years.

For the last few years of Edward II's reign municipal affairs were overshadowed by the growing threat of civil war. Desperately anxious to keep control of London, the king in 1321 suspended the mayoralty for a few months and maintained restrictions on the freedom of elections until 1326.[78] Despite all his efforts, the city became one of the chief storm centers of the revolution that ended in his deposition. The mayor elected in 1326, Richard Betoyne, was an open partisan of the queen.[79] In reward for his services the city was granted a new charter within a few months of Edward III's accession.[80] This temporarily allayed many grievances by emphatic guaranties against abuse by royal officials and by granting the mayor the office of royal escheator within the city. It also strengthened his judicial power by permanently investing him with the right of Infangthef, that is, with the power to hang thieves who had been caught with the goods they had stolen; the mayor had formerly exercised this power only by virtue of special commissions as Justice of Gaol Delivery of Newgate. The charter did not tread on the delicate ground of constitutional change.

76. Riley, *Chronicles*, pp. 251–52. According to Stow, he and some others in 1319 fled the city "for thinges laid to their charge" (II, 163). He had regained the royal favor by 1324 (*Cal. P. & M. Rolls*, I, 24).

77. See *Lib. Alb.*, I, 141–44. John Wengrave, mayor in 1318, is said to have opposed the charter (Riley, *Chronicles*, p. 252).

78. Sharpe, *Cal. L. Bk.*, E, p. x. In 1321 the royal warden removed 4 of the aldermen, including John Gisors and Stephen de Abyndon (*ibid.*, pp. 138–39).

79. See *Cal. P. & M. Rolls*, I, 11–19.

80. *Lib. Alb.*, I, 144–48.

In the new reign radical reform hung in abeyance. By diplomatically avoiding the choice of unpopular names, the aldermen contrived to keep the mayoral elections in their own hands; assemblies were summoned but merely to hear the decision announced.[81] In the years of profitable wartime trade and finance, indeed, few of their number were anxious to devote time to the steady duties that the mayoralty involved, so that to accept office came almost to wear the aspect of gracious public service. The doctrine that office was a duty had therefore to be stressed, and it was extended also to service on citizens' committees and assemblies. Aldermen became liable to a fine of £20 for absenting themselves without reasonable cause on the day of a mayoral election and, along with commoners, to a fine of 2s. for every neglect to obey a summons to other meetings at the Guildhall.[82] In 1342 the king granted the mayor and aldermen the right to amend city customs, but they did not presume to exercise the power without consultation with other citizens.[83] Policy in the main followed lines agreeable not only to merchants but to the majority of citizen masters. Repeated efforts were made to suppress the competition of the petty dealers who set up unauthorized street markets.[84] The crafts were brought under judicious control.[85] During the king's absence in France the mayor was intrusted with authority to inflict the death penalty for breaches of the peace. This was used on only one occasion, on the command of the regent, and the mayor took the precaution of summoning the extraordinarily large assembly of 528 citizens to give assent to the executions.[86]

Aldermanic elections were in this period conducted at the Guildhall but do not appear to have aroused much excitement.[87] Al-

81. See description of the procedure, given on one occasion when the first choice—Hamo de Chigwell, a former supporter of Edward II—proved unpopular and a second choice was made (*Cal. P. & M. Rolls*, I, 72–73). The size of the election assemblies was reduced in 1346 by scaling down the quotas of the smaller wards (*Cal. L. Bk., E*, p. 174).

82. Ordinances of 1346 and 1354 (*Cal. L. Bk., F*, p. 305; *G*, pp. 22–23). It was also ruled that any suitable candidate for the office of sheriff who absented himself from the city at the time of an election should pay £100 to the man who accepted election in his place and also forfeit his citizenship. This was not enforced.

83. *Lib. Alb.*, I, 153.

84. See Thomas, *Cal. P. & M. Rolls*, I, 1, n. 2.

85. See below, pp. 92 ff.

86. See Thomas, *Cal. P. & M. Rolls*, I, xxvii–xxviii, 128–29.

87. See notices of seven elections between 1342 and 1372, made by unspecified numbers of good men of the ward at sessions of the court of husting for common pleas and pleas of land, on Mondays and Tuesdays, and of two others made at meetings in the chamber of

though family influence lessened, men continued to serve for long terms, running up to twenty-eight years; the average tenure of office, about eleven years, was very little less than the average in the thirteenth century.[88] To what extent the mayors permitted criticism of the conduct of individual aldermen to be ventilated in the meetings of citizen committees and councils at the Guildhall is not known, but criticism outside these meetings was likely to be stamped as malicious or disrespectful and as such was punishable by imprisonment. Extremist opposition and criticism of corrupt practices could thus readily be throttled.[89]

City politics would no doubt have been much livelier if the craft, with its permanently active executive organization, had been allowed to replace the ward as the unit of representation. The experiment was tried on four occasions after 1312—once in 1326, again in 1351 and in 1352, and once at the royal command for a meeting with the king in 1371.[90] One reason for hesitating to adopt it as a regular plan lay in the existence of jealousy and hostility between crafts that enjoyed differing degrees of privilege or economic advantage; several serious intercraft riots had occurred.[91] Again, should the smaller crafts demand representation, the character of the councils would begin to alter. This was far from the desire of the merchants, who felt that they should be in the majority. In 1351, only three of the lesser crafts—the saddlers, cordwainers, and butchers—were allowed to participate, as against ten merchant companies, with the result that the merchants had a majority of forty-two to twelve.[92]

---

the Guildhall on Saturdays (*Cal. L. Bk.*, *F*, p. 71; *G*, pp. 48, 50, 51, 94, 291). In 1350 Ralph de Lenne was elected for Billingsgate by vote of only 12 men. This small attendance was probably owing to the plague. The election was confirmed two years later, presumably by a larger vote (*Cal. L. Bk.*, *F*, pp. 225, 247).

88. Aldermen elected between 1260 and 1300 averaged nearly thirteen years in office. The figure for those elected between 1301 and the 1360's would have been the same had not several of their number been mowed down by the Black Death.

89. A street-sweeper named Straw had been imprisoned in 1299 for saying that the mayor and aldermen embezzled the orphans' money in their charge (Riley, *Memorials*, pp. 40–41). A dyer was imprisoned in 1343 for calling an alderman names (*Cal. P. & M. Rolls*, I, 162). Some of the instances on record may have been merely cases of drunken insolence (*ibid.*, I, 197; II, 28).

90. *Cal. P. & M. Rolls* I, 15; *Cal. L. Bk.*, *F*, pp. 237–38; *G*, pp. 3, 280.

91. In 1268, 1327, and 1339 (see Unwin, pp. 81, 86).

92. *Cal. L. Bk.*, *F*, pp. 238–39. It is probable that merchants had always dominated the citizen assemblies. The following figures are significant if not conclusive: Attendance of 20

The only really strong common front that can be discerned before 1376 is that formed by the employer interest. The more prosperous artisans and retailers were united with the merchants in a common desire to keep dependent workers out of politics and in a feeling that the public authority should at least hinder them from achieving effective organization. On both these points they had the central government behind them. The police register that was planned under the royal warden's regime in 1297 would have served as a means of blacklisting unsatisfactory employees.[93] The civic proclamation that was issued in 1326 in an effort to cope with the disorders produced by the queen's revolution contained a significant order to employers to report all cases of rebellion among their servants and apprentices for punishment, and the following year wardens of misteries were made responsible for keeping men at work and for reporting all cases of disobedience to the mayor.[94] In 1349 the mayor and aldermen became justices of laborers, fully empowered to punish all demands for higher wages with imprisonment. There was trouble in that year between master-bakers and their servants, and a number of cordwainers' men and winedrawers were imprisoned for trying to obtain higher wages.[95] In 1350 a civic code of prices and wages was drawn up, to be enforced by a panel of two to four good men in each ward.[96] Ordinances granted to the whitetawyers, the glovers, the shearmen, and the braelers between 1346 and 1355 all provided for the disciplining of hired men.[97]

Other anxieties besides fear of labor unrest were always present in the minds of citizen politicians and help to explain the weakness of the reform movement. All the cherished local "liberties" hung upon the Londoners' success in satisfying the king that they were able to govern themselves without friction. Moreover, they had the honor and the duty of setting an example to the smaller

in 1305; total whose occupations can be identified, 15; number of merchants included, 12. Names of 33 attending in 1320; total whose occupations can be identified, 22; number of merchants included, 17. Attendance of 167 in 1356; total whose occupations can be identified, 136; number of merchants included, 86 (*ibid.*, *C*, p. 143; *E*, pp. 136–37; *G*, pp. 58–61).

93. See above, p. 63.
94. *Cal. P. & M. Rolls*, I, 16, 34.
95. *Ibid.*, pp. 225–26, 228–29, 231–32.
96. Riley, *Memorials*, pp. 253–58.
97. *Ibid.*, pp. 232–33, 246, 247–48, 277–78.

self-governing cities. London, they were reminded in the procla-mation of 1326, was "a mirror to all England." Among responsible citizens, therefore, the necessity of public order was probably the dominating political idea, dwarfing all others. Large public meet-ings were regarded with nervous apprehension, lest they stir up latent private feuds. The size and density of London's population were felt to enhance the problem to an abnormal degree.[98]

Yet the mass of the citizens could be content with the existing form of civic government only while they were satisfied that the aldermen were in the main acting in the public interest. Toward the end of Edward III's reign they became more and more fearful that this was not so. Rising prices made them suspect that the great merchants were battening on the community, and news of intrigue and corruption at court, doubtless exaggerated many times in the telling, aggravated hatred of the financiers. In 1364 three merchant companies, the vintners, the fishmongers, and the drapers, managed to buy royal charters granting them monopo-listic rights. Immediately a rumor sprang up that the drapers' competitors in the lesser textile crafts were preparing to take up arms and kill all the city magnates and officials. On investigation the story was stamped as a slander, but it is evidence of a state of frayed nerves.[99] The next year brought an entirely new and sinister development in the shape of a monopoly obtained by an in-dividual citizen, the vintner courtier-politician, Richard Lyons.[100] This must have spread alarm and jealousy in merchant circles. Lyons, a man of illegitimate birth, divorced from his wife, flam-boyant in his style of living, and a favorite of Lord Latimer, who threw government business in his way, was not a popular figure in

98. A thirteenth-century writer had defended the citizens' objection to serving on inquisitions by pointing out how much more crowded they were than upland people; hence they were more likely, he argued, to fall to quarreling over their drink (M. Bateson, "A London Municipal Collection of the Reign of John," *EHR*, XVII [1902], 719–20).

99. On the circumstances in which these charters were obtained see Grocers of London, pp. 259–61. For the drapers' charter, dated July 14, see Herbert, I, 480–81. On August 1 a group of tailors, fullers, and members of other textile crafts sought an interview with the king. They were committed to Newgate prison but were released on condition that they inform the city officials of any conspiracies made in taverns or other secret places. On the same day information was laid by a tailor, who alleged that a fuller had told him of plans for an insurrection. The latter cleared himself by oath of a jury from Cornhill, and the tailor was sentenced to the pillory and to a year in Newgate (*Cal. P. & M. Rolls*, I, 276–77; Riley, *Memorials*, pp. 315–16).

100. *Cal. L. Bk.*, G, pp. 192–93, 199. Lyons' public career is eloquently treated in G. M. Trevelyan's *England in the Age of Wycliffe* (1899), pp. 10–11, 24, 30.

the city. In 1374, nevertheless, he was made both sheriff and alderman. It was intended that the operation of his monopoly in sweet
wines be supervised by the city authorities, but from the fact that
a member of the committee appointed for this purpose, John
Peche, procured letters patent associating him with Lyons in the
monopoly,[101] one would infer that the supervision was lax. Peche,
who had been alderman of Walbrook ward since 1349, was known
as an aggressively acquisitive man; he had bought a landed estate
in Kent, was bringing up his son to become a knight, and obliged
a reluctant but rich young ward to marry his daughter.[102] Other
old-established members of the court of aldermen had been making personal enemies. In 1373 an alderman had been assaulted,
and another had been sued at Westminster by a horner who complained of extortion and wrongful imprisonments of citizens of
Farringdon ward.[103] The suit was a futile move, since it was illegal
for any citizen to sue another outside the city without permission
from the mayor and aldermen.

For the time being the discontented elements found it impossible to unite on any policy of protest. Demonstrations at mayoral
and shrieval elections merely called forth a renewal of the royal
prohibition against attending these without a summons.[104] A citizen assembly in 1375 plucked up courage to petition for a reduction
in the sheriff's staff of serjeants[105] but apparently did not lodge any
complaints against the aldermen. Without the bold leadership that
was injected into the situation by the Good Parliament, the citizens might conceivably have done no more than grumble and
debate. The impeachment of Lyons and Peche and Adam de Bury
made it essential for the city authorities to do something to mollify
public opinion. Yet nearly four months elapsed between the parliamentary trials and the convening of a council to deprive these
men of their rank as aldermen.

101. Lyons had obtained a lease of the only three taverns in which the wine could be
sold (*Cal. L. Bk., G*, pp. 205, 318, 320).

102. On coming of age this son-in-law obtained a divorce but was obliged to pay £100
for the support of Peche's daughter. The sheriffs had to put pressure on Peche before he
would settle accounts owing by him to his ward (*ibid., H*, pp. 141–42). In 1374 Peche had
to be distrained for services he owed the duke of Lancaster for some land held from him in
Kent (*John of Gaunt's Register*, Camden Society, 3d ser., XXI, 213). After his death
the duke bought some of his leasehold property in London (*Cal. C.R., 1377–81*, p. 461).

103. Aldermen Walter Forster and John de Chichestre, *Cal. P. & M. Rolls*, II, 150, 154.

104. In 1370. L. Bk., *G*, fol. 254*b* (the same order as in 1315; see n. 69, above).

105. *Cal. L. Bk., H*, p. 12.

The disunity and delay arose from latent opposition between the artisans and the merchants. While the more politically minded of the former were anxious to use the crisis as a means of gaining a share of power, few if any of the merchants were liberal enough to sympathize with their ambition. In the end the situation was skilfully exploited by that enigmatic figure, John Northampton, draper, who set to work to build a party from the lesser crafts. With the help of a handful of associates among the drapers and mercers, he persuaded the mayor to appeal to the citizens through the crafts instead of through the wards. Representatives of forty-one crafts were accordingly assembled as a council on August 1, 1376. They met in a spirit of reformist indignation, deposed the three delinquent aldermen, and laid down the principle that reason demanded more citizen participation in the government: nothing should be done by mayor and aldermen in secret. Councils (from this time usually styled "common councils") were to be elected annually from the crafts, were to meet at least twice a quarter, and were in addition to be responsible for the mayoral and shrieval elections. The mayor and aldermen, most of whom had been implicated in the abuses of the wine monopoly, had no recourse but to give their assent to these changes, and the other merchants present, being in a minority, had to be equally acquiescent.[106] In a fresh council that was promptly elected under the new plan, from fifty-one crafts, the merchants were in a still smaller minority. This council aimed at forcing aldermen to retire after a single year's service and in November was successful in obtaining a royal charter to that effect.[107] If interpreted so as to mean that no man could serve more than once, the rule would obviously have opened their office to wide and democratic rotation, in time giving men of the lesser companies, even artisans, a chance to take their turn. Here merchant opinion balked and Northampton himself drew back. He was present at a small council, representing only thirteen crafts and therefore dominated by merchants, which met just before the first general election in March, 1377, and issued a conservative interpretation of the charter. Unless they had been guilty of misconduct while in office, aldermen were to be allowed

106. *Ibid.*, pp. 36–41.
107. In November of 1376. Recorded in art. 468 of Henry IV's *inspeximus* charter (Beaven, II, xix; Sharpe, *Cal. L. Bk., H*, p. ix, n. 1).

to stand for re-election after a year's interval.[108] On this ruling, the circle of candidates for magistracy would be very little widened. In the election that followed, only two of the new men chosen were members of lesser crafts, and during the whole of the seven years for which the rule remained in force, only two other aldermen came from outside the circle of the great companies.[109]

Northampton must already have made it known that he intended to play on the consumer interest and to work for stricter regulation of the victualing trades, for it was immediately evident that the men with large interests in these trades, fishmongers, grocers, and vintners, were in league to check him. From 1376 to 1381 they contrived to maintain a majority in the court of aldermen. The elections of 1377 gave them only half the votes in the court, but they regained control within ten days by obtaining a royal writ for the deposition of the mayor who was a mercer and by procuring the election in his place of Nicholas Brembre, grocer.[110] To insure a majority in the common council, however, was not so easy. Under the system of election by crafts, and under the practice, which had followed, of voting by crafts, the fishmongers, grocers, and vintners would necessarily have been in a very small minority, even if they had had the support of the lesser victualers.[111] With control of the court of aldermen, this was not a fatal matter, since the council had not learned to assert much power of initiative. But it was unsatisfactory, and the situation inevitably hastened constitutional reaction. In 1379 the elected council was arbitrarily enlarged by the addition of "others of the more powerful and discreet citizens," and the next year there was a partial return to

108. *Cal. L. Bk., H*, pp. 59–60. It was added that any councilor guilty of misconduct should cease to be eligible either for re-election to the council or as an alderman.

109. John Marbone, elected for Tower ward, 1377. A man of this name was an official of the fullers' company and had possibly served as undersheriff under Lyons (*ibid.*, pp. 37, 77; *Cal. P. & M. Rolls*, II, 272). Roger Elys, waxchandler, elected several times for Aldersgate, was a man of wealth, at his death having property in five parishes (*C.W.C.H.*, II, 323). Symon Wynchecombe, armorer, and Thomas Carleton, broiderer, both elected twice, were also well-to-do men.

110. The victualers had been strong enough to put up half the members of the committee of 8 appointed by the council of August 1, 1376, to recommend revisions in the city ordinances (*Cal. L. Bk., H*, p. 41). On another committee appointed early in Brembre's regime to oversee matters of policing and defense and the prices of victuals and armor they took only half the membership; but on a third, set up in July, 1378, ostensibly to supervise the city's liberties, 20 members out of 38 were victualers (*Cal. P. & M. Rolls*, II, 243).

111. Distrust of the lesser victualers is indicated by the omission of the poulterers from both the councils of August, 1376, and of the brewers and bakers from that of August 1.

election by wards. Further reaction was postponed by Northampton's capture of the mayoralty in 1381. He held it for two years, partly by means of influence at court, partly by strategy in appealing for popular support, and partly, his enemies alleged, by keeping armed men at hand on his second election day. He used his power with unflagging energy in the enforcement of price regulation and in attacking profiteers and usurers. This unfamiliar zeal soon aroused fears of social revolution. He is said to have made

TABLE 6*

COMMON COUNCIL MEMBERSHIP

Date of Council	Total Membership	Total Members Whose Craft Affiliation Is Known	Members Identified as Members of Merchant Companies	Members Identified as Members of Other Companies
a) August 9, 1376.....	153	153	57	96
b) March 6, 1377.....	64	64	46	18
c) 1381–82...........	138	138	56	82
d) June 11, 1384......	60	60	44	16
e) July 30, 1384......	268	251	169	82
f) October, 1384......	94	94	70	24
g) July, 1385.........	140	123	86	37
h) 1385–86...........	97	97	69	28
i) March, 1386.......	174	146	98	48
j) 1386–87...........	98	98	72	26
k) August 31, 1388....	209	171	107	64

* Identification of the councilors' craft affiliations has been checked from as many sources as possible. The lists are printed, as follows: (a) *Cal. L. Bk.*, *H*, pp. 42–44; (b) *ibid.*, p. 59; (c) *Cal. P. & M. Rolls*, III, 29–31; (d) *ibid.*, pp. 53–54; (e) *Cal. L. Bk.*, *H*, pp. 237–40; (f) *Cal. P. & M. Rolls*, IV, 85–88; (g) *Cal. L. Bk.*, *H*, pp. 269–71; (h) *Cal. P. & M. Rolls*, III, 122–24; (i) *Cal. L. Bk.*, *H*, pp. 280–81; (j) *Cal. P. & M. Rolls*, IV, 132–33; (k) *Cal. L. Bk.*, *H*, pp. 332–34.

inflammatory speeches to the poor, telling them "that ever the grete men wolden have the poeple be oppression in lowe degre," and to have planned to "put owte of the town al the worthiest" by prosecution for usury. Unhappily, his fear or hatred of Nicholas Brembre, who succeeded him in the mayoralty, led him to keep up an armed following. This not only brought about his own disgrace but discredited the lesser crafts on whose backing he had relied.[112]

Brembre resumed his former policy with the general approval of merchant opinion. In the summer of 1384 a large council, packed for the occasion with a merchant majority, voted for returning to

112. *Cal. L. Bk.*, *H*, pp. 137, 155.

the system of election by wards. The avowed purpose was to insure, as a preliminary committee had recommended, that the
council "be composed of men qualified by means and understanding," and the effect, as Table 6 illustrates, was to establish merchant majorities.[113] The change increased the victualers' representation but did not give them control.[114]

4. THE CITY CONSTITUTION IN THE FIFTEENTH CENTURY

The wealthy merchants soon regained a complete monopoly of
judicial office. Brembre allowed aldermen to stand for re-election
in successive years; and in 1394, "for better government," the
formality of re-election was abolished by parliamentary authority.[115] As had been the traditional custom until 1376, men were
now to hold office for life or at will, subject only to removal for misconduct. The next step was to deprive the citizens of the right of
direct election when vacancies occurred. To avoid "headstrong,
partial and imprudent elections," they were by an ordinance of
1397 restricted to the right of nominating two candidates in any

113. The constitutional changes of this period have been summarized by Tait (*op. cit.*,
pp. 310–13); the economic conflicts with which they were associated were analyzed by
Unwin (pp. 129–51); and the importance of the personal issues between the leading men
concerned is well brought out in Miss Ruth Bird's unpublished M.A. thesis, "Civic Factions
in London—Their Relation to Political Parties" (University of London, 1922). Cf. H. J.
Mills, "John of Northampton's Pardons," *EHR*, LII (1937), 474–79. Some extracts from
the charges made against Northampton at his trial are printed in E. Powell and G. M.
Trevelyan (eds.), *The Peasants' Rising and the Lollards* (1899), pp. 27–36, and in *A Book
of London English*, ed. R. W. Chambers and M. Daunt (1931), pp. 23–31. It had been
decided in February to have a trial election by wards, the size of the council not to exceed
96 (*Cal. L. Bk., H*, p. 227).

114. In councils elected by crafts the victualers had, on August 9, 1376, 35 seats out of
153; in 1381–82, 39 seats out of 138; and, in a smaller council, on March 6, 1377, 18 seats out
of 64. Under election by wards they had, in the councils of medium size, roughly 30 per cent
of the seats: 35 out of 94 in 1384; 32 out of 97 the next year; and 30 out of 98 in 1386–87.

E. F. Meyer, interpreting this period primarily in terms of intergild conflict, assumed
that Brembre was still acting for the victualing interest. Pointing to the rule made in
February, 1384, which barred the admission of more than 8 councilors belonging to the same
craft, he added, "The victualling gilds though few in number were large in membership
and might by use of the ward system obtain continuous control of the council" ("Comments on the Observations of Tait on the Common Council of the English Borough,"
Speculum, VII [1932], 250). This is too narrow a view. The merchant fishmongers, grocers,
and vintners were well outnumbered by their fellow-merchants, and the lesser victualers
were too much distrusted to hope for many seats. Since most great merchants, however,
dealt on occasion in foodstuffs, opposition between the victualing and the consumer interest may have heightened the class antagonism between merchants and the small manufacturers and dealers whom Northampton had organized.

115. Beaven, I, 399; *Cal. L. Bk., H*, pp. 409–10.

ward, the mayor and aldermen having the right of final selection.[116] Any hopes there may have been of achieving a more democratic structure within the wards were thus defeated.

Meanwhile the general state of unrest among the laboring poor, the revolutionary spirit that had given Northampton his opportunity, gradually subsided. Although isolated groups of journeymen periodically organized and agitated for better wages and working conditions in their particular trade, the "smale people" whom he had sought to intrench in the common council lacked leadership and lost their political ambition. Throughout the fifteenth century, London appears to have been stolidly content with merchant government.

The fifteenth-century aldermen were consistently drawn from the wealthiest men in the city and remained in office at pleasure for terms averaging over a dozen years. In these respects their position was much the same as that of their thirteenth-century predecessors, except that they were not fortified by family influence; they were seldom closely interrelated or of old London families. In the exercise of their magisterial powers they were directly responsible only to the mayor, who was of their own number and virtually of their own choice. Otherwise their authority had diminished only to the extent that the traditional custom of consulting representative citizens when it was expedient had hardened into a legal obligation. The conservative regime of 1384 had both confirmed the elective basis of the council and admitted the need of at least four meetings a year. The nature and powers of the council, however, remained extraordinarily indeterminate. The practice grew up of referring to all sessions of the court of aldermen at which commoners were present, even small select committees, as meetings of the mayor and aldermen in common council. Since in 1425 it was ruled that "all substantial persons" who had been allowed to resign from the office of sheriff or alderman should

116. *Cal. L. Bk., H*, p. 436. In John Carpenter's time, *ca.* 1419, it was the custom, when an aldermanry fell vacant, for the mayor to summon all the freemen of the ward to a meeting place within the ward in order to nominate a candidate; if the name proffered was not acceptable, they had the right to make a second nomination within fifteen days, but the mayor and aldermen could reject this also if they saw fit and make their own choice (*Lib. Alb.*, I, 39–40). Sometimes the wardsmen nominated an alderman of another ward, who could then be translated, or transferred to their own. In 1480 it was ruled that no more than 2 aldermen and 2 commoners could be nominated and that no one could be present at the final election but the mayor, the aldermen, and the town clerk (Journals, 8, fol. 234*b*).

sit in all councils, there may often have been very few elected
members present, and these may have been picked quite arbitrarily.[117] Again, the meetings for the shrieval elections, at which the
elective council was supplemented by as many other citizens as
the mayor and aldermen chose to summon, sometimes transacted
business like an ordinary council.[118] How many full council sessions were held in a year, that is, meetings to which the whole
quota of members elected in each ward was summoned and no
others, is not clear. Like the king and lords in parliament, the
mayor and aldermen formed an integral part of the council; the
elected members could take the initiative by submitting petitions
but could never reach binding decisions independently. Sometimes they appear as merely assenting to ordinances that were
made by the mayor and aldermen. Yet it is probable that free discussion was the rule, for ordinances and administrative decisions
made with the assistance of commoners were usually recorded as
the work of the mayor, aldermen, and commonalty or simply of
the common council. On the whole the status of the commoners in
council seems to have been rising. A petition drafted by the sheriffs in 1440 was addressed jointly to the mayor and aldermen and
to "þe right sad and discrete Commoners of þe Cite of London in
þis Commone councell assembled," and other petitioners later
followed their example.[119]

The referring of business to the council was governed by custom
and expediency. The most important right that it exercised, dating from at least 1300, was that of sharing in the responsibility of
checking city accounts. In the fifteenth century the larger sessions of the council regularly took part in the election of the
chamberlain, or treasurer, of the two wardens of London Bridge,
and of two aldermen and four commoners who annually audited
the chamberlain's and the Bridge accounts.[120] Some of its members
were usually present when Guildhall fees were revised or pensions

117. Journals, 2, fol. 54b. The minutes taken ordinarily name the aldermen who were
present but seldom count or name the commoners. A minute of 1440 names 15 commoners,
all merchants (ibid., 3, fol. 766). A large attendance was indicated by reference to "a congregation" or to "an immense commonalty."
118. See Cal. L. Bk., I, pp. 204, 226.
119. Ibid., K, pp. 241, 268, 269, 276, 314, 318; L, pp. 77, 158, 180, 207, 226.
120. It was ordained at a common council in 1491 that the mayor and aldermen should
nominate 2 chamberlains and 4 bridge wardens, from the council would make the final
choice (ibid., L, pp. 279–80).

granted. Vital questions of city privilege were brought before full councils in order to enlist wide public support. As the sheriffs pleaded in one case, ". . . . this cause is every Fremannys cause and þe gode and true kepyng and defendyng of the libertes of this famous Cite is þe welfare of every man þat is inhabitant theryn."[121] Councils also had a share in legislation on other issues in which the citizens at large were normally interested, such as brokerage, public morals, and control of the sale of beer. Yet the mayor and aldermen acted alone in all supervision of crafts and in a great variety of other legislative and administrative work, and the council acquired no new specific rights.

The only open constitutional change made during the century concerned attendance at the elections of the mayor and the sheriffs. In 1467 the wardens of liveried companies, as well as the common councilors, were allowed to attend by virtue of their office; and in 1475 the mayor and aldermen apparently relinquished to the wardens the privilege of selecting extra members, on condition that these be drawn from liveried members of the companies.[122] The new rule was obviously a reform in that it minimized the possibility of partisan packing of the electoral assemblies. It may also have enlarged the attendance, which hitherto had not always filled the great hall of the Guildhall.[123] But it was not a democratic reform in the sense of extending political rights to any new social class. The prosperous mercantile element in the more important of the lesser companies already had a minority representation in the common council. Full council panels ran to about two hundred members, and there was a wide rotation of membership from year to year, which, while insuring that the council should be dominated by merchant members of the greater companies, probably gave all company liverymen a chance to

121. *Ibid.*, *K*, pp. 242–43. A council was summoned immediately on receipt of Henry VI's unconstitutional request that Estfeld be elected as mayor for a third term, and Boleyn's exemption from jury service by royal writ was deliberated in council (*ibid.*, pp. 302, 308).

122. *Ibid.*, *L*, pp. 73, 132.

123. At the mayoral election of 1384 the common council of 94 members had been supplemented by 238 others (*Cal. P. & M. Rolls*, III, 84–88). The largest attendance recorded at any Guildhall congregation was that of 528 in 1340. The capacity of the great hall was probably not much above this. Reference to the figures given above, p. 108, will show that by the end of the century the total number of liverymen was more than twice this figure, and in the merchant companies alone they must already have exceeded it in 1475.

The mayor + aldermen included commoners in the council for decisions in which they needed popular support.

participate.[124] The only additional right conferred by inclusion in the electoral assembly was that of voting for one of the sheriffs, the other being appointed by the mayor; as for the mayor, the commoners could make two nominations, both of aldermen who had served as sheriff, the choice between these two lying with the mayor and aldermen.[125]

The two and a half centuries ending in 1500 had thus seen little alteration in the distribution of power as between social classes. The city government had been controlled throughout by a merchant élite, with the acquiescence and assistance of the rank and file of the wholesale merchants. The mercantile element in the miscellaneous lesser trades, the only other group displaying political ambition, had been held to a much smaller representation in councils and electoral assemblies in proportion to its numbers. It was tacitly accepted that the right to vote must be restricted to the number of voters who could be simultaneously packed into the Guildhall. Had there been any real wish to extend the vote, some balloting technique could surely have been devised. This, however, with its potentially democratic implications, making it possible for all citizens to vote, would have seemed in that age unnecessary and undesirable. It was sufficient that the poorer citizens were legally free to vote in their wardmotes, if they were interested and could be accommodated, at the annual elections of common councilors and at the occasional elections of aldermen. In developing a council on an elective basis London had indeed been exceptionally liberal; save in the few towns that in the fifteenth century copied this part of its constitution, the poorer freemen had as a rule no vote at all. Yet the restrictions upon attendance at mayoral and shrieval elections did not pass altogether without challenge. Northampton's followers complained when Brembre made partisan use of them,[126] and they were defied in the

124. Only 38 of the 202 councilors elected in 1458 appear in the panel of 189 for 1460. Of the 162 in the former list whose company affiliation can be identified, 133 belong to the great merchant companies and 29 to lesser companies; for the 148 whose affiliation can be identified in the second list, the corresponding figures are 112 and 36. Each time there were 20 to 30 members from each of the companies of mercers, grocers, and drapers (L. Bk., *D*, fols. 70*b*–76*b*).

125. The right of making two nominations was mentioned in 1384 and the limitation to former sheriffs in 1406. In the latter year the custom of a pre-election mass was instituted, and elections were sometimes said to have been made by the Holy Spirit (*Cal. L. Bk., H*, p. 241; Riley, *Memorials*, pp. 565–66).

126. Parliamentary petitions No. 7484.

fifteenth century when merchant tailors were seeking support among the lesser textile crafts in their recurrent quarrels with the drapers.[127] Other sporadic disturbances early in the century were said to have been deliberately organized by wealthy men who hoped to escape office by inciting apprentices and journeymen to demonstrate in favor of other candidates. In terror of the revival of intercraft faction, disorder, and labor unrest, the authorities in 1416 therefore prohibited the holding of any political meetings in connection with elections.[128] Sharing these fears, the small free masters were probably quite content to efface themselves and accept their subordinate political role.   *Year of civil unrest*

5. CIVIC TAXATION

Much of the internal civic discord in the thirteenth century was due to the fact that, except in regard to the city ferm, authority in the raising and administration of public revenue was not yet clarified by law. Before the mayor and aldermen could impose direct taxation, they were by custom bound to obtain both the royal assent and that of the principal citizens, and they were not supposed to alter any assessments made in the wards. The liberal charter of 1319 upheld the commoners' control over assessment and also over money produced by direct taxation but did not actually concede autonomous powers of taxation. When these were finally granted by Edward III, they were vested not in the mayor and aldermen alone but in the corporation, that is, in the mayor, aldermen, and commonalty; the corporation was also in charge of a trust which had been set up in the time of King John for the maintenance of London Bridge.[129] The common ownership of other property was not recognized by royal charter, perhaps because no considerable revenue was involved, until 1444.[130]

127. See incidents of 1425, 1442, 1443, 1452: L. Bk., *K*, fols. 40*b*, 205*b*, 214; *The Brut* (E.E.T.S., old ser., No. 136), p. 509. Intruders on the last occasion were committed to Newgate, "where they abode a gret while, and were wel ponysshed."

128. Riley, *Memorials*, pp. 635–37. There seems to have been no excitement over the elections of members of parliament. These took place usually either in the court of husting or in the common council but were sometimes simply managed by the mayor and aldermen (see McKisack, *op. cit.*, pp. 14–15, 30–32, 48–51).

129. *Lib. Alb.*, I, 152; C. Welch, *A History of the Tower Bridge* (1894), pp. 29–33.

130. Pollock and Maitland stressed the appreciation in value of wastelands during the fourteenth century as the chief influence in developing "the notion of a true corporate ownership of town lands" (*History of English Law* [2d ed., 1898], I, 685). In London this development occurred in the previous century, stimulated by the selfishness with which

The sheriffs raised the city ferm, of £300, partly from the perquisites of justice and partly by means of indirect taxation which, falling largely on food and fuel, was regressive in incidence.[131] Their staff of serjeants was unpopular, but dissatisfaction was kept within bounds by the common knowledge that, far from making a profit out of their office, the sheriffs often had difficulty in meeting their full account. Even their serjeants were supposed to be men of independent means.[132]

In the early part of the fourteenth century the ordinary costs of civic administration ran to not much over £100 a year.[133] Mayor and aldermen served without salary, being allowed small privileges, such as that of enrolling their apprentices free and of getting their water supply free; the mayor was also traditionally allowed to admit six men to citizenship, a right that was in 1434 converted into a present of four casks of wine.[134] The most highly paid official was the recorder. In order to obtain the services of an expert lawyer, the city had to pay a salary commensurate with the earnings that such a man could command in the courts; an early figure of £10, augmented by enrolment fees, was in 1310 raised to £15 and before 1419, reflecting the enlargement of professional opportunities, had reached 100 marks. The salaries of the common pleader and the town clerk were in the meantime raised from £5 to £10; that of the chamberlain and his serjeants remained fixed at £10 and £2, respectively. Retaining fees, further, were paid to more than a dozen pleaders and attorneys in the king's central courts.[135] The only other regular expenses were the small salaries of the

the greater property owners tended to block lanes and alleys at their private convenience. See the reservation of a right of way in a grant of license to inclose in 1327 (*Cal. P. & M. Rolls*, I, 46; cf. *ibid.*, II, 174; Thomas, *Cal. P. & M. Rolls*, III, 163 n.; *Cal. L. Bk., F*, p. 159).

131. *Lib. Alb.*, I, 123–48. The reformist council of December, 1312, accused the sheriffs of committee extortion on people bringing victuals to the city (*Cal. L. Bk., E*, p. 13). The form of oath administered to the undersheriffs shows that they were allowed to farm the customs (*ibid., D*, p. 203; *Lib. Alb.*, I, 317).

132. *Cal. L. Bk., K*, pp. 345–46. The undersheriff of Middlesex was supposed to have property in London and Middlesex of the value of 10 marks a year (*ibid., L*, p. 196).

133. Chamberlains' accounts (*ibid., E*, p. 292; *F*, pp. 3–5, 16, 54–55).

134. *Ibid., D*, p. 158; *K*, pp. 180, 372.

135. *Ibid., D*, pp. 233, 313–15; *Lib. Alb.*, I, 43, 47–50. All these payments were supplemented by the issue of liveries. The recorder complained in 1378 that the fees for enrolment of wills and deeds did not amount to the sum of £10, as had been represented, and that a recent prohibition of the acceptance of fees and robes from lords had diminished the profits of his office. His salary, at that date £40, was accordingly raised by 40 marks, but he was no longer to take the enrolment fees (*Cal. L. Bk., H*, p. 100).

ward officers and the upkeep of the Guildhall, the city walls, and the conduits.

This outlay was secured by income from a variety of sources, including the fees charged at the Guildhall; a half-share in amercements in the mayor's court; the customs dues known as murage and pontage; the ferm of the piped water supply; a ferm of 50 marks paid by merchants from Amiens, Corbie, and Nesle; and rentals of city property. It was a fortunate increase in the value of the last item that made it possible to meet the fourteenth-century increase in legal fees. The only part of the regular expenditure that was ordinarily raised by direct levy on the citizens was the relatively unimportant item of the ward officers' pay.

Other taxation was resorted to from time to time as need arose. The heaviest demands were occasioned by the purchase of charters, the payment of the large sums that represented the price of the king's favor, and the expediency of offering gifts to other members of the royal family, as well as to lords and officials. Edward I took £1,000 as a "courtesy" in 1289 and 2,000 marks for restoring the city's liberties ten years later.[136] Edward II took 1,000 marks as a gift in aid of his Scottish campaign in 1311 and another of 600 marks three years later in lieu of tallage, and he is said to have exacted £1,000 for the charter of 1319.[137] The sum of £1,000 was raised in 1371 for a gift to the Black Prince and his consort; Edward III was content with smaller gifts but demanded enormous loans as well as taxes and military and naval contributions for the war with France.[138] Richard II was reported to have wrung the unprecedented amount of £10,000 out of the citizens for the restoration of their liberties, after two years suspension, in 1392.[139] Such demands, coupled with military emergencies, kept problems of taxation well to the fore.

Like all civic problems, these were approached in the light of tradition. It was a principle that all householders should share

136. *Cal. L. Bk., A*, p. 224; *Cal. E.M.C.R.*, p. 38. The initial offer was £500 plus 500 marks (Riley, *Chronicles*, p. 252).

137. *Cal. L. Bk., D*, pp. 257, 307.

138. *Ibid., G*, pp. 275, 331. A petition sent to the king in 1357 claimed that citizens had already lent him £137,000 (*ibid.*, pp. 85, 242–45). Between 1337 and 1369 the city supplied 31 ships, 500 archers, and about 600 armed men for the French war, besides sending 200 men to Scotland (Riley, *Memorials*, pp. 196–99; *Cal. L. Bk., F*, pp. 10–15, 25–27, 32–34, 51–52, 130, 206, 217; *G*, pp. 242–45; *Cal. P. & M. Rolls*, I, 133, 140, 170, 221–22).

139. On Walsingham's authority. Cited by Sharpe, *Cal. L. Bk., H*, p. 381 n.

public responsibilities as equally as possible. All were liable to
special police duties, and all were liable to assessments and even
to labor conscription for the purpose of keeping the city ditches
clear and the conduits in repair.[140] In both cases proxy service
was allowed, but in view of the nature of the work, this was
reasonable enough. When small money levies were required, there
was not much discrimination in rates; for example, when money
was needed in 1310 for police work by the wards, only two rates
were set, of 1d. and 1½d. per household.[141] Tradition also favored
indirect taxation. In the form of murage it was sanctioned by the
king, and it had also the administrative advantage, from the point
of view of the mayor and aldermen, that it could be farmed. The
murage customs, instituted by royal grant in 1276, made it possible to rebuild several sections of the city wall. It is true that they
were unpopular with the merchants, who claimed that they drove
trade to other centers. On these grounds they were in 1319 discontinued, but for lack of any means of raising an equivalent regular revenue they were revived two years later. Although their value
must have been diminishing, as the king persisted in selling exemption to the merchants of both English and foreign cities, they were
in 1330 farmed for 200 marks. At some time during the next generation they were again allowed to lapse.[142] Indirect taxation was
resumed in 1344 through a highway toll at Aldgate and was increased in 1356 by a tax levied in the wards on brewers and retailers and others for military purposes; in the following year tolls
on carts and pack horses entering with goods for sale were taken
at all the city gates to pay for road repairs.[143] It was obvious
that both of these, in particular the latter, were highly regressive
in incidence; the rich used the roads to bring in goods by the cart-
load for their household use, yet were exempt from the road toll.

140. On the history of the city police watch see Thomas, *Cal. P. & M. Rolls*, III,
xxxvii–xxxix. By the fourteenth century, night patrolling of the streets appears to have
been normally left to the beadles and constables, but in all emergencies ward watches were
assigned to duty. Citizens who refused to serve were fined at the mayor's general court
of wardmote (*ibid.*, I, 133; II, 87; Journals, 7, fol. 2b). Common councilors were in 1384
exempted (*Cal. L. Bk.*, *H*, p. 241). In 1379, when no more money could be raised by taxation, householders were conscripted for one day's labor in five weeks on the ditches and
conduit (*ibid.*, pp. 127–28; cf. *E*, pp. 146–47).
141. *Cal. L. Bk.*, *D*, p. 214. It is possible that the salaries of ward officers were raised in
somewhat the same way.
142. See Thomas, *Cal. E.M.C.R.*, and *Cal. L. Bk.*, *E, F, passim*.
143. *Cal. L. Bk.*, *F*, p. 100; *G*, pp. 62, 81.

Indirect taxation, however, could not provide the very large sums of money of which the city was intermittently, often very suddenly, in need. It was therefore absolutely necessary to impose tallage. As in the case of royal taxation, this was measured in units of a fifteenth, worth from £700 to £750, and was normally assessed on goods and chattels. In 1302 assessment was at a flat rate of 18*d.* in the pound; shortly afterward it was increased, being set in 1314, for the second time, at 13*s.* 4*d.*[144] There were serious difficulties in collecting the amounts assessed. Some of the wealthiest and most influential men in the city neglected to pay, with the result that citizens of middle rank, who found themselves distrained and, if they abused the collectors, punished, were likely to feel the whole procedure to be unjust. A taverner who was assessed at 2*s.* toward a gift for the Prince of Wales when he was knighted in 1306 was sent to prison on his admission in court that he had desired the devil to curse and hang the assessors.[145] Refham made a check of arrears in 1311, enforcing at least one distraint, of a horse, on a wealthy citizen and obliging an alderman to pay sums that were owing. But he did not bring all the wealthy tax-evaders to book. Three years later there were several aldermen on a list of those whose pledges for tallage lay unredeemed, and John de Triple, a fishmonger who died in 1324 in possession of property in two parishes and was laid in a tomb he had prepared for himself in his parish church, at his death still owed £50 on various tallages that dated back past Refham's mayoralty. Jurors at the Iter of 1321 swore that Wengrave and a number of the aldermen had been in league to levy tallage only "de mediocri populo," paying nothing themselves, and, further, that in two instances they had kept a third and more of the sums collected.[146]

A third plan of taxation remained open in the shape of an income tax on rents. In 1322, when city debts, accumulated in the recent Iter, amounted to well over £1,000, it was finally decided to tap investment income. A tax of 3*s.* in the pound on rents, calculated to produce £1,000, was combined with assessments on

144. *Cal. E.M.C.R.*, p. 126; *Cal. L. Bk., D*, p. 307.
145. *C.W.C.H.*, I, 311–12; *Cal. L. Bk., D*, pp. 243, 246–47, 257, 273; *E*, p. 198; Riley, *Memorials*, pp. 108–10; M. Weinbaum, "London unter Edward I und Edward II," *Verfassungs- und Wirtschaftsgeschichtliche Studien zur Vierteljahrschrift für Sozial- und Wirtschaftsgeschichte*, Beiheft 29 (1933), p. 175.
146. *Cal. E.M.C.R.*, pp. 126–248.

1. indirect taxation
2. tallage
3. income tax on rents

goods and chattels totaling 500 marks.[147] The merits of this scheme were probably hotly debated, for both merchants and other citizens were divided; some had invested in house property, some had not. The clash of interest among them may have had the effect of drawing more attention to the problem of just distribution of burdens. How the next few tallages were assessed is not recorded, but it was prescribed that a levy of £300 in 1324 be taken "with as little hurt as possible."[148] As early as 1318 the king's military demands had done something to redress the balance of the hitherto regressive taxation, 168 of the wealthiest citizens having had to undertake the equipment of a contingent of soldiers for the Scottish war.[149] A similar arrangement was made in 1340 for the French war.[150] In 1358 citizens were given the opportunity to come forward with voluntary contributions, only those who proved unwilling being liable to assessment.[151] In three assessments on goods and chattels in 1339, 1346, and 1376, exemption levels were set at 40s., £10, and 10 marks, respectively.[152] The rate, in a levy of £1,000 in 1371, was set at 6d. in the pound and in another the next year, for naval purposes, at 3s. 4d.[153]

The democratic interlude that began in 1376 coincided with critical strain on the tax system. The French invasion scare caught the city with inadequate means of defense and no reserve funds. Sir John Philpot's munificence saved the day in 1377, but to put the walls and ditches in proper condition took several years and several thousand pounds of public money. The first levy for the purpose was assessed on chattels and the second on rents.[154] Toward the end of 1378 the withdrawal of a part of the court from London brought about a trade decline that aggravated popular unrest. In order to complete repair of the defenses, there had to be recourse to another levy, of 12d. in the pound on chattels. The committee of aldermen and commoners, mostly merchants, who recommended it, however, did so only on condition that an effort be made to discover some way of raising money that would not in-

147. *Cal. L. Bk., E*, p. 148.
148. *Ibid.*, p. 187.   150. *Cal. P. & M. Rolls*, I, 131–33.
149. *Ibid.*, pp. 93–94.   151. *Cal. L. Bk., G*, p. 103.
152. *Cal. P. & M. Rolls*, I, 116–18; II, 226; *Cal. L. Bk., F*, pp. 143–52.
153. *Cal. P. & M. Rolls*, II, 134; *Cal. L. Bk., G*, pp. 302–3.
154. *Cal. L. Bk., H*, pp. 84, 85. The rate on rent was 21d.

volve taxation of victuals for sale in the city.[155] It is not clear whether this referred to the tax levied in the wards in 1356, which was described as falling partly on brewers and retailers, or to the fact that stocks of victuals were included among the merchandise that was ordinarily tallaged along with other chattels. In either case that part of the tax that fell on victuals would naturally tend to be passed on to the consumer. A gift fund of over £600, subscribed by fewer than two hundred citizens, brought the lords back to town before the end of 1379. During the next two years the equivalent of two-fifteenths was levied on chattels, as well as two rental income taxes of 6d. in the pound, and the road tolls were reimposed. Northampton, who then became mayor, gave the people a respite. The common council of 1385, in which merchants were in the majority, had to face the problem of ways and means again. It fell back on the taxation of victuals, but it also produced a new idea, in the form of a roughly graduated income tax, at 6d. on the pound in citizens' rents and a shilling on noncitizen *rentiers*.[156]

From this time there seems to have been an uneasy consciousness that royal and civic taxation combined to bear very unjustly on the poor. A city chronicler writing a hundred years later remarked that "at every ffyfftene ar Chargid pore people."[157] A few wealthy citizens left money for the relief of poor taxpayers, and others made handsome bequests to the city.[158] One city rector organized a pool of £18 out of which taxes due the king by the poorest of his parishioners should be paid.[159] Although extraordinary expenses were still met from household levies and assessments of chattels as well as by income tax, there were attempts to make the rich shoulder a greater share than in the past. An extension of the Guildhall was begun in 1410 on a basis of voluntary donations; when these ran short, three years later, the work was financed by such means as raising the Guildhall fees for enrolment of wills and deeds, registration of apprentices, and use of the mayoralty seal,

155. *Ibid.*, pp. 108, 116. Northampton sat on this committee as a commoner.

156. *Ibid.*, pp. 123–26, 137, 155, 271.   157. *The Great Chronicle*, p. 245.

158. *C.W.C.H.*, II, 61, 307, 418, 514, 575, 577. A mercer who died in 1374 had left 500 marks toward conduit work (*Cal. L. Bk., H*, p. 108). Smaller bequests had been made for this purpose earlier, and the maintenance of London Bridge had always been a popular charity.

159. The parish of St. Michael, Bassishaw, in 1481 (*Cal. L. Bk., L*, p. 189).

and by drawing on the revenues of the Bridge.[160] Payment of parliamentary expenses and other debts was sometimes met by doubling these fees.[161] An old injustice, in the custom of compelling people who lived beside the conduit to pay for its repair, was condemned.[162] Funds for repairing the city walls were raised in 1478 by weekly subscriptions of 5d. from citizens who could afford it; the mayor energetically solicited contributions for alms from all executors and widows whom he knew to have money and carried a collection box about with him on the street.[163] Military expenses were thrown more and more on the larger and wealthier crafts. As early as 1431 the grocers were equipping and paying part of a contingent sent to Calais;[164] in 1450 the leading crafts subscribed a fund of some hundreds of pounds for the city's defense, and in emergency they mustered up to two hundred armed men apiece.[165] A loan demanded by the king in 1486 was assessed by crafts rather than by wards, "for the more ease of the pore people";[166] and when a household levy of 5d. was considered necessary to pay for cleaning out the city ditches, the collectors' instructions ended with, "sparying all poore men by your discretion."[167]

6. THE MECHANISM OF CONTROL OVER
TRADE AND INDUSTRY

The unique feature of medieval urban administration lay in the jurisdiction that city authorities claimed over trade and industry. It was in this sphere that the merchants of Continental cities are held to have shown their most constructive and original ability. The composite code of regulations in which economic policy was embodied in London was similar in its basic principles to Continental codes and may, indeed, have owed something to their ex-

160. Also from fines on absentees from wardmotes and by raising the fines inflicted on delinquent victualers (Riley, *Memorials*, pp. 589-91). This was done for nine years (*Cal. L. Bk.*, *I*, pp. 111-12).

161. *Cal. L. Bk.*, *K*, pp. 292, 331.

162. In 1430. Reference was to the conduit in West Cheap (*ibid.*, p. 110).

163. Mayor Josselyn (*The Great Chronicle*, pp. 225-26).

164. See Herbert, I, 112.

165. Journals, 5, fol. 42. Further grants were made for the purchase of arms (*ibid.*, 6, fols. 199, 207, 208, 209). In 1477 the companies raised money for repairing the city walls. The mercers scaled their members' contributions from 20d. to a mark, but they had difficulty in reaching their quota (*Mercers' Acts*, pp. 96-98, 101, 105, 107). On musters of men in 1453 and 1483 see Journals, 7, fol. 221; Herbert, I, 405; Prideaux, I, 27.

166. *The Great Chronicle*, p. 240.   167. Journals, 8, fol. 154 (1477).

ample. The primary aim, to insure an adequate food supply at reasonable prices, was sought through market supervision; secondary aims included the enforcing of certain standards in manufacture, in protection of the consumer's interest, the prevention of monopoly among merchants and of collective bargaining among hired workers, and the control of brokerage rates. The operation of these policies involved a triangular division of power among king, mayor and aldermen, and elected craft officials. The mayor derived from the king a direct authority over all retailers of victuals and, with the aldermen, assumed by custom the right of veto over all private craft legislation. As has been described above, most of the crafts in time sought direct authorization from the king, not with the intention of disputing the control of the mayor and aldermen, but to secure certain advantages that could not be obtained in any other way.[168] For the most part the relationships between the crafts and the mayor and aldermen were quite harmonious, the crafts fitting conveniently into place as organs of administration, not only in economic policy, but in police work and defense, in community pageantry, in taxation, and ultimately in the matter of elections.

Control of the victualing trades was one of the worst of a mayor's problems, a searching test of his good judgment and integrity. The aim in view was apparently to peg prices, so far as was possible, to traditional levels that were associated with standard qualities of product and to minimize tendencies for retail prices to rise when goods were in short supply.[169] The mayor periodically set official prices for standard grades of ale, beer, and wine and, after inspection of supplies in the market, for meat and poultry; in the case of fish he was supposed to inspect each shipload. The difference in quality in all these commodities and the enormous number of sellers that were concerned made control a very difficult matter. To simplify administration the vintners were intrusted with supervision of the retailing of wine by taverners. The brewers, being independent, were not trusted at all. Aleconners were elected in each ward, whose pleasant duty was to

168. Such as rights of supervision in the suburbs or at fairs or the right to contest competition from other crafts in the city. Unwin's account, dealing somewhat sensationally with internal city conflict, overemphasizes it.

169. A full study of prices and price control in the city was reserved for a volume on the economic history of London in the middle ages, work on which was suspended by the war.

taste every brewing made for sale and to assign it to one of the grades priced by the mayor. Beadles checked the measuring-vessels and were allowed to confiscate a third of any ale that was being sold dishonestly. Despite all these precautions, there were constant complaints that brewers and caterers sold above the official price. Presentments in seven wards in 1422 and 1423 all concern breaches of the assize of ale. This situation was partly due to the fact that the latter made no allowance for differing qualities of service. In sedulously offering presents to the mayor, as their early fifteenth-century books show was their custom, the brewers were perhaps in the main merely buying a general license for the higher class of business, carried on in more attractive surroundings than the alewives who supplied the poor could provide. More serious offenses were punished by imprisonment; and when brewers combined to raise the prices of ale and beer in 1478, country brewers were invited in to compete with them.[170] The sale of meat, poultry, and dairy products, being concentrated in market places, was easier to supervise. The butchers were trusted to co-operate in observing price levels that were considered reasonable, but the poulterers, after complaints raised at the Iter of 1321, were for a long time placed under outside control.[171] The price of bread was controlled by tying it, through a test of baking costs conducted at the expense of the craft of bakers, to the price of grain. In theory the baker was allowed a sufficient margin above the cost of materials and labor to enable him to live as well as the community expected. In practice the tests were not conducted frequently enough to keep an even ratio between the price of bread and the price of grain.[172] The latter had inevitably to be allowed to fluctuate, subject only to the control of publicity, all transactions being supposed to take place in the city's corn market. Practices that were at all secretive, such as forestalling, buying by sample, and the offering of commissions to country dealers, were suspected of leading directly to the "enhancement" of prices and were subject

170. *Cal. L. Bk., G*, p. 124. Victuals confiscated for any breach of regulations were normally sheriffs' perquisites (*Cal. P. & M. Rolls*, III, 119, 121, 131, 135, 136, 138, 139, 158, 159; Brewers' Records, Accounts, 1418–40, fols. 32–35). Some extracts are translated in Herbert, I, 56–58; *Cal. P. & M. Rolls*, I, 246; *Cal. L. Bk., L*, pp. 157, 179.

171. P. E. Jones, *The Worshipful Company of Poulterers* (1939), pp. 3–4.

172. For details see S. L. Thrupp, *A Short History of the Worshipful Company of Bakers of London* (1933).

to punishment by the pillory and by imprisonment and in heinous cases by loss of the franchise.[173] The subordinate officers through whom these controls were administered were under oath to be honest and impartial and to abstain, as mayor, sheriffs, and aldermen were also bound to do, from any retail trade in victuals on their own account. City serjeants and their yeoman assistants nevertheless sold ale, and in 1485 the practice was legalized.[174]

The only price regulations that seriously affected any of the merchant companies were those in the retail fish trade. Prices were here a vital public concern, because, next to bread, fish was the most important food of the city poor; but it took a strong mayor to undertake much interference with the fishmongers. The latter were proud of their own court and preferred to deal with offenders in their own way. Their wardens were sworn to search for evidence of forestalling, to prevent dealers from handling Thames fish, which were supposed to be sold by fishermen and their families, and also to preside over the fair division among members of the craft of all shipments that did not belong to citizens, in order that the retailers should sell "with owte takyng of excessif wynnyng."[175] In the first half of the fourteenth century, groups of fishmongers were several times prosecuted before the mayor for selling outside the prescribed market places and for using baskets of short measure; Hamo de Chigwell, himself a fishmonger, had one of his fellows deprived of the freedom for persisting in the latter offense.[176] By the middle of the century the fishmongers were growing alarmed at the amount of business that outsiders, peddling fish about the poorer quarters of the city or bringing small boatloads to sell at Billingsgate, were building up.[177] Since no mayor would grant them a monopoly of market stands, they appealed to the king, representing that the trade would be more reasonably governed if it were entirely under their control; and in 1364, as has been seen, they obtained a grant of retail monopoly.[178] How

173. See *Cal. L. Bk.*, *C*, pp. 58–59; *E*, pp. 56–57; *F*, pp. 165–66; *G*, pp. 170–71, 201; *Cal. P. & M. Rolls*, II, 196.

174. L. Bk., *G*, fol. 259*b*; *Cal. L. Bk.*, *D*, pp. 3–13, 192–94, 200–204; *H*, pp. 209–10; *L*, pp. 182, 226.

175. *Cal. L. Bk.*, *D*, pp. 198–99. Text of oath as administered in the fifteenth century.

176. *Ibid.*, *E*, pp. 179–80, 184, 189–90; cf. *C*, pp. 157–58; *E*, pp. 42, 46, 200; *Cal. E.M.C.R.*, p. 63.

177. See Regulations of 1351 (Riley, *Memorials*, pp. 267–68).

178. Herbert, II, 118–19; cf. above, n. 99.

far they were able to go in enforcing this is not certain, but the fishmongers were at least successful in keeping the price of herring twice as high in the city as in the country. Their first vigorous opponent was Northampton, who forced down the price of herring, planted country dealers in the main fish market to compete with them, set a fishmonger in the pillory, and obtained parliamentary legislation annulling the privileges of their charter.[179] In some respects he pressed them too hard, as in an act of common council forbidding any fishmonger or other citizen to advance money to country victualers or to provide them with nets or boats;[180] this confused the issue. Yet he won the main battle—none of his successors in the mayoralty dared sanction the exclusion of country fishmongers, and mayoral supervision of the company was maintained through the fifteenth century.[181]

Although the grocers enjoyed a closer monopoly of the retail trade in spices than the fishmongers could ever have hoped to maintain in fish, they were not called to account in the same way because spices were considered a luxury. Parliament made one attempt to peg the price of pepper, in 1411, but the city authorities did not interfere of their own accord until 1466, when it was ruled that the mayor should in future fix the price of figs and raisins as he did for other victuals.[182]

With the exception of the fishmongers and, in this one instance, the grocers, none of the merchant companies was actually kept under mayoral supervision. Their wardens' oath of office acknowledged the formal authority of the major and aldermen over all their activities, but in practice they were left to frame what bylaws they chose. The only general exception to this rule occurred in 1487–88, when, as a result of complaints in parliament about the high prices charged by the London crafts, the mayor called in all sets of ordinances for scrutiny.[183] Although lesser crafts, it is true, had often

179. Riley, *Memorials*, pp. 467–70; *Cal. L. Bk.*, *H*, pp. 190–91, 192–93, 202–3; 6 Ric. II cap. xi.

180. *Cal. L. Bk.*, *H*, p. 191.

181. The fishmongers did obtain a royal charter to this effect in 1399, but it was annulled within a year (*ibid.*, pp. 447–48 n.). The mayor's right of setting prices on each newly arrived shipload of fish, in consultation with the owner, was affirmed by ordinance in 1416. In 1462 the fishmongers were ordered to bring in their company ordinances for inspection and to enforce none in future unless they had been approved (*ibid.*, *I*, p. 169; *L*, p. 16).

182. *Ibid.*, *I*, p. 98; *L*, pp. 61–62.

183. "Where at the last parlement, grete grudge and displeasure was had ayens corporacions of Felishippes of this Citie for sellyng of dere stuffe excedyng price resonable,

been left alone for long periods, supervision not being consistently energetic, most of them had had their chief regulations placed on record at the Guildhall long before this date. The lesser crafts were also less independent in exercising the right of search; their wardens did not venture to condemn goods as defective on their own authority but had them brought before the mayor and aldermen. The latter then sometimes accepted the wardens' oath, sometimes summoned a jury of the craft. The merchants fell back on the public authority only when they felt in urgent need of its support. They co-operated with the mayor and aldermen in the appointment of brokers in order to keep out untrustworthy men;[184] and whenever their own methods of discipline broke down, they brought their problem before the city courts. The mercers in 1341 appealed for a mandate to prevent Norfolk agents from selling mercery in the city,[185] and other merchant companies occasionally brought obstinate members before the mayor and aldermen, who in such cases always inflicted a heavier punishment than was normally inflicted in the company's court.[186]

7. THE MERCHANTS' OUTLOOK ON GOVERNMENT

In thinking out their governmental problems the Londoners had no very clear body of political theory to guide them. This was not because they had any aversion to abstract ideas. On the con-

---

saying that by mean of ordenances whiche that everyche withyn them self by reason of theire corporacions do make ordenances and statutes in comen hurt of the Kynges liege people, with muche saying on the same more to grete rebuke of this Citie" (*Mercers' Acts*, p. 183 [October 15, 1488]). A general court of the mercers' company proved "agreable" to complying with the mayor's order to send in their book of ordinances but prudently appointed a committee to make any alterations beforehand that might seem necessary (*ibid.*; cf. *Cal. L. Bk.*, *L*, pp. 246, 274).

184. The profession of brokerage was kept under public supervision primarily in order to check the spread of usury through "feigned" sales of goods and to control the number of alien brokers. In London, brokers were licensed by the mayor and aldermen and were also sworn to the service of a company. They were allowed a portion of the fines inflicted on unlicensed brokers; in the fifteenth century they had a fraternity (see *Rot. parl.*, II, 332*a*; III, 541*a*; IV, 193*b*; *Cal. L. Bk.*, *C*, p. 17; *G*, pp. 313-14; *H*, pp. 198-200; *I*, p. 63; *K*, p. 351; *L*, pp. 162, 233).

185. *Cal. P. & M. Rolls*, I, 134-35.

186. Cases of goldsmiths, *ibid.*, pp. 62, 242; II, 228, 236, 255; Prideaux, *Memorials*, I, 7; of a grocer, *Cal. P. & M. Rolls*, III, 219-20; of drapers, *ibid.*, p. 220; Herbert, I, 429; of skinners, *Cal. P. & M. Rolls*, II, 18-19; *Cal. L. Bk.*, *G*, p. 274; of a tailor, Merchant Tailors' Minutes, 1488-93, fol. 46; of a fishmonger, *Cal. P. & M. Rolls*, I, 126. Sentences ran up to five months' imprisonment; and the grocer was fined £200, of which he paid £50, whereas forty days was the normal limit for disobedience to wardens and £10 was the limit of fines imposed in company courts.

trary, it was a convention to frame public policies in the name of general principles, such as the nurturing of love, the common profit, the profit of the realm, the honor of the city, justice, or reason. In themselves these principles were universally accepted, unassailable, axiomatic. To advance a special interest, it was almost a necessity to declare that it coincided with the public interest, a claim that might or might not be taken at its face value. The charters by which FitzThomas had planned to extend craft powers were attacked as tending only to the particular advantage of the wealthier men in each craft. Fourteenth-century craft ordinances were indorsed as "just and consonant with reason," "for the profit of the people," "for the honour and saving of their trade and the profit of the commons," or as providing a remedy for practices deceiving the people to their great loss, damage, or peril; yet, outside opinion, as expressed in pulpit and parliament, was skeptical. Personal ambition had to adopt the same high principles as group interests. Taunted with coveting the office of mayor, Hervey defended himself by swearing that he was acting only from the love of God and charity and to help the poor resist oppression.[187] Sir John Percevall, a late fifteenth-century candidate put forward by the tailors, who allowed himself to be too openly ambitious, was on that account for several years passed over—"the bench concideryng his hote apetyte which he hadd yerely to that offyce dyspoynted hym."[188]

Every effort was made to bind the city officers to observe the highest morality in all the personal relationships in which public business should involve them. From the mayor to the aleconners they were sworn to eschew all temptations to show favor or malice. Although the law embodied special privileges for citizens, the mayor and sheriffs were under obligation to do right to all comers; and a scale of moderate fees was set for the services of attorneys. In short, the administration and the law both sought to minimize the special influence of the rich and to weaken the possibilities of patronage.

If the search for morally satisfying solutions to more complex

187. *De antiquis legibus liber*, fol. 133a.
188. *The Great Chronicle*, pp. 245–46. The chronicler claimed that Percevall represented a coalition of the tailors, fullers, shearmen, and dyers and that he was finally elected in 1499 only by invoking the influence of the king and the bishop of London (*ibid.*, p. 288).

problems, involving the pressure of conflicting group interests, seems to have been less straightforward, it must be remembered that there were certain difficulties peculiar to the time and place. One of these was that chronic fear of incurring the royal displeasure through failure to maintain high enough standards of law and order, with consequent loss of the city's liberties. Mayor, sheriffs, and aldermen were like the rulers of a nation engaged in a war for existence, who dare not throw too many controversial issues open for public discussion lest disagreements should weaken the unity that is for the moment so vital. Routine police work taxed all their resources, for a mobile and ingenious underworld made its headquarters in the city, recruited and led by fugitives and outlaws from other parts of the country and from the Continent and by desperadoes who occasionally broke out of Newgate prison.[189]

Having no adequate means at their disposal for insuring the orderly conduct of large public meetings or for coping with local riots, the authorities clung to policies of repression. No criticism was permitted save by action at law against a city officer. There was nothing in such an atmosphere to prevent the governing élite from dealing honestly with the hundred and one concrete details of day-to-day administration—with the mesh of fishing nets, the price of eels, or even the rates of brokerage; but there was insufficient incentive to probe to the bottom of the larger issues of government.

The one leader who had squarely broken with this timidity was John Northampton, and the end of his public career brought inevitable reaction. In 1391 all discussion of his opinions or of those of his rival, Brembre, was forbidden for the honor of God, the king, and the realm; everyone was to agree, on pain of a year's imprisonment in Newgate.[190] John Carpenter, our only fifteenth-century commentator on the city's constitution, had grown up under the influence of this reaction. To him old customs were the best, and the experiment of electing councils from the misteries had led merely to popular tumult and the despising of the great by the small. Unity before the king was the city's prime need; any

189. *Lib. Alb.*, I, 277, 281–83; cf. above, n. 44. On escapes from Newgate see M. Bassett, "Newgate Prison in the Middle Ages," *Speculum*, XVIII (1943), 234–36.
190. Riley, *Memorials*, pp. 526–27.

man who should stir up dissension at the time when pleas of the crown were being heard was a public enemy, to be disfranchised, with his heirs, forever. Public meetings are a danger, as a verse from Ecclesiasticus bears witness. Wardsmen who twice nominate for alderman candidates unacceptable to the mayor and ruling aldermen do so from a proud and malevolent spirit. The city is like a body, with the mayor for a head and the sheriffs for eyes and, along with other officers, for limbs.[191] Carpenter was learned in the law and custom of his city, but his political ideas spell mere passive acceptance of the social hierarchy as he found it.

Implicit in the citizens' political experience, however, was the basic idea of seventeenth-century liberalism, that political rights and obligations stem from property. The man who was in scot and lot could vote in his wardmote. When he had accumulated more property, he had a chance to be consulted on the affairs of the city, including its financial affairs; he might even have to assist in the auditing of public accounts or be appointed a warden of the Bridge, with trusteeship of public lands. If he had the wealth to afford it, he would be in line for still higher office, and it would not be "consonant with reason" to refuse to stand. These customs matured into law without encountering enough resistance to bring about full definition or discussion of the underlying principles[192] and without necessitating any breach with the conventions of hierarchical social theory.

Conflicts of interest failed to detach any permanent opposition theory that was entirely free from the dominant assumptions. The dependent workers who in 1327 took up arms "as equals and as commoners" against the saddlers' abuse of economic power had no revolutionary theory of human equality in mind; when brought into court, they rested their case on the fact that they were citizens who had always borne their share of tallage and that therefore they should not be compelled to sell only to the saddlers nor suffer the treatment of which they complained. This plea won

191. *Lib. Alb.*, I, 18–19, 39–42, 51.
192. Riley, *Memorials*, p. 635. It is remarkable that the principle of financial responsibility does not appear to have been contested. What the aldermen were accused of in the thirteenth century was tampering with assessments for royal tallage. They were also guilty of taking advantage of their own position to evade full payment of their own assessments in civic taxation. It would be the duty of the sheriff in such cases to place a sequestration on their goods; but unless he had the mayor's encouragement, he would probably not care to prosecute them if they broke it.

them an apparently fair arbitration, and nine of the saddlers were condemned for specific offenses.[193] The doctrine of the equality of taxpayers did not seem to find political expression except in vague dissatisfaction with the method of electing mayor and sheriffs. If it gave rise to other discontents, these must have been at least partially alleviated by the wide delegation of powers in the government of trade and industry.

The orthodox views were not openly challenged until 1376, when Northampton was undoubtedly acting on the theory that abuses of economic power and special privilege could be prevented only by enlarging the basis of political power. It is a matter for question whether this theory struck any deep root, even among those who stood to profit by it. The soil was not very favorable. Many of those who wished for craft representation on the common council were intent mainly on the consolidation of their own craft privileges. A petition for reform of the council in 1364 had proposed that all wardens of misteries should attend a monthly meeting with the aldermen to discuss the affairs of the city and in particular to insure restriction of the numbers of masters. No such meetings had been instituted, but the fee for admission to the freedom by redemption, that is, without apprenticeship had at the petitioners' request been raised to 60s. The immediate effect of this had been to drive men to set up in business in Westminster and Southwark.[194] The fourteenth-century citizens were most certainly not devoted to fair competition, as a general ideal, and it is not even clear to what extent they believed in a free market in foodstuffs as the best means of obtaining cheap supplies, for they relied also on the mayor's authority, exercised under orders from the king, to fix prices. The perversion of this system of control at the hands of the great fish and wine monopolists created an odious situation, but few citizens could have been persuaded that there was any logical remedy in departing from the usual property qualifications for common councilors. The problem was one of corruption at court and, perhaps, of too great secrecy in sessions of the court of aldermen. Why fly in the face of tradition by electing poor men, inexperienced in public affairs, to the council? In re-

193. Riley, *Memorials*, pp. 156–62.
194. The rate was made adjustable to the candidate's means in 1366 but in 1383 was again raised to 60s. (*Cal. L. Bk., G*, pp. 179–81, 211–12; *H*, pp. 162, 213.

pudiating this reform the merchants may not have been out of harmony with the second thoughts of the poorer citizens themselves, and they saw to it that no comparable crisis of oppression occurred again.

Limited though their ideas may have been and lacking in precision, the experience of the merchants, both in London and in the smaller towns, was one of the formative elements in the groping political thought of late medieval England. Both their knowledge of the details of government and their sense of responsibility in matters of finance were superior to those of the gentry who, owing to their higher social position, took the lead in parliament; the Londoners had no poll tax to their discredit. In their attachment to property as the foundation of political rights and duties they were not behind any of their contemporaries and were indeed in advance of all those sections of society in which public office was a matter of family right. No fifteenth-century London merchant would have asserted, as did Christine de Pisan, that public office in cities should go to men of ancient family.[195] Nor do any of the London chronicles of that period display the nervous and cutting disdain with which she lashes the "menu peuple"; their feeling for the community as a whole is too strong. Yet this local patriotism did not prevent the citizens from seeing their community as a model and as a part of the realm of England. The character of "lover of the commonwealth," given to one of the many merchants whose charities were bestowed in his country birthplace as well as in London, points forward to the ideals that in the Tudor age were to link municipal and central governments together in the construction of a common social policy.

195. *Le Livre de la paix*, cited in *Paris et ses historiens aux XIVe et XVe siècles, histoire générale de Paris*, ed. Le Roux de Lincy and L. M. Tisserand (1867), VI, 417–18.

Chapter III

WEALTH AND STANDARDS OF LIVING

MANY of the merchant fortunes of medieval London crowned a long family history of peasants and yeomanry, small handicraftsmen and country traders, devoted to the accumulation of property. Some grew out of large fortunes built up in trade in one of the smaller towns. In such cases the member of the family who was sent to London could start with a substantial capital and the invaluable asset of important trading connections. Young merchants who could step into a family business already established in London might also be well provided with capital. One fifteenth-century mercer, "of trust and because he wolde understonde the actifues and disposition of oon John Middleton his son in feate of merchandise," set him up independently with a stock of merchandise valued at £1,100; as it happened, this young man "profited not in feate of merchandise but decresid the seid stokke," finally absconding with a part of the goods and taking refuge from his creditors in sanctuary.[1] Few young men had so much to throw away, the portions with which sons of London merchants were launched in life ranging down to £10. The majority had between £20 and £200, some with landed property in addition. It is difficult to discover what capital the gentlemen's sons who entered trade were able to bring with them. One cannot but suspect that the young Richard Whittington had a good deal more than the penny with which he bought his legendary cat. Yet his early entry into the profitable business of supplying luxury textiles to the court may have been due less to any large initial capital than to the influence of aristocratic friends.

To open business in one of the greater companies, it was desir-

---

1. E.C.P., 64/836. The stock was mostly wool and woolfells.

able to have a stock of goods worth £40 to £50, although it was not essential to have so much. The grocers in 1480 fixed a minimum of £40 but did not long adhere to it. The mercers in 1503 set the minimum at £100 on the grounds that many members "for lack of a sufficient beginning have decayed and undone themselves," but young freemen were probably able to halve the requirements by forming partnerships.[2] Even so, it is clear that the smaller family portions would not take a young man far along the road to independence. Indeed, they sometimes barely covered the full expenses of apprenticeship in a merchant company.[3] Some apprentices emerged from their training with a debt to their master round their necks. This could soon be worked off, competent free servants being able to command wages of £5 a year and more. Top earnings ran to £20 a year with board and "othir avaylys," a rate paid in the mercers' company in times of prosperity; in the depression of 1493 even mercers' servants were considered lucky to earn 5 marks.[4] By paying generous wages the masters hoped to retain their servants' full loyalty, but the policy had sometimes the opposite effect of encouraging them to begin sporadic trade on their own account. In the mercers' company, in which this was forbidden, the young men hid their merchandise in taverns and other secret trading places; if it was discovered, they were fined. Other companies were less strict, one goldsmith being allowed to trade with a legacy of £100 while he was still an apprentice.[5] Wealthy men sometimes left handsome legacies to favorite apprentices or servants, and faithful service with the master's widow was often rewarded with the price of admission to the freedom, but most legacies of the kind amounted to not more than £5 or £10, as a wage for the work of collecting the master's debts.[6]

The ordinances of both the mercers and the grocers contem-

2. Grocers' Records, Vol. 300, fol. 52; *The Charters, Ordinances and Bye-laws of Mercers' Company*, ed. W. D. Selby (1881), ordinance No. 36. An ordinance of 1486 "for ii parsones takyng oon shopp to gether" insisted that each must pay the entry fee of 40s. due from shopholders, but half the payment could be deferred (*Mercers' Acts*, p. 293).

3. On premiums see below, p. 214.

4. *The Great Chronicle*, p. 249.

5. *Mercers' Acts*, pp. 77, 110; Wardens' Accounts, fol. 187v (1455); E.C.P., 235/71.

6. John Curteys, grocer, directed that, if his apprentice would serve his wife, he was to be made free at her cost and "when þt he purposith to sett up an hows" was to be given wares from the shop worth 10 marks (Comm. Lon., Sharpe, 246 (1458)).

plated that a new shopholder might obtain his initial stock of goods through the aid or favor of friends, that is, on credit. It may therefore be assumed that this was a common practice, family plate and other household goods and heirlooms serving as security. The youngest son of an aldermanic family in the grocers' company, "of good towardlyness," was alleged to have induced a friend to lend him 50 marks "to sette hym forward in his occupation" when he was only twenty, without any security; and a goldsmith was similarly able to borrow fine silver and implements to the value of £24 "to begynne his crafte" on trust.[7] For the man with few friends or relatives in the city, the way cannot have been so easy. A charitable fifteenth-century goldsmith provided that if his children died £100 of their portion was to be used for interest-free loans of up to 10 marks in value and a year's period of time to young men of his craft "begynnyng the world and by liklyhood disposed to thryve"; they were to lay "sufficiaunt plegge" at the company hall.[8]

The young man who was not inclined to save money from his wages and could not borrow might yet acquire enough capital to set up a business by marriage. The mercers' wardens, examining a young shopholder's finances, asked whether he had come by his merchandise "by service by favour or friendship by marriage or by taking of stock lawfully to his profit whereby of likelihood he may continue and prosper."[9] In any event, marriage was regarded as an important means of building up one's resources. The young merchant looked about carefully, made business-like inquiries, and was ready to pay a commission on the dowry to a broker. John Lyonhill, goldsmith, agreed to pay a clerk £10, out of a dowry of £80, for arranging his marriage with the daughter of a senior member of his company. Another goldsmith, "moved by frenshippe," married on a promise of £40. There was a great deal of bargaining. William Nightingale, draper, married on the promise of £100, a gold ring, a gray fur, a horse described as "an Irissh hevy," and a thirty-four-year lease of a quay. Thomas Bataill, mercer, being offered 40 marks with a niece of Sir William Plumpton, insisted that his wife's family should board them both for three years and

7. Edward Hill, grocer, E.C.P., 186/98 (1493–1500); E.C.P., 67/13.

8. Oliver Davy, P.C.C., Wattys, 11 (1473).

9. Selby, op. cit., p. 79.

lend him 100 marks during that period for his business. The husband was often required to assure his wife's security by settling landed property on her and their heirs to the value of the dowry. Such settlements went far to dispel any reluctance that gentlemen might have felt in accepting merchants as their sons-in-law. John Godyn, grocer, received £100 with the daughter of a judge, Sir Hugh Huls, on condition that he entail property of that value on their heirs, but he was not obliged to arrange the entail immediately and on putting up goods as security was allowed to use the money in his business. Marriage settlements were also common between merchant families.[10]

If his business prospered, the man who could defer marriage until later in life had a proportionately greater bargaining power in the matter of dowries. Whether he sought a rich young heiress, however, or an older woman, a widow, he would meet keen competition, and widows were well able to play one suitor off against another. According to the story told by a draper, he had made a contract of marriage with a widow, before witnesses, and had subsequently for three years spent much of his time and money on her business, "entendying it shuld have been for his owne wele and profite in tyme comyng." In the same spirit he sent her a series of gifts of which he kept careful account, as shown in Table 7. In addition, he stated, she had caused him to spend £20 on herself and her friends and had allowed him to buy merchandise for her in Spain worth over £400. Then, while he was absent, she had turned to a rival, and when he came home from Spain, "not feryng the dompnacion of her soule," she refused to marry him or even to see him. Ultimately she died unmarried with a fortune of £2,000, to which, on the strength of the alleged marriage contract, the draper laid claim.[11]

Widows with young children were less obdurate. If the new husband was allowed to take charge of his stepchildren's inheritance, such a marriage might be a great prize. Some of the greatest fortunes the city could boast were created through the merging

10. E.C.P., 64/271, 74/17, 216/68, 48/416; L. Bk., *I*, fols. 261*b*, 277. For examples of marriage settlements between merchant families see *Cal. P. & M. Rolls*, III, 103; IV, 47, 59. A goldsmith marrying the daughter of a widow of St. Albans with dowry of £40 agreed to settle on her London property to the value of 10 marks (E.C.P., 108/13).

11. Case of Elizabeth, wife of John Kyrkeby, goldsmith, widowed by 1484, and George Bulstrode (*Cal. L. Bk., L.*, p. 216; F.C.P., 115/34).

of businesses in this way. One fifteenth-century grocer, marrying as his second wife a widow with dower of £764, was appointed guardian of her six children and allowed to trade with their patrimony, of an equal amount; in other words, he was able to use two-thirds of the assets of a large business. Another grocer, later knighted, acquired control of nearly £3,000, while he was a comparatively young man, by a similar marriage.[12]

It was not necessary to assume the guardianship of orphans in order to borrow their money. A court of orphanage, composed of the mayor and aldermen and the city chamberlain, had charge of

TABLE 7

a peir of great bedes gauded wt gold............................	£ 2	2s.	
a great Ryng of fyne gold wt a grete poynted diamant price.........	10		
a smal cheyne of golde wt a litel agnus dei of golde................	3	6	
a signet of golde wt her armes grave in stone & a ruby & an emeraude sette in same...	3	2	6d.
a great ryng of fyne golde sette wt a Turkesshe whiche I did do make for her in Syvyle.......................................	3	5	2
a popingeay which I might have sold to my lady hungerford for 5 marks	2	6	8
for 7 plight & a quarter of figne laune...........................	3	12	6
for 6 elles of fyne holand cloth for kerchiefs......................	1	16	
for a ffure of fyne bogye......................................	2	2	
for 18 pampilions at 20d. & 60 tavilleons at 2d....................	2		
for a venyce corse of golde & a Sivile corse & ribanys & laces.........	1	5	8
for diverse deyntees as ffiges & reisin dates almonds prunes capres Suge & other spices lampreis conervais pomegranats & orangs..........	6		
for ypocras whiche she caused me to make for her & for her frends at diverse tymes 8 galons for a hoggeshede of white wyne in all......	2	11	8
for yeres giftes at diverse yeris to her servaunts & to her frendes & kynnesfolk...	1	18	8

children's shares in many citizens' estates and administered the proceeds as a commercial loan fund from which merchants with sound security could borrow at annual interest rates of 10 per cent.[13] The only other institutional sources of large commercial loans were the merchant companies. The grocers in the fifteenth century sometimes lent their corporate funds, and other companies probably did the same.[14]

12. Cases of John Wells and George Irlond (see Appen. A).

13. L. Bk., Journals, *passim*. In 1491 it was ordered that "all suche persones whiche be bounde for any Orphanes goodes" be bound by their recognizance to report to the mayor and aldermen every year on the Monday after mid-Lent Sunday "that it may appere . . . . whether the said persones . . . . be on lyve or dede or abydynge within the said Citee or not" (Journals, 9, fol. 287).

14. Grocers of London, p. 253.

Another means of augmenting trading capital was the exaction of loans from the families of apprentices.[15] Members of the lesser companies were more anxious to turn their money over themselves than to intrust it to merchants, but they could furnish occasional loans.[16] So also could the gentry. The wife of Sir Robert Knolles, one of the generals who made a fortune from the French wars, invested £2,000 with Adam Chaungeour, grocer, on the agreement that profit and loss be divided between them equally. This was an exceptionally large amount. Chaungeour, incidentally, lost the entire sum.[17]

Throughout their career, merchants frequently pooled their resources in partnerships of a temporary and shifting nature. This circumstance, coupled with the scarcity of series of accounts, makes it difficult to judge the amount of capital with which a man was operating at any particular period. Leading importers might ship in goods up to £2,000 in value at a time; how much they would have in other enterprises there is usually no means of knowing.[18] From this level the scale of enterprise ranged down very widely. In 1474 thirty-two mercers, a third of the livery, were reported as being worth more than 100 marks in goods but less than £100. The report was submitted at the command of Edward IV who, for the purpose of raising a benevolence, desired to know how many citizens had £5 or more in rents or £100 in goods.[19] The returns made by other companies are not known, but it is likely that the proportion of members who were operating with a comparatively small capital was in most cases larger than among the mercers.

Other sources show the scale on which merchants had accumulated wealth at the time of their death. By the custom of London a citizen was obliged to leave his wife a third of his movable property, another third being divided among his children, and the re-

15. See below, p. 214.

16. Gilbert Prince, painter, invested money with one of the Frowyks (*Cal. P.R., 1377–81*, p. 286).

17. *Rot. parl.*, III, 258*b*.

18. Grocers of London, p. 264; C, 160/24; for some analysis of the financing of English trade see M. M. Postan, "Credit in Medieval Trade," *Ec. H.R.*, I (1928), 234–61; on the wool trade see Eileen Power, *The Medieval English Wool Trade* (1941). Financing of the cloth trade will be dealt with in a forthcoming book by E. M. Carus Wilson.

19. *Mercers' Acts*, pp. 78–80, 84. The return gave 106 names, including 6 lawyers.

mainder being spent for the good of his soul. If the wife had died, the children received half his movables; a widow had the same if there were no children. There are admittedly certain defects in the evidence of wills. The valuations set on property might err on the side of optimism. Bequests based on the book value of outstanding debts had sometimes to be drastically reduced. The executors of William Lynne, wool merchant, were obliged to reduce the amount of his legacies to his children by a third; debts owed to Richard Toky at his death constituted 40 per cent of his assets, and none of them could be realized.[20] Again, the wills of which copies are on record are likely to be weighted with those of men who were above the average in wealth and particularly with those of landed men. When it was directed that land be sold to cover the bequests made in the will, the sums named are an indication of the total value of the estate; but when land itself was bequeathed, there is no such complete indication.

The records of the court of orphanage are free from all but the last of these objections.[21] In 245 instances of merchants' estates, set out in Table 8, there is record of the exact amount of money paid over to children representing, according as their mother was alive or not, a third or a half of the value of movables and lands that the executors had sold to meet the provisions of the father's will. The selection of cases for record was determined not by the size of the estate but by the fact that there were one or more children and that the father had neglected to provide guardians for them. Scattered though they are in date, from 1350 to 1497, they serve to show the range of variation in business success and give some indication of the proportions in which men fell along the scale. For comparison, approximate estate valuations from a group of wills are set alongside; the wills are selected on the basis of membership in the company of grocers, which by reputation of wealth ranked second only to the mercers. As one would expect, the percentage of grocers in the upper brackets is higher than the percentage in the general sample. But the range of variation is the same in each series, and the proportion of men who left less than £100 is 25 per cent; in each case, moreover, the median estate value at death was less than £300. Estate value at death would on

20. *Cal. P. & M. Rolls*, III, 208–16; L. Bk., *K*, fols. 16*b*–17.

21. L. Bk., *G–L, passim.*

the average naturally tend to be higher than the average level of wealth among young and old taken together, as it would appear in a cross-section of the merchant class. It is significant that as many as 11 to 12 per cent left less than £50, some barely £20. In every company there were men who had a struggle to keep their heads above water and died without materially increasing the small property with which they had started business.

The scale of wealth among men in livery in the lesser companies began, in the case of the younger men, at about 20 marks.

TABLE 8

Value of Estate	Merchant Estates from Orphanage Records		Estates from Grocers' Wills (1386–1506)	
	No.	Per Cent	No.	Per Cent
Up to £50............	26	11 ⎫	8	12 ⎫
£ 50–£ 100........	32	13 ⎬ 69	8	12 ⎬ 54
£ 100–£ 200........	52	21 ⎪	12	18 ⎪
£ 200–£ 400........	59	24 ⎭	8	12 ⎭
£ 400–£ 600........	15	6 ⎫	11	16 ⎫
£ 600–£ 800........	16	6 ⎬ 17	5	7 ⎬ 28
£ 800–£1,000........	12	5 ⎭	3	5 ⎭
£1,000–£2,000........	21	9 ⎫ 14	3	5 ⎫ 18
Over £2,000..........	12	5 ⎭	9	13 ⎭
	245	100	67	100

This was the property qualification set for admission to the livery among the fullers and the carpenters in ordinances registered late in the fifteenth century.[22] No representative series can be obtained to illustrate accumulation in the course of a career. But it could run well above the median level for merchants. A glover who died in 1475 estimated the value of his debts and stock in hand in the "houses of office" in his garden at over £360,[23] and payments were made in the court of orphanage from four similar estates that had realized over £400.

An ordinary small master required only the value of tools and

22. Fullers' ordinances of 1487, Journals, 9, fols. 144b–247; L. Bk., L, H, fols. 232b–233. Carpenters' ordinances of same date, transcribed in E. B. Jupp and W. W. Pocock, *An Historical Account of the Worshipful Company of Carpenters* (1887), p. 350.

23. Will of John Wode (P.C.C., Wattys, 20).

equipment and a stock of materials. One young glover successful-
ly set up shop on London Bridge with only £2 8s. 4d. in cash; a
goldbeater valued his tools, for sale to a friend, at 6 marks; a dyer
valued his utensils at 10 marks; and an impartial valuation of a
tanner's implements came to £8 9s. 2d.[24] Heavy fixed apparatus,
such as was needed in bakehouses and breweries, was very commonly rented. A master-baker was supposed to have 40s., but
there was no such regulation with regard to brewers; one who fled
for murder left behind him no movable goods but a quarter of
barley, a hundred flasks of beer, a shilling's worth of fuel, a little
pig, four geese, a cock and a hen, and a dice box. The metal
trades, in which both materials and implements were expensive,
required most capital. An armorer wishing to establish an apprentice in business left him 20 marks in money and pieces of
armor. Two pewterers in partnership in 1428 had tools and apparatus valued at £19 16s. 5d.; half of this belonged outright to
one of the partners, and the heavier molds were shared among as
many as six people.[25] Some idea of requirements in the fifteenth
century may be gathered from craft ordinances by means of which
the older masters were trying to keep their ranks closed against the
entry of "simple young persons." The fullers forbade anyone to
set up a shop or "wirkynghous" unless he "be demed and knowen
to be of Substance of his own propre goods" to the extent of 10
marks; the graytawyers and the turners set similar property
qualifications of £5 and 5 marks; and the cutlers refused to allow
young men to start business in partnership unless each of the
partners had sufficient means to operate independently.[26]

The more ambitious young men were impatient to set up their
own shops as soon as they had finished their apprenticeships. If
they could not draw on legacies or family assistance, they would
begin, as the fullers' ordinances complained, with "borrowed
wares," applying to friends or to charitable loan chests. Others
continued in service. Information as to the wage rates that pre-

24. L. Bk., *H*, fol. 146; *C.W.C.H.*, II, 202 (1377); will of John Hicheman, dyer (P.C.C.,
Rous, 16 [1451]); *Cal. L. Bk.*, *F* (1340).

25. Will of John Perfay, armorer (Comm. Lon., Brown, 27; L. Bk., *K*, fol. 49). The
will of John Selle, pewterer, bequeathes capital lent him by a woman, "the Stoke which I
have of my maisters Agnes Crowde accordying to the writings made be twynne her and
me" (Comm. Lon., Lichfield, 43 [1485]).

26. L. Bk., *L*, fols. 149*b*-50, 212, 232*b*-33, 242*b*-44.

vailed in the fourteenth century is hard to collect. Tradition appeared to favor customary rates for different types of work, which craft officials, supported by the mayor and aldermen, sought to enforce. The servants, however, had the advantage that there was a chronic scarcity of competent skilled hands. Masters were therefore tempted to offer more than the usual rate in order to attract a good workman, although such an act was considered contrary to the ethics of craft membership. Between the years 1308 and 1389 eleven industrial crafts registered ordinances forbidding masters to "entice" apprentices or servants away from a fellow-member, with penalties for breach of the rule up to £2.[27] If this prohibition was respected, the servants must surely have had an added incentive to organize and back each other up in demands for higher pay. All open organizations of the kind were sooner or later banned by order of the mayor and aldermen, but it cannot have been easy to break them up altogether. The men would seek to continue their meetings secretly or under the guise of a drinking-club. The scanty evidence available suggests that, at least in the latter part of the century, when the ravages of plague were creating a general shortage of labor, efforts to peg wages within the London crafts were unsuccessful. Although the fullers and dyers in 1353 elected a joint board of eight masters to prevent any increase in wages, the fullers were, ten years later, still faced with the same problem and were holding the threat of a year's imprisonment, as well as fines, over servants who should combine to demand higher wages.[28] The only recorded instance of punishment of masters for yielding to pressure from their men occurred in 1349, when two bakers were summoned before the mayor and sheriffs for breaking an ordinance made for their trade to the effect that wages should be paid only at the conclusion of a quarter of a year's service.[29] The occasional punishment of servants for receiving too high wages could hardly have sufficed to keep the rates down. Ten brewers' men were imprisoned in 1372 for taking wages of 32s. by the year, 10s. by the quarter, and 4d. by the day, with board. The next year two others were arrested, one for tak-

27. The craft ordinances in question were registered at the following dates: fusters (1308), fullers (1314, 1363), whitetawyers (1346), pewterers (1348), glovers (1349), furbishers (1350), braelers (1355), verrers (1365), blacksmiths (1372), cordwainers (1375), and founders (1389).

28. *Cal. L. Bk., G*, pp. 14, 160.   29. *Cal. P. & M. Rolls*, I, 225–26.

ing the still higher rate of 3s. 8d. by the week, but they were released after a few days' imprisonment and the payment of a fine amounting to no more than a week's wages.[30] The cutlers were lamenting in 1380 that they were paying excessive wages, even to men who had not served a full apprenticeship. As a remedy they determined that in future the craft officials would put such men through a test and set their wages by conscience, according to their skill; no increases were to be allowed without proof of an improvement in skill.[31] Men who had completed an apprenticeship and been admitted to the freedom of the city could apparently not be subjected to these tests. Yet the wages of the free servants doubtless varied likewise with different types of work and skill. When the sheathers in 1375 set a flat rate of 30s. and board,[32] they were probably allowing for variations in the value of the food and drink offered. During the next two decades money wages among the saddlers, whose servants were well organized, were said to have risen 200 and 300 per cent, from £2 and 5 marks to 10 or 12 marks or even to £10. In response to the masters' complaints, the mayor and aldermen in 1396 ordered the dissolution of their men's fraternity, but it is not known whether the order was any more effective than previous prohibitions, in 1362 and 1380, of their "covins" and assemblies.[33] The money wages of masons, set by the civic authorities at 6d. a day, seem to have risen above the official rate by at least a third, and the same was probably true of carpenters and other workers in the building trades.[34]

The scarcity of skilled labor may have been to some extent alleviated in the fifteenth century, although the crafts themselves sought to maintain it artificially by limiting the number of apprentices that any master might enrol.[35] The brewers still had

30. *Ibid.*, II, 148, 160.

31. Riley, *Memorials*, p. 439.   32. L. Bk., *H*, fol. 22b.

33. *Cal. L. Bk., G*, p. 143; *Cal. P. & M. Rolls*, II, 264; Riley, *Memorials*, pp. 542–44; cf. n. 35, below.

34. See D. Knoop and G. P. Jones, *The Medieval Mason* (1933), pp. 123–29. The authors believe that official rates may have been enforced before 1350 but not after.

35. The following crafts penalized masters for "enticing" apprentices or servants: blacksmiths (1408), braziers (1416), glovers (1482), bowyers, cappers, lorimers, plumbers (1488). Ordinances of the following dates provided for limitation of apprentices: girdlers (1435), founders (1456, 1490), paviors (1480), tilers (1481), brewers, glovers (1482), shearmen (1483), cutlers (1485), barbers, fullers, plumbers, graytawyers, woolmen (1487–88), and curriers (1493).

trouble with their men, appealing to the mayor and aldermen in 1406 for power to arrest all who demanded more than 3*d.* a day in winter or 4*d.* a day in summer, with board. In 1427 they were trying to restrict the wages of their foremen to 53*s.* 4*d.* a year, plus meat, drink, clothing, and some other unspecified "avauntages," but four years later they were complaining that no "servant chief Brewere" could be hired by the year and that demands ran to 2*s.* or 20*d.* by the week, with board in addition. In 1475 one of their men was sentenced to several weeks' imprisonment for having urged his fellows to assemble at the company hall with swords and daggers to protest against wage regulations; a similar armed demonstration had been staged once before.[36] Rates set by the dyers in 1433 and the blacksmiths in 1452 were only 40*s.* a year, with board and clothing in addition in the case of the dyers; and a pewterer's will of 1451 refers to a servant who was receiving only 40*s.*; money wages paid to the bakers' men in 1441 were somewhat higher, running in a scale of 12*d.*, 13*d.*, and 16*d.* a week for different types of work, with a penny a day extra for drink but no mention of food.[37] It was said that these had been the prevailing rates for "tyme oute of mynde." It was also remarked that most of the masters in the craft, who were condemning a fraternity that their servants had formed, had at one time belonged to it themselves. One may therefore infer that, for a trade that did not require very much capital, the wages named were a satisfactory prelude to mastership. In the metal trades maximum wages were higher. A plumber who died in 1463 directed his wife to pay their servant from 4 to 6 marks a year, "with covenable Reward above that if he deserve itt," rather than to lose him; plumbers' servants, however, were supposed to provide themselves with three of their tools, a hammer, a knife, and a "shavyng-hooke."[38] The wages of unenfranchised workers may have been kept lower than those of

36. L. Bk., *I*, fol. 53; Brewers' Records, 1418–40, under dates of mayoralties of Gedney and Welles; Journals, 8, fol. 124*v.* The masters' word as to traditional rates of wages cannot be regarded as very trustworthy; for example, their petition to Mayor Welles states that "in time passed" foremen had received 40*s.* a year and second and third brewers 30*s.* and 20*s.*, all with meat and drink, figures which seem to refer to some time too far back for accurate memory.

37. L. Bk., *K*, fol. 133*b*; H. C. Coote, *Ordinances of Some Secular Guilds of London, 1354–96* (1871), pp. 41–44; will of John Paris (P.C.C., Logge, 19; L. Bk., *K*, fols. 198*b*–99).

38. Will of John Kirkeby (P.C.C., Godyn, 6–7; L. Bk., *L*, fols. 252–53*b*).

WEALTH AND STANDARDS OF LIVING 115

freemen; one rate found is that of 20s. a year and board, paid to a broiderer in the employ of a vestment-maker.[39]

A rough indication of the general distribution of wealth in the form of movables among the citizens of the early fourteenth century is contained in two surviving subsidy rolls. The first of these relates to the collection of a twelfth in 1319. Specific directions had been issued that the assessors were to report on all merchandise owned by citizens, no matter whether it were in the country or abroad or on the seas, and also on all clear debts and all jewels of gold and silver. The only goods to be exempt were those appertaining to lands owned outside the city, a limited list of personal belongings comprising one gown each for a man and his wife, one ring and bracelet, silk girdle and drinking goblet for each, and one bed for the two of them, and all property of less than half a mark in value.[40] The plan followed was in all probability to exempt everything except merchandise actually on hand in city shops and warehouses and to take a twelfth of this by lenient valuation. The exact procedure is described in only one distance, that of Roger Chauntecler, a merchant of Farringdon ward, who either would not or could not make any payment at all. Discovering twenty-four sacks of wool that belonged to him, in Billingsgate, the collectors confiscated two and sold them for 10 marks.[41] The highest sum collected was £40, from John de Triple, a fishmonger, which made up practically half the taxation of the ward in which he lived, Walbrook. Two other merchants were assessed at 40 marks, three at £20, one at 25 marks, and seven at £10. These thirteen sums, with Chauntecler's two sacks of wool, made up more than a third of the city's tax, the ward of Vintry excluded. The second roll relates to the levy of a tenth and a fifteenth in 1332.[42] By rights this should have produced twice as much as the twelfth, but it was so carelessly handled that it brought in less. Although it lacks the returns for Vintry, the 1319 roll is therefore a better guide to the numbers and wealth of taxpayers. The returns are

39. E.C.P., 66/398.

40. *Cal. L. Bk., E*, pp. 122–24; cf. J. F. Willard, *Parliamentary Taxes on Personal Property, 1290 to 1334* (1934), pp. 88–90, 138.

41. Marginal notes on the roll, E, 179/144/3.

42. Printed and analyzed in M. Curtis, "The London Lay Subsidy of 1332," in *Studies in Finance and Trade under Edward III*, ed. G. Unwin (1918), pp. 61–92.

analyzed in Table 9 by wards, and the general gradation of payments is set out in comparison with those of 1332.

The distribution was no doubt distorted by the haphazard methods of assessment, which obviously allowed of much unfairness. The line of exemption, for example, must have been drawn somewhat erratically. In 1332, when it was supposed to stand at 10*s.*, there were more small taxpayers than in 1319, when it was set at 6*s.* 8*d.* On both occasions there was outright evasion, and there is no means of checking its incidence. In 1332 seven of the aldermen failed to make any payments. Although none of the al-

TABLE 9

ASSESSMENTS FOR THE TWELFTH OF 1319

Ward	£4 and Over	£1–£4	10*s.*–£1	5*s.*–10*s.*	16*d.*–5*s.*	Under 16*d.*	Number of Assessments Illegible	Total Number of Taxpayers	Total Contribution		
Aldersgate	....	....	....	6	24	10	....	40	£ 5	8*s.*	4 *d.*
Aldgate	....	1	....	6	14	2	....	23	4	18	9¾
Bassishaw	....	....	1	5	10	20	....	36	4	9	7¾
Billingsgate	3	8	5	4	21	11	3	55	45	15	6
Bishopsgate	....	....	....	5	19	41	....	65	4	16	8
Bread Street	2	8	5	23	32	16	....	86	35	17	10
Bridge	1	5	6	24	35	9	....	80	41	9	4¼
Broad Street	2	4	4	8	24	28	....	70	37	18	4¾
Candlewick	....	5	5	15	18	23	....	66	17	12	2¾
Castle Baynard	....	3	8	8	26	14	....	59	16	1	7
Cheap	1	13	18	25	63	53	....	173	57	6	4½
Coleman Street	....	....	3	1	31	23	....	58	6	19	1
Cordwainer	5	15	12	13	23	3	....	71	73	15	0½
Cornhill	1	....	69		28	14	....	58	21	16	10
Cripplegate Within	4	3	11	10	39	43	....	110	77	4	11
Cripplegate Without	1	2	7	8	27	35	....	80	16	5	4¾
Dowgate	5	6	8	12	20	6	....	57	106	3	0
Farringdon Within	1	9	12	19	68	63	....	172	41	4	8¾
Farringdon Without	1	....	6	24	56	17	....	104	25	19	8
Langbourn	2	....	7	9	16	34	....	68	25	4	10
Lime Street	....	....	....	1	3	7	....	11	1	4	3
Portsoken	....	....	1	2	18	23	....	44	3	19	1¼
Queenhithe	1	16	9	8	27	11	4	76	41	9	6
Tower	3	21	8	17	18	5	....	72	67	13	8
Vintry	....	....	....	....	....	....	....	....	94	10	11¼
Walbrook	1	14	15	16	28	2	....	76	80	19	2
Total	34	133	160	275	688	513	7	1,810	£851	13*s.*	8¼*d.*
Assessments of 1332	16	172	141	253	502	543	....	1,627	£670	7*s.*	5¾*d.*

dermen had been able to escape in 1319, it is extremely doubtful whether all merchants had contributed, for out of twenty-one pepperers known to have been in business in Sopers Lane in 1316, the names of only thirteen appear on the roll. Unless population had decreased in the interval, which is unlikely, the figures of 1332 are therefore even shorter in the middle sections than they appear. Since those of 1319 are short in the lowest category, the total population capable of paying taxes must obviously have been well over two thousand.

The unenfranchised were not liable to taxation. One of the names entered on the 1319 roll is struck off with the note, "Cancell qe non liber ville." Several other names were entered with the note, "Nichil quia pauper." Three of these exemptions were for women, possibly widows, and the names of the men—Hug' le Wyrdrawere, Stephen le Nayler, Roger le Brewere—are suggestive of lower-class occupations and servingmen. The smallest sums collected, between $6\frac{1}{2}d.$ and $13\frac{1}{2}d.$, were paid by many of the poorer members of prosperous crafts, by working tailors, cordwainers, girdlers, chandlers, and brewers, also by taverners, colliers, fusters, metal-workers, and by people who probably followed the humble occupations after which they were named—William Lymbrenner, Patrick le Ymager, Adam le Lokier, William le Milleward, Nicholas le Glaswright, William Wyndrawere, Ralph le Bowestrengere.

Practically all the taxpayers of 1319 who by assessments of 16s. 8d. or more were credited with the possession of goods worth £10 or more were merchants, the proportion who were members of lesser companies, 5 out of 182, being less than 3 per cent. This is a smaller proportion than appeared in 1347, when out of 414 resident citizens assessed on goods worth £10 or more for the purpose of raising a gift and a loan for the king, 20, or nearly 5 per cent, were members of the lesser companies.[43] On the other hand, the smaller merchant payments of 1319 were scaled down as low as 2s., representing an assessed value of merchandise of only 24s., a level assigned to a great many members of industrial crafts, men such as cutlers, tanners, tawyers, joiners, and others. Many members of the more predominantly commercial of the lesser com-

43. *Cal. L. Bk.*, *F*, pp. 143–53. Unless the line of exemption was actually higher than £10, this list, too, is incomplete, for it includes only 26 out of the contemporary roll of 107 freemen in the mercers' company (Mercers' Register of Freemen, entries for 1347).

panies, men such as saddlers, fullers, cornmongers, and wax-chandlers, paid between 5*s.* and 10*s.* or more. The two rolls concur in giving on the whole a rather modest impression of merchant wealth. A system of assessment based only on merchandise that could be inspected on city premises, however, would inevitably have favored the merchants, because they always had much of their stock in movement to or from other ports or centers of distribution. This interpretation does not rule out the possibility that they were unduly favored by the assessors, as against citizens of other classes; again, the merchant companies of this period may have included more members who were struggling along on a very small capital than they did later.

2. LANDS AND RENTS

London citizens were in the market for landed property of many kinds from an early date. Enrolments made in the husting court enable one to trace transfers of city property back to 1258; and surviving deeds in other series, going back into the twelfth century, show the great citizen families accumulating houses, shops, and quays in London and country property also in the home counties, East Anglia, and in Northamptonshire. This process continued throughout the thirteenth century. Edmonton and Enfield were favorite Middlesex locations, where citizens bought country houses, manors, and plots of woodland and pasture and agricultural land.[44] Some of this property was held for several generations; some was but a temporary investment. A garden in Westminster descended for three generations in the Bucointe family, five acres of corn-growing land in Southwark were passed on from a merchant in the Eswy family to his brother, who sold it to an Irishman for the high price of £10; a manor in Northamptonshire passed to Stephen of Cornhill by mortgage and was sold by him to a knight. Similarly, large and small properties in London were bought and sold again or passed on to heirs.[45]

44. On twelfth-century purchases see W. Page, *London, Its Origin and Early Development* (1923), pp. 239–63; also deeds in the Bridge House collection, and others in the possession of the drapers' company. For thirteenth-century purchases in Middlesex see W.A.M., 140, 247, 252, 264, 283, 287, 297, 299, 300, 1235, 4216. On East Anglian purchases see J. H. Round, "An Early Citizen Squire," *Ancestor*, II (1902), 58–62; Blomefield, V, 185; *Norfolk Feet of Fines*, ed. Walter Rye (1885), pp. 310, 385.

45. W.A.M., 17481; *Chart. St. Thomas*, p. 122; *Henry of Pytchley's Book of Fees*, ed. W. T. Mellows ("Publications of the Northampton Record Society," Vol. II [1927]), pp.

The extent of this acquisition can be read more plainly in the fuller records of the fourteenth century. A typical merchant estate was that of Ralph de Honilane, alderman and vintner, who in 1306 failed for debts of £91. In one city parish he held two messuages worth £18 a year, out of which £5 annual rent was owing to another citizen and 20s. to St. Giles's Hospital; 16 per cent of the remainder had to be allowed for repairs, leaving him a clear income of £10. In a second parish he held two cellars, one being under the church of all Hallows in Honey Lane, and two shops; the depreciation on these was only 6 per cent, leaving him further clear income of £4 16s. Under the terms of statutes staple, all the property was handed over to be held by his creditors until they should have recovered the amount of their claims.[46] The very high rate of depreciation does not speak well for contemporary methods of building, although in these circumstances, in order to guard against abuse of the property by the creditors, it may have been set higher than was actually necessary.

As was normally the case in medieval cities, the church was a great ground landlord; it also, in the late thirteenth century, owned more than half the flourmills in the city and vicinity.[47] Lighter construction on the sites in its possession was largely left to citizens, who, paying comparatively small quitrents, were allowed to reap most of the benefit that accrued from improvements.[48] New construction was continuing in the early fourteenth century, with merchants building and enlarging houses for their own use and shops to be rented. Another form of investment was the purchase of rent charges, that is, the securing of annuities on house property, a practice that was very common in Continental cities.

The incomes that were drawn from freehold and leasehold

63–64, 70–71 n. Thirteenth-century transactions in the city are recorded in many of the deeds in the possession of the Dean and Chapter of St. Paul's and in the P.R.O. series of Ancient Deeds, as well as in the other series mentioned above.

46. *Cal. L. Bk.*, *C*, pp. 245–48. The same rate of 16 per cent depreciation was allowed on a house, two shops, and two solars seized for debt in 1307 (*ibid.*, p. 243). A Ralph de Honilane, son of Elias de Honilane, had in 1279 received a bequest of a garden in the parish of St. Giles Without, Cripplegate, from a citizen friend (*C.W.C.H.*, I, 42).

47. Of 26 millowners named in city records of this period, 16 were of ecclesiastical and 2 of knightly rank; the king and 7 citizens completed the list (*Cal. L. Bk.*, *A*, p. 2).

48. This was the normal policy; see M. Hemmeon, *Burgage Tenure in Medieval England* (1914), pp. 149–51.

property and rent charges in the city ranged over a wide scale. One vintner midway in his career, in 1327, had three houses, two breweries, a tavern, and several blocks of shops, worth £36 a year; another, holding a wharf in the Vintry and the advowson to a chantry, was able at his death in 1397 to assign his wife an income of £80 from city property.[49] A grocer, serving as city chamberlain, had in 1376 a rental of £118, derived from over forty shops, five woolhouses, four gardens, three breweries, and other tenements and rents in London and Westminster and the suburbs.[50] Sir Nicholas Brembre's London property, valued at £58 10s., included, besides two large houses and several blocks of shops, four cellars, eleven chambers, two stables, a wharf, and a crane; his rival, John Northampton, had seventy pieces of property scattered about the city, worth, in all, over £120 a year.[51] The Grantham family, grocers, had accumulated a still larger rent roll, its heiress in 1370 having an income of £153.[52] It should be added that it is not certain whether these valuations allowed for depreciation.

Country holdings were equally diversified in nature and value. Large lump sums were paid for manors or portions of manors, and small pieces of land were acquired as opportunity offered. East Anglia was a popular field, but manors within easy riding distance of London, which not only could serve as investments but also provided pleasant country residences, were the most eagerly sought. William Cosyn in 1305 bought the manor of Great Sutton in Kent, with the advowson of the church there, for £200; a dozen years later he is found buying a neighboring messuage for £5, and he apparently settled down to live there.[53] Hugh de Garton, mercer, was at the same period buying property in four parishes in Norfolk, and another family of mercers had mills at Mitford in that county.[54] Ralph Nontey, draper, was settled at the time of the

49. Reginald de Conduit, E, 199/25/33; and Henry Vanner, Hust. R.W.D., 126/76.

50. William Eynesham, E, Rentals and Surveys, 1/21. He seems to have held about the same amount at his death in 1394 (Hust. R.W.D., 123/58).

51. E, 136/108/1 (London escheats, 10–12 Ric. II).

52. L. Bk., *G*, fol. 252*b*.

53. *Cal. P.R., 1301–7*, p. 312; *Feet of Fines for the County of Essex*, II, 123, 169. Will of William Cosyn of Sutton, dated 1340, is either his or his son's (*C.W.C.H.*, I, 479–80).

54. Rye, *op. cit.*, p. 244. Garton's will (1327) mentions only London property (see Appen. A). John Hauteyn paid his parents an annuity of £4 in return for enfeoffment of lands and mills at Mitford (*Cal. L. Bk., C*, p. 203 [1306]).

Black Death at Halstead in Essex and had more lands and fisheries at West Greenwich; other merchants had inland fisheries in Kent and Hertfordshire.[55] Richard Preston, grocer, bought a wharf and a grange in East Greenwich and had lands at Sandgate, in Kent, several water-mills in that county and elsewhere, and property in Calais.[56] William Causton, mercer, was one of those who kept up the London ties with Edmonton. He bought a whole knight's fee there and shared another with a fellow-mercer, Roger de Depham, and, in consequence of advancing money to local people on the security of their lands, he was constantly adding to his possessions.[57] One of the largest citizen landlords of the century was Sir John Pultney, who at his death in 1349 held twenty-three manors, in five counties; his favorite one was Penshurst, where he made his country home. He had also bought a disused fulling-mill at Stepney and restored the channel supplying it with water-power, and he owned two other mills in East Smithfield.[58]

Many of the landed citizens of this century retained personal charge of the management of their estates. One goldsmith had to be sworn before the mayor and aldermen that he would train his apprentice properly and not waste his time sending him out into the country to thresh his corn and do field work.[59] The produce he raised might form an important part of a merchant's business assets. The store of grain alone on Pultney's manors at his death was valued at £258, and there were also stores of meat. The handling of any large quantity of produce of his own was likely to draw a citizen into the produce trades. John Wade, whose crop of wheat on his manor of Bromley in 1307 sold for 50 marks, owned granaries in London; and Roger de Depham bought up growing crops that were for sale on a knight's estate near his own lands at Ed-

55. *Chart. St. Thomas*, pp. 146, 147; W.A.M., 4363, 5183.

56. Hust. R.W.D., 120/16 (1391).

57. See Appen. A. He acquired his knight's fee from William de Ferynges; the other was shared by Depham and Robert de Plesyngham (E, 179/141/114). He bought other pieces of property from other citizens, a tanner, a grocer, a fishmonger, also from a knight (W.A.M., 164, 166, 237, 341). Among those to whom he lent money were John Patrick, who held woodland, Thomas Squiler, John de Chilterne, and John le Venour. Some of the loans were said to be for purposes of trading for Causton's benefit (W.A.M., 175, 189, 218, 231, 233, 235, 5036). Venour mortgaged property also to Depham (W.A.M., 305, 308). Chilterne was a man of considerable property, with an armorial seal (W.A.M., 47).

58. *Cal. Inq. p.m.*, Vol. IX, No. 183; *Cal. Inq. Misc.*, Vol. III, Nos. 77, 189; E, 149/222/12; E, 101/508/12 (Accounts Various).

59. *Cal. P. & M. Rolls*, II, 18 (1365).

monton.[60] John de Bernes was lord of a market and an annual fair at Colworth in Northamptonshire.[61] Grain and stock were frequently bequeathed in wills. A fishmonger who had retired to his lands at Lindfeld in Sussex left a friend his best cow; and another fishmonger, who raised sheep in Surrey as a side line, left twenty of them to maintain a light in Cheam church; Walter Sibyle, an alderman belonging to the same company, kept a large flock of sheep on his lands in Suffolk.[62] Merchants' lands were probably kept well stocked with other animals as well. A holding of thirty-eight acres at West Greenwich that Ralph Nontey bequeathed to the Hospital of St. Thomas in Southwark carried with it two horses and two oxen for work, seven cows, thirty-four pigs, forty-nine sheep, and ten lambs.

In the hands of merchants both rural and urban property did constant service as security for business loans. A series of particulars of lands seized for creditors under statutes staple in the last decade of the century shows that very small holdings were so used and that a great many London merchants had only small pieces of property, perhaps only a few scattered acres; these were often, no doubt, inherited from country parents. Members of the lesser companies also had small rural holdings, mostly in the home counties, and made use of them for credit in the same way.[63]

One of a merchant's chief motives in acquiring real property and rents was to provide for the future of his wife and children in the event of his early death. As has been shown, many purchases were made under the pressure of marriage settlements; another urgent incentive was the desire to leave a source of income out of which chantry priests could be hired to sing for the family souls. Under favorable conditions the returns were probably not much below average trading profits. In the mid-fourteenth century it was possible to expect from 6 to 8 per cent; in the fifteenth century the market price of country property rose, pushing the returns down

60. *Cal. L. Bk., B*, p. 199; W.A.M., 146 (1335).

61. *Cal. Ch. R.*, V, 229.

62. Wills of Ralph Double and William Maihewe (P.C.C., Rous, 6 [1392]) and Laurence de Wyght (Comm. Lon., Courtney, 147 [1386]). Sibyle once had 212 sheep stolen (P.R.O., *Duchy of Lancaster Miscellanea*, 10/47). John Northampton's will refers to the grain in his granges; he had lands at Shoreditch and Tottenham (Hust. R.W.D., 126/18).

63. C, 131, Extents on Debts. On the use of the lands for this purpose and on the temporary acquisition of land see Postan, "Credit in Medieval Trade," *op. cit.*, pp. 248-49.

to about 5 per cent on investments. Rent charges were assumed to represent about 4 per cent; annuities paid by religious houses ran to 10 per cent.[64]

Standing for security in both this world and the next, the lands and the houses in a citizen's possession wore a symbolic importance that was independent of their market value. To husband them carefully and increase them became a part of the cult of family status. The mixed spirit of piety, pride, and acquisitiveness in which the accumulation of property was pursued is well illustrated in the papers left by John Lawney, a broker of the early fifteenth century. Compiled about 1430, they form the earliest family book of the kind that has come to light. In 1422 Lawney had married a stockfishmonger's widow who came of a propertied merchant family in Lynne. This marriage set him on the path of accumulation. His injunctions to his heirs cannot be better expressed than in his own words from the introduction to the book of deeds he left for their guidance:

Be hit knowen to alle my childerin and here Eyris þat cumyn of me Jon Lawneye citezin & grocer of London & of Mergrete my Wyef þe towto' of Philip Wyth of Lynne, þat þe forseyd John Lawneye p'chasid in fee symple þe place of Lynne Wyth þe tenementis þer aboute by fore seynt Mergret Cherche. First þe modir of my Wyf Margrete Wyth þe Wyf of Philippe Wyth þe fadir of my forseyd Wyf eche hadde of me for here state for þe terme of here lyf. ii. Marke and Sir Youn Wyth, her son hadde of me for his state for þe reversyn of his modir. iiii. marke//And þanne y made newe þe parlour & al þat syde þat coste. C.l. marke. And treweli y myyth have had mykil more faire good for þe same tenementis i for gret cherischete & love of oure children and kynredin of my forseyde Wyf, We John Lawneye & Mergrete my Wyf have done Entalyid þese forseyd tenementis be Fine at Westmynster lyke as ye schal fynden yt Writun in þis Book after clereli as hit was doon.

Also of ye tenementz in London & in Southwerke þat were parteynynge to Mergrete my Wyfe the terme of here lyf & aftir here dissese to be sold. þanne y þe forseyd Jon Lawney purchasid here reversiun of þe feffez and payde þer fore liche as ye schul see in þis same book so þat þe fee symple was in me to gyf hit & selle hit And for þe grete love þat my Wyef & y hadde to oure childrin. We dede

64. William Thorneye instructed his executors to use £400 in buying land and rents worth £40 or 40 marks a year (Hust. R.W.D., 77/141 [1349]). The earl of Arundel in 1375 left 1,000 marks for the purchase of lands yielding 97 marks a year, for the support of the College of Arundel (Dugdale, VI, 3 [1377]). Trading profit of 8 per cent was at the end of the century considered satisfactory. Adam Chaungeour made this on his first year's trading with Lady Knolles's money. The grocers' average profit on fifteenth-century trade in spice with company funds was 10 per cent. Thomas Bataill in 1455 left 100 marks for the purchase of a rent charge of 4 marks (P.C.C., Stokton, 6). William Estfeld bargained in 1437 to receive 50 marks for life on the sum of 500 marks paid to the convent of Waltham Holy Cross (*Cal. C.R., 1435–41*, p. 124).

entayle hit to oure eiris. like as ȝe may see aftur in þis book, And copiid þe dedis
of þe forseyd tenementis of London and of Lynne in þis book for a Kalender to
alle oure eyris. (And chargin alle oure childrin up on oure blessynge & alle þe
eiris þat hit fallir to: þat ȝe preye & do preye for me þe forseyde. Jon. & Mergrete
my Wyef. & for alle oure goode coeris and doy for us in almus dede everi of ȝou
þat hit fallir to. to your' powere wir outin ani fayntise or fraude. As ye Wil
answere by fore god at þe day of doom. & consydere ye þat ye be mikul bound-
in þer to for alle þese forseyd tenementis boþe in Lynne and in London þe
Which was oure be my purchas to give and to selle. And for grete love to you
oure eyris: We wolde nat selle hit. but Entaylid hem to you. And þer fore schewe
ye as moche love to oure soulis. And hit is Entaylid so clerli & so sykerli: þat yer
may no creature disseyve you þer of. nor non of you disseyve oþir

Also ye schul fynde folwinge in his book bi þe copie of þe testament of olde.
Philip Wyth. þat þe forseyde Philip hath Entaylid bi þe forseyd testament to
alle oure eyris a feyre place wyth a keye be þe Watir. syde. þe Whiche place is
called þe rose. in dampgate. þe whiche place þe modir of my Wyf hath sinfulli
sold aȝens þe ryth. And ye same testament of þe forseyd Philip is EnRollid In
þe gyldehalle of Lynne By þe whych ye þat be oure eyris schal rekwer hit wanne
ye lust to sewe hit by þe wri of lynne.

Also ye schal fynde a monge mi dedis mani dedis þat is nat Writin in þis
book of a place at Watlingeston be syde lynne and of .xx. akris: & a Rood of
lond wiþ þe same place þe Whyche longys to oure Eyris be good Ryth. & þer
for ye þat cum aftir us; save ye hit.

Also ye schal fynde mani dedis þt is nat wrytin in þis book of a place in lynne
þat is in hogge mannes wey that is callid Wenteworthis place þer to have ye
riȝth also. þer which Sewith for youre riȝth for y was so chargid wiþ purchas þt
y myȝth nat sewe hit// And also y hadde a losse by a fals felaw of . ii. Mark up
on o day—And þer for ye þat cum aftir me parforme þis goodis þat y have nat
toon. And prayth for þe soulis of us for þat we have doon to you.

PRAYETH FOR þE SOULIS OF JON LAWNEYE AND MERGRETE
HIS WYEF & FOR ALLE CRISTIN.

. . . .

This testament nex folwynge is þe testament of old Philip Wyth. of Lynne be
þe whych testament he hath Entayled to us. and to alle our Eyris. þe feyre
place with a keye on þe Waturside þt is callid þe rose in dampgate. And Mergrete þe modir of my Wyef solde the same place to Blakeneye of lynne. And he
Wyste Wel þat hit was nat clere. And þer for he made þe modir of my Wyef
and here husbond herre loveliche bowndin to him by obligacion in a gret some
þat yif ye Eyris put him owt þer of þey to forfete ye summs of here obligacion
/ And for as moche as noydir. i. nor my Wyf myȝth nat of ryȝth nature Seen
her modir at Myschef.// by þis bond þer for we forbar and Wolde nat entre
duryng here lyef. But y charge you alle myn Eyris as ye Wil aunswere bifor god:
þat ye sewe youre ryȝth & recovere þe same place for hit is Enrollid in þe gilde
halle of lynne & þat þis be don In savinge of þe soule of my Wyfes modir for bi
here live sche hadde moche sorwe for þis matir And mykil fayre þyng sche sold
aWey aȝens ryȝth & conc̄nce And serche well ye þis testament & yif ye to so hit
Wil turne you to profyt.[65]

65. City of London archives, Lynne MS.

The number of citizen freeholders in Lawney's day is fairly accurately known through a lay subsidy assessment roll of the year 1412.[66] Nobles, knights, esquires, officials, clerks, and chantry trustees aside, this gives the names of 771 men and 111 women. Three of the latter were wives of citizens, apparently holding property in their own right, 10 were widows of knights and aldermen, and 28 were widows of ordinary citizens. Seventy were single. Probably many of these were independent householders in business, like one, with a shop worth 5s., who was a chandler. Others, like "Elena commorans cum Thoma' Chaucer," were probably gentlewomen, and still others may have been orphan heiresses of citizen families. Since the roll relates to city property only, one must look elsewhere for information as to the number of people whose holdings lay entirely outside London. To judge from the evidence of contemporary wills, about 15 per cent were in this position.[67] The number of citizen households that were backed by landed property, then, must have been between 900 and 1,000.

The commissioners of the subsidy reported cautiously that, owing to lack of tenants and to dilapidations resulting from fire and water, the valuation of city property could not be exact. The assessments were based on inquiries made under oath. On estates yielding less than £20, which were not liable to taxation, they may have been very close to current annual values; but on the larger properties it is likely that there was a more generous allowance for depreciation. Only one citizen estate was assessed as worth over £100 a year, that of Sir John Philpot's widow, set at £122 odd, and the nearest two figures to this were £93 and £78. The general distribution, if all the women's holdings are included, and also the seventeen estates in the hands of executors, was as follows: under £1, 103; £1–£5, 468; £5–£10, 172; £10–£20, 80; £20–£50, 25; and £50 and up, 10.

In 1436 all citizens with lands and rents in or out of London worth £5 or more became liable to payment of a subsidy. The

66. E, 179/144/20; printed in *Archaeological Journal*, XLIV, 56–85. Seventeen figures were given for the estates of recently deceased citizens, still in the hands of their executors. The particulars of account, giving the names of those whose property was assessed at £20 and above, who alone were called on to contribute to the subsidy, are contained in E, 179/144/19, printed in *Gentleman's Magazine*, May, 1839, pp. 497–98. For discussion of the levy see R. Sharpe, *London and the Kingdom*, I, 251–52.

67. From a sample of 172 wills proved between 1401 and 1410, referring to lands. The same proportion holds among those listed on the 1436 subsidy roll (see Appen. B).

commissioners of 1412, indeed, had been directed to assess holdings outside the city and had professed to find the task impossible. This time no such excuse was allowed, but resentment probably gave rise to a good deal of evasion and underassessment. In spite of the fact that 61 people, gentry and clergy excepted, were described as having property entirely outside the city, the number returned, 320, was only 3 more than the number listed in 1412 as having property above £5 in value in London alone. The total assessment on the 320 estates came to £6,080. Adding the assessed values of the London properties that had been set below the £5 line in 1412 gives the figure of £7,290 as a conservative estimate of the total value of the citizens' freehold lands and rents; this leaves many small country holdings out of account.[68]

TABLE 10

	£100 and Up	£50– £100	£20– £50	£10– £20	£5– £10	Total
Merchants, including widows..	5	12	67	61	53	198
Members of lesser companies, including widows.........	....	....	3	14	26	43
City officials................	....	1	2	1	3	7
Unidentified................	....	2	8	24	38	72
Total................	5	15	80	100	120	320

The majority of those who on each occasion were assessed at £5 and above can be identified as belonging to the merchant class. The assessments of 1436 give the picture of the distribution of landed wealth shown in Table 10. Representatives of over forty of the lesser companies, however, are to be found on the 1412 roll, one of them, a saddler, being assessed at just over £50. If all the owners of one or two small shops or houses or a few acres in the country could be included, it is more than likely that the merchant freeholders would be outnumbered by other citizens, yet the amount of property in merchant hands was undoubtedly greater in value than the sum of the smaller holdings.

Paradoxically enough, some of the wealthiest merchants in the

68. For names on the roll of 1436 see Appen. B. For discussion of this subsidy see H. L. Gray, "Incomes from Land in England in 1436," *EHR*, XLIX (1934), 607–39. Comparison with the figures there printed will show that the figure of £6,080 (which excludes holdings of gentry and clergy), represented about 4 per cent of the total national assessment of property above the £5 exemption line.

city had little or no landed property. Men who had their warehouses regularly filled with several hundred pounds' worth of merchandise did not seem to feel the possession of lands essential to
their security. A mercer who died in 1462 worth over £800 had no
lands at all; and Simon Eyre, draper, who at his death had 7,000
marks invested in his business, was content with investments in
urban property yielding only £10 a year and lived in a rented
house.[69] After the property qualification for the office of alderman
had been defined, in 1469, as consisting in £1,000 in goods and
good debts, it was believed that some men had bought lands simply in order to reduce their business capital below this level.[70]
Being well able to arrange profitable marriages for their children,
the more successful merchants were not so deeply concerned about
the future of their families as were John Lawney and his wife; even
when they bought lands, they would not necessarily trouble to entail them. On the other hand, success might induce in a merchant
a driving ambition to establish his son as a country gentleman; in
that case he would make a practice of buying country property
and would seek to entail at least one large manor.

The merchant who was both successful and socially ambitious
might by the time of his death have a third to a half of his fortune
or more in the form of lands. John Hende, draper, estimated that
his debts and merchandise would realize between £4,000 and
£5,000; his income from manors in Kent was £41, he had property
in Essex, including several manors, a mill, and the reversion of a
quay in Colchester, worth possibly as much again; and his income
from London property had been assessed in 1412, six years before
his death, at £54 14s. 7d. Thomas Wilford, fishmonger, left legacies of about £700 and property in London, Surrey, and Nottinghamshire; his widow, who had received most of the property in
London, but not all of it, was assessed in 1412 as having drawn an
income there of £44 9s. 11d. Robert Chichele, grocer, drawing up
his will in 1439, bequeathed only £360 in cash apart from that

69. John Chacombe (Jacombe), Journals, 7, fol. 31. On Eyre see Appen. A. Cf. case
of Thomas Dyster, mercer, whose goods and debts were worth £2,590 and his lands not
quite £150 (*Cal. P. & M. Rolls*, IV, 18–20, 21–24). Another merchant's goods came to
£2,842, including £14 as a year's rent from London property he had owned (E.C.P., 43/
273). Cf. case of Sir Thomas Hill, Appen. A.

70. Beaven, II, xxxix. For some use of material on this period see Mary Albertson,
London Merchants and Their Landed Property during the Reigns of the Yorkists (Phila-
delphia, 1932).

arising from the sale of his lands, which had been assessed for the recent subsidy as yielding £81 a year. William Wetenhale's legacies in 1457 came to £500, less than the value of his Essex lands and London property, which were judged by inquisition to be worth 64 marks a year. Another example is that of Sir Geoffrey Boleyn. According to Leland, Boleyn "got together about an 100 markes of land" and "died a great rich man." By the official extent made after his death in 1463, he had considerably more than this; with manors in Kent, Sussex, and Norfolk, as well as London property, he was worth £115 a year in rents, representing an investment of over £2,000. He had left £1,000 in money and plate among his children and possibly as much again to his wife.[71]

The subsidy roll of 1436 shows that the citizens' country properties were widely scattered, every county in the kingdom being mentioned except Worcester, Rutland, Lancashire, and those in the extreme north. Many of the more distant holdings had probably been acquired by inheritance or marriage, but the citizens' radius of acquisition by purchase continued, as in the previous century, to include East Anglia, and the market was active enough to justify the licensing of brokers of lands and rents.[72] Like his predecessors, the fifteenth-century merchant was interested in all forms of revenue-producing property, in mills, quays, fisheries, woodlands, and gardens, as well as in sheep pastures and arable land. A purchase of a third share of two mills at Staines called "Le Newmylles" is on record, and one man refers in his will to the recent building of a brick warehouse for wool in his "grete garden" in Calais.[73] There are a great many references to the suburban gardens that helped to produce London's food supply, in the parishes outside Bishopsgate and Aldersgate, in the meadows to

71. On the affairs of these men, all of them aldermen, see Appen. A. Cf. Stephen Brown, Staundon, Merlawe, Parker, Wyfold, for similar cases.

72. L. Bk., *I*, fol. 276, and list of brokerage rates in the Mercers' Wardens' Accounts, I, fol. 167; E.C.P., 77/38. There was apparently little purchasing in Staffordshire before the sixteenth century (see F. G. Davenport, "The Agricultural Changes of the Fifteenth Century," *Quarterly Journal of Economics*, XI [1896], 207–10). The same manor might be bought and sold among merchants repeatedly. See an instance in P. & M. Rolls, A 98, m. 3*b* (MS cal.); the manor in question was in 1479 worth 400 marks. Cf. case of a carpenter in Southwark selling the manor of St. Maryehalle in Kent with land for 157 sheep and two adjoining sheepfolds to William Lemyng, grocer; purchase price £100 (*Cat. Anc. Deeds*, I, 395 [C 100]; II, 567 [C 2864] [date, 1468]).

73. W.A.M., 16801 (1448); will of Robert Twygge, mercer (P.C.C., Milles, 45 [*ca.* 1491]).

the north of the city, in Southwark, and, farther out, at Chertsey and Bermondsey, at Broomfeld in Middlesex, and Radclive in Berkshire; gardeners, who might be women, were engaged to work them.[74]

Charges were made and may in some instances have been true that merchants abused their position as creditors and mortgagees to obtain possession of property that they coveted. Two such charges were brought against Thomas Cook, draper, his alleged dishonesty being in one case explained by the fact that the lands in dispute were "nygh the contre and shire where the said Thomas Coke was born."[75] William Wetenhale was accused of ingratiating himself with a young landowner with the object of getting the manor of Clapham in Surrey for 300 marks instead of 500. As the latter's story goes, Wetenhale had feigned "to be of amyte," ready to do all he could for the boy for his mother's sake, called him "cosyn," invited him often "to com to London to dyne with hym," and so "wt fayre promysse and gay disseyvyng langage hadde the seid manor."[76] Another accusation was that merchants who leased lands or had temporary possession of them for recovery of the amount of a debt were guilty of felling too much timber.[77]

Throughout the century numerous bequests of sheep and cattle and wheat indicate that the landed merchant took a direct interest in the management of his property.[78] In the Cely family, when

74. Henry Cantelowe left half a mark "to John my gardyner at Radcliffe"; and Rob. Parys 20s. to "Eleanore muliere custodienti gardinum meum de ultra Thamisiam" (P.C.C., Milles, 26; Archdeaconry, London, 165). See also wills of John Hoo and William Henore (Comm. Lon., More, 204v, 377), Richard Hakedy (P.C.C., Stokton, 15), John Dommers (P.C.C., Luffenham, 26), John Sussex (P.C.C., Marche, 7), John Love (P.C.C., Wattys, 29), John Fysh (P.C.C. Vox, 7), Thomas Babham (P.C.C., Milles, 36), Richard Lee (P.C.C., Horne, 27), and Sir William Taylor (Appen. A; Anc. Deeds, C 5214). For similar references of the previous century see Anc. Deeds, A 1873; Hust. R.W.D., 30/93; *Chart. St. Thomas*, pp. 51, 52, 58; *Chertsey Cartularies* ("Publications of Surrey Record Society"), XXXIV (1933), Part III, 369. For references to merchant ownership of garden property in the thirteenth century see H.M.C., *Ninth Report, Appendix*, p. 8.

75. *Cal. C.P., Eliz.*, I, lxvii, lxviii (the charge was not proved); E.C.P., 191/10, 60/183, 108/70.

76. Robert Weston *vs.* William Wetenhale (E.C.P., 39/129 [1433–43]).

77. See cases involving Cook and Wetenhale, nn. 75, 76. Lord Hastings, leasing the manor of Willoughby at Tottenham and Edmonton to a London fishmonger, reserved the woods (H.M.C., Hastings MSS, I, 215 [1473]).

78. For examples see wills of Brampton, Doget, Evot, Staundon (references in Appen. A). John Develyn kept swans on property in Cambridgeshire (P.C.C., Milles, 14 [1487]). Case of theft from a grocer's fisheries in Essex, K.B., 27/620, Rex, xiv (1417).

the sons stayed long abroad, their father had not only the buying
end of the business to manage but also their country estate in
Essex: "I may not dele wyt woll and fell and my hosbanry in the
contre bothe but I may have helpe," he wrote in one appeal for
their speedy return.[79] In another family a mercer with lands in
Bedfordshire left his mother to manage sheep and wool.[80] As landlords, merchants were perhaps inclined to be more business-like
than gentlemen. Thomas Knolles's purchase of the manor of North
Mimms in 1428 led to an upward revision of rents. When one of
the tenants complained, however, Knolles agreeably observed that
he wished all men well and promised an adjustment. It was not he
who had ordered the increase, he said, but his "dame," who with
the help of their granddaughter's husband and a hired auditor took
all the responsibility for managing the estate.[81] In a number of
other instances the merchant farmed out his lands.[82]

3. STANDARDS OF COMFORT

The standards of living of the different classes in the city were
at many points in sharp contrast but nowhere more so than in the
vital matter of housing. The poor had to crowd their families into
single rooms in alley tenements that rented for a few shillings a
year, carrying on their crafts there, if they were domestic workers,
as best they could. Sanitation, ventilation, light, and cooking
facilities were of the worst. The shopkeepers were better off, having a separate place in which to work, but the majority had
probably only one living-room, built either behind their shop or as
an attic or solar above it. The smaller shops, wedged into corners
or huddled against the great merchants' warehouses, measured as
little as five or six feet by ten. The larger ones were built in long
rows, with solars above them, identical in design. The street frontage was ten or twelve feet and the depth about twenty feet; some-

79. *Cely Papers*, p. 43 (1480).

80. John Muscell (P.C.C., Logge, 19 [1485]).

81. P. & M. Rolls, A 81, *m. 5b* (MS cal.). The tenant was a London tallow-chandler,
who had inherited a holding of 100 acres from his elder brother. Sir John Fortescue, who
later acquired this holding, found it necessary to have the matter investigated.

82. This arrangement is mentioned in the deed of sale of Robert Clopton's Cambridgeshire lands and in several wills in 1445 (Anc. Deeds, C 3584); wills of John Bolle (Hust.
R.W.D., 191/23 [1459]), Lady Margaret Leynham (P.C.C., Logge, 6 [1482]), and James
Framlode (P.C.C., Milles, 3 [1485]). Bolle's lands were in Kent; the last two references are
to Gloucestershire.

times there was a garden of equal length at the back, where craftsmen could take the more cumbrous or obnoxious processes of their
work.[83]

Merchants, on the other hand, and other substantial citizens
occupied the urban equivalent of the manor house. In its most
compact form this could be built on sites no wider than were
needed for an ordinary shop. The ground floor of the house would
consist of a shop, with warehouse space behind it; the main room,
the hall, would be on the first floor above, with kitchen, larder,
and butlery adjoining, and a third story would contain sleeping
chambers. The need for economy in space and materials led to
duplex construction. A contract of the year 1310, for the building
of "a place" in Cornhill, called for three shops on the ground floor,
two halls, with chimneys, on the first floor, with kitchens, but-
leries, and pantries, and on the top floor "deus beles chaumbres
ove chaumbres curteyses."[84] Another contract, a century later in
date, outlines the plan of a triplex house that was to be erected
over adjoining stalls and cellars in Friday Street, in the ward of
Farringdon Within. The halls were to be nine feet high, with
"speres," or screens, as a protection against draughts from the entrance, and kitchens and larders. The top floor was to be larger
and more elaborate than that of the older Cornhill place, providing three rooms for each household, eight feet in height and at
least partly ceiled, "une principal chambre, une drawyng chambre
et une forein."[85] A second type of design was similar to the old

83. Rent accounts in company records and elsewhere give many details, e.g., "of a
waterman a chaumbre by yer vis viiid . . . . of William Paris joynner a chaumbre and
the schopp under it . . . . vis viiid . . . . of a waterman a schopp wt an inner chaumbre
by yer . . . . xs" (rental of 1485, in St. Mary Hill Lane, *Mediaeval Records of a London
City Church*, E.E.T.S., No. 125 [original ser., 1878], p. 91). Thirteenth-century records
show 15 shops between old Jewry and ironmonger Lane occupying 150 feet (A. H. Thomas,
"Life in Medieval London," *Journal of the British Archaeological Society*, XXXV [new
ser., 1929], 125). A row of 20 shops to be built near the bakehouse of the Dean and Chapter
of St. Paul's in 1369 was to occupy 86 yards (H.M.C., *Ninth Report, Appendix*, p. 50).
Examples from the reign of Henry IV show 4 shops, with gardens, covering an area of
40 feet 10 inches × 43 feet 8 inches; 2 shops 8½ yards deep with total frontage of 6¼ yards;
1 shop 4 yards 11 inches × 2 yards; 2 shops each 12 feet × 20 feet; 1 shop in West Cheap
3¼ yards × 1½ yards 8 inches, height to solar 2¾ yards; 3 shops and a garden, with
frontage of 44 feet 3 inches on Candlewick Street, and lengths of 60 feet 16 inches to 67
feet (Hust. R.W.D., 130/44, 45; 132/24, 133/32, 133ˣ/47, 139/56). Four shops in West
Cheap described in 1498 as "lately rebuilt" had a frontage of 49 feet 4 inches and lengths of
32 feet to 43 feet 7 inches (Grocers' Records, Vol. 386, fol. 47).

84. H.M.C., *Ninth Report, Appendix*, p. 20.   85. *Ibid.*

twelfth-century style of manor house, which centered in the gabled, bay-windowed hall, built over cellars, but with no other story above it. In one example, as indicated in a skinner's plans for adding to an older house, in 1308, there was a two-story addition at one end of the hall, consisting of a larder, a chamber with a fireplace, and a solar above; another chamber jutted out on one side of the hall. After an old custom, the kitchen was in a separate building in the yard, in this case over a stable.[86] Such a design was capable of indefinite variation and expansion. At first there seems to have been more desire for small extra sitting-rooms than for privacy in sleeping quarters. In a fishmonger's house, described in 1373, there was a parlor (*interloquitorium*) off the hall, leading into a small chamber furnished with three chairs and a cupboard, but there was only a single family bedroom; this was either over the parlor or over the kitchen and the larder, which were both at the other end of the hall; a servants' chamber, with a "prentises-chaumbre" above it, formed another extension or wing.[87] An inventory taken in a grocer's house in 1390 refers to a counting-house and storehouse off the hall, as well as pantry, buttery, and kitchen, but there was still only one bedroom for the master and his wife and their family of five children, two of whom were daughters.[88] The greater houses of the next century made more provision for privacy, but there was no general separation of sleeping quarters except between family and servants. A wealthy mercer of the reign of Edward IV had only one chamber in which he and his wife and seven children could have slept, and his three servants had presumably to be content either with a clothes cupboard, the "presse chambre," or with a little room under the gallery of his hall, the "nether Autepaas." An inventory taken in a haberdasher's house in 1499 similarly shows only two bedrooms in use, one containing two beds, the other five.[89]

The cost of building these medium-sized houses appears to have run from about 50 to 100 marks, and they were rented for about

---

86. Riley, *Memorials*, pp. 65–66, printed also in G. G. Coulton, *Chaucer and His England* (5th ed., 1930), p. 84. For a succinct account of the evolution of house forms see A. Hamilton Thompson, *The English House* ("Historical Association Pamphlets," No. 105), p. 136.

87. *Cal. P. & M. Rolls*, II, 154–56.

88. *Ibid.*, III, 209–13.   89. Journals, 7, fol. 31; E, 154/2/7.

2 marks and up. The finest type of house, the "great house" in which the richest of the merchants lived, might be worth ten times as much.[90] A part of this value inhered in the wharfs that were attached to waterfront sites and in the clusters of "tenauntries," or little shops, that were built around the edges of other large sites, but the houses themselves were more elaborate and in some cases were built of stone; the Gisors' place, in Basing Lane, in part was of stone from Caen.[91] Usually there were stone cellars, either under the hall or elsewhere; at a mercer's house in Coleman Street the cellar began under a two-story addition in front of the hall and extended under the street.[92] In either case the house plan tended toward a quadrangular form, with the hall at one side, a two-story wing thrown out to front the street, cut by an arched gateway into the courtyard, another wing of two or three storys at the back, and warehouses and outhouses completing the square. William Servat, a Caorsin who bought a house of this kind in Bucklersbury at the beginning of the fourteenth century, added a stone tower to guard the gateway, obtaining the king's permission to crenellate it; his tower was still a landmark in Elizabethan London.[93] Sir John Pultney had two grand houses, "Cold Harbour" and "Pountney's Inn," both of which passed into the hands of nobility.[94] It is

90. Case of a carpenter's contract to build for a merchant in 1313 for £36; for a mercer in the mid-fifteenth century, a house with a chapel, for 100 marks (*Cal. L. Bk., E*, p. 21; E.C.P., 66/370). For a tenement on a site in Basing Lane measuring a little over 14 feet × 52 feet a tailor agreed to pay 40s. a year for nineteen years, and a vintner bought a tenement in the parish of St. Bride's, Fleet Street, for £62, to be paid in instalments of 8 marks a year (Hust. R.W.D., 153/57, 26 [1424]). Carpenter's charges of 94 marks for workmanship alone in building two houses for Whittington's executors in Basinghall (*Cat. Anc. Deeds*, I, 543 [*C* 1570]). The rent accounts of the grocers' company show merchants paying rents of 2 marks to £4 for dwelling-houses. Quayside tenements and those surrounded with "tenauntries" rented for from £5 to £20. Askham's place, which was built on a site just above London Bridge, with 26-foot frontage on Thames Street and a depth of 233 feet to a quay and which included a stone wall and a rambling house with a tower, was bargained for shortly after 1434 at figures of 700 and 800 marks (E.C.P., 11/527). For description of the site see Herbert, II, 51–64.

91. Stow, I, 348.

92. Merchant Tailors' Deeds, C, XIX, 1 (1455). The cellars under John Grantham's house in Dowgate measured 22½ feet × 33⅔ feet × 8¾ feet (*Cat. Anc. Deeds*, I, 212 [1329]).

93. *Cal. C. Warrants*, I, 592; Stow, I, 52, 71, 260; II, 329. Known as "Survetistour," it was used for a time for Edward III's Exchange; in 1355 the king rented it to two merchants from Lucca for £20 a year. In 1365 William Holbech, alderman, drew up his will there.

94. The Cold Harbour, in Dowgate, which he rebuilt of stone, was rented in his lifetime to the earl of Salisbury. His own residence, Pountney's Inn, was later used by the Black Prince and was not reacquired by merchants (Stow, I, 236; II, 321; R. A. H. Unthank,

possible that these famous houses were at first chiefly remarkable for the size of the halls and the solidity of their structure rather than for leading the way in facilities for privacy. Servat's house must have had at least one very large room, for the grocers rented a portion of it for their company meetings, before they built their hall, and the hall in which Henry Picard was said to have entertained five kings was considered very fine.[95] John Malewayn, one of the great financiers of the middle years of the century, followed the ordinary custom of having only two bedrooms; he had three other rooms, however, besides his hall.[96]

The earliest indication of any concern for privacy is a little later, in the house of Richard Lyons, the hated monopolist and speculator. Besides hall and office and a well-equipped kitchen, pantry, buttery, and larder, he had four bedrooms, two wardrobes, a parlor, and a chapel. Descriptions of three great merchants' houses of the latter part of the next century reveal about the same amount of accommodation. John Norman's place in Honey Lane had no more than three bedrooms, but at least one of them was apparently assigned to an individual member of the household.[97] John Olney's place in the parish of St. Mary Magdalen Milk Street had eight rooms available for bedrooms and parlors.[98] At Brown's Quay, near the Tower, where there was a fine oak hall forty feet long and twenty-four feet wide, there were two parlors, a chapel, and three other chambers on the ground-floor wings, in addition to three small garrets and a larger room on a rambling second story.[99] Sir Thomas Cook continued to cherish the privacy of separate small rooms even when he could no longer afford a great house; after losing much of his fortune he built himself "a lytyll mancion fforeagayn the Est ende of the Frere Augustyns" without

"Some Cold Harbours," *Home and Counties Magazine*, XIV, No. 54 [1912], 82–83; C. L. Kingsford, "Historical Notes on Medieval London Houses," *London Topographical Record*, XI [1917], 74; cf. *Archaeologia*, X, 94-97).

95. Kingdon, I, 96; C. L. Kingsford, "The Feast of the Five Kings," *Archaeologia*, LXVII, 119–26.

96. E, 101/508/21/2. The rooms with beds were the "pryncipal camera" and the "garderob" (Accounts Various).

97. Lyons, E, 199/25/70; Norman, Drapers' Deeds, A. VII, 176.

98. Assize Rolls, FF, 10* (1470); MS cal.

99. C. L. Kingsford, "A London Merchant's House and Its Owners, 1360–1614," *Archaeologia*, LXXIV, 137-58.

any hall but with five rooms for himself, including a study and counting-house, further chambers for his wife, and a chapel.[100] Toward the end of the century Italian influence may have been encouraging these leanings toward privacy. The Conterini and their partners, merchants of Venice, who held a great house of the courtyard type in Botolph Lane on lease, were in 1485 using ten of its rooms as individual bedrooms and two as offices and were apparently content with two parlors; the traditional hall is not mentioned in their inventory.[101]

The nobility and the wealthier gentry were by this time well ahead of the city merchants in their tastes. Pultney's Cold Harbour, when in the hands of nobility, contained forty rooms. The country house that Sir Thomas Urswyk maintained at Dagenham had nine bedrooms, including private rooms for the family priest and Sir Thomas' clerk and a nursery for the children; there was the usual parlor by the hall, and one extra sitting-room.[102] Robert Morton, gentleman, had a fifteen-room house in the parish of St. Nicholas Olave's and a still larger place at Standon in Hertfordshire.[103] Dudley's house in Candlewick Street, at the end of the century, was built with long, well-lighted galleries connecting the main rooms in the different wings.[104]

If the merchants were more conservative in their architectural tastes than the gentry, it was partly because so much of the space at their disposal was required for the unloading and storage of their merchandise. The cellars under their halls were used mainly for wine, and other storehouses had to be set around the courtyard for cloth and miscellaneous goods. There had also to be room

100. *The Great Chronicle*, p. 222; Cook's will (P.C.C., Wattys, 3).

101. *Medieval Records of a London City Church*, p. 28. None of the rooms contained more than one bed, and one was called "Antonyes Chambre."

102. E, 154/2/2.

103. See will and inventory, printed in *Journal of the British Archaeological Association*, XXXIII (1877), 308-30. Three of the rooms at Standon were named after individual occupants: "Master Mortons chambre, ... masteres Dorothes chambre . . . . John Cookes chambre." His town house was very similar in accommodation and arrangement to the house in Cornhill where Sir John Rudston, merchant, died in 1531; both included a "Maydyns chambre," a "brusshyng chambre," presumably where clothes were brushed and cleaned, and a special larder for fish (see Book of the Funeral of Sir John Rudston, Harl. MSS, 1231). Morton had married an alderman's daughter (see Forster, Appen. A).

104. C. L. Kingsford, "On Some London Houses of the Early Tudor Period," *Archaeologia*, LXXI, 17, 39-42.

for stables and for feed for the horses, and a large household might have a special "boulting house," where the meal needed for its baking was sifted. The shops and chambers that were rented were usually outside the gate, but a desire to draw as much income from the property as possible might allow them to intrude further, into the courtyard itself.[105] Moreover, it was a custom to keep poultry and to save a small stretch of the yard for a garden. The latter had its practical use, yielding herbs and fruit, but was also designed for "consolation and pleasure." The care taken of the sunny garden at the grocers' hall shows how much the outdoor domestic life was appreciated. Hedged with whitethorn, it boasted a fig tree, some whortleberries, a melon bed, a little vineyard trailed against the parlor wall, and an abundance of flowers, the favorites being primroses, lavender, and roses. There were butts for archery practice, "a fayr erber" for rest, and "six water potts of tyn for byrds to drynke of." Gardeners and laborers were hired to dig and weed, to nurse "dyvers delicate sedis" and potted plants, to trim the vines and clip the "lory" (laurel) trees.[106]

The church was the pioneer in the city's domestic sanitation, at least two of the thirteenth-century ecclesiastical foundations having their own supply of water from sources outside the city.[107] There was no municipal water system until about the middle of that century, when Tyburn water was piped to a conduit in West Cheap. Other outlets were added from time to time, and an auxiliary source was tapped at Highbury before the middle of the fifteenth century to serve the thickly populated district of Cripplegate.[108] On account of the heavy demands on it by brewers and

105. See C. L. Kingsford, "Historical Notes on Medieval London Houses," *London Topographical Record*, XII, 5.

106. Each liveryman had a right to two or three clusters of grapes a day, when they ripened (Kingdon; Grocers' Records, Vol. 401, *passim*). The private gardens were very small (see C. L. Kingsford, *Prejudice and Promise in Fifteenth Century England* [1925], p. 139, and in *Archaeologia*, LXXIV, 154). Roof drippings hindered plants (Cal. Rolls A.N.D. [MS], DD, *m.* 3; FF, *m.* 21*d*, 35). Two wills refer to dovecots in gardens.

107. One was St. Mary's Hospital, Bishopsgate (V.C.H., Lon., 531). Another was the Franciscan convent (C. L. Kingsford, *The Grey Friars of London* [1915], and P. Norman, "Recent Discoveries of Medieval Remains in London," *Archaeologia*, LXVII [1916], 18–26; cf. *ibid.*, LXI, Part 2 [1909], 347–56). The charter-house obtained a license to lay a private aqueduct from Islington in 1431 (H.M.C., *Fourth Report, Appendix*, p. 84; see also E. A. Webb, *The Records of St. Bartholomew's Priory in Smithfield* [1921], II, 191]).

108. Stow, I, 16–19, 293; cf. A. H. Thomas and I. Thornley, *The Great Chronicle*, p. 420 n.

dyers, the supply was quite insufficient to allow piping to private houses. In 1478 a waxchandler dug through his cellar to the Fleet Street pipes and pierced them for the benefit of his own household and his neighbors. Since this caused the conduit to run low, he was discovered, sentenced to imprisonment, and paraded through the streets as an object for ridicule and abuse, dripping wet from a little model conduit set on his head, "in Example of all other which wold take a boldnes of his deds if he were unponysshed."[109] It is likely that Edmund Dudley was taking advantage of his immense political influence in the city when in 1507–8 he applied for permission to lay "a pype of leade of the quantite or compas wtin Forth of a Swannes quyll," from one of the conduits into his house, although he promised that he would make use of it only when there was an overflow and never when water was short.[110] Ordinary citizens had to make shift with rainwater cisterns, from which they sometimes ran gutters through their kitchens. Many of the wealthy merchants were better off than their neighbors in having wells on their premises, and those who occupied the great houses on the riverbank were also fortunate, except for the circumstance that neighbors swarmed down their alleys and quay steps to water horses and wash clothes.[111]

No very fastidious standards could be expected in this environment, yet conditions may on the whole have been better than in later centuries, when the city was more crowded and its cemetery problem was a serious matter. The larger medieval houses were properly equipped with cesspits having exit pipes, which should have rendered the sewage innocuous. In the smaller houses nextdoor neighbors shared the use of a privy, and there were street privies for the poor.[112] Liquid refuse of all kinds, it is true, was

109. Journals, 8, fol. 184b.

110. Ibid., 11, fol. 21. The taps at conduits were ordinarily described in those terms, as at Coventry, where it was the rule that "ther be no pype more then a swan penne" (Coventry Leet Book, E.E.T.S., original ser., No. 134, I 108 [1426]). Thomas Cromwell later had conduit water laid to his house in Throgmorton Street (Herbert, I, 471).

111. An ordinance of the common council in 1417 forbade those in possession of wharves and stairs at the river to extort money from people coming to fetch water and wash clothes (Riley, Memorials, pp. 648–49).

112. Details regarding cesspits in Cal. Rolls of Assize of Nuisance (MS), DD, passim. They were sometimes placed too close to cellars, and the stone lining was not always thick enough. For the regulations see Lib. Alb., I, 323–24. One woman put a latrine in her solar, connecting it by a wooden pipe with a street gutter in Queenhithe; she was ordered to remove it. On the regulation of latrines set over the streams see E. L. Sabine, "City

emptied from buckets and kitchen gutters into open channels in the streets and into the streams that drained the city area; and in the early fourteenth century pigs were able to root about in garbage piles. Later the public scavenging service became more efficient, superseding the pigs, and it was supplemented by private enterprise in shipping stable refuse off in dung boats, to be used as fertilizer on the citizens' fields and gardens up and down the river.[113]

Well-to-do households did not lack facilities for washing. All inventories included metal basins and ewers and often the more elaborate *lavatoria*, hanging basins with drainpipes that could empty into gutters. Sir John Pultney had six of these of silver and three of copper and dozens of basins, ewers, pots, and tubs. John Malewayn had five *lavatoria* of silver, four other basins, and three tubs. Richard Lyons had a tent to put up around his bathtub (*1 pavilon pour 1 bathfatte*). How often bathtubs were in use is uncertain. During the first century or so of recurrent plague medical opinion was doubtful of the wisdom of bathing in the winter months or of opening the pores with hot water at any time when an epidemic was in progress, but in spring and summer frequent herb baths were normally prescribed, especially for elderly people with pain in their limbs.[114] The doctors may have been more cautious than the urban public, for in all large medieval cities the bathhouse was a popular institution. In early fifteenth-century London there were at least three respectable ones for women and two for men.[115] It is probable that these were of

Cleaning in Mediaeval London," *Speculum*, XII (1937), 33–34. On construction of 10 privies in a row of 18 shops see D. & C. St. Paul's, Deeds, A/11/1074 (1371). Bequests toward repair of public latrines occur in wills. Leaden urinals were kept in the great courtyards.

113. On the whole question of sanitation see E. L. Sabine, "Butchering in Mediaeval London," *Speculum*, VIII (1933), 335–53, and "City Cleaning in Mediaeval London," *op. cit.*, XII, 19–43. In 1365 a tanner was given a week to remove his pigs and was bound in £100 not to breed them in the city again (*Cal. P. & M. Rolls*, II, 39). Poor owners of one or two pigs, however, were not penalized.

114. Advice of John de Cornhout and John of Bordeaux is contained in a fifteenth-century English manuscript, Society of Antiquaries, MS 101, fols. 18, 91, 92b. Cf. G. Henslow, *Medical Works of the Fourteenth Century* (1899), p. 100. Pultney inventory, E, 101/508/12 (Accounts Various); Lyons inventory, see n. 97 above; Malewayn's, n. 96.

115. *Cal. L. Bk., K*, pp. 75–76, 95. Known as "stews," they were likely to be confused with the brothels that went by that name. Brothels had been established in Southwark since at least as early as the twelfth century. Some of the "stews" there may have combined the functions of brothel and bathhouse. See case of a boy employed in one to carry

service chiefly to the people of moderate means, the larger house-holds making their own arrangements. The apothecaries' shops sold castile soap and sponges, and every garden grew some of the herbs that the doctors recommended. In between baths there was piecemeal washing. A merchant's widow bequeathed a friend "a bolle basen . . . . to wash his fete in."

The heavy furred woolen clothing that was worn must have grown extremely dirty. Servants and professional laundresses, however, washed everything that could be washed—table linen, bed linen, women's headdresses, and other linen clothing. Apprentices had to be given clean clothes and clean bedding. Part of a charge of neglect and ill-treatment of an apprentice that sent a tailor to prison dwelt on his having forced the boy to sleep in a bed "foule shirtyd & full of vermin."[116]

In the heating and lighting of their houses, as in their sanitary and washing arrangements, the citizens had all the modern conveniences of their age. The better two-room dwellings were constructed with wide fireplaces in the shop; the larger houses had kitchen fires for cooking, as well as fireplaces in the hall or first chamber or in both; and wheeled braziers were at hand to take the chill off other rooms.[117] Fear of burglary led to the darkening of street-front windows by iron bars, but long rows of windows in the hall sides show a craving for brightness. One citizen giving next-door property to his daughter in 1321 specified that she should erect no building within ten feet of his house, lest the light of his glass windows, two on the west and others on the north, be obstructed. In 1369 a merchant in the parish of St. Botolph without Aldgate had sixteen windows overlooking a neighbor's garden; and another in Southwark, in the next century, planned to have eighteen windows in each of the two upper storys of a new wing,

---

heavy vessels of water (*Cal. P. & M. Rolls*, II, 54 [1366]; cf. Stow, II, 54, 366). On public baths in French and German cities see L. Thorndike, "Sanitation, Baths and Street-cleaning in the Middle Ages and Renaissance," *Speculum*, III (1928), 197-98.

116. Merchant Tailors' Court Minutes, 1488–93, fol. 41*v*. Names of laundresses occur throughout the city records, e.g., Beatrice le Wimplewasher, Massiota la Lavendere.

117. For building regulations forbidding use of wooden chimneys see Lib. Alb., I, 333. A mason's contract specifies that chimneys serving adjacent shops were to be 5½ feet wide between the jambs and "desus dez mantles de Flandrisch tyle et desouth les mantles de perez et tylesherd" (H.M.C., *Ninth Report, Appendix*, p. 12 [1370]). A "petit chymene de feir" in Richard Lyons' kitchen weighed 4½ cwt., 24 lb., and was valued at 34*s*.

sixty-six feet long, that he hoped to add to his house.[118] For artifi-
cial lighting most people relied on candles; out-of-doors they used
torches or oil-burning lanterns. The rich kept large stocks of fine
wax and lit their great halls with heavy hanging chandeliers.

Fourteenth-century houses blazed with color. Whitewashed
plaster walls set off red, blue, purple, orange, and green hangings
which, being made of wool, added materially to the comfort as
well as to the brightness of the rooms. The same brilliant colors
were repeated in the profusion of cushions and canvas-lined draperies that were spread upon benches and chairs. Stripes, ermine
dots and checks, floral and heraldic designs and figured scenes,
stained or embroidered or worked in tapestry, sometimes in softer
colors, added variety. Sir John Pultney's halls were hung with the
arms of Pultney and Montague, set off by drapery spangled with
butterflies and white stars. The curtains and coverlets that en-
veloped his beds were patterned with lions' heads, eagles, fleur-de-
lis, violet popinjays, and striped "appelblom"; the least valuable
were of red or green worsted wreathed with white roses; the most
valuable was a set from Germany worked with leaves and griffins;
the oldest, nearly worn out, was stained with the story of Tristram
and Iseult, on a background of green; and among other stained
figures were the apostles, on worsted. Richard Lyons had a cloth
described as of Arras in his hall, leopard skins and ermine in his
chamber, and bed curtains of red and blue worsted embroidered
with lions. John Coggeshale, a grocer, had cushions made with his
merchant's mark, others of tapestry in a peacock design, worsted
hangings stained with animal figures, and bench covers worked
with angels and knights. Some tastes were more subdued, but the
favorite themes were the crude heraldic figures. In house after
house merchants and their families sank to sleep among fantastic
visions of dragons, boars' heads, unicorns, or leaping dolphins.[119]

In the next century a liking for painted wooden paneling developed,[120] and softer shades, such as "lilady," "applebloom,"

118. Cal. Rolls A.N.D. (MS), DD, *m.* 33; Cal. Rolls of Assize, Miscellaneout, FF, *m.*
21*d.; Cal. C. P.,* II, liv. Because of a dispute over the cost of preparing the foundations,
this last house was never built.

119. Appen. C; *C.W.C.H.,* I, 670; II, 97, 186, 207, 214, 221, 250, 262. John Malewayn
had two dorsers "de armis de Garreyne," and there is a bequest in 1361 of another showing King Richard and "Ector of Troye."

120. The parlor of the goldsmiths' hall was wainscoted and painted with oil in the

mulberry, and gray, were more often chosen for cushions and draperies. Flowers and the traditional animal figures still appeared in tapestry and embroidery and in dark coverlets and hangings stained in white that were made at Bury,[121] but there was more tapestry than formerly, and artists were becoming more ambitious. There were bequests of crude portraits, as of a worsted bedcover, embroidered "cum le Fader & quatuor filiis," and one of a man and his wife, on stained cloth, with his merchant's mark and the arms of the merchants of the staple for decoration. Other bequests were of "a steyned cloth of Mary Magdalene," an arras of the Passion, a stained cloth picture of the fight between Lord Scales and Fauconbridge, cushions "with gentilwomen and pecockes" and parlor hangings "wt fenne Countreys and boudred wt histories of the bible."[122] In collecting tapestries the merchants were but following a fashion set by the nobility. It was said that the duchess of Bedford brought about Sir Thomas Cook's ruin out of pique that he would not sell her, at her own price, a scene of the siege of Jerusalem worked in gold thread, for which he himself had paid £800.[123]

Furnishings remained otherwise very simple. Dining-tables were on trestles, ship's chests and little portable lockers held clothes and other valuables, the canopied beds served as couches, and carpets were not in general use. At the end of the fourteenth century, Flemish and German influence was evident in chairs, chests and boxes, and carved bedsteads "of beyond see makyng." Individuality showed itself in the choice of round chairs, little painted tables, three-leaved folding tables, clothespresses, stools, and

fourteenth century; the drapers' parlor was painted green in 1495 (Herbert, II, 224, 465). Mention of a painted chamber with a paneled ceiling in 1428 (*C.W.C.H.*, II, 464), also in 1472 in a mercer's house (Drapers' Deeds, A VII, 176).

121. Bequest of a coverlet "of Bury Werk with white lyons and a Chamberynd stayned according to the same werk," in will of Katherine Swetenham (P.C.C., Godyn, 6 [1464]). Other animals and birds on articles bequeathed were elephants, squirrels, dogs, pelicans, and falcons.

122. Wills of John Godyn (P.C.C., Godyn, 22 [1465]; *Archaeological Journal*, CLXVII [1885], 317); John Lamberd (P.C.C., Milles, 10 [1487], P.C.C., Vox, 7 [1493]); Hugh Brice (P.C.C., Horne, 2 [1496]). The drapers paid £10 15s. for an arras for the parlor in their hall (*Transcripts*, p. 47 [1431]). The ironmongers had two hangings "withe pecokkes vynis and wellis with the vii planettys countersette" (Register, fol. 48 [1489]). These may have been native work. See description of "tapytys of Aras" of London work at Ewelme manor in 1467 (H.M.C., *Eighth Report, Appendix*, I, 628).

123. *The Great Chronicle*, p. 207.

furniture made for children.[124] In view of English skill in carving,
the wooden furniture may well have been among the most artistic
of the contents of a merchant's house, yet it was relatively cheap,
the kitchen pots and pans and pewter dishes being as a rule worth
much more. These again were barely half the cost of the textiles,
including the stocks of table linen and sheets with the draperies
and cushions. The improvements of the fifteenth century lay in
the addition of wrought-iron hearth backs, possibly of better
flooring, and above all in the architectural harmony that cul-
minated in Crosby Hall.[125]

The careful husbanding of resources that was necessary at the
outset of so many merchants' careers made for a tradition of
economy in household management. The cost of bringing up
daughters, according to guardians' accounts of the second half of
the fourteenth century, ran from £1 a year to £2 13s.; the sum of
£60 was spent on one mercer's son over a period of eighteen years,
and an average of nearly £5 each was spent on another mercer's
son and daughter throughout the years of their childhood. Other
well-to-do citizens' standards were within the same range, expenditure on a currier's son being about £2 7s.[126] These figures are close
to minimum standards of decent subsistence in the fifteenth century, when university students and elderly people were expected
to manage on from 4 to 6 marks a year.[127] Higher standards ran to
20d. a week for board and lodging alone, as measured by a bill one
grocer presented another, £10 a year for the board and lodging of an
esquire's wife and her woman servant, staying with a London

124. C, 131/48/25, 131/62/1, 131/164; Hust. R.W.D., 94/150. The drapers in 1495
had mats in a chamber at their hall for women, but in their banqueting-hall they spread
rushes (Herbert, I, 464, 466). For other London inventories see nn. 96, 97, above, also
E, 154/2/15 and E, 194/2/7.

125. Sir John Crosby is believed to have paved his hall with unpolished Purbeck
marble (A. W. Clapham and W. H. Godfrey, *Some Famous Buildings and Their Story*
[1913], p. 137). The drapers had tiled their hall and put a parquet floor in the kitchen
(*Transcripts*, pp. 48–49 [1430]).

126. L. Bk., *G*, fol. 4; *H*, fols. 117*b*, 121, 142*b*, 215; *I*, fol. 18. Other instances, covering
shorter periods and perhaps including more abnormal expenses, are of £39 spent on a
fishmonger's son over four and half years and £7 19s. 3d. on a vintner's daughter in two
years (L. Bk., *H*, fols. 64*b*, 118*b*).

127. Inmates of Elys Davy's and the Ewelme almshouses were to be discharged in the
event of inheriting income of these amounts (A. C. Ducarel, *History of Croydon* [1783],
cited in J. Nichols, *Bibliographia topographica Britanniae*, II [1790], No. 12; H.M.C., *Ninth
Report, Appendix*, p. 220). The grocers boarded out one of their almsmen in London, in
1443–44, for 6d. a week (Kingdon, II, 283).

alderman, 3s. 4d. a week, or 13 marks a year, for board and lodging of a woman and her maidservant in Cambridge, with £2 a
year as a dress allowance for the mistress and 1 mark for the maid;
these last were claims put forward in a breach-of-promise suit.[128]
The widow of a mercer who had been worth nearly £1,000 kept
house for thirty-six weeks after his death, in 1464, with seven children and three servants, on £24 9s. 8d., that is, on 1s. 2d. a head
per week; out of this she had needed £2 9s. 6d. for clothing and
other necessaries for the servants and £1 5s. 6d. for "hoses shoes
Cappes Scolehire shavyng and other necessaries" for the children.[129] The men usually allowed a little more than this. Wills of
various dates from 1408 on instructed executors to set aside sums
for household expenses during the first few months after the testator's decease that, counting children and servants on the same
basis, allowed from 1s. 4d. to 4s. a head per week. Aldermanic families of the latter part of the century were probably more extravagant, for two retired aldermen who had no children allowed their
widows £100 for the first year's household expenses.[130]

4. SYMBOLIC ELEMENTS IN STANDARDS OF LIVING

In deciding how to spend his income the merchant was impelled
by a tangle of motives. The quantity of cushions about his house
and the equipment of his kitchen testify to love of ease and comfort and good living. This had to be harmonized with the furthering of his business. Need of warehouse space curtailed the size of
house and garden. Supplies of ready money were low. "I pray you

128. E.C.P., 46/70; P. & M. Rolls, A 73, m. 9b. (MS cal.); E.C.P., 61/584 (this suit was
against a law student who had gone to Padua for two years and stayed for ten). A retired
vintner with property worth 10 marks a year expected it to yield him a cash income of
20d. a week above the cost of food and clothing (E.C.P., 39/41). Cost of board and lodging
of an old lady and her maid staying with a servant of the duke of Clarence in the building
business in Kent was set at 4d. a day (E.C.P., 67/93). A woman lodging with a London waxchandler was charged 16d. a week (E.C.P., 64/764).

129. Chacombe accounts, Journals, 7, fol. 31 (1464).

130. John Wodecok, alderman, allowed £50 for his widow, 4 children, 8 servants, and
2 apprentices over six months (P.C.C., Marche, 17 [1408]). John Petit, grocer, allowed £20
for widow and 6 others over three months (Comm. Lon., Sharpe, 183 [1455]). William
Laurence, grocer, allowed his widow a maximum of 6s. 8d. a week for food and drink and
"hire"; the household consisted of 1 young kinswoman and 5 servants (P.C.C., Wattys,
27 [1476]). Robert Goodwyn, draper, allowed his widow, 5 children, and 2 servants £40
for one year. William Dere and Geoffrey Feldyng, ex-aldermen (P.C.C., Godyn, 2 [1459];
Comm. Lon., Wilde, 70 [1469]), and William Holt, mercer, allowed 100 marks (P.C.C.,
Godyn, 6).

144 THE MERCHANT CLASS OF MEDIEVAL LONDON

make money in all the hast after my decesse," begged a mercer in
his will, referring to the collection of his debts; and a wealthy
grocer directed his executors to raise money by selling his sword
and his jewelry.[131] Again, wishing to be thought "estatly of his
gouvernaunce," the merchant in many ways modeled his habits
on those of the gentry, yet, as the use of trade-marks in decoration
bears witness and the frequent use of fish in fishmongers' coats of
arms, he was proud of his business world. Perhaps his clearest aim
in adding to his possessions was to establish his position in the city
community more firmly by demonstrating the soundness and success of his business.

All these motives entered into the expenditure on houses. Business convenience and pleasantness set a premium on sites by the
river or on the main city thoroughfares.[132] The tradition that gave
the hall its central importance in the house was common to town
and country and linked with the desire to entertain guests as handsomely as possible. The fondness for startling heraldic themes in
the decoration of the main bedroom, which was often used as a
"withdrawing chamber" after dining, is in part to be explained by
this same desire to impress. The gateway towers and the great
arched gates that gave entrance to the courtyards were obviously
conceived with the same intention.

The merchants' country properties satisfied the same mingled
love of business, pleasure, and display. Robert Hardyng, goldsmith, combined the first two by leasing all his Surrey property to
a local yeoman with the exception of the north wing of the manor
house, an orchard, a garden, and a stable "and all other sportyng
plases there," which were to be reserved for his use whenever he
should choose to come out with guests.[133] One simple attraction

131. John Boton (P.C.C., Godyn, 6); William Burton (P.C.C., Luffenham, 24).

132. The mercers were in 1474 scattered in at least eighteen wards; of 65 liverymen
whose ward address is given in that year, 21 were in Cordwainer, 17 in Cripplegate, 13 in
Cheap; only 9 were in waterfront wards (*Mercers' Acts*, pp. 78–84). The drapers were more
closely concentrated, 77 of their wealthiest members in 1421 living in the three wards of
Candlewick, Cheap, and Cornhill (A. H. Johnson, *A History of the Worshipful Company
of Drapers* [1914], I, 292–94). The goldsmiths' total membership was more scattered, but out
of 157 in 1493 there were 59 in Cheap, 11 in Lombard Street, 10 in Foster Lane (Minutes,
1492–99, fols. 28–29).

133. Harl. Ch., 86, H 22 (1497). This was after Hardyng had retired from an aldermanry and only three years before his death. Thomas Wood, a contemporary, also an
alderman and goldsmith, bequeathed his leasehold rights in "Mote Place" to members of
his family "for their recreations" (P.C.C., Holgrave, 2 [1503]).

that the country held was its greater safety in time of epidemic. "I undyrstonde they dy sor in London," wrote Richard Cely in 1487, urging his brother to join him at their place in Essex.[134] Another attraction was the hunting. A love of hunting was natural to all classes and heightened the value of rights over game. During the fourteenth century the area of the royal forests, within which no one might hunt without the king's license, was shrinking, but at the same time increasing numbers of landowners were being allowed to inclose parks for deer and also to reserve for themselves the right of hunting smaller game in uninclosed warrens. This growth of private monopoly was much resented, the rebels of 1381 demanding that hunting rights be open to all. In an endeavor to check poaching, the government in 1390 made it illegal for greyhounds or other dogs to run loose unless they belonged to laymen with lands worth 40s. a year or clerks with salaries of £10; hunting, it was stated, whether of deer, rabbits, or any other kind of game, was "the sport of the gentle."[135] Although the citizens of London had hunting rights reserved for them by charter in Middlesex, Surrey, and the Chilterns,[136] some of the wealthier merchants were among the new monopolists. The Swanlands obtained rights of free warren at North Mymmes in 1316, and Sir Thomas Cook was granted the right to inclose a park of two hundred acres.[137] Whether such men hunted in quite the same style as the nobility and wealthy gentry is uncertain. "The sport of the

134. *Cely Papers*, 158.

135. See C. Petit-Dutaillis, *Studies and Notes Supplementary to Stubbs' Constitutional History*, trans. W. T. Waugh ("Publications of the University of Manchester Historical Series," No. XXII, 1915), II, 210–11, 246–48.

136. Lib. Alb., I, 129–31, 133, 136, 140, 155, 164, 165. Fitz-Stephen, writing in the third quarter of the twelfth century, stated that the privilege extended in Middlesex, Hertfordshire, all Chilterns, and in Kent as far as the Cray. Henry III extended the area by exempting the warren of Stanes from forest law. It is possible that the process of creating private parks and warrens gradually encroached on the citizens' rights. Throughout the fifteenth century the official known as the Common Hunt was retained at a salary of £10 a year and livery. He kept horses and a pack of hounds and watched over the citizens' hunting and fishing rights. The names of 9 appointees between 1379 and 1463 are recorded in the letter books (*Cal. L. Bk., H*, 121–22, 309, 388; *I*, 179; *K*, 321; *L*, 36; cf. Stow, II, 370).

137. Cussans' *Hertfordshire*, Parts XII–XIV, p.282, *Cal. Ch. R.*, VI, 214. Similar grants to John Peche and Nicholas Brembre (*ibid.*, V, 169, 231). Sir Henry Colet had rights of free warren in his manors (*Hist. Parl. B.*, p. 205. See Thomas Knolles's dispute over hunting rights with the abbot of St. Alban's (*Chronicles of St. Albans, John Amundesham* [R.S., No. 28 (1870)], I, 59). Sir William Estfeld had the right to hunt in any royal park in Essex or Middlesex (*Hist. Parl. B.*, p. 304).

gentle" was properly an expensive cult, pursued with highly bred horses, dogs, and hawks, creatures costly to buy and requiring the tenderest care. George Cely, who loved good dogs and horses and frequented the horse fairs in Flanders, had little sympathy from the older members of his family. After one unsuccessful experiment in breeding greyhounds, his father refused to allow any dogs in the household but spaniels, and he objected to keeping more than one hawk. The elder son, Richard, would take care of animals left in his charge, but he, too, disapproved of George's extravagance. "I undyrstonde that ye have sowlde your grehyt gray hors and I am ryught glad therof for ii ys as good as xx," he wrote.[138] Private parks and warrens nevertheless offered ideal opportunities for combining a favorite recreation with aristocratic habits of display in hunting parties. The improvement of old manor houses or the building of new ones would also attract favorable attention from the local gentry. Leland noted that Sir Geoffrey Boleyn had built himself a "fair house of brike" at Blickling. Sir Thomas Cook obtained permission to put up a crenellated stone wall about his manor of Gidihall. With a more dramatic gesture still, one man bought an old castle.[139]

A universal form of indoor display was the exhibition of plate. Every merchant and substantial citizen had at least one or two mazers—wooden cups bound with silver—and the wealthiest men had magnificent collections worth several hundred pounds. Orphans sometimes received more than half their inheritance in silver cups and spoons, spice dishes, and basins. These articles were cherished as much for their beauty as for any other reason. English merchants were behind some of their contemporaries in the appreciation of painting, but they were connoisseurs of good goldsmiths' work. Decoration was usually either heraldic or religious in theme, enameled or wrought in silver or gold, as in a

---

138. *Cely Papers, passim.* Hawks cost as much as horses. George sold two horses at 4 and 5 marks and a hawk for £2 6s. 8d. An agent of Francesco Sporza, duke of Milan, being commissioned to procure some English dogs for his master, reported that the only people owning fine dogs were lords, who would not sell (*Calendar of Milanese Papers*, I, 100). Another man commissioned to buy a goshawk in Calais reported that Lord Hastings had bought up all that were any good (*Cely Papers*, 23, 74, 79, 81–82, 118). See case of a grocer in 1357 importing thirty-nine falcons from Germany (*Cal. L. Bk., G,* p. 90).

139. Leland, II, 9; V, 233; *Cal. Ch. R.,* VI, 214. Richard Bonifaunt, mercer, bought the old "Castle of the Ston" at Stone, Kent (Weever, p. 126).

powder box "silver and gilt with an eagle," "a litill standing cup covered of silver blak aneled wrought with the passion of our lord god," "a cup of serpentyne covered garnesshed wt gold stones and perles with a panter of gold." Coats of arms were copied to order, and representations of St. John the Baptist and St. Katherine were common. The sculptured and enameled pieces were especially beloved and were given names, like little household gods—"belle-cuppe," "the grete grubbe," "Peregrin." These collections were valued also from another point of view, as a business asset. They were always readily convertible into cash and always acceptable as security for a loan. In time of need they were drawn upon like a savings account. Sir John Young explained in his last will that he was unable to leave his daughters as much silver as he had promised, on account of the great expenses he had incurred in a lawsuit.[140]

Dress was perhaps more purely a symbol of status than any other item in medieval standards of living. Although the merchant had the eye of an expert for the intrinsic beauty of the color and texture of cloth, in the imagination of the age scarlet and other bright dyes and the smoothness and sheen of fine fur and the softer materials were associated with power and importance, drab colors and coarse fabrics standing for poverty and insignificance. Conservative opinion attributed the introduction of rapid and extreme changes of fashion to the influence of the Hainaulters who came over with Queen Philippa. It was only in respect of the new styles in tailoring, however, that the opinions of the older and the younger generations differed, both alike admiring expensive cloth and fur. The same chronicler who condemned the styles of 1328 as "destitu and desert fram al old honeste and good usage" and complained of Mortimer's pride in dressing "oute of al maner resoun," betrayed a touch of wistful admiration in referring to the earl's

140. Plate is described in innumerable wills. Examples of other types of design occur, as in a gilt cup "with a water flower and a horse sculptured in the base" and a mazer cup made like a ship. Some work was imported. Sir John Pultney had a covered silver basin "de opere Paris annielat'" bearing his arms (E, 101/508/12); and Sir Hugh Wyche's widow, in 1475, presented the mercers' company with "a garnysshe of new sylver vessel whiche was bought by yonde the see" (*Mercers' Acts*, I, 82). Sir John Crosby directed that his wife was to have part of her dower in plate valued "at such reasonable price as that plate . . . . shall be worth reasonable to be bought and sold for ready money between merchant and merchant." Sir William Taillour valued his plate, for part payment of his wife's dower, at 4s. an ounce. Sir Thomas Cook's plate and jewels were worth £700 (*The Great Chronicle*, p. 207).

clothes as "wonder ryche."[141] Sumptuary legislation governing dress was attempted in 1363, partly because habits of extravagance were believed to be responsible for the rising cost of food and partly because fashion was tending to obscure class distinctions. Ermine and cloth of gold were to be reserved for knights and others who had lands worth over 400 marks a year, silk and cloth priced at 5 marks for gentry worth £200 a year and merchants worth £1,000 in goods, and cheaper grades of cloth were prescribed in turn for gentry worth £100 a year or citizens worth £500 in goods, for yeomen or craftsmen and for agricultural workers, servants, and other people worth less than 40s.[142] The impractical nature of these provisions is shown by the fact that in 1379 silk and fine furs were allowed to knights and gentry having incomes from land of £40 and up. The parliaments of 1402 and 1406 narrowed the privilege of wearing fine fur and ornaments of gold to knights and to mayors and former mayors of London, York, and Bristol and their wives. Not until 1463 was it legal for lesser merchants and then only for aldermen and sheriffs in these and other cities to dress with the same degree of luxury as esquires and gentlemen with incomes of £40. Since there was no means whatever for enforcing any of these laws, it is probable that their net effect, if they had any influence at all, was contrary to their intention. No one was likely to covet furs and silk and jewelry the less because the law regarded them as a sign of high rank. Bishop Brunton was distressed that he could not tell the difference between a countess and the wife of a citizen, and it was in vain that Hoccleve warned lords that it was unbecoming to dress their retainers so well, for in popular opinion fine liveries advertised the power of the lord who bestowed them.[143]

Wills and inventories show that London citizens had always loved to dress as richly as possible and to adorn themselves, as

141. *The Brut*, E.E.T.S., original ser., No. 131, p. 261; No. 136, pp. 296–97. Compare the sneers at Henry VI's repeated public appearances in the same gown "as thowth he hadd noo moo to chaunge wt" (*The Great Chronicle*, pp. 214, 217).

142. See F. E. Baldwin, *Sumptuary Legislation in England* (1926). The law was amended in 1379, 1402, 1406, 1453, 1463, 1477, and 1482. Maximum tailors' charges were also set in 1363 but could easily have been raised by charging for trimming (*Cal. L. Bk., G*, p. 150).

143. Cited in G. R. Owst, *Pulpit and Literature in Medieval England* (1933), p. 406 (reference to sermon of 1390). "If twixt yow and youre men no difference Be in array, lesse is youre reverence" (*Hoccleve's Regement of Princes*, Stanza 64, ed. F. J. Furnivall, E.E.T.S., extra ser., No. 72, p. 17).

well as their wives, with gold and silver rings and buckles. Although feminine fashions called for brooches and bracelets and gold circlets, frequent changes in the colors of company liveries gave the men even more excuse for extravagance. Fourteenth-century magnates were resplendent in tunics of samite and velvet, silk-lined hoods trimmed with fur or gold-thread embroidery, and outer robes of purple or scarlet or green, furred with ermine, beaver, and marten. Their fingers sparkled with jeweled rings, their silken girdles were set off with taffeta bags and crystal-hafted knives, their hats were fur-trimmed, and their shoes variegated in color. On state occasions, following French fashions, they moved to the musical tinkle of little gold and silver bells sewed about their hoods and sleeves. Even lesser merchants of the period wore silk, and their best robes were always furred.[144] Fifteenth-century men might have as many as nine gowns worth giving away or selling at their death. Rich furs and striped silks were in use, and bright colors and silk girdles were essential. Poets and chroniclers never tired of describing the vivid color schemes with which citizen liveries filled the streets on days of pageantry or royal entries into the city. The mayor's robes outshone all, "in rede Crymsyn velwett, and a grete velwet hatte furred royally, and a girdell of gold aboute his mydell, and a bawdrik of gold aboute his neck, trillyng down behynde hym."[145] A man would buy violet cloth for his wedding gown, with violet hose to match. Women seem to have had fewer gowns than their husbands, but their jewelry continued to be more elaborate. One widow had five gold rings, two "herts" of gold, a gold rose "powderid with perle," gold and coral beads, and four girdles with gold and silver fastenings; and Lady Lee bequeathed her daughter a "coler of gold with stones" and a golden brooch "made like a maid sitting on an erber set with stones and perles." Women also needed stocks of kerchiefs for their headdresses. One man left his mother-in-law £5 "to buy her kerchives with." The families of the poorer merchants and of other citizens had to fall back on black and russet cloth and lamb's

144. For Pultney, Malewayn, and Lyons see above, nn. 96, 97, 114. An inventory of the goods of Richard Toky, grocer, taken in 1391, includes a silk nightgown, vest, and cap (*Cal. P. & M. Rolls*, III, 209–13); and a grocer bankrupt in 1398 had two short silk slops (outer garments) (C, 131/47/25). Furred robes are mentioned in numerous wills.

145. At Henry VI's entry into London in 1432. *The Brut*, No. 136, p. 462. See also Lidgate's verses on the same occasion, cited in *The Great Chronicle*, p. 157.

wool for everyday use, but in their holiday clothing they vied with the fashions of the rich as best they could.

The older merchants set store rather by the richness of their dress than by subtlety of cut or passing fancies of fashion. In this they differed both from their wives and the younger men, who liked to copy the fashions of the London gentry and the courtiers. A funeral brass of 1485 represents an ordinary merchant's wife dressed exactly like a knight's lady, in a low-cut gown and high headdress.[146] Although the women may have been able to do as they pleased, the young men were subject to discipline through their companies. Several tailors were fined a shilling each in 1463 for wearing their cloaks too short, and the mercers in 1479 admitted a young man as shopholder only on condition "that he sadly dispose hym and manerly bothe in his arreye & also in Cuttynge of his here/ & not to go lyke a gallaunt or a man of Courte/." Masters were supposed to keep apprentices neatly dressed, with gowns over their doublets when they went out, and were to have the lads' hair cut regularly. For refusing to have his hair cut a draper's servant was sent to prison. Such drastic action, however, could not be taken often. In 1478 the mercers appointed a committee to "conceyve & provide for a convenient remedy, to Reforme the inordinate aray used & worne by covenaunte servauntes."[147] It would seem, on the whole, that the only people connected with citizen society with whom the sumptuary legislation was enforced were the pensioners in the almshouses they endowed. Elys Davy's regulations for the almshouse that he founded at Croydon laid down that the inmates should wear clothes "darke and broune of colour, and not staring neither blasing and of easy price cloth according to ther degree."[148]

It was characteristic of the merchant to be appreciative of food and drink and to have a fine sense of hospitality. The author of *The Great Chronicle* relates feelingly that the first mayoral banquet served at the Guildhall was "Ful Rawe" and dwells in disgust upon an incident in which good wine was left opened to spoil.

---

146. See C. Belcher, *Brasses of Kent*, No. 49. A broker's servant who married an Italian merchant ordered 40s. worth of furs for her wedding clothes; neither her master nor her husband would pay for them (E.C.P., 66/408).

147. Clode, p. 520; *Mercers' Acts*, pp. 121, 108; Ironmongers' Register, fol. 33 (1498); Fishmongers' Records, fol. 16b; Goldsmiths' Minutes, 1492–99, fol. 345; E.C.P., 48/107.

148. See below, p. 179.

Household inventories show stocks of red wine, bacon, salt fish, and sides of beef in cellars and larders. Despite Sir John Fortescue's boast that the English drank no water and lived in plenty, the fourteenth-century London water supply was designed to provide the poor with water for drinking, the rich and the *mediocres* using it only in cooking; and there was a keen demand among the poor for the cheap fish that country dealers peddled about the city. Although the *mediocres* drank beer and ale and were in a position to buy meat, they could not afford trained cooks. Beer and ale were probably the staple drinks in the wealthier households and were much used in the miscellaneous entertaining that was incumbent on the mayor; fancy breads, cheese, and fruit were served for light meals at the company halls. Wine and lengthy dinners, however, were the accepted means of entertaining important guests.[149]

Like a gentleman or a nobleman, a merchant considered it essential to his dignity and that of his wife to be waited on. In order to demonstrate that they were in this happy position, the older people were accustomed to have a servant in attendance whenever they chose to go out. Among the demands made by a retired tailor on his son was this, that ". . . . at all due tymes whan that I or my wyf walketh oute that my said sone shall late me have an honest man chyld to wayte upon me & an honest mayde chyld to wayte upon my wyf at his own propre coste yef we desire it."[150] The mercers, when they appeared on horseback at one of Edward IV's entries into the city, were each attended by "a clenly man or Childe," also mounted but dressed in black and russet instead of in red.[151] Aldermen competed with each other in the number of attendants they brought to hold their gowns at civic ceremonies. It was finally ruled that at mayoral and shrieval elections they bring only one servant each.[152] The majority of merchants

149. Sir John Fortescue, *De laudibus legum Anglie*, ed. S. B. Chrimes, pp. 86–87. Conduit regulations, L. Bk., *F*, fol. 107*b* (1345). Company records contain a good deal of information on dietary habits. A bill for £50 was submitted to Robert Bassett for beer and ale bought during his mayoralty, in 1475 (E.C.P., 89/31).

150. Merchant Tailors' Minutes, fol. 21. The agreement was made in 1467. The business, which the son was taking over, was worth £220. Out of the proceeds he was to provide his parents with food, drink, and clothing to the value of £10 a year, and he was to reserve for them two rooms, "the White Chambre and the Rede Chambre," in their Bucklersbury house, held on lease.

151. *Mercers' Acts*, pp. 90, 91.   152. *Cal. L. Bk., L*, p. 133 (1475).

had probably no more than one or two servants, but the great houses required a staff of five or more, several of whom, including the cook and the undercook, would be men and boys. Sometimes, in imitation of the great noble households, they were given the titles of chamberlain, butler, page. The women and girls acted as children's nurses and personal maids, kitchen work being, if possible, left to boys. In the late fifteenth century the women were paid about a pound a year;[153] the men presumably had more than this, and the young girls and boys may not have received anything beyond their board and clothing. Often they were relatives of the family or else adopted waifs. The servants were often remembered by name in the wills, as "to Cicile the maide to pray for my soule 12*d.* and oon of my old gowns to make hir a kirtell" or, more generously, 40*s.* "to Alice my mayde that was given me to fynde for almes" or £3 6*s.* 8*d.* "to my lytel maiden" for her marriage. Sir Richard Lee left his cook a life pension; a merchant friend of the family left small sums to Stephen Forster's cook and to other servants in that household. A grocer's household staff in 1410 consisted of Joan, the "ancilla"; a woman butler called Margery; Agnes, "servant in my house"; and Gerard "de Coquina." The kitchen boys were engaged on long-term contracts, perhaps apprenticed to the cook. One man left money "to lytell Jak of my kechyn he to serve oute his termes"; another left "Hankyn my duche child" a new suit of clothes.

The final problems in expenditure that perplexed the merchant arose out of the question as to how he should be buried. The size of the torches and tapers that should be set about his body on the hearse, the length of the procession that would follow it to the grave, the quality of the tombstone to be ordered, the number and rank of the guests to be invited to eat and drink at his house after the funeral, the cost of the mourning garments to be worn by his family and servants, the nature of the feast to be held after the memorial service, or "month's mind," a month later and again after the anniversary service or "obit," and the amount of the alms to be given away on each of these occasions would all reflect

153. The accounts of a draper in 1526 note payment of an annual wage of 13*s.* in money plus 10*s.* for gowns to a "maydyn servant." The money was doled out in pennies as it was needed "for showis & offyryngs" (Drapers' Howell MS, fols. 19*b*, 20, 27). A fifteenth-century contract made by a woman servant with the chief serjeant of the mayor of Exeter named a wage of 4*d.* a week with food and drink (E.C.P., 60/168).

upon his status. For any man who cared about his social position it was therefore logical to wish for as splendid a funeral as could be arranged without working hardship to his heirs. On the other hand, his priest would tell him that worldly standards should at this point give way before humility and piety: he should spend his money on alms, not on vain display. Torn between the habits of a lifetime and a fear that his priest might be right, the merchant either compromised or left the problem to his executors. William Thorneye, alderman, dying in the year of the Black Death, set aside £80 to be spent on his funeral and for his soul. This is the highest sum named in any of the surviving fourteenth-century wills, three other aldermen suggesting figures of £20, £30, and £40. Richard Toky's executors spent almost £25 on funerals for Toky and his wife and son, with "month's mind" and anniversary services; and it cost John Heylesdon's widow £17 simply to transport her husband's body to his native village of Hellesdon in Norfolk, where he had wished to be buried.[154] Some wealthy men, however, firmly set a limit of £4 or of 10 marks or of 20 marks for funeral and alms to the poor who would attend it.

In the fifteenth century, funerals became still grander and more expensive, mainly through displays of wax torches and shields of arms, the giving-away of mourning gowns, the hiring of a horse-drawn hearse, and lavish entertainment. John Doget in 1403 ordered twenty-five torches for his hearse besides authorizing 20 marks' expenditure on other items. He requested that no one wear black for him but his wife, his executors, his servants, and his feoffees, almost as though it were customary to thrust all the deceased's friends into mourning. No commercial organization of the funeral as a whole developed to force expenses up, and it was still possible in the reign of Edward IV for a merchant to bury his son for half a mark and for the grocers' company to bury an almsman respectably for less than 9s.[155] In a £50 funeral there was therefore a generous allowance for ceremonial display as well as

---

154. *Cal. P. & M. Rolls*, III, 214–15; Add. Ch., 19, 915.

155. A draper in 1475 paid church fees of only 6s. 8d. for the burial of a son (*Records of the Parish of St. Michael Cornhill*, p. 52). Cost of burying an almsman of the grocers' company: "for þe wyndynge clothe ii ells xiid. for the cofyn & the clothe iiii d. for the preste viii d. for iiii torcheholders xvid. & for the Knylle xiid. for prestis & clerks iis" (Grocers' Records, Vol. 401, entries of 1468). Bill for burying "Maistresse Hoggyns," *ca.* 1526, 6s. 8d., exclusive of the priest's fee (Drapers' Deeds, A III, LIV).

for alms. Yet the executors of a grocer could spend this sum on his funeral, in 1499, when it amounted to almost an eighth of his estate and there were three children to be provided for.[156] Wealthy merchants, while professing a distaste for worldly show as unprofitable to the soul, made a still more ample concession to it. Nicholas Wyfold, directing that he be buried "without any grete hers poni ponis oost or other vaine glorie of the Worlde," set aside 100 marks for the expenses; and Sir William Tayllour requested that "only" £100 be spent. Excess, it is true, brought common-sense reaction in its train. Not every merchant was gratified to think of his company brethren and neighbors descending like locusts on the family larder after his memorial services. "I warne you I wol noon monethis mynde have," wrote one mercer, who also specified that he be buried "in easy honest wise" with only three torches; and another made it clear that his "fellowship of the mercery" was not to be invited to any "solempne dyner nor fest."[157] When an alderman died, it was more difficult for the family to cut down expense because the community expected a show and hospitable entertainment. Sir Thomas Hill himself wished enough ceremony to mark his "degree" as an alderman and a knight and insisted only on temperance:

I will that my body be brought over erth in honest wise according to my degree wt owte eny pomp or blandise of the world. . . . . I utterly forbedde any moneths mynde to be kept solempnely for me after the guyse of the world in any maner place but in the seid sent Thomas of Acres I woll that brede drynk and chese of the saasen therto be ordeyned for the preests & clerks ther & other comers thedir in honest wise utterly forbeding any solempne dyner to be kept or ordeyned for my cause except onely a convenient repast for my wif my children executers & myn old ffrendis such as they will call unto them.

Lady Lee likewise forbade the giving of "eny solempne dyner for eny asstates" after her death; yet she wished there to be "at my monethis mynde an honest repast of mete and drynke" at her house, "for brethern and sustern of my executours and neighburs of the parish of St. Stephen and for other my frendys and lovers." Lesser citizens, outside the merchant class, were torn in the same way between desire for a show and desire for economy; a typical compromise was in prohibition of any "magna mangeria" at the month's mind.

156. Journals, 10, fol. 157b.

157. John Boton and John Shelley, mercers (P.C.C., Godyn, 6 [1464]; Logge, 27 [1486]).

Chapter IV

THE CONDUCT OF LIFE

I. FORMAL EDUCATION

THE merchant's craft demanded some degree of literacy, with the consequence that he at least had access to the knowledge of his age. In building up his views of life and in formulating them for his children he was not necessarily restricted to his own experience. One of the motives in seeking education was to have direct access to the Scriptures. From the thirteenth century, platitudes had been current in Continental writing about the importance of education for developing children's reason and acquainting them with right beliefs lest they resemble the dumb beasts. In a version of these sayings translated by Caxton it was the duty of every Christian man to cause his children and his friends to read the Scriptures. Otherwise they would suffer the vengeance of God,

> For ignorance
> Shall nothyng excuse hem.

According to Pecock, English heretics were already demanding universal education for both sexes in order that they should be able to read Scripture in the original language in which it was written and also, as he reported vaguely, for the sake of "myche othir good."[1]

Secondary education, in Latin, was a monopoly of the church. No one could set up a grammar school in London without the approval of the bishop of London and of the chancellor of St. Paul's, on pain of excommunication. The ostensible object of control was to preserve high standards of learning, typical church-school statutes requiring that only masters of arts be allowed to teach

---

1. *Dialogues in French and English*, E.E.T.S., extra ser., No. 79, pp. 9, 37; *The Repressor of Overmuch Blaming of the Clergie* (cited hereafter as "*The Repressor*"), R.S., I, 91.

grammar. Until the middle of the fifteenth century, when their number was increased to six, London was served by three approved church schools, all probably dating from the twelfth century. Nothing is heard of competition until 1392, when a man named Richard Exton is known to have been taking pupils. In the following year several people were ordered out of the field on the charge of conducting "escoles generales de gramer" without being properly qualified. Again in 1446, this time with the backing of the royal authority, competitors were served twelve days' notice to close, on pain of excommunication. It is hard to believe that they were all unqualified, because four city rectors who in 1447 obtained the royal permission to open schools in their parishes and who would surely have known how to select competent teachers were frustrated in their aim. Moreover, a private school of high standing in Cornhill, where John Seward, a distinguished humanist scholar, had taught for a time, had been unable to continue, and a bequest of 3,000 marks for the foundation of a grammar and writing school in the chapel attached to the Leadenhall market, left by a draper in 1458, was for some undisclosed reason never implemented. The restrictive policy cannot be explained by a wish to limit the right of teaching to the priesthood, for unordained men were employed in the cathedral school. The four rectors who were prevented from opening new schools believed the ban to be due to nothing but a selfish desire to monopolize fees.[2]

In elementary and commercial education, however, the field was open. The extent of it cannot yet be judged before the reign of Edward IV. Out of a series of 116 male witnesses who gave evidence in the consistory court in that reign, between the years 1467 and 1476, the clerk in charge registered 48, or 40 per cent, as literate. This proportion tallies with that found in two much smaller groups of witnesses in 1373 and 1466. The standards for witnesses may not have been so high as those set for allowance of benefit of clergy, by which a man found able only to "spell and put to-

2. A. F. Leach, *The Schools of Mediaeval England* (1915), pp. 143, 260–67, based largely on *Rot. parl.*, III, 324a; V, 137a; *Cal. P.R., 1441–46*, p. 432. See also *Cal. P. & M. Rolls*, III, 182; and V. H. Galbraith, "John Seward and His Circle," *Mediaeval and Renaissance Studies*, I, 85–104. The Cornhill school was apparently still running in 1439–41, when "Morton the scoldmaister is sone in Cornhille" was admitted to the grocers' company for £5 (Kingdon, II, 257). There may have been some teaching at Leadenhall, for Eyre's will refers to the "chapel and scholes" there. His bequest was contained in a codicil proved under the seal of Cardinal Thomas in 1474 (Draper's Deeds, A III, 135).

gether" was denied purgation as a clerk, but let us presume that in most cases it meant the ability to read a little Latin.[3]

The occupations of the London witnesses were as listed in Table 11. The group is broadly representative of the city laity, except that it contains no members of their professional groups—the lawyers, the physicians and surgeons, the scriveners, and the lay schoolmasters. If any of these had been included, the percentage showing would have been slightly better. As one would

TABLE 11

Occupation	Literate	Illiterate	Occupation	Literate	Illiterate
Baker		3	Haberdasher	1	1
Barber-surgeon	4	5	Hosier	1	
Bargee		1	Ironmonger	1	2
Bladesmith	1		Joiner		2
Brazier	1		Laborer		3
Brewer	1	5	Mercer	2	
Broiderer	2		Merchant	2	
Butcher		1	Ostler		2
Butler (mayor's)	1		Patenmaker		2
Capper	1	2	Pewterer	3	1
Cook		1	Pinner	1	
Cooper		1	Saddler		1
Cordwainer		1	Salter	1	
Cutler		1	Shearman	5	2
Dauber		1	Skinner	2	4
Draper	4	1	Smith		4
Dyer		1	Spurrier		1
Founder	1	2	Tailor	6	9
Fuller		1	Tiler		1
Glover		1	Tinner	1	
Goldbeater	1	2	Whitetawyer		1
Goldsmith	1	1			
Graytawyer		2	Totals	48	68
Grocer	4				

expect, the test was beyond the powers of laborers, sawyers, ostlers, and men of similar lower-class occupations; and it further disclosed a wide fringe of ignorance among citizens who were above this level. Although most of the eighteen members of the greater companies who were described as illiterate may have been artisans or servants, at least one of them, a haberdasher, can be identified as a merchant.[4]

3. Dicta testium in Consist 1467 . . . . , *passim;* J. W. Adamson, "The Extent of Literacy in England in the 15th and 16th Centuries," *Library*, X (1930), 167; C. B. Firth, "Benefit of Clergy in the Time of Edward I," *EHR*, XXXII, 183; cf. L. C. Gabel, *Benefit of Clergy* (1929).

4. Stephen Smyth, aged 33. Since the name was not then a common one in the city, it is likely that he was the same man who by 1481–82 was important enough to be made

If 40 per cent of the lay male Londoners of this period could read Latin, it is a fair guess that some 50 per cent could read English. Latin having been taught in English since the second half of the fourteenth century, all successful grammar-school pupils would have been able to read both languages, and it was possible to study English alone. The goldsmiths had a rule, in force by 1478 and reissued in the 1490's, forbidding any member to take an apprentice "wtout he canne writte and Rede"; in one curious case it was found that a man who had learned the craft in Banbury and was expert in engraving letters could not read them. The skinners must have had a similar rule, for two of their apprentices who came up from the provinces in 1496–97 were to be sent to school to learn to read and write. They were allowed only three months, which would hardly have given them time to learn Latin. The ironmongers' rules, as copied in 1498, merely required that apprentices register their names "with theire owne handes, yf they can write." The brewers' wardens had decided in 1422 not to have their records kept any longer in Latin, which none of the members could read, but in future to use English, which some of them, it was stated, could both read and write. There is other evidence of the inability of poorer citizens to read Latin. A skinner's servant pleaded in chancery that he was "a simple persone and not lettred," unable to read the terms of a bond; and a fuller "by innocency as a man not lerned" had sealed a bond thinking that it was a receipt. In a study circle formed in the reign of Henry IV by seven Londoners of humble rank who were interested in heretical writing, six of them had to depend on the other to read to them aloud.[5]

The chief obstacle to the extension of elementary education was probably the fact that the poorer people either required the labor of their children in the workshop or else saw no advantage in schooling that could arouse their interest. There was little free education to encourage them. The more generous of the chantry priests may have been willing to take pupils for nothing, but the

---

an assessor for subscriptions to a loan to the king and to be a trustee for the son of a wealthy draper (*Cal. L. Bk., L*, pp. 176, 191).

5. Goldsmiths' Book A, fol. 237; Prideaux, I, 26–28; Skinners' Register of Apprentices, date, 1496–97; Ironmongers' Record Book, fol. 32; Brewers' Accounts, passage printed in *A Book of London English*, ed. R. W. Chambers and M. Daunt (1931), p. 16; E.C.P., 80/94, 64/532; J. H. Wylie, *History of England under Henry IV* (1884), I, 289–90.

only regular free places known to have been offered were in the song school attached to the church grammar school at St. Antony's Hospital. Although school fees may not have run much above 2*d.* a week, they would normally have been beyond the means of those "poor householders burdened with children" who figure in the wills of the rich as objects of charity.[6]

From the circumstance that schooling could be delayed until apprenticeship or limited to a grounding in the three R's just before a boy was indentured, one would infer that the attitude toward education could be utilitarian rather than religious. Even a hermit priest in London, apprenticing an adopted son to a tailor, was content to have him taught merely "to rede write and lay Accomptes suffisauntly." A haberdasher who had promised to send a boy to school for the first two years of a twelve-year apprenticeship, a year and a half to learn grammar and six months for writing, neglected to send him at all.[7]

Small private schools offered the mixed elementary education that was required, some perhaps attached to the grammar schools, some run independently by priests, some probably by scriveners. There were two complaints in chancery about clerical schoolmasters. One was accused of having beaten a goldsmith's son too hard; the other, running his school on Squeers' system, had offended a draper's apprentice by sending him into the kitchen "to washe pottes pannes disshes and to dight mete."[8] Scriveners were developing high-pressure methods of education. In a manual of commercial French which advertised the tuition offered by William Kyngesmill, about the year 1415, a twelve-year-old boy declares that in three months at Kyngesmill's hostel he had learned to read and write, to cast accounts, and to speak French and was now ready for a London apprenticeship; there was a scrivener of this name in London.[9] Writing schools, to which goldsmiths' ap-

6. On song schools see Leach, *op. cit.*, pp. 137–38, 196, 300.

7. E.C.P., 66/66, 19/491. Another case of neglect of promised schooling, coupled with ill-treatment of the boy, for which the master was imprisoned, Merchant Tailors' Minutes, 1488–93, fol. 41*v*.

8. E.C.P., 19/33, 46/162.

9. K. Lambley, *The Teaching and Cultivation of the French Language in England during Tudor and Stuart Times* (1920), pp. 40–42. Text of the manual (from Add. MS, 17716), printed by P. Meyer, in *Romania*, XXXII (1903), 49–58. Harl. Ch., 45, F 34, a deed of February 1, 1422, contains a scrivener's signature of *Kyngesmyll*, and in 1409–10 a Florentine gave a bond for 40*s.* to William Kyngesmyll, citizen of London (H.M.C., *11th*

prentices were being sent in the 1490's, may have been run by scriveners.[10]

In many merchant families, however, as also in some families that remained attached to the lesser companies, the second generation received a much more thorough education, one that was informed by more than commercial interests. Legacies left to boys for their "finding to school" were of 5 to 10 marks or more, which would have kept them at city day schools from the age of seven or eight until they were considered old enough to be apprenticed. Although they needed some Latin for the understanding of legal instruments, this would have given them more than was strictly necessary for business purposes. Parents were genuinely anxious for their sons to be initiated into that world of Latin learning over which the church presided. A baker could order that his son be brought up "in all lernyng," just as an alderman desired his brought up "to connyng lernyng & erudition."[11]

The wealthier merchant families had always adopted much the same attitude to education as the more cultivated gentry. An alderman who died in 1312 had wished his sons to stay at school until they could compose reasonably good verses; this might mean staying until they were twenty, as William Tonge specified later in the century.[12] Most of these boys would probably have attended the city grammar schools, living at home, but some, like country gentlemen's sons, were sent to boarding schools. At the end of the

---

Report, Part III, p. 77). See note of Kyngesmill's adaptation of teaching material worked up by Thomas Sampson of Oxford in H. G. Richardson, "Business Training in Medieval Oxford," *American Historical Review*, XLVI, 276. I find no mention of the study of Italian. See case of a draper taking a bill "endented in lombardy" which he could not read (E.C.P., 27/329 [1459]).

10. Goldsmiths' Book A, fol. 53. The fishmongers possess a fine early-sixteenth-century copy of a set of ordinances ending "Written by me rychard felde the Sone of Maister Jhon Felde then beinge Warden and the said rychard being of the age o xii yeres at the fynishing here of."

11. The baker was Henry Narburgh, squire; his son went to school until the age of 15, when he died in an accident (C. Misc., 68/9/191; and Narburgh's will [P.C.C., Wattys, 11]). The alderman was Bledlow. See Thomas Cornton, haberdasher, directing his son to attend school until the age of 15 *causa addiscend' literaturam* (Comm. Lon., Broun, fol. 172v [1408]); see also John Treguran, vintner, urging "necessary scolys" to the age of 16 (P.C.C., Godyn, 29 [1469]).

12. H.M.C., *6th Report, Appendix*, p. 408; Riley, *Memorials*, pp. 378–79; L. Bk., *H*, fol. 254; cf. wills of John Nicholl and William Newport (P.C.C., Wattys, 36 [1477]; P.C.C., Milles, 12 [1488]). See case of a roper in 1357 providing for a cousin in his household to be sent to school only until he should learn to write.

century a grocer had two boys in his charge at a school kept by the
vicar of Croydon, and two mercers' sons had lately been sent to
Oxford for periods of eleven and thirteen years.[13] One of these
came back to London to be apprenticed in his father's company.
His case was probably exceptional, most merchant's sons who had
so long a formal education being naturally tempted to go on into
one of the learned professions. The proportion of men in the merchant class who had stayed at school past the age of sixteen must
have been very small.

To limit the picture to the merchant class, then, it is clear that
all the men read English and that most of them had some training
in Latin, and, as will be shown, there is reason to believe that most
of the intelligent women had found ways of learning at least to
read and write English. The question now arises as to whether
these skills were put to much use save in the handling of business
transactions and in following the liturgy. It is of no use to object
that other opportunities depended on the local supply of books,
for the merchants' own demand for books was one of the chief
factors conditioning that supply. No one was in a better position
than they to tap foreign sources or to organize local production.
The fact that the book trade remained largely in the hands of
aliens and that as late as 1520 the mercers were classing books
among the "tryfylles" of their import trade does not speak well
for the London merchants' intellectual curiosity or initiative.[14]

The only merchant known to have spent any considerable
amount of money in collecting books was Sir William Walworth,
who bequeathed nine religious books to churches, as well as a law
library, worth £100, to his brother. About 20 per cent of the fifteenth-century wills of personal property mention a few books; in
half the cases they were all liturgical and devotional—massbooks,
missals, psalters, and primers. For purposes of bequest, however,
there was no doubt some selection on the basis of cash value,
which depended on the binding and the quality of lettering and

13. E. Rickert's description of Gilbert Maghfeld's account-book (*Modern Philology*,
XXIV, 250–52; Riley, *Memorials*, pp. 378–79; *Cal. P. & M. Rolls*, II, 175; L. Bk., *H*,
fol. 74).

14. Demise of houses and an alley off St. Clement's Lane to Henry Franckenbergh and
Barnard van Stonto, merchants of printed books, 1482 (*Cat. Anc. Deeds*, I, 491). Suit by
Joyce Pylegrome of London Bokeseller, "a Straunger" (E.C.P., 218/2). Bookbinders occur
with English names (see *Cal. P. & M. Rolls*, I, 143; *Cal. Inq. Misc.*, III, 156; E, 136/
108/26).

illumination. A finely illuminated massbook, for example, could be worth up to £10; or an antiphonary, with musical notation, double this amount; objects of art, such possessions made munificent gifts. It was natural, too, that books with a sacred use should be singled out as heirlooms. Shelves may not have been quite so bare as the evidence of legacies alone would suggest, for books could be produced to order, without a binding, quite cheaply and were on sale in this condition. The stocks of two grocers who became bankrupt in the 1390's contained four *libros de romaunc*, valued at 11s. 4d. for the lot, two *libros de Englysshe* valued at 8d., a calendar worth 8d., and a primer worth 16d.[15]

Bequests from public-spirited merchants were gradually building up a library at the Guildhall, but this may not have been easily open to citizens outside aldermanic circles. There were also collections of devotional books and Scripture at some of the larger parish churches and at St. Paul's. These may have been more generally accessible than the Guildhall library, for people wandered in and out of church buildings on all sorts of business. The best libraries in the city were probably those at the religious houses, to which access must have been limited.[16]

The intellectual life that was germinating in this environment fed primarily upon religious interests. Among the twenty odd books contained in sixteen bequests made between the years 1403 and 1483, liturgical manuals and primers excluded, there were three Bibles; three sets of legends of the saints, one bound with the Gospels; a copy of the Book of Job; an English translation of Bonaventura (1439); a treatise called *Speculum ecclesie;* a copy of the Franciscan moral treatise, *Fasciculus morum;* one dictionary;

15. C, 131/12/24, 131/42/2. On the multiplication of small manuscripts written in unbound quires in the fifteenth century and on the low cost of copying see H. S. Bennett, "Caxton and His Public," *Review of English Studies*, XIX (1943), 114; and H. E. Bell, "The Price of Books in Mediaeval England," *Library*, 4th ser., XVII, 314–21.

16. See E. M. Borrajo, *The Guildhall Library, Its History and Present Position* (1908). A mercer in 1368 bequeathed St. Lawrence Jewry a missal, a portifory, a Bible, and the legends of the saints (Harl. Ch., 58 G 20). Repair of the library at St. Peter's Cornhill by Crosby's executors mentioned in Newcourt, I, 523. Mention of new library begun at St. Paul's in *Cal. P.R., 1452–61*, p. 201. An inventory of books at St. James Garlekhithe, worth over £154, included a chained French Bible, "an oþer boke of holy Wrytte compiled in frensshe," "a prikkid song boke," etc. (W.A.M., 6644 [1449]). Mention of the library at Elsyng Spital in 1448 in A. W. Clapham, "Three Medieval Hospitals of London," *Transactions of St. Paul's Ecclesiological Society*, VII, 154. Whittington contributed £400 to the building of the Grey Friars' library.

a group of books of grammar; a book entitled *Svdrak;* several volumes vaguely referred to as English books; and one of *Prikked Songs.* Philosophy was represented by a Latin version of *The Consolation of Philosophy* of Boethius and history by a Brut and two copies of a *Polychronicon.*[17]

The interest in history is significant. Because of their strong sense of political and legal continuity, merchants had in this one direction been able to play an important intellectual role in the community. They had not directly composed all the city custumals and chronicles, but they had at least given patronage and encouragement to those city officials and other writers, some of them perhaps secretaries in their employment, who had done the work and should thus have some credit for that interpretation of the city's political experience and linking-up of its story with the story of the nation at which the chronicles aimed.[18]

There was little other literary patronage with which the city merchants can be credited. Robert Chichele, following a fashion of the day, commissioned Hoccleve to write him one of his labored religious ballads, and it was Sir Hugh Brice, goldsmith, who set Caxton on the enterprise of translating "The Mirrour of the World" for presentation to Lord Hastings; but it is well known that Caxton found his patronage mainly among the aristocracy and gentry.[19] It must even be admitted that the merchants showed no great zeal for the extension of education. They were generous in giving scholarships to theological students; but in spite of their interest in the country communities from which so many of them came, there is record of the founding of only three new country schools through their agency.[20] When business affairs were laid aside, they could listen with interest to preaching; otherwise they preferred convivial relaxation to intellectual discussion.

17. Other bequests give incomplete descriptions of books. Several apothecaries left medical books in English and Latin.

18. On the possibility that Fabian's chronicle was written by a secretary in his household see A. H. Thomas, *The Great Chronicle* (1938), pp. xlvii, lxvii. References to merchants' secretaries include an admission to the freedom of the city in 1311 and a legacy of £40 in 1407 on condition of serving his master's widow (*Cal. L. Bk., D,* p. 73; Comm. Lon., Broun, fol. 88). John Northampton left a legacy to send his secretary to the university.

19. *The Minor Poems of Hoccleve,* E.E.T.S., extra ser., No. LXI, pp. 67–72; *Caxton's Mirrour of the World,* E.E.T.S., No. CX (extra ser., 1913), p. 6.

20. Leach, *op. cit.,* pp. 244–46.

2. MORAL DISCIPLINE OF BOYS

The church schools stressed the teaching of virtue along with that of grammar. To the merchant this was of supreme importance; at a pinch, his children could go through life without much knowledge of Latin, but it was essential that they be brought up virtuously, well instructed in *bonis moribus*. In his mind this referred not only to the inculcation of abstract moral values but also to a training in all those social attitudes that were by convention suited to their role in the community. The two kinds of training had to be interlinked, the one reinforcing the other. This part of the children's education, in the nature of the case, could not be surrendered entirely to priests or to any other schoolmasters, for it was carried on continuously through pressure exercised by all the older members of a household.

In the first place, the child had to learn that the world was organized by authority. Linked, through religious teaching, with the idea of divine authority, this was further impressed upon him by lessons in deference and obedience to elders and superiors, which were taught with rather more rigor than immediate disciplinary ends could always have required. The child's state of subordination, involving liability to corporal punishment, was prolonged throughout apprenticeship, the master's part in the matter being set out in the indentures as though chastisement of his charge was a duty rather than a right. Boys who wished to protest against ill-treatment had to prove that they had been beaten more constantly or with more severity than was considered reasonable.[21] Whatever psychological complexities may have lurked in this particular relationship, there was obviously a sense of urgency in the teaching of respect for authority that would have served to give it broad social implications. The boy learned that there were gradations of status and that these had to be accepted.

Along these lines he was gradually led to comprehend his own role as member of a governing and employing class. One of the arts he had to acquire in this capacity, the art of good manners, depended primarily upon a sensitivity to differences in status. The

---

21. Chastisement intended after "reson and the comon usage" (Goldsmiths' Book A, fol. 69). That his mistress should run a needle through his thumb, one apprentice complained, was "ayens all reison & lawefull demeanyng" (E.C.P., 155/43).

code of good behavior was not elaborate; indeed, it could almost be summed up in the necessity of restraining the temper, especially before inferiors or superiors. Being an avoidance of the sin of anger, this restraint had a moral aspect. It had also the value of bestowing a personal dignity that the merchant felt to be peculiarly fitting to his station. In the presence of superiors, calmness of manner betokened respect; in the presence of inferiors, on the other hand, it symbolized superiority, for loud voices and undignified quarreling in public were typically associated with the lower classes. Any public quarreling among merchants was felt to be a disgrace to their companies. When a mercer once "broke the hed" of another with his dagger, in the climax of an argument in the company hall over some merchandise, the company wardens fined both of them £10 and bound them in £200 not to repeat the disgrace. To go on quarreling in the presence of wardens, the representatives of authority, made the offense still more heinous. The mercer who had drawn his dagger later fell into this further disgrace, refusing to let the wardens pacify him in a violent quarrel with his brother. The clerk who recorded the incident set him down as behaving "full ungoodly & unworshipfully . . . . full unmanerly and not as a man of worsship." A similar incident is more fully recorded in the minutes of the tailors' court, one of the parties to the quarrel continuing to rail in the presence of the wardens, the other restraining himself in a vein of self-righteousness:

Master Heed . . . . in ungoodly wise reviled rebuked & spake unto the seid Derby unmanerly . . . . wt an unmeeke spirit a rude voice unsad demeanure & irreverent maner—Thou liest falsely lyke a falsse harlot as thou arte. Whereunto the seid Derby answered soberly wt a well advised mynde and sad demeanure and seide / Sir I wote and remembre in what place and whose presence that I am in and if I were in an other place and from hensse and worshipfull company I wold speke as playne English unto you as ye have don unto me. . . . .

Self-control before the representatives of authority is here clearly assimilated to that character of prudence and discretion in which the merchant liked to conceive himself; the prudent man is always mindful of the opinion of others. At the same time, respect for authority is viewed in a strongly moral light, for rudeness shows "an unmeeke spirit," that is, a breach of Christian virtue. It is interesting that the only use made of the aristocratic term "courtesy" in company records is in regard to this matter of respect for superiors, the grocers' apprentices being told to be "lowly and curteis" whenever they met a liveryman of their company.[22]

In private there was little formality in merchant manners, consciousness of minor differences in status being normally concealed under a jovial friendliness. Use of the French tongue bequeathed an ambiguous intermingling of the terms of love and friendship. Business letters from one merchant to another could begin, "Salut & bon amour Treschier amy . . . ." or "A son tres chier & grant amy—salus & treschiers amistees . . . . ,"[23] and members of an intimate circle would be dubbed "good frendes and lovers." Yet the smooth surface would break; it is significant that even the well-haved tailor, Master Derby, would have felt free to give way to his anger in a private interview and bandy what he called plain English. There was little originality in the merchants' language of abuse, which revolved about such points as probity, fortune, intelligence, ancestry, on which they felt themselves to be jockeying for public esteem. "Harlot" was the favorite, most inclusive epithet of insult. In the episodes mentioned above this was varied by "carl" and "whoreson"; in the family quarrel the mercer had called his brother "fals harlott knave & dryvyll / and said that he was never his true brother / but as oon founde & Chaunged at the londes ende with moche other more ungodly & inconvenyent langewage moved & spoken."[24]

Much of the moral teaching addressed to the young was focused upon the need of making what was considered prudent use of money. The wasteful character was undeserving. A boy would be left a legacy, for example, on condition that he grow up "of good verite and sad governaunce" or that he be "thriving and toward the world and of no riotuose disposition." The same qualities would serve him in good stead when he was seeking a bride with a good dowry, for parents and guardians preferred to intrust these only to promising businessmen. As one draper directed in his will, his daughters were to be married to "suche sadde and discrete persones . . . . as seme convenyent and profitable."

Although thoughts thus tended to gravitate to the making of

22. *Mercers' Acts*, pp. 60, 85–86; Merchant Tailors' Minutes, 1488–93, fol. 45; Kingdon, Vol. II, date of 1431.

23. Harl. MS, 4971, fol. 15v, 44.

24. *Mercers' Acts*, p. 86.

money, the medieval merchant class does not seem to have generated a gospel of hard work. It was probably the practice to keep apprentices well occupied in waiting upon customers and carrying messages, but there was no great pressure of office work to harass them, nor were they enjoined to spend all their days on earth at labor.

Nor was there any extreme puritanical ban upon amusement, although there were strong reservations on the score of expense. The love of hunting has been referred to already, and the love of pageantry and theatricals is too well known for comment. Commercialized amusements, however, were looked on with distrust as so many incitements to extravagance, and there was grave concern lest young men grow up in habits of dissipation. An instance occurs of a grocer who married under age having to promise that he would not become "a Comen Riotour" and to restrict himself to an amusement allowance of 20s. a year; he was bound to this by a bond of £500, drawn by a relative of his wife, a wealthy pewterer, who hoped by this means to keep him "in awe and ffere to lose or mysspend his goods." There was a very acute fear of the temptation of gambling. Apprentices were forbidden to play with cards or dice, but these and other forms of gambling retained their fascination. Robert Cely was reduced to borrowing right and left to pay his dicing debts and was unmoved by his eldest brother's disgust at his "onstedfastness." A number of organized amusements persisted that must have given occasion for betting. The butchers made a double profit out of bulls by having them baited before they were killed, and bear-baiting, cock-fighting, and wrestling matches were popular.[25]

The physical exuberance of youth could find plenty of outlet in other exercises and sports besides hunting. Military exercises were encouraged. Young men of the merchant class, it is true, may have taken less part in these than the poorer citizens; for, although it was the duty of every citizen to provide himself with what armor and weapons he could afford, in order that he might take his turn in the city watch or in levies for the royal service, wealthy men were privileged to hire others to serve in their place. Men of mer-

25. E.C.P., 197/5; *Cely Papers*, p. 14; *Cal. L. Bk., K*, p. 10. Yet in 1349 the butchers' overseers had admitted on oath that the flesh of unbaited bulls was more wholesome (*Cal. P. & M. Rolls*, I, 22).

chant families had nevertheless volunteered to serve with the levies that were raised in the city for service in the Scottish and French wars of Edward II and Edward III,[26] and the tradition of responsibility did not die. In the fifteenth century, merchants took a lead in local efforts to cultivate skill in use of the longbow. Governmental efforts to build up reserves of amateur archers by proclaiming all other sports illegal had not been generally successful, for the reason, as Sir John Fortescue pointed out, that archery was a sport "wich may not be done without ryght grete expenses, as every man experte þer in knowith right well."[27] It was impossible for workingmen to take it up unless men of property would give them the equipment. By the 1430's the grocers had practice butts in the garden of their hall, and in 1456 a salter bequeathed a new bow to each of twenty of his neighbors in the parish of St. Michael's Cornhill "that useth the sport of Shotyng." Near the end of the century a grocer named William Steyde, who had served for a short period as alderman, personally organized a body of bowmen among the poor shopkeepers of London Bridge, who came to be jocularly known as "Steyde's Knights." By bequests of the year 1506 his son renewed their equipment and bequeathed bows also to the porters of the grocers' weighhouse. Typical of the spirit of truly national patriotism in which the movement had grown was his bequest to a scrivener of "my bowe called England."[28]

Meanwhile the young and vigorous of all classes had continued to practice the other sports that had been forbidden. The grocers promoted wrestling, and a mercer lost his life in a wrestling bout at Blackheath.[29] Tennis had a great vogue. The author of *The Great Chronicle* mourned the execution for treason of Richard Steris, a former member of the skinners' company, because he had

26. V. B. Redstone, "Some Mercenaries of Henry of Lancaster," *Transactions of the Royal Historical Society*, VII (3d ser., 1913), 154–60; and C. Stephenson, "The Aids of the English Boroughs," *EHR*, XXXIV, 463–66. In 1338 and 1340 men with the names of Gisors, Thorney, Elsing, Swanland, served in person (*Cal. L. Bk., F*, pp. 21–23; *Cal. P. & M. Rolls*, I, 130–33).

27. *The Governance of England*, ed. C. Plummer (1885), p. 138.

28. Wills of William Lyndesey (P.C.C., Stokton, 7) and Thomas Steyde (P.C.C., Horne, 17).

29. Journals, 6, fol. 260b; Kingdon, II, 226; *Historical Collections of a London Citizen*, Camden Society, new ser., No. 17, p. 89. Case of death from a fracture received in wrestling (*Cal. Coroners' Rolls*, p. 20 [1301]).

been " .... oon of the cunnyngest players at the Tenys in England, ffor he was so delyvyr þt he wold stand In a Tubb that shuld be nere brest hye, and lepe owth of the same, bothe standyng at the hows and at Rechace, and wyn of a good player. . . . ."[30]

The pleasures of eating and drinking were so well savored as to form lifelong habits of relaxation. Although gross gluttony and drunkenness were regarded as both sinful and undignified and to be so "oft overcharged wt drink" that one could not attend to business, as was reported of a certain vintner, was reprehensible, occasional tipsiness was probably regarded as natural enough, like Noah's, and a little amusing, and the drinking songs of the day found their way, along with prayers and hymns, into fifteenth-century commonplace books. Pecock, while warning of the dangers that arose from excess, seems to have indorsed enjoyment of wine, ale, and cider as "meritorie."[31]

The discipline that was exercised over apprentices included prohibition of sexual relations. The indentures drawn for a Cirencester boy who was apprenticed to Drew Barentyn, wealthy goldsmith, in 1382, specified that he should not commit fornication either in his master's house or elsewhere, that he should not marry, and that without his master's permission he should not even become engaged. Nor was he to play at tables or chess or other forbidden games or to go to taverns except on business for his master. A tailor brought an apprentice into his company's court to be reproved for the waste of time that was consequent on falling in love; he "used the company of a woman which was to his grete losse and hynderyng for asmoch as he was so affectionate and resorted daily unto hyr," and the drapers punished an apprentice's misconduct with a maidservant by a cermonial flogging in the company hall, inflicted by masked men.[32]

3. THE WOMAN'S ROLE

In the training of girls the end in view was to make them grow up useful, with a sense of economic responsibility toward the family of which they were a part, and at the same time to keep

30. *The Great Chronicle*, pp. 207, 430.

31. *The Repressor*, I, 121. Yet see G.R. Owst, *Literature and Pulpit in Medieval England* (1933), pp. 425–41.

32. W.A.M., 5059; Merchant Tailors' Minutes, 1488–93, fols. 60v–61; Herbert, I, 423. On apprentices' behavior and on age of marriage see below, p. 193.

them gentle, so that they would be amenable to male authority. The relative emphasis that was laid on these ideas varied with the wealth and personal disposition of the parents. Wealthy landed merchants, who might look forward to marrying their daughters into the gentry, sometimes engaged a governess or mistress to look after them or intrusted them to nuns until they should be married; the girls would thus have maximum shelter from roughening influences and would learn at least to use a needle.[33] But it was not uncommon to encourage girls to learn a trade in order that they could be self-supporting or of assistance to their husband. Pecock wrote that it was a wife's duty, if her husband wished it, to use her spare time in contributing to the support of the household,[34] and among the poorer classes in the city the custom was general. There were also independent women householders among all classes. Four per cent of the city taxpayers of 1319 were women, some of whom were wealthy *rentiers* but most of whom were identified by name with a trade.[35]

In the merchant class married women's business activities were less often an economic necessity than an outlet for surplus energy or a means of earning additional money to spend. Margery Kempe was the wife of one of the wealthiest merchants at Lynne, yet she took up first brewing and then "a new huswyfre," the grinding of corn in a horsemill, because she had time on her hands and because, in her own words, she was envious that any other woman in Lynne "schuld be arrayd so wel as sche." In London a fishmonger's heiress who was four times married went in both for tailoring and for brewing. A fishmonger's widow bequeathed a male apprentice all the "anavildes & Slegges" of some kind of metal-working shop that she had directed. Dame Elizabeth Stokton had cloth manufactured for export to Italy. The favorite trades were embroidery, the "garnishing" of cloth and wearing apparel with jewelry, and the manufacture of silk; this last was

33. Wills of Johan Drew, Thomas Mareschal (Comm. Lon., Broun, 55; *C.W.C.H.*, I, 620; cf. Eileen Power, *Mediaeval English Nunneries* [1922], pp. 261, n. 3, 265, 576–77).

34. *The Reule of Cristen Religioun*, E.E.T.S., No. 171 (original ser., 1926), p. 319.

35. E.g., Elena la Juelera, paying 8*d*.; Matilla la Bracereste, "man' in dom' sua," 10*d*.; Petronilla la Brewere, 12*d*.; Margeria la Sylkewymman, 13*d*.; Alic la Stocfysshmonger, 14*d*.; a coifer, a leach, and a saddler, each 20*d*.; a spurrier and a girdler, each 3*s*. 4*d*.; Dyonisia la Bokebyndere, 6*s*. 8*d*. (E, 179/144/3). There were occasional charitable bequests to poor women householders.

managed almost entirely by merchants' wives, some of them having their raw silk imported by their husbands.[36]

Illiteracy would have hampered a woman's efficiency in business matters. It followed that girls were recognized as in need of at least some elementary education for the same mixed reasons, economic and religious, as their brothers. They were admitted to the elementary schools, though not to grammar schools. Pecock advocated the sending of "femawlis" to school in order that they should be able to read treatises such as his own, which were written in English; liberal though he was, he did not urge that girls be taught Latin. Yet they could learn a little Latin in an elementary school and get more by private tuition. The story of Rahere tells of a twelfth-century priest in the suburbs with a daughter "whome he lovynge with fadirly affeccionn / yn yonge age put her to lernynge /." In 1390 there is a note of 25s. spent on school fees for a chandler's daughter, the ward of a broiderer, between her eighth year and her thirteenth, when she was married; and a century later a mercer gave instructions for his daughter to be sent to school for the same length of time as her brothers, four years. A woman could become a teacher, a wealthy grocer in 1408 leaving the sum of 20s. to E. Scolemaysteresse. One of the earliest London deeds found bearing a signature as well as a seal was drawn between two women, in 1478, signed by a wool merchant's widow. Bequests of devotional primers, which contained parts of the liturgy in Latin together with prayers in English, were made to women as well as to men. This evidence is not enough to show whether education was actually as general among the women as it was among the men of the merchant class, but one may infer that it was quite commonly within their reach.[37]

In the silk industry and sometimes in other trades, women trained their assistants through a formal apprenticeship. Terms ran from

36. *The Book of Margery Kempe*, E.E.T.S., No. 212 (original ser., 1940), pp. 9–10. Will of Mazera Aghton (Archdeaconry, London, 137 [1405]; E.C.P., 137/33, 67/307, 351, 354, 110/125). Rose, wife of John de Bureford, merchant, in 1316 sold the queen a cap ornamented with coral for 100 marks (F. Devon, *Issues of the Exchequer* [1837], p. xxxv). Cf. Thomasina Parker, "garnisshster," one of the recipients of a deed of gift from John Parker, draper (*Cal. C.R., 1435–41*, p. 428; M. K. Dale, "The London Silkwomen of the Fifteenth Century," *Ec. H.R.*, IV, 324–35).

37. *The Reule of Cristen Religioun*, p. 363; *The Book of the Foundation of St. Bartholomew's Church in London*, E.E.T.S., original ser., No. 163, p. 48; L. Bk.,*H*, fol. 162*b*; wills of William Rows (Comm. Lon., Lichfield, fols. 62–63) and of William Cresewyk (Comm. Lon., Broun, fol. 88*v*; Harl. Ch., 49, I, 35).

seven to fifteen years, and up to £5 was paid as premium. If the mistress was a married woman, the indentures were made out in her husband's name as well as in her own, but they would specify that it was her trade, not his, that was to be taught. It was expected that a girl apprentice would receive more consideration than a boy, for the indentures might include an agreement to treat her "pulcrior' modo."[38]

Two fifteenth-century handbooks dealt in doggerel verse with the role of the wife. Addressed by a "goode wyfe" to her daughter, they referred to town society, although to people of slightly lower status than the London merchant class. The model they upheld was that of the sweet and prudent woman, "evermore of mylde mode," who would regard her husband as her "lord," would not try to dress as richly as a lady, and would be content to stay at home instead of running about to wrestling matches and cock-shooting, where people might take her for a strumpet. To be sure of going to heaven, she would always return borrowed articles. Finally, she would cultivate an inner sense of resignation, accepting the loss of friends and the deaths of her children without rebelling against God. A corresponding set of verses written for the benefit of a young man, however, hints that he had better put up with less than perfection. If he beats his wife, she will despise him. He must remember that

> Tho sche be servant in degre
> In som degre she felaw ys.[39]

By some such modification of the principle of authority the merchant family managed to retain its equilibrium even when the wife became a successful businesswoman and a forceful personality. There is no need to look to the fictitious Wife of Bath for this quality of force. It stands out in every line of the large draped fe-

---

38. Cases of apprenticeship of orphan daughters of merchants (L. Bk., *G*, fols. 73*b*, 120*b*; *H*, fols. 136, 143, 145*b*, 240, 254, 289*b*; *I*, fol. 247*b*; P. & M. Rolls [MS Cal.], 72/3). Loan of £10 in place of premium, paid for a Henley girl apprenticed to a purser and his wife in shepstry (E.C.P., 155/10). Indenture of apprenticeship of daughter of John Eland of Lincolnshire, esquire, to a London tailor and his wife, for seven years (date of 1454; Anc. Deeds, D 1176). Model indentures to a London mercer and his wife, silkwoman, for seven years, in Add. MS, 17716.

39. *A Book of Precedence*, E.E.T.S., extra ser., No. 8, pp. 43–46; "How the Wise Man Taught His Son," ll. 131 ff., *Ancient Popular Poetry* ed. J. Ritson (1884).

male figure that "Roesia la custurere," wife of William of the king's chamber under Henry III, had placed on her business seal.[40] Dame Agnes Forster, in the fifteenth century, has left the impression of a masterful character. Lending some lawbooks, she had a deed drawn to the effect that the borrower should return them "when her ladyship will Comaund hym." Chancery proceedings of the same period represent a hatter merchant's widow as a hard-headed dealer who was trying to tie the business of a former apprentice to her own.[41]

The London women were teased and privileged. Sir John Fortescue took the same low view of women's capacities as Aristotle, remarking that they had not the powers of concentration that were required in business. They were privileged, in that they had the choice of trading alone, with the legal rights and responsibilities of a citizen, or of sheltering behind their husband's credit. The silkwomen early petitioned parliament for statutory protection for their industry, the product of which was inferior to foreign silk; they diplomatically claimed that their work pleased God and the gentry, and the petition was granted. Women could obtain minor offices of profit. One of the assayers of oysters, for example, made a practice of farming his office to women. A Queenhithe ward inquest objected that this derogated from the city's "worship," because women could not effectively suppress the frauds of the trade.[42]

City women had a great deal of freedom in recreation. At the social level for which the good wife's verses were intended, they had to be warned not to be seen drunk and not to sit up too late at home drinking ale. In the merchant class it is probable that they followed the custom of gentlewomen in the city, learning to hunt and going freely to taverns.

In the family the mother enjoyed a respect that enabled her at her husband's death to succeed to his authority even over grown sons. Children were enjoined by their father to be "lowly and obedient" to her, "gentil and lovyng."

40. W.A.M., 13845. Another remarkable seal, of the next century, shows a female figure in a short pleated skirt, apparently dancing, arms flung above her head. It belonged to a mercer's widow, Alicia Fraunceys (W.A.M., 415).

41. Harl. Ch., 50, D 24; E.C.P., 61/540.

42. Sir John Fortescue, cited in E. F. Jacob, *Essays in the Conciliar Epoch* (1943) p. 115; Dale, *op. cit.*; *Rot. parl.*, V, 325, 506; *Cal. P. & M. Rolls*, IV, 138–39 (1423).

There could nevertheless be extreme nervous tension and break-down. The illness that preceded Margery Kempe's development as a mystic is an example. There are some confused details of a case in London, in which a woman wandered away from home to hide "in a foxborow." The immediate occasion of strain was grief at the death of her child. It was apparent also that she had suffered from being pushed into one or more of her four marriages, on account of her property. Although rich, she had not lived in leisure but had been carrying on business as a tailor and an ale-brewer. In repudiation of a charge that she was insane it was urged that she had conducted these and her household *bene et sapienter*.[43]

4. THE STEWARDSHIP OF WEALTH

The merchant achieved a very happy justification of his pursuit of wealth as approved by God. The wealthy were fond of texts and mottoes that expressed confidence of divine approval. A four-teenth-century citizen's wife encircled her seal with "God help þat best man." A lighthearted letter written by a mayor of Exeter, assuring his friends that an enemy's charge of impurity in his private life was false, adds, "therefore y . . . . sey sadly *si recte vivas*, etc., and am right mery and fare right well, ever thankyng God and myn awne purse." Late fifteenth-century aldermen displayed such mottoes as "I trust in God," "dextra Domini exaltavit me," "A Domine factum est istum." Wills of the same period, drawn "of such goodes of fortune as god hath sent me and lent me," show confidence buoyed up by the doctrine of the stewardship of wealth.[44]

God approved of newly accumulated wealth, it was understood, only on condition that it was honestly won. Preachers would warn merchants against too much love of wealth, "for goodes þat ben evel goten beryn witnesse ayenst þe soule, and to þe perdycyon of hem that have falsely goten yt."[45] More specifically, they would reprove the giving of short measure, misrepresentation, trading on

43. C. Misc., 68/4.

44. Anc. Deeds, AS 294; *Letters and Papers of John Shillingford, Mayor of Exeter, 1447–50*, ed. Stuart A. Moore, Camden Society, II (new ser., 1871), 16; Draper's Deeds, A VII, 107; Simon Eyre's motto in Newcourt; Sir John Young's "proverb" in his will; wills of Sir William Taylour, Hugh Shaa, aldermen, of John Heyward, haberdasher (P.C.C., Godyn, 32).

45. Harl. MS, 149, fol. 239.

holidays, and usury. In London these came under the jurisdiction of the mayor and aldermen, who held a general authority to punish all trade offenses at their discretion. On minor matters, as has been seen, this authority was largely delegated to the crafts; otherwise the severity varied with the temperament of the mayor in office. For example, there was spasmodic sabbatarian legislation, spasmodically supported. The grocers in 1429 renewed an old company ordinance, "þat no man selle no ware uppon no sonday nor uppon none halydaye þet vygyll is uppon by no maner off colour. . . . . This ordinance is Renovelyd on þe Reverence off God & amendment off owre selffe." Yet they left themselves a loophole in the excuse of "Grete hye nede"; and a chronicler reported that a city ordinance to the same effect, issued in 1443 by Thomas Catworth, one of the stricter mayors, "was holdyn but a short whyle afftir this mayers tyme."[46]

Jurisdiction in the more difficult problem of usury lay in the area of authority that was disputed between church and state. The central government in 1363 upheld the claim of the mayor and aldermen to control it without interference, and in 1421 this control was described as being part of the immemorial custom of the city. Action under it, however, was spasmodic. Northampton threatened to prosecute usurers but did not carry out his threat. The chief prosecutions on record were in 1421 and 1434.[47]

The scope of this book does not allow of any full illustration of the circumstances in which interest was taken in English trade at this period or of the rates to which the London merchants were accustomed. It may be noted in passing that one of their regular forms of investment was that of lending to the monastic houses, on a variety of terms. William Estfeld obtained the grant of a rent of 50 marks for his life and that of his wife in return for the loan of 500 marks to the abbot of Waltham Holy Cross, the grant to be void if the loan was repaid within a year. The house of the Knights Hospitalers at Clerkenwell and the abbey at Westminster both borrowed heavily in London, repaying partly by pensions and corrodies. A mercer obtained an eighty-year lease of a garden and

46. Kingdon, II, 190; *The Great Chronicle*, p. 177; cf. Journals, 4, fol. 27; *Rot. parl.*, V, 152.

47. *Cal. L. Bk.*, *G*, pp. 160–63; *H*, pp. 23–25, 200, 206–7, 261–62, 302; *K*, p. 374; *L*, p. 249; Liber Dunthorne, fol. 244; *Cal. P. & M. Rolls*, I, 279–80; III, 25; IV, 95–109, 285–87.

wharf in Rochester from the abbess and convent of Denney, in Cambridgeshire, for the very low annual rent of 8*d*. Some of these transactions troubled conscience. A number of merchants at death renounced continuing rights to monastic corrodies. One Londoner left the sum of 10*s*. "to the Covent of our Blissed lady in founteyns so that I may be assoiled of alle the offences þat I have doon to that place"; another canceled debts owed him from the abbeys of Lesnes and Begham and renounced corrodies that he had taken at Begham in payment.[48]

Conscience dictated other acts of direct restitution, arising mostly out of qualms about the collection of debts from the poor. Sir Edmund Shaa was troubled:

> Whereas a kynnysman of mine called Richard Shaa caused me xl winter passed . . . . to go wt hym to a mannys ground in the peke in derbyshire to take a distresse . . . . and we toke ii oxen . . . . the which I am suer cam never again to his possession that ought them . . . . and be cause that dede was doon in my wanton dayes whanne I lakkyd discresyon therefor I have a remorce therof now in these dayes being better advysed. . . . .

His executors were to try to trace this man, in order to restore to him or to his family or executors the amount of which he had been defrauded, 20*s*.; if this should prove impossible, they were "to consult of some sadde doctours of dyvynte to understand what is best to do wt the said xxs for the wele of the soule of the said man that was distraynyd and for the discharge of my consciens." One mercer had nothing of the kind on his conscience but a memory of having caused loss to his master; he bequeathed him £5, "for neclygent servyse that y dyd to hym in the tyme of my prentyshode yf he wyl take hyt." One man was worried only that he had sold goods of bad quality or overcharged; his executors were to make an allowance to all debtors who should complain of "any lose in my waris." Sir John Wyngar made a general offer of restitution: "If any man or woman that ever I bought and sold wt all if they fynde theym agrevus dew prove made to recompense theym according to good conscience I trust in Jesu they shall fynde few or none." Several men wished money distributed among all poor people with whom they had traded. Sir Thomas Hill said that he

48. Rot. cl., 15 Hen. VI, *m. 8d. The Knights Hospitallers in England*, Introd. by J. M. Kemble, Camden Society, No. 65 (old ser., 1857), pp. lix, 98–99, 206–8. W.A.M., 28048, 5728, 5891, 5898, 5899, 5900, 5909, 28170–76, 30400, 30403. Harl. Ch., 44, D 17. Wills of Thomas Porter, William Lemynge (P.C.C., Godyn, 28, 31 [1469–70]; *Cal. P.R., 1340–43*, p. 227).

had made out a list of people among whom his executors were to distribute sums amounting in all to £649. The restitution could be in the form of prayers, John Stokker ordering that the priest who was to sing and pray for his soul for five years should pray also "for all thos persones þat ever I toke any good wrongfully of prevy or part." A mercer left £14 for a divinity scholarship at Cambridge, "forasmoche as I fynde myn consciens aggrugged that I have deceived in this life divers persons to that amount." In one instance, that of William Dere, financier, a general offer of restitution led to a claim against his estate in chancery on grounds of usury. Dere's widow left £500 among the city poor "for a cause that chargith my conscience and movith me for to doo."[49]

In many dealings it was difficult to determine whether usury had been committed or not. Fortunately for the merchant, he could still justify his gains by charity. In Langland's comforting picture there is at first some doubt whether the merchants can be forgiven their "covetyse of wynnynge," because they have ignored holidays and sworn presumptuously that God was helping them. But truth finally assures them that if they will but put their profits aside into pious and charitable uses they may die in certainty of heaven:

> And ich shal sende ȝow my-selve . seynt Michel myn angel,
> That no devel shal ȝow dere . ne despeir in youre deyinge,
> Ande sende ȝoure soules . ther ich my-self dwelle,
> And there a-byde body and soule . in blisse for evere.[50]

Charity had thus a magic virtue. The only difference of opinion concerned the question whether a man should give alms throughout his life or could safely wait until the division of his estate after death. By long-standing custom it was usual for a man to assign from a third to a half of his movables to uses that would benefit his soul. It is significant that in London this custom was followed quite strictly and that there was a tendency to extend it to immovables, land often being sold for pious and charitable objects.

Many of the charitable provisions in the merchants' wills remind one of the primitive belief in the power of a gift to nullify some po-

49. For aldermen named, also Hammond, Parker, Wyfold, see Appen. A; other wills, Robert Scalton (P.C.C., Marche, 41), William Hill, Thomas Rawson (P.C.C., Wattys, 12, 14), Robert Goodwyn, Richard Gardener (P.C.C., Milles, 22, 35), Richard Roos (Comm. Lon., Broun, 75v); Dere's case (E.C.P., 26/196, 31/527).

50. *Piers the Plowman*, C, Passus X, ll. 1–40.

tential threat to the donor. Maximum safety would lie in the distribution of a maximum number of gifts, no matter how small they might be. The man who tried to reach more people with his charity than anyone else in London was Philip Malpas, who was one of the most popularly hated of the city magnates of his time. He left close to £1,800 to charity, most of it to be scattered in gifts of half a mark each to five thousand poor city householders. Dere, the financier, left £300 to be given away at his funeral in the form of black bread. Some ordered pennies given away at the grave's side. One fund of 100 marks was to be spent "for the easement of poure men in lones and taskes set be neth seven pence," another in dowries for poor country girls, with 4*d.* each to poor householders in a list of nearly twenty towns and villages. The acts of giving might be spread out over a long period of time, as in a bequest of a penny a week for ninety years to each of the poor tenants in a certain building. Smaller sums were doled out in the same way. One man left a shilling's worth of fruit as an annual treat for forty years "to be deled among yong children which can spek and sey god have mercy of my godfaders soule." Others wished 10*s.* given away in coal every winter for twenty years and three pennyworth of bread every Friday for a year.[51]

The beneficiaries most frequently named were small debtors in prison, patients in the city leper-houses, and the inmates of the asylum of St. Mary's Bethlehem, known as "goddes prisoners." There may still have been some superstition mixed with the sympathy felt for these people. Special local bequests showed more imagination, as in the disposal of £100 among poor fishermen and plowmen of the Sussex coast to make up for their liability to suffer from French raids, the assignment of £702 for the pensioning of thirteen poor people over sixty, in Tower ward, and the underwriting of taxation in the testator's birthplace.[52]

Some men were constructive in their imagination, their charities being designed as more or less permanent contributions to the community. They built granaries, market-place shelters, water-

51. Wills of Thomas Borden (Comm. Lon., Harvey, 218 [1500]), William Waltyngfeld (P.C.C., Wattys, 12), Robert Marshall (Register, Stafford, 152), of aldermen Wyngar, Cook, John Stokton.

52. Wills of Robert Byfeld, alderman; Richard de Kislingbury, draper (*C.W.C.H.*, II, 39 [1361]); William Holt, mercer (P.C.C., Godyn, 6 [1464]); John Norlong, mercer, born at Wyberton, Lincolnshire, executors to pay fifteenths due there "at oon or at dyvers tymes" (P.C.C., Godyn, 13 [1466]).

supply systems, or endowed hospital service. One named an expert "weymaker" to make use of a legacy for road repair. Thomas Knolles left money for the piping of the first water supply into Newgate and Ludgate prisons, "Consideryng alwey the miserie & povertie off the prisoners that have no Rychesse nor liberte to plede neyther complain off their wrongs."[53] The founder of Elsing's hospital for the blind expressed himself as torn with pity for blind people (*viscera mea gravius torquentur*), and the same spirit informed a mercer's bequest of £25 toward providing free medical attention for the London poor: "I will that Thomas Thorneton, surgeon, contynewe his daily besynes and comfort of the poure sore and seke peple lakkyng helpe and money to pay for their lechecraft. . . . ."[54]

Some of the people who made bequests of this nature had shown constructive social sympathies during their lifetime. Whittington's great reputation for piety and generosity rested partly on donations made during his life. Stephen Forster and his wife, among others, took an interest in the beginnings of a prison reform movement.[55]

In his capacity as a man of property the merchant's attitude toward the poor was curiously mixed. The superstition in his desire for the prayers of as many poor people as possible was allied to a feeling that the poor were somehow blessed. This comes out in the statutes of the almshouse that Elys Davy founded at Croydon. He concluded with the hope that the almsfolk would live together in charity "and that after thende of this life they may comme to the hous of the kyngdome of Hevin, the which to poure people is promised by the mouth of our Lord God. Amen."[56] The allusion, apparently, was to the Sermon on the Mount. Again, there was uneasiness as to whether economic relations with the poor were really just. Executors were often cautioned not to trouble old people when they were collecting debts or to do "hurt or damage to any poure and nedy person." One mercer wished debts owing from tenants on property he had inherited in Lincolnshire to be

53. Grocers' Register of Freemen and Apprentices, fol. 105 [1467].

54. Dugdale, VI, Part 2, 706; will of John Don (P.C.C., Logge, 2 [1480]).

55. On prison reform see M. Bassett, "Newgate Prison in the Middle Ages," *Speculum*, XVIII, 233.

56. A.C. Ducarel, *Some Account of Croydon* (1783), printed in J. Nichols, *Bibliographia topographica Britanniae*, II (1790), No. 12, 35.

pardoned "if they may not be had wt fairenesse."[57] This uneasiness was complicated by the feeling that people were degraded by doing dirty manual work. A goldsmith who felt himself unfairly penalized by the company wardens for some trade offense called out that he would rather be dwelling at Croydon among the colliers than be treated as they were treating him.[58] Women had the same attitude. The good wife advised her daughter not to be hard toward poor people or to shrink from them: "Of pore men be þou not lothe." Pity, however, was only for the industrious poor, not for those who were astute enough to stop working in order to live by the indiscriminate almsgiving that went on at funerals. Some of the wealthy men tried to insure that no "comen torch bearers" should be employed at their funeral and that no beggars or "rynners aboute in toune" receive their alms. It was usual to restrict admission to almshouses to those who had fallen into poverty through some misfortune and not through their own misjudgment or idleness.

5. THE MERCHANT AS PARISHIONER

Every phase of life in the merchant class had some customary connection with the imagery and beliefs of the Christian faith. Angels competed with heraldic beasts in the decoration of the household. Sacred emblems were the normal foundation of the marks set on merchandise. The sign of the cross was inked into account-books. The mercers appended a prayer to their company accounts. Children were named, at their christening, from a list of popular saints' names, and such pious names as Pentecost and Baptist occurred.[59] A man would wish church bells rung after his death "in encreasing the more devotion and praiere . . . . to the honour of almighti God and profit of my soule." Three fifteenth-century merchants had the theme of the Resurrection represented on their tombs, and another expressed hope in the intercession of St. Albion, on whose day he had been born:

Tresting by preyer celestiall, joy to be my judgment.[60]

57. William Hille (P.C.C., Wattys, 12).   58. Prideaux, I, 27 (1480).

59. Pentecost Russel, fourteenth-century fishmonger (Liber de assisa Panis [Guildhall], fol. 35v; Herbert, II, 54–55); Baptist Pynchon, of Little Wakering, Essex, gentleman alias citizen and fishmonger of London (*Cal. P.R., 1476–85*, p. 58).

60. "Credo quod Redemptor meus vivit . . . . ," Simon Seman ("Holles Church Notes," *Lincoln Record Society*, I, 78); will of Thomas Muschampe (P.C.C., Wattys, 14); Richard Payn (Weever, p. 198).

The demand for chantry priests in 1345 exceeded the supply. The private endowment of permanent chantries fell off during the next century, but short-term endowment persisted.[61] Both men and women went on pilgrimage or paid others to do so for their benefit. A fourteenth-century magnate would spend £40 or more on a tour of Continental shrines with his wife and their servants. A woman of the Fraunceis family traveled abroad on pilgrimage with no company but two servants and her chaplain. Matilda Toky, the wife of a wool merchant, visited Rome after her husband's death. William Purchase, mercer, had visited the Galician shrine of St. James "for his soul hele" some twenty years before his mayoralty. Popular shrines nearer home, besides the great one at Canterbury, were St. John's at Bridlington and two of the Virgin Mary at Walsingham and at Muswell, near Highgate. A salter in 1456 bequeathed half a mark "to myn neyboures in their going a pilgrimage unto the devout place at Muswelle."[62]

There is evidence also of meditative and reflective interest in matters of faith. London shared in the general trend of the fifteenth century toward improving the intellectual level of instruction in the church, doctors of divinity being appointed, in preference to mere bachelors, in the few parishes that were under civic or company patronage. The procedure was to take the advice of the four best-known rectors in the city, either in nominating a panel of candidates or in making the final selection. Pecock, who spent fourteen years in London as master of Whittington College, wrote in 1456 that both men and women had often come to ask his opinion about the views of some doctor or preacher who had impressed them. A draper's will begs his wife to keep God daily before her eyes. Streamers given to the church of St. Margaret Pattens near the end of the century bore the mottoes, "Know thyself" and "desyr reste."[63]

61. V.C.H., London, 205–8.

62. *Cal. P.R., 1348–50*, pp. 543, 560; *ibid., 1354–58*, p. 645; *ibid., 1367–70*, pp. 55, 56, 70, 71; Drapers' Deeds, A VII, 271; H.M.C., *9th Report, Appendix*, pp. 21–22; *C.W.C.H.*, I, II, *passim*, for bequests for pilgrimage. An example in bequest of £20 by a skinner to a former servant of a nobleman to go to Jerusalem for him and his friends, he hoped, without fraud, in will of Robert Scalton (P.C.C., Marche, 41 [1418]). Letter of John Chircheman from Rome (B. H. Deeds, F. 88 [1388–92]). Purchase's pilgrimage (E.C.P., 64/167). Will of William Lyndesey, salter, (P.C.C., Stokton, 7).

63. V.C.H., London, 228; Journals, 2, 4, 8, *passim*; Grocers' Register of Freemen and Apprentices, fol. 17; *The Repressor*, I, 91; will of William Breton, P.C.C., Luffenham, 22); "Inventories of St. Margaret Pattens," *Archaeological Journal*, CLXVII (1885), 320, 329.

The only evidence of heretical leanings in the city's merchant class concerns women. Sir John Yonge's mother-in-law, Joan Boughton, was burnt as a heretic in 1495, at the age of eighty, defying all the doctors in London to shake her faith in the tenets of Wycliffe, and a few years later Lady Yonge followed her to the stake. Pecock had complained of women "which maken hem self so wise bi the Bible," who would insist on disputing with the clergy and would admit no practice to be virtuous "save what thei kunnen fynde expresseli in the Bible." But he did not say who they were nor what their husbands thought or did about their unorthodox habits in argument.[64]

Inequalities in taxation as between lay and ecclesiastical landlords led to resentment of the latter's wealth in London. In 1312 it was estimated that they held a third of city rentals, and a petition of 1357 asking for relief from royal taxation suggests that the proportion had risen, since many of the richer citizens had lately died of pestilence, and their property, it says, had fallen into the hands of Holy Church.[65] In 1412 about 19 per cent of the London freehold property and rents assessed for national taxation was in the hands of the church, representing values of £1,865 out of £9,530. The list of ecclesiastical owners, however, which in 1291 had included seventy names from outside the city, was very incomplete. Correction for omissions would bring the total above £10,000, with the church's share about 25 per cent. The figure is still an understatement, for it does not cover the value of buildings used for ecclesiastical purposes or of the gardens and orchards that were attached to several of the religious houses or of the income from parish offerings.[66]

64. V.C.H., London, 234–35. Horribly mocking account of Joan Boughton's end in *The Great Chronicle*, p. 252. *The Repressor*, I, 123. The original following of the Lollard movement, both in London and elsewhere, had been chiefly among artisans. Evidence for the year 1415 in J. H. Wylie and W. T. Waugh, *The Reign of Henry V* (2 vols., 1914–29), I, 260–85. A London heretic burned in that year is described in one source as a skinner, but he was not a liveried merchant.

65. H. M. Chew, "Mortmain in Mediaeval London," *EHR*, LX, 3; *Cal. L. Bk.*, G, p. 85.

66. For details of endowment see Newcourt, I, 235–565; *Taxatio ecclesiastica Angliae et Walliae auctoritate P. Nicholai IV*, Record Commission (1802), pp. 8–13; V.C.H., London, 407–585; A. G. Little, "A Royal Enquiry into Property Held by the Mendicant Friars in England in 1349 and 1350," *Historical Essays in Honour of James Tait* (1933), p. 183. The assessment for the priory of Holy Trinity decreased between 1291 and 1412. For the college of St. Martin's le Grand and St. Bartholomew's Priory, rent accounts of 1392 and 1306, respectively, show totals above the 1291 figure (W.A.M., 13311; and E. A. Webb, *The Records of St. Bartholomew's Priory* [1921], I, 322).

Most of the original endowment of the older religious houses in the city had been due to piety at court, and royal and noble patrons continued to contribute to all types of ecclesiastical foundation. Donations from the merchant class also flowed freely, going most generously to the friars, to the enlargement of parish churches, into hospitals, and to the newer types of collegiate foundation.

Their business connections brought many London merchants into close touch with the higher members of the church hierarchy. The wealthy men who negotiated loans to the government became well-enough acquainted with the great political churchmen to claim them as friends and patrons. Sir William Estfeld and Sir Thomas Cook named the bishop of Lincoln among their executors. Other dignitaries who were asked to supervise the execution of London wills included Adam Moleyns, who became bishop of Chichester and lord privy seal; Thomas Rotheram, as archbishop of York; and Cardinal Morton, as archbishop of Canterbury. One of the more useful patrons in London was the head of the semi-monastic military order of the Knights of St. John. As prior of the whole order in England, he had control over a revenue of £600 and a seat among the lords in parliament. Sir John Weston, who held the position in the 1480's, at that time had Richard Cely and his sons, London merchant staplers, in his following. The correspondence of the Celys, full of anxious reference to the wishes of "my lord," shows how important the relationship with such a patron could be. They had gowns of his livery, a sign that they were under his protection. When a charge of poaching in the royal forest threatened them with serious trouble, his influence was of material help. He was personally friendly to them, inviting the brothers to stay with him at holiday seasons and once lending them a hawk and the services of his falconer. For their part, they acted as his financial agents in Bruges, furnishing him with foreign exchange at need, filled small commissions for him in the markets abroad, and kept him informed of foreign news. The father complained that George Cely, who handled their business in Calais and Bruges, was not sharp enough in scouting for news: "I thynke ye mythe wryt myche more nor ye doe for my lorde of Send Johnys send to me for tyyngs every weke . . . . wryt moche the more of tyyngs for my lordys sake for in good faythe he is a curtes lorde to me and to you and Richard Cely. . . . ." The bond made for an identification of interests with the patron. When Sir John was in difficulties, one brother wrote to another: "whe ar grehtly enoyed I trwste Jhesu whe schaull be abbull to wythstonde owre enmys Syr John ys in grehyt trobull and God knowys full wrongfowlly and parte of them whe gawhe gownys to labors moste agayne hym."[67]

Connections of this kind served to set a merchant in a rather lofty vantage point in relations with the city's parish clergy. A number of other circumstances contributed to the same end. Like nobility, many of the wealthier merchants had their own private chapel at home, richly furnished, with a family chaplain in permanent employment. At the master's death the chaplain would receive a small cash bequest. One draper who left his chaplain half a mark gave considerably more to his butler and his women servants and twenty times as much to his cook. There were usually two or three city advowsons in the hands of private merchants, and several more came into the corporate hands of the mayor and aldermen and of the companies of tailors and grocers.[68] In their capacity as chantry trustees a great many private merchants were in a position to offer employment to priests and to dismiss them if their conduct was displeasing.

The economic position of the parish clergy was in general, in all towns, unsatisfactory. In the smaller parishes the incumbent's income would not run above 10 marks a year, and it was paid with a grudging irregularity. Pecock urged people to conceive of a priest as having a right to a regular income: "his luflode schulde not hange upon her plesaunce oonli."[69] There is no certain evidence of any endowment in London for the payment of rectors. Subsidy assessments in 1412 and 1436 credit fifteen of the parsons with incomes running from £2 7s. to £34, but these may have been from

67. Cely Papers, passim; H. E. Malden, "An Unedited Cely Letter of 1482," Transactions of the Royal Historical Society, 3d ser., X, 159–65.

68. Details in Newcourt, I, 235–565. Most of the city benefices were in the gift of about 30 ecclesiastical patrons, headed by the archbishop of Canterbury and the Dean and Chapter of St. Paul's; the others included many monastic and collegiate foundations outside the London and Westminster area.

69. The Repressor, II, 393. K. L. Wood-Leigh (in Studies in Church Life under Edward III [1934], p. 122) argues that frequent interchange of benefices between parochial clergy and chantry priests in the country at large in that period suggests similarity of salary; the minimum for chantry priests was 10 marks.

private sources or from land held in trust. The taxable values of land belonging to two of the richest parishes, St. Michael Crooked Lane and St. Michael Cornhill, given in 1436 as £55 and £30, respectively, were in that year assigned entirely for chantries. Current income for the payment of rectors must therefore have come entirely from tithes and offerings. A portion of the receipts would have gone to the owner of the advowson. In 1291 and 1303 patrons were drawing from 2s. to 10 marks a year from London benefices, sums that represented on the average nearly a third of their taxable value.[70]

In spite of the fact that the clergy were entitled to call upon the spiritual courts for the excommunication of delinquents, difficulty in the collection of tithes and offerings was chronic. Praedial tithes, due on grain crops, had early been commuted for levies based on the value of dwellings, to be offered in instalments at festivals throughout the year. As originally framed, the official scale of assessment had not taken into account houses worth more than 10s. in rent; and, when the scale was extended, a succession of disputes ensued, in which the mayor and aldermen fought to minimize the obligations of the wealthier citizens. The authority of a papal bull, issued to settle the question in 1453, was not accepted for over twenty years. Personal tithes, on the other hand, were not subject to any exact assessment. Due from trading profits, their estimation hung necessarily upon conscience, and the Austin Friars and Franciscans had spread the doctrine that they need not go to parish clergy who were unworthy but could lawfully be disposed in works of charity, including donations to themselves. Uneasy conscience was salved by compensatory payments at death. About seven out of every ten citizens' wills open with a bequest to the high altar of the testator's parish church "in payment of tithes and offerings witheld," ranging from the artisan's 4d. or 6d. to the great merchant's £10 or £20.[71]

70. Figures for 1291 from *Taxatio .... P. Nicholai IV*, pp. 8–13; for 1303 from Lib. Cust., I, 133–36; for 1412 see above, chap. iii, n. 66; for 1436 see Appen. B; cf. taxable values of 1428, E, 179/144/31; *Feudal Aids*, III, 383–88; *Cal. L. Bk., K*, pp. 71–75.

71. The tithe disputes are summarized in V.C.H., London, 187, 200, 248; and in A. Gwynn, *The English Austin Friars in the Time of Wyclif* (1940), pp. 80–89, 216–24. On the right of enforcement through the spiritual courts see G. B. Flahiff, "The Writ of Prohibition to Courts Christian in the Thirteenth Century," *Mediaeval Studies*, V (1943), 201–313.

Effective control of the business affairs of a parish lay with the wardens, who were elected by the parishioners from the merchants or other substantial citizens among their number. If a parson abused his trust in regard to the property of the church, the wardens could prosecute him in the city courts. The parson of St. Martin Oteswich was brought before the mayor and aldermen in 1376 for having for thirteen years appropriated to his own use a certain rent that had been bequeathed to the church for the support of an assistant chaplain. Found guilty, he was ordered to make up the whole amount, and steps were taken to prevent him from using burial fees for the purpose or from selling church valuables. A few months later he was again in court, because the assistant whom he had inducted to serve at mass and hear confessions had disappeared with some of the vestry goods. The parson was held responsible for the theft and was in consequence ordered to pay the wardens the sum of £5, which it was assumed he could do only by instalments. In the next century the wardens of St. Margaret Pattens sued their parson in the sheriff's court for the sum of 20 marks, the amount of offerings on St. Margaret's Day, which they claimed he had wrongfully retained for his personal use. In this case the parson asserted his right to the money and appealed to the chancellor.[72]

The parish clergy, together with chantry priests, were also under the jurisdiction of the mayor and aldermen in regard to minor breaches of the peace and offenses against sexual morality. Procedure was partly by presentment in wardmotes, which ventilated gossip about abuse of the confessional, personal violence, and resort to women. Fines and imprisonment could be inflicted. A priest employed at the Guildhall chapel was imprisoned simply for idleness. After arrest for sexual offense a priest could be exposed to public ridicule on his way to prison. Between 1401 and 1440, 44 arrests were made on this ground. In a clerical population that in 1381 had numbered nearly 700, including 102 rectors and vicars, 513 chaplains, and 75 clerks, this does not represent a high annual proportion of convicted offenders. But the whole situation, in particular the ease with which imprisonment could be inflicted,

72. *Cal. P. & M. Rolls*, II, 212, 241. The last-mentioned appeal printed by C. T. Martin in "Clerical Life in the Fifteenth Century, as Illustrated by Proceedings of the Court of Chancery," *Archaeologia*, LX, Part (1907), 368.

emphasized the low social position that the lesser clergy occupied. A chantry priest employed at the Guildhall was committed to Newgate prison simply for neglect of his duty.[73]

If the great merchant had no private chapel, he would attend his parish church, keeping a special seat, sometimes a pew fitted with a lock. The parson, unless he was a man of exceptional ability or had a reputation for learning, was to him merely someone hired to perform customary set duties. He was not a man of authority and had to be careful not to offend his important parishioners. In 1375 the parson of St. Michael at Corn was brought into court before the mayor and aldermen and the city recorder on the charge of having spoken disparaging words of a group of his parishioners who belonged to the goldsmiths' company and was forced to bind himself in £10 not to do so again.[74]

With the lesser citizens and with the less prosperous merchants, those who had little or no landed property, the parish clergy were able to establish relations of trust. At the beginning of the fifteenth century about one merchant's will in ten named a city priest as one of the executors. One service that priests could do was to help in getting an education for boys. There is an example of a priest standing as surety for a mercer's apprentice, of an anchorite apprenticing a boy he had adopted to a tailor, lending the latter £20 from some church funds he held in trust, and also of a mercer's widow leaving 40s. "to William the parsons childe in helping him to his scole."[75]

It was by their preaching that the better-educated rectors and friars were able to catch the merchants' interest. They must somehow have been able to enlarge their world of thought and feeling. To retain their sympathy, however, they had to be cautious in referring to city politics. One of the men speaking in an annual series of sermons at St. Mary's Hospital outside Bishopsgate was in 1442 severely reprimanded for an attack on the ruling mayor, Henry Frowyk, and was forbidden to speak there again.[76] Series of sermons, particularly those given at Paul's Cross, remained so popu-

73. *Cal. P. & M. Rolls*, II, 49; IV, 127, 154; *Cal. L. Bk.*, *I*, pp. xlii–xliv, 273–87. Clerical subsidy rolls, E, 179/42/4a, 11; Journals, 1, fols. 24–25.

74. *Cal. P. & M. Rolls*, II, 204.

75. E.C.P., 66/66, 92/46; will of Johanne Bataille (P.C.C., Stokton, 12).

76. Journals, 3, fol. 145b.

lar that they became a means of making announcements about such business matters as repayment of debts.[77] In the latter half of the fifteenth century a number of merchants left money for the education of divinity students who would become "the prechers of Criste is faith" or "prech the Worde of God for the helth of manys soule." One left a fund of £100 to be distributed among friar students at the universities, of all the orders, each to be "of wille witte and speche . . . . somewhat to comfort and chere him to his boke and learnyng"; another left a few pounds to provide fees of 4*d.* to the Sunday preachers at St. Paul's. Philip Malpas, mindful of his soul's need, left 20 marks for a graduate priest to travel about the country for a year to preach to the people "exhorting hem among other to pray for my soule."[78]

6. THE MERCHANT'S ATTITUDE TO THE RELIGIOUS LIFE

No instance has come to notice of any London merchant being so overcome by religious emotion as to give up his way of conducting life and enter a religious order. Nor, on the other hand, is there any evidence of disapproval of the monastic life. The Londoners had, indeed, so many business dealings with the monasteries, selling them supplies, buying the produce of their lands, farming their tithes, and lending them money, that one might say they had literally a vested interest in the whole system of monastic endowment. A late fourteenth-century collection of model business letters contains one from a prior to a merchant, addressed "A son tres chier & graunt amy Guillaume W. de Londres" and offering him the refusal of the wools and tithes of farm produce on a manor.[79]

A few of the merchants' sons became monks. The mayor and aldermen allowed an orphan in their charge to enter the priory of Lewes at the age of ten because he begged permission *maximo cum fervore*, and three other orphans were allowed to enter provincial monasteries at ages between seventeen and twenty. Later, in 1468, an only son's insistence on entering the priory of Hurley caused family distress. His father was so concerned lest the prior treat the

77. An example in E.C.P., 87/61.

78. Wills of John Don, mercer, and Thomas Northlonde, grocer (P.C.C., Logge, 2, 23); also of several aldermen: Estfeld, Wyche, Taylour.

79. Harl. MS, 3988, fol. 53; cf. *Literae Cantuarienses*, R.S. (1887), I, 356–57; III, 272.

boy too "streightly" that in a codicil to his will he asked the wardens of his company to convey money to him or somehow to procure his release—"Or els that they wolle putte away from hym his abite and livyng of a Monke there whiche he hath chosen to hym."[80]

The girls of merchant families were much attracted by the pleasantness of the monastic life and the high social esteem it enjoyed. Nunneries were founded for gentlewomen and seldom accepted the daughters of lesser tradesmen, yet London merchants' daughters were able to gain entrance to all the more fashionable houses in the south of England. There is no evidence of any parental objections. Although dowries were exacted and small annuities were necessary to buy them comforts, their fathers could find it cheaper to put girls into nunneries than to marry them. One mercer offered his daughters £20 and a silver cup if they should marry, with the alternative of £10 and "a les Cuppe" if they should "entre in to Religion." But the dowries given ran as high as £100, and legacies of jewelry, fur, and furniture would follow. A draper with a daughter in the minster of Sheppey left £200, to provide her with an annuity of £5, or to be available as a lump sum for her advancement should she have any opportunity of becoming prioress. A liking for the life seemed to run in families. A fifteenth-century mercer had two aunts and two sisters in East Anglian nunneries and had nieces who were apparently thinking of following their example.[81]

There was a high regard for the Carthusian order. A fourteenth-century grocer had endowed the London house to the extent of over 1,000 marks, and this and the house at Sheen were favorite objects of charitable bequest. Legacies were left to many other monasteries, in all parts of the country, in the form of used funeral torches or of sums of money up to about £10, with or without special requests for prayers. There was also purchase of letters of confraternity, permitting the owner to share in the benefit of the

80. L. Bk., *H*, fols., 46*b*, 229*b*, 317; *K*, fol. 139*b*; *Cal. L. Bk.*, *I*, pp. 231, 263. Will of Henry Jordan, printed in J. C. L. Stahlschmidt, *Surrey Bells and London Bell-founders*, p. 69.

81. Power, *op. cit.*, pp. 11–13, 16–24; wills of John Frost (P.C.C., Godyn, 13) and Sir John Stokton, alderman, £100 to daughter whether she married "or if she have bestowed her self to lyve in any devoute place to serve god ther to lead her lyfe in clennesse" (E.C.P., 150/28); will of John Trussebus (P.C.C., Luffenham, 27 [1439]).

monks' prayers. Sir William Estfeld in this way styled himself a capitular brother of five religious houses. A good many merchants arranged to be buried in monastic or collegiate churches, either in London or elsewhere. Lady Lee, as a widow, retired to live as a guest with the nuns of Stratford. In all this there was probably some social satisfaction. Monastic society was exclusive, its benefactors for the most part belonged to the world of aristocratic wealth, and letters of confraternity were issued chiefly to the gentry.

The merchants were not critical of the comfortable and easy life that the monks of the time were leading. They gave abbots feather beds, embroidered draperies, silver cups, and fruit and left legacies of the same kind and in cash to friends and relations among the monks. There was some exchange of intellectual interests. One man left the abbot of St. Osithe a French book, and another left a canon of the priory of Hales the sum of £4 to pay his expenses for a year at a university.

The friars appear to have worked more among the lesser citizens than among the merchants. "Godds blissyng and myn" was part of a fuller's legacy to two sons in the Dominican order in 1484. But they were in constant receipt of bequests for the recital of prayers and masses for the souls of merchants, and those were sometimes preceded by personal contacts. A draper left 3s. 4d. to a friar minor who had been visiting him in his last illness; a mercer left 10 marks to be given to a certain Austin friar when he should become a doctor of theology; and an alderman's widow appointed a Carmelite as her executor.

Chapter V

THE FLUIDITY OF THE MERCHANT CLASS

IT WAS William Caxton's belief that merchant families retained a high status for a much shorter span of time in London than was commonly the case in the cities of the Low Countries, sons somehow failing to inherit the business capacity of their fathers and consequently tending to sink in the social scale:

> I have sene and knowen in other londes in dyverse cytees that of one name and lygnage successyvely have endured prosperously many heyres / ye a v or vi hondred yere / and somme a thousand / And in this noble cyte of london / it can unnethe contynue unto the thyrd heyre or scarcely to the second / . . . . fayre ne wyser ne bet bespoken children in theyre yongthe ben nowher than ther ben in london / but at their ful rypyng ther is no carnel ne good corn founden but chaffe for the moost parte /.[1]

In his opinion, no matter how much capital they were given to start with, barely two out of ten merchants' sons prospered. These sweeping judgments need not be taken too seriously, for they were adduced out of Caxton's desire to sell his new translation of the precepts of Cato, a book which he represented as an invaluable guide to success in life. It is nevertheless interesting that he should have drawn such a contrast between English and Continental conditions, and his estimate that London families rarely held a leading position in the merchant class for as many as three generations is not altogether without value as evidence. The question arises, however, whether many merchant families survived in the male line for so long.

At first glance it would seem that the chances were very favorable, for the marriage rate was consistently high, only about 4 per cent of London merchants choosing to remain bachelors. There was

---

1. W. J. B. Crotch (ed.), *The Prologues and Epilogues of William Caxton*, E.E.T.S., No. 176 (original ser., 1928), pp. 77–78.

not the same compulsion to force unions in childhood as existed among the nobility and the wealthy gentry—who felt that they had to plan far ahead to make sure that their children would make marriages befitting their rank—because the court of orphanage relieved citizen parents of this anxiety. The court would not permit children to be married without suitable disposition of property or before they were old enough to give their consent freely.[2] There are a few instances of the marriage of London boys of the merchant class under the age of twenty-one, most of them in the fourteenth century. One was a case of kidnapping and forced marriage in order to get control of the boy's property; another was a case of a guardian inducing a boy to marry his daughter, for the same reason. A wealthy grocer making his will in 1398 sought to keep his executors from putting pressure on his son by ordering that the boy should not be married before he was fourteen. Only one instance has been found in which the father arranged his son's marriage as a minor.[3]

There is no means of judging the age at which young merchants normally married, however, until the fifteenth century. Family authority and the influence of the merchant companies then ordinarily combined to delay marriage until the twenties. Many wills left money to be delivered to sons at ages between twenty and twenty-four "or when married," as though marriage was likely to occur by the ages named. Two merchants expressed the desire that their sons should not marry until they were twenty-six; one of them was directed to live at home in economic dependence upon his mother until that age, although if a particularly good match presented itself, for his "avayle and furthering," he might be married earlier.[4]

Parental control in the matter was reinforced by the master's authority over his apprentice. It was customary to insert a clause in indentures of apprenticeship prohibiting marriage during the term of service, and a youth who broke his contract on this point was liable to arrest on a writ of trespass. Desire for delay in

2. On action by court of orphanage to prevent child marriage see L. Bk., *E*, fol. 34; Liber Dunthorne, fol. 352; *Lib. Alb.*, I, 488–90.

3. L. Bk., *E*, fols. 58, 225*b*, 226; *H*, fol. 53*b*; Journals, 2, fol. 15*b*; *Cal. Proc. C.*, I, xv; kidnapping case in Frowyk family, Appen. A. Will of William Hide (P.C.C., Marche, 2).

4. Walter Stalworth (P.C.C., Milles, 17 [1487]) and John Bolle (Hust. R.W.D., 191/23 [1459]).

marriage was further reinforced, in the wealthier and more exclusive companies, by an attempt to prolong apprenticeship to the age of twenty-five or twenty-six. The mercers at some date before 1457 had made a ten-year term compulsory and by 1501 were refusing to enrol any apprentice under the age of sixteen. A check of names and dates in the registers of freemen of the companies of mercers and grocers with wills and inquisitions shows the age of admission to the freedom between 1463 and 1493 to have been twenty-one, twenty-two, and twenty-three in two cases each, in one case twenty-four, and in another twenty-six. The grocers in 1496 made it a rule that no apprentice should be freed until he was twenty-five or twenty-six. Two cases of defiance of these company rules are on record. An apprentice who had married on his master's death asked the mercers' court to make him free, on the grounds that he had served seven years, the traditional period set by city custom; the court held him to his ten-year term but compromised by granting him wages. Another case was that of a mercer's son, Antony Pontisbury of Cheapside, early in the sixteenth century, who, "havynge an inward love to a young woman . . . . and the yonge woman havynge the same unto him intendying they both to live under the lawes of god," found himself imprisoned, on his master's writ of trespass, on his wedding day. He petitioned the chancellor to free him on the double grounds that he had served for seven years and that the prohibition of marriage was "contrary to the lawes of godde and causeth moche fornication and adultery to be wtin the said citie." The only other evidence is from cases in which marriage was being delayed until after the age of twenty-six. Three young mercers, sons of aldermen, were still unmarried when they died at this age, another did not marry until five years after his admission to the freedom, and one of the Shaas did not marry until he was twenty-nine. The same delay occurred outside the aldermanic families: Elys Davy married at about the age of twenty-eight and Caxton not until he was about thirty.[5]

5. Mercers' Wardens' Accounts, fol. 193; Acts, pp. 186, 382; Grocers' Records, Vol. 300, fol. 50; E.C.P., 154/60. A haberdasher pardoned an apprentice for marrying on condition that he serve his mistress for one year beyond the term of his apprenticeship. Will of John Herdewyk (Comm. Lon., Brown, 31v [1403]). Case of a master fined for taking an apprentice already married and cancellation of the indentures (Journals, 5, fol. 140b). A draper's apprentice was imprisoned in 1436 for making a runaway marriage with a young silkwoman (L. Bk., K, fol. 163). Families of Parker, Boleyn, Shaa, Mathews, Irland, Frowick, Appen. A. Crotch, op. cit., p. lxxxi.

In the fifteenth century, men who had reached their middle or late twenties had a fair expectation of life. Length of life is known approximately in the case of ninety-seven London merchants who had been admitted to the freedom of a company and who died between the years 1448 and 1520. There are grounds, in the eight cases mentioned, for assuming that the first of these events occurred at the age of twenty-two or twenty-three. The date of admission to the freedom can then be compared with the date of probate of a man's will. If the probate was within a year of the dating of the will, the time of death is fixed. As it happens, the

TABLE 12

Age at Death	Number of Cases	Age at Death	Number of Cases	Age at Death	Number of Cases
22–23	1	40–41	1	62–63	3
23–24	1	42–43	3	63–64	1
24–25	2	43–44	3	64–65	1
25–26	2	44–45	4	65–66	2
26–27	1	45–46	2	66–67	5
27–28	2	46–47	3	67–68	2
28–29	1	47–48	3	69–70	2
29–30	1	48–49	2	70–71	4
30–31	1	49–50	1	71–72	1
31–32	1	51–52	4	73	1
33–34	2	52–53	2	75	1
34–35	3	53–54	2	77–78	3
35–36	1	54–55	3		
36–37	1	55–56	2	Total	97
37–38	2	57–58	1		
38–39	3	59–60	5		
39–40	2	60–61	3		

limited set of cases in which both of these events can be dated is heavily weighted with landed merchants whose wealth was above the average. It is possible that these men had slightly better life chances than less prosperous men, since they were more likely to have country estates to which they could take their families in time of plague. The number of cases is too few to justify exact calculation of the average expectation of life at each age; nevertheless, it is significant that the median age at death was from forty-nine to fifty. *But not enough evidence to make a case*

In other late medieval English groups that have been investigated the chances of life appear to have been very similar to those shown by this table. Professor J. C. Russell has assembled information as to the length of life of 581 male tenants-in-chief who had reached the age of twenty-one and who died between the years 1250 and 1358. The choice of these dates isolates his sample from the influence of bubonic plague. His table shows the median age at death to have been forty-nine. A second point in his table seems to have been closely applicable also to fifteenth-century members of parliament. Wedgewood estimated that the average length of life that these men attained, a mixed group of country gentlemen, lawyers, officials, and merchants, was fifty-eight. The figure has to be related to their age at election. Among 47 London merchants, who were elected at ages ranging from thirty-five to seventy-six, the median age at election was forty-four. The median age at death in this sample was the same as Wedgewood's general average, fifty-eight. By Professor Russell's calculation, the expectation of life of tenants-in-chief at the age of forty-four, before the plague era, was fifteen, only one year greater. Another fifteenth-century group for which information is available is that of the monks at Canterbury. They would have reached the age of about nineteen before being professed, and life thereafter was very leisurely and comfortable. It is estimated that they lived on the average to about the age of fifty.[6]

There are fifteenth-century English complaints that the fifties saw the onset of old age. Caxton was only just past fifty when he wrote that "age crepeth on me dayly and febleth all the bodye," and Hoccleve saw "ripeness of death" hastening upon him fast at the age of fifty-three. Both may have been striving for literary effect, although they were not on this point tied by any set literary convention. On the periodization of life there was a wide choice of literary conventions. Jean le Bel, rather arbitrarily, regarded middle age as lasting only from thirty to thirty-five. An English manuscript marks off four periods by the differing constitution of the body: childhood, hot and moist, lasting to twenty-five; youth, hot and dry, to thirty-five or forty; manhood, cold and dry, to fifty or sixty; and "elde," cold and moist, to the end. Writers agreed only in typing old age as cantankerous. There seems to have been familiarity with the possibility of long life.[7]

6. See J. C. Russell, "Length of Life in England, 1250–1348," *Human Biology*, IX (1937), 528–41; *Hist. Parl. B., passim*; H.M.C., *9th Report, Appendix, p. 127.*

7. Crotch, *op. cit.*, pp. xxviii, 7. *Hoccleve's Minor Poems*, ed. F. J. Furnivall, E.E.T.S., No. 61 (extra ser., 1892), pp. xii, 31, 119. Jean le Bel, "Li ars d'amour, de vertu et de bo-

Women were married young. It was known that too early child-bearing was dangerous and that there were other disadvantages to marrying young girls; as one writer observed, "there is gret suffraunce yn marryage yn lasse than both partyes be ryght wise . . . . but many be dysseyved for be cause they take her wives at xii yere age or ther a boute. And what they wyl be aftyrward no man can knowe/."[8] Yet, since many London merchants willed property to be delivered to their daughters at the age of thirteen or fourteen or else upon marriage it was apparently considered proper for girls to be married by that age. Guardians may sometimes have put pressure upon orphans to marry sooner than their parents would have wished. One widow, intrusting a small daughter to the charge of a friend, begged him in her will "to be unto hir as verray a fader And that she be not married unto the tyme that she be of reasonable age of yeres for to have discretion and understanding to govern and rule hereself in such things as longith to womanhode."[9] In forty-one cases in which the age at marriage is known or the wife's age at the date when her husband appeared before the court of orphanage to claim her property, it varied from eleven to thirty-four, the median being seventeen. In seventeen other cases it is known only whether the bride was of age when the marriage took place, and in fourteen of these she was not.[10] It is therefore likely that girls were usually married, for the first time, before they were seventeen.

There is little direct information as to the fertility of marriages. A family of four children orphaned in 1389 were all under the age of five, but in two examples of marriages that lasted nineteen and twenty years, in the fifteenth century, a child was born on the average only once in two years; in a marriage that took place

---

neurte," Académie Royale de Belgique (1867), pp. 47–48. Society of Antiquaries MSS, 338. For a summary of literary conventions regarding periods of life see C. R. Coffman, "Old Age in Chaucer's Day," *Modern Language Notes*, LII, 25–26; LIII, 181–82.

8. Harl. MSS, 149, fols. 231*b*–232. Egidius Colonna, following Aristotle, enlarged upon the danger of too early childbearing (*De regimine principum*, lib. I, cap. 16 [1607 ed.], p. 265).

9. Will of Katherine Swetenham (P.C.C., Godyn, 6).

10. L. Bk., *G–L, passim*; Journals, 8, fol. 189*b*. In 20 cases of Bristol girls orphaned in the period 1385–1485 marriage occurred at ages from 10 to 20, the median age being 17 (city of Bristol archives, Tolzey Court, Orphans' Recognizances, 04422).

earlier and lasted sixty years, there were nineteen children.[11] Less than two-thirds of the men, however, in the wealthiest section of the class were married continuously for so long as twenty years: in the cases of thirty-five out of ninety-seven aldermen none of the marriages that they made lasted so long. Ten out of sixty aldermen who died in the period between 1448 and 1520 had outlived their wives, one, who died at fifty-eight, by twelve years. Many widowers remarried but not all and not immediately, and some men lost two or three wives. A woman who outlived a husband was almost certain to marry again if he had left much property; there was a premium on well-dowered widows. This preference may have raised the proportion of wives who were past the age of maximum fertility.[12] Again, although almost nothing is known of the conditions of health among married women, there must have been some incidence of sterility from infections and from other causes. Lady Eleanor Cobham pleaded that she had resorted to witchcraft only "forto have borne a child by hir lord," and prayers were offered at shrines to the same end. Finally, there was not entire ignorance of contraception. Bishop Pecock, outlining the obligations of matrimony, explicitly condemned the prevention of child-begetting: intercourse between husband and wife would be free from sin on the condition that they "lette not witingly bitwixe hem in her bodily knowing eny child bigeetyng." This passage might conceivably refer to abortion, but the bishop returned to the point more explicitly. Although it was preferable for mankind in matrimony to have intercourse only for the sake of children, in the absence of this purpose it was still lawful "so þat whilis he lettiþ not neiþer werneþ child-bigetyng"; on a literal interpretation his words refer to the prevention or denial, forbidding, of conception. He would hardly have felt it necessary to dwell upon the subject unless abortion and contraception were matters of discussion; the latter may have been credited with effects that were actually due to sterility.[13]

11. L. Bk., *H*, fol. 243*b*; Appen. A, Knolles; will of Richard Awbrey gives dates of birth of 9 children between March, 1449, and December, 1469 (P.C.C., Wattys, 18).

12. On this point see Marcus Rubin, "Population and Birth Rate, Illustrated from Historical Statistics," *Royal Statistical Society Journal*, LXIII (1900), 609–10. Eighty-two aldermen dying in the period 1448–1520 had entered into 122 marriages.

13. *The Brut*, E.E.T.S., original ser., No. 136, p. 480; Reginald Pecock, *The Reule of Cristen Religioun*, E.E.T.S., original ser., No. 171, pp. 341, 342.

It is still possible that the average merchant had about twenty years of marriage or a little more and could have fathered about ten legitimate children. This impression is confirmed by the evidence of epitaphs and by the long rows of children who are depicted beside their parents on tombstone brasses. Thirteen London merchants who died between 1463 and 1511 laid claim in this public manner to families of from three to twenty-two, the average lying between ten and eleven to a father.[14] The objection could be raised that an old or sick man drafting instructions for his executors might not recall the exact number of his children, especially if many had died young. But it was becoming a custom of the time to keep a written record of the growth of the family tree. If the tombstone figures err, it is probable through representing a selection of families larger than the average. To have obeyed the biblical injunction to multiply and be fruitful was cause for pride. A man whose showing was good was more likely to desire the total set out on his monument than one whose family had been small. It is therefore quite improbable that the number of children born in the average London merchant family of this period exceeded ten or eleven.

Monuments are too scanty to illustrate conditions before 1460. Indeed, the only way in which one can draw any comparisons between one citizen generation and another is by using the information contained in wills. This has certain obvious defects. It is not a measure of total births, for children who had died are rarely named or counted; and married daughters, who had received their portion as dowry, are not always named. Although legacies were made openly to bastard sons and daughters, the roll of illegitimate children is probably incomplete. Moreover, although the interval that elapsed between the drafting of a will and the testator's death was usually not more than a few months and often only a few days, it sometimes ran to several years. Other births and deaths, besides the birth of posthumous children, could thus escape the record. Yet the cases in which the wills are supplemented by records of the court of orphanage reveal that very few births and deaths occurred during this interval, that posthumous births were infrequent, and

14. See Appen. A, Colet, Croke, Crosby, Fabian, Feld, Horn, Lambard. On Amondesham, Gilbert, Hoore, see Haines, II, 81, 122, 127. On Payne see Weever, p. 198. On Abbot and Matton see Mill Stephenson.

that testators gave an accurate count of their children under age. A study of family histories shows also that the wills rarely overlooked any adult sons; even if they had already received their share of the father's property, he was likely to remember them with the gift of some heirloom or to name them as standing in line of succession to landed property. Grandsons, too, if by the sons, were likely to be similarly remembered. In short, the wills enable one to estimate, within a reasonable margin of error, the average number of male heirs that citizens dying at different periods left behind them.

Long series of merchants' wills are available in the form of copies enrolled in the court of husting and in the various ecclesiastical courts of probate. Enrolment was not essential but was useful for purposes of record, especially if there were bequests of land or houses. The figures set out in Table 13 refer solely to men with real property and are sufficiently weighted with aldermanic families to represent, definitely, the wealthier half of the merchant class.[15] The figures have been grouped by thirty-year generations, the year of the onset of the Black Death, 1348, being selected as the key dividing line.

The number of cases obtainable is unfortunately too small to permit of reading a trend. But it is unmistakably clear that at no part of the period did the average number of heirs that a mer-

15. This weighting is relatively heavier for the fifteenth century, the number of aldermanic families included in the samples used being for the 8 generations as follows: 32, 41, 43, 44, 31, 31, 41, 22. The remainder of the wills have been taken, for the fourteenth century, from the court of husting; these, being less numerous later, have from 1408 been supplemented by a random selection of wills from the records of the ecclesiastical courts. In three cases the omission of one son from the father's will, presumably on account of estrangement, has been rectified (see Appen. A, Corp, Finchingfeld, Rawson). Five of the 1,001 heirs in Table 13 were described as illegitimate. Negative evidence has been sifted with caution. Very brief wills of personalty, leaving the bulk of the estate to the widow without referring to children, and wills referring only to estate in lands, not mentioning children, have been discarded. Sometimes there is positive evidence that children had been born but had died, the testator asking to be buried beside them. Again, if personal property was to be divided into two parts, one for the widow and one for the benefit of the testator's soul, it is certain that there were no children in existence and none expected at the time the will was drafted, because it was customary, if there were children surviving, as well as a widow, to assign them a third share. On the prevalence of this custom and on the tendency in London to extend it to the division of immovables see E. F. Jacob (ed.), *The Register of Henry Chichele*, II (1938), xxxv–xl. Other details are often indirectly conclusive. If it is plain that all the estate in lands was left to other branches of the family or to friends or to the church or for the endowment of a chantry or if there were substantial bequests of money or goods to brothers, sisters, nieces, nephews, or apprentices, without mention of children, then it is reasonably certain that the testator was childless.

chant left behind him in the direct male line reach two. With a sinister uniformity the figures hover close to the figure one. A striking feature of the table is the high proportion of men who died leaving no heirs at all in the direct male line. This was at no period due to distaste for marriage. Out of the entire aldermanic group included, 295 men, there are not more than 9 who may have been bachelors. Some men married twice, a few three times, only to die childless. Whatever the incidence of sterility, it is an inevitable conclusion that the rate of child mortality was tragically high. At least one of the aldermen in the tables suffered the same experience as that gentleman of the Barentyn family in the early

TABLE 13

GENERATION	NUMBER OF TESTATORS	LACKING HEIRS IN MALE LINE		TOTAL NUMBER OF SONS	GRANDSONS BY SONS	TOTAL HEIRS IN MALE LINE	AVERAGE HEIRS IN MALE LINE PER MERCHANT
		No.	Per Cent				
1288–1317....	99	36	36.6	130	1	131	1.3
1318–47......	109	23	21	146	2	148	1.35
1348–77......	209	80	38	252	4	256	1.2
1378–1407....	111	50	45	102	....	102	0.9
1408–37......	83	33	37	88	2	90	1.0
1438–67......	80	31	38.7	105	7	112	1.4
1468–97......	85	24	28	117	8	125	1.5
1498–1527....	29	9	31	35	2	37	1.2

fifteenth century of whom Leland laconically reported that "he had very many children, but in contynuance they died."[16]

The imagination of the age was harassed by the frailty of child life. Wycliffe castigated mothers who gave way to grief in bereavement, arguing that it was "gret mercy" of God to take a child out of this world. The same theme reappears in the play of Abraham and Isaac, the plot of which drives home the moral of submission, of not "grochyng." It is cast partly in stoic form, with the argument that it is in nature for children to die, and they are thereby spared from harm:

> And thys women that wepe so sorowfully
> Whan that hyr chyldryn dey them froo,
> As nater woll, and kynd.
> Yt ys but folly.....

16. Leland, V, Part X, 232; cf. Appen. A, Colet, Sir William Horne.

The owner of a fifteenth-century commonplace book had the play copied out. In the Dance of Death the theme is lifted above such scolding. An English version of the fifteenth century gives a child these terse lines:

> I am full yong / I was born yisterday
> Deth is ful hasty / on me to ben wreke.[17]

That the hazards of child life were so high throughout the age was largely due to the number of epidemics, of which bubonic plague was only one variety. Other diseases had always heightened in danger with the famine conditions that had been recurrent in the thirteenth century and the early years of the fourteenth century. After its first onset in 1348–49 plague, too, was recurrent, flaring up intermittently with results that may occasionally have been as fatal, in some localities, as those of the first outbreak. The 1360's saw three terrifying outbreaks, the second of which a chronicler described as "such a pestilens, that nevere non such was sene in no mannes tyme alyve." Another disease distinguished by "pokkes" spread at the same time. Few, if any, of these more serious epidemic waves spared London. One writer guessed that in 1407 thirty thousand people died in London alone. Since this would virtually have eliminated the population, it may be assumed that he set the figure down at random; yet to make such an impression, the year must have been a bad one. The 1420's brought a severe form of influenza, and during the third and fourth decades of the century London suffered six times from plague. Between 1450 and 1470, however, conditions improved: only two major epidemics struck locally. Between 1471 and 1474 a dangerous disease known as the "styche" and another, a flux, said to be new in England, carried off many victims in different parts of the country, and during the next three years plague returned: "peple dyed myhtely in every place, man, woman and chylde." A London chronicler reported for 1479–80 "an huge mortalyte. . . . . To the grete mynysshyng of the people of all maner of agys"; and in 1485 the fever named the "sweating sickness" swept through the city. Two years later there was a plague in Westminster, and the cen-

17. *The English Works of Wyclif*, ed. T. Arnold (1869–71), III, 199; *The Boke of Brome*, ed. L. T. Smith (1886), p. 69; *The Dance of Death*, E.E.T.S., No. 181 (original ser., 1929), p. 71.

tury closed mournfully, with "grete deth in london and othir partis of this Realm."[18]

Under these conditions it is probable that the population of the country as a whole was for long stretches stationary or declining. Yet favored sections of the population might have been holding their own or even increasing in numbers. Was this true of the London section of the merchant class? How many of the heirs in the direct male line that men left behind them had safely reached the age of majority, when they would have a fair expectation of life ahead of them? How many of the rest, those who were not yet of age at the time of their father's or grandfather's death, lived to

TABLE 14

	Number of Sons Living at Time of Father's Death	Number of These Who Were under Age at Time of Father's Death	Percentage Who Were Orphaned under Age
1318–47..........	55	44	80
1348–77..........	33	20	60
1378–1407........	44	17	39
1408–37..........	36	24	67
1438–67..........	43	29	67
1468–97..........	76	31	41

grow up? These questions cannot be answered as exactly as one would wish, for the information is elusive except in small series of cases. Split up by thirty-year periods as before, however, these can serve as checks upon one another and can roughly indicate the limits within which the situation varied.

Information as to how many sons were of age at the father's death is not available for many of the families used in the last table except for those in which the father was an alderman. In Table 14 the proportions are therefore illustrated from the aldermanic families alone. Since so large a proportion of the sons were under

18. For a survey of the recurrence of plague see J. Saltmarsh, "Plague and Economic Decline in the Later Middle Ages," *Cambridge Historical Journal*, VII (1940), 23–40. On the sweating sickness see J. F. C. Hecker, *The Epidemics of the Middle Ages* (1844), pp. 177–353. The following refer to contemporary evidence: K. Vickers, *England in the Later Middle Ages* (4th ed., 1926), pp. 183–86, 423–24, 500; A. Abram, *English Life and Manners in the Later Middle Ages* (1913), chap. xiv; W. Denton, *England in the Fifteenth Century* (1888), pp. 96–105. For citations see *The Brut, op. cit.*, pp. 314, 316, 321, 604; and *The Great Chronicle*, pp. 226, 239, 294.

age when their fathers died, it is very important to know what happened to them. Again the information is elusive. What happened to families of small children is rarely on record unless the disposal of their property was being handled by the court of orphanage. The figures in Table 15 represent families in which it is quite certain that the fate of all the male children is known. They include some of the aldermanic families used in Table 14 but also other merchant families. There is now some basis for computing how many of the heirs in the male line that were shown in Table 14 as surviving the father's death may be supposed to have reached their majority. For example, in the period 1408–37, 24

TABLE 15

	Male Orphans under Age at Time of Father's Death	Number of These Who Died before Age 21	Percentage Who Died under Age
1318–47	13	3	23
1348–77	51	17	33
1378–1407	36	15	42
1408–37	33	8	24
1438–67	31	5	16
1468–97	39	19	49

per cent of the heirs were minors and 67 per cent of these died in childhood or adolescence, that is, 16 per cent of the total. In other words, only 84 per cent of the heirs, counting sons who were already of age at their father's death, had any life as adults and any likelihood of marrying. Merchants who died in this period left, on the average, one heir in the direct male line; they left only 0.84 who had any chance of reproducing themselves in their turn (Table 16).

It must be repeated that these calculations are too narrowly based to give the contour of a trend. They do, however, compel the conclusion that over the period as a whole the merchant class was barely reproducing its numbers; indeed, there are two reasons for believing that they put the situation in too favorable a light. In the first place, the selection of the information from the wealthier families means that the children concerned were those who could have had maximum protection in time of epidemics; there is no adverse factor, such as lesser fertility, to offset this advantage. In the second place, the reliance upon wills as the basic source of information involves neglect of the possibility that when plague was rampant it could wipe out entire families in a few brief days that were far too full of misery and horror to allow of anyone's sitting down to compose a will. There is good reason to believe that the degree of intestacy was higher than usual at these times, withdrawing some of the heavier losses from written record. A fuller record would almost certainly have made the figures dip much more severely after 1348. If they were compiled by decades instead of by thirty-year periods, it would be seen that the dip

TABLE 16

	Average Number of Heirs in Direct Male Line at Father's Death	Proportion of These Who Died under Age		Number Who Died under Age	Average Number of Heirs in Direct Male Line Who Survived to Age 21
1318–47.......	1.35	80% of 23%		0.25	1.1
1348–77.......	1.2	60	33	0.24	1.0
1378–1407.....	0.9	39	42	0.15	0.8
1408–37.......	1.0	67	24	0.16	0.8
1438–67.......	1.4	67	16	0.15	1.25
1468–97.......	1.5	41	49	0.3	1.2

lasted for a full century; in the decade of the 1440's eleven out of nineteen testators died without leaving any children at all.

The reasons for questioning Caxton's view that the failure of London merchant families to hold their social position for more than three generations was due to young men's incapacity and proved the need of education are now apparent. In his day, there were sons enough to take their fathers' places if they were so inclined. But for many generations before, this had not been the case.

Still more important in depleting the ranks of the merchant class was the fact that it had never been a universal custom for the son to follow his father's occupation. Official careers, the church, the law, life in the country, if possible as a gentleman—all beckoned to the young Londoner who did not care for trade. Family pride, seemingly gratified by prospects of success in any direction, did not ordinarily stand in his way and might push him on. This is true of the whole period. A Chigwell had entered the royal service in Queen Philippa's household.[19] The priesthood and the religious orders held a strong attraction. Young boys were known to set their hearts on a religious life after they had been apprenticed and would be allowed to cancel their indentures. A man who died in 1361 leaving two sons made the younger one's inheritance conditional on his becoming a chaplain before the age of twenty-five, and another who died in 1381 had allowed both his sons and his only daughter to enter the church.[20] Toward the end of the fourteenth century the law was obviously growing in its appeal as a profitable profession. William Tonge, vintner and former alderman, directed in his will that his elder son should take up the study of common law and that the younger one should either go to a university or, if he wished, enter trade; there was no compulsion. A fifteenth-century vintner of more moderate fortune left his son entirely to his own choice. His guardian was either to apprentice the lad "or els to set hym other wise in vertuous disposition as my said sonne can agre unto."[21]

Barely two thirds of the aldermen's sons followed their fathers into trade. Of twenty-six sons of fourteenth-century aldermen sixteen became merchants, three entered the church, two became known as gentlemen, and five were knighted. Of seventeen in the first half of the fifteenth century ten entered trade, one of them in Bristol; five became gentlemen and esquires, two of them in the king's service; one became city chamberlain; and one a lawyer. Of fifty-two in the latter part of the century only twenty-six entered and remained in trade; sixteen came to be known as gentlemen or esquires, although at least five of these continued to be connected with merchant companies; four were knighted, two of them in the king's service and one after becoming a successful lawyer; two others practiced law; and five chose careers in the church. Two of the latter studied canon law in Italy, one became a doctor of divinity and rector of a rich London parish, and one rose to be prior in the military order of Rhodes.

It is not likely that sons of the less prominent merchants had so many opportunities to seek a career outside the merchant class as the sons of aldermen. Table 17 sets out the situation that would

19. Appen. A.

20. *C.W.C.H.*, II, 52, 225.   21. John Treguran (P.C.C., Godyn, 29 [1469]).

have resulted, in each generation, according as two-thirds of the young men of the class as a whole had entered trade or 80 per cent of them or 90 per cent. It will be seen that even if 90 per cent of the sons had entered trade, they could have taken their fathers' places only in two of the six periods; if 80 per cent had entered trade, they could have taken their fathers' places only in one period; if only two-thirds had entered trade, the class would rapidly have died out unless new men had been joining its ranks. In any event, it is obvious that the class could not have maintained its numbers without outside recruiting.

TABLE 17

	Average Number of Heirs in Direct Male Line	Number Available To Succeed Father if 66% Entered Trade	Number Available To Succeed Father if 80% Entered Trade	Number Available To Succeed Father if 90% Entered Trade
1318–47	1.1	0.7	0.9	1.0
1348–77	1.0	0.7	0.8	0.9
1378–1407	0.8	0.5	0.6	0.7
1408–37	0.9	0.6	0.7	0.8
1438–67	1.25	0.8	1.0	1.1
1468–97	1.0	0.7	0.8	0.9

2. IMMIGRATION TO THE CITY

Merchant families were far from being below the average in vitality. Orphanage records show that other citizens left even fewer children than the merchants,[22] and it is unlikely that the poor unenfranchised workers were any better off in this regard. Without a fairly steady stream of immigration, the population would therefore rapidly have dwindled. There may well have been times when neither the merchant class nor the citizen body was quite maintaining its numbers from year to year, although

22. Figures from L. Bk., G–L, *passim*, and Journals, 1, 2, give the following picture (these figures include daughters).

	MERCHANT FAMILIES		OTHER CITIZEN FAMILIES	
	No. of Families	Average No. of Children	No. of Families	Average No. of Children
Orphaned 1350–1400	66	2.36	52	1.9
Orphaned 1401–1500	170	2.61	90	2.35

there is no mention of the prolonged surplus of housing that a shrinking population would have created, and company records point to a growth in the second half of the fifteenth century greater than can be accounted for by so small a rate of increase as the merchant families registered.[23] Yet it is impossible to find out exactly what proportion of any class or group, at any period, had been born outside the city. Only two sets of entries in the surviving merchant company records mention where the parents of newly enrolled apprentices lived. Nine out of 72 lads enrolled by the tailors in 1486–87 and 15 out of 115 of the apprentices taken by the skinners between 1496 and 1500, that is, practically the same proportion, were of London families, including 1 son of a member of the tailors' company and 4 sons of skinners.[24] Possibly some of the country boys who came to London to be apprenticed went home again to set up in business, leaving a larger proportion of native Londoners to remain as freemen of the companies. Between 1481 and 1500, 9 per cent of the freemen admitted by the mercers and the grocers were sons of members.

Immigrants to the city had often no other surname but one taken from their place of origin. These place names, significantly, were the commonest type of citizen surname. Being passed on as long as a family survived in the male line, however, they are obviously not proof of recent migration. Nor are they an infallible guide to an immigrant's actual origin, for the identity of very young and small apprentices could easily be swamped under that of their master's family. Peter, called "Dabyndone," a young draper named in a deed of 1325, was the son of a man of Gosberton in Lincolnshire called Warin Cullul, but people had given him the same name as his late master, Simon de Abyndone.[25] Yet the place

---

23. Admissions to the freedom in the companies of mercers and grocers varied as follows:

	Mercers	Grocers		Mercers	Grocers
1392–1400.....	72	....	1451–60.......	114	189
1401–10.......	90	20 over 3 years	1461–70.......	132	124
1411–20.......	83	14 over 3 years	1471–80.......	175	144
1421–30.......	97	16 over 2 years	1481–90.......	110	107
1431–40.......	104	11 in 1432	1491–1500.....	157	155
1441–50.......	117	46 in 1448*			

* Many probably deferred owing to plague.

24. See Appen. D. Less than a seventh of the citizens newly enfranchised in 1551–53 had been born in London (see A. H. Thomas, *Cal. P. & M. Rolls*, II, xxxiv).

25. *Cal. L. Bk., E*, p. 190.

names prevalent at any time are probably broadly indicative of the regions from which population had been drawn over the last generation or two. They at least make it clear that, from the earliest years of the fourteenth century, London was drawing on the entire kingdom, any large sample of names conjuring up a map of the length and breadth of England, dotted with villages and towns. In a sample of 564 taken from the subsidy roll of 1319 a little less than half the names relate to places within the immediate circle of the home counties. This is less than is indicated in statements of the origins of a series of apprentices who were enrolled between 1309 and 1312. By counties and by regions the distribution was as shown in Table 18.

Many of the recruits from the home counties entered trades that were largely supplied from that area, becoming butchers, dealers in corn or malt or wood, or workers in wood or leather. Similarly the connections with East Anglia ran through the fish and cloth trades and such industries as the making of gloves, purses, and caps. The relatively small contribution of the west and the south reflects both the lesser density of population there and also the local importance of Southampton, Salisbury, and Bristol. These and other towns, no doubt, absorbed most of the surplus ambition of the surrounding regions.

As time passed, London drew less upon the home counties and became more truly a national melting-pot. Of eighteen merchants' apprentices who ran away from their masters between 1351 and 1369 only seven were from the home counties.[26] Perhaps boys from more distant places were more likely to run away, because of homesickness, than others who had been born near London, yet in another sample of thirty-eight whose origins are on record for various reasons between 1350 and 1450, there were only twelve from the home counties.[27] The testimony of merchants in their wills, in which they often left money to the country church where they had been baptized or to the poor of the village where they had been born, points to a still greater drop in the contribution of the home

26. *Cal. Letters of the Mayor and Corporation of the City of London*, Vols. I, II, *passim*.

27. Their origins are mentioned in the course of legal proceedings or on the occasion of transfer to a new master (E.C.P., 15/165, 39/221, 61/413, 476, 575, 183/13; Liber Dunthorne, fols. 390, 391, 397; P. & M. Rolls, *passim*; Journals, 4, fol. 84*b*; *Cal. L. Bk., I*, p. 157; *K*, p. 224; *C.W.C.H.*, I, 637; W.A.M., 5959).

counties, the chief increase being in the quota from the midlands
(Table 19).

The evidence of the wills is naturally weighted by the more
prosperous men, who alone were in a position to leave money for
repairing and beautifying village churches or to scatter legacies
among poor country relatives. Almost the only auxiliary evidence

TABLE 18*

REGION	TAXPAYERS OF 1319		MERCHANTS' APPRENTICES, 1309-12		APPRENTICES IN LESSER CRAFTS, 1309-12	
	No.	Per Cent	No.	Per Cent	No.	Per Cent
Home counties (including Berkshire, Buckinghamshire, Essex, Hertfordshire, Kent, Middlesex, Surrey)....	270	48	29	54	40	61
East (including Lincolnshire with Cambridgeshire, Norfolk, Suffolk)..	111	20	15	28	11	19
Midlands (including Bedfordshire, Huntingdonshire, Leicestershire, Northamptonshire, Nottinghamshire, Oxfordshire, Shropshire, Staffordshire, Warwickshire, Worcestershire).........................	71	12	6	11	4	....
North (including Cheshire, Cumberland, Derbyshire, Durham, Lancashire, Northumberland, Westmoreland, Yorkshire).............	44	8	3	....	2	....
West (including Cornwall, Devonshire, Dorsetshire, Gloucestershire, Herefordshire, Somersetshire, Wiltshire).	44	8	1	....	....	....
South (including Hampshire, Sussex)..	24	4	....	....	1	....
Total	564	....	54	....	58	....

* The 1319 selection was intended to include all place-name surnames having the particle "de," which
might indicate more recent country origin than in cases in which it had been dropped, but in 132 cases the
name was either so common or referred to so obscure a hamlet that its location could not be identified. The
sample of apprentices of 1309-12 includes only those whose master's trade was given (*Cal. L. Bk., D*, pp. 35-
179).

free of this bias is the sample record of the origins of the skinners'
and tailors' apprentices, toward the end of the century. This suggests that the contribution of the north came to be greater than
that of any other region. Fifteen out of 34 provincial boys apprenticed to skinners who were in the livery of their company or
about to enter it were from the north, and the proportion in 155
cases, including boys enrolled under poorer freemen in the two

companies, who were not necessarily destined to be merchants, was about the same (Table 20).

The immigration of women is harder to trace but was obviously essential to the maintenance of the city population. Many London merchants married the widows of provincial merchants. Other women came to the city as young girls, to enter domestic service or to be apprenticed in various trades. References in wills and

TABLE 19*

REGIONS OF BIRTH OF MERCHANTS	MEN DYING 1350–1450		MEN DYING 1450–1515	
	No.	Per Cent	No.	Per Cent
Home counties..........	22	23	34	24
East....................	30	31	38	27
Midlands...............	19	20	39	28
North..................	9	10	14	10
West...................	14	15	13	9
South..................	3	....	....	....
Ireland.................	....	....	1	....
Total	97	....	139	....

* *C.W.C.H.*, I, 674; II, 27, 32, 40, 98, 101, 104, 109, 173–74, 249, 266, 293, 303, 309, 324, 328, 330, 340, 381, 405, 407, 419, 501, 535, 544, 546–47. Wills of Neve, Walington, Marcheford, Chivaler, Sutton, Tikhill, Clerke (P.C.C., Marche, 3, 4, 28, 38, 43, 44, 53); of Crysshefeld, Chamber, Chynnore, Aleyne, Hawkyns (P.C.C., Rous, 11, 13, 15, 18); of Kyng, Tatersale, Curteys, Bacoun, Bosom, Redyng, Chertsey, Toft (P.C.C., Luffenham, 6, 11, 12, 21, 25, 31, 33, 34); of Hilton, Herne, Abbey, Bataill, Colby, Dounton (P.C.C., Stokton, 2, 4, 6, 9, 19); of Payne, Boton, Elys, Norlong, Frost, Gregory, Fulbourne, Skrayngham (P.C.C., Godyn, 1, 6, 11, 13, 15, 18, 23); of Blaunche, Everley, Syff, Gryme, Laurence, Overey (P.C.C., Wattys, 4, 11, 24, 25, 27, 38); of Don, Goldwell, Haynes, Thomas, Cras, White, Goodwyn, Northlonde (P.C.C., Logge, 2, 16, 17, 19, 21, 23); of Gardyner, Haryes, Ryngbell, Hill, Moton, Smyth, Agmondesham, Babham (P.C.C., Milles, 2, 22, 23, 26, 28, 30, 33, 36); of Nonelay, Petit (P.C.C., Horne, 15, 20); of Payntour (P.C.C., Adeane, 17); of Drew, Barnewell (Comm. Lon., Broun, 55, 103*v*); of Macchyng, Warner (Comm. Lon., More, 246, 394); of Chesham, Halmar, Person (Comm. Lon., Sharpe, 59, 179*v*, 253); of Abyn (Comm. Lon., Wilde, 73); of Trappys, Turvyle, Higden, Chambre (Comm. Lon., Lichfield, 34*v*, 41*v*, 66, 127); of Hungerford (Drapers' Deeds, A VI, 297); of Potter (Grocers' Register of Freemen and Apprentices, fol. 14). See also Appen. A, *passim*. The bias in favor of wealthy men is partially counteracted by including evidence from notes of retirement from jury service, from deeds, and from early chancery proceedings (see *Cal. L. Bk.*, I, pp. 25, 56, 68, 94, 99; nn. 28, 29, below; Rot. cl., 7 Hen. VI, *m.* 6*d*, 18 Hen. VI, *m.* 25*d*; E.C.P., 38/255, 48/2).

deeds and stray notices of apprenticeship show that they came from as far afield and from as many different regions as the men.[28]

3. THE SOCIAL ORIGINS OF IMMIGRANTS

Speaking every English dialect, the London apprentices also represented almost every social group in the kingdom, paupers and

28. Notice of girl apprentices from Henley, Bristol, Leicester, Sussex, Norfolk, Lincolnshire (E.C.P., 155/10; *Cal. P. & M. Rolls*, IV, 71; Anc. Deeds, D 1176; W.A.M., 5966; H.M.C., *8th Report, Appendix*, Part I, p. 420).

nobility excepted. Among the merchants' apprentices on the chamberlain's lists for 1309–12 were a nephew of Sir John de Sandal, the king's treasurer, and sons of Bartholomew le Cryour of Westminster, of Richard le Mattere of Lambeth, of Richard le Fisshere of Denham, of John le Forester of Rippele, of Gilbert le Smyth of Mereworth, Kent, and of John le Taillour of Messyngham, Lincolnshire. The aldermen, both at this time and later, were also of mixed origin. Roger de Frowyk, goldsmith, was the son of a Middlesex landowner whose antecedents are not known. Simon de Paris came of Norfolk bondmen. William Thorney, one of the great importers of the early fourteenth century, came from the

TABLE 20*

	No.	Per Cent
Home counties.............	29	18.7
East Anglia................	12	....
Lincolnshire...............	15	17.6
Midlands..................	17	10.9
North.....................	72	46.4
West......................	2	....
South.....................	3	....
Wales.....................	2	....
Ireland....................	3	....

* See Appen. C. A stray sample of 12 members of lesser companies of the first half of the fifteenth century includes 3 each from the home counties, the midlands, and the east, with 1 from each other region—west, south, north (*Cal. L. Bk., K*, pp. 121, 169, 202, 235, 277, 279; Hust. R.W.D., 170/19; *Cal. P. & M. Rolls*, IV, 70; C. Misc., 122/31).

borders of Lincolnshire and Cambridgeshire, where he had four acres of land. John Lovekyn, stockfishmonger, was the son of a prosperous Surrey figure, probably a merchant, who had built and endowed a chapel at Kingston-on-Thames. Sir John Pultney was the son of a Sussex landowner who had married into Leicestershire gentry. Thomas Canynges, in the next century, belonged to the celebrated Bristol shipowning family.

The majority of these provincial-born merchant citizens seem not to have inherited any property at their birthplace or, at least, none that they considered worth keeping. This circumstance is not in itself any clue to their social origin, since it was the custom among all classes to cast younger sons on their own resources. Both among the landed and the landless there was a sprinkling of younger sons, cousins, and nephews of gentlemen, some of them inheriting, or hoping to inherit, whole manors or other valuable pieces of property. Thomas Cressy, mercer, complained of two relatives making an armed attack to oust him from his manor of Kyngeshawe, in Nottinghamshire, of which he and his ancestors had been seized, he claimed, "dauncien temps"; in another instance a tailor brought suit against a yeoman, a gentleman, a squire, and a knight for refusing to give him possession of one hundred and forty acres in Huntingdonshire of which, he alleged, his father had enfeoffed them in trust.[29] Some inherited substantial holdings of land without apparently having any close connection with gentry; these must have been sons of well-to-do peasants or yeomen or country traders. One wealthy grocer, from Kent, had inherited two hundred acres there and another a "grete place" with lands in two parishes that he let. Other descriptions refer vaguely to lands lying in the vills, fields, or marshes of adjacent parishes in various counties. John Cornewe, vintner, claimed that according to the custom of the manor of Brampton, in Devon, he would have inherited his father's holding of fifty acres there in preference to his elder brother, had not his father's feoffee refused to give him possession. Another complaint was against an uncle in Devonshire, who had thrust aside John Lappe, haberdasher, while he was a boy, and taken possession of twenty acres of pasture and two pieces of arable land, of twelve and twenty acres, at Ugborough. Some had mere scraps of family property, such as a house "holden by copy" in Bloxham, Oxfordshire; two acres of land "with appurtenances" in Leek, in south Lincolnshire; two crofts with six acres in Essex; a messuage in Middlesex consisting of a garden, three roods of arable land, one rood of meadow, and a "parcell of land." At the time of his death Thomas Dounton, wealthy mercer and pewterer, held no property at Shirbourne in Dorset, where his relatives lived, but five acres and one "clausum terre" given him by his mother shortly before. John Herne, stockfishmonger, was one of those surplus sons who, although obliged by custom to leave the family holding, yet retained some rights to the income that it produced: in his will he

29. E.C.P., 6/40, 18/37. Any series of fifteenth-century deeds or records of legal proceedings concerning land and Londoners will yield examples in which London merchants were associated as mainpernors or feoffees or were engaged in litigation with gentlemen and esquires bearing the same surname (see the E.C.P., the deeds enrolled on dorse of the close rolls, the chancery miscellanea, the records of the court of common pleas).

required a brother to supply his widow with a "sufficient" income from their property at Brampton in Huntingdonshire.[30]

Many came from the trading and artisan elements in the villages and small towns. Richard Moton, skinner, who had a brother in Wales and lands on the border, at Oswestry, and Robert Wollehous, mercer, who acted with a landless husbandman of Lincolnshire also named Wollehous in buying merchandise, may have risen by means of the wool trade. Richard Marchall, haberdasher, who executed a deed of gift to a tanner of Shropshire bearing his name, may have come from some village family mixing mercantile and handicraft enterprise. John Abyn, grocer, was from Taunton, where he had a cousin in the cloth industry as a "toker." At his death he left a gold ring to a mercer in Yeovil and a gilt cup inherited from his father to a brother in Taunton; another brother was a cutler in London. Robert Gryme, grocer, desired to be buried beside his father in the chapel of the friars minor in his native town of Shrewsbury. In both these cases, as the gilt cup and the chapel burial indicate, there had been some preliminary foundation to the family fortunes before a son was sent to London.[31]

Still others came from the larger towns, either as boys to be apprenticed or as young men already trained and experienced in trade and in a position to buy the freedom of the city. The leading provincial merchant families were too deeply rooted in local inter-

30. E.C.P., 61/24, 161; 76/42, 100/34, 108/86, 137/52. Rot. cl., 18 Hen. VI, m. 7d; 23 Hen. VI, m. 7d; 16 Hen. VI, m. 12d. Wills of Bolle, Chamber, Goldwell, Dounton, Herne (Hust. R.W.D., 191/23; P.C.C., Rous, 11; P.C.C., Logge, 16; P.C.C., Stokton, 19, 4). A grocer claimed that "his auncestres before hym tyme owte of mynde" had been seised of a certain messuage in Holme, Nottinghamshire; this may have referred to two or three generations (E.C.P., 208/42). Cf. name of William Tenacre, fifteenth-century mercer.

31. E, 13/141; Rot. cl., 1 Edw. IV, m. 36d. Wills of Moton, Abyn, Gryme (P.C.C., Milles, 30 [1480]; Comm. Lon., Wilde, 73 [1460]; P.C.C., Wattys, 25 [1473]). See also wills of John Don, mercer, whose father was born in Kidwelly, in Wales, and who had relatives there and in Dorset, the latter including a baker and a tanner; and Thomas Parker, tailor, who left money to repair the road by Wigan and a legacy to a cousin there, a cordwainer (P.C.C., Logge, 2 [1480]; P.C.C., Godyn, 31 [1470]). A fishmonger wrongfully challenged as a serf in 1371 was able to prove himself the great-grandson of a small landowner, possibly a miller, Elias atte Mille of Chesthunt (H.M.C., 6th Report, Appendix, I, 410–11). For emphasis on the early importance of mercantile and handicraft elements in village life see E. A. Kosminsky, "Services and Money Rents," Ec. H.R., V, 36 ff. Both were probably often combined with working of land. A mercer of the village of Walden who died in 1488 left a stock of malt, a pack horse, a hackney horse, a copyhold croft of three acres "enclosed wt hedges," another inclosed acre "sett wt saffron hedys," and freehold and copyhold lands in a neighboring township (John Harvey [P.C.C., Milles, 11]).

ests and responsibilities to wish to transplant themselves entirely, but they sometimes liked to send one or two members to London. Thus, one member of the Payne family, which had branches in both Southampton and Salisbury, moved to London, where he joined the grocers' company; his son, however, remained in Southampton.[32]

Before a master enrolled an apprentice, he would do his utmost to extract a premium from the boy's family, the amount of which was supposed to represent the cost of board and maintenance, with a charge for instruction. In 1393 the goldsmiths ruled that no member should accept an apprentice for a term of less than seven years with less than 10 marks or for ten years with less than £5 on pain of paying £5 to company funds. In actual practice the rates were set by a kind of sliding scale according to the means of the family in question. Sir William Capell took 20 marks with one gentleman's son, an abbot in Chester paid £10 to place a boy with a London tailor, and a miller's son from Hertfordshire sold a piece of land left him by his father in order to pay the 30s. demanded of him by a master in the skinners' company. For apprenticeship in merchant companies city orphans paid from 4 to 10 marks. Instead of paying a premium, some parents preferred to make the master a loan for the duration of the apprenticeship. From their point of view, this was intended to serve the same purpose, that of insuring that their boy would receive good care and training. As one woman expressed it, she had lent £20 to her boy's master, a London girdler, "to thentent that heir seid sone shulbe hadde more in favour." The loans were interest free and ran from 10 marks to £100, sometimes taking the whole of a boy's patrimony without adequate security for repayment. One merchant, providing in this way for his godson, felt it necessary to insist upon security for the loan, "that the child may have hit agayn to his owne behove at the ende of his terme and not to be dissayved thereof." Again, a master might require an apprentice's father or some other sponsor to protect him by a personal obligation for perhaps as much as £100 against the risk of loss through the boy's dishonesty or carelessness.[33]

32. *C.W.C.H.*, II, 558; Anc. Deeds, B 9479; E.C.P., 73/145.

33. Prideaux, p. 15. One goldsmith in 1372 had paid only 5 marks to apprentice his son to another master in the company (Wardens' Accounts, A, fol. 25). E.C.P., 94/22, 125/2; W.A.M., 4237 (1310). For bequests by London merchants of sums of 5 marks to

Unfortunately for the masters, the supply of labor able to pay for apprenticeship fell short of the demand. One of the pepperers' ordinances of 1345 refers to the custom of accepting some apprentices "saunz argent on autre avoir rienz." Lack of payment could be made an excuse for prolonging the term of service, but unfulfilled promises to pay were sometimes remitted by the master's will. Masters might also have to lend an apprentice the sum that was needed to buy his freedom.[34]

Indirect evidence that London companies drew apprenticed labor from the poorer strata in both town and country arises from the city's opposition to the statute of 1406 which made it illegal to take apprentices from families that had not at least 20s. annual income from land or rent. The mayor and aldermen, upon whom responsibility for enforcing the statute devolved, completely ignored it until 1428, when one of the king's clerks brought a bill for contempt and trespass against a prominent city scrivener for having taken an apprentice from a family with less than the stipulated income from land. They then adopted the cavalier view that the law referred only to parents, leaving children free to apprentice themselves as they chose. The next year, however, during the mayoralty of William Estfeld, a petition was drawn up asking that citizens of London be exempt from the provisions of the statute

£5 for putting sons to a trade see *C.W.C.H.*, I, 401; II, 119, 270; L. Bk., *G*, fol. 302; *H*, fol. 115; *I*, fol. 7*b*; *K*, fol. 173*b*. On loans to masters see E.C.P., 64/358; L. Bk., *H*, fols. 279*b*, 282*b*; *I*, fols. 32, 197; *K*, fols. 40*b*, 43, 85*b*, 130, 173*b*. In only one case on record was it stipulated that anything beyond the principal be returned; the loan in question was the patrimony of an orphan apprenticed to his guardian and was thus on the usual terms sanctioned by the court of orphanage (L. Bk., *I*, fol. 38*b*). One premium, of £22, was paid only on condition that if the boy died under age it was to be regarded as a loan, repayable to his family (*Cal. P. & M. Rolls*, II, 125). In another case a premium of 50s. was supplemented by a loan of equal value (will of W. Wircestre [Comm. Lon., Courtney, 122 (1384)]). On security for loans see D. & C. St. Paul's, Deeds, A 68/66. Sir John Percevall, tailor, sued on an obligation of £100 guaranteeing that a certain boy "shuld truly behave hym . . . . as a prentes ought to . . . ."; and there is record of similar suits for this amount and less, both in London and in provincial towns (E.C.P., 48/527, 528, 61/366, 446, 67/319, 68/94, 72/66, 94/22, 106/8, 206/55, 208/63).

34. In the only two cases on record in 1345 a pepperer's apprentice who had paid a premium was bound for a term of 8 years, while another who had not paid was bound for 14 years (Kingdon, I, 26). Grocers of London, pp. 255-56. Both the apprentices serving a corder who died in 1357 owed him money, one £20, one 20s., described as being for his apprenticeship (Hust. R.W.D., 86/14). The master's will remitted both debts; cf. will of Thomas Goldwell, forgiving an apprentice "thoo three pounds I shulde have had with hym of his fader" (P.C.C., Logge, 16). The cost of the freedom, including the Guildhall fee and a company fee, might run to about £2 or £3. Case of a tailor's apprentice bound to his master for £3 13s. 4d., for the purpose of making him free (E.C.P., 60/216).

and be authorized to accept as apprentices the children of any person of free condition. Although a very similar petition from the mayor and burgesses of Oxford had been rejected, new legislation promptly confirmed the Londoners in the liberty requested.[35]

The ban upon accepting the children of villeins as apprentices, which thus received statutory sanction, was not of long standing and may have been introduced solely to placate influential noblemen. It first appeared in a city law of 1387 requiring foreigns to swear that they were not bondsmen before being enrolled as apprentices or admitted to citizenship. Deception was punishable by fine or loss of the franchise, "saving always the liberty which appertains to the soil of the city." This saving clause, presumably referring to the custom of regarding a man as of free condition if he had lived undisturbed in the city for a year and a day, must largely have nullified the effect of the regulations. At the same time, to obviate all risk of high city officials being claimed as villeins, which would have compromised the dignity of their office, it was laid down that no citizen could stand as alderman or mayor unless he was clearly free, that is, unless his father has been free at the time of his birth.[36] Whether having to fight a lord's claim involved any personal indignity is doubtful. Villeins had long carried on such a variety of occupations that their legal status did not coincide with any set economic or social status. The mercers, however, probably wishing to boast that every one of their members was potentially

35. 7 Hen. IV, c. 17. The text admits that an earlier statute (12 Ric. II, c. 5) forbidding the apprenticeship of children who had been engaged in field work before they were 12 had been a failure. The citizens of Oxford interpreted the new condition as referring to income "in freehold" (*Rot. parl.*, V, 205). The law was amended by 8 Hen. VI, c. ii. See L. Bk., *K*, fols. 79–83*b*, and *Cal. L. Bk.*, *K*, pp. 87, 105. The grocers' accounts note 40*s.* paid to Estfeld "for costes of our parte off Repelyng off ye statut off prentyshodys" (Kingdon, II, 204).

36. *Cal. L. Bk.*, *H*, p. 309. H. S. Bennett (in *Life on the English Manor* [1937], p. 301) overlooks the saving clause. For a case of successful appeal to city custom on this point in 1428 see L. Bk., *K*, fol. 56. The men whose status was called in question were fishmongers who were said to have lived in the city for 40 years. As late as 1373 a parliamentary petition had complained of the difficulty of reclaiming villeins who had gone to London (*Rot. parl.*, II, 319). A citizen cornmonger had in 1361 endowed a fraternity of villeins with house property in Smithfield (*C.W.C.H.*, II, 33–34). Mutual assistance in fighting the claims of lords may have been the main purpose of such an organization. The names of the members reported in 1389 are illegible (C, 47/42/206). John Carpenter believed that villeins had been excluded from citizenship by ancient custom, but his only evidence, besides the rules of 1387, is the disfranchisement in 1305 of four butchers who held land in villeinage of the bishop of London at Stepney and lived outside the liberties; this hardly proves his point (*Lib. Alb.*, I, 33; cf. Alice Green, *Town Life in the Fifteenth Century* [1894], I, 196).

eligible for city office, had by 1404 agreed that no apprentice should be accepted among them until the masters of the craft had ascertained that he was "a fre man born and fremannes sone." The grocers made no such discrimination until 1429, when it had become a legal necessity. They then hastily classed unfree birth along with lameness, leprosy, and loss of an eye as disqualifying a boy for apprenticeship in their company. Nine of the lesser craft ordinances that were submitted to the mayor and aldermen for approval at this time or later required apprentices to be of free birth, but several others asked only that, like the heroes of popular novels, they be "clene of lymmes."[37]

Any previous connection with an unsavory occupation might disqualify a lad for apprenticeship. The mercers banned country peddlers, who were in general under suspicion of handling stolen goods. Association with vagrant beggars was equally damaging. The goldsmiths' wardens rejected two younger brothers of a member because one had for a time made his living by leading a beggar about the country; later they relented and admitted them but only on payment of a fine of £10.[38]

Toward the end of the fifteenth century it is likely that from a third to a half of the immigrant apprentices being accepted in the greater London companies came from families already engaged in industry and trade, mostly in the smaller towns and villages. The proportion in the companies of skinners and tailors is shown in Table 21. It is by no means certain that all the men who were classified as yeomen or husbandmen derived their livelihood only from the land; indeed, when they gave town addresses, as some of those in Table 21 did, they may have been much more closely connected with trade or industry. Clerks attempting to set down a man's status or occupation often fell back on the label "yeoman"

37. Mercers' Wardens' Accounts, fol. 9; Kingdon, II, 180. See rules of the barbers, fullers, brewers, carpenters, graytawyers, coopers, and saddlers as they were approved between 1482 and 1490. The shearmen's rules, as registered in a spiritual court in 1452, required apprentices to be freeborn; later rules brought before the mayor and aldermen asked only that members take "as nygh as they can apprentices comen of good kynrede." The cutlers had apparently amended their rules to comply with the statute of 1388. The skinners' rules at the end of the fifteenth century required free birth (Journals, 8, fols. 9, 145v, 269v; 9, fol. 19v. L. Bk., L, fols. 182–85, 230b, 243, 249, 281; I, fol. 259. Skinners' Register, art. 14. H. C. Coote, Ordinances of Some Secular Guilds of London, 1354–96 [1871], p. 52).

38. Mercers' Ordinances of 1404; see above, n. 37. Goldsmiths' Wardens' Accounts, A, fol. 55 (1411). The other young brother had been first a miller and then a cobbler (souter).

when they were in doubt as to his main occupation but estimated
that he was of middling rank, and they likewise used "husbandman" as a generic description of a somewhat lower status. Towns-
men of the merchant class, even Londoners, could on occasion be
described as yeomen.[39] Among liverymen's apprentices, from
whom it is probable that the majority of the merchant class was
formed, the proportion of gentlemen's sons was higher than in the
companies at large but was less than that of the humbler rural
recruits and hardly any greater than that of the mercantile and
artisan elements combined. The opinion once put forward, that
commerce was at this period reserved for the sons of gentlemen

TABLE 21

OCCUPATIONS OF APPRENTICES' FATHERS*

	Crafts-men and Merchants	Yeomen	Husband-men	Miscel-laneous	Gentry	Total
Sons apprenticed to skinners and tailors..............	48	45	29	5	25	152
Sons apprenticed to skinners in the livery or about to enter it	8	4	11	....	10	33

* See Appen. C.

and prosperous city merchants, clearly misjudged the breadth of
its base and the vitality of village enterprise.[40]

The lesser companies competed with the greater in drawing
upon rural and town families that had a little property and were
willing to pay one or two pounds to give a son a start in London.
Masters in the chief metal- and leather-working trades demanded,
and were sometimes able to obtain, premiums of this amount or

39. John Payne, a liveried London grocer and a citizen of Southampton, was indicted
in the court of king's bench with the alias "nuper de Westminster . . . . yoman"; another
figure, described as late tailor of Thornbury, Glos., was given the alias "nuper de London
yoman" (K.B., 27/792, Rex roll, m. 98, 27/806, m. 84). A burgess and merchant of Great
Yarmouth was pardoned as "late of London yoman," and another burgess of Great
Yarmouth was described as "husbondman" (Cal. P.R., 1446–52, p. 398; 1422–29, p. 510). An
unenfranchised shopkeeper in London was described as "yomon" (P. & M. Rolls, A 50/6).
Country chapmen could be classed as yeomen (Cal. P.R., 1429–36, p. 320). The term "laborer" was similarly ambiguous. A Cornwall man "possessed of a tin work" and employing
other laborers there was so described (Cal. Proc. C., I, xiii–xiv). Cf. pardon to a Newcastle-
on-Tyne man described as "yoman, alias laborer alias marchaunt," and revocation of a
protection granted to an Essex yeoman with aliases as chapman, draper, and husbandman
(Cal. P.R., 1476–85, p. 198; 1452–61, p. 237).

40. See A. F. Pollard, Wolsey (1929), p. 303.

larger sums as loans. They would take land if it was near the city. One young man, binding himself to a bowyer for ten years, was obliged to convey his late father's lands at Tottenham to his master for this period, on the understanding that they would then be entailed on his heirs by a marriage with the latter's daughter.[41] Other instances occur of families in possession of about a hundred acres in the vicinity of London and elsewhere sending a son into one of the lesser companies.[42]

In all classes there was a sprinkling of Welsh and Irish immigrants of varied social origin. Some of the Welsh merchant families seem to have spent more than one generation in migration, trading and acquiring land on the way, yet retaining a connection with relatives in Wales.[43] Some of the Irish had landed or mercantile fortune behind them and perhaps enjoyed influential connections through service with nobles and high officials.[44]

There was also some infiltration of immigrants from the Continent. In the early fourteenth century the surname "de Paris" was common. Two French financiers in the service of Edward II, William Servat, pepperer, from Cahors, and William Trente, a wine merchant from near-by Bergerac, stepped into the city's ruling class as aldermen. Simon Corp, pepperer, another alderman of that period, may have come from the same region; and his

41. H.M.C., *9th Report, Appendix*, p. 30 (1331–32). On thirteenth-century demands for premiums see Unwin, pp. 83, 85, 91. The spurriers in 1300 ruled that no one might take an apprentice for less than 10 years or with less than 40s. (*Cal. E.M.C.R.*, p. 52). For payment of 30s. premium to a saddler, loan of £20 to a girdler, and more extreme demands by a cutler see *Cal. L. Bk.*, D, p. 103; E.C.P., 64/358; *Cal. P. & M. Rolls*, III, 14–16. Evidence of artisan origins in apprenticeship of a son of Richard "Hendyman" de Grene to a smeremonger (*Cal. L. Bk.*, D, p. 112). The desire for land near the city is shown in the will of a pouchmaker entailing 10 acres at Hackney and leaving his daughter another acre as dowry "that I bowth wt my peny" (Comm. Lon., Lichfield, fol. 48v [1486]). Roger, son of Richard le Shepdryver of Amwell, inherited lands there, acquired more from sons of another sheepdriver, became citizen and butcher (W.A.M., 4213, 4215). His deeds are sealed with a sleeping lion.

42. See case of a winedrawer from Shoreditch and of a pewterer and tallow-chandler with property at North Mymmes (*Cal. C.R., 1381–85*, p. 232; W.A.M., 4127, 4128; above, chap. ii, n. 81). See will of William Smyth, of London and of Bedingfeld, Suffolf, where he was a customary tenant with over 100 acres inclosed and had bought four separate small holdings; these were bequeathed to his son, a London joiner (P.C.C., Wattys, 8 [1472]).

43. See case of John Don, n. 31, above, and wills of Elys and Oliver Davy (P.C.C., Stokton, 4; P.C.C., Wattys, 11; and *Home and Counties Magazine*, VI, 160).

44. See Brice, Appen. A. Robert Fitz Robert, grocer, whose grandfather had come from Ireland, left a bequest for the soul of Joan, countess of Ormond (Register, Chichele, fol. 445; Hust. R.W.D., 153/74; *Cal. L. Bk.*, I, p. 100).

brother-in-law, Reymond de Burdeus, son of a citizen saddler of that name, was one of the original founders of the pepperers' fraternity of St. Antony. Burdeus married into the family of a goldsmith named Robert le Convers.[45] The vintners' company was always ready to admit a few Gascons, but none of these played any prominent part in the fifteenth-century city.

Italians had made more of a mark on the merchant class. Two of the ruling city families of the twelfth and thirteenth centuries, the Bucointes and the Buckerels, are thought to have sprung from Italian settlers of the late eleventh century, and the Legges, later, are credited with some such remote Italian ancestry.[46] This early immigration was probably of merchant families that had already moved into business in France, the extension of the spice trade and financial operations carrying them on into England. The Vans of Lucca settled in London in the early fourteenth century in this way. John Van, an associate of the Ballardi, money-changers to Edward II, was favored by a royal grant of exemption from all taxation; by swearing to forgo this privilege and to contribute to all the city's charges, he was in 1313 made a citizen of London, where he had settled with his wife and children.[47] Peres, one of his five sons, was among the first members of the fraternity of St. Antony. Three other Italian spice merchants were taken into this fraternity when it later expanded,[48] and several, one from Lucca, one from Florence, were admitted into the skinners' fraternity of Corpus Christi.[49] Others settled down as spice dealers or apoth-

45. *Cal. L. Bk., A*, pp. 24, 69; *B*, pp. 70, 127; *D*, p. 185; *C.W.C.H.*, I, 253.

46. See W. Page, *London, Its Origin and Early Development* (1929), pp. 236–42. For fine equestrian seals of early Bucointes see D. & C. St. Paul's, Deeds, A 1/543; Drapers' Deeds, A V, 3.

47. *Cal. L. Bk., E*, pp. 16, 75, 76; *C.W.C.H.*, I, 264–65.

48. Bartholomew Myne and John and Lewis Donat. Myne had become a citizen, with a family in London, before he was able to obtain exemption from paying alien rates of customs (*Cal. P.R., 1358–61*, p. 550). John Donat was in 1358 granted royal assurance that he should enjoy all the liberties of a citizen on the grounds that he had lived in London from his youth and married there. He had possibly appealed for protection; in the same year the city authorities imposed on him the severe fine of 20s. for having had a wax torch of inferior quality made in his house. He did business in Ireland, acquired lands in Kent, was assigned a legacy by a son of Sir Walter de Cheshunt, and left a son Nicholas who by 1393 had reached the age of 20 and received a patrimony of £40 (*Cal. P.R., 1358–61*, p. 48; *1374–77*, p. 97; *Cal. L. Bk., G*, p. 92; *C.W.C.H.*, II, 229; *Cal. Anc. Deeds*, III, 120, 161; L. Bk., *H*, fol. 273).

49. Bartholomew Thomasyn of Lucca had citizenship before 1346, acquired London property, and passed it on to his son Nicholas, who was in turn admitted to the skinners'

ecaries but, either because they were not rich enough or on account of prejudice, were not welcomed into the liveried societies.[50] Prejudice, jealousy, and suspicion were kept alive by the ease with which Italians bought royal favor and by their connection with the suspect profession of brokerage. When John de Marconovo, a Venetian broker, paid £5 for honorary membership in the grocers' fraternity and began to make presents of wine for the company feasts, one of the wardens noted in the margin of his accounts, "Hit is to drede we bye þylk pipe full dere."[51] Only four other Italians joined the grocers in the fifteenth century, and only three are listed as entering the skinners' fraternity. Few could have had any wish to become naturalized. Gerard Caniziani accepted free letters of denization from Edward IV, joined the mercers' company, and married an alderman's widow, but he was soon afterward seeking special royal protection against indignant fellow-Florentines.[52]

Flemish and German immigration mainly affected strata lower

fraternity (Anc. Deeds, C, 87, 905; *Cal. C.R., 1318–23*, p. 489; *1346–49*, pp. 139, 235). John Adam, from Lucca, settled in London early in life, married there, obtained citizenship and exemption from the alien customs, acquired land at Hakham, Surrey, from a Genoese citizen of London named John Pynselegle and came to be called Hakham, although in his will he called himself "de Montecatuin." He died in 1358, leaving 4 children, one of them illegitimate (*Cal. P.R., 1350–54*, p. 196; *Surrey Fines* ["Surrey Archaeological Collections," Extra Vol. I], p. 121; Hust. R.W.D., 86/60; *Cal. Inq. p.m.*, XII, 433). Peter Jacobi of Florence was admitted to the freedom early in the century after apprenticeship to another Florentine, Bartholomew Muscardi, spicer (*Cal. L. Bk., D*, p. 153). John Donat, grocer, was also in the skinners' fraternity.

50. It is not clear whether these obtained citizenship through companies, as nonliveried members, or through the royal favor. Nicholas Guillelmi of Lucca, apothecary, who with his brother Brunettus supplied the king's wardrobe, had a son, John William, who became a citizen and spicer; cf. John Falcoun of Lucca, John Gouche of Florence, Lodewicus Francis, and Bette Bosan, "lumbard," who was sentenced to the pillory in 1376 for forging a bond and may have been the Bartholomew Bosan of Lucca who fifteen years later paid £50 for letters of naturalization, granted on condition that he should not belong to any society of foreign merchants (*Cal. C.R., 1313–18*, p. 448; *1354–60*, p. 240; *1360–64*, p. 133; *Cal. P.R., 1358–61*, p. 99; *1370–74*, p. 263; Recognizance Roll, 12, *m.* 9; Riley, *Memorials*, pp. 404–5; H.M.C., *9th Report, Appendix*, p. 57). Several of the surnames among visiting Italian merchants, e.g., Francis, Norman, Michel, were common also among London merchants, but no family alliances have been traced.

51. Kingdon, II, 180–81, 186, 193. Eight Italian brokers subscribed to the building of the grocers' new hall, 1428–31 (*ibid.*, p. 10). The suspicion of brokers is illustrated also by a note against the names of 13 English brokers of grocery: "the mo schrowez þe worse company her is a Covent mo nor lase ffor theme many man ffarys þe worse" (*ibid.*, I, 178 [1428]).

52. *Cal. P.R., 1467–77, passim.* See Stokton, Appen. A. One other Italian joined the mercers, Thomes Guenes, of Lucca, in 1500.

than the merchant class. In addition to groups of weavers, gold-smiths, and brewers, the first two of which were conspicuously set apart by gild and fraternity organization, there was throughout the whole period a trickle of immigration, from Bruges and Cologne and neighboring regions, into such trades as tailoring, embroidering, woodworking, the making of paternosters, and the cheese trade. Although the process of full assimilation may have been slow, many of these people were admitted to citizenship.[53]

4. PATTERNS IN FAMILY HISTORY

Heavy odds against the survival of male heirs do not preclude the chance favoring of individual families for successive genera-tions. Despite the continued need of new recruits, the merchant class at all times contained a small core of families that had be-hind them a long tradition of London life.

Some of these had worked their way up from the lesser com-panies. Of four generations of Dogets who continued in the wine trade, the first was represented by a taverner who died in 1282 leaving two sons, the other three by vintners, the last of whom died childless in 1403; two more vintners of the name, who lived to 1456, may represent a fifth generation, descended from the tavern-er's other son. Both branches were attached to the parish of St. Leonard's, Eastcheap, held property in that neighborhood, and left their monuments and inscriptions in the church. One of the sons of Gilbert Prince, a fourteenth-century painter who invested in trade, became a mercer and left a son who became a tailor. Many sons of workers in the base metals became goldsmiths, and a number of vintners and grocers came from families in the lesser victualing trades. Behind the ambitious parents who thus enabled their sons to push upward there may in turn have been several generations of London shopkeeping.[54]

53. The admissions to citizenship may be traced, two or three at a time, in the records of the husting courts. Some of the immigrants were wives or children of Englishmen who had married while in Flanders; see case of a cheesemonger whose son was thus born in Bruges (E.C.P., 38/276). Cf. Margaret Roos, a Fleming, late wife of a mercer, granted letters of denization for 40s. (*Cal. P.R., 1436–44*, p. 352). See case of the "evil disposed person" from Bruges, claiming to be an illegitimate son of John Pykering, mercer (E.C.P., 229/19). Two "Easterlings" entered the skinners' lesser fraternity in 1438.

54. On the Dogets see Appen. A; on the Princes, Hust. R.W.D., 171/8. Case of a vintner grandson of a brewer (D. & C. St. Paul's, A/3/665 [1430]) and of a girdler, son of "Mariote la Bokeler" and grandson or still more remote heir of a buckler of Bread Street (D. & C. St. Paul's, A/1/1628 [1332]).

Other families make their first appearance in city records with the transactions of some fourteenth-century merchant, whose sons and nephews and grandsons and grandnephews kept the name and the business alive throughout all the worst periods of plague. A single branch of the Elsyng family covered a span of some hundred and twenty years as well-to-do mercers. Although the first who appears, William, devoted a substantial sum to founding a hospital for the blind, his son was prosperous enough to add to the endowment; the grandson, Thomas, followed the lead of his guardian, Jordan de Elsyng, mercer, in buying country property but was living in London when he made his will and died, childless, in 1431. The son and grandson of Richard Odyham, grocer and chamberlain, succeeded him in his company, and there were three generations of Claverings in the drapers' company in one direct line. Such a record was rare enough to justify a certain pride. The grandson of the first Clavering, dying childless in 1421, ordered his descent, with his father's arms and a plea for prayers, to be embroidered on white vestments for his parish church. The most remarkable record yet discovered is that of the Gisors, presumed to be of Italian origin, who had settled in London by the beginning of the thirteenth century. Owing to the chance survival of five brothers in the generation immediately preceding the Black Death, they were still represented by at least one line in the sixteenth-century city. Yet, on the whole, astonishingly few names recur in company membership lists: of ninety-seven on the mercer's list for 1347, for example, only eleven recur between 1392 and 1420. It is true that sons did not have to join the same company as their fathers or even, unfortunately for the researcher, necessarily bear the same surname, names derived from trades sometimes alternating, in a disconcerting way, with place names. Nevertheless, the percentage of the members of the greater companies who represented a third generation of successful trade in London can never have been very large.[55]

55. On the Elsyngs see *C.W.C.H.*, I, 562, 637; II, 456; *Cal. P. & M. Rolls*, I, 182, n. 3; *Cal. L. Bk.*, *G*, p. 238. Comm. Lon., More, 3 , 274; *Norfolk Feet of Fines*, pp. 334, 360; E, 179/141/14. For three other citizens of the name see *Cal. L. Bk.*, *F*, p. 48; *E*, p. 146. On the Odyhams (who also used the name of Hatfield) see Hust. R.W.D., 134/106, 143/32; P.C.C., Marche, 31; *Cal. L. Bk.*, *I*, *passim*. On the Claverings see Weever, p. 123; Harl. Ch., 48/B35; *C.W.C.H.*, II, 383, 429. On the Gisors see Appen. A.

1) Sons didn't join the same trade as their
   fathers always

2) Sons changed their surnames.

In the story of such long-lived and wealthy families as clung to the city the curve of fortune was usually downward. The inheritance of rent-rolls could make for the neglect of trade, although young men did not grow up looking forward to a life of idleness. Merchant guardians and relatives would have frowned on this as "unprofitable," nor were there yet enough upper-class diversions in the city to lend such a life much attraction. Some turned their energies into civic affairs. William Eynsham, for example, the son of an alderman and one of the greatest landlords in the fourteenth-century city, took the office of chamberlain. John Northampton may have lived mainly on his rents during his active political career. But families did not keep to a tradition of civic service, nor did they long retain large city rent-rolls intact; these became split up as daughters required dowries. Again, if much money was invested outside the city, it tended, as will be seen, to draw the heirs after it. The leisured section of the community was made up chiefly of elderly merchants in retirement, wealthy widows, and unmarried women. The subsidy roll of 1412 lists forty-two citizens who claimed the rank of esquire, but less than a dozen of these were credited with over £15 in London rents, only one had over £50, and most had such very small city incomes that they must either have had property elsewhere or have had some employment. At least two representatives of the fourth generation of old merchant families were included, but neither was rich in city rents. John Hotoft, an esquire in the queen's household, whose great-grandfather had been one of the leading wool merchants of his day, was assessed at only £2. Thomas Farndon, with £18, could have lived in comfort and security but not in the style of his grandfather and great-grandfather, who had enjoyed long terms as aldermen. The Gisors family, which had for three generations, up to 1336, put domineering men into the court of aldermen, had likewise fallen on quiet and undistinguished days. Thomas, the most prominent of its members in the latter part of the fourteenth century, once headed the vintners' company but politically rose no higher than the common council. His son Edward, a grocer, held no office in his company and possibly rested in content on his London rent-roll, assessed in 1436 at £37. He was followed in turn by a John Jesors, either a son or nephew, a gentleman, who remained apart from public life, married his rent gatherer's daughter, and died in 1501. After him came another John Jesors, gentleman, and another Edward Gysors, grocer.[56]

The slackening of political ambition on the part of the older city families was a very marked feature of the fifteenth century. In part this may have been due to lingering fears of family compacts in the court of aldermen, in part to the greater wealth and the valuable business connections of new immigrants from provincial centers of trade and industry. In a sample of twelve aldermen serving early in the century, four can be identified as sons of London merchants; among thirty-seven serving after 1450 only two were sons of Londoners.[57] Another element in the situation was the fascination that the legal profession was coming to hold for wealthy citizens' sons. The elder son in the fourth generation of the Coventry family, which had migrated originally from Coventry and had bought its way from the pinners' company up to the ranks of the mercers, in 1432 entered Gray's Inn. A little earlier the grandson of William Wodehous, alderman, defied his guardians by marrying outside the merchant class at the age of fourteen and began legal studies; he was perhaps urged on by an aunt who had married a successful lawyer. In two other instances merchants are known to have encouraged grandsons, who were their sole surviving heirs, to take up the study of law. In some families one branch might take to the law and another remain in trade. In the Costantyn family, for example, three generations of drapers and aldermen were succeeded by a well-to-do citizen esquire whose second son, in the fifteenth century, became a fellow of Gray's Inn. The branch that remained in trade was exceptional among the older merchant families in achieving re-entry of the court of aldermen, a contemporary of the lawyer, either his brother or a nephew, serving in it for six years. The alderman's son became a grocer but passed also as a gentleman and esquire of Kent. The lawyer's sons may have remained more loyal to the family's urban traditions than the merchant's. The eldest inherited ancestral property in

56. On the Costantyns, Farndons, and Gisors see Appen. A. John Costantyn, whose son used the alias Peche, may have been the John Pecche, esquire, who was assessed in 1412 at £51. On the Hotofts (Hotots) see Hust. R.W.D., 146/26, 153/29, 59, 167/30. A Hamo de Hotot had held land in Westminster in the time of John (W.A.M., 17324; Gisors, Appen. A).

57. Of 42 aldermen in the first half of the fourteenth century 13 had certainly been sons of London merchants and 19 more probably so; of 25 in the latter part of the century 6 can be identified as sons of Londoners, and 5 more were related to citizen families.

London, the second was apprenticed to a draper, and the third was educated as a priest.[58]

Although family roots could strike so deeply and firmly into the London community, there are no records to voice any sharp sense of preference for town life in opposition to country life. Possibly the most genuinely urban types in London were among wage-workers who were without hope of finding better working conditions elsewhere and had not the means to travel or visit in the country merely for recreation. In the upper citizen classes the situation was very different. The only vehement cry of attachment to London comes from a woman's reluctance to move to a small provincial town. A vintner's widow, she was courted in the latter years of the fourteenth century by a member of her late husband's company who came from Chichester and still held citizenship there. She accepted him only on condition that he would not try to make her leave London, where she had been born and wished to stay until her death; and, not trusting his word alone, she made her brother-in-law bind him by an obligation of £100 to this effect. After the marriage she was nevertheless persuaded to settle in Chichester.[59] A few instances occur of fifteenth-century London merchants moving to smaller towns, presumably for some business advantage.[60] The country, however, exercised an attraction of its own. For many of the well-to-do it was bound up with childhood memories; some parents intrusted babies to the care of village nurses or sent children to school in Stratford or Croydon, and all who could do so took them off for country vacations when serious epidemics swept the city.[61] A young Londoner might therefore

58. See Coventry, Costantyn, Wodehous, Brice, Appen. A. On the purchase by Coventry and his sons of membership in the mercers see Wardens' Accounts, fol. 39v. The grandson of William Michell, grocer, member of parliament for the city in 1415, was intended to study law (see Michell's will [P.C.C., Luffenham, 6]).

59. Alice, widow of John Walworth, marrying William Neel. Her sister sued Neel on the obligation (E.C.P., 6/234). Neel's will (*C.W.C.H.*, II, 427; Register, Chichele, 149–50).

60. See Knolles, Seman, Welles, Appen. A. Hildebrand Ellewell, grocer, moved between London and Wells (Kingdon, I, *passim*; and *Cal. P.R., 1422–29*, pp. 245, 308, 397). Case of another grocer's moving to Bristol (E.C.P., 29/541). Cases of a draper and a grocer described as alias of Hadley, Suffolk, draper and clothmaker, and of a London mercer pardoned as alias of Oxford, mercer (Rot. cl., 20 Hen. VI, *m.* 31d; *Cal. P.R., 1452–61*, p. 264; *1467–76*, p. 321).

61. William Sampson, fishmonger, left small bequests to two nurses of his children, one living in West Ham, one at Stratford Langthorn (P.C.C., Luffenham, 16 [1432]). A girdler left his baby of 23 weeks with a foster-mother in Kingston-on-Thames for half a year; he claimed the child was then lamed and "utterly undon forever" by neglect and lack

grow up, like George Cely, passionately fond of sport and with some familiarity with the work of the countryside. Some, like his father Richard, became so fond of a country house a day's ride from London that they preferred, so far as was possible, to manage their business from this point. So many of the aldermen were staying out of town on their estates at the time that Henry V was leaving for the Agincourt campaign that he felt it necessary, out of concern for the defense of the city, to order them to return.[62] Apprentices who had been gentlemen's sons, born and brought up on a manor, sometimes never became habituated to city life and established themselves in country houses near London as soon as was feasible. Even after his election as mayor in 1485 John Warde proposed to continue living in his native county of Hertfordshire, in the hope of sheltering from the sweating sickness and the political troubles of that year, and only the threat of a fine of £500 induced him to assume his full responsibilities and to bring his family with him to town. Such men and many others naturally felt no permanent bond of association with a city parish, planning to be buried in the church nearest to their country home. The tombs of these retired London merchants are scattered about the whole circle of the home counties.[63]

---

of nourishment (E.C.P., 60/173). Two Venetian merchants did no business in London from Michaelmas to Easter, 1442–43, "par cause de pestilence, qi fuist en loundres qar ils demoyent en pays" (E, 101/128/31). Case of a draper "departed wt alle his houshold frome the said Citie for this dethe" (E.C.P., 64/323) and case of an apprentice sent to relatives in Hereford for the same reason (E.C.P., 61/478).

62. L. Bk., *I*, fol. 198v. In 1380 it was reported that over a dozen prominent citizens had been out of town for so long that they had escaped recent taxation; these can be distinguished from some two dozen others who were citizens and merchants of other towns or woolmen staying in Calais not professing to be London residents (*Cal. L. Bk., H*, pp. 146–47). In 1432 the mayor appealed to nonresident citizens for voluntary contributions toward repair of the city walls (*ibid., K*, pp. 131–32). Despite protests against nonresidence, provincial merchants continued to obtain citizenship (see Journals, 8, fol. 127v; and case of William Redehode, mayor of High Wycombe in 1475, citizen and salter of London [H.M.C., *5th Report*, pp. 554, 564]). In 1431 the grocers alone had seven provincial members, "men off Countre" (Kingdon, II, 201).

63. On Warde see Appen. A; *Cal. L. Bk., L*, p. v; and Journals, 9, fol. 78b. Although more monuments survive from the fifteenth century (see Mill Stephenson, *passim*), the dating of many wills of the previous century from country places shows that retirement to the country was already popular in that age. For examples, including places in Northamptonshire and Cambridgeshire, see *C.W.C.H.*, I, 327, 352, 365, 377, 576, 608; II, 104–5; Appen. A, Bury, Dolseley, Lacer, Pyel. A few of the fifteenth-century examples are from Northamptonshire, Leicestershire, and Oxfordshire, the rest from the home counties. See John Bacon, woolman (P.C.C., Luffenham, 21); Richard Hylle (P.C.C., Stokton, 18; Haines, II, 114; Appen. A, *passim*; and Mill Stephenson, *passim*).

Family ties with relatives in remote provincial towns and villages remained surprisingly close. Letters or messages must have been exchanged, for not only parents but uncles and aunts, brothers and sisters with their wives and husbands, nephews and nieces, and cousins with country addresses were all mentioned by name in London wills and were often assigned quite generous legacies. Sometimes an interest in family land or the borrowing of money from the London brother may have been the chief link in the ties, but evidence of continued affectionate regard is not lacking. One man left money to be delivered to his sister secretly, without her husband's knowledge, and another willed that his sister in Sudbury should have a ten years' pension and two good gowns and kirtles to be made at his expense. Others left their best furred gowns to father or brothers living as far off as in Lincolnshire, apparently contemplating no difficulty in the dispatch of parcels. Some remembered their old nurses. A few belonged to provincial fraternities.[64] Bequests for the education of yeomen's sons or for "a drinking for men of the cuntre" point to a friendly mingling with country neighbors. Some of the provincial-born Londoners lost touch with their birthplaces yet would direct their executors to distribute money among poor relations still living there or to the poor of the neighborhood; this was still their "country," their *patria*.[65] All this was true of both merchants and members of the lesser companies, the latter often renewing their provincial ties by intermarriage.[66]

Occasionally Londoners' sons struck out into business in the

64. Cases of membership in the great fraternities of Coventry and Lynne (Hust. R.W.D., 142/20; and Drapers' Deeds, A VI, 297 [1482]). A London apothecary belonged to a fraternity at Brokham (Brookham Green, Surrey?) in 1301 (Hust. R.W.D., 121/204). Thomas Elys, Bedfordshire-born draper, left money to fraternities at Ashwell and at Baldok, where his mother was living, in Hertfordshire (P.C.C., Godyn, 11 [1479]).

65. The will of Thomas Fulbourne refers to "parentela mea apud Fulborn .... et alibi in patria" (P.C.C., Godyn, 18). John Hilton, grocer, requesting burial beside his mother in London, left lands to endow a scholarship at Oxford for a Shropshire boy and money for bridge repair and poor people in two places in that county (P.C.C., Stokton, 16).

66. E.g., a London shearman's daughter married in Essex, a currier's in Kent, a chandler's in Lincolnshire, a brewer's in Colchester to the son of a London founder, a barber's widow in the Isle of Thanet, a malemaker's widow to a wheeler in Essex (Hust. R.W.D., 142/8, 148/21, 146/22, 155/6; Drapers' Deeds, A VIII, 129; Journals, 8, fol. 175). Late fifteenth-century country tomb inscriptions include those of two London victualers and a fuller, at Bethersden in Kent, Farley in Surrey, and Ewelme in Oxfordshire (see Mill Stephenson).

provinces.[67] More often, especially in time of trade depression or if for any other reason they found business distasteful, they turned their back on it and settled on family property in the country. The move may not always have been of their own volition. A merchant's last resource in dealing with a wayward son who ran into debt was probably to follow the example of an early fifteenth-century draper who paid the youth's debts, bought his wedding clothes, married him, and stocked one hundred and ninety acres of land for him at Fulbourne, in Middlesex.[68] There were others who moved out to small country properties in happier but equally un-ambitious fashion, with the intention of eking out their living by London rents. This arrangement did not always satisfy the next generation, yet, if the heirs wished to go back to the city, they would find that the family had lost caste there by its spell of obscurity. Two of the Hardels, one of the old governing families, abandoned trade in this way early in the fourteenth century to live quietly in Surrey and Essex. Later both estates fell to a single heir who took up citizenship in the lowly company of the tapicers.[69] The Sely family underwent a similar experience. John Sely, skinner, successor to four generations of distinguished members of that company, at the end of the fourteenth century settled in Wilt-shire, where the family had perhaps originated. There he brought up two illegitimate sons, who went off to Buckinghamshire, one as a tailor, one as a mere husbandman. His only legitimate son re-turned to London but had to be content with taking up citizenship through the brewers instead of through the skinners.[70]

The sons of city magnates who had been able to build up coun-try estates comparable in value with those of important local

67. For case of a grocer's son going to Bristol see Knolles, Appen. A. Case of a gold-smith's son setting up his trade in Maidstone (W.A.M., 5206 [1491]).

68. The only surviving son of John Olyver, who made three marriages (*Cal. P. & M. Rolls*, IV, 6–7). The deeds enrolled in the husting court records contain many references to merchants' sons and grandsons in country places, without specifying their occupation; e.g., cases in Suffolk, Surrey, and Oxfordshire (Hust. R.W.D., 133/30, 138/40, 159/52). Case of an ironmonger's son settling in Glaston, Somerset, shown by wills of John and Ste-phen Lane (P.C.C., Godyn, 31; P.C.C., Vox, 23; L. Bk., *L*, fol. 101*b*).

69. This heir was William, great-grandson of Robert Hardel, alderman. His father had appointed a tapicer as his guardian (*C.W.C.H.*, I, 429). Details of his descent and property in London and Surrey in Escheat Rolls, *m*. 67*d*, and W.A.M., 1907, 1908.

70. Appen. A.

landowners were in a very different situation. By settling down on their manors they stood to gain in status, not to lose, for the head of the family was before long likely to be drawn into the influential circle that controlled the administration of the county. The strategic steps that assured a son's entry into the leisured landowning class required a patient watching of the land and marriage markets and were probably all more or less motivated by social ambition. An extreme instance in point is that of a member of the grocers' company, under Richard II, who acquired land in Essex held in chief by service at the king's coronation; although he was not allowed to perform this service in person, he retained the property, bought an heiress' marriage for his son, and settled him there.[71] By his time a number of London families had established a senior branch on estates near by, junior branches continuing in trade in the city. Even so tenaciously urban a family as the Gisors had by the early years of the century planted a line at "Gesoresplace" at Edmonton. In the same period the Swanlands put out two country branches, one at Harefield in Middlesex and one which held the mannor of North Mymmes, on the border of Hertfordshire, for four generations. The last heir let this manor pass into the possession of Thomas Knolles, grocer. Knolles, securely seated in the court of aldermen for over forty years, was in no mind to leave the city or to see his wholesale business abandoned. He placed an agent in charge of the manor and cannily bred both his sons to trade, keeping the elder in London, sending the younger to Bristol. Not until the third generation, in this case, did the heir retire to the country and move into the squirearchy. If the hold on civic honors had been less firm, the move might not have been so long deferred. Sometimes the rise was more impatient and ostentatious. One of the most decorative pictures of an esquire of the reign of Edward IV is to be found at Staundon, in Hertfordshire, on the monumental brass of John Felde, showing him with long, curled hair, in conventionally designed heraldic dress. Yet only a few years before his death Felde had been associated with his father, a former alderman, in the wholesale business of a stockfishmonger and wool merchant.[72]

Very often the evolution from merchant to gentleman was but a

71. John Wiltshire (see *Cal. P. & M. Rolls*, III, 292).

72. On Gisors, Swanland, Knolles, Felde, see Appen. A.

small step, signifying merely the knitting-up of family traditions that had been temporarily broken or the assimilating of younger sons into ways of living long customary with the senior line. Many fifteenth-century families, for example, the Lovelaces of Kent and the Babhams of Cookham,[73] put only a single member into trade in London, a younger son, whose eldest son in turn reverted to the country gentleman's life. There was in all probability much similar stock, represented by grandsons and nephews of gentlemen rather than by sons, among the young provincial merchants who migrated to London.

The problem of providing for younger sons could not have been generally acute among the gentry, for wills indicate that frequently only one son, and sometimes not even one, survived childhood. Among professional men the tendency was probably to marry late. A fifteenth-century parent, asking for a friend's co-operation in the discipline of his son, who was about to enter Lincoln's Inn, laid it down "yn especialle" that the youth was "to be not conversant ne neere amonge women as I was kepte from her company xxx yeres or any such were of my councelle."[74] Funeral brasses suggest that fewer children were born among landed and careerist gentry than among merchants. Seventy-three of them, mostly of late fifteenth-century date, display on an average only nine children, as against an average of eleven on London and provincial merchants' brasses.[75] Even before the plague era there was a high turnover among military tenants, no doubt due largely to the dying-out of families in the direct male line. F. M. Nichols, analyzing the returns for Oxfordshire in Palgrave's *Writs*, found that out of the fifty-eight names of tenants in the country in 1296 only eight recurred among the forty-one tenants of 1322.[76]

Among the more prolific gentle families there might be sporadic recourse to trade throughout the two centuries. The country line of the virile family of Frowyks twice reared three sons, each time in the height of a plague period, and each time one of the three

73. On the Lovelaces, *Archaeologia Cantiana*, X, 184–220; XX, 54–63; E.C.P., 31/285–89, 44/67–69, 53/275; P.C.C., Godyn, 13; Hust. R.P.L., 168/39d. On the Babhams, E.C.P., 64/101; P.C.C., Milles, 36.

74. H.M.C., *7th Report, Appendix*, I, 536.

75. Derived from Mill Stephenson, *passim*.

76. *Archaeologia*, XXXIX, 221.

entered the mercers' company in London. The first of these was an illegitimate son, whose heirs have not been traced. The second had a long and distinguished civic career; his descendants made their way as gentlemen, not by trade.[77]

All the seemingly disparate elements within the merchant class were linked together by a complex pattern of intermarriage, which grew up and was maintained the more readily from the circumstance that many of the families dying out in the male line survived through daughters. These London women, remaining for the most part attached to city property and city ways and marrying within their class, must have contributed immeasurably to the stability of its culture. Another circumstance tending toward the same result was the fact that, when sons failed to grow up, their places were often filled by nephews or cousins or by the children of friends in the provinces who were taken in tutelage as apprentices. Country immigrants therefore did not necessarily represent so much alien raw material to be assimilated only through the process of education offered in apprenticeship but often fitted in a most welcome and intimate way into some family situation.

The types of citizen family history that have been illustrated here could without a doubt be duplicated from the archives of any medieval city comparable in size with London. Everywhere in Europe the same underlying conditions of fertility and mortality made for fluidity in the composition of the upper urban classes. Yet Caxton, returning from abroad, became aware of some lack of depth in London culture, and it struck him as peculiarly English. As regards the longevity of patrician families on the Continent, his imagination may have outrun his powers of critical observation. He may have been misled, as local patriots with whom he talked about the history of Bruges may have been, by mere coincidences of name, or he may have been thinking of instances in which great families had contrived to prolong their lives, when sons failed, by the adoption of heirs. This practice had never taken root in London. The Faringdon family, in the early fourteenth century, offers almost the only certain example of it.[78] But the question immediately arises and surely occurred to Caxton: Why had the practice of adoption, on failure of heirs, not become cus-

77. Appen. A, Frowyk generations Nos. 4–11.

78. Appen. A.

tomary in London? Why was there so little pride in preserving a long record of high family status in the city?

The question calls for more careful statement and much longer consideration than can be given it here. But the answer would probably lie in the circumstances that conditioned citizens' opportunities for careers. In the great Continental cities patrician groups held aloof from active participation in trade, concentrating on government and finance. In London the work of government was limited and specialization in finance was slow to develop. In consequence young men of ambition who did not care for trade looked elsewhere for careers, and those who were merely restless sought the only other life they knew that was easy of access, life on the land.

Chapter VI

TRADE AND GENTILITY

I. THE CRITERIA OF GENTLE RANK

IT IS one of the commonplaces of English social history to remark upon the successful merchant's traditional ambition to
become a gentleman. This tells only a small part of the story of the
social relations between merchants and gentry. In the earliest
period in which these relations have been traced, the fifteenth century, they were already complex and were far from being governed
in all respects by clear-cut attitudes of superiority on the one side
or inferiority on the other. Mrs. Green, touching on the subject in
her survey of town life in this century, went so far as to write of a
class fusion as in process on a national scale between the two
groups.[1] Before one can judge of the meaning or truth of such a
generalization, however, or interpret any of the evidence, one
needs to know the exact senses in which medieval terms referring
to gentle rank were descriptive.

Nineteenth-century historians were inclined to assume that
England had always produced gentle families in a middle-class
position. In Stubbs's picture of the later middle ages these families
formed a hereditary landed class which acted as a connecting and
balancing mean between the baronage and the yeomanry. Cul-
turally, its members were assimilated to the former, imitating
baronial habits in their way of living as far as their means would
allow. Social gradations among them ran according to income and
influence, upward from those who had only a single manor to
those who held a great many, scattered in several counties. These
wealthy men, who almost invariably took up knighthood and wore

1. Alice Green, *Town Life in the Fifteenth Century*, II (1894), 78–79.

it with an air, verged in public estimation upon the dignity of lords.[2]

The picture was realistic enough in its outline, but detail was lacking and long remained scanty. As late as 1902 it was possible for an essayist in the field to be taunting historians with the charge that, despite all their work, the structure of medieval English society was still "a dark and mysterious subject."[3] This critic, Sir George Sitwell, inclined to the sweeping view that in the thirteenth and fourteenth centuries the whole body of barons, knights, and other free tenants formed, at least "in theory," a single social group, divided only by gradations of rank, not by any lines sharp enough to be regarded as class lines. The younger sons in the wealthy families, he believed, were in the habit of settling down to an agricultural life, with some such rank as franklin, on terms of virtual equality with other rural freeholders. Differentiation of the nonbaronial gentry as a separate class was delayed until the fifteenth century and was due, it was argued, to the introduction of stock- and land-leasing, which divorced younger sons from the land. Thrown on their own resources, with nothing to boast of but their status as gentlemen of birth, they naturally set a new value on this, emphasized it by calling themselves gentlemen, and thus helped to bring new class lines into existence. Plausible as it may seem, this theory rested on a series of suppositions, none of which yet has any certain support. The implied social importance of free tenure, in the earlier period, is a matter of doubt, the status of franklins is obscure, and far too little is known of family histories to enable one to predicate that the spread of stock- and land-leasing either pauperized younger sons or in any way affected their choice of careers. The only concrete evidence adduced was the new use made in the fifteenth century of the various terms—French, Latin, and English—that indicated gentility. Whereas formerly they had applied indiscriminately to all grades of titled nobility as well as to knights and esquires and to others whose military rank might be simply that of *valet*, or yeoman, they now came to denote a specific gradation intermediate between that of esquire and yeoman. Record of the change dates from 1414, a

---

2. See W. Stubbs, *The Constitutional History of England* (5th ed., 1898), III, 568; and T. F. Tout, *Collected Papers*, II, 180.

3. Sir George Sitwell, "The English Gentleman," *Ancestor*, I (1902), 58–103.

statute of the previous year (1 H. V, c. 5) having required that in all original writs and appeals concerning personal actions and in all indictments in which process of outlawry lay, the defendant's place of residence and his "estate degree or mystery" be given; this tended to bring about similarly precise identification of individuals named in other types of records, including quasi-legal documents such as wills. The appearance of the new gradation, of gentlemen, may have been due in part to the appearance of the type of man of whom Sir George Sitwell was thinking, the younger son returned from the French wars "to idle about his brother's hall, or to be a hanger-on at the castle of some great peer." It may also have been due to current shifts in the hierarchical organization of great households or in military organization. Again, it may have been mainly a matter of shifts in language, of splitting the category of *valet*, one of the changes promoted by the growing trend toward the use of English in place of French. It is certain only, as will be shown, that its connotation was not restricted to the idea of birth.

Although Sir George Sitwell thus failed to substantiate his views on the medieval class structure, it was a service to focus attention upon the contemporary terminology of rank as a source of evidence as to social grouping. This gives a useful starting-point, for it allows one to identify groups in such definite terms as income and occupation.

The sumptuary legislation of 1363, for example, indicates the scale of wealth with which the leading nonbaronial gentry were at that time associated. The statute distinguished two groups of knights, those with lands worth from 200 to 400 marks a year and those with more; along with "esquiers & gentils" and "esquiers & gentils gentz" with incomes from land of £100 and £200, respectively. All these were officially granted permission to wear the most expensive qualities of woolen cloth, all but the £100 group were allowed the use of silk, and the wealthier knights were allowed cloth of gold and miniver.[4] There is a clue to the numbers of these people in the subsidy returns of 1436, when a little over a hundred and fifty knights and esquires were assessed as having incomes from land of £100 and up. The assessments of a few of the knights, running up to £400, exceeded those of a few of the

4. *Statutes of the Realm*, I, 381.

barons, which ran as low as £200 and £300.[5] From an economic point of view these leading knights, esquires, and "gentils" may be regarded simply as an extension of the baronage, which was directly rooted in the land system of the age.

But the great majority of the landowning esquires and gentlemen of the fifteenth century, who amounted in all to several thousand in number, had estates of very modest size. In the wealthy counties of Cambridgeshire, Huntingdonshire, and Lincolnshire there were esquires who in 1436 were assessed at only £5, £6, and £8. In Derbyshire, a poor county, in that year, seven esquires were assessed at £5, £13, £16, £16, £26, £27, and £60, five gentlemen at £5 each, one at £7, and one at £28; and there is reason to believe that there were other gentlemen living in the county at that date who escaped taxation, presumably because their rents came to less than £5, which had been set as the exemption line.[6]

Gentlemen who had no other source of income but these small properties must have lived as simply as many of the neighboring yeomen. An income of £5, Sir John Fortescue reckoned, adding up the fees and perquisites of a parker in the royal service, was "a feyre lyvyng for a yeoman."[7] In the richer counties a man could have considerably more than this and still keep the unpretentious name of yeoman. In a census of Hertfordshire landowners worth £10 a year and above, taken by the College of Heralds at some date between 1461 and 1485 and listing seventy odd names, ten are those of yeomen, some of them credited with as much as £20 of income.[8] If it was not wealth, then, that marked off the poorer

5. See H. L. Gray, "Incomes from Land in England in 1436," *EHR*, XLIX, 613–39. The scale of baronial incomes outlined by these figures is very similar to that set out in Professor S. Painter's figures from the thirteenth century (see *Studies in the History of the English Feudal Barony* [1943], p. 174).

6. See Gray's figures: 183 nonbaronial incomes of over £100, 750 between £40 and £100, 1,200 between £20 and £40, 1,600 between £10 and £20, and 3,390 between £5 and £9; these groupings include merchants, artisans, and yeomen as well as gentlemen (*op. cit.*, pp. 620–39). There may have been a few landless knights with high incomes from annuities; see grant of £100 to Guy of Warwick until his father should die or provide for him and of £200 to a newly created knight banneret (*Cal. P.R.*, *1354–58*, p. 314; *1345–48*, p. 473). Comparison of names printed by Gray with those listed in the special commissions of the peace for 1434 suggests that some gentlemen may have been exempt (see *ibid.*, *1429–36*, pp. 381–82, 385–87, 410–13).

7. *The Governance of England*, ed. C. Plummer (1885), p. 151.

8. Harl. MSS, 1546 (a copy, dated 1620).

country gentlemen and esquires from their nongentle neighbors, what was it that distinguished them?

There is no single formula that can cover all the possible answers to this question. In some cases there may have been a family history of misfortune and decline in the social scale, the claim to gentility resting on descent from men who had belonged among the greater gentry. At some point in the decline the claim would be disputed. A Yorkshire knight wrote to a cousin that he was "a poore gentilman borne thof he never werr taken heir bot for a yoman."[9] In other cases the story may have been just the opposite, the small property being the fruit of recent prosperity and the owner's status having risen with his income and expenditure. He could perhaps have assumed a coat-of-arms or obtained one from a herald.[10]

Again, the emphasis may have lain neither on birth nor on any particular form of display or expenditure but simply on an attitude of distaste for manual labor, which the yeoman would not yet have affected. There was some current conception of a gentlemanly way of living. A cadet in the Ardern family begged his elder brother for a settlement on the grounds that "he had no levyng to leve upon lyke a gentilman," and the widow of a gentleman of Bermondsey accused his executors of nonfulfilment of instructions "to bie for her . . . . a competent lyvelode to lif by as a gentilwoman."[11] These two presumably wished to live with a minimum of effort; the young Ardern complained that the world was "full casuell." But the small country gentleman, if he really tried to live on property worth as little as £5, could certainly not have enjoyed complete leisure. He could not have afforded to employ a bailiff to manage his affairs. He could, however, have drawn the line at manual labor; in this one respect his life may have resembled that of the great gentleman.[12]

Many of the gentlemen who owned these small properties may have had some other source of income. In the service of a lord a

9. *York Civic Records*, Yorkshire Archaeological Society ("Record Series," CIII [1941]), Part I, 169 (date, 1486). On birth and poverty see below, chap. vii, sec. 2.

10. *Ibid.*

11. *Cal. Proc. C.*, pp. lxxii–lxxiii; cf. case of knight sued by younger brother for annuity of 10 marks (E.C.P., 153/40).

12. E.C.P., 74/95.

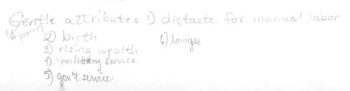

Gentle attributes 1) distaste for manual labor
(& poorer) 2) birth   6) lawyers
3) rising wealth
4) military service
5) gov't service

number of occupations were honorable enough to support gentle
rank without the backing of any landed property at all. The provisions made for graduating the poll tax of 1379 singled out for
special consideration the landless esquire who lived by household
service or by soldiering. The rate for esquires with £40 a year in
rents was 20s., for those "de meindre estat" it dropped to half a
mark; and for each esquire "nient possessionez," lacking land,
rent, and chattels, who was "en service ou ad este armez," it was
half this again, 3s. 4d. This last was the amount due from such
people as lesser merchants, graziers, "artificers q'ont la gaigne de
la terre," and leaseholders.[13]

Gentility was associated with the four military ranks of knight,
banneret, esquire, and man-at-arms; "jentilmen" spearmen were
among London reinforcements sent to Calais in 1448–50.[14] Early
fourteenth-century scales of pay ran from 6d. a day for mounted
archers and men-at-arms, the same rate as was paid to masons
serving with the army, to 1s. a day for esquires and 2s. for
knights.[15] Given the notorious irregularity of army pay, a gentleman who was dependent on the wage of a man-at-arms could at
this time have been little better off than an ordinary skilled craftsman. As to knights and esquires, they were in their turn more
heavily burdened by expenses in maintaining their equipment.
Their chief economic advantage lay in superior claims in the division of loot and the appropriation of ransom money from enemy
officers taken prisoner. During the victorious phases of the French
wars prudent officers, such as Sir Robert Knolles, were able to
bring fortunes home for investment. But conventional extrava-
gances often made away with a great deal of these gains as fast as
they were accumulated, leaving the landless soldier facing poverty
both in periods of unemployment and in old age. For the man of
knightly rank and influential friends there was some prospect of
rescue through royal favor. Edward III opened a home at Windsor
for twenty-four poor knights.[16] Sir Hugh de Lymme, a contempo-

13. *Rot. parl.*, III, 57–58.

14. Kingdon, II, 307.

15. The scale at Calais in 1346 (cited in J. W. Fortescue, *A History of the British Army*
[1899], I, 24–25). These rates remained traditional in the next century. See rates for indentured service in France in 1416 (H.M.C., *Hastings MSS*, I, 299).

16. Dugdale, VI, Part 3, 1353. Admission of an esquire of the king's household (*Cal.
P.R., 1476–85*, p. 270).

rary of Knolles, obtained a crown pension of £20 just in time, so he represented, to stave off ruin by his creditors; and pensions of up to £40 were sometimes granted at the time of promotion to knighthood.[17] Another welcome source of security was the practice of indenturing for military service with a nobleman. John of Gaunt contracted in this way with over a hundred esquires, guaranteeing them a fixed annual salary of 20 marks, with extra wages and expenses in time of war, on condition that each found his own man-at-arms as attendant.[18] Lesser noblemen possibly paid less but for long and faithful service might hold out hope of a small pension or of a legacy in the form of land. Failing security from any of these sources, the landless soldier out of employment was soon in difficult straits and, whether he considered himself of gentle rank or not, as a last resort might turn for subsistence to robbery. A parliamentary petition of 1376 complained of organized robbery by men "qi se sont par lour dit Gentils & Hommes d'armes ou Archers & sont devenuz a meschief par les Guerres," although it was suspected that some of them were merely craftsmen ("gentz de mestier"); and in 1458 a royal commission was appointed to deal with the problem of gentlemen robbers in the county of Hampshire.[19]

Senior posts in all important departments of estate and household service automatically carried with them titles of gentle rank. Estate administration, charge of the parks and warrens, maintenance of buildings, chamber and garden work, care of the family health, and the skills of the kitchen, pantry, buttery, confectionery, and laundry all had parallel ladders of promotion. John of Gaunt's butler, master-cook, and master-carpenter each had the rank of esquire, as did his steward, his seneschal, and underseneschal and some of his porters, constables, and wardens of fees. Next below the rank of esquire was that of serjeant,

17. *Ibid.*, *1343–45*, pp. 380, 382; *1345–48*, pp. 228, 274; *1350–54*, p. 536; *1354–58*, pp. 320, 465, 492, 580; *1364–67*, p. 312.

18. *John of Gaunt's Register*, I, xvii–xix, 9–26 (1379–83).

19. *Rot. parl.*, II, 332; *Cal. P.R.*, *1452–61*, pp. 411, 442–43. Records of the court of king's bench for this period contain numerous cases of gentlemen arrested for disturbance of the peace. Many of them gave London as their place of residence and were associated in their activities with people described as yeomen or craftsmen of London. Tale of a landless knight who "had geton moche good yn werres. And when he hadde all spend out . . . . ," on his fiancée's advice killed and robbed a merchant (*Myrk's Festiall*, E.E.T.S., extra ser., No. 96, p. 88).

traditional at court, or, in the fifteenth century, that of gentleman and gentlewoman. Sir John Fastolf's household at Caister consisted of nine pages, grooms, and maids; twelve other servants with the rank of *valet*, including his baker and his cook, his butler and his bailiff, a gardener and two lady's maids; and eight *generosi*, among whom were a supervising clerk, the family chaplain, the seneschal, and the laundress. At court the king's apothecary might rank as yeoman, serjeant, or esquire and his surgeon as either yeoman or esquire; heralds had rank as esquires.[20]

The salaries paid at court, 6*d.* a day for yeomen, 1*s.* for serjeants and esquires, augmented by miscellaneous fees and perquisites, probably enabled mere yeomen to live and dress as well as or better than many country gentlemen. Favored esquires with royal appointments might be granted life-annuities of up to about 40 marks a year, and two of Edward III's physicians were assigned regular salaries of £50 and £100. Service with noblemen was less remunerative but gave comfortable security. John of Gaunt's physician, for example, enjoyed a retaining fee of £10 a year for life, with 3*s.* a day in "gages" and two horses and a boy at his disposal while he was in actual attendance on the duke.[21]

Some of the skills that were traditionally associated with gentility in baronial households were in demand also in the service of municipalities. The dignity of the mayor of London, in his public official appearances, was upheld by the attendance of ceremonial guards to carry his sword and mace. These guards ranked as esquires or as gentlemen. Their money fee was only 40*s.* a year, but they were supplied with rich liveries and were entitled to take food and drink in the mayor's house, and each had a personal servant at his disposal. Another London office held by a gentleman or esquire was that of the Common Hunt. This official watched

20. *John of Gaunt's Register, passim;* H.M.C., *Eighth Report, Appendix,* p. 268 (Fastolf's steward's account roll, 1431–32); grant to the heralds of Christmas issue of livery "lyk to other squiers of the Kynges court . . . . in honneur of gentilesse . . . ." (1439), *Proceedings and Ordinances of the Privy Council of England,* V, 114. For a complete list of the royal household in 1331, counting 669 members, see T. F. Tout, *Chapters in the Administrative History of Medieval England,* IV (1928), 414, n. 1. For its formal regulations see *A Collection of Ordinances and Regulations for the Governance of the Royal Household,* ed. J. Nichols (1790).

21. *John of Gaunt's Register,* I, 214 (1372). *Cal. P. R., 1334–38,* p. 117; F. Devon, *Issues of the Exchequer* (1837), I, xl. So far as is known, the wealthiest of the royal surgeons was Thomas Morstede, esquire, in attendance on Henry IV, Henry V, and Henry VI, who had lands in London, Surrey, Essex, Suffolk, and Lincolnshire (*Cal. C.R., 1429–35,* p. 305; *1436–41,* pp. 199, 545; will, P.C.C., Rous, 12 [1450]).

over hunting rights and arrangements, having charge of the stables and kennels that were maintained for the common use of the citizens; he received a salary of £10 a year and issues of clothing.[22]

Administrative service under the crown, although in chancery appointments and other secretarial work long monopolized by clerks, was also honorable in nature. Important clerks had equivalent rank with lay gentlemen and esquires,[23] and the barons of the exchequer included knights.

The practice of conferring knighthood on judges brought the legal profession within the sphere of honorable recognition. By the latter part of the fifteenth century, attorneys were beginning to be recognized as gentlemen, a distinction of rank being drawn between qualified professional men and those who hung about the courts in less reputable capacities; this is evidenced by the charge of a defendant in chancery that the plaintiff was no gentleman but only "a supersedeas monger."[24]

Popular opinion may have exaggerated lawyers' earnings, as Sir John Fortescue, remarking that some of the merchants of his day surpassed all the judges in wealth, was in his turn inclined to exaggerate the takings of trade. Despite their fees and salaries, when judges took up knighthood, they usually represented that they could not support the dignity without the help of a pension, and many of the landed lawyers who lived in London appear to have had no more cash in hand at the time of drawing up their wills than gentlemen in modest circumstances living in the country.[25]

22. Earliest reference to a Common Hunt of gentle rank is in appointment of an esquire in 1392; his livery was to be the same as that of a serjeant of the chamber (L. Bk., *H*, fol. 276). Later appointments, L. Bk., *I*, fol. 194; *L*, fol. 19*b*; Journals, 2, fol. 8*b*; 4, fol. 214*b*; 6, fol. 118; 7, fols. 40*b*, 155*b*. Reference to sword-bearers and a serjeant-at-mace of the mayor, in the decade of the 1440's, as gentlemen or "squiere" (L. Bk., *K*, fols. 202, 230*b*, 231); entry of John Metford, "Jentylman & Swerdberer of the Cite of London" as a freeman of the grocers' company, 1469.

23. See description of Thomas Kent as "gentyllmane, alius .... clericus consilii domini regis" (*Political Poems and Songs*, ed. T. Wright [R.S., II (1861), lvii, *n.*]); and knighthood, with annuity of £50, to John de Sordich, formerly a clerk, holding office of the chirography in the common bench (*Cal. P.R., 1343–45*, p. 458). Occurrence of knights among lay wardrobe officials (T. F. Tout, "The Chief Officers of the King's Wardrobe to 1399," *EHR*, XXIV, 498).

24. "John of Boteler of London pretendyng hym selfe Gentilman bot in dede he is a supersedeas monger," charged with forging an obligation (E.C.P., 46/470).

25. J. W. Fortescue, *De laudibus legum Anglie*, ed. S. B. Chrimes (1942), p. 130. Judges' pensions of £20, £40, 100 marks (*Cal. P.R., 1343–45*, p. 464; *1354–58*, p. 8; *1358–61*, p. 163; B. Wilkinson, *The Chancery under Edward III* [1929], p. 115).

Although rents, military pay, and salaries and fees received for household and professional services were the chief and regular source of income of the several types of medieval gentry, these were sometimes supplemented by poaching on the merchant's ground. Far from regarding this with any disdain, gentlemen of all types seem to have been alert for opportunities to make money by trade, both as silent partners with merchants and by active wholesale dealing on their own account. In the great staple-commodity–producing regions these practices were found from the higher nobility and the wealthy landed gentry downward. Lords with East Anglian estates obtained government licenses in the fifteenth century to export wool directly, and others shipped cloth with merchant adventurers of London. Sir John Fastolf, one of the richest knights of his time, having in 1436 an income of £600 from his estates in Norfolk and elsewhere, and Lord Cornwall, a Norfolk baron, both took part in the export of barley and malt. Sir Henry Brounflete, of Yorkshire, who became Lord Vescy, owned merchant ships and sought membership in the grocers' company in London. The west of England franklin in a version of "The Childe of Bristowe" who was "a grete tenement man," counting his wealth in horses and cattle, jewels and other treasure, was represented as having also "many a shyp." In Dorset the Russells and other families turned indifferently to trade, political appointments, and the nursing of their estates, and it is unlikely that the gentry of that county stood entirely aside from the local smuggling of wool. From Lincolnshire there comes the story of a late-fifteenth-century dispute between two gentlemen, one of whom intrusted the other with £10 and a thousand "saltfisshes" to be used in trade at Bordeaux:

Robert Langton of Lincoln Gentilman . . . . oftymes juparded unto dyvers partes beyond the see wt merchaundises and so contynually used to make many viages there came on ffraunces Meryng of Lincoln Gentilman and oftymes entretyd Robert Langton to take and Jupard both merchaundises and money of his into suche places as he used beyond the See sayng to hym to doo his best likyng therwith and if it proved well that then Robert Langton shuld after consciens somewhat restore hym and if not that the seid ffraunces shuld byde thextremyte of the losse thereof. . . . .

There are many records of gentry of the home counties and elsewhere trading in London, sometimes in partnership with citizens, shipping wool, buying raw silk; sometimes in what may have been

stray deals that came their way, as in trading "good and mer-
chaundable" scythes for bowstaves, cloth for alum, or buying and
selling wine; sometimes lending money, in one instance, in the form
of a small loan, partly in the form of dye, in another instance
making a large loan, in partnership with a merchant, to a priory.
Gentlemen also competed with merchants in the victualing of the
army and in construction contracts for the government and took
part in the acquisition of mineral rights. When the leasing of land
became profitable, they became "fermours." Some made their
daughters learn to support themselves. The silkwomen stated in
1455 that there were "many Gentilwymmen" in their industry,
and there is record of the apprenticeship of country gentlemen's
daughters in this and in other London trades.[26]

The gentleman's attitude to wholesale trade differed from the
merchant's merely as it was a secondary or intermittent interest.
The only discernible prejudice concerned retail trade. Readers of
the Paston letters will recall the disgust with which the family
learned of Margery Paston's engagement to their bailiff, Richard
Calle, who apparently managed a chandler's shop as a side line.
Even if his mother and his elder brother should consent to the
marriage, wrote John Paston, Calle "should never have my good
will for to make my sister to sell candle and mustard in Framling-

26. I. Haward, "Economic Aspects of the Wars of the Roses in East Anglia," *EHR*,
XLI (1926), 174. R. H. Mason, *History of Norfolk*, I (1882), 93. Brounflete was at first
exempt from London taxation on the grounds "quod non est communis mercator," but he
was later adjudged liable (Journals, 3, fol. 38b). *Remains of Early Popular Poetry of England*, ed. W. C. Hazlitt (1864), p. 132. G. Scott Thomson, *Two Centuries of Family History*
(1930), chap. ii, "Dorset Merchants and Squires." E.C.P., 211/62, 212/12, 9/324, 43/50,
45/381, 59/69, 61/190, 64/660, 66/373, 76/68, 157/27, 241/29. *Cal. P.R., 1422–29*, p. 457.
Case of an official in the Tower trading in Tower ward (*Cal. L. Bk.*, G, pp. 308–9). Case of
John Beauchamp, esquire of the king's chamber, paying £20 to a fishmonger, in the guise
of apprenticeship dues, obviously for the right to trade (Drapers' Deeds, A VI, 107).
For indications of Edmund Dudley's interest in the spice and cloth trades see D. M. Brodie,
"Edmund Dudley, Minister of Henry VII," *Transactions of the Royal Historical Society*,
4th ser., XV, 143. Case of an esquire licensed to trade in Bristol (1453), *Great Red Book of
Bristol* ("Bristol Record Society Publications"), IV, 188. Numerous grants of protection
for victualing on the patent rolls. For other forms of enterprise see *Hist. Parl. B.*, pp. 22,
32–33, 94, 104, 132, 140, 391, 583, 649, 687, 735. Indication of a Gloucestershire squire's
interest in mining is a crest on his brass (date, 1443), representing a miner, candle in mouth,
bag for ore on his back, pick in hand (Mill Stephenson, p. 153). On gentlewomen in silk
trade and apprenticeships see *Rot. parl.*, V, 325, 506; *Cal. P. & M. Rolls*, IV, 12; W. Blyth,
Historical Notices and Records of the Village and Parish of Fincham in the County of Norfolk
(1863), pp. 113–14. On large investments *ad mercandizandum* at 5 per cent by Sir John
Fastolf see K. B. McFarlane, "Loans to the Lancastrian Kings: The Problem of Induce-
ment," *Cambridge Historical Journal*, IX, 62. Many more instances could be given, but
there is no means of making a statistical check of their significance.

ham." Yet this very episode should guard one against assuming that the prejudice was equally strong among the lesser gentry. As an efficient bailiff, who had come to the family recommended by no less a patron than the duke of Suffolk, Calle may well have felt that his employment entitled him to rank as a gentleman.[27]

In short, gentle rank was not conceived in such a way as to be tied to any fixed economic criteria, not even to the possession of land. But was there, in the middle ages, any single generalized conception of it? The question reaches beyond the scope of this book. Let it suffice to suggest that whatever tradition may have been attached to the notion of being a gentleman, it must at some point of time have acquired a good many different overtones in these different contexts of activity, wealth, and power. With the barons and the great nonbaronial landed families gentility was a matter of the secure enjoyment of power and influence and of the attributes that flowed therefrom; these people were associated with the stability of the land itself. With the gentlemen in their service and in the royal service gentility could be derived solely from the function exercised on the lord's behalf. It could be bestowed simply by promotion—a chronicler refers to a servant whom the queen "hadde made bothe yeman and gentylman"—and, according to legal opinion of 1448 and 1450, could be lost on dismissal from office.[28] Rank was bestowed not for skill or knowledge in its own right but for making it of use to the lord, for filling positions of responsibility. The gentleman servant was one who contributed in some special way to the lord's power. Socially, he was identified with the lord's following. Gentility, in his case, was derivative, a small reflection of his lord's status; he was literally a satellite of the great man.

The case was different, again, with the landed gentleman of moderate or small means. Behind the idea of his gentility there may have been a long tradition of respect for mingled civil and military reasons. He could provide himself with better arms than his poorer neighbor and could free himself from manual labor. He might be able to imitate, on a small scale, the hospitality and household customs of the great. His relative ease could perhaps

27. *The Paston Letters*, ed. J. Gairdner (1910 reprint), Introd., p. 76, and Vol. II, Letter 607 (1469).

28. *Collections of a London Citizen*, p. 209 (1460); Sir John Doderidge, *The Magazine of Honour* (1642), pp. 145–46.

have been regarded as a personal achievement. In this light the attitude toward him would have merged into the feeling with which the gentility of professional men was regarded. With the honoring of achievement and of skill and knowledge among laymen, apart from their service to king or nobles, new types of gentlemen were to emerge and new overtones in the conception of gentility. Recognition of the professional man was still, in the fifteenth century, rather grudging. Judges were honored with knighthood partly because they personified the king's justice, and physicians and surgeons were so honored only if they won the king's favor in his service. Sir John Fortescue's observation that there was scarcely any learned lawyer in his time who was not a gentleman "by birth or by fortune" shows an ambiguous attitude toward the achievement of learning for its own sake, and a reference to a certain surgeon as "calling him self Gentilman" shows the insecure status of that profession.[29]

Frequently all these conceptions of gentility became mixed, being represented in the same man. A son of a landed gentleman who took to service or the law and inherited some land united the several traditions. Chivalric literature, casting a certain glamour over the condition of being born a gentleman's son, helped both to clarify the situation and to subordinate the lesser types of gentility to the stable and courtly culture of the great.

Poets' and chroniclers' allusions to the relative rating of individual gentlemen indicate that this rested on a nice balancing of considerations of birth, lands, and type of service. Enjoyed in combination, wealth and birth outranked all else. When they occurred separately, the rating depended on circumstances; now the *nouveau riche* would be honored more, and now the poor man of good birth. Grades of service were identified by generally recognized differences in the quality of livery issued and also by distinctions within the household, concerning precedence, diet, and bedding. Menial household offices were less honorable than service in a lord's retinue. Edward IV's household bodyguard, of forty esquires, was specially picked from leading county families, "to be chosen men of theyre possession, worship and wisdom . . . . from sundry sheres"; yet in the popular story of the squire who loved the daughter of the king of Hungary, the hero, who "was

29. *De laudibus legum Anglie*, ed. Chrimes, chap. xlix; E.C.P., 64/626.

not ryche of gold and fe" but was "a gentylman borne for sothe" and served the king in the highly responsible office of marshal of his hall, was still typed as "a squyer of lowe degre."[30]

2. CULTURAL AFFINITIES BETWEEN MERCHANTS AND GENTLEMEN

Merchants shared many customs with gentlepeople of similar means. The material setting of domestic life was very much the same. Another bond was interest in education. Merchants formed the only other group that was impelled to take an interest in secular education and could afford to indulge it in the same way as gentlemen could. It is true that many of the latter had far more formal education than the average London merchant, notably the lawyers and those wealthy men's sons who rounded off their years in grammar school by residence at a university or in one of the inns of court. On the other hand, successful merchants were probably at least as cognizant of law as the average gentleman of other types and may sometimes have been better informed as to the current of political events. In any case, they need not have been at a disadvantage, in ordinary social intercourse, for lack of book learning or for incompetence in reading Latin. An esquire who was accused in London, in 1378, of forging a bond, defended himself with the plea that he was illiterate, meaning that he could not read Latin; although it was not accepted, the plea was presumably a plausible one. It might have been heard in more respectable circles also, for a few years later Chief Justice Cavendish had his will drawn up in French rather than in Latin, in order, as he explained, that his friends should understand it more readily.[31]

Caxton looked to his own class for patrons and customers in the book trade, as well as to noblemen and gentlemen. Slight as is the evidence of intellectual stirring among merchants, they had long formed an important proportion of the country's small lay book-owning public. The only lay groups that may be suspected of any

30. *A Collection of Ordinances and Regulations for the Governance of the Royal Household,* p. 45; *The Squyr of Lowe Degre,* ed. W. E. Mead (1904), pp. 19–20. Case of identification of a man as "habitum praeferens alicujus armigeri generosi," *Gesta abbatium monasterii Sancti Albani,* II, 176 (1308–26). See Lydgate's characterization of a man of high rank in *Political, Religious, and Love Poems,* ed. J. Furnivall (E.E.T.S., original ser., No. 15, p. 27):

> "And for he was / a man of high degre
> Born of good blood / and notable in substaunce."

31. *Cal. L. Bk., H,* p. 67; F. Bickley, *The Cavendish Family* (1911), p. 5.

marked attachment to books were the professional men—the doctors, lawyers, and wealthy men's secretaries—and their interests could be rather narrow. Some lawyers had no books that they valued sufficiently to bequeath except the few treatises and compilations that made up their professional library. Sir Thomas Urswyck, chief baron of the exchequer and recorder of London, who died in 1479, made no book bequests at all, and the inventory of his household at Dagenham lists only six volumes, kept in the chapel. John Carpenter, town clerk of London, who died in 1442, was quite exceptional in leaving over twenty-six books among his friends, and others to the Guildhall library. Carpenter's collection was larger than that of one of the wealthiest knights of the century, Sir John Fastolf, who left only nineteen books and in all his great house at Caister had no better place to store them than in the "Stewehous," or bathroom.[32]

Some gentlemen's reading took them by preference into the world of romance and poetry, a world that lay open also to the women in their families. Sir Bartholomew Bacon, dying in 1389, left his book called *Romaunc* to his wife for life, then to be sold for his soul; and Sir Thomas Cumberworth in the next century bequeathed his only nondevotional book, the "talys of cantyrbury," to a niece. Chaucer, Mandeville, and Froissart lay in Urswyck's chapel, along with a lawbook and two devotional works. Three "Englysshe bokys," the *Canterbury Tales* again, a "troyles," and a version of *De regimine principum* were found among household goods confiscated from Sir Thomas Charlton. A generation earlier, in 1443, a Norfolk squire had bequeathed three books—a copy of Hoccleve, a book of statutes, and "a little quire of paper with the Kings of England versified." Four romances were the only books among goods left by Sir James de Audeleye in his Bristol house in 1352. These slender finds hardly entitle one to think of gentlemen as very greatly excited by imaginative literature. Even in the fifteenth century, when appreciation of Chaucer was growing, an immoderate literary enthusiasm stood out as a little peculiar, as in the figure of William of Worcester, Sir John Fastolf's secretary, of whom a friend wrote that he was "as glad and as feyn of a good

---

32. E, 154/2/2; T. Brewer, *Memoir of the Life and Times of John Carpenter* (1856), pp. 121–44; H.M.C., *8th Report, Appendix*, p. 268 (date, *ca.* 1456); and *Paston Letters*, ed. Gairdner, I, 475–90.

boke of Frensh or of poetre as my Mastr Fastolf wold be to pur-
chace a faire manoir." Fastolf's small collection was more historical than poetic, with six histories, including a Livy and a
Caesar, only one French poem, a translation of the ancient treatise
on the art of war by Vegetius, and only two romances. Nicholas
Hotot, a gentleman of an old London family, in 1404 was bequeathing history and devotional works but no romance, and
Carpenter's tastes ran almost entirely to moral and devotional or
technical works; he had a copy of the *Philobiblon* but only one
history and bequeathed no romances.[33]

The interpenetration of culture between merchant class and
gentry was further expressed in the adoption, by the older and the
wealthier families in each, of armorial bearings; these served a
double purpose in identifying families and individuals and in asserting a claim to status. The commercial community had a comparable symbolic code of its own in the form of trade-marks, which
identified merchandise and personal property and could also, in
the case of a well-known business, acquire a secondary connotation
of status. All through Europe, however, the greater merchants
sought to impress their importance on the noncommercial world
and, perhaps, to heighten their standing in their own communities
by borrowing the symbolic code that was used by noblemen and
gentlemen, the language of heraldry.

English writers have often stated that the medieval merchant
was not allowed to bear arms, but there is no medieval authority
for this view.[34] In London it was customary for aldermen to bear
arms in the same manner as any military commander of high rank,
as in "coat-of-"

33. *Norfolk Archaeology*, IV, 320–21, 331–32; *Lincoln Diocese Documents*, E.E.T.S.,
original ser., No. 149, pp. 48–49; W.A.M., 6630; *Cal. Inq. Misc.*, III, 37, No. 109; *Paston
Letters*, ed. Gairdner, I, 431; Hotot's will, Archdeaconry, London, fol. 127. William of
Worcester became the historian of Bristol.

34. For the view that early merchants were forbidden to bear arms see, among others,
W. Newton, *A Display of Heraldry* (1846), p. 395; H. W. Macklin, *Monumental Brasses*
(3d ed., 1913), p. 107; W. E. Gawthorp, *The Brasses of Our Homeland Churches* (1923), p.
53. This idea may well have arisen from the ambiguity of Francis Thynne's account of the
duties of a king herald: "He shall prohibit any merchant or other to put their names marks
or devises in escutcheons or shields; which belong and only appertain to gentlemen bearing
arms, and to none other" (*A Discourse of the Duty and Office of an Herald of Arms* [1605],
printed in *A Collection of Curious Discourses Written by Eminent Antiquaries*, ed. T. Hearne
[1775], p. 153). There is no evidence that heralds had ever used their authority to challenge
the validity of arms that conformed to the conventions of heraldic art. On London visi-
tations of the sixteenth century see A. R. Wagner, *Heralds and Heraldry in the Middle
Ages* (1939), pp. 118–19, 139–46.

and there is no record that their right to do so was ever challenged or ridiculed. Carpenter believed it to be an ancient tradition that aldermen should be buried with baronial honors, having their armor and their coats-of-arms displayed at the funeral by men on horseback; the custom had fallen into abeyance by his time, but as late as 1386 city regulations had required that in assembling the general watch every alderman should lead the citizens of his ward with his pennon of arms flying.[35] The heralds went to great pains in keeping copies of the coats borne by London city officials. Tudor and seventeenth-century compilations ascribe arms to about half the aldermen and sheriffs of the fourteenth century and to all but two of the fifteenth-century aldermen. If it stood alone, this testimony would be unconvincing, but its general validity is corroborated from earlier sources. In twelve of the fourteenth-century cases the men's monuments or surviving impressions of their seals supply an exact confirmation of the heralds' record, and in several more there is similar evidence that the arms were at least in the family, near relatives having used them on seals. In a few instances the heralds were in error as to the charges or their arrangement; the man whose name they gave had sealed with a different escutcheon. In addition, seals and monuments of this century depict twenty other aldermanic coats that are not represented in the books of arms. For the fifteenth-century aldermen there is archeological confirmation either of the fact that the man bore arms or of the exact charges as given in the books, in at least seven cases, and in a few others there is some contemporary allusion to their possession of arms.[36]

But it was not necessary to be an alderman in order to possess a coat-of-arms. Several of the fourteenth-century aldermen had been making use of armorial escutcheons on seals long before they were elected,[37] and impressions of nearly eighty other shields of

35. *Lib. Alb.*, I, 33; *Cal. L. Bk.*, *H*, p. 286.

36. Stowe MSS, 860; Harl. MSS, 1349, 1464; 1464 Plut. LVII E (compiled in 1634). Errors include the attribution to Henry Darcy of arms actually used by Johanna, daughter of Hugh de Wygorn, skinner, and wife of John de Thunderle, merchant (D. & C. St. Paul's, Deeds, A, 6/77, 81). The record is erroneous also in the cases of Picard, Pike, and Stable and doubtful in the case of Cavendish. See Appen. A on these and also on arms of Barton, Boleyn, Chichele, Crosby, Framlingham, Gardener, Hatherley, Knolles, Lambard, Melreth, Norton—aldermen of the fifteenth century.

37. Cornwaleys, Exton, Adam Fraunceis, Secheford, Thorpe, Tornegold, Vanner, Weld, Appen. A.

arms have been found from the seals of London merchants who never arrived at aldermanic rank. The fifteenth-century record is not so full, but over a dozen merchant citizens of nonaldermanic rank referred in their wills to some form of armorial display, and at least as many more left imprints of armorial seals that still survive in London collections of deeds. On the whole there can be little doubt that the use of arms was fairly widespread among London merchants in both centuries, and provincial deeds and monuments indicate, in the same way, that the custom was also common among the greater provincial merchants.

Merchants must have acquired their arms by one or other of the same means as were open to gentlemen. One means was by inheritance. Some of the armorial merchants in London may have inherited their arms from ancestors of gentle rank; in view, however, of the large proportion of London families that were not of gentle origin, it is unlikely that this was the rule. Another means was by grant from the king. This would have been a rare honor, in reward for unusual services. According to his epitaph, Sir William Walworth was so honored, receiving a coat-of-arms when he was knighted for his services in the Wat Tyler crisis. Yet Walworth's arms had been engraved on his seal at least four years before the date of his knighthood. If he received a royal grant of arms on this occasion, it would have been merely in the nature of a special authorization, like a kind of blessing, investing his coat with a higher status value.[38] A third way of acquiring arms was to purchase an official patent from a herald, whose expert knowledge would assure one of correct and unique blazoning. Only one such grant to a London merchant has been found, a copy of a patent made out by Clarenceux king-of-arms to Nicholas Mattock, a fifteenth-century mercer. It describes him not as a citizen or a merchant but as a resident of Hitchin, in Hertfordshire, where he retired and was buried.[39] Since it included the grant of a helm and crest surmounting the coat-of-arms, it is possible that Mattock already possessed the latter and had sought a patent only for the sake of these extra embellishments; for there was a fourth way

38. On the rarity of royal grants of arms in England see Wagner, *op. cit.*, p. 67.

39. Harl. MSS, 1507, fol. 6, printed in Sir James Lawrence, *On the Nobility of the British Gentry* (1824), pp. 8–9; on Mattock see *Hist. Parl. B.*, p. 581; Gough, II, Part 3, 378.

of acquiring arms—simply by assuming them.[40] Many merchants who had no family arms may have saved the herald's fee, relying on a painter or a seal-cutter to devise a coat of conventional design.

The Londoners were fond of choosing the same predatory creatures for their emblems as had traditionally appealed to noble families as symbols of power. Pultney and Stodey bore leopards' heads; Andrew Aubrey and his son, four griffins' heads; Walter Sibile, alderman and stockfishmonger, "a chevron between three eagles displayed"; and John Northampton's shield carried the fantastic device of a crowned leopard with two seated bodies, joining at the neck.[41] In contrast with these were religious symbols. William de Elsyng, founder of Elsyng Spital for the blind, abjured family pride by selecting a shield of the Passion, like an ecclesiastic. Catherine wheels appear on the fishmonger's shield used in 1336, encircled on his seal with the invocation, "Katerina Beata ora pro me." John Churchman, grocer, had pilgrim's scallop shells at the base of his shield, perhaps added after his journey to Rome. The most popular of religious symbols, both among merchants and among gentlemen, was the fish, usually in the form of dolphin or pike. About three out of every four fishmongers, when they adopted arms, took this opportunity of combining pious reference to the name of Christ with honor to their company. Fish lent themselves to blazoning in simple but picturesque fashion. One fishmonger's shield bore two pike, saltire-wise; this was an unusual arrangement that drew attention to the owner's name, Pyke. Another member of the company signified his ambition by the device of a lion passant above a fish swimming. The only exclusively commercial emblems that merchants attempted to fit into conventional heraldry were the clove, found occasionally in the arms of grocers and mercers, in allusion to their spice trade, and the goblet or the buckle, standing for the craft of the goldsmith. Both blended easily with noncommercial devices, cloves as background on the field, the goldsmith's handiwork as balancing charges. An odd juxtaposition of the symbols of trade and feudal power appears

40. On this point see below, p. 307.

41. Appen. A; Northampton's arms are illustrated in Harl. MSS, 2169, reproduced in *Ancestor*, IX, 168. For note on two somewhat similar examples see *Archaeological Journal*, XV (1858), 289.

on the armorial seal of an early fourteenth-century goldsmith; divided by a fess, the shield shows the figure of a lion rampant cut off in the middle to make room for two buckles and a covered goblet.[42]

The merchants' arms that have been referred to up to this point all conformed to the conventions that had been developed in the thirteenth century concerning symmetrical division of the field and placing of the charges. To these must be added a few that were slightly unconventional, using stars and crescents in irregular arrangement on an undivided field, sometimes with a bird or a boar's head; again, the owner's initials might form the charges. Such variants were just as common in gentlemen's arms as in merchants', and there is no reason to suppose that they were not regarded as properly armorial.[43]

There were other deviations, however, that were not accepted as armorial but turned the whole shield into a mere trade-mark. A specimen is sketched in one of the documents connected with the indictment of a London mercer for complicity with John Northampton. Fearful lest his merchandise abroad should be confiscated, he was said to have ordered his factor to stamp it with a new mark; this was a shield incorrectly divided, the upper half cut vertically by a single line, with a ring on either side of it.[44] An illustrated heraldic treatise compiled in 1454 or 1455 gives three more examples, two of blank shields with asymmetrical divisions and one of an ordinary merchant's mark set on an undivided shield; all are laconically condemned as "non armys."[45] Examples similar to these can be found in abundance among impressions of fourteenth-century London seals, usually with a cross or the streamered head of the staff that was associated with the sacred lamb extending above the shield. One series of deeds shows the evolution of a crude mark of this kind into armorial form. Richard de Lambeth, fishmonger, sealed alternately with his commercial mark, a sacred lamb and banner, in the base of a shield, and with the banner alone set upright in the center of the shield, flanked by two pike; his son

42. Elsyng, *B.M. Cat. Seals*, 9452, D. & C. St. Paul's, Deeds, A/9/422, 488; Anc. Deeds, B 4290; *B.M. Cat. Seals*, 11, 369; Pyke, Anc. Deeds, DS 55; Long, goldsmith, D. & C. St. Paul's Deeds, A/10. 1011.

43. For examples see W. H. B. Bird, "Seals and Arms," *Ancestor*, X (1904), 84.

44. C. Misc., 68/12/357.   45. Harl. MSS, fols. 110, 119*b*, 139*b*.

retained the lamb and banner and contrived to use it as a charge in the base of a shield of arms properly divided by a chevron and surmounted by the honorable distinction of helm and crest.[46]

On seals, the unorthodox, trade-marked shield was relatively more common in the fifteenth century than earlier. This was probably because it was simple to cut, the design consisting chiefly of narrow, straight lines, for the art of seal-engraving was noticeably on the decline. Whereas a great many London citizens had formerly possessed very beautiful seals, the detail of armorial charges or of religious pictures and surrounding tracery being cut with extreme delicacy, little survived but coarser types of work such as monograms and single initials or figures and heads which were obviously copied, rather clumsily, from antique signet gems.[47] The fact that he sealed with a trade-mark on a shield therefore did not mean that a merchant had no coat-of-arms; often a man had two shields displayed about his house, one with his trade-mark and one with his arms.

Simple pictorial seals remained popular both in gentle and in merchant families, representing one of the constituent charges of the owner's coat-of-arms or one of the predatory animals of heraldry, whether or not this figured on the owner's arms, or part of a deer-hunting scene. A sleeping lion, curled up in a tree or under a bush, was a favorite choice, as in the seal of a goldsmith's widow, in 1331, with the militant motto, "Wake me no man." More original examples of the predatory theme are a curious eagle on a mercer's seal in 1382, the body drawn as transparent, showing some small animal in its maw, and the picture of a crested kingfisher with a pike in its beak, on a draper's seal of 1460. There were a few allusions to trade; vintners sometimes used a wine tun, one fishmonger's wife sealed with the head of a woman with a pike leaping over her, and another, Hugh Fastolf's widow, had ·the device of a lobster.[48]

The names by which houses were known in London reveal no distinction between those occupied or owned by gentlemen or

---

46. Drapers' Deeds, A VIII, 195, 258, 259 (dates, 1337–52).

47. Bird (*op. cit.*, pp. 83–85) makes some reference to the influence of antique gems on signet-ring design, though only with reference to arms.

48. H.M.C., *20th Report, Hastings MSS*, I, 213; Simon de Reynham, W.A.M., 13998; Harl. Ch., 79/A4; Drapers' Deeds, A VI, 225; V, 104; Anc. Deeds, C 472.

merchants or other citizens. Indeed, few houses were generally known by a name except the great "places," with courtyards, taverns, and breweries, to which there was public resort, or those that had some peculiarity attracting notice. The great houses were named more often from their appearance, as "La rouge sale," the "Copped Hall," "Ivy Hall," or after their original owner, than from any heraldic emblem that might be on display. Taverns and breweries were known from their pictorial signs, which bore any striking emblem that a painter could produce, heraldic or otherwise, horses, elephants, ships, and woolsacks or a picture, presumably intended to be humorous, of a Scot or a Welshman; the sign might tally with the owner's arms, as in the case of one tavern under the sign of the goat, but there was no necessary correspondence of the kind.

Outside the merchant class, citizens were in general too poor or too closely identified with their trade to develop many of the traits of culture that were associated with gentle rank. Those who required a seal for business purposes were often content with one of round or oval shape depicting the tools or material of their craft, a knife for a barber, an ax for a carpenter, cauldrons for a potter, the head of an ox for a tanner. Some had shield-shaped seals but by preference either filled them with simple graphic trademarks or else contrived a coat-of-arms from pictorial devices of their trade: a bowyer would present a crossbow as his arms, a barber his tools, a mason his compasses placed like a chevron. There is no reason to suppose that the heralds would have challenged these as not armorial, for one of the shields blazoned in the treatise of 1454, bearing two T squares, crossed, was obviously a mason's.[49] A few, however, broke into the more aristocratic armorial tradition, one glover bearing a lion's mask, a brazier a lion rampant, a brewer two dragons; and well-to-do cordwainers, chandlers, and others would follow the fashion of placing the predatory and fantastic creatures of conservative heraldry—the lion, the eagle, the griffin—on seals of other shapes. Moreover, when they had the means to do so, citizens of these lesser companies practiced many of the same forms of conspicuous consumption as

49. Harl. MSS, 2259, fol. 164b. Two good examples of masons' arms in D. & C. St. Paul's, Deeds, A/6/1, 5, t. Edward III; two potters' seals of 1308 in W.A.M., 28050. Most of the other examples referred to are from the Drapers' Deeds or from the Bridge House Deeds.

were common to merchants and gentry; they employed domestic servants, treasured silverware, and on gala occasions appeared, with their wives, in brightly colored gowns adorned with fur and jewels.

3. SOCIAL RELATIONS BETWEEN MERCHANTS AND GENTLEMEN

London merchants met almost every type of gentleman in business or in other formal relationships. Contemporary documents show their names linked with those of gentlemen in buying and selling, borrowing and lending, standing as surety for each other in bonds, associated with deeds of gift, in obtaining the keeping of lands that were in the king's hands, and as feoffees of lands. Even a confirmed rustic like John Throkmorton, who set down in his will that he had spent all the days of his life in his "Countree," meaning his native county of Worcestershire, if he had large amounts of produce for sale, might be in touch with Londoners, for wool merchants would ride out into the country to take personal charge of valuable consignments.[50] Allegations that embroider the facts with controversial detail are drawn out at interminable length in the legal records of the time. Late fifteenth century chancery proceedings disclose the picture of a London gentleman offering to act as a broker in the land market and taking advantage of his position to buy up a fishmonger's property in Kent that lay conveniently near an estate of his own; in another case a grocer claimed to have lent a large sum of money and household goods to a gentleman, "for the specyall acqueyntaunce" that he and his wife had with the gentleman's wife, the daughter of a Middlesex knight, with no repayment but "a litell tymber," the gentleman's widow hotly denying that there had been any such transaction.[51]

Gentlemen of high connections were much sought after. Influential government officials, both noblemen and others, were frequent guests at company banquets and were invited to join merchant fraternities. The mercers took in over thirty members of gentle rank between the 1430's and the end of the century, including one of the Mortons, who was admitted free, on account of his

50. Throkmorton's will (P.C.C., Luffenham, 31); case of a mercer's riding into Oxfordshire for eight sacks of wool (E.C.P., 123/9).

51. E.C.P., 117/27, 191/53.

being a kinsman of the great bishop of Ely; with the same eye to influence, the goldsmiths admitted another gentleman because he was "a man of substance and in great favour with lords." The popular religious fraternities of the tailors and skinners, which enjoyed the patronage of the royal family, were able to attract scores of gentleman members. Incomplete records of the fifteenth century give the names of nearly two hundred who joined the fraternity of St. John the Baptist; some of these were high officials of the wardrobe or of the exchequer; some were noblemen's servants, such as the earl of Huntingdon's receiver, who may have had to spend a good deal of time in London on business; some were lawyers and men of fashion, such as Sir John Paston; some were great county knights, such as Paston's patron, Sir John Fastolf; and some were obscure provincial gentlemen described as of Exeter, Reigate, Gloucester, Shropshire, and other counties.[52]

Merchants were in a position to do a number of favors for gentlemen of their acquaintance. Their services to men who were rich and powerful enough to stand to them in the relation of patron have been illustrated already from the relations between the Cely family and Sir John Weston, head of the order of the Knights of St. John. Another type of favor was to give a young man sponsored by the patron some experience in trade, in order to discover whether he was suited for it; a grocer who did this to please the king's treasurer found that the young protégé took advantage of an expedition to Bruges to borrow money there illegally, in his name.[53] Gentlemen in need might feel it worth while to ingratiate themselves with influential citizens in the hope of appointment to one of the salaried and fee-taking offices that were under the city government or in the gift of a merchant company. Richard Norman bequeathed £40 in plate to his company, the drapers, on the condition that a squire friend of his be given a life appointment to the keepership of Blackwell Hall, and it was a matter of vexation among the mercers that members would "labour" with lords to indorse candidates for the offices connected

52. Mercers' Lists of Freemen, Wardens' Accounts; Drapers' Wardens Accounts; Merchant Tailors' Lists of Freemen; Skinners' List of Founders, Book of the Fraternity of Our Lady's Assumption; Grocers' Register of Freemen and Apprentices. Prideaux, I, 27. Fastolf was also a member of the company of St. George, in Norwich (Blomefield, IV, 349–50).

53. *Cal. P. & M. Rolls*, I, 217.

with weighing and measuring that were in their gift.[54] For lawyers, acquaintance among citizens might lead to profitable business in the city courts. A more general reason for seeking acquaintance was the circumstance that to hold secure title to London property it was desirable to take out citizenship, and for this it was necessary to have either strong noble patronage or citizen sponsorship.

Once he had taken out citizenship, a man was under the jurisdiction of the mayor and aldermen; the fact that he was a gentleman gave him no right to call for preferential treatment. This was made very clear in the case of Master Peter Peckham, a prominent lawyer of hasty temper. Summoned before the court of aldermen to account for having spoken disrespectfully to one of its members, he refused to appear and signified his intention of resigning from the freedom of the city by tearing up his certificate of citizenship. Neither action helped him at all; his attempt to resign his citizenship was interpreted as subversive of the municipal government, and in punishment for his disrespect he was imprisoned in Newgate and fined 100 marks, a sum that was reduced, on the mediation of the chancellor of England, but remained at the substantial figure of £20.[55]

Although firm in the defense of its own disciplinary powers, for reasons of expediency the city government had to be sensitive to all causes of offense on the part of private citizens against courtiers or other gentlemen of importance. A mayoral decree of the year 1478, cautioning citizens "not to provoke any affray" upon members of the king's household or of any lord's household, was relayed among the citizens by their company wardens. Companies had to undertake that none of their members create offense by taking "any gentilman or other comyng by the way by the sleve goun or otherwise"; even the mercers entered the caution in their court minutes. Some years later the merchant tailors were concerned that "a grete Cryme & defamation" was attached to their fraternity on account of their members' lack of manners, and they proceeded to bind one man in £40 to be "of honest demeanyng."[56]

54. Norman's will (P.C.C., Wattys, 7). *Mercers Acts*, p. 50 (1461). In 1467 an ordinance of the common council forbade any freeman to accept the livery of a lord (*Cal. L. Bk., L*, p. 73). One of the gentlemen admitted as an attorney in the sheriff's court brought letters from the king and queen (*ibid.*, p. 61).

55. *Ibid.*, p. 89.

56. *Mercers' Acts*, pp. 106–7; Merchant Tailors' Minutes, fol. 18.

The great merchants of the fourteenth century had apparently won themselves a reputation for too eager social ambition. Flattered by noblemen who wished to borrow their money, some were perhaps led to hope that they might repeat William Pole's unique success at court. So, at least, a sermon of Friar Bromyard insinuates:

> Merchants and moneyed men reckon themselves "ennobled" and on the road to enrichment, when they are seen to have friendships with the nobility, when they can wear their robes and are summoned to their banquets, and when they can go a-hunting with them. But the end of all these things is that, when they ask for . . . . the money back, which (after it has been acquired with much labour) they bring and lend to them, they will be friends no longer.[57]

The friendship of the greater nobles may well have been condescending and somewhat incalculable. The clerk who kept John of Gaunt's register, entering a record of currency exchange services rendered by the great London financiers, Brembre and Philpot, referred to them casually by their nicknames, as "Nichol" Brembre and "Jankyn" Philpot. The duke himself, when presiding as steward of England over the court of coronation claims, severely snubbed another citizen, John Wiltshire, a grocer, who by purchase of half the manor of Heydon in Essex had become a tenant-in-chief, holding by the service of handing the king a towel before dinner on his coronation day. Although conceding that his claim to appear at Richard II's coronation was valid, the court awarded that his service be delegated to the earl of Cambridge. The objection, obviously, was to an individual merchant's enjoying such an honor, with the fee that was attached to it, by mere right of purchase. No objection was raised to the claim of the mayor of London to serve the king with a goblet of wine before he dined or of a selected group of citizens to help the chief butler at the coronation dinner. This claim, however, was a point of London custom dating from the previous century, and the coronation roll sets out the political considerations behind the royal consent quite candidly:

> . . . . the kynges highnes consideryng the great kyndenes & subsidie that his Progenitours habundantly tyme paste had founde of the Cytie of London trustyng tyme commyng to have like kyndenes & subside amongst the said Citezens &

57. As translated in G. R. Owst, *Literature and Pulpit in Mediaeval England* (1933), p. 352. Estimates of the date of composition of these sermons vary between the late 1320's and 1390 (*ibid.*, pp. 224, 596).

to make ther hartis merier and well willyng to doo hym true service & to helpe hym hereafter in his necessites. . . . .[58]

A merchant had, nevertheless, a recognized place of honor in any nobleman's hall. According to a manual on the duties of a marshal, "worshipful" merchants were to be seated alongside gentlemen and esquires, and another version omits the qualifying adjective, stating that all merchants and gentlemen may be seated at a squire's table, with the exception of mayors and former mayors of London, who, as everyone knew, sat higher. The mayor sat nine degrees above an esquire, side by side with a chief judge, higher than a knight, a knight banneret, or an abbot without a miter, with only the mitered abbots and the ranks of the nobility above him; and in London he took precedence of all nobles except those of the blood royal.[59]

The high-ranking officials and other wealthy gentlemen who lived in London were divided in their attitude to the citizens, some having little close association with merchant neighbors, others being on very friendly terms with them. The greatest land-owner living in the city in 1436, according to the assessments of that year, was William Venour, esquire, warden of the Fleet prison, who had estates in seven counties yielding him an income of £166. Next to him came the widow of a Berkeley, with £160; Simon Camp, esquire, at one time treasurer and receiver-general for Henry IV's queen, with £120 in lands and a royal pension of £40; and Thomas Morstede, esquire, court surgeon, with £154 from lands. Gentlepeople so wealthy as these did not hold themselves entirely aloof from citizen society—Venour, for example, joining the grocers' fraternity—yet their wills suggest that official and family connections tended to keep them in the environment of court and county gentlemen. Richard Bokeland, another London squire with estates assessed at £100, named a number of friends in his will, including Lord Cromwell, but no citizen; and his wife's will, although it assigned £20 "to the poer men of ffyshmonger craffte in London," referred otherwise only to "my Skryvener at

58. *John of Gaunt's Register*, I, 79. J. H. Round, *The King's Serjeants and Officers of State with Their Coronation Services* (1911), pp. 125–29, 168–70; Harl. MSS, 1309, fols. 7b–8b, 13–14.

59. John Russell's *Boke of Nurture* and Wynkyn de Worde's edition of *The Boke of Keruynge*, printed in *Early English Meals and Manners*, ed. F. J. Furnival, E.E.T.S., original ser., No. 32, pp. 72–73, 170–71; Society of Antiquaries MSS, No. 287, fols. 125–25b.

london," in the manner of a patron.[60] The pull of professional, court, and family connections could prolong an aloofness irrespective of material superiority in wealth. In total income the gentlemen just mentioned could have had little if any advantage over the wealthier aldermen, five of whom were in 1436 enjoying rents of from £120 to £150 in addition to business earnings; and some of the lawyers, men at much lower income levels, may have been equally exclusive, their wills naming only friends of gentle rank, either in their profession or in the country.

High officials of the exchequer and of the royal household and well-known lawyers were sometimes asked to stand as supervisors of citizens' wills. This points to a relationship of patronage. More often, however, they were named as executors, which argues a more equal friendship. So also does the active concern that Avery Cornburgh, esquire, a careerist royal official, showed in Sir Thomas Cook's trouble and disgrace. Cornburgh's friendships among the citizens were not limited to aldermen. A former sheriff's widow whom he helped in payment of her husband's debts observed gratefully that he was "of gentill & good disposicion."[61] Many less prominent London gentlemen were appointed as executors of merchants' wills, some of them city officials, some of them probably family lawyers, one, named Leche, at Elsing's hospital for the blind, presumably a doctor.[62] Gifts of a customary nature—money, drinking-cups, rings, gowns—were bequeathed to these executors and sometimes to other friends of gentle rank.

Relations of this kind were reciprocal, London gentlemen not infrequently appointing merchants as their executors. Thomas Lute, a clerk of the king's bench, named a merchant of the staple along with Sir William Hody, chief baron of the exchequer. Thomas Bowes appointed a goldsmith who had held office with

60. On Simon Camp, Roll of Royal Grants, E, 163/6/35; for his arms, Anc. Deeds, RS 364; his wills, Comm. Lon., Prowet, 92; P.C.C., Rous, 14. On the Buklands (Bokelonds), Hust. R.W.D., 180/1; P.C.C., Luffenham, 21; *Early Lincoln Wills*, ed. A. Gibbons (1888), p. 181. Morstede's will, P.C.C., Rous, 12.

61. E.C.P., 87/61; *The Great Chronicle*, p. 204.

62. Robert Leche, gentleman, of Elsyngspitell; will of John Wade, fishmonger [1463] (P.C.C., Godyn, 22). "Maister William Smithers gentilman commone clerk of the citee of London," executor for Sir William Taylour, 1483. John Moor, "gentilman of Court," executor for John Cras, mercer (P.C.C., Logge, 21 [1480]). George Assheby "de domo Regia," supervisor of will of William Ederyth of East Greenwich, mariner, citizen, and haberdasher (P.C.C., Stokton, 1 [1454]).

him at the mint, leaving him his Bible and his best signet; he also
left bows and arrows, indicative of sport shared together, to three
other merchant friends. Richard Forster, of the Temple, who had
done a great deal of legal business among citizens, named four
mercers among his executors and left money to three merchant
fraternities.[63]

The willingness to do each other services usually stopped short
of the guardianship of children. This was not due to lack of trust.
One of the city attorneys, entering his young son at Davy's Inn to
prepare him for law, placed him under bond in £20 to a fishmonger,
to be paid if he behaved "otherwise than well." Nor was it due to
aversion for each other's occupations. A merchant's son might
take up the study of law while under merchant guardianship; and
gentlemen, as has been seen, did not necessarily look upon trade
with any personal disapproval. There is an instance of a London
attorney whose wife kept a shop in Sopers Lane and another of a
man who, having taken up the freedom of the city as an attorney,
turned to wholesale trade and had to be re-registered on the city's
record as a grocer. The eldest son of Alexander Anne, city recorder, followed his father's profession, at Gray's Inn, but the
second son was apprenticed to a city merchant; in his case an
exception was made in that he was placed under his master's
guardianship. The normal bond between the brothers seems not to
have been affected by the difference in choice of a career; for, when
the lawyer died young, he made the merchant his residuary legatee,
referring to him, in a phrase which was not so common as to require
dismissal as a mere convention, as his "beloved brother." Another
family which remained united in spite of differing careers was that
of the Fennes. John Fenne, stockfishmonger, making his will in
1474, left £200 to his brother Hugh, described as "Clerke," and
£100 to his "worshipful cousin" Hugh Fenne, gentleman, an
official of the royal household, to be an executor and to act as
guardian of two children.[64]

63. Lute (P.C.C., Milles, 6; *Hist. Parl. B.*, p. 548); Bowes (P.C.C., Logge, 12; *Hist. Parl. B.*, p. 97); Forster (P.C.C., Marche, 23).

64. E.C.P., 94/14. John Bally, of the sheriff's court, deputy-coroner; wife Isabella's merchandise stored partly in his house in the Poultry; she and Everard Flete, mercer, his executors; property in Lincs. sold to fulfil his will (*Cal. L. Bk.*, *H*, p. 85; *I*, p. 21; P.C.C., Marche, 40). Raulyn Stokes, translated to grocers, paying them £10 for admission (*Cal. L. Bk.*, *K*, p. 61; Kingdon, I, 165). Will of William Anne, of North Aston, Oxon., and parish of St. Andrews Holborn, London, 1451 (P.C.C., Rous, 17); his monument inscribed "gene-

Merchant families enjoyed great freedom of intermarriage with London lawyers and with the minor resident officials. The greater lawyers, who lived in the best houses that were available in the city or else in peaceful retreat a few miles away in the country-side, putting their clients to the trouble of riding out to find them, made alliances with the families of aldermen and other wealthy merchants. Thomas Urswyck, elected city recorder "for his prudence and affability," soon afterward married, as his second wife, a daughter of Richard Rich, a well-to-do mercer; and his friend Sir Humphrey Starkey, who succeeded him, married one of his daughters to a son of Thomas Bledlow, alderman.[65] Lesser gentlemen, whose homes were to be found in most parts of the city, more particularly, perhaps, in the river-front parishes and in the outlying suburbs,[66] were content with alliances involving smaller dowries. One of Richard II's *valets*, or esquires, took the illegitimate daughter of a woolmonger with only a little over £10; the daughters of a serjeant of the mayor, who could have had little more, readily found merchant husbands; and a tailor married the sister of a London gentleman mainly, or so a statement of his implies, "for old love and fancy that was betwene them."[67]

The country gentry were less prepared to match with merchant families since they were more sensitive, at least on behalf of their daughters, to the prestige of birth and lands. At a pinch they could forgo the advantages of birth, but they could not bear to surrender a daughter to the insecurities of life without land. When a clerk of the king's counting-house had kidnapped a little heiress, not yet twelve, and forced her into marriage with him, the crux of her father's complaint in chancery was that this man had "no fote lond of his owne"; the blow was the harder in that he had expected,

---

roses de Grays Inne" (*Chronicle of the Grey Friars of London*, Camden Society, No. 53 [old ser., 1852], p. 86); on his brother John, his executor, L. Bk., *K*, fols 247, 282. Will of John Fenne (P.C.C., Wattys, 17).

65. J. M. Neale, *Illustrations of Monumental Brasses* (Cambridge Camden Society [1846]), pp. 99–100; T. A. Urwick, *Records of the Family of Urswyk* (1903), chap. xii; Bledlow, Appen. A. Evidence from year 1500 that it was customary for counsel to receive clients at their country houses (H.M.C., *9th Report*, p. 147).

66. A sample of 70 London gentlemen named as sureties between 1444 and 1452 lived in seventeen parishes, 6 of them in St. Clement Danes, 4 in St. Andrews Holborn, 3 in St. Botolph's outside Aldgate, 2 each in All Hallows Berkyng, St. Katherine Crichurch, St. Dunstan's in the East, and the rest scattered (C. Misc., Bundles 115, 116, 117).

67. L. Bk., *H*, fol. 276; *I*, fols. 187*b*, 188*b*, 211*b*; E.C.P., 64/321.

he said, to marry the girl "to such dyvers notable persones as myght exspend C li of enheritaunce be yer," who would have paid 200 marks "of money" for his permission.[68] If a daughter of such a father happened, as the accepted freedom of manners made quite possible, to fall in love with a merchant, she would raise storms of indignation. An item in a correspondence formbook of the middle of our period tells of an esquire's daughter who was summarily turned out of a knight's household for having engaged herself to a London citizen and who went for help and shelter to an aunt. The letter in which the aunt informs the girl's father of the affair is included in the collection as a model of the soothing manner in which a woman should write to a brother of the rank of esquire. The tact with which it minimizes the girl's offense and leads up to an appeal for money to pay her expenses allows one to suspect, on the assumption that it is taken from a set of actual family correspondence, that the writer herself was not much prejudiced against a citizen marriage:

Treschere & tres honeuree sire & tresamee frere ie me recomande au vous en tant comme ie puis aux tous honeurs & reverences Et mon tres honeuree frere ie vous remercy entierment de cuer de tous les bienfais bontees & naturesses qe on temps passee de votre grant gentilesse & courtoisie vous mavez fait & monstree sans le mien desiert / et encores me ferez sil dieu plaist comme iay esperance de vous / Daultre part tres honeuree frere vous plaise assavoir qe ma dame de S. sen est bien marry & coroncee de votre fille & ly a hors bontee de son hostel a cause qe Guillam de B. Citezein de Londres ly donna un anel pour lamour qe votre dicte fille est de laffuncee de sa famme Car vrayement beau tres doulz frere ie say bien qe ma dicte dame navoit poynt daultre cause envers ly dont tres chier frere ie vous empri cherement qe vous ly vueillez avoir tout plainement escusee de son dit departir Car pour avoir secour & aide de ses parens elle saherdoit vers noz parties & orest elle repeirant & demourant avecque moy tanqe dieux en aura ordennee meulx pour ly Par quey vous ensuppli tant chierement comme ie puiș beau frere & comme ie maffi soveraynement de vous qe vous ly plaise envoier ar tant de monoye comme il vous plerra de votre grace deia a sa grant necessitee Tres amee frere sil es chose qe par moy puist estre fait a votre plaisir & consolacion mandez le a moy comme a votre humble baissellete & ie le ferai voulontiers & de bon cuer Je ne vous sai plus qe mander a present mais vous plaise ceste matiere gracieusement prendre au cuer. Mon tres honeuree sire & tres amee frere le saint Esprit vous maintiegne & accrese en honeur & joye & vous doint saintee & paix. . . . .[69]

If he had lands to recommend him, a merchant who wished to marry into a gentle family had a fair chance of dispelling prejudice against his person on the grounds of his occupation or his ancestry. If he also had some blood relationship with landed gentry and could play up his regard for birth, as William Crowmere, alderman and draper, did, stipulating that his son should marry someone "de bono sanguine," the way was easy. A quarter of the wives of fourteenth-century aldermen whose parentage is known were the daughters of country landowners, the proportion in the fifteenth century rising to a third; and at least some of these, as in the oft-cited cases of Whittington and Boleyn, Pultney's second wife, and others, were from families ranking by birth. The proportion of wives of gentle birth among landed merchants who had not the ambition to take aldermanic office was only about half this and in the merchant class as a whole was very much lower.[70]

Although prejudice from the side of the gentle families may have limited the degree of intermarriage between merchants and gentle-women, it did little to check the marriage of gentlemen with mer-chants' daughters and widows. Indeed, gentlemen were so un-ashamedly eager in their search for fat dowries, wherever they could sniff them out, that they may sometimes have aroused some caution and reluctance on the side of the merchant family. Among the matrimonial prospects that excited the Paston brothers were the widow of a merchant of Worsted who was estimated to be worth 200 marks in goods and to have £10 a year in rents, a draper's daughter in London, and one of the Boleyn daughters. The Boleyn family, looking for somewhat better marriages, was discouraging: "What if he and sche kan agre," wrote the mother, of John Paston's suit, "I wyll not lette it, but I will never advyse hyr therto in no wyse."[71] The parents of a young Canterbury widow hesitated to approve her courtship by the marshal of the archbishop's hall, a report that they would prefer to see her married to a merchant raising the hopes of one of John Hende's servants in London.[72] Sir Hugh Brice, making arrangements in his will for the future of a granddaughter, hoped indifferently that she would be married "to some discreet citizen of London or a gentleman."

Gentlemen were nevertheless persistent and shrewd enough to

70. Appen. A, and above, p. 28.

71. *Paston Letters*, ed. Gairdner, II, 300; III, 109, 278.

72. *Anglo-Norman Letters and Petitions* ("Publications of Anglo-Norman Text Society," No. 3), pp. 118–19.

win a fair proportion of the heiresses and widows with shares of merchant fortunes who came on the marriage market. To speculate upon the devious ambitions that may have helped to bring these matches about would be rash in the extreme, yet surely many a London girl must have dreamed of marrying her way up in the world. One of the Gisors, left a widow by Henry Picard, married Sir Bartholomew Burghersh, courtier. Margaret atte Lee, a chandler's daughter, married William Walderne, who became an alderman almost as soon as he was out of his apprenticeship to a mercer, and after his death she married a Norfolk gentleman who had been appointed guardian of her four children. Matilda Fraunceys, daughter of another fourteenth-century alderman, went further. Her first husband was John Aubrey, one of the richest young merchants in London, with an inherited fortune; her second was Sir Alan Buxhill, courtier; and finally she married John de Montacute, who became third earl of Salisbury. In the next century there were several more London marriages into noble families, among them that of Estfeld's daughter to a Bohun; Thomas Bledlow's widow to Sir Thomas Bourchier, younger son of Lord Berners and one of eleven royal favorites singled out for exemption from a sumptuary law forbidding the wearing of fine furs; and John Stokker's widow, who had lost three merchant husbands in three years, to George Neville, fourth lord Abergavenny.[73]

About a third of the marriages made by daughters of fourteenth-century aldermen were to gentlemen and ten of fifteen remarriages by aldermen's widows; in the fifteenth century more than half the daughters' marriages were to gentlemen, and the widows were equally fond of merchants and of gentlemen or noblemen for their second and third husbands.[74] The exact proportions are not very significant since the samples known are small and the choice may often have been decided by the wife's original background. In the Capell family, for example, in which both of the two daughters who grew up were married to men who received knighthood, the mother was a daughter of Sir Thomas Arundell; and a number of the widows who married wealthy men of birth, as in the case of

73. Also widow of Thomas Ilom to Lord Ferrers and of Robert Drope to Viscount Lisle (Appen. A).

74. Thirty-four marriages by daughters of fourteenth-century aldermen to merchants, 18 to gentry; in the fifteenth century 19 to merchants, 28 to gentry, 13 remarriages of widows to merchants, 13 to gentry (counting a woman's third marriage) (*ibid.*).

Lady Pultney, who married Nicholas de Lovaigne, and of John Hende's widow, whose second husband became Lord Sudeley, were themselves of gentle family. In a few instances, as in that of Pultney and of Sir Ralph Josselyn, draper, whose second wife, an esquire's daughter, married a son of Lord Clifford for her second husband, the alderman also was of gentle family. The same may have been true of Ralph Verney, one of whose daughters married Sir Edward Raleigh, and of John Wodecok, of Yorkshire origin, whose widow and daughter both married gentry of that county. Richard Gardiner took steps to insure his daughter a husband of rank by buying the wardships of a young esquire and his brother, arranging that if the elder boy should die before the marriage was consummated, his brother, if the girl liked him ("if the same children can so aggre"), was to take his place. Whether through the influence of relations or by mere personal preference, Gardiner's inclinations here coincided with those of his wife, who after his death looked about for a man of rank for her next husband, marrying Sir Gilbert Talbot. High ecclesiastical distinction in the family could also help to make good marriages possible. Both the Chicheles in the court of aldermen married their daughters well, William's daughter Florence taking a knight for her first husband and a gentleman of Yorkshire descent, John Darrell, esquire, who was steward to her uncle, the archbishop of Canterbury, for her third.

It is not suggested that all the gentlemen seeking these unions were men of birth. Men such as Richard Forster, of the Temple, and Thomas Morstede, the court surgeon, who each married a daughter of an alderman, may sometimes have derived their rank from their office or profession rather than from their family.[75]

Similar types may be distinguished among the gentlemen who married into lesser merchant families. Some were men of ancestry who were accustomed to exercise authority in county affairs. Sir Thomas FitzNicholl of Gloucestershire married the widow of a skinner. Sir Nicholas Stukeley of Cambridgeshire married a draper's widow with the comparatively small dower of £100, the

75. Forster to Knyghtcote's daughter; his will (P.C.C., Marche, 23). Morstede married Elizabeth, daughter of John Michell and widow of William Fitzherry, esquire; after his death she married John Wode, Sr., esquire (Hust. R.W.D., 160/26; Anc. Deeds, B 12057). Morstede, named as supervisor of a haberdasher's will in 1408, was then described simply as "Master" and "medicus" (Comm. Lon., Broun, 171v). By 1431 a deed refers to him as both Master and esquire (Hust. R.W.D., 160/3).

guardianship of her two children giving him control of another £100. Sir Thomas Vaughan, high in Edward IV's service, married a grocer's widow. Provincial town gentry were represented, another grocer's widow becoming the wife of an esquire who lived in Ipswich. There were also professional men of the rank of gentleman, such as Thomas Kent, clerk of the king's council, in close touch with London financiers, who married the widow of Thomas Dounton, mercer.[76]

Friendships and intermarriage with gentry can indeed be traced as far down in citizen society as records of landed property extend. The executors of Gilbert Prince, a painter who had made money in trade, intrusted his son to the guardianship of the king's herberger, Master Thomas Sy. The daughter of a well-to-do cofferer could marry first a mercer and then a knight; a broiderer's daughter married an Oxfordshire knight; and a brewer who left his daughter lands in Northamptonshire worth £20 a year as well as property in London was able to marry her to a gentleman. The widows of a pinner and a pewterer married London gentlemen. A fuller, a carpenter, a pointmaker, and a cutler appear as supervisor and executors of the wills of four other gentlemen who wished to be buried in London parishes. Some of these ties may have grown out of neighborliness, but some were based on blood relationship. John Mollesley, a citizen and drover who died in 1445, leaving only a little over £40 among his four children, asked his brother Thomas Mollesley, of Staffordshire, "gentilman," to be co-executor with his wife, under the supervision of another Thomas Mollesley, kinship unspecified, who was a citizen and butcher.[77]

In circles in which these cross relationships with the gentry, either by marriage only or by blood, were frequent, differences of outlook arising from tradition were naturally at a minimum. One would suspect the existence of mutually convenient economic connections within the Mollesley group, and the interests of some of the gentlemen who took wives in London were such as to keep them in constant touch with trade. John Darrell's property included a mill and two boats at Northfleet and a wharf, with a

76. Hust. R.W.D., 126/11 L. Bk., K, fol. 51b; E.C.P., 107/5, 57/46; will of Alice Tymperley (P.C.C., Milles, 5); Drapers' Deeds, A/V/172.

77. L. Bk., H, fol. 317b; Hust. R.W.D., 129/28. Wills of Orchard (P.C.C., Wattys, 9); Maister (P.C.C., Luffenham, 29); Martyn (P.C.C., Stokton, 3–4); Leversegge (P.C.C., Luffenham, 20); Mollesley (P.C.C., Luffenham, 30).

crane and warehouse, at Faversham.[78] The Fynchams, a Norfolk family of mixed traditions, tried to combine loyalties to all of them. Laurence, a London fishmonger dying in 1481, sacrificed all his lands in order to spread legacies among his relatives, leaving his son only the salthouse at Winchelsea that they used in their trade. William, the son, who died a few years later without an heir to carry on the business, set aside 400 marks for the purchase of lands to support his wife and daughter, after whose deaths they were to be divided among the "heris male of the Fynchams" in general and in his wife's family. Both men showed their loyalty to the fishmongers' company by leaving money among its young men.[79]

Men who were conversant with such mixed family backgrounds could hardly have thought of gentlemen as necessarily having any generic superiority to merchants. Wealthy landed merchants were probably conscious of the poorer gentry only as deserving objects of charity. John Berby, a mercer who died in 1464, left 40s. between "ii pour gentilmen" for whom a clerk of his acquaintance had pleaded; and among the general charitable causes recommended to the executors in charge of his estate was the "Relevyng of pour gentilmen and other nedy people" who had lost their goods by some accident that could not have been their own fault. John Warde's sympathies were more especially for a "Pouer gentleman attorney in the Guildhall," to whom he left 10 marks; and Sir Bartholomew Rede, endowing a grammar school at Cromer, specified that the pupils admitted should be "gentlemen's sons and others and poor mens children."[80]

4. THE GENTLEMAN MERCHANT

A puzzling figure, who emerges in records dating from soon after the act of 1415 had made it obligatory to give a man's occupation or status in specified classes of legal documents, as though he had been already on the scene, is the person who laid claim to dual status as a merchant and a gentleman. Was it possible to belong in both of these spheres at the same time?

The explanation is in some cases very simple. The man was a merchant who for the time being held a household appointment

78. Darrell's will (Register, Chichele, 568–70).
79. Fyncham wills (P.C.C., Logge, 3, 24).
80. Berby's will (P.C.C., Godyn, 22). On Warde and Rede see Appen. A.

that carried the pay and rank of a gentleman or esquire. Richard Hakedy, who held the appointment of apothecary to the king, used the description of the rank he reached in that capacity, king's esquire, together with reference to his status as a citizen of London and member of the company of grocers; or he might use only one description, either one, as he chose. Members of lesser companies could be in the same position. William Wodeward, the gunfounder, held the rank of king's esquire.[81]

Often the only evidence of the claim is in the wording of a writ of protection issued on the grounds that the person named was about to go abroad, as, for example, to Walter Wode, fishmonger, alias late of London gentleman, said to be going abroad in the company of the mayor of the staple of Calais. The purpose of the journey, it was often stated, was to arrange for army supplies. It is conceivable that this was sometimes the object in view and that a victualing contract might be obtained in such a way as to give a merchant a rank equivalent to that of gentlemen in the army. But very frequently the journey was fictitious, the writ having been sought simply to stave off creditors. In this event it was likely to be revoked before it had run its term. The question arises as to whether descriptions of status in writs that were obtained under false pretenses are of any value as evidence. If it was so easy a matter to procure a writ of protection for an imaginary journey, it would surely not have been difficult to have inserted in it a fictitious description of status, in order to make the document look more impressive. But it would not thereby have become legally any more effective, and sometimes a third description was added which detracts from the impressiveness. Thomas Plouden, who obtained a writ of protection in June of 1484 on the pretext that he was going to Picardy on victualing and defense work at the Castle of Hammes and lost it in November because he had not left London, is described in it as citizen and grocer of London, alias "gentilman," alias brewer.[82]

The same strings of aliases occur in indictments and pardons. The clerks were in all cases aiming at a complete identification of the person before them. If he had lately lived in more than one

---

81. *Cal. Fine Rolls*, t. Henry IV, II, 148.

82. P. & M. Rolls, A 101/2 (MS cal.); numerous writs of protection and revocations of same are to be found in the calendars of the French rolls and patent rolls.

place, how was he publicly known in each? Had he lately been known in more than one character in the same place? It would be understood that it was to a man's interest to describe himself correctly, lest he be confused with someone else and be held responsible for that other person's acts. It is therefore likely that there were some literal grounds for each alias. John Nicholson, "yoman" of Westminster, acquitted of a charge of housebreaking and theft there, had been indicted with the alias lately of London stationer, "Gentilman," and brewer. His will, drawn up a few years later, shows that he was both a stationer and a brewer; he is described in it as citizen and stationer, and he left his wife a brewery. Citizens of London were often officially designated as yeomen in Westminster. Why he was indicted also as a gentleman is not clear. There is a possibility, however, that he had held a household appointment. As a stationer, he would have been qualified to act as a copyist or secretary, and in that capacity he could have been assigned rank as a gentleman servant.[83]

If a man had been known elsewhere as a gentleman before he entered trade in London, having come there as an adult and taken up the freedom by redemption, he would have been bound, for complete identification, to mention the status that he held in his former place of residence. If he had been apprenticed in the city as a boy, gentle birth alone would not lead a merchant to assert dual status. Some of these gentlemen merchants may have come from those resourceful and versatile gentry who were either rising for the first time by means of trade or were taking to it to revive drooping fortunes. Thomas Stevenes, a London mercer whose commission of appointment as a customs inspector gave him the alias Thomas Stevenes of Gloucester, "gentilman," and John Kebbyll, stockfishmonger of London and Sandwich, who obtained a writ of protection with the alias of gentleman of Sandwich, may have been in this category. An instance of the type, in industry, is Robert Colyns, who was indicted for various felonies as dyer and gentleman of Thaxted, in Essex; since he had not taken out citizenship in London, his alias there was that of yeoman.[84]

83. K.B., 27/793, Rex roll, *m.* 138*d* (37 Hen. VI); P.C.C., Godyn, 15 (1466). He left his father, who is not referred to as gentle, 5 marks and his best gown; feoffees of his lands were a scrivener, a gentleman, and a brewer. Case of a Cambridge graduate's serving a Yorkshire knight, his cousin, as "my Clerc and Secretarie in the rowme of a gentilman" (*York Civic Records*, I, 176 [date, 1486]).

84. *Cal. P.R.*, *1416–22*, p. 356; *1429–36*, p. 284; K.B., 27/840, Rex roll, *m.* 49*d* (1462–63).

A third possible reason for asserting dual status lay in the fact that in some localities a merchant who enjoyed a large and regular income was regarded by some, at least, of his neighbors in much the same light as a gentleman of equivalent wealth. The brewers of Canterbury recalled in a memorandum of the year 1507 that each of four merchants who had been elected to the mayoralty of their city afterward "toke uppon him the occupation of makying of cloths and lyved like a gentleman" and that a fifth, who before his election had been a baker, sold the business, let his house, and "lived after as a gentleman," presumably on either clothmaking or rents or on both. These Canterbury men were known to their fellows as Master.[85] Evidence of the same attitude comes from Norwich, where an inscription in a chapel begs the passer-by to "Pray for the sowl of Robert Thorp, gentilman citezen and alderman of Norwich"; and the epitaph of Thomas Elys, three times mayor of the city, who died in 1487, contains the curious formula, "prudens mercator et nobilis istius urbis."[86] Women of the merchant class were sometimes referred to as gentlewomen, both by men of their own class and by gentlemen who were courting them. Richard Cely described a sister of his family's business employee, Dalton, as "a ꝫenge gentylwhoman," and Edmund Paston, looking out for a wife for his brother William, spoke in high recommendation of "a fayr jantylwoman" in Worsted, the widow of a merchant, who had £10 a year as well as 200 marks in money and furniture.[87]

A merchant who had a country estate might gain the reputation in that neighborhood of being a gentleman mainly from his way of living when he visited the place. If he was related to gentry in the neighborhood, this was all the more likely to occur. If he had a clothmaking business there, putting out material in the villages, he might still have the reputation with the Canterbury mayors of living "like a gentleman." All the while he could be spending part of his time in London as an ordinary merchant citizen and might have no serious intention of severing his ties there and turning himself into a country gentleman until the latter years of his life when he felt inclined to retire from active business.

An early example of a merchant who claimed gentility in a county, though not in London, was William Covele, goldsmith,

---

85. H.M.C., *9th Report*, pp. 174–75.

86. Weever, pp. 530, 528.   87. *Cely Papers*, p. 59 (1481).

described in the revocation of a writ of protection in 1429 with the alias of gentleman of the county of Oxford; Covele was in the market for land, being at one time in negotiation for the purchase of "a place Ikallid Covele with the appurtenances" from a gentleman of Godstowe. Another example is John de Stratton, who between 1417 and 1435 sued several provincial merchants for debt in his capacity as citizen and mercer. He had bought a manor and other lands near Norwich twenty years before, but a transaction with a salter suggests that he had not yet retired from trade. Augustine Stratton, who finished his apprenticeship with a London mercer in 1425, may possibly be identified with the Augustine de Stretton, esquire, who ten years later was made a commissioner of array in Suffolk. William, one of several Kempes on the mercers' list of freemen, who finished his apprenticeship in 1431, appears after thirty years with the alias, late of Thetford in the county of Norfolk, "gentilman." Similarly Richard Thorp, who had been an apprentice of Thomas Fauconer, an alderman in the mercers' company, appears later with the alias, late of Weston in the county of Lincoln, esquire. Other examples of men who were living part of their time in the country as gentlemen, though still engaging in business, are Geoffrey Yermouth, late citizen and draper of London, alias of Wargrave, Berkshire, draper alias gentleman; and John Shirwode, merchant of Coventry, alias of Alspathe, Warwick, esquire, and late of London, grocer. Shirwode was found to be living at Alspathe instead of attending to the victualing business in Calais that was mentioned in a writ of protection he had obtained.[88]

The only details that are available about the gentleman-merchant's life in the country come through the records of legal proceedings; these show him, like other gentlemen of the countryside, energetic in the pursuit of quarrels. Elys Davy is an example. An apprentice of Thomas Fauconer, Davy was known in London as a citizen and mercer from the time that he took up the freedom in 1407 until his death in 1455. In 1428 he was indicted for felony with the alias of gentleman of Twyford. At that time he had a house in Harrow. The indictment was for having assaulted three

88. Covele (*Cal. P.R.*, *1422–29*, p. 537; E.C.P., 16/347); Strattons (*Cal. P.R.*, *1416–22*, *1422–29*, *1429–36*, passim; C. Files, Treasury Series, No. 171; *Feudal Aids*, III, 262, 274, 593–94; Blomefield, VIII, 150). Other instances, *Cal. P.R.*, *1452–61*, pp. 268, 269, 285, 384; *1422–29*, p. 372; *1467–76*, p. 440; *1476–85*, p. 58.

men there, including one of his own servants and another whom he was alleged to have left in despair of his life. He was indicted a second time for stealing stock and a third time for aiding a dyer of Harrow to harbor a common thief, and a sensational charge was brought against him of complicity with a Canterbury mercer and a London attorney in a plot to destroy the king and his uncles by magic. A St. Neots man gave information that the group had met in a tavern in Cheap and over their drinks had hired him to take them to a clerk who knew the art of making people waste away. Not finding the clerk at St. Paul's, as they had expected, they had arranged to meet again in Davy's house at Harrow the following Christmas. Davy was cleared of all these charges; in his turn he had a husbandman of Kingston imprisoned for knocking out his left eye and tried, unsuccessfully, to have him convicted also of cutting off his tongue, robbing him, and leaving him for dead on the highway. The reasons why he was the target of so much enmity may have been purely personal, but it will be noticed that his quarrels were not with the great but with poorer people. He was an exporter of cloth, and the connection with the dyer at Harrow suggests that he may have had industrial interests in the country. He was not one of the large Middlesex landowners. He had some lands at Totenham, possibly acquired through his wife. He was fond of Croydon, where he bought a small property from a bowyer, founded an almshouse, and was buried. At his death he had only London property and a sixty-year lease of a manor at Acton.[89]

A few merchants claimed gentility in London. Among these were men who were admitted to the freedom by redemption and gave their status on entry as gentlemen or esquires. The goldsmiths once swore in a gentleman among their "allowes," or hired servants. Jankyn Parke, admitted to the grocers' livery in 1403, was twenty-nine years later on their lists as "Squyer"; in the interval he had served at least once as mayor of Calais and had perhaps acquired some other office that carried rank. Thomas Clarell, grocer and owner of a soaphouse, described himself in his will as a gentleman. There is no discernible reason for this except the prob-

89. K.B., 27/666, Rex roll, *m.* 16. 70*d*, 71*d*, 142, 165; 27/667, Rex roll, *m.* 92*d*, 98;27/668, Rex roll, *m.* 93*d*; Add. Ch., 40,571; Reg. 17 B XLVII, fol. 133*b*–34; *Cal. P.R., 1441–46,* p. 318; will, P.C.C., Stokton, 4.

ability that he was a member of the noted Buckinghamshire family of that name. A member of the wealthy family of Fetplaces, which had branches in both trade and landed gentry, made his will in 1464 as "Squier and draper of London"; several other squires in the drapers' company may have been of the same type. One of the wealthier men who bought Middlesex property, William Yorke, fishmonger, by 1461 described himself as a gentleman both of Twickenham and of London; before his death he was called esquire.[90]

Finally, there was the merchant who took up knighthood. This step was very different from the process by which he would acquire the reputation of living "like a gentleman" or of ranking among the new substantial landowners of a country. Except among the wealthiest of the gentry, with whom it was a matter of tradition and pride for the head of the family to be a knight, and among professional soldiers, for whom knighthood represented a promotion in their career, there was no general desire for the title. It was very generally felt that the burdens attached to it, in the shape of liability for military service and for service on public commissions, were out of all proportion, in tedium and expense, to the honor that was involved. Thirteenth-century government policy had experimented with the hope of consolidating all nonbaronial landowners above specific income levels into a national order of knighthood whose members could be drafted to organize defense and to do the work of local government but had not succeeded. Men preferred to pay fines of up to £20 to be excused from the honor. Enforcement of distraint of knighthood therefore became primarily a means of raising revenue. The income level on which it bore was raised once during the reign of Edward II to £50 and was thereafter fixed at £40 in income from rents. Once, in 1410, it was given as covering income from all sources, if so much as £40 had been received for three consecutive years; the qualification that the property must be in the form of land was then restored.[91]

90. See city recognizance rolls, which give a record, not complete, of admissions by redemption; Goldsmiths' Records, Book C, fol. 151 (1475); Kingdon, II, 220; wills of Clarell (P.C.C., Vox, 7 [1493]); Fetplace (P.C.C., Godyn, 5); "Robert Hyll of London Gentilman otherwise called Robert Hyll Citizen and Taillour of London" (P.C.C., Milles, 13 [1488]). Yorke's name on list of staplers receiving a pardon (Cal. P.R., 1461-67, p. 351); deed by his executors (Cat. Anc. Deeds, VI, 357).

91. F. M. Nichols, "Feudal and Obligatory Knighthood," Archaeologia, XXXIX, 189-244; C. Moor, Introd., Knights of Edward I ("Publications of the Harleian Society,"

Sheriffs' returns for 1322 and 1324 for thirty-three counties give a total of 1,119 landed knights at the latter date, suggesting a total of not much above 1,200 for the country as a whole. A century later the number had apparently fallen to barely a quarter of this figure. The very extensive commissions of the peace that were appointed in 1434 named only 73 knights in fourteen counties. This was not necessarily a full roster, but it was probably not far short of the total. Lay subsidy returns for 1436 name only 24 knights as worth above £5 in lands in the five counties of Derbyshire, Essex, Lincolnshire, Middlesex, and Warwick. Essex, for which the sheriffs had in 1324 returned 68, now had only 6, the number in Middlesex had fallen from 13 to 2, in Warwick from 42 to 5, in Derbyshire from 17 to 5. Yet the same subsidy returns indicate that there were still about a thousand men in the country who could have met the property qualification. Many paid fines to be exempt; many escaped unnoticed. Toward the end of the century the threat of fines may have been inducing more people to take up knighthood. Wedgewood believed that in 1491 there were about half as many again as in 1434, an estimate which, however, by his own reckoning yields a figure of only 375. This is consistent with the evidence of inquisitions post mortem, which for the first three years of Henry VII's reign show about 10 knights dying each year. The ideas associated with knighthood were still failing to kindle enthusiasm for the governmental work of the counties. They retained life, indeed, only as they were deliberately fostered at court and dramatized by the young men of the baronial class.[92]

Merchants who had £40 in rents were in no more haste than the gentry to volunteer for knighthood. In London the royal writs ordering the sheriffs to report the names of citizens who had the requisite qualifications regularly met with evasive returns to the effect that since tenements were often empty and were subject to

---

Vols. LXXX–LXXXIV [1929–32]); J. H. Wylie, in *History of the Reign of Henry IV* ([4 vols. 1884–98], III, 321–22), found no proved case of knighthood traceable to the order of 1410 yet inferred, from "the flood of knighted names" in the military records of the next few years, "that the wealthy and untitled classes took up the honor greedily." This conclusion is not borne out by evidence of the numbers of knights.

92. Palgrave, II, Part II, 587, 637, 643, 648, 652, 657. The number of 13, for Lancaster, is the same as that found in 1305, when, for appointment to the great assize, "plus de chivalers ne poeynt en le conte trover" (*Year Book*, 32–33 Edward I [R.S.], pp. 387–89). Commissions of the peace (*Cal. P.R., 1429–36*, pp. 370–413). Returns of 1436 analyzed by Gray, *op. cit.*, pp. 607–39. Wedgewood's estimates, *Hist. Parl. Register*, p. lxxxvii.

damage by fire and wind, citizens never knew the value of their property and that in any event they did not hold by knight service. It was largely from anger at the citizens' refusal to pay fines for not taking up knighthood that Richard II in 1392 suspended the city's liberties, but the collective attitude on the question did not alter.[93]

Before 1381, when Richard II knighted five of the aldermen for their services in suppressing the rebellion, there were never so many as five merchant knights living in the city at one time, and there were never so many again until the reigns of Edward IV and Henry VII, who courted the aldermen with honors. In the early years of the fourteenth century there were three, a Basing, a Blund, and a Banquell. In 1322 there was only one, Richer de Refham. Henry de Bidyk, two years later, paid £20 to be excused. John Pultney accepted it only with a pension of 100 marks and Richard de la Pole only on retirement. Two other aldermen were knighted later in the royal service, Robert Aleyn, fishmonger, who accompanied Sir John Fernande to Portugal, and John Wroth, fishmonger, who also went abroad. Other wealthy citizens, at the end of this century and in the next, were buying blanket exemptions from the liability to take up knighthood, to serve on juries, or to take a variety of public offices. Neither in 1412 nor in 1436 were there any merchant knights in the city; Estfeld and Whytingham seem to be the only two cases before 1461.[94]

Most of these men were knighted by the king himself, and several shared in the ceremonial procedures which were ordinarily open only to young noblemen of the court or to picked soldiers. John le Blund was invited to join a group of nearly three hundred young men of noble and gentle family who were knighted with the Prince of Wales in 1306. Edward IV, at his coronation and that of his queen, made six of the aldermen knights of the Order of the Bath, "a grete worschyppe unto alle the cytte," as a city chronicler

---

93. A series of fourteenth-century returns to the writs is preserved in the Chancery Miscellanea, Bundle 1, Nos. 8/16, 12/37–38, 13/32, 15/4–5, 16/16–17. Similar returns from Bristol in the *Little Red Book of Bristol*, ed. F. B. Bickley (1900), I, 100–101. On the incident of 1392 see Tout, *Chapters in the Administrative History of Medieval England*, III, 479–81.

94. On Refham, Bidyk, and Aleyn see Palgrave, II, Part II, 587; Part III, 507; *Cal. P. & M. Rolls*, III, 23. On the others see Beaven, I, 255–56, and Appen. A. Fines for exemption on receipt rolls of the exchequer and grants of exemption on patent rolls.

commented. Henry VII knighted Sir Ralph Astry, while he was mayor, at a court dinner at which he and the aldermen were entertained in a friendly style, the king's players staging an interlude and a ballet for them; Astry went home "by brekyng of the daye and . . . . kissed his wife as a dowble lady." It was not until the reign of Henry VIII that it became a matter of custom to knight the mayor during his term of office.[95]

Knighthood given by the king himself could not be ridiculed; indeed, it carried a maximum degree of honor. In the fourteenth century, conservative aristocratic opinion was probably critical of giving knighthood to merchants, for chroniclers seemed to seek justification for it in the men's military capacities. Philpot was referred to, with a suggestion of surprise, as "miles fidelissimus quamquam mercator." Walsingham had high praise for his public spirit in equipping vessels for naval defense; he had acted "nobilissime." Walworth was "vir incomparabiles animositatis et audacie." John Wroth was "miles strenuus et valens," stock epithets of the good knight that had been on John Gisors' tomb in the Grey Friars' church.[96] The same justification for honor in having contributed to national defense could have been found in the case of most of the merchants whom Edward IV knighted. The honor usually came too late in a merchant's life to make much difference in his own social relations. Yet the fifteenth-century merchant-knights looked higher than most merchants for their friends and patrons. The archbishop of York was named as overseer of Sir John Percyvale's will and the archbishop of Canterbury of Sir Hugh Brice's; Lord Hastings was overseer of Sir John Plomer's will, Lord Ferrers an executor for Sir John Young, the earl of Ormond a feoffee for Sir John Brown, and "my right especiall ffrend sir Rainold Bray," architect to Henry VIII, was an executor of Sir Edmund Shaa. Such connections stood the merchant-knights' children in good stead, helping them to marry out of their own class. The social importance of merchant-knighthood showed itself chiefly as it facilitated the movement of merchant families into the upper ranks of the landed gentry.

95. On the history and significance of the ceremonial procedures see W. A. Shaw, *The Knights of England* (1906), pp. xiii–xiv; *The Great Chronicle*, pp. 251–52.

96. *Chronicon Anglie, 1328–1388*, Chronicles of St. Albans, R.S., pp. 359, 367; Walsingham, *Historia Anglicana*, I, 370, 465; C. L. Kingsford, *The Grey Friars of London* (1915), p. 80.

5. MOVEMENT FROM THE LONDON MERCHANT CLASS
INTO THE LANDED GENTRY

Movement from the merchant class into the landed gentry is difficult to define in such a way that the extent of it can be checked. Opinion will differ as to whether the kind of movement that occurred within one generation should be counted. As they have just been described, the types that were concerned could be called indeterminate, hybrid. The merchant who lived a part of his time on a country estate or retired there in his latter years would in the eyes of the older families of the county always be a *nouveau riche*. He remained closely connected with London and with trade. Unless he was already related to these older families by blood, his absorption into their circle would be incomplete. If he was related to them by blood, would his case genuinely illustrate movement from one class to another?

These arguments are inconclusive. A London merchant could not very well entirely sever his connections with the city. Once he had taken out his citizenship, he could not finally lose it except by some serious breach of city law. If he had any property in the city, it was to his interest to remain continuously in scot and lot, that is, to bear his share of city taxes. He remained a member of the liveried fellowship of his company, with a right to participate actively in London trade. If he discontinued active trade, his former associates would no doubt try to enlist his co-operation as a sleeping partner. In view of the interest that the gentry themselves took in trade, it cannot be maintained that the man who still directed some wholesale trade in staple commodities from his country home was thereby disqualified to rank as a gentleman; still less was this the case if he was merely investing money in another man's business. If he had held office in London as sheriff and alderman, this would enhance his reputation; it meant that he was a man accustomed to authority and experienced as a magistrate, a fit candidate to be named for administrative work in the county. If he had been mayor, his reputation in this regard would stand still higher.

Admittedly, the situation would have varied from region to region. Aristocratic opinion in the north looked askance on Londoners, professing to regard them as of servile birth. Testimony was given that the north rebelled against Henry IV because he had been chosen king only by the "Villanos" of the city of London.[97] This opinion would not have been shared at large among the gentry of Yorkshire, who, as has been seen, sent sons to be apprenticed in London and who also made incidental investments in trade; there is an example of the latter from the fourteenth-century papers of one of the older families in the county, the Calverleys.[98] But Londoners did not retire to the extreme north or even, unless they inherited lands there, to Yorkshire; they went to the Cotswolds, to Lincolnshire, to East Anglia, and to the home counties immediately encircling the city. In all these regions the gentry were well accustomed to trade, to the purchase of land by Londoners, and to their settlement among them.

It may be granted, at least, that the possession of a country house could set a city merchant on the way to changing his class status. If, as many of the wealthier men are known to have done, he then assumed the social role of a gentleman in his county, serving on public commissions, acquiring private hunting rights, modernizing his manor house, making arrangements to marry his daughters into gentle families, and preparing at least one of his sons for one of the careers that were associated with gentility, the degree of change was certainly significant. In so far as can be judged from office-holding and marriage into older families, assimilation to the landed gentry was still further advanced in the second generation after such a move, and in the counties more distant from London there might be a severance of all formal ties with citizen life. There are comparatively few families in which all these points can be checked in both first and second generation of change of status, but all can be amply illustrated.

Special circumstances would tend to encourage the move. Undoubtedly one of the chief of these was blood relationship with gentle families of good standing. Sir John Pultney, who played the role of magnate in town and country alike with luxurious aplomb and whose son left the city for life as a landowner, had some assistance also from the inheritance of family lands. The patronage of a relative who rose high in the church could be of assistance.

97. *Chronicque de la traison et mort de Richart Deux roy Dengleterre*, ed. B. Williams ("Publications of the English Historical Society" [1846]), p. 268.

98. *The Calverley Charters* ("Publications of the Thoresby Society," Vol. VI [1904]), p. 167. Investment of £40 "ad marcandizandum" by Sir John de Calverley (1351).

John Chertsey, draper, who retired to Hertfordshire, reputedly as a gentleman, and whose grandson called himself a gentleman of Rochester, may have benefited by being brother to Archbishop Sudbury.[99] Both of Archbishop Chichele's London merchant brothers remained in the city, as did his nephew John, who was for eleven years city chamberlain; but one of John's sons became a king's esquire, and one, settling as a squire in Cambridgeshire, established a landed family that continued in the male line until the eighteenth century.

Another circumstance that facilitated withdrawal from the city was the acceptance of knighthood, either in the first generation of movement into gentility or in the second. Stephen Aswy, said to have accepted knighthood at some time during his long tenure of the aldermanry of Cheap, between 1274 and 1298, left a son Stephen, who also was knighted; neither the second knight nor his son took part in city affairs. John Banquell, an alderman who was knighted in the early years of the fourteenth century, left a son who was known as lord of the township of Lee in Kent and was summoned for military service in that county; the grandson appeared before the city court of orphanage but was assigned to the guardianship of a knight, Sir Guy Brian. If the family property was close to London, it was natural to keep up connections with citizen friends for the sake of younger children. Sir Thomas Bidyk, who inherited the manors of Finchley and Aldermanbury from his citizen father, left his elder son provided with seven parcels of title deeds to property; the younger son he placed under the guardianship of a mercer, and his daughter married a goldsmith. In some of the other fourteenth-century families with knighthood there was a more complete absorption into the life of gentry of the home counties. Sir John Philpot's two younger sons were apprenticed, but at least one of them followed the eldest son into the life of the country esquire. Sir Thomas Salisbury, son of a grocer, left his son in the guardianship of an alderman's widow, but the youth, inheriting an Essex manor that had come to be named after the family, was known as an esquire. The descendants of Adam Fraunceys, mercer, who bought the manor of Edmonton, all struck

99. For note on Chertsey see C. L. Kingsford, "A London Merchant's House and Its Owners," *Archaeologia*, LXXIV, 138, 155; Anc. Deeds, A 1780, 1861, B 3149; Rot. cl., 9 Hen. VI, *m. 3d*.

root as gentry, his son, who further acquired the rich manor of Cobhams in Essex, being knighted. Sir Adam's sister married into nobility, his son followed him at Edmonton, his daughter married into the older Middlesex family of Charleton, and her son was knighted. In the Peche family there was a variation from the usual pattern. For several generations these people were small Middlesex landowners. In the middle of the fourteenth century John Peche then consolidated his fortunes by the joint means of marrying an heiress to property in London and Middlesex and three other counties and by trade as a fishmonger. His descendants, who inherited the manor of Lullingston in Kent, lived there as knights but through the fifteenth century took out membership in London companies.[100]

The purchase of an estate where it would be suitable to live, the acceptance of the social role of a gentleman in that neighborhood, the making of good marriages and the arrangement of good marriages for the next generation, the cultivation of the favor of patrons and of relatives of gentle blood—these were the obvious means, adopted in varying proportions, by which a merchant left his class and launched his family in a new way of living. Unless the father took one or more of these steps, the son was not likely to reach the upper ranks of the landed gentry. This is not to say that the son could not otherwise become a gentleman. He could do as Chaucer did, enter the royal service and take up the versatile career of king's esquire. But king's esquires had no more than a comfortable living; unless they inherited lands or married brilliantly, they were not likely to establish families with any standing in a county. Throughout the fifteenth century the names of gentlemen and esquires of citizen parentage occur in city deeds; some probably derived their rank from service at court or with members of the nobility and others may have been lawyers. Among them were sons of citizens of lesser companies as well as sons of merchants, as Thomas Pyryman, "gentilman," whose father and brother were spurriers, and William Taverner, esquire, son of a

---

100. Aswy (Beaven, I, 375; W.A.M., 9, 62; E. Williams, *Early Holborn and the Legal Quarter of London* [1927], I, 706). Banquell (Palgrave, II, Part 3, 477; L. Bk., G, fol. 98). The boy was of age by 1368. Bidyk (pedigree in William, *op. cit.*, II, 1038). Sir Thomas' shield of arms and crest impressed on seal (D. & C. St. Paul's, Deeds, A/19/329). On Alexander see *Cal. P. & M. Rolls*, II, 146. An earlier Alexander was a pepperer (C. Misc., 109/6).

girdler.[101] But the only citizens' sons who entered the royal service and achieved social eminence were sons of wealthy merchants like William Crowmere or Sir Robert Whytingham, who had enjoyed every advantage that money could buy. Again, the only member of a citizen's family to achieve an outstanding success in law was Thomas Marowe, grandson of a grocer who had settled Thomas' father as an esquire in Middlesex.

The wealthy merchant's son who inherited land and did not take up a career was not necessarily swallowed up in rustic isolation with no pleasure but hunting. The role of a well-to-do young gentleman, in the fifteenth century if not earlier, allowed of a certain amount of fun in town. Robert Marshall, a grocer who died in 1446, showed disapproval of excess by making his son Alexander's inheritance of lands conditional on abstention from "ryoth and vices"; at the same time he betrayed sympathy with a young man's desire to cut a figure by leaving him a velvet doublet and a sword with silver fittings. Alexander's sisters tried to bar him from his inheritance on the grounds that he was not abstaining from vice. He had stolen a saltcellar, they alleged, and a woman had been seen sitting in his room; but for lack of credible witnesses they lost their case. Robert Rocheford, a grocer who died near the end of the century, wrote that his eldest son William "hath in Ryot and in other ungoodly demeanyng mysspente my goodes . . . . to my grete hurte and hynderance and grete heveness to my herte." William, who called himself alternatively gentleman and grocer, had run through £600 before he was thirty, and though his father left him £200 and a manor in Dorset worth £10 a year, he was shortly afterward arrested for debt.[102]

The multiplication of scattered instances that appear to be typical can tend to give an impression of larger total numbers than may be justified. The lay subsidy returns of 1436 show only two hundred citizens as worth £10 a year in lands, including property in London. The proportionate amounts of city and country property are not known or the degree of underassessment and evasion. But it seems unlikely that more than half of these had £10 a year

101. Drapers' Deeds, A VII, 64; Hust. R.W.D., 204/28 (1474); cf. Master Nicholas Baron, buried beside his father William, citizen and dyer of London, at Northfleet, Kent (1429) (*Archaeologia Cantiana*, XXXII, 51).

102. Marshall (P.C.C., Stafford, 152; P. & M. Rolls, A 90, *mm.* 1–2 [MS cal.]). Rocheford (P.C.C., Horne, 4; *Cal. Inq. p.m.*, t. Henry VII, II, 58; *Cal. P.R.,1494–98*, p. 170).

or more solely from country property. On this reckoning only about a hundred people, representing at this time not much more than 10 per cent of the merchant families in the city, would have been in any position to contemplate a move to the country on a social level above that of yeoman. Raise the figure to £20, and the number is halved again. Distribute these at all evenly among the number of counties in which the Londoners were interested, and it will be seen that there could scarcely have been enough new immigrants from London in that generation to make much impression on the character of the landed gentry of any one county. Nor, given the rate of child mortality, could one expect London immigration to produce much cumulative effect from generation to generation. Even in the home counties one could not expect to find more than a small proportion of London names at the higher social levels.

Two of the citizens' favorite counties, where their purchases of land were most frequent, were Middlesex and Surrey. Over the period as a whole the number of London merchants who bought or sold land in Surrey by the instrumentality of feet of fines almost equaled the number of gentry whose names occur in these deeds.[103] An inquisition held in Middlesex in 1353 lists 7 London names among 30 holders or groups of holders of knights' fees and fractions thereof.[104] Another, of 1402, lists 26 London names among 110 who had property in the county worth from a mark and a half upward in annual value; these London names include such descendants of merchants as William Swanland at the manor of Harefield; Sir Adam Fraunceys; John Hotoft, esquire, with £5 of land at Heston; William Comberton, kinsman and heir of John Northampton's son James. They also include several whose property was in the town of Westminster, not out in the country, and several whose country holdings in Middlesex were too small to provide any basis for gentility.[105] A list of 16 jurors presented in the hundred of Edmonton during the reign of Richard II contains the name of only one London citizen, John Gedney, alderman; with three manors, however, he was by far the most considerable owner of property in the hundred. One other name in the 16,

103. See analysis by Ralph Nevill, "Surrey Feet of Fines," *Surrey Archaeological Collections*, XIII (1897), 130-40.

104. *Feudal Aids*, III, 374-76.   105. *Ibid.*, VI, 486-91.

Thomas Frowyk, esquire, may be counted as a descendant of London merchants, and one, William Wroth, esquire, was of a family that had sent sons to London.[106] An assessment for the hundred of Ossulstone taken in the same reign gives 30 lay names, the valuation of their lands running from £5 to 40 marks. The name of David Sely, Westminster merchant, occurs and of John Croucher, a London vintner; and there are two other possible identifications with London merchants.[107] A more comprehensive list, that was drawn up either in the reign of Henry V or not later than 1427 and covered all the Middlesex suburbs of the city, gives 40 names of lay owners of land valued at from £5 to £40. Ten of these, counting two Chicheles, were citizens.[108]

These lists refer only to ownership of land in the county, not to residence there. The assessment for the lay subsidy of 1436 is indicative of residence.[109] It gives the names of Middlesex residents who had land worth £5 or more either in Middlesex or elsewhere. There were thirty-seven of them, all knights, esquires, and gentlemen who were of old Middlesex families or were courtiers or lawyers, with the possible exception of two who may have been citizens or sons of citizens; in addition there was a Frowyk and a Wroth and the Westminster merchant, David Sely or Selly.

Two generations later the proportion was still about the same. The college of heralds kept a record of fifty-two names of lords, knights, esquires, and gentlemen who were "resyent" in the county in the reign of Henry VII. Again the list includes prominent lawyers and officials—Lovell, Fortescue, Elsyngton, Fenne. The old county name of Danyell continued and Worthe, probably intended for Wroth. There were three Frowyks and a John Philpot, gentleman. Not more than four or five of the other names can be identified with any probability with families of contemporary or recent prominence in the city. There were omissions, some possibly of gentlemen who had not yet taken coat armor, and also random omissions. The existing list is one compiled in 1601 from "an old book imperfect,"[110] and it does not include all who were styled gentleman in an account of a benevolence raised among inhabitants of the hundred of Ossulstone during the same reign.[111] But

106. W.A.M., 309.
107. W.A.M., 12,356.
108. W.A.M., 12,357.

109. E, 136, 238/90.
110. Harl. MSS, 6166.
111. W.A.M., 12,358.

there is no reason why the mice or other hazards that had damaged the heralds' book should have preferred the names of Londoners to others. If the London families had disappeared from view, it was by all odds due to the old story of the deaths of their sons.

The picture in Kent, Hertfordshire, and Norfolk leaves the same general impression. A sixteenth-century copy of a list of 183 "Gentils of Kent" in the reign of Henry VII includes not more than half-a-dozen names that recall London families.[112] One was Richard Lee, presumably the son of the alderman knight of that name. Included on account of his lands and his rank as squire, as son of a knight, Lee is an example of a Londoner who had not fully identified himself with country life. In his will he described himself as a parishioner of St. Stephen's Walbrook, and in case he died "ferre from the citie" he wished his body brought back there for burial. For Hertfordshire there is a list in a copy made in 1600 or 1620 and referring to the time of Edward IV or Richard III of "Al maner of persons Resydent wtin Hertfordshire yet mei despend X li by yere and above."[113] There are 79 names, including 1 London merchant and 1 goldsmith of Watford, 1 maltman, a number of yeomen, several widows, and several men who had moved in to London. Among the 54 who are described as gentlemen and esquires there are 5 London names, Knolles, Feld, Josselyn, Croke, and Penne, with a few others, Braughing, Bassingbourne, Swan, Forster, which may have belonged to relatives or descendants of London merchants. Of these, Knolles and Feld had certainly risen by trade. The names of Pulter and Vynter, among the other gentlemen, suggest a recent origin in trade but whether in London is not known. In the more distant counties the proportion of Londoners probably dropped. In a list of 111 lords, knights, squires, and gentlemen said to have been resident in Norfolk in 1501 there are some half-dozen names that recall London merchant families; but identification is very uncertain.[114]

In addition to the movement of merchants and their sons and grandsons into the landed gentry, there was also the giving of daughters and their dowries. In all these respects there was interchange between the two classes, but the movement from the mer-

112. Printed in *Archaeologia Cantiana*, XI, 394.
113. Harl. MSS, 1546.
114. R. H. Mason, *History of Norfolk*, I (1882), 110.

chant class into the landed gentry exceeded the reverse movement. In many of the instances in which a merchant is found to be a brother or other close relative of a gentleman, the latter may have achieved his rank not long before, through service or the law or through the enlargement of a small family property by some lucky purchase. Even in the home counties, where its investment in land was so considerable, the London section of the merchant class was only one of many tributary streams by which the landed leisured class was maintained. As Thomas Fuller, who also essayed this subject, summed it up, "it is not onely difficult but impossible to anatomize the English gentry so exactly, as to shew where every smallest vein thereof runs."[115]

115. *The Holy State and the Profane State*, ed. M. J. Walten (1938), II, 148. On the joint effects of war-profiteering opportunities and depression of agricultural prices in giving rise to new men, leaseholders on the greater estates, see M. M. Postan, "Some Social Consequences of the Hundred Years' War," *Ec.H.R.*, XII (1942), 1–12.

Chapter VII

A GENERAL VIEW OF THE MIDDLE
STRATA OF THE NATION

I. VARIANT CONTEMPORARY VIEWS OF THE SOCIAL ORDER

ENGLISH preachers and didactic writers of the later middle ages kept their public constantly in mind of the two basic ideas of traditional Christian social doctrine, namely, that society was organic and hierarchical. The ordinary sermon or vernacular treatise did not present these in any systematic intellectual context but emotionally, with stress upon the individual's obligations to perform his allotted duties and to obey his superiors. The organic nature of society was held to be sufficiently demonstrated by metaphors that could be varied to suit the occasion. Preaching in London on the theme of the body politic and its needs, Bishop Brunton gracefully likened citizens and burgesses to the body's heart, adding that faithful mechanics were its left hand.[1] The same type of metaphor, by arranging the functions that were associated with typical social groups in order of importance, served also to drive home the lesson of the hierarchical nature of society; but it did so persuasively, emphasizing the need that each rank or group had of the others.

More frequently, these doctrines were simply taken for granted, being contained by implication in the conventional picture of society as composed of three estates. "There be in þis world þre maner of men, clerkes, knyȝthis, and commynalte," a preacher would remind his audience, as though the fact were self-evident.[2] The picture took on life and reality through subdivision of the two lay estates into the smaller groups with which people were familiar. The second estate thus became that whole series of ranks that

---

1. G. R. Owst, *Pulpit and Literature in Mediaeval England* (1933), p. 554.
2. *Middle English Sermons*, E.E.T.S., original ser., No. 209, p. 237.

stretched from royalty to esquires and gentlemen, condensed sometimes into lords and other "gentles"; and the commons broke down into occupational groups. The broad division of function between them was then obvious, the one standing for defense and government, the other for the work of production and exchange. Knights, however, and the function of defense were often taken as symbolic of the one, giving it the name of the estate of chivalry, and manual labor of the other. A preacher could speak of "the comyne peple, whose occupations stondeth in grobbying aboute the erthe," taking field labor as representative of the estate of the commons.[3] Heretical writing of a mystical turn, such as *The Lantern of Light*, which expounded the mystical identity of society with the church, embraced the same orthodox scheme. The order of knighthood was made up of persons "havyng powere and drede," and it stood for the might and the power of God the father; "symple laburers" are named as typical of the commons.[4]

This tendency to single out laborers as typical of the commons made for a certain sense of incongruity in placing the merchant class in the same estate. The primary association of the phrase "the common people" came to be with the poor and the low. Walsingham wrote of the urban poor and of the rebel elements in London in 1381 as the *vulgus*, or as *vulgares*, terms which appear in an early fifteenth-century dictionary as the equivalent of "comoune pepylle"; and Capgrave, referring to an item in the sumptuary legislation of 1363 that had been drafted to apply to people with less than 40*s.* worth of goods, described it as applying to "the comoune puple."[5] The duties that corresponded with these conditions were interpreted as diligence, submission, and contentment, qualities that a priest would not suitably choose as the subject of a sermon to an audience of well-to-do merchants. Nor would he tell such people that they were oppressed. Yet it was admitted that the common people were subject to oppression. One preacher, asking why this was so, found the answer in their failure to be submissive enough: ". . . . for þer synnes and unthrifty lyvyng and evell will

---

3. Owst, *op. cit.*, p. 553.
4. E.E.T.S., original ser., No. 151, pp. 19, 33–35.
5. *Historia Anglicana*, R.S., I, 457, 466; *Promptorium parvulorum*, Camden Society, old ser., No. 25, I, 89; John Capgrave, *Chronicle of England*, R.S., p. 222; *Rot. parl.*, II, 279, No. 31. Walsingham referred to this item as affecting the *plebii operarii et agricultores* (*Chronica monasterii S. Albani*, R.S. [1863], I, 299).

to holychurche and to þer lordes, þei ben oppressed." To identify the common people with the whole estate of the commons may have been loose and inexact, yet it occurred, very plainly, for example, in this sermon, in which they are contrasted with "men of holychurche" and with "gentilmen."[6] The first systematic English treatise on the three estates to place the merchants firmly in the estate of the commons was Edmund Dudley's *The Tree of Commonwealth*, which was not written until 1510, when Dudley lay in the shadow of the executioner's block, repenting of his past life and forging rules of conduct and policy. Members of the estate of the commons were to labor in sweat without resentment and to remember to pay their rent, if need be going hungry rather than imprudently selling "their necessare." It was made clear, however, that this applied only to the lower members of the estate, for very different rules were laid down for "the chief of theis folkes; as the substantiall merchants, the welthie grasiers and farmers." They were not to "use nor covet over great lucor," they were to beware of usury and manipulation of prices, and they were to be kind to lesser folk and to "their underlinges."[7]

Social description was not necessarily tied to the three-estate framework; both in satire and chronicles and in documents without literary form, writers might describe any groups that interested them without direct reference to the estates. When religious interests were strong, there was likely to be either open reference or indirect allusion to the estates. The fraternity of St. Christopher at Norwich prayed in its fourteenth-century meetings for all the component ranks of the estate of chivalry, adding citizens and burgesses, franklins, tillers of the soil and artificers ("alle trewe tyliers and men of craft"), shipmen, pilgrims, and "all þe communalte and cristen peple."[8] The three-estate scheme also appealed to the baronage and to gentlemen, since it provided an admirable background and support for theories of aristocracy.

Other secular interests tended to produce alternative views of the structure of society. An early fourteenth-century writer, author of that vigorous outline of world history, the *Cursor mundi*, gave lay society a threefold stratification by subdividing the com-

6. *Middle English Sermons*, pp. 254–55.
7. *The Tree of Commonwealth* (printed for the Brotherhood of the Rosy Cross, 1859), pp. 19–20.
8. Toulmin Smith (ed.), *English Gilds*, E.E.T.S., No. 40 (original ser., 1870), pp. 22–23.

mons into the free and the unfree. A northerner, he may have been influenced by Scandinavian sources, but his scheme is drawn out of Scripture, each class being provided with a biblical ancestry. His theory was grounded on the two beliefs, first, that after the flood the world had been repopulated by Noah's three sons and, second, that in consequence of Ham's disrespect to his father, all his descendants had been born under a servile curse. This curse gave him at the same time a historical origin for the institution of bondage and a clue to the ancestry of the unfree. What was more natural than to assume that the other two sons of Noah had given rise in the same way to two other classes, Japhet to knights and Shem to an intermediate class of freemen? It was no matter that each brother had been assigned a separate continent, Ham having been given Africa to populate and Shem, Asia, while Europe had been Japhet's. The movement of their descendants and the ultimate scattering of the strains to form the stratified society of Europe are not described but are taken for granted as a mysterious part of the historical process. The conclusion is presented as clear of all doubt:

> Knyth and thrall and freman
> Oute of þer thre breþer bigan
> O Sem freman, o Japhet Knytht,
> thrall of Cham þe maledight
> O þis thre com all, als þou sais
> Has bene in werld and yeit beis.[9]

This ingenious theory must have been widely noted, for the *Cursor mundi* was very popular. But the idea of a middle class of free descent did not openly gain general currency, no doubt because the distinction between free and unfree was already ceasing to be of much social importance. A habit nevertheless existed of regarding lay society as roughly divided into three groups, corresponding to the extremes and the mean of power and wealth. All discussions of power had reference to the extremes of wealth. Preachers, encouraged perhaps by a reading of the prophets, would denounce the oppression of the poor by the rich. They would class "lordes and þe grette men" together and dwell on their collaboration in corrupt use of the law courts to wrest the goods of the poor from them: the poor man was "helpelissh in þis cause," for "commonly þe gret holdeþ togeþur."[10] Between the extremes of rich and

9. E.E.T.S., original ser., No. 57, pp. 126, 128, 130.
10. *Middle English Sermons*, pp. 202, 238, 311.

poor came the *mediocres*. In London documents, as has been seen, this referred to people of a status between that of the merchants and the laboring poor. In the broader context of national society it had a broader connotation, although one that was realized to be very loose and vague. When shipowners were licensed to carry pilgrims of middle condition, defined as those having no great estate, it was felt to be necessary to add that the license did not permit the admission of clerks, knights, esquires, or others of noble condition on the expedition.[11] A tale in the *Gesta Romanorum*, tilting against the unscrupulous use of power, laments that "the wytty men of this world" have power over poor gentlemen and people of middle degree; some uncertainty appears here as to whether the notion of middle degree would be understood, or should be understood, as including poor gentlemen or not.[12] Walsingham used it of those who were neither poor nor of high rank: describing the grief that followed the death of William Ufford, the earl of Suffolk, he wrote that his mourners were "non tantum . . . . proceres, set et omnes mediocres et pauperes."[13]

Parliamentary experience tended to push thought further in the same direction. Had the early practice of summoning merchants for separate or additional consultation on the problem of supply persisted, it might conceivably have become the custom to describe them as a separate social estate, as some French and German writers did in the fifteenth century, dividing the estate of the commons into the two estates of trade and of labor.[14] As it was, when they were spoken of in parliament, it was with due regard for the national importance of their wealth and with concern for their share in economic difficulties. Sir Peter de la Mare regretted that they were not as able as formerly to be "seigneurs et maistres" of their own shipping, and Archbishop Scrope spoke of the great poverty of the merchants in 1405, "in whom was wont to be the substance of the riches of alle the land."[15] But there was only one formal reference to them as a separate order. This was in a pedantic sermon before parliament in 1442, given by the chancel-

11. *Cal. P.R., 1367–70*, pp. 134–35, 137, 140.
12. The passage cited in Owst, *op. cit.*, p. 341.
13. *Op. cit.*, II, 49.
14. Ruth Mohl, *The Three Estates in Mediaeval and Renaissance Literature* (1933), p. 80.
15. *Rot. parl.*, III, 5b; *An English Chronicle of the Reigns of Richard II . . . . Henry VI*, Camden Society, No. 64 (old ser., 1856), p. 31.

lor, Bishop Stafford. Comparing the kingdom of England to the throne of Solomon, he cast about to find some political and social significance in the six steps that led up to the throne and hit on the idea that they stood for the orders of society. To make six orders, he split the estate of clergy into two, the bishops and the ordinary clergy (*clerimonia*); and the estate of the commons into three, into merchants, cultivators (*culturis*), and artificers and common people (*ac communitate populosa*); leaving the estate of knighthood as one (*militia*).[16]

The net effect of parliamentary experience was to encourage people to associate the merchants and gentry together as significant middle strata in society, with certain similar functions. It had early become parliamentary practice to address the members for the shires and the boroughs together as "Vous mes Sires de la Comune d'Engleterre" or "Vous de la Commune" or briefly as the king's "comunes," the lords being the "Grantz," or "Mes seigneurs."[17] Used in the singular, the word "comune" referred plainly enough to the nation as a commonalty or corporate unity. In the plural it may have had some overtones of reference to the fact that the members came from the separate commonalties or communes of the shires and boroughs, but its use in this way was ambiguous enough to begin to confuse and obscure the three-estate pattern of thought. In his sermon before the parliament of 1433 Bishop Stafford had employed a novel metaphor which linked the merchants and the gentry together as a middle group of vital importance to the state.[18] His discourse ran on the thesis that the people had to be given peace and justice. The people were the cultivators, the artificers, and, vaguely, the *vulgares;* their sole political duty was to obey. For the gift of peace they could rely on the bishops and the *magnates*, whom he likened together to mountains. For equity and justice they must look to the knights, the esquires, and the merchants, or, as he put it in repeating the point, to the knights and the middle people (*mediocribus*); these were compared to hills. Fifty-one years later his successor, Bishop Russell, took much the same position before Richard III's parliament:

16. *Rot. parl.*, V, 35.

17. *Ibid.*, Vols. II, III, *passim*. Petitions alternated between including all as "communes" (*ibid.*, IV, 8) and distinguishing the various groups of petitioners.

18. *Ibid.*, p. 419a.

In thys grete body of Englonde we have many diverse membres undre oone hede. Howe be hyt they may alle be reduced to iii chyef and principalle, whyche made thys hyghe and grete courte at thys tyme, that ys to seye, the lordes spiritualle, the lordes temporalle, and the commens.

The language, reminiscent of the mystical analysis by which the three estates were interpreted as parts or members of the church, is borrowed directly from Paul's exposition of membership in the body of Christ. Already the state takes the place of Christ and the church, and at the same time the knight and the gentleman are made to stand beside the merchant. In the estates of Christendom gentlemen had been classed with lords; now, in this secular thought, in the community of the nation, they become commons.[19]

Legal phraseology recognized the same divisions as parliamentary language did, regarding all who were not lords as common persons. Lyttleton noted that, in the event of an appeal against him, a lord and peer of the realm must be tried not by his peers but "comme un comen person."[20]

Another habit in the use of language that may have contributed to blur the dividing line of the three-estate scheme between merchants and gentry was the London custom, followed also in other cities, of distinguishing the mayor and aldermen as above the condition of ordinary commons or commoners. These terms were applied to members of the common council and to the population of the city at large but not to the presiding magistrates. One late chronicler went further, distinguishing wealthy merchants from commoners: "many Ryche Marchaunts and Comeners," he wrote, had died of the sweating sickness of 1484.[21]

The evidence of a dictionary is of more significance than any of these special usages. The *Catholicon Anglicum*, compiled about 1483, gives the word "commontye" (commonalty) the meanings of *vulgus, populus, plebs*, and *gens*, the first three of which were terms hitherto used only of people below the status of merchant, people associated with manual labor; it seems to regard these as filling the

19. *Grants from the Crown during the Reign of Edward V, etc.*, Camden Society, old ser., No. 60, pp. lviii–lix. Reference was to I Corinthians, chap. 12.
20. *The Year Books of Henry IV* ("Publications of the Selden Society"), XLVII (1931), 63. The term "commōner" was not yet used in this sense. The phrase "peers of the realm" dates from the time of Edward II (see T. F. Tout, *Chapters in Medieval Administrative History* [6 vols., 1920–33], III, 137).
21. See *New Oxford Dictionary* on "commoner"; Elyot's remarks there cited, of date 1531, apply also to the fifteenth century; Harl. MSS, 2252, fol. 6.

commonalty or estate of commons. "Gentylle men," moreover, is given the translation of *proceres, medio correpto*. This pays tribute, in the word *proceres*, to the traditional idea that gentlemen were noble, while at the same time it insists, in the phrase *medio correpto*, that they occupy only a middle position.[22]

The sense of sharp differentiation between baron and gentleman, relegating the latter to a middle position in society, comes out in a versified treatise on "The Active Policy of a Prince," written about 1460 or 1470 by George Ashby, once clerk of the signet to Queen Margaret of Anjou. He urged the king to be slow in creating new peers, "lest the Realme be charged"; many folk, he said, were of this opinion. For the same reason, the king should never appoint a temporal lord as his treasurer or receiver but should prefer a person of mean, that is, of middle, station, who would be both more competent and less greedy:

> For a lordis rewarde is infinite,
> A mene personne may be content with lite.[23]

Meanwhile the three-estate theory was receiving more notice than formerly. In the fourteenth century it had been expounded only from the pulpit and as an incidental theme in narrative or didactic writing that circulated in manuscript. In the fifteenth century it made its appearance in treatises on heraldry and chivalry. The professional heralds were more closely organized than before. Regulations alleged to have been drawn up for them about 1417 required them to read widely in chronicles and the literature of deeds of arms,[24] and there was a desire to summarize and preserve the lore that they collected. In other quarters, too, there was a deliberate cult of chivalry, the promoters of which were influential in the early use of the printing-press.

One of the heraldic treatises of the latter part of the fifteenth century seems to have been directed in part against the historical theory of the free middle class that is found in the *Cursor mundi*. Its argument was destined to have a very long life by being incorporated in the miscellaneous collection of lore that was printed in 1486 under the name of the Book of St. Albans. The book was reprinted a number of times in the next two centuries, and the sec-

22. E.E.T.S., original ser., No. 75, pp. 73, 153.
23. *George Ashby's Poems*, E.E.T.S., extra ser., No. 76, pp. 32, 38.
24. See A. R. Wagner, *Heralds and Heraldry in the Middle Ages* (1939), pp. 59, 138.

tions dealing with gentility were frequently plagiarized, both in print and in new manuscript treatises. The argument in question is set out with a bare but dramatic dogmatism. A twofold division of society into gentlemen and churls is traced to the blessing that Adam and Eve bestowed upon Seth, on the one hand, and to Cain's sin, on the other: "A brother to slay his brother contrary to the law where myght be more ungentelnes." The division thus begun was deepened by Noah's curse upon his son Ham for ir- reverence: "Now to the I gyve my curse wycked kaytife for ever." Ham and his descendants had been assigned not to Africa but to the north, to Europe, "where sorow and care cold and myschef as a churle thou shalt have . . . . Europe that is to say the contre of churlys." Japhet and Shem, on the contrary, had received their father's blessing; they and all their descendants were gentlemen. Japhet had been rewarded with "the weste parte of the world . . . . where as welth and grace shalt be," interpreted as Asia. Shem had been given Africa, where he was to multiply the blood of Abel. A modern reader might wonder how gentlemen were supposed to have reached northern Europe, but there was a casual allusion to the siege of Troy, which to the medieval reader would have made the whole story plain. Chronicles and romance had kept alive the legend of progressive Trojan migration to the west and north, led by nobles. This was accepted lore, the burden of proof lying on those who would deny it, and there were no grounds for denial. The Book of St. Albans emphasized the nobility of the Trojan leaders by linking them with the scriptural figure Japhet. Not only was he their ancestor, being the father of Asiatic peoples, but he had set the first example of interest in armorial art. He had drawn a ball on a shield, "in token of all the worlde." After this, the author remarks, coat armor was first used at the siege of Troy.[25]

The book then distinguishes nine "maner of gentylmen," the number corresponding to the nine orders of angels and to the nine colors used in blazoning arms. The first two distinctions given, between gentlemen of ancestry and blood and those only of blood, may have been borrowed from Continental usage. The lengths of

25. Facsimile edition, *The Boke of St. Albans*, ed. W. Blades (1881), no pagination. The heraldic treatise compiled in 1454–55, which bears the name R. Strangways, had also placed the origin of arms at the siege of Troy. At first called "marks," they were not called arms, it says, until after "brute and his knyghtis" had settled in England (Harl. MSS, 2259, fols. 11, 11b).

The story of Ham used to explain classes in English society.

pedigree required were not specified and were supplied only by much later English commentators as three generations from a grant of arms to constitute gentility of blood and four, on both sides of the family, to constitute ancestry.[26] Three more grades of gentlemen are described according to the way in which they received their arms—from the king, with or without a grant of land, or by killing a Saracen. The sixth and seventh are cryptically named gentlemen "untrial" and "ypocrafet," defined by Adam Loutfut, a Scottish heraldic author writing in 1494, as "divers gentlemen maid of gromes that bene not gentilmen of cote-armur nother of blood." Gerard Legh in 1562 identified the first with boys brought up by abbots or bishops and addressing them as "uncle" and the second with servants in the royal palace.[27] The total of nine is reached by absorbing the first estate. All priests are by virtue of their office spiritual gentlemen, but some, it is pointed out, are temporal gentlemen as well.

The Book of St. Albans in effect reduced the old three-estate theory to a theory of aristocracy, an incomplete one, clipped and allusive, omitting any reference to wealth, but one very agreeable to readers' tastes. The myth of Trojan ancestry to which it alludes had already proved to be of almost universal appeal through northern and western Europe. In spite of his fanciful matching of distinctions among gentlemen with the mystic number nine, the author was realistic enough to rate three of the main grounds of gentle rank, namely, birth, achievement, and service, in the order of importance that they would assume, considered apart from wealth.

Caxton, too, lent his press to propagation of the cult of chivalry. The only London merchant to leave us his views on the divisions in society, he fell under the spell of the romances and treatises on chivalry that formed part of his stock in trade as a publisher. Far from wishing to dignify the merchant class or to draw the middle

26. Gerard Legh, *The Accedence of Armory* (1562), p. 25; Francis Markham, *The Booke of Honor* (1625), pp. 47–48.

27. Legh, *op. cit.*, p. 25. John Fern added to gentlemen "untrial" those brought up in the service of a baron and those who were addressed as Master on account of having taken a university degree or of having held office in a city; he also counted students of the common law who had no coat armor as gentlemen "apocrafat" (*The Blazon of Gentrie* [1586], p. 90). Loutfut's *Liber armorum*, Harl. MSS, 6149, fols. 59–60. On Loutfut see A. T. P. Byles (ed.), *The Book of the Ordre of Chyvalry*, E.E.T.S., No. 168 (original ser., 1926), Introd., p. xxvi.

social strata closer together, he wrote like an arch-aristocrat. The French version of Ramón Lull's book on the order of chivalry that he translated allowed that men "de nouuel lignage, honnourable et gentil," could be admitted to knighthood; Caxton turned the point so as to condemn the dubbing of squires who were "vylayns," which would mean knighting "peple of lytyl lygnage lowe and vyle." He referred to "marchantes and other comone people" as though, like Dudley, he would place the merchants in the estate of commons.[28]

The object of the cult of chivalry as Caxton thought of it was to arouse interest in military training. His ideas, expressed in a vehement prologue to the Lull treatise, were in line with the simple preaching on the second estate that had long been heard from the pulpit. The social function of the knight was fulfilled in the military life, and the modern knight was degenerate. Rarely nowadays did he keep himself in training or have armor ready and a horse broken to his hand, "that he knoweth his hors and his hors hym"; he would prefer to spend his time lazily at the baths or dicing or in other dissipations.[29]

Although in Caxton's own view the knight's vocation was essentially military, he included in his translation a passage in which Lull urged that if knights had studied law they were peculiarly fitted to be judges and that kings ought in any case to appoint them to administrative offices, "for the kny3t is more worthy to have the seygnorye over the peple than ony other man. . . . ." A previous English writer, author of *The Boke of Noblesse*, had allowed himself to be so carried away by the glamour of war as to object to knights' taking any part in civil affairs. At one time in the entourage of Sir John Fastolf, he had been fascinated by his stories and especially by what Fastolf had heard of the training in chivalry that Duke Henry of Lancaster had given some foreign noblemen's sons. He produced his book in manuscript in 1475 with the hope of fanning enthusiasm for the reconquest of France. Men of noble blood, he believed, should hold the soldier's life superior to any other and should be trained for it in their "grene age." It

---

28. *Ibid.*, pp. xxxix, 57–58.. J. W. B. Crotch (ed.), *The Prologues and Epilogues of William Caxton* (1928), p. 60.

29. *Ibid.*, pp. 82–83. The theme of degeneracy was conventional. See Owst, *op. cit.*, pp. 320, 331–34.

was deplorable that gentlemen of birth should wish to study law or should seek office under the government. He could tolerate this in cadets "havyng not wherof to lyve honestly," but for their elder brothers it was a waste of time, motivated only by desire to oppress the people and "to kepe and bere out a proude countenance at sessions and shires holding." Yet such was the fashion. The gentleman "who can be a reuler . . . . is, as the worlde goithe now, among all astatis more set of" than the brave and experienced soldier.[30]

The writer attached to aristocratic circles was not necessarily so inflexible. Malory went so far as to recognize three divisions in lay society, his hero, Sir Tristram, having worked out means by which "all men of worship may dissever a gentleman from a yoeman and a yoeman from a villaine."[31] He was too intent on teaching the importance of gentle birth to note any differences in status, on other grounds, among gentlemen. But he was not so prejudiced as to class everyone else as churl or villein; there was room for a middle group.

This brief sampling of works that contained a view of the social order would suggest that the three-estate theory, as expounded in England between 1300 and 1500, had not been concerned to define status relationships in any detail. The philosophical thought that lay behind it was content with an ideal picture. The set hierarchy that it demanded was not actualized except in the higher ranks of the nobility. The theory was most easily expounded by presenting dramatically contrasted types, such as the lord or the knight, on the one hand, as against the manual laborer. In consequence the relative status of groups intermediate between these was left altogether ambiguous. This made it necessary for people to think also of a threefold stratification of lay society, posed in secular terms. The middle division was conceived of as including the lesser types of gentry, the merchant class, country yeomanry cherishing a tradition of free ancestry and perhaps also the more substantial semimercantile elements in London and other cities. But there was obviously little cohesion among these assorted groups, not even a common theory of a middle class.

30. *The Book of the Ordre of Chyvalry*, pp. 29–30. *The Boke of Noblesse*, ed. J. G. Nichols ("Publications of the Roxburghe Club," No. 77 [1860]), pp. 76–78.

31. *Le Mort d'Arthure*, ed. T. Wright (1865), II, 6.

2. ATTITUDES TOWARD SOCIAL ASCENT

The traditional social teaching upheld the virtues of meekness and contentment and tried to minimize the competitive spirit but did not attempt to smother social ambition entirely. Contentment, for the commons, was interpreted partly as a negative political attitude; they were to "hold hem contente with þe questions and þe sotelte of þer own labour," leaving matters of government to the second estate. The exhortation, "let us not change of oure estatis," drawn from the comparison of life to a chessboard, on which by the rules of the game every piece had its set function, did not explain the rules by which a man would know the precise occupation and rank with which he was to stay content. According to Dudley, in his *Tree of Commonwealth*, people were allotted their station by God and the king, but he does not say in what way or at what time of life the choice was made. For the commons, he disapproved of any considerable rise in status during one generation. Yet even Dudley, the most rigid of all English exponents of the three-estate theory, did not insist that people should remain in the same station as their parents. Some late fifteenth-century verses on the conduct of life assume that the children of working people should do so:

> And gef þer faderis war servandis or husbandis
> Lat þam ga seike sic laboris in þe landis
> Batht tel and saw and dyk and delff þe erde
> Or use sum craft. . . . .

The verses are a paraphrase of a twelfth-century source in which there is an assumption that rank is hereditary. The question under discussion was whether, on the death of a father, sons should divide his property. Nobles should not divide family property. Merchants might find it advisable to do so. Workers could do as they chose: "Si laboratores sunt, faciant quod volunt." The four lines quoted, an expansion of this bald sentence, may reflect some contemporary feeling. But they are not evidence of English thought; for, as his language shows, the versifier was a Scot.[32]

The ambition to rise was ordinarily censured only when formerly privileged families felt their interests to be threatened by the upward currents of social circulation. Then, it is true, indignation

---

32. *Middle English Sermons*, p. 224; cf. Owst, *op. cit.*, pp. 558–59; *Bernardus de cura rei familiaris*, ed. J. R. Lumby, E.E.T.S., original ser., No. 42, pp. v–ix, 11.

could take on a moral tone and may have drawn upon the doctrine of contentment. Langland protested against the opening of ecclesiastical promotion to "Bondmen and bastardes and beggers children." He seemed to feel that it should be a preserve for "poure gentil blod" or, at least, that gentlemen entering the church should have preference over men of lower birth. Wycliffe similarly sympathized with "pore gentil men" who were being ousted from office and favor with lords, he claimed, by pharisaic clerks and friars. He also attacked lowborn ambitious clerics for spending church revenues on building up the fortunes of their families in order to pretend that they had come of noble blood: "þus ben many in englond maad riche fro ful symple staat."[33]

The greater gentry for long looked askance on the profession of law, another of the channels of mobility through which men of lower birth could rise to positions of power. A witness in a court of chivalry in the reign of Richard II gave evidence to the effect that his father had heard someone say that Sir Richard Scrope "nestoit my gentil homme par cause qil fuist Justice de Roy," the implication being that no man of really good birth would become "un homme de la ley."[34]

Resistance to social ascent thus gained emotional force from feelings that clustered about the idea of good birth. Poor gentry should not have to compete with men of lower birth nor should they seek to exceed in power the better-born. Belief in the superiority of people born into landed families that had been able to maintain their position for several generations was very deeply rooted. It was perpetually challenged but to no effect; the defense was elastic and impregnable.

The age was not without radical doubt, and not everyone would believe in the superiority of the great. The doubter offered only a weak and grumbling challenge, but for fear of revolutionary intent he was taken seriously and arguments were marshaled against him. The Book of St. Albans testifies to the obstinate appeal of the nongentle to common descent from Adam; hence its insistence, countering the appeal, that Adam's stock had been unequally endowed from the beginning. Other defensive arguments could be

---

33. *Piers the Plowman*, C vi, ll. 65 ff.; *The English Works of Wyclif*, E.E.T.S., original ser., No. 74, pp. 13, 439.

34. *The Scrope and Grosvenor Controversy*, ed. Sir N. H. Nicolas (1832), I, 181–82; II, 426–27.

drawn from the animal world as viewed at second and third remove through the fourth-century treatise of Vegetius on the art of war, which was made familiar by a number of translations. Citing Virgil as authority for the statement that there are two kinds of bee, "a gentil and a vile," this worked its way through various examples of timidity and fighting spirit among animals to the conclusion that only landed knights of noble birth could be relied upon to show courage in warfare. They will develop shame, which "wil refreyne hem not to fle."[35]

Another attack came from the moral angle, by way of revival of the ancient Roman saying that true nobility consisted not in blood but in virtue. Moralists used it to rebuke class pride. Yet when they interpreted *virtus* as Christian virtue, their own remarks tacitly admit that the appeal of nobility was the stronger. It was an incentive to the Christian to be virtuous, to tell him that he would then, in some mystic sense, be noble.[36] Moreover, there was no general agreement on the meaning of the term *virtus*. In this context it could refer also to the qualities appropriate to nobility, which were not necessarily identical with the Christian virtues. In spite of preaching on the subject, it was difficult to understand how it could include, for example, Christian humility. As Gower pointed out:

> In high astat it is a vice
> To go to low. . . . .

In eulogies of noblemen of the age and in romances there are endless examples of compromise between the ideals, but the compromise was always one that left belief in the superiority of men of birth intact. A typical position is well expressed in verses composed for a pageant in 1503:

35. *Of Knyghthode and Bataile*, E.E.T.S., No. 201 (original ser., 1935), ll. 235 ff., 271–75. Vegetius had been translated at least as early as 1400 (see H.M.C., *6th Report, Appendix*, p. 289).

36. See *The Ayenbit of Inwyt*, E.E.T.S., original ser., No. 23, pp. 87–88, a translation, dating *ca.* 1340, of *Le Somme des vices et de vertues*, composed *ca.* 1279 by Frère Lorens, O.P. On the history of the idea see G. M. Vogt, "Gleanings for the History of a Sentiment: *Generositas virtus, non sanguis*," *Journal of English and Germanic Philology*, XXIV (1925), 102–25; also G. Salvemini, "Florence in the Time of Dante," *Speculum*, XI (1936), 321–22; and J. E. Mason, *Gentlefolks in the Making* (1935), chap. i. For Chaucer's treatment of it see *The Tale of the Wyf of Bathe*, ll. 1109–76; *The Balade of Gentilesse*; his *Boethius De consolatione philosophiae*, Prose VI, Metre VI; and *Romaunt of the Rose*, B, ll. 2175–2342.

Vertu appartenyth unto every astate
As well to Noble, as ffolk of lowe degre
But yit the noble, afftyr an othyr Rate
Be applyed, of theyr Rygth propyrte
To be vertuous, and to have Regale,
Guyvyng the people, by strength for deffence
Of theym and theyrs, by singuler prudence. . . . .

In other words, everyone ought to be good, but the nobility have in any event a peculiar property of virtue which fits them to rule and defend the people.[37]

It might seem that the idea that courtesy was an essential attribute of the gentleman would have weakened respect for birth. Courtesy, consisting in manners and bearing, could not well be represented as innate; it was obviously a set of socially acquired characteristics and was indeed described as such, as a matter of nurture. The author of a dictionary compiled in about the year 1440 looked on manners as the very essence of nobility or gentility, translating *ingenuitas* by "gentry" and defining the latter as "nortore and manerys." Since it offered a common ideal of the cultivation of a dignified personality, the contemporary discussion of manners may have helped to blur distinctions among the various groups in the middle strata of society. The writer of a treatise on courtesy for boys, a type of manual that was to become increasingly popular, told his readers to "thinke in þi selve þat þou wold be a man"; he also represented his book as a useful guide to getting on in the world:

The child þat is curtas, be he pore or ryche
Yt schalle hym Avaylle, þer-off have no drede. . . . .

But the courtesy that was nurtured among the greater families remained of a different order and served as a subtle means of asserting superiority. It was not thought of as something that could be imitated or acquired quickly. Like courage, courtesy was a flower that came to perfection only after several generations. So the romances taught. Their heroes can disguise themselves only with difficulty. In Gower's tale of Apollonius of Tyre the king's daughter recognizes the hero as a nobleman almost at once.

He myte noght have such manere
Of gentil blod bot if he were,

37. Gower, *Confessio amantis*, ll. 1035–36. Pageant verses in *The Great Chronicle*, p. 300.

she cries, on hearing him speak and sing. The medieval reader who was familiar with the world of romance would not have objected that anyone could learn to speak politely and to entertain with a song or two; he would know that the great gentleman had a special facility for acquiring all the arts that pertained to courtesy and easily excelled in them. As Malory expressed it, "he that is of gentle blood will draw unto him gentle tatches."[38]

Ancestry was the most mysterious of the great gentleman's attributes. It connected him with the dead and with the universally recurring idea of magical properties in the blood; and the mythical chain of descent leading through the Trojans to Japhet and Seth, like descent from the gods, served to link him with divine grace. These may have been the only reasons why it dominated the descriptions of the great and the arguments in defense of their superiority. Families of the fourteenth and fifteenth centuries actually knew very little about their ancestry. They had few deeds or seals antedating the twelfth century, few hereditary arms ran back any further, and there were no early portraits. There is no genealogical information on the medieval rolls of arms. The pedigrees of which people boasted were passed on orally through the memories of the aged, a process which allowed fairly free play to the imagination. In the late fourteenth century several friends of the first baron Scrope testified on hearsay, without having seen any written record professing to prove it, that he was descended from great gentlemen of the time of the Norman Conquest. A Somerset knight, who was questioned, recalled that Scrope had once proved to the earl of Northampton that the arms dated from the Conqueror's reign; by the same method of proof a cousin of his own, from Cornwall, who bore the same arms as Scrope, had satisfied the earl that his right to them dated from the time of King Arthur ("Thomas Carmynau prova ces armes du temp le Roy Arthur"). A writer dedicating a romance to Sir Miles Stapleton in 1449 credited him with descent from fifty-two generations of "nobyl werriouris," a number chosen quite at random.[39]

This vagueness and arbitrariness caution one against assuming that there was much rational reflection about heredity. Eulogists

---

38. *Promptorium parvulorum*, E.E.T.S., extra ser., No. 102, p. 189. Gower, *Confessio amantis*, lib. VIII, ll. 793–94. *A Booke of Precedence*, E.E.T.S., extra ser., No. 8. Malory, *op. cit.*, ed. Wright, II, 6–7.

39. *Scrope and Grosvenor Roll*, I, 62, 92, 100, 134, 167, 169, 178.

touched on it but only with regard to qualities that were conventionally ascribed to the great. One reads of the earl of Warwick that he was "borne of a stock that evyr schal be trewe," and Stapleton's eulogist remarked that

> . . . . a gret rootyd tre
> Durabyl frute beryth,

but with reference only to the conventional qualities of worthiness, prudence, and discretion and to the wealth with which these were associated.[40] Despite imaginative fascination with the idea of descent, there was no clear notion of differing strains in human stock with fixed characteristics. It was only the social categories that were fixed, the estates and their component ranks. Human stock could move up and down through the ranks and from one estate to the other. Families were not conceived of as permanently gentle or common. They could fall from nobility, and they could rise into it.

The subject of social circulation was obviously distasteful to chivalric sensibilities. It might never have been discussed with any attempt at precision but for the development of a sense of property in coats-of-arms and the occurrence of disputes over their ownership. In England these were dealt with in a military court under the control of royal officers—the constable and the marshal. The chief of the professional heralds, the kings-of-arms appointed by the king, in the fifteenth century acquired more authority in matters of arms.[41] They and others who were interested were influenced in their views by Italian juristic thought, as formulated by Bartolo di Sassoferrato about 1356. But the so-called "law of arms," which the Book of St. Albans proudly describes as part of the law of nature, therefore older than the law of Moses, was compounded largely of uncertainties, and there was continual debate over its principles. Much of the debate circled about the question of the relation between arms and gentility or nobility, and it is in this connection that views on social circulation emerge.

There was general accord in England with the Italian view that a family lost the quality of nobility if its members fell to poverty or took to "artes viles." This is the phrase used by Nicholas Upton,

40. *Political Poems*, ed. T. Wright, R.S. (1861), p. 270; *The Works of John Metham*, E.E.T.S., original ser., No. 132, p. 78.
41. Wagner, *op. cit.*, pp. 21-24, 56-65.

canon of Salisbury and Wells, in reference to Italian custom; his treatise on arms, the outstanding work on the subject produced in England, was written about 1440.[42] Occupations were considered "vile" if they involved manual labor or menial service, except in the position of a gentleman servant in a royal palace or other great household. In the late fifteenth century a gentleman of higher rank could experience an immediate sense of disgrace if he were seen putting his hand to a vile task. A gentleman who apprenticed his son to Sir William Capell, London draper, asked the latter to give his word that the boy should not "be a keper of his horses berer of his tankardes nor to do any soche vyle and beseytous service the which shold be any abasshement to the seid apprentice considerying that he was a gentilman and alied to many worshipful." When the boy soon afterward suffered a severe illness, his father represented that this was due to the strain of having been compelled to help with stable and household chores. To his "gret shame" and "utter destruction" he had been obliged to carry tubs containing the Capell family's dirty linen from Cornhill to the Thames, where it was to be washed.[43]

But the fall of a family, even after catastrophic loss of fortune, was slow, the recourse to labor being postponed as long as possible. The Book of St. Albans sums up the process laconically in its story of the four evangelists, who were all supposed to have been descended from Judas Maccabeus. After this hero's defeat and ruin his descendants had gradually sunk in the social scale: "by succession of tyme the kynrade fell to poverty . . . . and then they fell to laboris and Ware calde no gentilmen."

Heraldic discussion shows that social ascent was taken for granted in the same way, provided that it was of a correspondingly slow rhythm. The spread of the custom of displaying arms posed a number of questions that bore upon the first acquisition of gentility. It was laid down early in the fifteenth century that arms were a necessary criterion of gentility. At a session of the court of chivalry held in the reign of Henry IV several of the older witnesses described themselves as gentlemen of ancestry although they had no arms. One, an esquire from Buckinghamshire with 20 marks worth of land, gave as an excuse that neither he nor his

42. *De studio militari*, ed. E. Bysshe (1654), pp. 3, 61.
43. E.C.P., 94/22 (1485); cf. E.C.P., 1/366, and Liber Dunthorne, fol. 392.

father had been to war. The court placed all this on record, together with a statement that the only people now accounted
gentle were those who possessed arms, either by inheritance or by
their own acquisition.[44] If they were not inherited, how were arms
to be acquired? It was agreed that the king had the authority to
grant them, but in England he very seldom did so. The earliest
English writer in the field, about 1394, ascribed some authority
also to kings-of-arms and other heralds; but Upton, not finding
any reference to this point in Bartolo di Sassoferrato, cast doubt
on it and ruled that people who were ennobled by virtue could
quite as properly assume arms on their own initiative as accept
them from a herald.[45]

A man was thus free to judge of his own ripeness in gentility,
subject only to the opinion of his neighbors. Heraldic writing was
not very explicit as to the kind or measure of virtue that he would
require. Upton wrote that many poor men had become ennobled
through service in the French wars, and he approved their action
in taking arms on their own authority. He could not have been
referring only to the winning of military distinction, for he mentioned prudence and energy and indicated vaguely that there were
still other relevant virtues, as well as valor. The Book of St. Albans,
paraphrasing the passage, omits the reference to the French wars,
as out of date, but remains vague: ". . . . in theys days opynly we
se . how many poore men by theyr grace favoure laboure or de-
servying . are made nobuls Sum by ther prudens . Sum bi ther manhood . sum bi ther strength . sum bi ther conyng . sum bi oder
virtuys. . . . ."

The duke of Clarence, who is supposed to have promulgated the
official rules for the guidance of kings-of-arms and other heralds, in
1417, had indicated bluntly that one of these other virtues was a
matter of property. Arms were not to be granted to the vile or
dishonest but could be given to anyone who was virtuous, honest,
and prosperous (*de bonne substance*).[46] In a dispute between two of
the kings-of-arms, Garter and Clarenceux, in 1530, it came out

44. "Quod notatu dignum duximus, quia hac nostra aetate illos solos generosos reputa-
mus quibus a majoribus, sive ex propria adquisitione, arma sive insignia sunt, generositatem
indicantia" (*An Account of the Controversy between Reginald Lord Grey of Ruthyn and Sir
Edward Hastings in the Court of Chivalry in the Reign of King Henry IV* [1481], p. 29).
45. The arguments are summarized in Wagner, *op. cit.*, pp. 67–69, 72–73.
46. *Ibid.*, p. 137.

that this rule had long been interpreted as justifying a precise property qualification, namely, an income of £10 from lands or else movable goods to the value of £200 or £300.[47] In the wording of their patents, however, the heralds refrained from any allusion to property, dwelling instead, in a flowery style, on the applicant's courage and virtue. Their grants to individuals were of three types. The first affected merely to confirm a man's right to bear arms which had belonged to his ancestors but had been forgotten: "consideringe the worshipfull disposition of his persone and of his habilite in gentilnesse, I . . . . have founde owte the Armes of his progenytours which been suche. . . . ."[48] A second type begged the question of the applicant's virtue more briefly, merely certifying that the arms he proposed to bear, and had, perhaps, already been displaying, were "trulie his and to his heires."[49] The third type was frankly a new creation, based on some such formula as this, from a grant of the year 1460:

> Equity requires and reason ordains that men virtuous and of noble courage be rewarded for their merits by renown and that not only their persons in this mortal life so brief and transitory but after them those who shall issue and be procreated of their bodies may be in all places of great honour perpetually shining before others by certain signs and shows of gentility. . . . .[50]

The phrases dealing with virtue were painfully labored in their avoidance of any reference to prosperity. A confirmation of arms made out in 1443 professed to be rewarding the courage of a gentleman who had been to France under Henry V, that is, over twenty years before.[51] The virtue and truth of an exchequer clerk who was given arms in 1479 consisted in his having "sadly and honourably gyded and governyd himselfe," and another gentleman's recommendation lay in the fact that he was "couragiously moeved . . . .

---

47. *Ibid.*, pp. 78–79, 83–99, giving the figure of £300, from State Papers. MS Faustina, E, 1, fol. 249, gives £200.

48. *Miscellanea genealogica et heraldica*, V (4th ser., 1914), 121 (grant dated 1443). Copies of similar fifteenth-century grants in Harl. MSS, 69, fols. 55*b* (1507), 3–5, 10*b*, 205; Society of Antiquaries MSS, 511, Roll No. 11; College of Arms, *Register of Nobility and Gentry*, Vol. II, fols. 639, 668, 676; *A Collection of Miscellaneous Grants* ("Publications of the Harleian Society"), LXXVI (1925), 31, 70.

49. Harl. MSS, 69, fols. 55 (1507), 7*b*; College of Arms, *Register of Nobility and Gentry*, Vol. II, fol. 633.

50. *A Collection of Miscellaneous Grants*, LXXVI, 3. Similar formulas, 1479 and 1481, *ibid.*, p. 92, and in College of Arms, *Register of Nobility and Gentry*, Vol. II, fol. 635.

51. Harl. MSS, 69, fol. 55; cf. MS Faustina, E, 1, fol. 12, and *A Collection of Miscellaneous Grants*, LXXVI, 3; LXXVII, 149–50.

to atteigne unto honure and wourshipe."[52] The wording of a patent of the year 1481 half admits that the general certification of ancestry it conveys is fictitious. Other people, it hopes, will be encouraged to follow the grantee's example, spending their lives in honorable works and virtuous deeds "for to purchase and gett thereby the renoune of Antient gentleness."[53]

Gossip would surely have spread knowledge of this situation. An intelligent person who contemplated the assumption of arms would have known further that, if he was of low origin or of very recent prosperity, he ought not to hurry the step; it would perhaps be best to leave it to his sons. The heralds were supposed to refuse arms to men "vyle borne" and to rebels, and to denounce as invalid any arms that these might assume of their own accord.[54]

Fifteenth-century evidence nevertheless tells of determination to be counted among the lesser gentry as soon as possible. Nicholas Newetymbyr, buying land in Surrey in 1431, did not allow his name to deter him from adding the title of "gentilman," and from the same period there is a case of a gentleman villein in Oxfordshire. The latter was a man of some education, having been brought up as a boy at New College, but he had only a few acres of land and, when the abbot of Abingdon claimed him as a bondman, had difficulty in raising the sum of 50 marks that was the price of manumission.[55]

Once he had entered the lesser gentry, a man's further efforts to rise encountered the full pressure of conservative opinion. For himself he would have to rest content with accumulating more land and arranging good marriages for his children; it would be for his sons or his grandsons to reap the benefit. There was no short cut into the ranks of the higher gentry except by the favor of the king, and even then the older families would be hostile to the new. Froissart paints a picture of one of the soldiers knighted by Edward III, Sir Robert Salle, as a paragon of chivalric skill, valor, and beauty, yet he represents the rebels of 1381 as tempting

52. College of Arms, *Register of Nobility and Gentry*, Vol. II, fols. 537, 635; cf. *A Collection of Miscellaneous Grants*, LXXVII, 192.

53. *Ibid.*, LXXVI, 92.

54. This was the tradition as interpreted in 1530. A roll of grants going back to the time of Edward IV was apparently submitted in evidence that the rule had not been broken (Wagner, *op. cit.*, pp. 79, 90–91).

55. *Surrey Fines* ("Publications of the Surrey Archaeological Society," Extra Vol. I), p. 180; E.C.P., 44/4.

him to join them because, being only the son of a mason, he will never be accepted as a gentleman.

The great gentleman's jealousy of the new man who had won the favor of the king was mixed with a conviction that only those who had inherited wealth could be trusted to observe old ways. Bishop Russell gave bitter and imaginative vent to these feelings in the draft of an attack on the Rivers family that he had intended to deliver before Edward V's parliament, if this had met. If there was any firmness under heaven, he wrote, it was in the firm land around which sea and rivers flow, not "in eny grete Ryvers." The land, the islands, stood for the nobility, endowed with riches. Lower people were necessarily unstable, like the wavering, running water, because there was not enough wealth for everyone ("for lacke of suche endumente, not possible to be departed amonges so many"), and they had therefore to live "by ther casuelle labours." This metaphor of stability as found only in the noble rich epitomizes much of the social thought of the age. To bring out more sharply his point that to give a man true stability his wealth should be inherited, Russell added a familiar definition of nobility as "vertu and auncienne Richesse," which had the authority of Aristotle. In other words, ascent into the highest ranks must be slow.[56]

The idea of social stability, approved by all authority, was the most natural and the simplest guide that chivalric and popular moral thought could have accepted. Change was something fortuitous that by definition could not be reduced to order. Unless it should assume disturbing proportions, why, then, discuss it? Thus the movement of individuals and families across the supposedly fixed ranks of society was not a subject of much discussion except as it recalled the ancient idea of Fortune or as it might appear to threaten some established interest.

Ascent into and within the middle strata of English society was accepted with little question. Among the lesser landed gentry it was cloaked with the fiction of ancestry. The recruiting of new men as gentlemen in service, as officials, or as military knights was justified by the lord's need or the king's need. The wide recruiting of the merchant class was similarly justified by the usefulness of the class. A Yorkshire knight who had a grievance against an alderman in York in 1500 could write of him rudely to the mayor as "a

56. *Grants from the Crown during the Reign of Edward V*, pp. xl–xli.

carle which ye knowe is comen lightly up and of smale substance and wilbe maid glade shortly to knawe his neghbours for his better." One would gather that respect for his wealth would ordinarily keep in check any latent disapproval of a merchant's quick ascent. The great merchant had also to be respected as a deserving candidate for magistracy. It was on this score that the mayor of York defended his brother alderman from the knight's insult: "all this Citie knoweth that he wurshipfully hath been and born the charge as the Kyngs lieutenant within this Citie."[57]

3. CONCLUSIONS

In every aspect of the life of London merchants and their families, the detail lends itself to emphasis upon elements which are the opposite of static. Customs that stand out as fixed were fixed in a pattern that fostered ambition in the individual and often impelled him toward goals that were not his father's. Wealth that was accumulated was quickly dispersed. New families were constantly appearing for a generation or two, by the end of which time either they were physically extinguished or else surviving members had moved to new scenes and a different social position. These facts lead insistently beyond the local context and demand a broad background for summary and interpretation.

Business conditions of the time account for some of the flux and insecurity. The hand-to-mouth methods of public finance, the risks from piracy, interruptions in the flow of foreign trade by war and of the home demand by epidemics—all bore upon the merchant with urgency. He was pushed into a scramble for influence and favor in army contracting and for the temporary security of such appointments as the customs service and the royal household offered. The wise merchant cultivated political patronage and flexibility of interests because he could not safely plod in a rut. He fed commercial capital into the cloth industry, which could find both home and foreign outlets, but he could not trust to industrial expansion in other directions. In towns there was a wide demand for the finer consumers' goods in which he dealt, but the same was not so true of rural districts, which contained the mass of the population, and there was no promise of rapid change in this con-

57. *York Civic Records* ("Yorkshire Archaeological Society, Record Series," Vol. CIII [1941]), Part II, p. 156.

dition. To nurse increasing accumulations of capital for industrial purposes did not ordinarily suggest itself as a prudent family policy; scattered holdings of land, with mixed produce, were by all odds of more appeal as an investment.

But, however fully they are analyzed, business conditions alone will not account for all the behavior that has been described. Custom and circumstance, arising out of the pattern of family life and its integration with religious belief, contributed to the instabilities. The custom of setting aside at least a third of a man's movables, including the value of merchandise and debts, as a kind of voluntary death duty for pious and charitable purposes considerably hindered the accumulation of capital. Investment in land could exempt a portion of the estate from these obligations, but only about half the class bought land and it, too, was sometimes devoted to pious uses. Since half the London merchant class, or more, left estates worth less than £200, the portions of heirs were often too small to provide them with the security of income adequate for support. The circumstance that more than half the sons were under age at the time of the father's death meant that the smaller portions were not available intact as trading capital but had to be eaten into for the children's maintenance and apprenticeship or other education. The same circumstance, the relatively early death of the father, could affect the sons' future in still another way, in that there was often no family business in existence by the time that they came of age. Sometimes the widow kept the business up or remarried in the same company with very little delay, so that the business of the one husband could be amalgamated with that of the next. But otherwise the young men, if they wished to enter trade, were obliged to make their own openings. If they had inherited capital, this may have been quite easy. Even if they had no inheritance beyond the amount needed as premium for apprenticeship, it would not have been too difficult. They would have their training, they could then earn wages, and they could ultimately borrow money for trade or acquire it by marriage. Probably no merchants' sons were left in literal economic insecurity; they would have enough at least to equip them for making their own way. But they did not necessarily have the kind of fixed hereditary security that would come of being able to enter a family business and succeed to the father's position. This could be true in the richer families as well as in the less successful. Elder and younger sons alike could be left quite free in their choice of a career.

These circumstances lie behind the apparent restlessness of ambition, the frequent disinclination to follow tamely in the father's course of life. The lack of continuity in the families composing the class was due partly to the high death rates but also to this restlessness. If all surviving sons had been content to follow in their fathers' footsteps, the class would not have been nearly so fluid.

But why were sons not content to remain in a class in which the rewards could be so high? The lack of fixed hereditary security in the same status as the father, due to the discontinuity of firms, explains only why it was not a binding custom to follow the father; it does not explain the frequency of movement into other careers. Moreover, many boys who were orphaned very young went into apprenticeship, and many of the sons who turned their backs on trade were of age before their father died and could quite well have chosen to go into partnership with him.

There is another angle to the problem. Merchants' sons would hardly have been left so free in their decisions had not their fathers and their fathers' friends been able to find apprentices elsewhere. The boys who came to them, who could pay for their training, were in their turn obviously restless, either unable or unwilling to follow their fathers. Mostly from the country or from provincial towns, they represented all other sections of the middle strata of the nation. They were not obliged to come to London any more than the London boys were obliged to leave their fathers' class. There was some common quality of ambition in this whole area of society that is far too interesting to be taken for granted. The situations that gave rise to it call for analysis and comparison.

The social thought of the time dealt with it only indirectly. Traditional social theory could not grapple with such phenomena as insecurity and mobility and had tended to ignore them. The most commonly expressed views of the social order dwelt on the landed aristocracy and the agricultural laborers, two groups that were characterized by a fixed hereditary security. Although in the former only one son could succeed to the father's niche in the social hierarchy, there was always wealth and influence enough to assure younger sons of a high place in the service of a noble or of the king.

Among the peasantry there were several different customs of inheritance, but the strong demand for labor in the later middle ages assured all sons of security in a status very close to that of the father. In the middle strata of society these conditions did not hold.

There is no need to look for sharp edges of contrast, because there were no sharp lines of social demarcation. The lesser landed gentry and the yeomanry merged, respectively, into the greater gentry and into the peasantry. Again, among both lesser landed gentry and yeomanry, if only one son survived, he could succeed securely enough to the father's land and social position. While there was a prospect that more than one son would survive, however, the future of the younger ones constituted a graver family problem than could have been the case at either extreme of the social scale. For the son of a gentleman or yeoman to take to wage labor like one of the poorer villagers would bring disparagement to his family. To solicit influence from a patron to help him in some other direction might not be easy. Younger sons had to be prepared to shift for themselves with no more help than a small cash legacy. Quarreling over the amounts of these could bring anxiety to bear also on the heir, to whom the small property left him was the sole guaranty of independence in a position equal to that of the father. The sense of insecurity, with consequent need of careful husbanding of resources and of toadying to patrons, was probably higher among gentlemen in service, officials, and lawyers, for in none of these groups could even the eldest son succeed automatically to his father's position.

The pattern no doubt took on many variations in different environments. The common core is the fact that early family relationships could have impressed the individual with notions of economic and social insecurity in his formative years. This made for a widespread cultural similarity among all sections of the middle strata of society.

Moralists, feeling it their duty to check the individualistic and family ambition that resulted, are among the witnesses on whom one can call. A mid-fifteenth-century moral treatise that decried the "avauntyng of godys" named four objects of boasting in this order: riches, "nobylte of kyn," friends, and strength. The last three of these add up to influence, the means to advancement, and the secure acquisition of property. Another writer divided the goods "whare-of a man enprydes hym" into three classes: those "of kynde," wherewith he is endowed by nature, such as wit and noble kindred; those "of purchase," that he has to strive for, such as "cunnynge" and "dygnyte or office"; and "erthely gude," including clothes, houses, rents, servants, horses, and "honour of þis worlde."[58] These writings were not addressed to the peasantry, who were shut out from all honor of this world, or to the great, who, being manifestly noble themselves, would not have to boast of noble kindred. It was in the area intermediate between the great and the peasantry that ambition was so petty, restless, and insidious.

Apart from these conventional warnings against worldly pride and cautions against the other sins, popular religious teaching had no special help for the man whose family pushed him into making his own way. The influences arising from economic and social insecurity were not yet connected with any clearly thought-out theory of the individual's place in the universe, as was to occur later with the absorption of Calvinist thought in Puritan culture. They were formalized only in the traditional kind of wisdom that was embodied in proverbs on the themes of prudence and thrift and discretion. Some of these were handed down orally and some were found in the Old Testament and in such books as the sayings attributed to Cato, which Caxton valued so highly. They supported family and professional discipline and, as the clichés of conversation, perhaps helped people to understand each other. But they did not constitute a bond of unity of the positive force that fully developed religious or political ideas can provide.

Chivalric literature is significant in marking one of the lines of disunity within the middle strata but is misleading by exaggeration. By convention it singled out the merchant as the type of avarice and ambition, narrowly absorbed in the pursuit of money and power, in contrast to the noble, who, in the romantic world, made life an art. Burgess and merchant are the least courageous of the tragic figures in the Dance of Death. Their hearts "ai frette with covetise," they clutch miserably at their treasures and cannot reconcile themselves to giving up their powers of city government

58. *Jacob's Well*, E.E.T.S., original ser., No. 115, p. 149; *Religious Pieces in Prose and Verse from Robert Thornton's MS*, E.E.T.S., original ser., No. 26, p. 23.

to others. They make a poor showing beside the types of chivalry—
the baron and the knight, the amorous squire and gentlewoman—
who move to their death living to the full, "Lusti fre of herte / and
eke desyrous," the very air about them enlivened by tournament
trumpets and dance music.[59] Charles of Orleans unkindly stretched
the contrast to cover citizens' wives and daughters. You win their
favor only by gifts, preferably by something rich "to fresshe them
in a-ray," whereas the way to please gentlefolk is "by sewte of
curteys speche."[60]

It is unlikely that people were conscious of any difference between one group and another on this score. All were acquisitive.
Langland's figure of Avarice confessed to an impartial influence
over knights and merchants:

> Ich have mad meny a knyght . bothe mercer and draper
> Payede neuere for here prentishode   nauht a payre gloues

and Wycliffe condemned lawyers as well as merchants for getting
rich quickly, "now ben þei pore, and now ben þei ful riche, for
wronges þat þei done."[61]

In wit and gaiety the merchant would perhaps not have shone
beside a polished courtier, but neither, one imagines, would a rustic
gentleman. Chaucer might insinuate that the merchant was a
bore, talking always of his gains, but talk of crops and hunting
could surely be quite as monotonous. Both merchants and gentlemen were, in fact, touchy on the score of heaviness of wit. The
author of *The Great Chronicle* regarded it as scandalous that a
mayor of London, Onlegreve, once fell asleep while presiding at an
important treason trial; he was "a Replete and lumpysh man" is
the comment.

Generosity was supposed to be a gentlemanly characteristic.
Hoccleve, spending freely in the London and Westminster taverns,
felt that he was looked on as "a verray gentleman"; and a herald,
angry with a man who had protested against the high scale of fees
charged at a ceremonial bestowal of knighthood, put him on record
as "not willing never to doo as a gentilman shulde doo. I

59. *The Dance of Death*, E.E.T.S., original ser., No. 81, pp. 20, 26–27, 29, 38, 40, 44, 54,
56.
60. *The English Poems of Charles of Orleans*, Roxburghe Club (1827), pp. 6–7.
61. *Piers the Plowman*, C VII, ll. 250–51; *Select English Works of Wyclif*, ed. T. Arnold
(1871), III, 153.

pray god lerne him better." Yet as between the wealthy sections of one group and another there was little difference in spending habits; all were extravagant.

It was chiefly in its aspect of command over luxury consumption that the literary imagination of the age conceived of the power of money. A jingle in handwriting of the late fifteenth century paraphrases the old saying that manners make the man:

> Yt ys all wayes sene now a days
> That money makythe the man.[62]

The reference would seem to be simply to "conspicuous consumption." In this aspect the power of money was associated with all wealthy groups and, generally, with worldly success of any type. Popular gossip would link any prominent man with the idea of great fortune. In illustration of untrue opinion, Pecock alludes in passing to the fact that people might believe a London alderman to be "miche riccher than in trouthe he is." A London chronicle notes the death of John Franke, an ecclesiastical pluralist in the king's service, with the remark that he "was holde the rychist man that dyed in many yers."[63] In all English literature there can be no more longing and anxious eulogy of money than occurs in the doggerel verses that Peter Idley, a gentleman falconer in the service of the king, in the mid-fifteenth century addressed to his son. Money is the key to all that a man can desire. It will bring him friends, protect him from enemies; it will "purchase blisse," make him "a Godde undre God."[64]

The conception of money as capital, as a new nexus of power, was not absent but was dim. In the tale of King Edward and the shepherd a merchant rides about the country in the background, a dominating and vaguely sinister figure:

> He is a marchande of gret powere
> Many man is his trespere
> Men owe hym mony a pounde.[65]

But this was only one aspect of the power with which a great merchant was associated. He was not yet wholly identified with it; he

62. Reg. MS, 17B, XLVII (British Museum).

63. *The Great Chronicle*, pp. 173, 422.

64. *Peter Idley's Instructions to His Son*, ed. C. d'Evelyn ("Modern Language Association of America, Monograph Series," No. 6), lib. I, ll. 684-90.

65. *Ancient Metrical Tales*, ed. C. Hartshorne (1829), p. 59.

was also the landlord, the city magistrate, the man with patrons in the government. The abbot of St. Albans came to terms with Thomas Knolles in a dispute over hunting rights adjacent to the latter's manor of South Mimms because he reckoned him as too powerful and subtle an adversary to sue at law.[66]

The ambition of fifteenth-century gentle families appears to have been directed with much more intensity toward the profession of law than toward trade. In the tale of the Childe of Bristowe the son of a rich landed squire of the west country is for some inner reason anxious to take up a career and proposes to become apprenticed to a merchant in Bristol. His father objects; trade, he warns him, "is but caswelte."[67] Peter Idley was determined that his son should study law as a means to riches and success:

> To grete worshippe hath the lawe
> Brought forth many a pouere man

was his theme. It is an escape from economic insecurity. The boy must realize this, must study hard, and be "stable." Otherwise his father will cut off his allowance and so far as possible disinherit him; poverty will hang over him, with its menace of "disease and derke desolacion." Another stern parent, Margaret Paston, urging a younger son, Clement, toward the law, ordered his tutor to thrash him; she would rather see him dead, she declared, than a failure.

The detail that would fill out this broader context and substantiate comparison between one group and another is still to be sought. On a general view, it is clear only that there was a driving search for success in any direction that for the time being held promise of economic security and good social status. There was nothing to isolate the London merchant class from such a tendency. Kinship ties were widely ramified among all the other socially ambitious groups, and London was a center of new opportunity. Merchants did not hold their sons to the discipline of business but encouraged them to make a free choice of a career. They could follow a profession, enter the service of a patron, or move into the country, either

66. ". . . . quomodo dictus dominus de Mymmys dominus erat in operibus potens, in operibus valde subtilis; secundo, quomodo contra talem dominum posset de facili commoveri placitum, sed nequaquam ita faciliter obtineri victoria contra eum" (*Chronicles of St. Albans*, John Amundesham, R.S., I, 255).

67. *The Childe of Bristowe*, Camden Miscellany, Vol. IV (1859).

at the level of gentility or below it. There was family discipline and family pride, but both were tempered by desire for the happiness of the individual. A goldsmith who had four shields of family arms to set on his seal added this motto, between two sprigs in leaf, "La Sal Joyous a lalagspousa."[68] Translate the cryptic language of the seal-cutter as one will, the meaning is intended to center on the word "Joyous"; the house and the family line it symbolized and those who married into it were to be happy.

Comparison with other groups might bring the elements of stability in the culture of the class into still more generous relief. It is significant that some families were able to hold their sons in the city, in trade, for several generations. The stabilities and satisfactions of the life were rooted in a creative tradition that had given fresh historic forms to the corporate sense, in the municipal community and the gild, and was not yet stagnant. London was still compact enough, too, to be familiar in all its parts, and affection could make of it a physical home for that notion of the commonwealth or welfare that echoes, often so abstractly, throughout medieval writing. The merchant may have been devious and limited in his conception of the common welfare. Yet public discussions of taxation and private plans of charity both show genuine concern and confusion over the presence of poverty in the community, a problem which, in that day, was insoluble.

68. Anc. Deeds, BS 34, William de Norton, 9 Edward III.

Appendix A

ALDERMANIC FAMILIES

ABYNDON, STEPHEN DE, draper, ald. 1312–21. Beaven, I, 380. Of a London family. Came of age *ca.* 1299, when his guardian, Thomas de Basinges, promised to render accounts of his lands. *Cal. L. Bk., C*, p. 53. In 1301 m. Johanna, dau. of Walter le Blund. Riley, *Memorials*, p. 44. Died 1336; portion of will enrolled names s. Richard, dau. Isabella, m. to Benedict de Dytton, dau. Margery, m. to John Torel. *C.W.C.H.*, I, 413. In the same year his s. Thomas d., naming a brother Stephen and sister Isabella his heirs. *Ibid.*, p. 416. Will of Benedict de Dytton, of Alveley, Salop, enrolled 1354, names late w. Isabella and one s. *Ibid.*, p. 677.

AGHTON, NICHOLAS, stockfishmonger, ald. 1415. Beaven, II, 5. Died 1415, leaving two s., five dau. *C.W.C.H.*, II, 413; L. Bk., *I*, fol. 156*b*. Seal, a merchant's mark and initials on a shield. D.&C. St. Paul's, Deeds, A 18/1452. One dau. m. Gilbert Beauchamp, fishmonger, P. & M. Rolls, A 46/3 (MS cal.).

ALLEY, RICHARD, skinner, ald. 1451–60. Beaven, II, 10. After election as ald. m. Margaret, formerly w. of Clement Lyffyn, draper. E.C.P., 16/574. Dame Margaret d. by 1479. E.C.P., 214/87.

ALWYN, NICHOLAS, mercer, ald. 1496–1506. Beaven, II, 19. Son of Richard and Margaret Alwyn of Spalding, Lincs. By his will ordered prayers there for their souls; other charitable and religious bequests in the neighborhood. P.C.C., Adeane, 2. Apprentice of John Broddisworth, mercer, free 1463; d. 1505–6, will naming s. Francis, under 26, and grandson, the latter's s., Nicholas. Property in Spalding. *C.W.C.H.*, II, 625–26.

ANCROFT, WILLIAM, mercer, ald. 1383. Beaven, I, 398. Son of Robert Ancroft, who was buried at St. Botolph's, Billingsgate; desired burial beside him; recipient of deed of gift, 1384, from a man of Ancroft, Northumbr.; d. 1390, survived by w. Alice, dau. of WILLIAM BYS,[1] who became a co-sister of the Minoresses without Aldgate. Property at Plumstead, Kent, to s. John, under age; land in Northumbr. to a brother, Robert; manor of Abingdon. *C.W.C.H.*, II, 285–86; P.C.C., Rous, 6; *Cal. P. & M. Rolls*, III, 83, 177; C. Misc., 111/20.

ANDREW, JAMES, draper, ald. 1363–74. Beaven, I, 389. Son of Richard Andrew, shearman, who with w. Matilda acquired London property 1320. Died 1374, devoting rents inherited from his father to foundation of perpetual chantry for parents' souls; one dau. *Cal. L. Bk., E*, p. 116; *C.W.C.H.*, II, 166.

ARMENTIERS, JOHN DE, draper, ald. 1300–1306. Beaven, I, 379. Twice m.; will, enrolled 1306, names three s., one dau. *C.W.C.H.*, I, 179.

1. Names in caps and small caps are those of aldermen listed elsewhere in Appen. A.

ASKHAM, WILLIAM, stockfishmonger, ald. 1395–1410. Beaven, I, 403. In 1395 m. widow of William Wight, stockfishmonger; d. 1413–15, w. surviving, no children. Leasehold interest manor of Walworth, Surrey. L. Bk., *H*, fol. 302*b*; P.C.C., Marche, 31, 32; *C.W.C.H.*, II, 437.

ASTRY, RALPH (Astrich, Ostrich), fishmonger, ald. 1485–94, knighted 1494. Beaven, II, 17. Son of Geoffrey Astrie of Hitchin, Herts. Twice m., d. 1494, survived by w. Margery, formerly w. of William Edward, grocer, son of the ald., and of a Revell; s. Henry and s. Ralph, gentleman, who d. 1501. Weever, p. 192; *Cal. inq. Hen. VII*, I, 453; P.C.C., Vox, 19; E.C.P. 184/61; Drapers' Deeds, A VII, 284. His brother, Thomas Ostrich, citizen and haberdasher, bought property in Herts., d. 1485; will, 1483, mentions one s., three dau., one m. to John Twygg, grocer, with a s. and dau. P.C.C., Logge, 21. For arms see *Royal Commission on the Ancient and Historical Monuments and Constructions of England*, Vol. IV (1929), Pl. XV.

AUBREY, ANDREW, pepperer, ald. 1333–55. Beaven, II, 384. Will, dated 1349, enrolled 1358, mentions parents, Roger and Dionisia, w. Joan, dau. of ROBERT LE BRET. S. John, of age. Thomas Aubrey, pepperer, a kinsman, one of the executors. Hust. R.W.D., 86/43. Property in Boston, Lincs., Herts., Mdsx. *Cal. C.R., 1349–54*, p. 399; *1360–64*, p. 173; *1364–68*, p. 92. Sealed with a shield of arms, a saltire between four griffins' heads erased. *B.M. Cat. Seals*, 7014.

AUBREY, JOHN, grocer, ald. 1370–77. Beaven, I, 389. Son of the above. Same arms on seal. Anc. Deeds, C 2416. Twice m., d. childless, 1380–81. Will dated at manor of Shenley, Herts. *C.W.C.H.*, I, 222. His w. Matilda later m. Sir John de Montague. Hust. R.W.D., 117/77; Grocers' Records, Vol. 386, fol. 15.

AYLESHAM, JOHN DE, mercer, ald. 1342–45. Beaven, I, 386. Died 1345, leaving one s., under age, who was dead by 1350 without issue, and three dau.; bequests to church of Marsham near Aylesham, Norf., and to poor kinsfolk in that county. *C.W.C.H.*, I, 483–84; *Cal. L. Bk.*, F, pp. 137, 201–2. Two of dau. m. RICHARD DE PRESTONE, WILLIAM DE WELDE. Other mercers of the name: John, Sr., warden, 1328, and Alan, member of the company in 1347.

BACON, WILLIAM, haberdasher, ald. 1480–83. Beaven, II, 16. Died 1492; will mentions one w., deceased, no children. P.C.C., Dogett, 10.

BADBY, WILLIAM, grocer, ald. 1379, 1380. Beaven, I, 395. Twice m., d. 1397–99, apparently without issue. *C.W.C.H.*, II, 337–38.

BAMME, ADAM, goldsmith, ald. 1382, 1384, 1387–97. Beaven, I, 396. His s. Richard, esquire of Gillingham and Dartford, Kent, m. Joan, dau. of John Marten, chief justice. She d. 1431, was buried at Gillingham. He d. 1452, was buried beside his father in London; left s. John, Richard, and an illegitimate s., three dau., one of them a nun. John, esquire, active in Kent affairs, d. 1488, leaving a s. Edmund, of age. Stow, I, 210; Weever, p. 110; P.C.C., Rous, 18; *Hist. Parl. B.*, p. 38.

BAMME, HENRY, goldsmith, ald. 1383, 1388–94. Beaven, I, 399. Twice m., first w. Margaret dying 1386 without issue; by second w. Alice three s., who all d. without issue. Property Mdsx., Suff. Comm. Lon., Courtney, 153; *C.W.C.H.*, II, 408–9; *A Calendar to the Feet of Fines for London and Middlesex*, ed. W. J. Hardy and W. Page (1892–93), 10 Ric. II, 162; E.C.P., 72/16. Dau. m. WALSYNGHAM.

BARENTYN, DRUGO (Drew), goldsmith, ald. 1392, 1394–1415. Beaven, I, 401. Apprenticed to Robert Oxenforde, 1354; m. Margery, widow of SIR NICHOLAS TWYFORD, 1391 or later; she was living 1413. Died 1415, survived by w. Cristiana, no issue. Heir was Reginald Barentyn, s. of his brother Thomas, aged 30 in 1416. Tenant-in-chief, property in Bucks., Oxon., Cambs., Suff. P.C.C., Marche, 31; Hust. R.W.D., 141/48; Escheator's Roll, E, 136/108/13; Inq. p.m., C, 138/20; E.C.P., 5/90; *Cal. C.R., 1413–19*, p. 466. Cristiana m. John Mannyng, coroner of Wilts. *Cal. C.R., 1419–22*, pp. 74–75. Reginald's s. Drew, esquire, a lawyer active in Oxfordshire affairs; three times m., d. 1453, leaving two s., five dau. *Hist. Parl. B.*, p. 40; *Early Lincoln Wills*, p. 179.

BARTON, HENRY, skinner, ald. 1406–35. Beaven, II, 3. Twice m., d. 1435, no issue. Provided for prayers for souls of parents, Richard and Dionisia. P.C.C., Luff., 18, 19. A Richard Barton, citizen and goldsmith, s. of Thomas Barton, was discharged from jury service in the city in 1414 on account of old age. *Cal. L. Bk., I*, p. 114. Henry bought manors in Herts., had property in Norf. *Norfolk Feet of Fines*, ed. Walter Rye (1885), p. 410. Bequest to poor of Mildenhale, Suff. Weever (p. 168) erroneously assigned him origin and burial here. Thomas, s. of his brother Thomas, inherited a claim to his property in Barton, Bucks. Rot. cl., 15 Hen. VI, *m. 5d.*

BARTON, RALPH, skinner, ald. 1416–36. Beaven, II, 5. Brother of the above, beneficiary under his will.

BASSETT, ROBERT, salter, ald. 1461–84. Beaven, II, 12. Son of Robert Bassett of Billericay, Essex. Stowe MSS 860, fol. 57. Married widow of Richard Naylor, citizen; she survived his death to marry again twice. See *Hist. Parl. B.*, p. 49. He left at least two s., Robert and Thomas. Guildhall MSS, Box 9, No. 1358; E.C.P., 85/41, 86/33.

BASYNGSTOKE, RICHARD DE, goldsmith, ald. 1348–49. Beaven, I, 386. Died 1349, leaving s. Thomas, aged 1, dau. Amy, w. Joan, who that year m. John de Depleye. Amy executed deed of release 1355. *C.W.C.H.*, I, 567; *Cal. L. Bk., F*, p. 193; *G*, p. 37.

BERKYNGE, RICHARD DE, draper, ald. 1335–48. Beaven, I, 384. Will, enrolled 1356, names two dau., one m. to Thomas de Kent, a purveyor of corn. *C.W.C.H.*, I, 687; *Cal. L. Bk., G*, p. 106.

BERNES, JOHN DE (Biernes), mercer, ald. 1360–75. Beaven, I, 388. Died 1375, survived by dau. Alice who had m. (1) Sir Thomas Belhous, by whom she had one dau., and (2) John Romesey, citizen. *C.W.C.H.*, II, 180–81. William Wolnet of Little Waltham, Essex, an heir. *Cal. C.R., 1377–81*, p. 90.

BERNEWELL, THOMAS DE, fishmonger, ald. 1433–37. Beaven, II, 7. Married Alice, widow of William Flete, fishmonger. L. Bk., *K*, fol. 57*b*.

BERNEYE, WALTER DE, mercer, ald. 1368–69. Beaven, I, 389. Died 1377–79; will drawn up in Norwich, no mention of w. or children, bequests to various Norfolk churches. *C.W.C.H.*, II, 205.

BETOYNE, WILLIAM DE (Bettone), ald. 1288–1305. Beaven, I, 377. Will, enrolled 1305, names three s., four dau. *C.W.C.H.*, I, 170–71. Apparently each of the s. left s. *Cal. P. & M. Rolls*, III, 63; *Cal. C.R., 1377–81*, pp. 206–7, 512. Robert Betoyne, goldsmith, one of the grandsons, d. 1409, leaving one s., two dau. *C.W.C.H.*, II, 384.

BETOYNE, RICHARD DE (Betoigne, Betonia), pepperer, ald. 1322–33. Beaven, I, 382. Eldest s. of the above, d. 1340–41, will naming one s., m., and a dau. *C.W.C.H.*, I, 445.

BILLESDON, ROBERT, haberdasher, ald. 1471–92, knighted 1485. Beaven, II, 14. Son of Alexander Billesdon of Queniborough, Leics. Stowe MSS 860, fol. 58. Died 1491–92, leaving a cope to the church of Queniborough; legacies to w. Jane, s. Simon, John, Richard, Thomas, the latter m., and dau. Alice. Property in Essex. P.C.C., Dogett, 29. Thomas Billesdon, haberdasher, d. 1501 and John Billesdon, grocer, between 1522 and 1532. *Hist. Parl. B.*, p. 75, n. 8; *C.W.C.H.*, II, 635.

BLAKDEN, JOHN, goldsmith, ald. 1422. Beaven, II, 6. Died 1422–23, leaving all London property to w., reversion for sale, no reference to children. *C.W.C.H.*, II, 31–32.

BLEDLOWE, THOMAS, grocer, ald. 1472–78. Beaven, II, 14. By his will (P.C.C., Wattys, 33) left 40*s.* to the monastery of St. Albans with a request for prayers for the souls of his parents. At his death John Bledlowe, Jr., tanner, of the town of St. Albans, was one of his feoffees in a quarter of a knight's fee at Chigwell, Essex, held of the duchess of Bucks. Inq. p.m., C, 140/66. A Lewis Bledlow of Arkesden, Essex, had been king's bailiff and deputy sheriff in 1398. His elder s., John Bledlow, esquire, inherited land in Arkesden, including the manor of Peverels. Anc. Deeds, C 1601, 2318, 2347, 3007, 5593. A John Bled- low of the town of St. Albans d. 1466, dividing his goods and the utensils of his craft among his w. and s. John and Thomas. Stoneham 116.

    Thomas, the ald., was apprenticed to STEPHEN BROWN, free 1451, m. three times, d. 1478, survived by w. Agnes and four s., all under 13. Property in Herts., Kent, Essex, Suff., London, and Southwark. Agnes later m. Sir Thomas Bourchier, younger s. of Lord Berners, and was still living, 1502. E.C.P., 85/12–15; *Hist. Parl. B.*, p. 95. Thomas, the eldest son, was from 1479 in- trusted to the guardianship of Sir Thomas Frowick, came of age 1488, was made free of the grocers' company by right of patrimony 1491, and was in that year and in a deed of 1500 described as gentleman. L. Bk., *L*, fols. 143, 286*b*; Journals, 9, fol. 161*v*; Hust. R.W.D., 226/1. He m. Elizabeth, dau. of Sir Humphrey Starkey, serjeant-at-law and chief baron of the exchequer, and had two dau. P. Morant, *The History and Antiquities of the County of Essex* (1768), I, 461. The third s., Richard, d. under age 1495. L. Bk., *L*, fol. 302*b*. The fourth s., Henry, draper, d. 1502, leaving property in Bury St. Edmunds, Southwark, and Herts.; will mentions w. but no children. P.C.C., Blamyr, 17.

BLUND, JOHN LE, draper, ald. 1291–1309, knighted 1306. Beaven, I, 377. On the various London families of this name see W. Page, *London, Its Origin and Early Development* (1929), pp. 259–64. Sir John's will, enrolled 1313, names w., five s., a dau., a brother, Roger. He was s. of EDWARD LE BLUNT, draper, ald. *ca.* 1266–71, king's butler and chamberlain, whose will, enrolled 1278, names four s., one dau. Beaven, I, 374; *C.W.C.H.*, I, 30–31, 236–37.

BLUND DE FULHAM, ADAM LE, fishmonger, ald. 1291–1307. Beaven, I, 377. Died 1308, will naming three s., two dau. *C.W.C.H.*, I, 198. There was a third dau., a nun. Page, *op. cit.*, pp. 263–64. The eldest s., Thomas, was trading in 1311. *Cal. L. Bk.*, *B*, p. 23. Heirs extinct by 1369. *Cal. inq. p.m.*, Vol. XII, No. 279.

BOLET, SIMON, ald. 1307–14. Beaven, I, 280. Seal, 1316, armorial impression of charges indistinct. D. & C. St. Paul's, Deeds, A 6/76.

Boleyn, Geoffrey, mercer, ald. 1452–63. Beaven, II, 10. Son of Geoffrey Boleyn of Sall, Norf. Stowe MSS 860, fol. 54. Will gives parents' names as Geoffrey and Alice. Brass of Geoffrey Boleyn, who d. 1440, with w. Alice, five s., and four dau., at Sall. Haines, II, 134. For pedigree tracing descent from Norfolk landowners of the thirteenth century see Blomefield, V, 386; cf. notes in the *Athenaeum*, 1887, Part 2, pp. 675, 747. The records of the skinners' company fraternity of Corpus Christi show the entrance of a Raulyn (Ralph) Boleyn in 1402 and of a Bennid de Boleyn, Lombard, in 1436.

Geoffrey, citizen and hatter, was admitted to the mercer's company in 1435–36 on payment of £5 13s. 6d. Purchased manor of Blickling, Norf., 1460. *Paston Letters*, I, 539. Twice m., d. 1463, survived by w. Anne, dau. of Lord Hoo and Hastings, and by two s. by her, Thomas, aged 18, and William, and three dau. His brother, Master Thomas Boleyn, an executor. Property in Kent, Sussex, Norf. P.C.C., Godyn, 1, abstract printed in Nicholas, *Testamenta vetusta*, I, 299, and portion of will printed in Daniel Gurney, *Supplement to the Record of the House of Gurney* (1858), pp. 831–40. Inq. p.m., C, 140/10. Seal, a bull's head. *B.M. Cat. Seals*, 7573 (1442); Anc. Deeds, C 240 (1455): Note that John, s. and heir of Thomas Boloyne of Magna Briche, Essex, in 1316 sealed with a device of three heads; impression indistinct. Harl. Ch., 46 F, 19.

His s. Thomas was admitted to the mercer's company in 1466 and d., unmarried, 1471. P.C.C., Wattys, 2, 5. In 1473 William came of age and was admitted to Lincoln's Inn. L. Bk., *L*, fol. 94, and note of special admission, Trinity term, in *Lincoln's Inn Records*, ed. W. P. Baildon (1897–1902). He was knighted 1485 and d. 1490–91, leaving two s., Thomas, who was ennobled, and William, who was knighted. See *D.N.B.*

Geoffrey's dau. Alice m. John Fortescu, esquire, by 1473; her sister Isabel in 1465 m. William Cheyne, esquire, later Lord Cheyne, s. of Sir John Cheyne. Anc. Deeds, C 1529; *Hist. Parl. B.*, p. 181; L. Bk., *L*, fol. 94.

Boseham, John, mercer, ald. 1377, 1379, 1381, 1383, 1385–87. Beaven, I, 392. A portion of will enrolled, 1394, devoting property in London to pious and charitable uses for good of his soul and that of late w. Felicia, etc. *C.W.C.H.*, II, 308–9.

Box, Martin, woolman, ald. 1285–1301. Beaven, I, 376. Will, enrolled 1301, names three s., four dau. *C.W.C.H.*, I, 154.

Box, Thomas (alias de Brinkele, Brenchesle), corder, ald. 1285–93. Beaven, I, 376. Will, enrolled 1301, names w., a niece, and a nephew, Thomas de Brencheslegh, who was a London merchant. *C.W.C.H.*, I, 149–50; *Cal. L. Bk.*, *B*, p. 135.

Boxforde, Robert, draper, ald. 1377, 1379, 1381. Beaven, I, 393. Died 1393, w. Clemence, no issue surviving. Bequest to John Prentis, his brother. *C.W.C.H.*, II, 297–98. Seal of a John Prentiz of London, probably the draper of that name, 1365, shows a shield of arms.

Brabazon, Adam (Brabason, Brabson), fishmonger, ald. 1346–58. Beaven, I, 386. Married Margery, sister and heir of Robert de Godyton, tenant by knight service in Isle of Wight. *Cal. C.R., 1349–54*, pp. 439–40. A s. John, fishmonger, predeceased him, 1343. Adam d. 1366–67, leaving s. Robert and dau., property in Hants. *C.W.C.H.*, I, 477; II, 102. A Robert Brabazon, stock-fishmonger, m. the widow of a paternosterer. *Cal. L. Bk., G*, p. 240. (A James

Brabazone, merchant of Siena, was lending money to the abbot and convent of Westminster, 1292. W.A.M, 28916.)

BRAMPTON, WILLIAM, stockfishmonger, ald. 1390–1406. Beaven, I, 400. Twice m., d. 1405–6, leaving s. James, of age. Bequest to church of Brampton, Hunts., stock of manor at "Scottys okolt" to w. Alice. Had bought property in Southwark. P.C.C., Marche, 13; *C.W.C.H.*, II, 368–69. Sixteenth-century Bramstons of Essex said to have been his descendants. F. Chancellor, *The Ancient Sepulchral Monuments of Essex* (1890), p. 380. James left a s. John, apprenticed to Stephen Salman, draper, 1431. L. Bk., *K*, fol. 85*b*.

BREMBRE, NICHOLAS, grocer, ald. 1372–77, 1378–79, 1380–81, 1382–83, 1384–88. Knighted 1381. Beaven, I, 390. Married Idonia, dau. of JOHN STODEYE. Was executed 1388, no issue surviving. Property in London worth nearly £60 a year, manors in Kent and Mdsx. Escheators' Roll, E, 136/108/1; *Cal. Ch., R.*, V, 231; W.A.M., 374. Seals, letter *B*, crowned, and shield and crest. Anc. Deeds, BS 53; Add. MS Guildhall, 36. Hasted described him as s. of Sir John Brembre. See *D.N.B.*

BRET, ROBERT LE, goldsmith, ald. 1331–33. Beaven, I, 384. Son of a London goldsmith of the same name; nonarmorial seal. Harl. Ch., 111, D 54. A will, dated 1334, mentions dau. Agnes. *C.W.C.H.*, I, 410. Another dau. m. ANDREW AUBREY.

BRETEN, THOMAS, ironmonger, ald. 1483–85. Beaven, II, 17. Died 1485, survived by one s., four dau., under age. Will provided for w., appointed John Storke, "my son," grocer, an executor. Dau. Joan later m. William Esyngton, gentleman. P.C.C., Logge, 15; L. Bk., *L*, fol. 273.

BRIAN, JOHN, fishmonger, ald. 1377, 1380, 1382. Beaven, I, 393. In 1375 had three s., John, William, and Thomas, and a dau., living. *Cal. L. Bk., H*, p. 3. A s. John, twice m., d. 1418, leaving property in London inherited from his father to his s. Robert, property in Essex to same, in Mdsx. and Bucks. to s. William, under age. P.C.C., Marche, 42; L. Bk., *I*, fols. 233–34. John Bryan, fishmonger, 1393, sealed with a shield of arms within tracery: a chevron, a fish above, three stakes below. Anc. Deeds, CC 952.

BRICE, HUGH, goldsmith, ald. 1476–96, created K.B. 1485. Beaven, II, 15. Son of Richard Brice of Dublin. Stowe MSS 860, fol. 59. Was granted exemption from regulations imposed on native Irishmen resident in England, 1477. *Rot. parl.*, VI, 192*b*. Died 1496. Will, drawn up that year, mentions that his parents were buried in the abbey of St. Thomas, Dublin, and that his w. Elizabeth was born in Ruston, Yorks. His s. James predeceased him, leaving a s. and dau., under age in 1496. Property in Essex. P.C.C., Horne, 2*a*. Was possibly some relative of Henry Brice, citizen and fuller, who d. 1467, leaving lands in Staff. to a s. Henry and appointing Hugh supervisor of his will. P.C.C., Godyn, 20.

BRICKLESWORTH, WILLIAM (CURTEYS) DE, woolmonger, ald. 1338–46. Beaven, I, 385. Endowed chantries at Brikelesworth (Brixworth), N'hants. Will, dated at that town, enrolled 1367. Property in town of Northampton bequeathed to his s. John. *C.W.C.H.*, II, 104–5. John, 1359, used an armorial seal. Sheriff in 1365, he d. 1368, leaving three s. and one dau., a nun, and two sisters, one a nun, at Sempringham. John's eldest s., Richard, citizen, d. 1389, leaving a dau. only. Comm. Lon., Courtney, 183; *Cal. L. Bk., H*, pp. 5, 350. Anc. Deeds, D 11293; *C.W.C.H.*, II, 119–20.

BROKE, JOHN, grocer, ald. 1488–1502. Beaven, II, 18. Apprentice of William Constantyn, free 1469.

BROKLE, JOHN, draper, ald. 1426–44. Beaven, II, 7. Son of William Brokle of Neuport Pagnell, Bucks. Stowe MSS 860, fol. 50. Claimed property in Suffolk by right of inheritance. E.C.P., 12/165. His widow Katherine in 1445 m. NICHOLAS WYFOLD. *Rot. parl.*, V, 129–30.

BROMER, JOHN, fishmonger, ald. 1465–74. Beaven, II, 13. Three times m., d. 1474, survived by w. Joan and s. Roger, of age; will mentions parents, William and Alice. Property in Sandwich and in Mdsx. P.C.C., Wattys, 18; *Hist. Parl. B.*, pp. 114–15; E.C.P., 123/17. Joan's will, proved 1476, refers to Richard Osborn, gentleman, as a kinsman. P.C.C., Wattys, 21.

BROUN, STEPHEN, grocer, ald. 1429–60. Beaven, II, 7. Son of John Broun of Newcastle-on-Tyne. Stowe MSS 860, fol. 51. Left pious and charitable bequests in that town; bought property in Bishop's Lynn; d. 1462–66, outliving three w. Hust. R.W.D., 195/48. A s. John, who had entered the grocers' livery in 1452, d. about the same time, leaving three dau., who d. under age. L. Bk., *L*, fols. 22, 26, 36*b*; Grocers' Records, Vol. 386, fols. 34–35. Stephen's seal, 1441, device of a bird. W.A.M., 484. A nephew Thomas, s. of his brother Robert, rose high in the king's service, was knighted *ca.* 1450, d. 1460. *Hist. Parl. B.*, pp. 123–24.

BROWNE, JOHN, mercer, ald. 1470–98, knighted 1487. Beaven, II, 14. Alias John de Werks, s. of John Browne of Oakham, Rutland. Stowe MSS 860, fol. 58. Twice m.; two s. became mercers, Thomas, free 1497, William, free 1499, and ald. 1505–14. Beaven, II, 21; *C.W.C.H.*, II, 640–41.

BROWNE, WILLIAM, mercer, ald. 1500–1508. Beaven, II, 20. A William Browne, from Coventry, was made free in the mercers' company by redemption in 1481. Another, apprentice of John Brown, was made free in 1486. The ald. d. 1508, appointing his kinsman William Brown, ald., s. of Sir John, an executor. His will, 1508, mentions w. Elizabeth, four s., three of them under age, and three dau., one of them m. to Thomas Hynde, mercer. Property in Mdsx. and Calais. P.C.C., Bennett, 1.

BUREFORD, JOHN DE, pepperer, ald. 1321–22. Beaven, I, 382. Survived by w. Roesia, dau. of THOMAS ROMAYN; and by s. James, under age, who at his mother's death inherited lands in Surrey, Kent, Sussex. *Cal. inq. p.m.*, Vol. VII, No. 229. James was a knight by 1358. Anc. Deeds, E 703.

BURY, ADAM DE, skinner, ald. 1348–76. Beaven, I, 387. Property in Calais; London property bequeathed for chantries; d. 1385–86. Will contested by dau. Roesia, w. of Sir Andrew Cavendish. *C.W.C.H.*, II, 254–55; P.C.C., Rous, 1; H.M.C., *Ninth Report, Appendix*, p. 48.

BYS, WILLIAM, stockfishmonger, ald. 1382. Beaven, I, 397. Wife Alianora, 1383, used armorial seal. *B.M. Cat. Seals*, 8000.

CALLERE, ROBERT LE, mercer, ald. 1321–23. Beaven, I, 382. One of four s. of Ralph le Callere. Left two s. and three dau., all m. to merchants. Died 1335–37. *C.W.C.H.*, I, 421.

CAMBRIDGE, WILLIAM (Cambrugge, Cauntbrigge, alias Warbilton), ironmonger, later grocer, ald. 1415–32. Beaven, II, 5. Three times m., in 1414 m. second w. Anne, widow of John Stapleford, grocer; survived by w. Editha, formerly w. of Richard Spencer of New Sarum. L. Bk., *I*, fol. 134*b;* Roll of Outlawries, KK, *m.* 7; Comm. Lon., Prowet, 117. Died 1432, leaving one s., John, and one dau.; provision for prayers for souls of his parents, Luke and Alice. *C.W.C.H.*, II, 463. Will concerning London property, in Latin, in Grocers' Records, Register of Freemen and Apprentices, printed in English in *Medieval Records of a London City Church*, E.E.T.S., No. 125 (original ser., 1904), p. 46. Property in Kent, manor of Warbiltons and tenement called Bassyngbornes or Cambridges at Teversham, Cambs. Rot. cl., 16 Hen. VI, *m. 7d.*; 17 Hen. VI, *m. 19d.*

CANTELOWE, WILLIAM, mercer, ald. 1446–61, knighted 1461. Beaven, II, 9. A John Cantelowe, free 1410, preceded him in the mercers' company. Twice m., William d. 1463–64, leaving w., three s., three dau., property in Kent entailed, interests also in Herts. and Bedf. P.C.C., Godyn, 4; Anc. Deeds, C 706, 1056, 489. His s. Henry, mercer, d. 1490, m. to Joan, dau. of NICHOLAS ALWYN. Henry's will mentions two s., under 11, his sister Lady Kateryn, w. of Sir James Crowmer, with a dau., and his brother Thomas, with a s. and a dau. P.C.C., Milles, 26; Weever, p. 440; *Cal. inq. Hen. VII*, Vol. I, No. 629. This Thomas described himself as gentleman. E.C.P., 126/4. William Cantelowe sealed, 1434, with a crest and helmet. Anc. Deeds, C 1458. Various other seals, nonarmorial, Anc. Deeds, C 1056, 2093; Add. Ch., 40052.

CANTERBURY, JOHN DE, ald. 1289–1304. Beaven, I, 377. Died 1304, will naming w., four s., three dau. *C.W.C.H.*, I, 162–63.

CANYNGES, THOMAS, grocer, ald. 1445–61. Beaven, II, 9. Eldest s. of John Canyng, he belonged to a family for four generations engaged in trade in Bristol. For pedigree see E. M. Carus Wilson, *The Overseas Trade of Bristol*, Bristol Record Society (1937), pp. 303–4. John was survived by three dau. and one other s., William, merchant of Bristol. Thomas was survived by his w., Elizabeth, who lived at Chigwell, Essex; by s. William, John; and dau. Isabel. De Banco Roll, Hillary term, 5 Edw. IV, *m.* 377; for s. John, known as esquire, of Bristol, see E.C.P., 43/83. William had one s., Thomas, who engaged in trade and was in 1478 described as "late of Bristol, knight and merchant." Hust. R.W.D., 208/10; E.C.P., 53/35, 64/181; and information from E. M. Carus Wilson. Isabel m. John Holden, baker, of London, and had one s. who died in infancy. On later history of the family see *D.N.B.*, article on William Canyngs. There were other Londoners of the name, besides the above, e.g., John, mason, John, mercer, and Thomas, apprenticed to Robert Tatersale, draper, 1425. *Cat. Anc. Deeds*, III, 316; Extents, C, 131/16; *Transcripts of Drapers' Records* (1910), p. 8.

CAPEL, WILLIAM, draper, ald. 1485–1515, knighted 1487. Beaven, II, 18. Second s. of John Capell, owner of property at Stoke Nayland, Suff. F. Chancellor, *The Ancient Sepulchral Monuments of Essex* (1890), p. 233; Weever, p. 202. (See John Capell of London, merchant, *Cal. P.R., 1441–46*, p. 360.) Married Margaret, dau. of Sir Thomas Arundell. Harl. MSS, 1546, fol. 5*v*. Died 1515–16; at time of making his will, 1515, his w. was living, his elder s. Giles, esquire of the body, had been knighted and had two s.; his dau. Dorothea was m. to Sir John Zouche and dau. Elizabeth to William Paulett, later knighted. Property in Essex, Herts., Suff. There was a younger s. Giles. P.C.C., Holder, 13; *Hist. Parl. B.*, pp. 153–54.

CARLETON, THOMAS, broiderer, ald. 1382, 1388. Beaven, I, 397. Will, dated 1382, enrolled 1389, mentions w., one dau., mother Emma, brother William, kinsman John Carleton, and directs that his shield of arms be placed on his tombstone. *C.W.C.H.*, II, 272–73; Comm. Lon., Courtney, 173*v*–4.

CARLILLE, ADAM DE, grocer, ald. 1377, 1379, 1390–97. Beaven, I, 392. Died 1399–1400, providing for two dau. and w. Alice; bequests to church and bridge of Romford, Essex. Comm. Lon., Courtney, 458.

CATWORTH, THOMAS, grocer, ald. 1435–51. Beaven, II, 8. Son of John Catworth of Rushton. Stowe MSS 860, fol. 52 (this gives the county as Northumbr. in mistake for N'hants.). Feoffee of Westhall manor there. Rot. cl., 17 Hen. VI., *m.* 14*d.* Twice m., d. 1454, desiring to be buried in Norwich next body of first w., no issue surviving. Kempe, 318 (Lambeth wills). Nonarmorial seals. W.A.M., 484; Harl. Ch., 111 G 27. A William Catworth preceded him in the grocers' company, being in the livery in 1400.

CAUSTON, WILLIAM DE, mercer, ald. 1320–21, 1332–54. Beaven, I, 382. From 1312 making purchases of land at Edmonton, Mdsx. See series of deeds, W.A.M., 8–341, etc., *passim*. Twice m., d. 1354 without issue; will mentions an uncle William. *C.W.C.H.*, I, 680–81. Seal of William de Causton, mercer, 1332, a shield of arms: a chevron and three rowels with two clasped hands below. Anc. Deeds, BS 59. Seal of Cristien, w. of William, the ald., also armorial. W.A.M., 122.

CAUSTON, JOHN DE, mercer, ald. 1323–50. Beaven, I, 383. Twice m., second w., Eva, widow of a London merchant; d. 1353, leaving a s. William; John Causton, Jr., an executor. Will mentions a kinsman, William Causton. *C.W.C.H.*, I, 672–73. Seal of John de Causton, 1324, a shield of arms: a chevron and three crosses; Eva, w. of John, ald., also had an armorial seal. Add. MS, Guildhall, 11.

There were nine other prominent London merchants of the name at this period, including three other mercers, two grocers, and a goldsmith. See *C.W.C.H.*, I, 142, 637; II, 94; Anc. Deeds, D 718; *Cal. L. Bk., G*, p. 70. The marriage of a niece of one of the mercers to a man of Causton, Norf., suggests an origin in that neighborhood. Hust. RW.D., 147/58.

CAVENDISH, STEPHEN (Caundish, Candysh), draper, ald. 1358–72. Beaven, I, 388. Died 1372; s. Roger a friar, dau. Cristina a nun. His will (*C.W.C.H.*, II, 149) refers to his father, Thomas, as founder of a chantry in the church of St. Mary Colechurch, London. It is therefore likely that he was some relation of Thomas de Cavendych, mercer or draper, s. of William atte Watre of Ewell, Surrey, who d. 1349, his only s., John, dying the same year, leaving issue Thomas and Margaret, under age. Margaret m. (1) Thomas Broun, merchant, (2) John Aston, fishmonger, and claimed, 1422, to be nearest heir of her uncle Thomas. *Cal. L. Bk., D*, pp. 167–68; *C.W.C.H.*, I, 547–48, 628, 632; Hust. R.W.D., 126/127, 151/28. Stephen's will, however, refers to his two brothers Pyek, Sr., and Jr., bequeathing rents to Roger, s. of the latter, remainder to Thomas, s. of the elder, and to Richard, s. of Richard de Cavendysh. A Richard Candysh, 1377, is described as s. of Margaret, relict of John Candysh. Hust. R.W.D., 106/91. Roger de Cavendish, skinner, whose will, dated 1373, refers to w. Leticia, s. John and dau. Agnes, both under age, desired to be buried in the church of St. Mary de Cavendish, Suff. *C.W.C.H.*, II, 159–60.

Stephen's widow, Matilda, d. 1391, leaving charitable bequests in Heston, Mdsx. Comm. Lon., Courtney, 170. Stephen's seals, 1358, 1360, were armorial: a shield divided quarterly, two cups in chief. D. & C. St. Paul's, Deeds, A 20/310; Drapers' Deeds, A VIII, 216 (Stowe MSS 860, Harl. MSS, 1464, both incorrect).

There were still other Cavendishes in London, their relationships and connection with Suff. or with the family of Sir John Cavendish, chief justice, not known. William Cavendish, mercer, who d. 1433, bought the manor of Cavendish Overhall, Suff. See F. Bickley, *The Cavendish Family* (1911), pp. 2–6; J. H. Round, *Family Origins*, ed. W. Page (1930), pp. 22–32; A. S. Turberville, *A History of Welbeck Abbey and Its Owners* (1938–39), I, 18.

CELEY. *See* SELY.

CHALTON, THOMAS, mercer, ald. 1433–52. Beaven, II, 7. Son of Thomas Chalton of Dunstaple, Bedf. Stowe MSS 860, fol. 53.

CHAUNGEOUR, ADAM (alias St. Ive), grocer, ald. 1376, 1378, 1382, 1384–93. Beaven, I, 391. Seal, 1379–80: in a cusped circle a shield of arms, a chevron, and three crescents, in the first on either side a cinquefoil. Anc. Deeds, 13S, 86.

CHAWRY, RICHARD, salter, ald. 1481–1509. Beaven, II, 16. Twice m., second w. Julia, widow of William Shosmyth, skinner. *Hist. Parl. B.*, p. 176. Died 1509; bequests to s. Perys, dau. Dame Margaret, prioress of Cheston, Margaret Ravening, and Johanna, also to dau. of his brother in Westerham, Kent; small bequest to Thomas Chawry, "living in the Poultry." Property in Mdsx. P.C.C., Bennett, 22. A Richard Chawry of Westerham d. 1471 and John Chawry, 1505. See *Index of Wills Proved in Rochester Consistory Court, 1440–1561*, Kent Archeological Society, Records Branch, Vol. IX (1924).

CHESTER, RICHARD, skinner, ald. 1484–85. Beaven, II, 17. In 1472 described as chapman alias woolman of Stowe St. Edward, Glouc. *Cal. P.R., 1467–76*, p. 347. His brother, William Chester, citizen, skinner, bellfounder, and merchant of the staple, left money to Thomas Chester of Stowe, ordered Southwark property sold to maintain a chantry at Stowe founded by his father Robert Chester, and made a bequest to an almshouse there. P.C.C., Wattys, 23; *Cal. P.R., 1467–76*, p. 347. He had property in Essex and Sussex. *Cal. inq. Hen. VII*, No. 793. William's s. John, skinner, wool merchant, d. by 1485, leaving two s., two dau., of whom all but one dau. d. under age. L. Bk., *L*, fol. 207. There was a merchant family of the name also in Bristol.

CHICHELE, ROBERT, grocer, ald. 1402–26. Beaven, II, 2. Son of Thomas Chichele of Higham Ferrers, N'hants., and brother of Henry, archbishop of Canterbury. Thomas was mayor of Higham Ferrers, 1383. H.M.C., *Twelfth Report*, Part IX, p. 530. For the graduated poll tax of 1379 Thomas was assessed at 6*d.*; another Thomas, also Hugh and Richard Chicheley, in the neighboring parish of Ringshead, were assessed as laborers, at the minimum figure of 4*d.* E, 179/159/36, *m.* 1. Thomas, the mayor, d. 1400; monument to him and w. Agnes set up in Higham Ferrers by their s. William. See *Bridges' Northamptonshire*, II, 169, 173, 175; reproduction in Gough, II, Part II, 80, Pl. XXVIII. John Chicheley, horner, elected to the common council of London, 1381, may have been a relation. *Cal. P. & M. Rolls*, III, 31. See also John Chychely, spicer of Bedford, imprisoned for debt, 1431. C. Misc., 113/35.

Robert m. three times: (1) Elizabeth, widow of WILLIAM MORE, vintner, (2) or (3) Agnes, widow of RICHARD MERLAWE, ironmonger, and niece of Sir William de Farendon. Died 1439–40. Hust. R.W.D., 132/1, 150/22. His wills printed in full, Register, Chichele, II, 564–68, 646 n.; *C.W.C.H.*, II, 489–90, 491–92; Comm. Lon., Prowet, 17*b*. Left London property to college and hospital founded at Higham Ferrers by his brother Henry; bequests to poor relations there and at Suldrop; desired his anniversary kept at church of Rumford, Essex. No children mentioned in will, but he is said to have had two dau., who may have predeceased him: Philippa, by w. Agnes, dau. of William Apulderfield, gentleman of Kent, m. to Valentine Chiche, and another dau. m. to a Roper. B. Buckler, *Stemmata Chicheleiana* (1765), p. x.

CHICHELE, WILLIAM, grocer, ald. 1407–20. Beaven, II, 4. Brother of the above; m. Beatrice, dau. of WILLIAM BARET, grocer; d. 1426–27; buried at Higham Ferrers. Dated his will of personalty (printed in full, Register, Chichele, II, 339–41) at his country place at Stanwell, Mdsx. See *Feudal Aids*, VI, 488. Eldest s. William studied at Bologna, became archdeacon of Canterbury 1420, papal notary 1422, d. at Rome 1424. R. J. Mitchell, "English Law Students at Bologna in the Fifteenth Century," *EHR*, LI, 270–71; John Philipot (*Villare Cantianum or Kent Surveyed and Illustrated* [2d ed., 1776], p. 135) assigns him another s. William, of Woolwich, who left a dau. only; he too may have predeceased his father. The will of personalty mentions w., s. John, and dau. Dame Florence, with her s. Thomas. Florence had m. (1) Sir Nicholas Pecke, (2) John Burton, (3) John Darell, esquire, steward to archbishop Chichele, who d. 1438. *Archaeologia Cantiana*, XXXVI, 137; Register, Chichele, II, 568–70, 649–50.

The s. John, grocer, executor of his father's will, was city chamberlain 1438–51. Journal, 4, fol. 5*b*. He m. Margery, dau. of Thomas Knolles, grocer; was said to have had twenty-four children. Stow, I, 133–34; Leland, IV, Part VII, 34. Five of these, their names being unknown, may have died before reaching maturity; in addition, four s. are known to have d. in infancy, and two dau., unmarried. Of the remaining six s., seven dau., three s. entered the church. Of the others, Henry, esquire of Wimpole, Cambs., m. Alice, dau. of Sir Robert Clopton of Suff., sealed with device of a lion rampant (Drapers' Deeds, A V 282) and founded a family of gentry continuing in the male line to the eighteenth century. Robert, king's esquire, m., descendants not discovered. *Cal. P.R., 1441–46*, p. 437; Anc. Deeds, B 4256. William, m., left two s., who d. without issue, and a dau. Of John's dau., Christiana m. Thomas Harvey of Bedf., had four s., six dau.; Editha m. twice, issue not known; Beatrice m. Sir William Peche, who d. 1487; Florence was m. twice, to gentlemen; Philippa m. Henry Kent, merchant; Elizabeth m. three times, each husband a knight, no issue (Stow, I, 134); Agnes m. (1) John Tatersale, esquire, (2) William Kene (*ibid.*; C. L. Kingsford, *Additional Notes to A Survey of London by John Stow* [1927], pp. 6, 17). Statements in this paragraph otherwise unsupported rest on the authority of Buckler, *op. cit.*, pp. x–xiii.

CHICHESTER, JOHN DE, goldsmith, ald. 1357–77. Beaven, I, 388. Died 1380–81. Property in London left to w. Alice, remainder entailed on s. William. *C.W.C.H.*, II, 219.

CHIGWELL, RICHARD DE, fishmonger, ald. 1305–6. Beaven, I, 379. By 1280 a Richard de Chigwell had m. dau. of Simon de Gardino, called "de Purtepole," citizen. *C.W.C.H.*, I, 48. The ald.'s widow, Joan, d. leaving property in Kent to s. Robert Chigwell, over 40. *Cal. inq. p.m.*, Vol. VI, No. 585. This Robert may have been the clerk of that name in the service of Queen Philippa. See B. Wilkinson, *The Chancery under Edward III* (1929), pp. 159, 186 n., 205. Alan de Chigwell, an apprentice of Richard, left s. Hamo and William. *Cal. E.M.C.R., 1298–1307*, p. 2; Anc. Deeds, A 2613, 2615. Richard's seal bore device of a stag pierced in the neck by a spear, Robert's that of a stag beside a tree. D. & C. St. Paul's, Deeds, A 2*a*, 624, 626.

CHIGWELL, HAMO DE (Alias Hamond de Dene), fishmonger, clerk, ald. 1315–29. Beaven, I, 380. Will, dated 1332, enrolled 1333, mentions Thomas and Cecilia, his parents, and Richard, Walter, and William, deceased, possibly his brothers. *C.W.C.H.*, I, 382–83. See Henry and William de Chigwelle, among the moneyers of the king's exchange, 1302. *Cal. L. Bk.*, *C*, p. 103. The name also occurred among the smiths, lorimers, cordwainers. *Cal. E.M.C.R.*, pp. 33, 112; *Cal. L. Bk.*, *B*, p. 231.

CHIRCHEMAN, JOHN, pepperer, ald. 1381, 1383–91. Beaven, I, 396. Son of Ralph Chercheman of Necton, Norf. *Cal. C.R.*, *1377–81*, p. 479. Blomefield took him for brother of Ralph, who was a clerk and citizen of Norwich and s. of Roger Chircheman of Necton. John had a house in Norwich and sometimes lived there. His family glazed the windows of the church of Necton, placing their arms therein: argent, two bars, in chief two pallets sable. Blomefield, IV, 175. (These arms bear no resemblance to the arms of the knightly family of Nectons of the thirteenth century. *Knights of Edward I* ["Publications of the Harleian Society," LXXX (1929)], 246.) John's arms, on seal of 1382, were as above, with addition of an annulet in the base. Drapers' Deeds, A V, 88. He used also device of a scallop shell with his initials. D. & C. St. Paul's, Deeds, A 6/819. He ordained a perpetual chantry in the church of Heylesdon, Norf., for souls of JOHN DE HEYLESDON and w. Joan, himself and w. Emma, WALTER DE BERNEYE and Edmund de Aldeford. Hust. R.W.D., 131/36.

CLOPTON, ROBERT, draper, ald. 1434–48, d. 1448. Beaven, II, 8. Son of Thomas Clopton of Clopton, Cambs. Stowe MSS 860, fol. 52. Property in above neighborhood and in Suff. Anc. Deeds, C 3584; Rot. cl., 23 Hen. VI, *m.* 15*d.* Wife Clarice, formerly w. of Thomas Scot, salter, d. 1436. *C.W.C.H.*, II, 476. Had a s. John. E.C.P., 19/257. Robert's seal, 1437, a heart surmounted by a cross. Merchant Tailors' Deeds, IX, 11.

CLOPTON, HUGH, mercer, ald., 1485–96. Beaven, II, 18. Born at Clopton, Warw., s. of John Clopton of Stratford-on-Avon. Stowe MSS 860, fol. 60; Harl. MSS, 1349, fol. 21. Associated with Thomas Clopton of Clopton, Warw., gentleman, in making a loan. E.C.P., 87/2. Died unmarried, 1496. Bequests to cousins Thomas Clopton and children and William Clopton. Houses in London, Calais, Stratford-on-Avon. P.C.C., Horne, 2. See *Hist. Parl. B.*, p. 198; *D.N.B.*

COLET, HENRY, mercer, ald. 1476–82, 1483–1505, knighted 1487. Beaven, II, 15. Apprentice of John Colet, free 1457. This John was an elder brother, Henry being the third or fourth of the four s. of Robert Colet of Wendover, Bucks. See J. H. Lupton, *A Life of John Colet, D.D.* (1909), pp. 3, 313. John's will, dated 1461, proved 1466, names a brother Thomas, three s., Robert, John, Geoffrey, and three dau.; charitable bequests at Wendover and elsewhere in Bucks. P.C.C., Stokton, fol. 23. All the s. survived, Robert and John being of age by 1475, Geoffrey by 1483. L. Bk., *L*, fol. 46. The Mercers' Register of Freemen shows three Colets besides the brothers Henry and John, namely, John, free 1473, John, free 1476, and Geoffrey, described as s. of John, free 1491.

Henry m. Christian, dau. of Sir John Knyvett, Norfolk landowner. Died 1505. Inscription on his tomb at Stepney states that he had eleven s. and eleven dau.; of these only one, John, D.D., survived his death. His widow was living in 1520. Property in Norf., Hunts. Lupton, *op. cit.*, p. 312; P.C.C., *Holgrave*, 41, 42 (printed in S. Knight, *Life of Colet* [1724], pp. 348 ff.); *London inq. p.m.*, p. 21; Sir J. A. R. Marriott, *The Life of John Colet* (1933), pp. 46–48.

COLWYCH, ROBERT, tailor, ald. 1474–80. Beaven, II, 15. Apprentice of RALPH HOLAND (see latter's will). Died childless, 1480; will mentions w. Alice, born in Melchebourne, Bedf., also refers to Robert's christening at Colwich, Staffs. Legacies to his brothers Thomas, William, and Sir Richard, the latter lately prior of the priory of St. Thomas at Stafford, and to three other brothers named Young. P.C.C., Logge, 1.

COMBEMARTYN, WILLIAM DE (Cumbe Martin), ald. 1304–18. Beaven, I, 379. Connection with Combmartin, Devon? In business, 1298, with Richard de Cumbe Martin, servant or junior partner. *Cal. L. Bk., B*, p. 69. His will, enrolled 1318, mentions w. Margery, three dau., a kinsman Henry, and manors of Alderton and Stoke Bruerne, N'hants. *C.W.C.H.*, I, 276. These and property in Shutlayn were acquired in 1315. Hartshorne (p. 92) ascribes knighthood to him without authority. The kinsman Henry was probably HENRY DE COMBEMARTYN, ald. 1326–38. Beaven, I, 383. See below, JOHN (DE) NORTHAMPTON.

CONDUIT, REGINALD DE, vintner, ald. 1321–39, 1346–47. Beaven, I, 382. Will, dated 1344, enrolled 1347, mentions three s. and two dau., one of them a nun. *C.W.C.H.*, I, 498. Probably related to William, vintner; Charles, rector of Coulsdon, Surrey; and to GEOFFREY DE CONDUIT, ald. 1307–12. Beaven, I, 379; *Cal. L. Bk., E*, pp. 73, 76–77.

COOKE, THOMAS, draper, ald. 1456–71, created K.B., 1465. Beaven, II, 11. Said to have been s. of Robert Cooke of Lavenham, Suff. See pedigree, F. Chancellor, *The Ancient Sepulchral Monuments of Essex* (1890), p. 239; E. Ogborne, *A History of Essex* (1814), p. 129. Relationship, if any, to Thomas Cook, who was warden of the drapers' company as early as 1414, not known. Property in Kent, Essex, Surrey. E.C.P., 66/400. Married dau. of PHILIP MALPAS; d. 1478, survived by w. and three s., one dau., Joan, m. to John Forster. P.C.C., Wattys, 36. Eldest s. Philip his executor, known later as esquire, later knighted, m. dau. of Sir Henry Belknap, left a s. John, esquire, and a dau. Hust. R.W.D., 216/11; E.C.P., 126/7; and pedigree referred to above. For descendants of John see *D.N.B.*, article on Sir Anthony Cooke. The ald.'s second s., William, gentleman, m., d. 1500 at Arkesden, Essex; no children named in his epitaph. Weever, p. 407.

Thomas sealed with a monogram and with a merchant's mark (Harl. Ch., 76, G 32; Anc. Deeds, B 2029), his s. Philip with a representation of St. Michael. Drapers' Deeds, A VIII, 121.

CORNWALEYS, THOMAS, vintner, ald. 1376, 1379, 1381, 1383–85. Beaven (I, 391) describes him as goldsmith, presumably on the strength of his holding a large sum of money in a strongbox for a vintner's widow. See *C.W.C.H.*, II, 241; cf. *Cal. L. Bk., G*, pp. 178, 259; *Cal. P. & M. Rolls*, Vol. II, *passim*. Seal, 1368, a shield of arms: a fess between three cinquefoils pierced. Add. MS, Guildhall, 30.

CORP, SIMON, pepperer, ald. 1313–21. Beaven, I, 380. Married dau. of Reymond de Bordeaux, saddler, *C.W.C.H.*, I, 253. Died 1329, leaving w. Joan and s. Thomas and John. Shops, etc., in London and leasehold property in Boston, Lincs. Thomas, pepperer, d. 1345, leaving two s. and a dau. under age. John, pepperer, d. 1332, leaving a s., Thomas, and a dau., who m. a pepperer. *C.W.C.H.*, I, 349, 377, 477; Anc. Deeds, C 2953. John refers to a brother, Gerard, who is omitted from Simon's will, either because he was a stepson or on account of troublesome conduct. See *Cal. P. & M. Rolls*, I, 115, 192.

COSTANTYN, RICHARD (Constantin), draper, ald. 1319–32. Beaven, I, 381. Married Alice, widow of Simon Godard, pepperer. *Cal. L. Bk.*, *C*, p. 205. Died 1332, leaving one s., Richard. See below and *C.W.C.H.*, I, 374.

COSTANTYN, RICHARD, draper, ald. 1336–43. Beaven, I, 385. Son of the above, d. 1343–45, leaving w., s. Richard, John, two dau. *C.W.C.H.*, I, 482, 584. Richard d. under age, his sister Margaret m. and d. under age, leaving a dau., Petronilla, who m., under age: (1) Ralph Blakeney, (2) JOHN (DE) NORTHAMP-TON. Margaret was disseised of certain property by John Costantyn, presumably her brother. Cal. Rolls A.N.D. (MS), BB, *m.* 22. The latter left a s. John. Hust. R.P.L., 140 (3 Hen. V). It is likely that he was the ald. of that name. See below.

COSTANTYN, JOHN, draper, ald. 1349–58. Beaven, I, 387. Probably second s. of the above. Died 1358–61, leaving w. Idonia, s. John, under age, and two dau. *C.W.C.H.*, II, 49, 56. The s. was m. to Philippa, the dau. of JOHN PECHE, his guardian, but in 1381, after he had come of age, a divorce was arranged. He received 438 deeds relating to his inherited property. *Cal. L. Bk.*, *H*, pp. 16, 141–42. Known as citizen and esquire, he was dead by 1416, leaving s. John, William; the latter used two surnames, Peche and Costantyn. *C.W.C.H.*, I, 464; Hust. R.W.D., 144/49, 69; 152/40. This William may have been the fellow of Gray's Inn, gentleman, who d. 1470–72, desiring to be buried in the church of St. Mary of Aldermanbury (where Richard Costantyn, the second ald., was buried) under a stone bearing his arms and a reference to his ancestors. He left s. William, heir to his property "accordyng unto the Willis of myn Auncestres enrolled in the gylde halle of London"; Ralph, apprenticed to a draper; William, a priest; another William; and a dau. m. in Kent. P.C.C., Wattys, 38.

COSTANTYN, WILLIAM, skinner, ald. 1463–69. Beaven, II, 12. Died 1469; was buried in church of St. Martin Oteswich, London, leaving one s., William, grocer. P.C.C., Godyn, 27. William Costantyne, citizen and grocer, "*alias* late of Westmallyng, Kent, gentilman, *alias* esquire," obtained a writ of protection in 1482. *Cal. P.R.*, *1476–85*, p. 323.

N.B.—The name Costantyn appears to have been widespread, so that there is little chance of tracing the origins of the London family. See Palgrave, I, 551–52; II, Part III, 722. A Geoffrey Costantyn held land in Ireland in the thirteenth century, and one of his s., Richard, obtained land in Lincs. *Knights of Edward I* ("Publications of the Harleian Society," LXXX [1929]), 234. There were already merchants of the name in London in the thirteenth century, and the name also occurs later in the lesser companies. *Cal. L. Bk.*, *B*, p. 69; *C.W.C.H.*, I, 46; *Cal. P.R.*, *1381–85*, p. 391; *Cal. C.R.*, *1429–35*, pp. 30, 96. See also Simon Costantyn, purveyor to the buttery, *Cal. P.R.*, *1330–34*, p. 538.

COTE, HENRY (Coote), goldsmith, ald. 1490–98, 1505. Beaven, II, 18. Twice m., d. 1513, childless; property in Herts. P.C.C., Fetiplace, 12.

COTTON, WALTER, mercer, ald. *ca.* 1409–16. Beaven II, 4. Married dau. of JOHN FRESSHE, *q.v.*

COTUN, JOHN, skinner, ald. 1319–30. Beaven, I, 381. Will, dated 1340, enrolled 1348, mensions w. and dau. *C.W.C.H.*, I, 504.

COUMBYS, WILLIAM, fishmonger, ald. 1437–52. Beaven, II, 8. Died 1452, survived by w. Katrine and s. George; property in Kent and Essex, the former acquired by purchase; parents, Simon and Agnes. P.C.C., Rous, 16; *Hist. Parl. B.*, pp. 210–11. George received his patrimony, 1455, aged 24. L. Bk., *K*, fol. 263*b*.

COVENTRE, JOHN, mercer, ald. 1420–29. Beaven, II, 6. Eldest s. of William de Coventre and grandson of Thomas de Coventre, citizen. William was made free of the city, 1367, as a pinner, but in 1401 was translated to the company of mercers, paying that company, in 1403, the sum of £22 8*s.* 8*d. Cal. L. Bk., I*, 15; Mercers Register of Freemen. Twice m., d. 1406–7, leaving four s., three of them of age; his widow, Alice, by 1409 m. John Colman, esquire. *C.W.C.H.*, II, 374; Archdeaconry, London, 171. One s., a mercer, had predeceased him, 1405, leaving a dau. Archdeaconry, London, 148. His s. Robert became a grocer, the other three, mercers.

John, the ald., d. 1429, his three brothers still living. Will (printed in full, Register, Chichele, II, 402–6) provides for s. Thomas and Henry, dau. Philippa, w. Alice, and a sister Katharine, not mentioned in their father's will. Left 2,000 pennies to the poor of Coventry to pray for his soul. His s. Thomas in 1432 was sent to Gray's Inn to study under Richard Hungate; he came of age 1434, Henry in 1441. L. Bk., *K*, fols. 78, 108, 196.

CREPYN, WALTER, ald. 1323. Beaven, I, 383. Known also as Walter of Gloucester. Son of Ralph de Alegate, called Crepyn, clerk in the service of the mayor and sheriffs. Left a s. Edmund. See H. L. Hopkinson, *The Site of Merchant Tailors' Hall* (1931), pp. 7–24; *Cal. L. Bk., B*, p. 177. Another s. Ralph. Edmund, as brother and heir of Ralph, s. of Walter Crepyn, used Ralph's seal, 1332: a shield of arms, two bendlets. Add. MSS, Guildhall, 16, 17.

CRESEWYK, WILLIAM, ald. 1392. Beaven, I, 401. Married to Alice, widow, by 1386; d. 1407, w. surviving, no issue. Wills refer to father Henry, mother Agnes, buried at Norton, Derbys., deceased brother Robert, cousin John Cresewyk of Sheffield, Yorks., s. of his uncle William; property in Mdsx. and Surrey. *C.W.C.H.*, II, 371–73; Comm. Lon., Broun, 88. His brother Robert, d. 1372, was an attorney. *C.W.C.H.*, II, 147; *Cal. P. & M. Rolls*, II, 60.

CROKE, JOHN, skinner, ald. 1470. Beaven, II, 14. Will, dated 1477, proved 1481, mentions w. Margaret and s. Thomas, John, Robert, Richard; property in Mdsx., Bucks., and Calais. P.C.C., Logge, 4. At the death of Margaret, 1491, Thomas was 34. *Cal. inq. Hen. VII*, No. 793. Brasses of the ald. and his w. in the church of All Hallows, Barking, showed seven s., five dau., also Margery's coat of arms. *Royal Commission on the Ancient and Historical Monuments and Constructions of England*, IV (1929), 179. John, the second s., gentleman, d. 1485, leaving property to his w. Elizabeth, dau. of the late Richard Coton, esquire of Warw., and naming his brother Thomas, skinner, as executor; John had lived in the parish of St. Clement Danes, was a merchant of the staple, and had formerly m. a dau. of SIR THOMAS HILL. P.C.C., Logge, 20; *Cal. P.R., 1461–67*; Drapers' Deeds, A VII, 288. The fourth s., Richard, was probably the draper of that name who joined Thomas in a dispute with John over property· Drapers' Deeds, A VII, 288. Thomas, 1509, sealed with a merchant's mark, John, 1484, with device of a griffin. Drapers' Deeds, A VII, 99, 261.

CROSBY, JOHN, grocer, ald. 1468–76, knighted 1471. Beaven, II, 13. Died holding manor of Hanworth, Mdsx., which had belonged to John Crosby, who d. 1376, and to his s. John. See *D.N.B.* Apprenticed to JOHN YONGE, free 1452. By first w. Agnes, who d. 1466, had four s., two dau. Weever, p. 205. Stothard, pp. 180–83. Of these only one dau., Joan, was living at the time he made his will, 1472. By second w. Anne, dau. of William Chedworth, had s. John. Dead by 1476. Will, P.C.C., Wattys, 24, printed in full by Gough, II, Part III, Appen., iv. Legacy to his kinsman and apprentice Peter Christemas. Seal, 1467, a merchant's mark. Anc. Deeds, C 3492. His widow Anne later m. John Rogers, esquire. His s. John came of age. P. & M. Rolls (MS cal.), A 96/4. For Sir John's arms, and his mark, carved on a shield, see *Royal Commission on the Ancient and Historical Monuments and Constructions of England*, Vol. IV (1929), Pl. XV.

CROWMERE, WILLIAM, draper, ald. 1403–34. Beaven, II, 2. According to Stowe MSS. 860, fol. 49, was s. of John Crowmere of Aldenham, Herts.; but his connections were with Cromer, Norf. He endowed a chantry there for two years and left £10 to the poor of Cromer; left £40 among poor relations. Twice m., d. 1434, leaving s. William, who came of age 1443. Will mentions kinsmen of the names Fenyll and Thomas. P.C.C., Luff., 22; *C.W.C.H.*, II, 550–51. Manors in Kent. His second w. Margaret, dau. of Thomas Squerie, esquire, of Westwick, Cambs., later m. Robert, Lord Poynings. G. Leveson Gower, *Parochial History of Westerham* (1883), p. 11. The s., king's esquire, twice sheriff of Kent, m. Elizabeth, dau. of Sir James Fiennes, Lord Saye and Sele, lord treasurer; executed by rebels, 1450. *Hist. Parl. B.*, p. 242. His father's seal, a hedgehog. Anc. Deeds, E 385 (1411); Drapers' Deeds, A III, 145 (1429).

CROYDON, JOHN DE, fishmonger, ald. 1347. Beaven, I, 386. Died 1347–48. Will mentions John his apprentice, s. of Hugh de Croydon his brother, and five dau., one a nun, one w. of a fishmonger; London property entailed on s. William. Bequests to church of St. John at Croydon. *C.W.C.H.*, I, 501–2.

CROYDON, RICHARD DE, fishmonger, ald. 1367–75. Beaven, I, 389. Died 1375, survived by w. and two dau., one the w. of JOHN PHILPOT, one the w. of Thomas Gysors, vintner; will mentions Thomas Colewell his brother. *C.W.C.H.*, II, 167–68. See John Colewell, alias Croydon, s. of the latter. *Cal. P. & M. Rolls*, III, 239 (1396). Richard, 1370, used a seal of arms: on a fess between three dolphins, three roundels. Drapers' Deeds, A VIII, 211.

DARCI, HENRY, draper, ald. 1330–49. Beaven, I, 384. A Henry Darcy "de Totehelle," draper, free by apprenticeship 1311. *Cal. L. Bk.*, D, p. 119.

DEPHAM, ROGER DE, ald. 1338–59. Beaven (I, 385) identified him with the common clerk appointed 1335 and acting as recorder 1338–59; this man was sheriff's clerk as early as 1307. *Cal. L. Bk.*, C, pp. 178–79. Died 1359, leaving all London property to provide chantries in the church of St. Swithin, Candlewickstreet, for souls of Thomas and Margaret, his parents, late w. Margaret, etc. *C.W.C.H.*, II, 7–8. Property in Essex, Herts., Cambs. W.A.M., 1232. Seal, a sleeping lion. W.A.M., 44, 1232. A John and a Ralph de Depeham were in the mercers' company in 1347, and Thomas de Depeham was in 1344 appointed, with the consent of that company, to the office of controller of the small balance. *Cal. L. Bk.*, F, p. 114.

DERBY, JOHN, draper, ald. 1444–54. Beaven, II, 9. Twice m., second w. dau. of John Caldebek, grocer; d. 1478–80. *C.W.C.H.*, II, 579–80.

DERE, WILLIAM, pewterer, ald. 1451–56. Beaven, II, 10. Will, dated 1459, proved 1464, mentions his brother Thomas Dere of Leicester; charitable bequests in that town and legacy of £100 to poor relations in Leics. Further charitable bequests in neighborhood of Foxton, Cambs., in order that parishioners should pray for his soul and the souls of his parents. No mention of children. P.C.C.,

Godyn, 19, 20. Will of his widow Elyn, proved 1467, refers to two m. dau. P.C.C., Godyn, 17.

Deumars, Bartholomew, corder, ald. 1343–52. Beaven, I, 386. Born at South Benfleet, Essex, twice m., d. 1352, leaving s. Laurence. Gave certain London rents to Thomas Deumars of Ebbesham, Surrey, s. of Robert Deumars, citizen and corder. Sealed with merchant's mark. *C.W.C.H.*, I, 662; Anc. Deeds, A 2465, 2470, 2472.

Doget, Walter, vintner, ald. 1380. Beaven, I, 395. Only s. surviving death of his father Thomas Doget, vintner; grandson of John Doget, taverner, who d. 1282, leaving two s. *C.W.C.H.*, I, 60, 659; *Cal. L. Bk.*, *A*, pp. 102–3; *D*, p. 266. Dead by 1388, five children having predeceased him by 1352; s. John, vintner, his executor. John d. 1403, m., but without issue living; directed property in Essex, Mdsx., and Kent to be sold. *C.W.C.H.*, II, 263–64; P.C.C., Marche, 5.

Walter's seal, 1353, a merchant's mark. B.H. Deeds, G 49. John's seal, 1397, a woman's head. Anc. Deeds, C 262. Through some other branch, possibly through the sons of William Doket, vintner, s. of John, who d. 1363, the family continued, two more vintners of the name dying in 1456 and 1480. See *C.W.C.H.*, II, 77–78; Stow, I, 212; II, 312.

Dolsely, Simon, pepperer, ald. 1348–62. Beaven, I, 387. Uncle of John, s. of Robert Dolsely of Winchester, a large property-owner in that city. Hust. R.W.D., 92/81; H.M.C., *Sixth Report, Appendix*, p. 598. At least one s., Thomas, pepperer, and two dau. predeceased him. Died 1362, survived by w. Joan and dau. Joan, a nun. *C.W.C.H.*, I, 516; II, 75–76. Will dated at manor of "Horleston," or Orlaston, Kent, held in chief by Sir John Orlaston, who granted Simon and Joan two-thirds of it, 1362. *Cal. P.R., 1361–64*, p. 184. His widow used a seal composed of four shields within branches and an inscription with the name Dolsely. Guildhall, Deeds, parish of St. Stephen's Walbrook, No. 2. (Impression of one shield effaced here; the others all armorial but do not resemble either of the coats attributed to Simon in Stowe MSS 860 or 1464 Plut. LVII E.)

Dolsely, Thomas, pepperer, ald. 1355–60. Beaven, I, 387. Son of Henry Dolsely of Farnham, Surrey, citizen, pepperer. Hust. R.W.D., 89/1. Died 1370, leaving s. Edward, aged 3, heir to manor of Bretinghurst, held in chief by knight's service, and other property in Surrey and Kent. Keeping of the manors and marriage of the heir granted to John Trop. Edward d. 1383, heirs John atte Pantrye and Simon Worstede, mercer, sons of Thomas' sisters. *Cal. P.R., 1370–74*, p. 22; O. Manning and W. Bray, *The History and Antiquities of the County of Surrey* (1804–14), III, 413, 415; Inquisitions, C 136/25, 6 Ric. II, 30; E, 149/90/4. Thomas sealed with a shield of arms: three martlets below a chief dancette, fretty. W.A.M., 5909 (1364).

Drope, Robert, draper, ald. 1468–87. Beaven, II, 13. Son of John Drope of St. Malo, Hunts. Stowe MSS 860, fol. 58. According to testimony of his will, was born at "Seint Neede" (St. Neots), Hunts. Left money to the church and convent there for benefit of his parents' souls; legacies to a John Drope, to a kinsman Sir William Drope, priest, and to Richard Drope. P.C.C., Milles, 4; Comm. Lon., Lichfield, 67–69. May probably be identified with Robert Drope, upholder (see *Cal. P.R., 1446–52*, p. 289; Journal, 5, 35v; C. Misc., 115/58), who made a deed of gift to Walter Drop, citizen and butcher, and others. Rot. cl., 18 Hen. VI, *m.* 15d. In 1471 John Eryk, upholder, obtained the use of the patrimony of Richard Drope, minor, orphan s. of the above Walter. *Cal. L. Bk., L*, p. 100.

Robert m. Jehane, widow of Master John Tregman. *C.W.C.H.*, II, 626. She survived him, m. Edward Grey, Viscount Lisle, and d. 1500. Her will refers to Drope's arms and her own and mentions that she was born at Nutley, Hants. P.C.C., Moone, 10; printed in full, *Kent Archeological Society, Records Branch, Publications*, III, 127–45.

DURHAM, HENRY DE (Dunelm'), ald. 1307–15. Beaven, I, 379. WILLIAM DE DU-REME, ald. 1263–83, left a w. Sabina and s. Henry, who was of age by 1284. *Ibid.*, p. 374; *Cal. L. Bk., A*, p. 83. Henry's will, enrolled 1315, enjoins his w. Joan to pay debts of his father, names a s. John and a dau., three sisters, and a brother, who was in business, 1309. *C.W.C.H.*, I, 258; *Cal. L. Bk., B*, p. 211. Matilda, dau. of John Durham, m. Thomas Frowyk of South Mimms (see FROWYCK, who d. 1374. His grandson, Thomas, esquire, bequeathed his place called Durham, with two dairies, to his w. P.C.C., Rous, 13.

EDWARD, WILLIAM, grocer, ald. 1464–80. Beaven, II, 13. Son of William Edward (of Houghton, Essex, Stowe MSS 860, fol. 57), a prominent salter. Died 1487, survived by w. Isabel and s. Philip and William, both free of the grocers' company 1481, and Edmund, who became a priest. William d. 1488, survived by w. and one s., Thomas, under age. P.C.C., Milles, 10, 36; *Cal. L. Bk., L*, p. 268. Thomas inherited property of the salter in London and Isle of Thanet. Drapers' Deeds, A VII, 284; A III, 78.

ELY, ROBERT DE, fishmonger, ald. 1329–33. Beaven, I, 384. By 1316 m. widow of Henry Gubbe, stockfishmonger. *Cal. L. Bk., E*, p. 68. Left all London property for payment of debts. *C.W.C.H.*, I, 390. Seal, 1333, shield of arms: a chevron, a fish in chief, roundel below. D. & C. St. Paul's, Deeds, A 16/1240.

ELYS, ROGER, waxchandler, ald. 1377, 1379, 1381, 1384–88, 1393–*ca.* 1396. Beaven, I, 392. A brother of Thomas Exton, goldsmith, and some relation of Martin Elys, minor canon of St. Paul's. Twice m., d. 1396–97, childless. *C.W.C.H.*, II, 304–6, 323, 447.

ESTFELD, WILLIAM, mercer, ald. 1423–46, knighted 1439. Beaven, II, 6. Son of William Estfield of Tickhill, Yorks. Stowe MSS 860, fol. 50. Presumably a younger s., for a William Estfeld in 1428 held a portion of a knight's fee in the liberty of Tickhill. *Feudal Aids*, VI, 279. In 1435 the ald. bought the latter's lands in Yorks., Notts., Derbys., from his widow, Joan. *Cal. C.R., 1435–41*, p. 31. Twice m., first w. Juliana still living 1437. *Ibid.*, p. 124. Died *ca.* 1447; charitable bequests in Tickhill; will mentions John and Humphrey Bohun, s. of his dau. Margaret. *C.W.C.H.*, II, 509–11. Seal, 1425, a merchant's mark. Harl. Ch., 56 B 9. Two other nonarmorial seals, later. Anc. Deeds, B 10171; B.H. Deeds, H, 77.

EVERARD, ALAN, mercer, ald. 1415–18. Beaven, II, 5. Probably s. of William Everard of Walpole, Norf. See will of Alan Everard, mercer, 1366 (*C.W.C.H.*, II, 97–98), and *Cal. P. & M. Rolls*, I, 268.

EVOTE, WILLIAM, draper, ald. 1393–1402. Beaven, I, 402. Married dau. of SIMON WYNCHECOMBE, d. 1404, providing for chantry at Ealding, Kent, in which parish he had land at "Evottes"; land also in Surrey. Three s. surviving, one of them illegitimate, and one dau. P.C.C., Marche, 5, 6. Two s. d. under age; the third, the illegitimate s., John, was apprenticed to a draper and d. without heirs, possessed of inherited property in London and Kent. *Cal. L. Bk., I*, pp. 32, 84; P.C.C., Luff., 20. William's seal, a merchant's mark, 1400. Drapers' Deeds, A VI, 272.

EXTON, NICHOLAS, fishmonger, ald. 1382, 1385–92. Beaven, I, 397. Married, *ca.* 1382, Joan, widow of John Gille, draper; d. *ca.* 1401, leaving two dau. under age, one of whom m. Thomas Dru, the other *m.*, aged 11, Robert, s. of Sir William Berdewell. L. Bk., *H*, fol. 130*b*; *I*, fols. 14*b*, 25*b*, 29*b*; Hust. R.W.D., 146/43. A will, dated 1393, refers to a brother, John Curteys. *C.W.C.H.*, II, 352. Seal, 1377, a shield of arms: a fess between charges now illegible. *B.M. Cat. Seals*, 9559 (arms given in Stowe MSS 860 differ).

EYNESHAM, WILLIAM, pepperer, ald. 1379. Beaven, I, 395. Will, dated 1391, enrolled 1394, refers to parents, Robert and Alice, entails London property on s. John, remainder to charity. *C.W.C.H.*, II, 313–14. A Robert Eynesham, skinner, had been prominent in the city. *Cal. L. Bk., F, passim.* Johan Eynesham is on the grocers' list for 1417.

EYRE, SIMON, draper, ald. 1444–58. Beaven, II, 9. Son of John Eyre of Brandon, Suff. Stowe MSS 860, fol. 52. Obtained citizenship as upholder, was translated to drapers 1419. Stow, I, 153–54. Twice m., second time, in 1418, to dau. of John Mullyng, late brazier; d. 1458. Will mentions parents, John and Amy; charitable bequests in parishes of Brandon Fereis and Wangford, Suff. P.C.C., Stokton, 13; L. Bk., *I*, fol. 232. His s. Thomas in 1446 m. dau. of ROBERT LARGE, who predeceased him; in 1458 two s. and a dau. by this marriage were living. Thomas d. 1464, leaving s. Thomas, aged 16, who d. 1466. Inq. p.m., E, 149/214/3; L. Bk., *K*, fol. 311; *L*, fols. 36, 42*b*.

FABYAN, ROBERT, draper, ald. 1494–1503. Beaven, II, 19. Married Elizabeth, dau. of John Pake, draper, who inherited lands in Essex from her grandfather. They had sixteen children, of whom six were living in 1511, when Robert made his will. See *The Great Chronicle*, ed. A. H. Thomas and I. Thornley, pp. xliv–xlv.

FARNDON, NICHOLAS DE, goldsmith, ald. 1293–1334. Beaven, I, 377. Married Isabella, dau. of WILLIAM DE FARNDON, goldsmith, ald. 1278–93, taking her name; d. 1334, leaving property to dau. Roysia and to her s. Nicholas and Thomas. Roysia had m. (1) Robert Convers, (2) David de Cotisbroke. Cal. Rolls A.N.D., AA, *m. 55d.* But both her s. took the name of Farndon and both were goldsmiths. Nicholas d. 1361, leaving London property to s. Robert, who might, he feared, go mad, remainders to his sister Katherine and her two dau. *C.W.C.H.*, I, 112, 397–98; II, 18 *n.*, 19. Robert d. without issue, and his aunt and her dau. were both dead without heirs by 1415. Hust. R.W.D., 144/11. Thomas had a s. Thomas, alleged to be illegitimate. Cal. Rolls A.N.D., AA, *m. 55d.*

FASTOLF, HUGH, grocer, ald. 1381, 1384–90. Beaven, I, 396. Of Great Yarmouth. On the Fastolf family, Norf. landowners, see *Norfolk Archeology*, IV, 319–20. Twice m.; will, 1392, provided for s. John and William, by w. Agnes, and s. Hugh, George, Edward, by w. Joan, granddaughter of SIMON DOLSELY, who d. 1417–19. H.M.C., *Fourth Report, Appendix*, I, 461; Hust. R.W.D., 147/60. His widow's seal, 1396, a lobster. Anc. Deeds, C 472.

FAUCONER, THOMAS, mercer, ald., 1402–35. Beaven, II, 2. Son of John Fauconer of Honing, Norf. Harl. Ch., 45 D 28. A dau., Katharine, in 1417 m. William, s. of Sir William Molyns, who enfeoffed them of the manor of Brehull, Bucks. *Cal. P.R., 1416–19,* p. 105. Thomas was survived by w. Philippa; property in

Berks. *Cal. P.R., 1436–41*, p. 12. Seal, 1398, merchant's mark on a shield. Harl. Ch., 45 D 28.

FELD, JOHN, stockfishmonger, ald. 1456–63. Beaven, II, 11. Possibly s. or grandson of John Felde of Staundon, Herts., who d. 1408 leaving w. Anne and sons and desiring to be buried in the entrance of Staundon church. This man may have been the John atte Felde, citizen and brewer, who made a will in 1405, disposing of London property to his w. Anne for life, remainder to his s. John atte Felde in tail and to three dau. in succession. Comm. Lon., Broun, 127; Hust. R.W.D., 141/99. John Felde, the ald., held property at Staundon, also bought land in Essex; was living in Staundon in 1465. Was described in 1470 as "late of London, gentleman"; d. 1474, his heirs and executors being his s. John Feld and the latter's w. Agnes. E.C.P., 43/171; Harl. Ch., 43 B 32, 44, I 30. Add. Ch., 16477; Comm. Lon., Wilde, 160. Another John Feld, d. 1474, was buried at Digwell, Herts. See Gough and Waller.

The ald.'s s. John, known as esquire, d. by 1478. Harl. Ch., 49, I 34. A brass at Staundon shows that the ald. had had two s. and a dau.; the esquire had two s., two dau. Gough, II, Part 3, 242. Reproduction in color in Waller.

FELDYING, GEOFFREY, mercer, ald. 1446–60. Beaven, II, 9. Son of William Felding of Lutterworth, Leics. Stowe MSS 860, fol. 53. A family of the name was granted land in this neighborhood in the reign of Henry III; in the fifteenth century it included both gentlemen and merchants. See A. H. Dyson, *Lutterworth, John Wyclif's Town* (1913), pp. 26, 64–66; *Hist. Parl. B.*, p. 314; Hust. R.W.D., 152/2. Geoffrey was made free of the mercers' company by apprenticeship, 1421; d. 1469–70. Will refers to w. Aungell; he desired that his three s., Thomas, Richard, John, the last-named under age, 1469, be admitted to the mercers' company. P.C.C., Wilde, 1. Richard was so admitted, 1472, and was alive in 1519. *C.W.C.H.*, II, 638–39.

FENKYLL, JOHN, draper, ald. 1485–99, knighted 1487. Beaven, II, 17. Died 1499, without issue. P.C.C., Horne, 36.

FINCHINGFELD, WALTER DE, goldsmith, ald. 1291–1307. Beaven, I, 128, 135, 377. Died 1307; portion of will enrolled that year names w., one s., William, and a dau. In the record of proceedings in the court of orphanage there is reference to a third child, not named. In 1310, after delay due to some dispute, the will of Albric de Finchingfeld, s. of the ald., unmarried, was enrolled. *C.W.C.H.*, I, 193, 214; *Cal. L. Bk., B*, p. 221; *D*, p. 232.

FISHER, JOHN, mercer, ald. 1481–83. Beaven, II, 16. Apprentice of John Adam, free 1454; d. 1485, will mentions w. and children, not named. P.C.C., Logge, 18.

FLEMYNG, RICHARD, ironmonger, ald. 1460–64. Beaven, II, 11. Died 1464, leaving w. Alianor, four s., two dau.; property in Kent. P.C.C., Godyn, 5.

FORSHAM, ROGER DE, mercer, ald. 1338–43. Beaven, I, 385. Property in Norf., Suff. Died 1348, childless, survived by w. and stepdaughters. Seals: a merchant's mark, also a shield bearing a chevron between three mullets, initials *R F* beside it. *C.W.C.H.*, I, 506; D. & C. St. Paul's, Deeds, A 3/673, A 9/345; Anc. Deeds, C 2387.

FORSTER, STEPHEN, fishmonger, ald. 1444–58. Beaven, II, 9. According to Stowe MSS 860, fol. 54, the s. of Robert Foster of London, stockfishmonger. According to statement in his will (P.C.C., Stokton, 15; printed in full, *Somerset Mediaeval Wills*, pp. 181–85), he was baptized at Staunton Drew, Somers., and had a brother Thomas, with a s. John and a grandson John, living there at the time of his death, 1458; will names another brother, William Ford, of Norton Hawk-field, and a kinsman, John Forde, of Norton Malreward, Somers. Richard Forster, burgess and merchant of Bristol, who d. 1450, entailing property in Somers. and Glouc. on s. Richard, with remainders to his brothers Thomas and Stephen, was possibly also a brother of the ald. P.C.C., Rous, 16. Both he and Stephen left charitable bequests in Bristol and in Staunton Drew. In 1453–54 a Stephen Forster was one of the deforciants in a fine concerning part of the manor of Ashton, Somers. *Feet of Fines for the County of Somerset*, ed. E. Green, Somerset Record Society, XII (1898), 117. A John Forster of Somerset had held property in London as early as 1385. *Middlesex Fines*, 8 Ric. II, No. 74.

Stephen was survived by his w., Dame Agnes, three s., and a dau. Agnes. John, of age at his father's death, is described as gentleman in a deed of 1469 and as esquire in the will of his brother-in-law, Robert Morton, gentleman. Hust. R.W.D., 199/28; P.C.C., Milles, 18. He d. without issue. E.C.P., 102/9. Robert was apprenticed in the grocers' company, free 1468; he d. between 1478 and 1484, his mother's will, dated in the latter year, referring to his widow Agnes and two dau., under age. P.C.C., Logge, 9. Stephen became a clerk and d., unmarried, 1478, bequeathing £10 to a kinsman, John Forster, for his expenses at Cambridge University. Harl. Ch., 58 G 11. Agnes m. twice, having a dau., Dorith Feld, mentioned in her mother's will, and s. Robert and dau. Letice by Robert Morton, gentleman, of Lincoln's Inn and of the family of Cardinal Morton. See E.C.P., 102/10; Morton's will; and note in *Hist. Parl. B.*, p. 614.

Signature of Robert Forster, grocer, and his seal, a broad arrow as a merchant's mark, 1478. Harl. Ch., 50 D 21. Stephen's arms, three broad arrows. Stow, I, 40.

FRAMLINGHAM, WILLIAM (Frenyngham), skinner, ald. 1401–4. Beaven, II, 2. Died 1407–8, m., but apparently left no children. Property at Enfield, Mdsx. *C.W.C.H.*, II, 376; Comm. Lon., Broun, 98*v*. Sealed with shield of arms. D. & C. St. Paul's, Deeds, A 27/175, 34/900 (1401–2, 1403).

FRAUNCEIS, SIMON, mercer, ald. 1336–58. Beaven, I, 385. Died 1358, leaving London property to s. Thomas, dau. Alice, and to Elys Fraunceys, mercer. *C.W.C.H.*, II, 5. Held manors in Mdsx. Lysons, III, 392; W.A.M., 359, 362, 367, 385, 414, 388, 392. His w. Matilda d. 1380, outliving both their children. Thomas d. by 1379, apparently without issue. Comm. Lon., Courtney, 114; *Cal. L. Bk.*, G, p. 273. The arms ascribed to Simon in Stowe MSS 860, a saltire between four quatrefoils, occur on a seal inscribed Fraunceys, t. Edw. III. *B.M. Cat. Seals*, 9922.

FRAUNCEYS, ADAM (Fraunceis), mercer, ald. 1352–75. Beaven, I, 387. Acquired manor of Edmonton, Mdsx. *Cal. P.R.,1367–70*, pp. 312–13. Will, enrolled 1375, provided for maintenance of Peter Fanelour's chantry at Edmonton; mentions w. Agnes and s. Adam, with w. Margaret, but not his dau. Matilda who m. (1) JOHN AUBREY and (2) John de Montague, afterward third earl of Salisbury and K.G. *C.W.C.H.*, II, 171–72; G. F. Beltz, *Memorials of the Order of Knights of the Garter* (1841), p. 366; Add. Ch., 40563. Adam, Jr., was knighted and d. 1416–17, seised of the manor of Cobhams, Essex, and enjoying a huge London rent-roll. E. Ogborne, *A History of Essex* (1814), p. 25; Escheators' Rolls, E, 136/108/14. Buried in chapel of his own building at Edmonton. Will mentions dau. Thomasia, minoress. P.C.C., Marche, 38. A s. Adam was buried at Edmonton, also dau. Elizabeth, who m. Thomas Carleton, landowner, and had a s. Thomas, knighted, and grandson Richard. Weever, p. 303; *Hist. Parl. B*, pp. 173–74. A third dau. of Sir Adam, Agnes, m. Sir William Porter, *E*, 149/207/9; Hust. R.W.D., 151/44.

Adam, the mercer, sealed, 1351, with a shield of arms: a bend, in sinister chief a lion's face, field diapered lozengy. Harl. Ch., 50 D 52. According to Stowe MSS 860 and Plut. LVII E, he bore a lion rampant. Edmund Fraunceys, grocer, who d. 1401, bore two lions rampant. Add. Ch., 20362.

FRAUNCEYS, JOHN, alias Godman, goldsmith, ald. 1383–1405. Beaven, I, 398. Wills, proved 1406, mention w. Elizabeth but no children. *C.W.C.H.*, II, 364. Archdeaconry, London, 148.

N.B.—The name Fraunceis occurred in many counties at the time and in many trades in London. It was borne by several Florentine merchants visiting London. See *Cal. Inq. Misc.*, II, 399; *Cal. L. Bk., G*, p. 46; *H*, p. 114.

FRESSHE, JOHN, mercer, ald. 1381, 1385–97. Beaven, I, 396. Married Juliana, widow of Nicholas Pluket, mercer. Three dau., one of whom m. a mercer, another m. WALTER NEWENTON. Manors of Northwokyndon and Doures. *Cal. L. Bk., H*, p. 24; *C.W.C.H.*, II, 338.

FRESTLYNG, BARTHOLOMEW, grocer, ald. 1352–77. Beaven, I, 387. With w. Sara acquired manor of White Rothyng, Essex, held in chief, 1364. *Cal. C.R., 1360–64*, p. 563.

FROWICK. F. C. Cass, in *South Mimms* (1877), pp. 60–94, established the connections between eleven generations of this family in the male line. His study made use of pedigrees drawn up in the seventeenth century but was based to some extent on wills, deeds, and inquisitions. See Harl. MSS, 1546, also *Middlesex Pedigrees* ("Harleian Society Publications," LXV [1914]), 88–89, and *Transactions of the London and Middlesex Archaeological Society*, IV, 260–61. The generations ran as follows:

1. Thomas de Frowyk of Oldfold, Mdsx., m. dau. of John Adrian, member of prominent family of London merchants with property in Surrey.

2. Their two s.:

HENRY DE FROWYK, pepperer, ald. 1272–86, who m. Isabel, dau. of Thomas de Durham, and

ROGER DE FROWYK, goldsmith, ald. 1312–24, who with w. Idonia had seisin of property in West Ham, Essex, 1303. W.A.M., 1230. Will disposes of property in London without mention of children surviving. *C.W.C.H.*, I, 334–35.

3. Six s. and three dau. of the above Henry and Isabel. Eldest s. John perhaps the John de Frowyk alias de Frothewic holding a quarter of a knight's fee at Frothewic and elsewhere in Essex, d. by 1313, leaving s. Lawrence, aged 15, heir to the property. *Cal. inq. p.m.*, Vol. V, No. 361. Stephen was a monk; Anketill d. without issue; Thomas and William m., but their issue cannot be traced; their brother, Reginald, goldsmith, continued the line.

ROGER was said to have had a s. John who d. without issue.

4. Henry, s. of Reginald, the goldsmith, left a minor in the care of his mother Agnes and heir to property at South Mimms valued at £80 a year, was abducted at the age of 14 and forced to marry Margaret, dau. of William Pounz, against his will and that of his mother. *Year Books of Edward II* ("Selden Society Year Books Series"), II, 162; *Cal. P.R., 1307–13*, p. 384. He took no prominent part in London affairs but served on commissions in Mdsx. and as knight of the shire. Died in 1377, at about the age of 80.

5. Thomas, s. of the above, played a similar role in county affairs, in addition holding the offices of clerk of the market and coroner of the household. Anc. Deeds, WS 45. He had two sisters, one of whom became a nun, and two brothers, both illegitimate—Henry, who became a mercer, and Oliver. Thomas m. a Durham, d. 1374, was buried at South Mimms. *Cal. P. & M. Rolls*, II, 111, 183, 214.

6. Henry, s. of Thomas, m. Alice Cornwall, a descendant of HENRY DE GLOUCESTER, played a part in county affairs, d. 1384–86, was buried at South Mimms.

7. Thomas, s. of the above, known as esquire of Mdsx., m. Elizabeth Ashe, d. 1448.

HENRY FROWYK, second s., mercer, ald. 1424–57. Beaven, II, 7. Apprenticed to John Otley, mercer, free 1411 or 1417. (Otley had two apprentices of this name, free at these dates.) Married Isabel, dau. of William Otes, mercer, 1422. L. Bk., *I*, fol. 279. Will, dated 1455, proved 1460, mentions w. Isabel, silkwoman, a nephew, Thomas Charleton. P.C.C., Stokton, 20; *C.W.C.H.*, II, 541. Owner of Gunnersbury manor, Mdsx.

Robert, brother of the above, occupation unknown.

8. Thomas, the esquire, had six s., thirteen dau., but only one s. Henry, esquire of South Mimms, is traced as surviving.

Henry, the ald., left a dau. Elizabeth, m. to Roger Appulton, Jr., and two s., Thomas, who m. Joan, dau. of Richard Sturgeon, gentleman (P.C.C., Stokton, 9), was knighted and d. 1485 with an income from property in London, Berks., Herts., Suff., Mdsx., set at over £77 (*Cal. inq. Hen. VII*, No. 159); and Henry, gentleman (Anc. Deeds, C 4610). Thomas was before his knighthood described as "gentleman, alias mercer." *Hist. Parl. B.*, pp. 357–58. He had been admitted to the mercers by redemption gratis in 1446.

9. Sir Thomas left two s., Henry and Thomas, admitted to the mercers' company in 1473 and 1485. Henry, aged 26 in 1473, m. twice, was knighted, 1501, d. 1505. Thomas became chief justice, m., was knighted, d. 1506. Contemporary with these was their cousin Thomas, s. of Henry Frowyk, esquire of South Mimms (see generation No. 8); he m. dau. of Sir Thomas Leuknor of Sussex.

10. Sir Henry left a s. Thomas, aged 11 at his father's death, who d. without issue. Sir Thomas left no s. Thomas of South Mimms left one s. Henry, who d. 1527.

11. Thomas, s. of the above Henry, d. without issue.

Others occur in the records as follows:

William de London, alias William Frowyk, s. of Ralph de Frowyk of London, buying land in Surrey, t. Henry III. *Chertsey Cartularies* ("Surrey Record Society Publications," No. 27 [1928]), Part II, pp. 170–73, 176.

Geoffrey de Frowic, attorney of the abbot of Reading, buying rents in London and Surrey in that reign and later. *A Calendar of the Feet of Fines for London and Middlesex*, ed. W. J. Hardy and W. Page (1892–93), No. 50; Anc. Deeds, A 7302; Add. Ch., 23323.

Peter de Frowyk, goldsmith, s. of Geoffrey, m. into the Hardel family, 1255–56.

John de Frowyk and Walter de Frowyk, clerk, witnessed the marriage settlement for the above. Harl. Ch., 50 E 33.

344   THE MERCHANT CLASS OF MEDIEVAL LONDON

Laurence de Frowyk, who had two dau. and a brother Reginald, bequeathed property in London, 1276. *C.W.C.H.*, I, 26–27.

LAURENCE DE FROWYK, ald. 1240, d. 1277 leaving s. Laurence, John, William, Reginald. *Ibid.*, p. 28.

Reginald Frowyk, draper, d. 1307 leaving s. Roger and John. *Ibid.*, p. 183.

Adam Frowich, 1282, acted as mainpernor for a miller. *Cal. L. Bk., B*, p. 14.

John de Frowik, rector of Great Horkesle, Essex, referred in his will, enrolled 1278, to a brother Stephen, children of a deceased brother Walter, and to John, s. of Peter de Frowyk. *C.W.C.H.*, I, 35.

Walter de Frowyk, debtor, 1282. *Cal. L. Bk., A*, p. 57.

Robert de Frowyk, apprenticed to a cordwainer, 1276, in 1300 warden of his craft. *Ibid.*, pp. 5, 39; *C*, p. 57.

John de Frowyk, prior of the Hospital of St. John in Ireland and chancellor of Ireland, mid-fourteenth century. *Cal. P.R., 1354–58*, p. 426; *Cal. C.R., 1360–64*, p. 39.

Roger de Frowyk, apothecary, owner of rents in five parishes, d. 1349. *C.W.C.H.*, I, 582.

Walter de Frowyk, grocer, d. by 1373. A warden of his company.

John Frowyk, hurer, executor for a friend, 1404. Comm. Lon., Broun, 46.

FROWYK ARMS

Peter, goldsmith, sealed, 1256, with shield of arms: a fess between two chevrons each between three round buckles, the tongues fesswise. *B.M. Cat. Seals*, 9968. Henry, of South Mimms, 1332, 1368, and HENRY, the fifteenth-century ald., both sealed with a shield bearing a chevron between three leopard's heads; Thomas, 1361, 1369, added a molet of five points on the chevron. Drapers' Deeds, A VII, 160; *B.M. Cat. Seals*, 9967; D. & C. St. Paul's, Deeds, A 6/144. The ald. also sealed with the device of a boy's head or a maiden's head. Anc. Deeds, B, 2095; D. & C. St. Paul's, Deeds, A 1/550, A 5/787, A 20/1552, 1553. Henry the fourteenth-century mercer (see generation No. 5 above), used a shield divided per pale, a bend broken in half. D. & C. St. Paul's, Deeds, A 20/1549.

FULSHAM, BENEDICT DE (Folesham), pepperer, ald. 1327–38. Beaven, I, 383. Married a widow of Bernard de Bruys, landowner; d. 1364, leaving s. Richard, aged 19, m. to a dau. of Master Thomas de Thornton, and at least one dau. *Cal. inq. p.m.*, Vol. IX, No. 558; Vol. XII, pp. 39, 175. Tenant-in-chief, holding manor of Great Delce, Kent, which by next century passed to heirs of his sister. *Cal. C.R., 1413–19*, pp. 417–18. Sealed with two different shields of arms: (1) 1327, a bend with three leopards' heads impaling a letter *b* with a molet below, two cloves and a roundel above; (2) 1353–54, bendy of six pieces, a border with eleven martlets. Anc. Deeds, WS 618, CS 29..

GARDYNER, RICHARD, mercer, ald. 1469–90. Beaven, II, 14. Apprentice of William Stevyns, free 1450. Son of John Gardener of Exning, Suff. Stowe MSS 860, fol. 58. Will, proved 1490, gives parents' names as John and Isabell, expresses desire to be buried at Exning if he should die in the country. Three m. sisters named; legacy to children of his brother John Parterich. Property Cambs. P.C.C., Milles, 35. Survived by w. Audrey, whom he had m. as a widow with three children (see will), and by a dau., Mary, under age. Audrey (Ethelreda)

m. Sir Gilbert Talbot. E.C.P., 110/30; *Hist. Parl. B.*, pp. 362, 838–39. Mary in 1504, aged 21, m. Giles Alington, esquire, who had been her father's ward. L. Bk., *L*, fol. 327*b*; H.M.C., *Various Collections*, II, 290.

GARTONE, HUGH DE, mercer, ald. 1319–27. Beaven, I, 381. Died 1327, leaving three s., two dau., under age. *C.W.C.H.*, I, 326. His s. John, a mercer, left a s. John, mercer, and the latter's s. John has been traced to the year 1401. See V. B. and L. J. Redstone, "The Heyrons of London," *Speculum*, XII (1937), 195. The alderman's second s., Hugh, m. Joan, dau. of Edmund Crepyn. Merchant Tailors' Deeds, I, 8.

GEDNEY, JOHN, draper, ald. 1415–49. Beaven, II, 4. Son of William Gedney of St. Neots. Stowe MSS 860, fol. 49. Acquired the several manors at Tottenham, Mdsx., m. Joan, widow of ROBERT LARGE, d. 1449, childless, property passing to Richard Turnaunt, s. of Joan by her first husband. Lysons, III, 522–24; Inquisitions, C, 139/134, E, 149/186; Add. Ch., 40564.

GISORS (Gisorz, Gisorcio, Jesors). This family continued in London for at least three hundred years. The following generations may be traced, with the help of C. M. Kingsford, "Notes on Mediaeval London Houses," *London Topographical Record*, X, 127; Stow, *passim;* and other sources as given.

    1. Laurence de Gysors.

    2. Peter de Gysors, probably s. of above.

    3. JOHN (I), s. of Peter, ald. 1243, twice mayor. Will enrolled 1282. Beaven, I, 372; *C.W.C.H.*, I, 57. Anketin, second s. of Peter, and two dau.

    4. JOHN (II), eldest s. of above, ald. 1282–96, pepperer. Beaven, I, 376. Will enrolled 1296. *C.W.C.H.*, I, 128. Wife Margery d. 1305. Will, *ibid.*, p. 171.

    5. JOHN (III), eldest s. of above, pepperer (member of fraternity of 1345), ald. 1306–10, 1310–21. Beaven, I, 378. Twice m., d. 1351, described in deed of 1402 as a knight. *C.W.C.H.*, I, 643–45; Hust. R.W.D., 131/12.

    ANKETIN, brother of above; ald. 1312–36. Beaven, I, 380. Dead by 1343, his widow Joan and s. James acting as executors. *Cal. P. & M. Rolls*, I, 199. The former m. Adam de Acres, common serjeant of the city. *Cal. L. Bk.*, G, p. 3.

    HENRY, vintner, another brother, ald. 1330–35. Beaven, I, 384. Property in Kent; his widow Joan m. a Kentish landowner. *Cal. C.R., 1341–43*, p. 479; *Feudal Aids*, III, 27.

    Thomas, another brother, was by the mother's will appointed guardian of the youngest brother, Richard. The will also names two dau., Beatrix and Mabel. According to a rough table of descent drawn up in 1454, there were also two other dau., Johanna and Isabell. Drapers' Deeds, A VIII, 20. A Johanna, dau. of John Gysors, received a bequest in 1362. *C.W.C.H.*, II, 76.

    6. Sons of JOHN (III), Thomas, Edward, Nicholas. Named in his will, also younger dau. Juliana. Two Julianas among his legatees, one the w. of John de Wendovre, one of his executors, one the mother of John Vynent. Hust. R.W.D., 78/248.

    Sons of ANKETIN: James, mentioned in the table of descent, 1454, and probably also Thomas, prominent vintner, who had a brother James. *Year Books*, 19 Edward III, R.S., pp. 444–45, n. 5; C. Misc., 68/3. Thomas had London property worth £44 12*s*. 8*d*. per annum. C. Misc., 68/3 (1382).

    Son of Thomas: Thomas, mentioned in the 1454 table, with an indication that he left heirs. Possibly he was the vintner.

    Son of HENRY: John, mentioned in the 1454 table.

7. Children of Thomas, the s. of JOHN (III): Margaret, m. to HENRY PICARD, and Felicia, named in their grandfather's will. A later heraldic source (Add. MSS, 38133) names also Juliana, m. to Vynent; Isabella, m. to Spycer; Johanna, m. to Belton; and gives Felicia as m. to Fraunceis. Margaret, widowed, m. a Burghersh, quarreled with her family, and d. without issue. Hust. R.W.D., 131/12.

Children of John, s. of HENRY: Henry and Johanna, named in the 1454 table. This Henry was perhaps the grocer listed in company membership in 1383. Agnes, widow of William de Wircestre, felmonger, dying 1371, left 100s. to her brother Henry Gysors. Comm. Lon., Courtney, 96v.

Sons of Thomas, the vintner, who had m. Agnes, dau. of RICHARD CROYDON, fishmonger: James, Edward, Thomas. Hust. R.W.D., 151/25, 167/34, 171/11.

8. Isabella Spycer (m. to Peter, s. of Matthew Spycer, goldbeater) had a s. Paul, a vintner, who took the name of Gysors but d. without issue; so also did Fraunceis Nicholl, s. of Felicia. Johanna, m. to Belton, a draper, left dau. only, Johanna, m. to STODEY and Idonya, m. to GUNWARDBY, both dying without male heirs. Hust. R.W.D., 131/12, and 1454 table.

Thomas the vintner's s., Edward, a grocer, inherited property from both his brothers. Still living in 1454, he left a s. John, gentleman. Hust. R.W.D., 151/25, 171/11, 217/5.

9. John Gisors, gentleman, s. of Edward and Joan, m. the dau. of Walter Mower, draper, his rent-gatherer, and d. 1515. Drapers' Deeds, A VIII, 88, 91, 92, 204; Hust. R.W.D., 214/15, 217/5; E.C.P., 138/56.

10. John, s. of the above. E.C.P., 138/56.

An Edward Gisors, grocer, d. 1541, leaving s. John and dau. Cristina. Drapers' Deeds, A VIII, 87. A John Jesors, gentleman, sealed with a merchant's mark, 1524. Drapers' Deeds, A VIII, 19.

There was another Anketin Gisors, a fourteenth-century citizen, not placed above, who left s. James, John, Edward, all living in 1408. Hust. R.W.D., 134/110.

Another branch of the family had Gesoresplace at Edmonton, Mdsx. Robert Gisors there, d. by 1326, left a s. John who left a s. William. W.A.M., 37302. John was possibly the esquire of that name of Castle Baynard ward who was assessed at 2s. on the subsidy roll of 1332. William sealed with a shield of arms bearing a covered cup, in chief, two lions' masks. D. & C. St. Paul's, Deeds, A 29/359.

The family may have been of Italian origin. See John de Gisors, merchant of Genoa, *Cal. C.R., 1385–89*, p. 17. The name was also that of a town in Normandy.

GLOUCESTER, RICHARD DE, ald. 1295–1323. Beaven, I, 378. Will, enrolled 1323, names s. Richard and two dau., nuns. *C.W.C.H.*, I, 302. Son, 21 at father's death, protested against the treasurer of the exchequer's selling his wardship and marriage, since his father held nothing of the king save lands in Blemondisbury (Bloomsbury), Holbourn, and Kentishtown. *Cal. inq. p.m.*, Vol. VI, No. 483. Was living, 1341. H.M.C., *Ninth Report, Appendix*, p. 14. Richard, s. of Richard de Gloucester, late citizen and draper, sealed, 1330, 1333, with a shield of arms, three bendlets. Add. MSS, Guildhall, 15, 18.

GLOUCESTER, HENRY DE, goldsmith, ald. 1300–1319. Beaven, I, 379. Sealed, 1309, with a shield of arms: two pales, on a chief a lion passant. *B.M. Cat. Seals*,

10115. A Henry de Gloucester d. 1332–33, will referring to parents, William and Willelma, s. John, under age, and two dau. *C.W.C.H.*, I, 381.

GLOUCESTER, JOHN DE, fishmonger, ald. 1350–56. Beaven, I, 387. John de Gloucester, executor of Robert Chigwell, sealed, 1327, with a shield of arms: a chevron between two leopards' heads, a fish upright. D. & C. St. Paul's, Deeds, A 12/1133. In Stowe MSS 860 these arms are attributed to the sheriff of this name, 1345, who became ald. Died 1355–56, leaving s. John who came of age by 1361, lent £200 to a vintner, made his will that year at Yarmouth, and d. by 1363, without issue. *C.W.C.H.*, I, 687–88; II, 64–65; *Cal. L. Bk.*, G, pp. 120, 124–25.

GODCHEP, HAMO DE, mercer, ald. 1315–24, 1325–27. Beaven, I, 381. Married Isabel, dau. of a woad merchant; d. by 1330, leaving a dau. and a s. Richard, a mercer, who m. a dau. of Jordan Godchep (sheriff, 1284) and had a s. Richard, living in 1349. *Cal. L. Bk.*, E, pp. 243, 282; *Cal. E.M.C.R.*, p. 216; *C.W.C.H.*, I, 90, 251, 581. Jordan used an armorial seal. D. & C. St. Paul's, Deeds, A 16/1231.

GOSSELYN, RICHARD, ironmonger, ald. 1423–29. Beaven, II, 6. Twice m., d. 1431, survived by five s., two dau., all under 13. Two elder s. of age by 1442; widow Beatrix m. John Bedham, fishmonger. *C.W.C.H.*, II, 464–65; L. Bk., K, fols. 94–95, 126b.

GRANTHAM, JOHN DE, pepperer, ald. 1323–44. Beaven, I, 383. Endowed a chantry in London for souls of his parents, John and Matilda, etc. Had four brothers, two of whom d. without male issue. John d. 1344–45, leaving three s., under age, and three dau. Property in St. Omer. London property descended through the female line. *C.W.C.H.*, I, 475–76, 648–49; *Cal. L. Bk.*, G, pp. 13, 264; Guildhall Deeds, Box 10, No. 4.

GREGORY, WILLIAM, skinner, ald. 1435–61. Beaven, II, 8. Son of Roger Gregory of Mildenhall, Suff. Stowe MSS 860, fol. 53. Will of personalty, dated 1465, proved 1467, mentions three late w.; dau. Margaret, m. to John Croke, gentleman, with five s., two dau.; dau. Cecilia, m. to Robert Mildenhale, s. of a skinner, with two dau. Desired obit to be kept at Mildenhall. P.C.C., Godyn, 16, printed in full, *The Historical Collections of a London Citizen*, Camden Society, No. 17 (new ser., 1876), pp. xlii–xlix, and in abridged form in W. McMurray, *The Records of Two City Parishes* (1925), pp. 10–14.

HADDON, RICHARD, mercer, ald. 1499–1516, knighted 1497. Beaven, II, 19. Apprentice of William Bufford, free 1473, d. 1516–17; will mentions w., Katherine, s. William, m., with six children. Lands in Kent, N'hants., Oxon. P.C.C., Holder, 129. His monument showed two w., two s., three dau., also his coat-of-arms. *Royal Commission on the Ancient and Historical Monuments and Constructions of England*, IV, 182.

HADLEY, JOHN, grocer, ald. 1375–77, 1378, 1380, 1382, 1384–92, 1394–1407. Beaven, I, 390. Endowed chantry at Hadleigh, Suff., for souls of Robert and Alice, his parents, and Laurence, his father's brother, etc., and left 40s. among poor relations at Hadleigh. Twice m., no issue surviving. Lands in Essex, Mdsx., Calais. P.C.C., Marche, 20; *C.W.C.H.*, II, 417–18. His widow, Thomasina, m. John de Boys, esquire. P. & M. Rolls, A 41, *m.* 8b. Seal, initials within two triangles, 1410. Anc. Deeds, B 1963.

HAKENEY, RICHARD DE, draper, woolmonger, ald. 1322–43. Beaven, I, 382. Died 1342–43; three s., one of age at his death, and five dau., one posthumous.

C.W.C.H., I, 468, 625–26. Nigel, the eldest s., m. a mercer's dau. related to Sir Thomas Moraunt of Kent and d. by 1352, leaving a dau. aged 4. *Cal. C.R., 1349–54*, p. 146; *Cal. L. Bk., F*, p. 248. Richard, the second s., d. 1362, m. but childless. *Cal. L. Bk., G*, p. 141; *C.W.C.H.*, II, 77.

HALLINGBERY, ADAM DE, skinner, ald. 1297–1300. Beaven, I, 378. Will, enrolled 1305, refers to two s., two dau. *C.W.C.H.*, I, 168.

HALTON, HENRY, grocer, ald. 1407–15. Beaven, II, 4. Died 1415. Bequests to church of Esthalton-on-Humber and to the poor of that district. P.C.C., Marche, 30. Left three s., three dau., all under 11. Had by 1403 m. Margery, formerly w. of John Osbarn, stockfishmonger; she later m. JOHN WELLES. L. Bk., *I*, fols. 26, 219. Second s., Robert, apprenticed to a grocer, d. unmarried, aged 20–21, 1433, bequeathing money to poor relations in East Halton; mention of four dau. of a sister. Comm. Lon., More, 378.

HAMOND, JOHN, pepperer, ald. 1335–48. Beaven, I, 384. Endowed chantry in Margaretting, Essex, for souls of parents, Hamo and Cristina; d. 1346–49, leaving w. Agnes, formerly w. of Adam de Salisbury, no children. Survived by two brothers, Thomas Hamond, with dau. at Stratford convent, and Henry Hamond, of Margaretting, who had one s., John Yonge, citizen and pepperer. John Hamond's property passed to the latter and to his s. Thomas Yonge, dean of the collegiate church of the Blessed Mary of Warwick. *C.W.C.H.*, I, 515–16; Hust. R.W.D., 149/23, 151/17.

HAMPTON, WILLIAM, ald. 1462–82, knighted 1471. Beaven, II, 12. Son of John Hampton of Minchinhampton, Glos. Stowe MSS 860, fol. 57.

HARDYNG, ROBERT, goldsmith, ald. 1483–90. Beaven, II, 17. Died 1503; buried with his w. Agas in the church of St. Nicholas, Cranleigh, Surrey. Marble tomb there with his arms and effigy showing one child. No children living at time he made his will, 1500. Bequests of land to churches of Cranleigh and Chelsham, Surrey, with request for prayers for souls of his parents. Extensive property, Surrey and Kent. Left manor of Cranleigh to nephew Thomas Harding, citizen and ironmonger; other estates after death of his w. to go to nephew Robert, Thomas' brother. P.C.C., Holgrave, 5; a full abstract of the will printed in *Surrey Archaeological Collections*, VI, 38–42. Thomas d. without male issue. O. Manning and W. Bray, *The History and Antiquities of the County of Surrey* (1804–14), I, 537.

HATFIELD, ROBERT, pepperer, ald. 1374–77, 1379–80. Beaven, I, 390. Died 1379–81, leaving s. Robert who claimed his patrimony 1390, aged 24; three dau. living, 1379. *C.W.C.H.*, II, 223–24; *Cal. L. Bk., H*, pp. 165, 171.

HATHERLEY, JOHN (Adderley), ald. 1434–60. Beaven, II, 8. Son of John Hatherley of Bristol. Stowe MSS 860, fol. 52. Will, dated 1459, enrolled 1466, mentions three w., deceased; Robert, s. of dau. Agnes, heir. *C.W.C.H.*, II, 552–53. Widow Joan, apparently fourth w., formerly w. of a Wydbury, m. William Brocas, esquire; see inscription at Peper-Harow, Surrey. Gough, II, Part III, 303; *Surrey Archaeological Collections*, XXXI, 109; *Cal. inq. Hen. VII*, 497.

HAUTEYN, JOHN, mercer, ald. 1322–36. Beaven, I, 382. Son of WALTER HAUTEYN, from Lincoln, mercer, ald. 1290–93, who d. 1292–93 leaving two s., under age, and three dau.; his w. had entered a nunnery. *Cal. L. Bk., C*, p. 10; Beaven, I, 377; *C.W.C.H.*, I, 108; *Cal. E.M.C.R.*, p. 144; *Cal. L. Bk., E*, p. 173. According to Blomefield, Walter was descended from Theobald de Hauteyn, Norf. landowner of the twelfth century. John sealed, 1332, with a shield of arms: a cross indented. D. & C. St. Paul's, Deeds, A 20/1536.

HAYFORD, HUMPHREY, goldsmith, ald. 1464–68, 1470–80. Beaven, II, 12. Son of Roger Hayford of Stratford, Essex, and descended from the Hayfords of N'hants. Stowe MSS 860, fol. 58. Married dau. of John Admonde, mercer. *Cal. L. Bk., K*, p. 268.

HENDE, JOHN (Heende, Hynde), draper, ald. 1379, 1381, 1384–92, 1394–1400. Beaven, I, 395. Twice m., (1) by 1385, to Katharine, widow of Thomas Baynarde, Suff. landowner. Harl. Ch., 86 H 25; *Cal. C.R., 1405–9*, p. 295. Second w. Elizabeth, dau. of Sir John Norbury, m. 1407–9. John d. 1418, survived by w., who m. Ralph Boteler, later created Baron Sudeley, and by two s., John, aged 9, 6. Extensive property, Kent, Essex. Buried at Bradwell, Essex. P.C.C., Marche, 42; Inq. p.m., E, 149/114/1; P. Morant, *The History and Antiquities of the County of Essex* (1768), II, 155; T. Wright, *The History and Topography of the County of Essex* (2 vols., 1831–35), II, 275. A grandson of his sister Anne figured later as John Basset, gentleman of Bradwell. Add. MSS, 18783, fol. 36. Hende's elder s. d. 1461 leaving dau. Jane, m. to Walter Writtle, esquire, lawyer, official. See *Hist. Parl. B.*, p. 973. The younger s., king's esquire, marshal of the hall, d. 1464 without issue. E, 149/213/9; *Hist. Parl. B.*, p. 458.

HERYOT, WILLIAM, draper, ald. 1469–85, knighted 1482. Beaven, II, 14. Son of John Heriot of Seagrave, Leic. Stowe MSS 860, fol. 58. As late as 1469 was a member of the shearmen's company. *Cal. L. Bk., L*, pp. 60, 67, 78, 85. Left plate to both the shearmen and the drapers. Died 1485; will refers to his birth at Seagrave. Bequest to the church of Booney, Notts., where his mother was buried; mention of his brother Sir John Heryot, vicar there, and of his brothers John and Edward Fenkell and Robert Rochester. Property in Mdsx., Essex, Suff. Survived by w., three s., of age, and dau. P.C.C., Logge, 2. Widow Joan m. Thomas Creme, draper. *Cal. P.R., 1494–1509*, pp. 26–27. William, as citizen and shearman, in 1465 sealed with a shield of arms: per pale a crescent between three mullets, in chief a file of five. Drapers' Deeds, A VI, 290. His youngest s. William, draper, in 1516 described as gentleman of Chingford, Essex, sealed with this shield: per pale ermine and ermines, three crescents countercharged. Drapers' Deeds, A VI, 167.

HEYLESDON, JOHN DE, mercer, ald. 1377, 1379, 1381, 1383. Beaven, I, 392. Citizen of Norwich; d. 1384, desiring to be buried next to his parents' tomb in the church of Hellesdon, Norf.; small bequests to poor relations in that neighborhood; survived by s. and two young dau., one of whom d. under age, one m. John Gournay. Had manor at Hellesdon and endowed perpetual chantry there. Blomefield, X, 426; P.C.C., Rous, 1; *C.W.C.H.*, II, 241–43; *Cal. P. & M. Rolls*, III, 100; *Cal. L. Bk., H*, p. 267.

HIDE, WILLIAM, grocer, ald. 1397–1401. Beaven, I, 403. Died 1402, leaving w. Albreda and s. William who in 1409 m. Elizabeth, dau. of William Parys of Ludlowe. P.C.C., Marche, 2; *Cal. P. & M. Rolls*, III, 291.

HILL, THOMAS, grocer, ald. 1473–85, knighted 1485. Beaven, II, 15. Son of William Hill of Helston, Kent. Stowe MSS 860, fol. 59. Apprentice of Robert Ragon, free, 1448; d. 1485, leaving w. Elizabeth, two s. of age and two s., four dau. under age; property Essex, Hunts. P.C.C., Logge, 17; *Cal. inq. Hen. VII*, Vol. I, Nos. 32, 120. All the s. living in 1498, when their sister Johane d. unmarried; dau. Alice had also d. unmarried; other two dau. m., 1490, 1491, John

Croke, draper, and Rauf Latham, goldsmith. P.C.C., Horne, 27; L. Bk., *L*, fol. 245. Three s. entered the grocers' company. John Hylle, apprentice of the ald., s. of his brother John, was free 1482. Sir William, kinsman mentioned in the will, was one of the brethren of the hospital of St. Thomas of Acon. Richard Hille, gentleman, in 1492 acted as one of the sureties for payment of patrimony to the ald.'s s. Robert. *Cal. L. Bk.*, *L*, p. 293. The widow d. 1501, leaving property in Glouc. to s. Robert, aged 23. *Cal. inq. Hen. VII*, Vol. II, No. 487.

HOLAND, RALPH (Holland), tailor, ald. 1435–44. Beaven, II, 8. Died 1452; will mentions late w. Matilda, a brother Robert with a s. Thomas, property in London acquired partly by inheritance; bequest to poor of Newington, Surrey. P.C.C., Rous, 11. Seal, 1438, a lion rampant. Merchant Tailors' Deeds, VII, 9. A s., Ralph, admitted to the tailors' company, 1435–36.

HOLBECH, WILLIAM, draper, ald. 1358–67. Beaven, I, 388. Died 1365–67, childless; property in Essex, Wilts., Lincs., and in town of Henley. Bequest to churches of Holbech, Lincs., and Fittleton, Wilts. Kinsman Thomas de Holbech, citizen and draper, heir. Wife Matilda m. Hugh Sutherne, alias Holbech. *C.W.C.H.*, II, 103–4; *Cal. L. Bk.*, *G*, pp. 235, 239.

HORN (alias Blake), fishmonger, ald. 1377, 1379, 1381. Beaven, I, 393; *Cal. P. & M. Rolls*, II, 232. Seal, 1401, a shield of arms: couché, a chevron between three bugle horns stringed. Crest on a helmet, lambrequin, chapeau, a bugle horn stringed, hanging within a ring. *B.M. Cat. Seals*, 10828.

HORNE, ROBERT, fishmonger, ald. 1444–56. Beaven, II, 9. Dead by 1468; two s., one of them posthumous, two dau., under age. L. Bk., *L*, fol. 57*b*.

HORNE, WILLIAM, salter, ald. 1480–96. Beaven, I, 16. Son of Thomas Horn of Snailwell, Cambs. Stowe MSS 860, fol. 60. Died 1497, directing that a window in the church of Snailwell, Cambs., where his father was buried, be painted with images of his parents, their twenty-four children, himself and w. and their twelve children, his arms and arms of w. No mention of children surviving; property, after death of w. Joan, to pious and charitable uses. Thomas Horne, bachelor of divinity, and Sir John Horne of London, chaplain, overseers of the will. P.C.C., Horne, 1.

HULYN, WILLIAM, fishmonger, ald. 1450–70. Son of Nicholas Hulyn of Fulham. Stowe MSS 860, fol. 55.

ILAM, THOMAS (Ilome), mercer, ald. 1478–81. Beaven, II, 15. Apprentice of Thomas Boston, free 1455. His widow, Jane, m. Lord Ferrers. E.C.P., 64/85.

IRLOND, THOMAS, skinner, ald. 1379, 1381. Beaven, I, 395. Three times m., d. 1395, directing all London property, after death of w., be disposed for pious uses. *C.W.C.H.*, II, 316–17.

IRLOND, GEORGE, grocer, ald. 1461–73, knighted 1471. Beaven, II, 12. Apprenticed to John Basyngthwayte, free 1452; in 1456 m. Margaret, dau. of RICHARD LEE and widow of Thomas Hawkyn, grocer; d. 1473, his eldest s. then aged 12. Property in Surrey. *Hist. Parl. B.*, p. 494; L. Bk., *K*, fol. 289*b*. Another s., George, apprenticed to John Halhede, grocer, free 1495.

ISAAK, WILLIAM (Iskke), draper, ald. 1487–1503. Beaven, II, 18. Died 1518–19, appointing his s. John executor; apparently no other children surviving. P.C.C., Ayloffe, 16.

JAMES, BARTHOLOMEW, draper, ald. 1465–81, knighted 1471. Beaven, II, 13. Son of Edward James of London, upholder. Stowe MSS 860, fol. 58. Twice m., d.

1481, survived by w. Alice, formerly w. of THOMAS OULEGRAVE. *C.W.C.H.*, II, 598–99.

JAMYS, NICHOLAS, described both as fishmonger and ironmonger, ald. 1420–33. Beaven, I, 234; II, 6. Will of Nicholas Jamys, ironmonger, dated 1433, proved 1434, executors three fishmongers, endowed chantry for parents, James and Margaret, three s., and other children; w. Joan, two dau., living, and a brother, Roger. Bequests to churches of Crowmer, Norf., and Croydon, Surrey, also to poor in two parishes in Berks. Property in Southwark to dau., remainder to Nicholas James, kinsman, and heirs. P.C.C., Luff., 18. A dau. of the ald. m. John Elmebrugge, esquire of Surrey. Mill Stephenson, p. 492.

JENYNS, STEPHEN, tailor, ald. 1499–1523, knighted 1509. Beaven, II, 19. Died 1522–23, will mentioning two granddaughters. P.C.C., Bodfield, 8.

JOSSELYN, RALPH, draper, ald. 1456–78, created K.B. 1465. Beaven, II, 11. Of a landed family, s. of Geoffrey Jocelyn of Sabridgeworth, Herts., who d. 1470. Stowe MSS 860, fol. 55; Weever, p. 317; W. F. Andrews, *Memorial Brasses in Hertfordshire* (1903), p. 108; Cussans, I, 102. Apprenticed to Thomas Aylisby, draper, 1429; m. (1) dau. of PHILIP MALPAS, (2) dau. of William Barley, esquire, who survived him to m. Sir Robert Clifford, s. of Lord Clifford. Cussans, I, 102; E. G. Reilly, *Historical Anecdotes of the Families of the Boleynes and Jocelyns* (1839), p. 104; *Hist. Parl. B.*, pp. 505–6. The pedigree given by Reilly assigns the ald. a s. Richard, but his heirs were nephews Ralph, gentleman, s. of his brother George, and George, esquire, s. of his brother Thomas. E.C.P., 67/390, 72/14, Drapers' Deeds, A VI, 317. Property in Herts.

KELSEYE, ROBERT DE, common pleader, ald, 1315–20. Beaven, I, 381. Died 1336, leaving a w. and three s., one of them under age, one a priest. *C.W.C.H.*, I, 412.

KISLINGBURY, RICHARD DE, draper, ald. 1346–52. Beaven, I, 386. Twice m., d. 1361, childless; two manors in Essex. *C.W.C.H.*, II, 39.

KNOLLES, THOMAS, grocer, ald. 1393–1435. Beaven, I, 402. Relationship, if any, to Alison Knolles, grocer in the 1380's, to Sir Robert Knolles, who appointed him an executor, or to Thomas Knolles, brazier, who borrowed from the grocers' company in 1456 (Kingdon, II, 376), not known. Acquired manor of North Mimms, Herts., by 1428. W.A.M., 4438, 4439, 4453; *Feudal Aids*, II, 452; V.C.H., Herts., II, 253. Died 1435, his epitaph in St. Antony's recording in part:

> "Here lyth with him his good wyff Jone:
> They weren togeder sixty yere
> And nineteen chyldren they had in feer."

Weever, p. 189; Stow, I, 251–52. All his wills printed in full, Register, Chichele, II, 519–26. Surviving his death were s. Thomas, grocer; William, grocer, burgess, and merchant of Bristol; dau. Beatrice, relict of Richard Gosselyn, ironmonger; two other dau. P. & M. Rolls, A 57, *m. 5b;* Rot. cl., 10 Hen. VI, *m. 5d.*

His s. William m. Katherine Keche, widow; d. without issue, 1442. P.C.C., Rous, 16. Elder s. Thomas in nineteen years of married life with w. Isabel had ten children; d. 1445, two s., two dau. surviving. Weever, p. 190; P.C.C., Luff., 30; Stafford (Lambeth wills), 154. His elder s., Robert, of North Mimms, esquire, m. Elizabeth, dau. of Bartholomew Seman, goldsmith, 1436; their s. Robert, esquire, m. dau. of William Troutbeck, late chamberlain of Chester. *Herald and Genealogist*, VII, 556 ff.; F. C. Cass, *South Mimms* (1877), p. 111.

Thomas' younger s. Richard inherited London property, may have been the draper of that name mentioned in recognizances, 1485. Journals, 9, fol. 99b.

KNYGHTCOTE, WILLIAM, mercer, ald. 1378, 1381. Beaven, I, 394. Died 1382; three or more s. and several dau. C.W.C.H., II, 237; Comm. Lon., Courtney, 94b–95. One dau. m. at 13, to Simon, s. of Thomas Sampson of Suff., another, at 11 or 12, to Richard Forster, citizen. L. Bk., H, fols. 221b, 225.

KYNG, WILLIAM, draper, ald. 1377, 1381, 1383, 1379. Beaven, I, 393. Son of John Kyng of Colman Street, citizen, who d. 1339, leaving three s., two dau. William d. 1393–94, charging maintenance of obits for himself and w., his father and grandfather on tenements called "le Kyngesaley." Will mentions a brother, Robert Luton, but no children. C.W.C.H., I, 433–34; II, 312–13.

KYRKETON, JOHN, stockfishmonger, ald. 1378, 1380, 1382. Beaven, I, 394. Died 1387–88; will refers to his w., s. William, of age, other children under age not named, a kinsman William Godesone de Kyrketon. C.W.C.H., II, 269–70.

LACER, RICHARD LE, mercer, ald. 1334–57. Beaven, I, 384. A citizen of this name admitted to the freedom by redemption, 1311. Cal. L. Bk., D, p. 58. Died 1361, leaving a s., under age, and two dau., m., one to John atte Pole, citizen, one to Sir William Bruyn, the latter taking, as her second husband, Sir Robert Marny. C.W.C.H., II, 59–60; Cal. P. & M. Rolls, II, 132 n., 133. Property in Kent; desired burial at Bromley. Chart. St. Thomas, p. 145. The name occurs among citizens of the previous century. Cal. L. Bk., B, pp. 31, 66.

LAMBARD, JOHN, mercer, ald. 1460–70. Beaven, II, 12. Died 1487, survived by w. Anne; both buried at Hinxworth, Herts. Weever, p. 314. Property at Plumstead, Kent, left to s. Robert, money to s. John; a third s. William, in 1487 parson of the church of St. Leonard, Foster Lane, London; a dau. Elizabeth m. Thomas Lyntham, gentleman. P.C.C., Milles, 10.

LAMBYN, JOHN, fishmonger, ald. 1312–19. Beaven, I, 380. Possibly s. of Robert Lambyn, fishmonger, whose will, enrolled 1294, names s., Edmund and John, and dau. Alice, with London property near the church of St. Magnus, a newly built dwelling-house near the Thames, and property in Southwark, Yarmouth, and in two vills in Kent. C.W.C.H., I, 111. A John Lambyn, fishmonger, d. 1348–49, leaving two s., Guy and Goscelin. Ibid., p. 582.

LAMBYN, EDMUND, fishmonger, ald. 1319–25. Beaven, I, 381. Possibly elder brother of the above. A William Lambyn with property in the parish of St. Magnus d. 1327–28, leaving s. Edmund, Robert, Thomas, and Edward. Ibid., p. 333.

LANE, JOHN, mercer, ald. 1410–14. Beaven, I, 380. Died 1427, leaving w., dau., illegitimate s.; pensioned the latter. C.W.C.H., II, 443.

LARGE, ROBERT, mercer, ald. 1429–41. Beaven, II, 7. Son of Thomas Large of London. Stowe MSS 860, fol. 51. Died 1442–43, leaving three s., two of whom d. under age; s. Richard of age, 1448, dau. Elizabeth m. s. of SIMON EYRE. Widow Joan m. JOHN GEDNEY. Property in Essex. P.C.C., Rous, 16, 19. Will printed in W. Blades, The Biography and Typography of William Caxton (2d ed., 1882), pp. 153–58; L. Bk., K, fols. 208–10, 228. A Richard Large, d. 1458, buried with w. Alice at Thaxted, Essex, said to have been Robert's brother. Weever, p. 385.

LAUNDE, ROBERT DE LA, goldsmith, ald. 1376, 1378, 1380, knighted 1381. Beaven, I, 391. Born at "Hempstede," Essex, d. 1382, childless. Wills refer to brothers Adam and William, the latter a boy studying for the priesthood; two m. sisters;

a niece at Haliwell, dau. of John Launde of Cambs. His w. Cristina d. same year, will refers to two dau. Comm. Lon., Courtney, 99, 102; *C.W.C.H.*, II, 236–37. Robert's seal, 1377–78, shield of arms: three trefoils and a chief dancety also diapered, possibly two stags' heads upon the chief. Anc. Deeds, BS 3, A 4968, 6333.

LEE, RICHARD, grocer, ald. 1452–72, knighted 1471. Beaven, II, 10. Son either of Simon Lee or of John a Lee, both of the city of Worcester. Stowe MSS 860, fols. 55–56. Sought the help of the grocers' company in obtaining the freedom of the city by redemption, 1431. Kingdon, II, 202. Will states that his father was buried at Walkingstead, Surrey, and his mother at East Grinstead, Sussex; mentions kinsmen named Hagelot, Beld, Alwyn, also a brother, William Lee, joiner, in debt to him. P.C.C., Wattys, 5. A joiner of this name became janitor of the Tower of London. Rot. cl., 1. Edw. IV, *m.* 21. Sir Richard d. 1472, survived by w. Letice, two s., four dau. Elder s., Richard, may have been the apprentice of that name taken by GEORGE IRLOND, grocer, 1458. By 1482 he was known as esquire; d. 1498, holding property in Kent, Essex, Surrey, Sussex; his s. and heir, Richard, gentleman, then 24. P.C.C., Horne, 27; Hust. R.W.D., 212/8; *London Inquisitions*, pp. 15–16; Guildhall Deeds, Box 10, No. 7. The ald.'s second s., John, took his doctorate in canon law at the University of Padua, 1461. See R. J. Mitchell, "English Students at Padua, 1460–75," *Transactions of the Royal Historical Society* (4th ser.), XIX, 105. Of his dau., three m. grocers (see IRLOND, STOKES); one of these, widowed, m. Roger Brent, gentleman, esquire, lawyer, of Canterbury; the fourth m. John Fogge, esquire, official, later knighted, s. of Sir John Fogge, treasurer of the household. The ald. sealed, 1464, 1472, with device of a deer under a tree; his s., with a lion's mask. D. & C. St. Paul's, Deeds, A 16/1204; Anc. Deeds, C 3492; Drapers' Deeds, A VIII, 282.

LEGGY, THOMAS (Legge), skinner, ald. 1343–57. Beaven, I, 386. Said to have been descended from an Italian family settling in England in the eleventh or twelfth century. Rev. A. G. Legge, "Some Account of the Legge Family Resident in East Anglia," *Norfolk Archaeology*, XIII, 101–5. Twice m., d. 1357, leaving London property to s. Simon, remainder in trust for sale for maintenance of chantries in London and Grinstead, Sussex. Simon, aged 5 at his father's death, d. 1372–75. *C.W.C.H.*, I, 699; II, 184. Thomas' will printed in full in *Book of Records of St. Christopher le Stocks*, pp. 6–8.

LEYRE, THOMAS DE, ald. 1327–31. Beaven, I, 383. Died 1331, leaving one dau. *C.W.C.H.*, I, 364.

LEYRE, WILLIAM DE, pepperer, ald. 1298–1320. Beaven, I, 378. Died 1322–23, leaving two s., four dau., two of these nuns, one m. *C.W.C.H.*, I, 300. His s. William sealed with a shield of arms. Guildhall Deeds, parish of St. Michael Wood Street, No. 3 (1351).

LOK, JOHN, mercer. ald. 1463. Beaven, II, 12. By will provided for a chantry for two years at Dalling, Norf., for souls of his parents, Richard and Agnes Lok; had land there and at Salle and had purchased land also in Mdsx. and Bucks. Left legacies to his brother John Alburgh and to children of brothers and sisters living in Norf. P.C.C., Godyn, 1. Married Elizabeth, dau. of Eustace Valerian, citizen and salter, owning land in Hunts. *Hist. Parl. B.*; *Cal. L. Bk.*, K, p. 41. Died 1463, survived by w., three s., three dau., all under age. One s. d. under age; one dau. at age of 17 m. a gentleman named Cokayn. L. Bk., *L*, fol. 20*b*.

LOVEKYN, ADAM, grocer, ald. 1377–78. Beaven, I, 393. Apprentice and executor of John Flaun, 1361; m. dau. of ROBERT DE ELY, d. by 1390. Hust. R.W.D., 89/177, 132/81; *Cal. L. Bk., G*, p. 159. Seal, 1376, a merchant's mark. W.A.M., 9266.

LOVEKYN, JOHN, stockfishmonger, ald. 1347–68. Beaven, I, 386. Son of Edward Lovekyn of Kingston-on-Thames, who founded a chapel in honor of St. Mary Magdalen there. John endowed it further. Twice m., d. 1368, childless, leaving some London property to nephew John; had a coat-of-arms. Major A. Heales, "Some Account of John Lovekyn," *Transactions of the London and Middlesex Archaeological Society*, VI, 341–70. Inscription to his memory at Walkern, Herts. *Transactions of the London and Middlesex Archaeological Society*, III, 133, 561.

LUCAS, ROBERT, goldsmith, ald. 1377, 1381. Beaven, I, 393. Three times m., twice to widows (relict of Richard de Sutton, not a freeman, and Margaret, widow of John Northwich, goldsmith); d. 1382, w. Margaret surviving, but apparently no children. *Cal. P. & M. Rolls*, II, 169–70, 269; *C.W.C.H.*, II, 230–31.

LYONS, RICHARD, vintner, ald. 1374–76. Beaven, I, 390. Birth illegitimate; m. Isabella Pledour, divorced 1363, executed by rebels 1381. Afterward Isabella, claiming her portion of his goods, alleged that the divorce had been annulled. *Cal. P. & M. Rolls*, III, 104, 151–53, 184–85. Property in Essex, Herts. Sheriff's Accounts, E, 199/10/42.

MALEWAYN, JOHN, ald. 1357–61. Beaven, I, 388. Married Margery, dau. of Augustine Waleys and w. Maud, previously w. of a Turk and of a Hunston; d. 1361, leaving s. John, born in London, aged 17–18, and two dau. Will mentions mother, Matilda, and brother, William, with a dau. Matilda. Bequests to churches of Bedwyn, Wilts., and Navenby, Lincs. Property in Essex, Kent, Berks., Wilts., London, Southampton, and the Isle of Wight. *C.W.C.H.*, II, 389; *Cal. inq. p.m.*, Vol. XI, No. 138; Escheat Rolls, EE, *m.* 58*d.* Daughter Joan m. William, s. of Peter Tebaud of Chesterton, Cambs. H.M.C., *Various Collections*, IV, 120. Son John, esquire (*ibid.*), m. Elizabeth, formerly Countess of Atholl, made his will before going overseas, 1375; no issue; administration of his goods granted to his executor Sir Robert Turk, 1379. Comm. Lon., Courtney, 56.

MALPAS, PHILIP, draper, ald. 1448–50. Beaven, II, 10. Mentioned as an apprentice of Thomas Glynyan, draper, in the latter's will, 1408. Comm. Lon., Broun, 146. By 1421 m. to Juliana, dau. of John Beaumont, wealthy chandler, and formerly w. of William Middleton, grocer. L. Bk., *I*, fol. 263*b;* Beaumond's will, P.C.C., Marche, 34; Hust. R.W.D., 164/25, 26. Died 1469, will of that year referring to his two dau., Philippa, late the w. of SIR RAUF JOCELYN, and Elizabeth, w. of SIR THOMAS COOKE, the latter having at the time four s., under age; property in Essex. P.C.C., Godyn, 27, abstract in *Hist. Parl B.*, p. 569, n. 9.

MARCHALL, NICHOLAS, ironmonger, ald. 1463–65. Beaven, II, 12. Died 1473–74, childless. London property inherited from John Hokley, grandfather of his late w. Elizabeth, lands also in Essex, Herts. Remitted debts of his brother John Marchall and left money to the latter's s., Master John, priest, and Nicholas; money also to Robert, s. of William Marchall; his clothing to be divided among poor kinsmen at the discretion of Master Roger Marchall, his brother and executor. P.C.C., Wattys, 16. A s. had predeceased him 1468–69, leaving a dau., under age in 1473. Ironmongers' Register, fol. 31. Master Roger was a doctor of medicine. *Cal. L. Bk., L.,* p. 103.

MAROWE, WILLIAM, grocer, ald. 1449–64. Beaven, II, 10. Said to have been s. of Stephen Marowe of Stepney, Mdsx., but may have been s. of William Marwe, smith, who d. 1430–33. See discussion of evidence by B. H. Putnam, *Early Treatises on the Practice of Justices of the Peace* ("Oxford Studies in Social and Legal History"), Vol. VII (1926), chap. v. Twice m., second w. Katherine, dau. of Richard Rich, mercer, and three s., three dau., under age, surviving his death, 1464–65. He bequeathed funeral torches to the churches of Chelmsford and Stepney and legacies to Thomas Marow, priest, and to the latter's brothers: John Marow, of Bristol; Richard, of Dunstaple; and Thomas, mason. Mention also of children of his kindred in "Breges" or Breltes; property in Mdsx. entailed. P.C.C., Godyn, 9, 11.

His eldest s., William, esquire, with property in Mdsx. and Essex, d. 1499, leaving a s. Thomas, under age, and daughters; second s., John, d. without issue, *ca.* 1465; third s., Thomas, eminent lawyer, acquired land in five counties, d. 1505 leaving one dau., Joan, m. into the Clopton family, Suff. gentry; dau. Katherine m. Sir Robert Throckmorton and had five s., seven dau. Thomas, s. of William, the eldest s., founded a family of Warwickshire gentry, d. 1538. See Putnam, *op. cit.,* and abstracts of wills in *Records of King Edward's School, Birmingham* ("Publications of the Dugdale Society," No. IV), I, xxv–xxxv.

On the Marwes of Norwich, masons, see Knoop and Jones, *The Medieval Mason* (1933), *passim.*

MARTIN, WILLIAM, skinner, ald. 1483–1505, knighted 1494. Beaven, II, 17. Son of Walter Martin of Herts. Stowe MSS 860, fol. 60. (In 1408 a Walter Martin gave four bushels of grain toward the building of the church of Hexton, Herts. Cussans, Part VII, p. 9.) Seal armorial, 1494. Drapers' Deeds, A VII, 358.

MARYNS, JOHN (alias Foot), grocer, ald. 1375–77. Beaven, I, 391. Possibly s. of John Fot, vintner, who d. 1340 leaving s. Thomas and John and w. Margery; the latter m. Ferand Manion, Spaniard, citizen of London. *C.W.C.H.,* I, 438; *Cal. L. Bks., E,* p. 191; *F,* p. 113. In 1372 John m. Marina, widow of Adam Carlile, draper. L. Bk., *G,* fol. 297*b.* Died 1381–85, leaving two s. under age, property in Cambs. *C.W.C.H.,* II, 248. The widow m. Ralph Parles; both s. reached maturity but d. without issue. L. Bk., *H,* fol. 205*b;* Hust. R.W.D., 162/83. Relationship to the following, if any, not known: Thomas de Maryns, apothecary, city chamberlain 1336–49; Simon de Maryns, grocer; Nicholas de Maryns, of the society of the Bardi.

MATHEW, JOHN, mercer, ald. 1482–99. Beaven, II, 16. Son of Thomas Mathew of Sherington, Bucks. Stowe MSS 860, fol. 60. A linen draper, he was admitted to the mercers by redemption, 1473; d. 1499; bequests to John Field and to young Barry, both of Sherington. Property in N'hants., Hunts., Surrey, Essex, Mdsx., Kent. Survived by w. Margaret and s. Robert Mathew, gentleman; legacies to each of the two s., three dau. of the latter. P.C.C., Horne, 29; *Cal. P.R., 1494–1509,* p. 284.

MELRETH, WILLIAM, mercer, ald. 1429–46. Beaven, II, 7. Married Beatrice, widow of Reginald Cokayn, esquire, s. of John Cokayn, chief justice. *Cal. P.R., 1429–36,* p. 324. Died 1445–46, leaving w., two dau., m. to mercers. Bequest to Thomas Key of Melreth (Meldreth, Cambs.) suggests an origin in that county.

P.C.C., Luff., 234–35; *C.W.C.H.*, II, 506–7. Seal, device of a woman with two pitchers. Anc. Deeds, A 4519.

MERLAWE, RICHARD, ironmonger, ald. 1403–20. Beaven, II, 2. Born at Marlow, Bucks., m. niece of Sir William Farndon, who after his death m. Robert Chichele; d. 1420–22, leaving s. Thomas under age. Land in Mdsx., charitable bequests in Marlow. *C.W.C.H.*, II, 428–29; P.C.C., Marche, 50; L. Bk., *K*, fol. 2*b*.

MICHELL, JOHN, fishmonger, ald. 1413–44. Beaven, II, 4. Died 1445, endowing chantry at Iklingham, Suff., for parents, John and Clemence, and his three w., etc.; w. Margaret surviving and two dau., m., one to Thomas Morstede, surgeon. Property in Herts. P.C.C., Luff., 29. The widow d. 1452. P.C.C., Stokton, 2.

MIDDLETON, JOHN, mercer, ald. 1456–62. Beaven, II, 10. Will refers to Barlborough, Derbys., as his birthplace; charitable bequests there. Twice m., d. 1477, survived by w. Elizabeth, five s., four of whom were of age, and one dau. P.C.C., Wattys, 30; *Hist. Parl. B.*, pp. 590–91. One s., John, entered the mercers' company, 1474. Elizabeth remarried twice, (1) to Guy Wolston, (2) to SIR WILLIAM HAMPTON. *Cal. P.R., 1485–94*, p. 186; E.C.P., 50/31, 54/386.

MITFORD, JOHN DE, draper, ald. 1366–75. Beaven, I, 389. Died 1375, leaving all London property to w., remainder to dau.; a s. John apparently predeceased him. *C.W.C.H.*, II, 181.

MOCKYNG, JOHN DE (de Somerset), fishmonger, ald. 1336–47. Beaven, I, 385. Twice m., (1) by 1318, to Idonia, dau. of Gilbert le Leche, citizen (Anc. Deeds, C 3583), and (2) to Nicholaa, sister of Thomas Sterre, fishmonger. By 1332 acquiring land at Tottenham; by 1341 had a ninth of the manor of Tottenham, held in chief. Property also in Kent, and London income at death nearly £50. Add. Ch., 40468, 40472; *Cal. inq. p.m.*, Vol. IX, No. 28; Escheat Roll, GG, *m.* 67. Died 1347, leaving s. Thomas, 13; Nicholas, younger; three dau., one a minoress. *C.W.C.H.*, I, 499.

Thomas d. at 15; Nicholas, m. under age to dau. of JOHN MALEWAYN, fishmonger, d. 1360 without issue, property passing to his sisters, Margaret, m. to Roger de Shipbrok, and Idonia, m. to Simon de Benington, draper. Idonia d. aged 27. *Cal. inq. p.m.*, Vol. X, No. 636; Vol. XI, No. 122; L. Bk., *G*, fol. 33; Escheat Roll, GG, *m.* 67; *C.W.C.H.*, II, 120–21. Nicholaa's will, 1349, refers to John Mockyng, s. of her s. John, not named elsewhere as an heir of the ald. or of his sons. *Ibid.*, p. 168.

John sealed, 1330, with a shield, impression of charges illegible; he also used device of a cross above a stag's head, star and crescent on either side. D. & C. St. Paul's, Deeds, A 7/891; Add. Ch., 40493.

There were at least six other merchants of the name Mockyng in fourteenth-century London.

MORDONE, WALTER DE (Mourdon), stockfishmonger, ald. 1335–36, 1343–50. Beaven, I, 384. Endowed chantry in Croydon church for souls of William and Avice, his parents, Gilbert de Mordon, his former master, etc. Died 1349–51, leaving a s., four dau. *C.W.C.H.*, I, 654; *Cal. L. Bk.*, *F*, p. 231. Sealed with a merchant's mark, 1347. Harl. Ch., 53 E 51. His father may have been the William de Mordon, leading bureler, named in a record of 1299. *Cal. L. Bk.*, *C*, p. 52.

MORDONE, SIMON DE, stockfishmonger, ald. 1364–74. Beaven, I, 389. Will, enrolled 1384, directs all London property to be sold for pious and charitable uses on death of w. *C.W.C.H.*, II, 243.

MORE, WILLIAM, vintner, ald. 1382, 1384–1400. Beaven, I, 397. Died 1400–1402; w. but no other heirs. Property Southwark, Rochester, and Cambs. *C.W.C.H.*, II, 352–53.

NASARD, HENRY, draper, ald. 1318–22. Beaven, I, 381. Seal armorial, 1314. Anc. Deeds, WS 365.

NAYLER, RICHARD, tailor, ald. 1482–83. Beaven, II, 16. Died 1483, survived by w., six s., one of age, one posthumous, three dau.; property in Kent. At least one s., possibly three, d. under age; the two others came of age. The daughters m. Robert Byfeld, ironmonger, Walter Robert, Richard Coulpepyr. P.C.C., Logge, 7; L. Bk., *L*, fol. 208.

NEEL, WALTER, blader, ald. 1338–46. Beaven, I, 385. Twice m., d. 1351–53, apparently childless, will mentioning kinsmen Robert and John Neel. *C.W.C.H.*, I, 674. See a purser and a goldbeater of these names. *Cal. L. Bk., F*, p. 180; *E*, p. 162.

NEUPORT, WILLIAM, fishmonger, ald. 1377, 1380, 1382. Beaven, I, 392. Bought manors of Clepton and Rous, held land in Kent and the castle of Lullingstone. Will, proved 1391, left property between w. Massie and dau., w. of John Poynaunt, fishmonger; small bequests to two brothers and to poor relations. P.C.C., Rous, 8; *Cal. L. Bk., H*, p. 87; cf. Weever, p. 444. Seal, a merchant's mark. Anc. Deeds, A 1899 (1374). Guildhall Deeds, parish of St. Mary Aldermanbury, No. 35 (1383).

NOKET, THOMAS, draper, ald. 1377, 1383. Beaven, I, 393. Manor of Rislepe and land at Coulsdon, Surrey; d. 1396–97, survived by w. Margery, no children. *C.W.C.H.*, II, 322–23.

NORBURY, RICHARD, mercer, ald. 1383. Beaven, I, 398. Married Imanya, widow of John de Enefeld, pepperer. *Cal. L. Bk., G*, p. 262.

NORMAN, JOHN, draper, ald. 1441–68. Beaven, II, 9. Son of John Norman of Banbury, Oxon. Stowe MSS 860, fol. 54. Died 1468; no mention of w. in will. Bequests to Margaret Norman, widow, of Banbury and to the s. of his kinsman William Broun of Banbury to pay his expenses at Oxford University. Richard Norman, his brother, an executor. P.C.C., Godyn, 25. The latter, a draper, d. 1462, leaving money to Thomas Norman of Weston, Bucks. P.C.C., Wattys, 7. The name not uncommon. Three early-fifteenth-century citizens named John Norman—a brewer, a horse-dealer, a goldsmith. *Cal. L. Bks., I*, pp. 88, 103, 233; *K*, p. 49.

NORTHALL, JOHN DE, skinner, ald. 1339–48. Beaven, I, 385. Called "clerk," d. 1349, leaving a grandson John, under age, s. of his dau. Wymarca and Bonaventure Bonentente of Florence. *C.W.C.H.*, I, 572–73.

NORTHAMPTON, JOHN (de), draper, ald. 1375–77, 1382–83. Beaven, I, 391. Died 1397–98; will names parents, Thomas and Mariota; Joan and Petronilla, his wives; s. James; three brothers, Robert, William, and Roger Comberton; William and John, his nephews; and three nieces, children of his brother William; two sisters; and a kinsman, John Comberton. Property in Mdsx. *C.W.C.H.*, II, 333–35. His s. James executed a deed of release, 1394. W.A.M.,

302. His brother William may have been the skinner who was released from jury service in 1404 on account of old age and d. 1410, leaving a dau. and s.; the latter, William, skinner, was living in 1432. *Cal. L. Bk.*, *I*, p. 28; Hust. R.W.D., 161/23; Comm. Lon., Broun, 177.

John's seal, 1396, a shield of arms: a crowned leopard with one head, two bodies. D. & C. St. Paul's, Deeds, A 27/174, 34/898. See Harl. MSS 2169, in *Ancestor*, VII, 194; IX, 168; Harl. MSS 1386, fol. 35*b*.

The family was possibly descended from HENRY DE COMBEMARTYN.

NORTONE, GEOFFREY DE, recorder 1298–1303, ald. 1297–1303. Beaven, I, 378. Will, enrolled 1303, names w., s. Gregory, a dau. *C.W.C.H.*, I, 157.

NORTON, GREGORY DE, alias atte Schire, recorder 1329–38, ald. 1327–38. Beaven, I, 383. Son of GEOFFREY DE NORTONE, d. 1337–38, leaving a s. and dau. *C.W.C.H.*, I, 429; Cal. Rolls A.N.D. (MS), AA, *m.* 12*d*; *Cal. L. Bk.*, *C*, p. 194.

NORTON, WILLIAM, draper, ald. 1406–20. Beaven, II, 3. First w. Alice, widow of Peter de Wottone, draper, and dau. of Agnes atte Hale and one or other of her three husbands, all London merchants. L. Bk., *I*, fol. 134*b*; *C.W.C.H.*, II, 378–79. Second w., Egidia, later m. Henry Rydall of N'hants., gentleman; was styled gentlewoman; was living 1448. Hust. R.W.D., 186/30; C, 40/723/533. In 1407 a s. Edmund and dau. Cristina living. In 1440 William, his s. and heir, gentleman of London, demised London tenements in "Norton Aley," using as seal, a stag couched, initials. Drapers' Deeds, A VII, 204; Rot. cl., 19 Hen. VI, *m.* 31*d*.

NOTT, JOHN, pepperer, ald. 1361–69. Beaven, I, 388. Will, dated 169, enrolled 1372, names w., no children; niece Agnes, w. of John Warde, pepperer, and her sons, among his heirs. *C.W.C.H.*, II, 145.

OLNEY, JOHN, mercer, ald. 1435–58. Beaven, II, 8. Son of John Olney of Coventry. Stowe MSS 860, fol. 52. A co-feoffee with Walter FitzRichard of Olneye, and others, of John Olneye, esquire, of Bishops Tachbrook of Warw., and of his w. Elena. Hust. R.W.D., 166/1. Seal, 1441, a stag coursing. Add. Ch., 40052. His father might have been from Coventry and yet a London citizen. There were three citizens of the name in the previous generation, one a grocer, one a woolman, one son of William Olneye, fishmonger.

OLYVER, EDMUND, stockfishmonger, ald. 1377, 1379, 1381. Beaven, I, 393. Dead by 1404, when his widow m. John Yonge, fishmonger. A grandson, Thomas, s. of his s. Edmund, d. under age by 1413. L. Bk., *I*, fol. 38*b*.

OTELEYE, ROBERT, grocer, ald. 1426–36. Beaven, II, 7. Son of William Otley of Ufford, Suff. Stowe MSS 860, fol. 50. Left property in Suffolk and Kent, including land at Bromley inherited from his father, William. Twice m., first w. Joan, dau. of Richard Horsham, esquire; second w. Katherine, formerly w. of Bartholomew Seman, goldsmith, surviving. Died 1436, no children. See wills, printed in full, Register, Chichele, 549–53; and *Chart. St. Thomas*, fol. 81. Seal, 1433, device of a lion. Harl. Ch., 111, G 27. (Arms ascribed in Stowe MSS 860: argent, three lions' heads erased, and bordure ingrailed sable.)

See John Otle, on the grocers' list, 1349, and Thomas Otle, in the 1370's. The latter was s. of John Otteleye of Ufford, Suff. *Cal. P. & M. Rolls*, II, 107. John Oteleye, grocer and mercer, d. 1404–5, survived by two brothers and a nephew, and leaving money to the church of Ufford, Suff. *C.W.C.H.*, II, 362; P.C.C., Marche, fol. 8.

OULGREVE, THOMAS (Holgrave), ald. 1458–70. Beaven, II, 11. Son of Thomas Oldgrave of Knutsford, Ches. Stowe MSS 860, fol. 56. Twice m., d. 1472–73, providing for chantry at Knutsford, "where I was born and cristened"; had a dau. Agnes, m. to John Mildenhale, gentleman, s. of Robert Mildenhale. P.C.C., Wattys, 8. His widow Alice later m. SIR BARTHOLOMEW JAMES. *C.W.C.H.*, II, 598.

OXENFORD, JOHN DE, vintner, ald. 1324–42. Beaven, I, 383. Died 1340–42, endowing a chantry for souls of Adam and Cristina, his parents; two brothers; etc.; will names three s., three dau. *C.W.C.H.*, I, 460–61. Eldest s., John, d. 1357 leaving a s. John under age, heir to property in Essex. *Ibid.*, p. 699; *Cal. L. Bk.*, G, pp. 95, 196; *Cal. inq. p.m.*, Vol. VIII, No. 366.

PADDESLEY, JOHN, goldsmith, ald. 1428–51. Beaven, II, 7. Son of Simon Paddesley of Bury St. Edmunds. Stowe MSS 860, fol. 51.

PALMER, ROGER LE, skinner, ald. 1320–26. Beaven, I, 381. Twice m., d. 1327–31, leaving daughers only. Tenant-in-chief, Berks. *C.W.C.H.*, I, 363; *Cal. P.R.*, *1317–21*, p. 590. The name was a common one in the city in this century.

PAPPESWORTH, WALTER DE, ald. 1324–27. Beaven, I, 383. A dyer of this name admitted to the freedom of the city, 1311. *Cal. L. Bk.*, D, p. 79. Will, dated at Pappeworth, Cambs., mentions w. but no children; rents in London for maintenance of two chantries, one in London, one in Sonde, Bedf. *C.W.C.H.*, I, 326.

PARIS, SIMON DE, mercer, ald. 1299–1319, 1320–21. Beaven, I, 379. A bondman from Necton, Norf., *Year Books of Edward II* ("Selden Society Year Books Series"), I, 11–13.

PARKER, WILLIAM, mercer, ald. 1393–1403. Beaven, I, 402. Twice m., second w. the dau. of John Norbury, esquire; will refers to his brothers Esmond Chimbeham, Jankyn Parker, and to Thomas Parker, bastard. Died 1403, leaving three s., one dau., property in Essex, Kent. P.C.C., Marche 6. Chimbeham's will, Register, Chichele, II, 376–77. Match arranged between his widow Joan and Sir Richard, lord Seint-Maur, 1404–5, but apparently the marriage did not take place. *Cal. C.R.*, *1402–5*, pp. 322–23; H. St. Maur, *Annals of the Seymours* (1902), p. 10. Eldest s. John d. during his apprenticeship to Richard Herry, mercer, age 25–26, unmarried; his brother Nicholas had predeceased him. L. Bk., *I*, fol. 44; P.C.C., Marche, 27. Second s., William, esquire, d. 1421, buried at Kingsnorth, Kent, where he had inherited a manor. P. & M. Rolls, A 51, *m.* 3*b*; Mill Stephenson, p. 239.

PECCHE, JOHN (Peche), fishmonger, ald. 1349–76. Beaven, I, 387. Bought manor of Lullingston from John, grandson of GREGORY DE ROKESLE, 1360. It was held by his descendants in the male line for four generations. John Philipott, *Villare Cantianum or Kent Surveyed and Illustrated* (2d ed., 1776), pp. 226–27. Died 1380, survived by w. Mary and s. Sir William. Sudbury (Lambeth wills), 105*b*. In right of his w., held property in London, Mdsx., Surrey, Cambs., Wilts. His widow m. Sir William Moigne, who was dead by 1410; his s. John, esquire, later knighted, was of age in that year and in 1427–28 joined the drapers' company. *Cal. C.R.*, *1409–13*, pp. 49, 177; *Transcripts of Drapers' Records*(1910), p. 45. His s. Sir William joined the grocers. Grocers' Records, Vol. 300, August 23, 1459. For his career and marriages see *Hist. Parl. B.*, p. 673.

PEMBERTON, HUGH, tailor, ald. 1491–1500. Beaven, II, 18. Died 1500, leaving two s. *Hist. Parl. B.*, p. 674.

PENNE, JOHN, skinner, ald. 1408–22. Beaven, II, 4. Will, dated 1422, enrolled 1434, mentions late w. Olive; all London property to pious and charitable uses. *C.W.C.H.*, II, 471.

PERCIVALL, JOHN (Percyvale), tailor, ald. 1485–1503, knighted 1487. Beaven, II, 17. Born at Macclesfield, Ches. Stow, I, 111. Charitable bequests there and elsewhere in that county and in Derbys. Died 1503, survived by w. Thomasina, born in Cornw., formerly w. of a mercer and of a tailor, no children. Richard Percyvall, nephew, 28, heir. Land in Berks. P.C.C., *Blamyr*, 23; R. T. D. Sayle, *Lord Mayors' Pageants of the Merchant Tailors' Company* (1931), p. 9; *Abstracts of Inquisitiones post mortem Relating to the City of London*, Part I, ed. G. S. Fry (1896), pp. 19–20; C. M. Clode, *Early History of the Guild of Merchant Taylors* (1888), II, 11–13.

PERVEYS, JOHN, fishmonger, ald. 1416–34. Beaven, II, 5. Son of John Parveis of Ersegeston, Berks. Stowe MSS 860, fol. 50. Died 1434, leaving w. Joan, two s.; endowed chantry for souls of parents, John and Alice. Bequest to a brother, Robert Perveys, living in Abingdon, Berks. Property in Surrey. *C.W.C.H.*, II, 496–97. Elder s. John d. 1436, leaving property to his w. and desiring burial beside his brothers in London. P.C.C., Luff., 21. Henry, the younger s., draper, was living, with two s. and a dau., in 1476. *C.W.C.H.*, II, 586.

PHILIP, MATHEW, goldsmith, ald. 1450–76, knighted 1471, apprenticed to John Philip, 1410, free 1417. Beaven, II, 10. Son of Arnold Philip of Norwich. Stowe MSS 860, fol. 55. Twice m., first w., Cristina, d. 1470, second w., Beatrice, formerly w. of William Lemyng, grocer. Died 1476, survived by w. and s. William, goldsmith, his executor. Property in Kent. P.C.C., Wattys, 27; E.C.P., 59/11, 12. Lemyng's will, P.C.C., Godyn, 31 (1470).

PHILPOT, JOHN (Philipot, Phelipot, Filpot), grocer, ald. 1372–77, 1378–79, 1380–81, 1382, 1384, knighted 1381. Beaven, I, 390. Three times m. First w. Lady Jane Stamford. Stow, I, 320. Second w. Margaret, dau. of RICHARD DE CROYDON, fishmonger. *C.W.C.H.*, II, 167–68. Third w., surviving to at least 1412, Margaret, dau. of JOHN STODEYE (*q.v.*) and widow of John Berlingham, mercer. *Cal. L. Bk.*, *H*, p. 49; *Feudal Aids*, VI, 489. Dead by 1389; provided for chantry at Gillingham, Kent; three s., two dau., one of them a nun. *C.W.C.H.*, II, 275–77. Property in Mdsx. Eldest s. Edward not traced. Second s. John was apprenticed to WILLIAM PARKER, mercer, free 1400, m. Idonia, dau. of Thomas Austyn, mercer. Hust. R.W.D., 134/112. He may have been the John Philpot, esquire, with goods at Gillingham, who d. intestate 1415. Register, Chichele, II, 30; cf. *Cal. C.R.*, *1405–9*, p. 246. John, s. of the mercer, living 1431. Rot. cl., 10 Hen. VI, *m.* 13*d.* Youngest s. of the ald., Thomas, may have been the apprentice of that name in the goldsmiths' company. He is said to have purchased land in Kent and left descendants there and in London. M.A.P., *Notes on the Philpott Families* (n.d.), p. 54; E.C.P., 73/38. The ald.'s dau. Margaret m. (1) John, younger s. of Sir John de la Hale of Dorset, (2) John Nelond. Rot. cl., 10 Hen. VI, *m.* 13*d.* There were numerous Philpots in fifteenth-century London. The family at Philpotts, near Tunbridge, in the fifteenth century, bore Sir John's arms. *D.N.B.*

PICARD, HENRY, vintner, ald. 1348–61. Beaven, I, 386. Survived by w. Margaret, a Gysors, who m. Sir Bartholomew de Burgherssh. *Cal. inq. p.m.*, XII, 86. Sealed, 1351, with shield of arms: a daunce and three trefoils (Stowe MSS 860 in error). Same used by John Picard, 1407. Anc. Deeds, WS 400, B 1999, B

2994. John Pikard of London, 1402, bore a fess indented and three trefoils. Anc. Deeds, DS 1.

PLOMER, JOHN (Plummer, alias Leynham), ald. 1464–68, created K.B., 1465. Beaven, II, 13. Son of John and Cristian Plomer of Halstede, Essex. E.C.P., 11/432. On grocers' membership list by 1448. Married Margaret, dau. of Sir John Fray. *Cal. P.R., 1467–77*, p. 471. Died 1479, childless. Property in Mdsx., Essex, Surrey, Herts., Berks., Oxon., Bucks., Glos., to w., who d. 1482. P.C.C., Wattys, 37; P.C.C., Logge, 6; *C.W.C.H.*, II, 578–79.

POLE, RICHARD DE LA, ald. 1330–40, knighted 1340. Beaven, I, 384. Eldest of the three s. of William de la Pole, merchant of Hull. Born *ca.* 1281, d. 1345, leaving s. Sir William, *ca.* 26, and dau. Joan, m. to Ralph Basset. *Cal. inq. p.m.*, Vol. VIII, No. 596, 329. Property in Yorks., Lincs., N'hants., Hunts., Cambs. Through his brother William's descendants the family survived in the male line for six generations. H. R. Fox Bourne, *English Merchants* (1886), pp. 33–47; *D.N.B.*, article on Sir William de la Pole.

POLLE, THOMAS, goldsmith, ald. 1397–1413. Beaven, I, 404. Twice m., first w. Joan, dau. of William Box, citizen. Died 1413, no w. or children surviving; bequests to brothers John and Peter Polle. P.C.C., Marche, 27.

POUNTFRETT, WILLIAM DE, skinner, ald. 1340–48. Beaven, I, 385. Will, enrolled 1349, mentions nephew John, no children. *C.W.C.H.*, I, 550. The name was common in the city in this century.

POURTE, HUGH, fishmonger, ald. 1300–1307. Beaven, I, 379. Died 1307, leaving one s. *C.W.C.H.*, I, 192, 196.

PRESTONE, JOHN DE, corder, ald. 1321–39. Beaven, I, 382. Died 1339. Will names parents, Walter and Margery; a brother, Peter; and one s., John. The latter, also a corder, m. (1) dau. of his guardian, John de Oxenford, vintner, (2) Margaret Costantyn and d. 1353, leaving three dau. *C.W.C.H.*, I, 435, 669–70.

PRESTONE, RICHARD DE, grocer, ald. 1378–79, 1384–87. Beaven, I, 395. Burgess of Calais. Three times m., left no children. London property to endow a chantry for souls of Richard and Isabel, his parents, Stephen de Preston, corder, etc. Buried in the same church, All Hallows at the Hay, as John de Prestone, above. *C.W.C.H.*, II, 291; Comm. Lon., Courtney, 234.

PRIOUR, JOHN, woolmonger, ald. 1322–35. Beaven, I, 382. Married, after 1317, Idonia, widow of William de Conduit, vintner. *Cal. L. Bk., E*, pp. 76–77. Died 1335, leaving a s. and three dau. A younger brother, John, also a merchant. *C.W.C.H.*, I, 408.

PULTNEY, JOHN (de) (Pulteney), draper, ald. 1327–35, 1336–38, knighted 1337. Beaven, I, 255, 383. Son of Adam Neale de Clipston, of Weston, Sussex, and grandson of Hugh de Pultney. Inherited property at Pulteney, Misterton, Leics. See *D.N.B.* Members of his mother's family, the Naptons, were tenants-in-chief in Warw. and Leics., also merchants. *Knights of Edward I*, pp. 245–46; *Cal. P.R., 1321–24*, pp. 112, 247. Married, as second w., dau. of John de St. John of Lageham; endowed a chantry in St. Paul's for souls of his parents, etc.; d. 1349, leaving a s. William, aged 8. Property in Mdsx., Kent, Cambs., Leics., Warw., Suff. *C.W.C.H.*, I, 609–10; H.M.C., *Ninth Report, Appendix*, p. 47; *Cal. inq. p.m.*, Vol. IX, No. 183. His widow m. Nicholas de Lovaigne, later knighted and governor of Ponthieu. *Cal. C.R., 1349–54*, pp. 296–97; *1354–60*, p. 186; *1367–70*, p. 71.

His s. m. but d. childless, 1367. Escheat Roll, GG, *mm.* 17, 18. Robert, s. of Sir John's sister Ellen Owen, succeeded to the property, taking the name of Pultney. His family is said to have continued in the male line until 1637. Cussans, Part XIII, XIV, p. 308.

The ald. sealed, 1335, with his arms: a daunce with three leopards' heads in chief. Anc. Deeds, WS 396.

PURCHASE, WILLIAM, mercer, ald. 1492–1502. Beaven, II, 18. Son of John Purchase of Gamlingay, Cambs. B. B. Orridge, *Some Account of the Citizens of London and Their Rulers* (1867), p. 121. A tailor, he was admitted to the mercers by redemption, 1466.

PYCOT, NICHOLAS, mercer, ald. 1298–1312. Beaven, I, 379. Died 1312, endowing chantry for souls of w. Alice, parents, John and Emma. London property to two s., under age, and dau., m. to Hugh de Waltham, clerk. *C.W.C.H.*, I, 233–34.

PYEL, JOHN, ald. 1369–77, 1378–79. Beaven, I, 389. Buried at Irtlingborough, N'hants.; extensive property in that county, land purchased also in Mdsx. and Essex. Note that the manor of Irtlingborough was acquired by a John Pyel as early as 1343. Hartshorne, pp. 93–94. Will, dated 1379, proved 1382, refers to w. and two s. *Early Lincoln Wills*, p. 66. London property to w. for life, remainder to dean and college of the church of St. Peter, Irtlingborough. A brother Henry, an executor, possibly the rector of Werketon of that name. *C.W.C.H.*, II, 228; *Cal. C.R., 1360–64*, p. 523. Arms on monument and seals: argent a bend between two mullets, pierced. Anc. Deeds, WS 398 (1329), BS 26 (1359–60); *B.M. Cat. Seals*, 12634 (1369).

PYKEMAN, ANDREW (Pykenham), fishmonger, ald. 1376–77, 1378–79, 1380–81. Beaven, I, 391. Twice m., one of w. the widow of Robert Furneux, fishmonger. L. Bk., *G*, fol. 97*b*. Will refers to parents, Richard and Margaret, two sisters, a brother Roger with three s. Died 1391–92, dau. Cecilia, w. of John Sibille, fishmonger, predeceased him; her dau., under age, heir to his property in London and Surrey. *C.W.C.H.*, II, 293; P.C.C., Rous, 8. Andrew's seal, 1386, a shield bearing a six-pointed pierced star, ends of the points feathery. D. & C. St. Paul's, Deeds, A 81/3070.

PYNCHON, JOHN, goldsmith, ald. 1389–92. Beaven, I, 400. Twice m., d. 1392 leaving one s., who came of age 1406. *Cal. P. & M. Rolls*, III, 201; L. Bk., *H*, fols. 284, 324.

RADEWELLE, WILLIAM, stockfishmonger, ald. 1404–6. Beaven, II, 3. Brother of Richard Radewelle, stockfishmonger, who provided for services for souls of their parents, James and Margaret, and two other brothers. Richard had property at Radwell and elsewhere in Herts., left money to repair Radwell church; will, dated 1411, enrolled 1417, mentions no children. *C.W.C.H.*, II, 411–12. William d. 1410–11, leaving w. Margaret, who later m. John Lawney, grocer, and one dau., under age, who m. Robert, s. of Robert Isham, esquire of Pitchley, N'hants. P.C.C., Marche, 23; L. Bk., *I*, fols. 5, 280*b*; P. & M. Rolls, A 55, *m.* 2*b*.

RAWSON, RICHARD, mercer, ald. 1476–85. Beaven, II, 15. Son of James Rawson of Fryston, Yorks. See *Testamenta Eboraca*, IV, 131 n. Apprenticed to John Olney, free 1463; d. 1483. Will, dated that year, mentions w. Isabel; s. Averey, Christopher, John, Richard; two dau.; three brothers, Robert, James, Henry; and three sisters, m. Bequest to church of Shirburn in Emet, Yorks. Legacy for poor relations. P.C.C., Logge, 16. His brother Henry, gentleman, of Bessacar Grange, Yorks., d. 1500, leaving three dau. and a s. James m. to dau. of Sir Brian Sandford. *Testamenta Eboraca*, IV, 173. Another brother, Thomas Rawson, mercer, d. 1473–74, leaving money to Richard, his executor, and to the other three brothers named in the latter's will, also to his mother Cicely Rawson. Bequests to the churches of Fryston-by-the-Water and Castleford, Yorks., and to poor kindred. Two s., one posthumous, and three dau. P.C.C., Wattys, 14; E, 150/289/11.

Richard's sons Averey, John, and Christopher were admitted to the mercers' company 1488, 1492, 1493. John is said to have become a knight of the Order of St. John, later created Viscount Clontarf. J. Maskell, *Collections in Illustration of the History of the Church of All Hallows Barking* (1864), p. 47. Christopher, merchant of the staple, d. 1518–19, his will mentioning three s., two dau., also two s. of his brother Nicholas, the latter not named in their father's will. *C.W.C.H.*, II, 627–28. Richard Rawson, who studied at Bologna, and Ferrara and in 1522 became chaplain to Henry VIII may have been s. of the ald. See R. J. Mitchell, "English Law Students at Bologna in the Fifteenth Century," E.H.R., LI, 279. The ald.'s two dau. m. John Fox, mercer, and Godfrey Darrald, merchant of the staple. L. Bk., *L*, fol. 239.

REDE, BARTHOLOMEW, goldsmith, ald. 1498–1505, knighted 1503. Beaven, II, 19. Second s. of Norfolk landowner. Blomefield, VIII, 107. Died 1505; will names w., parents, Roger and Katherine, and several brothers; provision for his obit to be celebrated at Cromer, Norf.; charitable bequests there. Property in Mdsx., Surrey, Berks., Hants., Oxon., Wilts. No children, heirs were s. of his brothers John and Esmond, also Thomas, s. of Master John Reed of London, gentleman. P.C.C., Holgrave, 40–41.

REFHAM, RICHARD DE (Richer), mercer, ald. 1298–1300, 1302–12. Beaven, I, 378. Died 1328, leaving a s. John, with a s. Richer and other children. *C.W.C.H.*, I, 339.

REFHAM, JOHN DE, fishmonger, ald. 1339–43. Beaven, I, 385. Possibly s. of the above. Died 1359, childless. *C.W.C.H.*, II, 10–11.

REMYNGTON, WILLIAM, fishmonger, ald. 1485–1511. Beaven, II, 17. Died 1511; w. and two s. predeceased him. P.C.C., Fetiplace, 4.

REVELL, ROBERT (Ryvell), grocer, ald. 1490–91. Beaven, II, 18. Apprenticed to Symkyn Smith, grocer, free 1458. Died 1491, leaving w. Margery, s. Thomas, made free in the grocers' company that year, and s. John, under age. *Cal. L. Bk., L*, pp. 277, 321. Thomas d. 1497, leaving two dau., under age, and a kinsman, Robert, his apprentice, free that year. P.C.C., Horne, 12, printed in *Medieval Records of a City Church*, I, 18.

REYNEWELL, WILLIAM, girdler, translated to ironmongers, 1399, ald. 1397–1403. Beaven, I, 403. Son of Thomas Reynwelle, of Bromley. *Cal. L. Bk., H*, p. 446. Freeman of Stratford-on-Avon. Twice m., second w. Cristina, widow of Robert Ryder, brazier. Died 1403–4, leaving three s., two dau., m. to Thomas Chacombe, mercer, and John Weston, ironmonger. London property to two elder s., land in Kent to youngest; property in Stratford and elsewhere in Warw. P.C.C., Marche, 5.

REYNWELL, JOHN, fishmonger, ald. 1416–45. Beaven, II, 5. Son of WILLIAM REYNEWELL and first w., Isabel (Stowe MSS 860, fol. 49, in error in stating he was s. of Robert Rainwell, haberdasher). Died 1445, leaving s. William, dau.

Fridiswida, a minoress. Stafford (Lambeth wills), 164; *C.W.C.H.*, II, 577; *Hist. Parl. B.*, p. 715.

REYNHAM, THOMAS, goldsmith, ald. 1378, 1380. Beaven, I, 394. Died 1388; only near relation mentioned in will a sister, Reyna. *C.W.C.H.*, II, 269. Seals, 1368, 1370, nonarmorial, religious themes. Anc. Deeds, RS 326, CS 5.

ROKESLE, WALTER DE, ald. 1294–97, 1308–12. Beaven, I, 378. Nephew of GREG-ORY DE ROKESLE, goldsmith, ald. 1265–91. *Ibid.*, p. 374; *C.W.C.H.*, I, 98; *Cal. Inq. Misc.*, Vol. III, No. 874; John Philipott, *Villare Cantianum or Kent Surveyed and Illustrated* (2d ed., 1776), pp. 190, 260; *D.N.B.* Seal, 1290, name inscribed in circle about shield of arms: three rooks. W.A.M., 28862. No resemblance to Rokele arms on the rolls of the thirteenth and fourteenth centuries. *Three Rolls of Arms of the Latter Part of the Thirteenth Century*, ed. W. S. Walford and C. S. Perceval (1864), p. 68; *Roll of Caerlaverock*, ed. T. Wright (1864), p. 30.

ROMAYN, THOMAS (Romeyn), pepperer, ald. 1294–1313. Beaven, I, 378. By 1288 m. to Juliana Hauteyn. *Cal. L. Bk.*, *A*, p. 169; *C.W.C.H.*, I, 161. Died 1312–13, willing property to w. Juliana, and four dau., two of them nuns, two m., one to John de Burford, woolman, one to William de Upton. *C.W.C.H.*, I, 238. Juliana left property Mdsx., Surrey. *Cal. inq. p.m.*, Vol. VII, No. 696.

ROTHING, RICHARD DE, vintner, ald. 1333–46. Beaven, I, 384. Twice m. A s. John, vintner, d. 1375–76, leaving a s. John and dau. *C.W.C.H.*, II, 187; *Cal. L. Bk.*, *F*, p. 233; Stow, I, 294; II, 326. Numerous citizens of the name from the late thirteenth century.

SADELYNGSTANES, HUGH DE, ald. and recorder 1359–61. Beaven, I, 388. Died 1361, will providing for two s., under age, the elder to be intrusted to the mayor of Newcastle-on-Tyne as guardian. *C.W.C.H.*, II, 57.

SALISBURY, ADAM DE, pepperer, ald. 1325–30. Beaven, I, 383. Inherited property in town of Salisbury from his father Martin; d. by 1330, leaving two s. and a dau. who m. SIMON DOLSELY. Hust. R.W.D., 58/113. His widow m. JOHN HAMOND. *C.W.C.H.*, II, 65. Elder s. John d. without heirs. Drapers' Deeds, A VIII, 329. Younger s. Thomas, possibly the grocer of that name on the company's list in 1349, was by 1365 a knight, owning manor of Salisbury at Walthamstow, Essex. Hust. R.W.D., 92/33; G. F. Bosworth, *The Manors of Low Hall and Salisbury Hall, Walthamstow*, Walthamstow Antiquarian Society (1920), p. 13. He m. Alice, dau. of HENRY COMBEMARTYN; d. 1376, leaving s. Paul, under age, in custody of Agnes, widow of ADAM FRAUNCEYS. Comm. Lon., Courtney, 44. Paul, esquire, d. 1398–1400. entailing the Essex property on his dau. Hust. R.W.D., 129/21. Note that John de Salesbury, citizen and grocer of New Sarum, in 1405 bequeathed his house in that town to a kinswoman Joan, dau. of another knight, Sir John Saresbury. P.C.C., Marche, 15.

SCOT, THOMAS, draper, ald. 1446–63. Beaven, II, 9. Son of Robert Scot of Dorney, Bucks. Stowe MSS 860, fol. 54.

SECCHEFORD, HENRY DE, mercer, ald. 1319–36, chamberlain 1328–36. Beaven, I, 381. Three times m., d. 1337–39, will naming a s. and two dau., one of them a nun. *C.W.C.H.*, I, 435. His widow, Alice, m. Sir John Frembaud. His s., Henry, d. by 1364. *Cal. P. & M. Rolls*, I, 114, 278. Related to Andrew, s. of Albin de Seccheford, called "de Caustone," mercer. *C.W.C.H.*, I, 589; *Cal. L.Bk.*, *D*, p. 155. Seal, 1313, a shield of arms, ermine on a fess three escallops. Drapers' Deeds, A VI, 242.

SELY (Cely). Five generations of one branch of this family may be traced, as follows:

1. THOMAS SELY, skinner, ald. 1297–1300, 1303–11. Beaven, I, 379. Will, enrolled 1312, mentions w. Alice, s. Robert. *C.W.C.H.*, I, 228.

2. ROBERT SELY, skinner, ald. 1319–*ca.* 1325. Son of the above. With w. Joan acquired a rent, 1310. Merchant Tailors' Deeds, XVI, 1. Dead by 1331, leaving two s. C. Misc., 109/2; Escheat Roll, EE, *m.* 60; Hust. R.P.L., 139. Seal.

3. Laurence Sely, skinner, son of the above; m. Agnes, dau. of Roger Hesebonde, cornchandler. B.H. Deeds, *G*, 13. Will dated 1349, enrolled 1353. *C.W.C.H.*, I, 671.

Bartholomew, brother of the above.

4. JOHN SELY, skinner, ald. 1379–80, 1382–83, 1384–85. Beaven, I, 395. Son of Laurence, above. In 1365–66 m. Sibil, formerly w. of (1) William Laurence, fishmonger, before 1349, and (2) Ralph de Cauntebrigg, merchant. Died without issue. *C.W.C.H.*, I, 590; II, 91; *Cal. P. & M. Rolls*, II, 63–64, 72.

John, s. of Bartholomew. Settled in Chesildon (Chisledon, Wilts.?).

5. Two illegitimate s. of the above John, and one legitimate s., John, who became a brewer in London. Hust. R.W.D., 83/2.

6. Simon, s. of John; by 1443 described as gentleman of London. Hust. R.W.D., 172/19. His sister Alice m. John Marchaunt, lorimer. Hust. R.W.D., 172/18. Edward Sely of Ditton, Bucks., husbandman, and Davy Sely of Horton, Bucks., tailor, sons of John Sely, husbandman, one of the illegitimate s. mentioned above, sought to dispute Simon's claims to inherit certain property in London and in Bristol, but in 1459 they certified that he was the true heir. Hust. R.W.D. 83/2.

Numerous other citizens of the name, e.g.:

William Seely, spicer, admitted to the freedom by redemption, 1312. *Cal. L. Bk., D*, p. 94.

William Seely of Henley in the same year apprenticed to a fishmonger. *Ibid.*, p. 168.

Thomas Sely, among the armed men and archers sent to the defense of Calais, 1369. *Ibid., G*, p. 244.

Laurence Cely entered the skinners' fraternity of Our Lady's Assumption, 1399, becoming warden ten years later.

Alison Cely, admitted to above fraternity, 1409.

John Sely, warden of the fraternity, 1472; w. Margaret.

John Cely, admitted to the freedom in the grocers' company, 1474.

Thomas Sely of London, merchant. Rot. cl., II Hen. VI, *m.* 13*d.*

Thomas Cely of London, dyer. E.C.P., 127/8.

John Sely "of Chepyngfaryndon, Berks., yoman or citizen and felmonger of London." *Cal. P.R., 1429–36*, p. 93.

Robert Sely, for eighteen years a servant of the household under Henry V, Henry VI. *Ibid.*, p. 336.

William Cely, in 1478 a servant of the bishop of Winchester. Add. Ch., 5225.

David Selly of Westminster, citizen and draper. Drapers' Transcripts. Seal, a chevron between three wolves' heads. Harl. Ch., 84 I 30, a shield of arms.

Connections between the above and the family of merchants of the staple whose letters are so well known have not been established. The name was prominent throughout the west country and also in the Cinque Ports.

SEMAN, JOHN, alias Ragenell, fishmonger, ald. 1381. Beaven, I, 396. Probably the John Seman, apprentice of William de Berkyng, 1354. Twice m., d. 1394–95 without issue, survived by a brother Robert Seman with a dau. *C.W.C.H.*, I, 683–84; II, 314–15.

SEMAN, SIMON, vintner, ald. 1422–33. Beaven, II, 6. Died 1433, buried at Barton-on-Humber, Lincs., brass there with arms: barry wavy a crescent. Gough, II, Part II, 105.

SERVAT, WILLIAM (Cervat), ald. 1309–19. Beaven, I, 380. From Cahors. See F. Arens, "Wilhelm Servat von Cahors als Kaufmann zu London," *Vierteljahrschrift für Sozial- und Wirtschaftsgeschichte*, XI, Part IV, 477–514. Seal, 1303–4, a merchant's mark. Anc. Deeds, RS 294.

SEVENOKE, WILLIAM, grocer, ald. 1411–26. Beaven, II, 4. Son of William Rumschedde of Sevenoak, Kent, apprenticed to Hugh Boys, ironmonger, translated to grocers, 1394. *Cal. L. Bk., H*, p. 439. No reference to w. in wills. *C.W.C.H.*, II, 462, 466, 467.

SHAA, EDMUND, goldsmith, ald. 1473–88, knighted 1483. Beaven, II, 14. Son of John Shaa of Dukinfield, Ches. Stowe MSS 860, fol. 58. Died 1488, survived by w. Juliana, s. Hugh, two dau. Charitable bequests in parish of Stopford, Ches., where his parents were buried, and in various parishes in Lancs. P.C.C., Milles, 12. Extensive property in Essex. *Cal. inq. Hen. VII*, Vol. I, No. 38. At least two brothers. Both dau. m. mercers; w. Juliana d. 1494. *Ibid.*, No. 985. Hugh, aged 22 at his father's death, was admitted to the mercers' company in 1489; d. 1491–92, unmarried. P C.C., Milles, 37; Inq. p.m., E, 150/290/5. Sir Edmund's goldsmith's mark, a device set on a shield, is reproduced in Sir James C. Jackson, *English Goldsmiths and Their Marks* (1921), p. 79.

SHAA, JOHN, goldsmith, ald. 1496–1504, knighted 1497. Beaven, II, 19. Nephew of Sir Edmund (see latter's will). Married dau. of THOMAS ILAM, 1479, when she was aged 12. Journal, 8, fols. 258, 273. Died 1504, survived by w. Margaret, three s., all under age, and dau. m. under age to his ward, John Wrikell. Will mentions his cousins Rauf and Robert Latham and his "brother," SIR RICHARD HADDON. P.C.C., Holgrave, 13. A sister, Elizabeth, m. William Poyntz, esquire, by whom she had six s., six dau. F. Chancellor, *The Ancient Sepulchral Monuments of Essex* (1890), Pl. LV.

SHADWORTH, JOHN, mercer, ald. 1383, 1385–1415. Beaven, I, 398. Died 1428–30, apparently no children surviving. *C.W.C.H.*, II, 452–53.

SHYRINGHAM, WILLIAM, mercer, ald. 1383, 1388–97. Beaven, I, 398. Died 1397, will naming late w., and a brother William, rector of Holtmarket, diocese of Norwich; London property to be sold for pious and charitable uses; apparently no children surviving. *C.W.C.H.*, II, 331.

SIBYLE, WALTER (Sibille), stockfishmonger, 1377, 1379, 1381. Beaven, I, 393. Lands in Cowling (probably Suff.), received from his father, William Sibile. *Cal. C.R., 1385–89*, p. 500. In 1381 m. Margaret, widow of John Hothom, grocer; d. before 1400, when his w. had m. John Grace (a citizen of that name, a pewterer, 1412). L. Bk., *H*, fol. 135. Walter's seal, 1382, a shield of arms: a chevron between three eagles displayed. Drapers' Deeds, A V, 88.

SKYNNARD, RALPH, skinner, ald. 1429. Beaven, II, 7. Dead by 1431, leaving two s. and a dau., under age. The two former came of age, 1438, 1443, the dau. became a nun, under age. *Cal. L. Bk., K*, p. 118.

SMELT, RICHARD, fishmonger, ald. 1355–61. Beaven, I, 387. Will refers to w., two s., a dau., and unborn child; d. 1361–62. *C.W.C.H.*, II, 74.

SOUTHAM, JOHN, fishmonger, ald. 1377, 1379, 1381. Beaven, I, 393. Will, dated 1382, enrolled 1395, left London property to w. for life, remainder to pious uses. *C.W.C.H.*, II, 315.

SPELEMAN, STEPHEN, mercer, chamberlain, ald. 1407–16. Beaven, II, 3. Gentleman, of Norf. family. Stow, II, 5. Died 1419, childless. Will mentions late w.; property in Herts., Beds., for sale, land in Essex to kinsman, John Spelman. P.C.C., Marche, 45; *C.W.C.H.*, II, 419.

STABLE, ADAM, mercer, ald. 1372–77, 1378–79, 1380–81. Beaven, I, 390. His widow, Katherine, between 1384 and 1386 m. Sir John Cyfrewast. *Cal. P. & M. Rolls*, III, 72, 127. Seal, 1359–60, a shield of arms: a fess between a cross and an annulet. B.H. Deeds, G 71, 72 (Stowe MSS 860 gives three boars' heads).

STAUNDON, WILLIAM, grocer, ald. 1383–90, 1392–1410. Beaven, I, 397. Twice m., d. 1410, desiring to be buried beside his late w. at Wimpole, Cambs. Property there and elsewhere in that county held in chief. Endowed chantry at Staundon for souls of John and Alice, his parents, etc.; bequest to a nephew at Staundon, John Hunte. *C.W.C.H.*, II, 393; P.C.C., Marche, 22. Survived by w. Agnes and dau., Elizabeth, who was aged 21 by 1425. Agnes m. Sir William Porter, who had been assigned the keeping of Staundon's lands. L. Bk., *K*, fol. 31; *Cal. Fine Rolls, Hen. IV*, II, 230.

STODEYE, JOHN DE, vintner, ald. 1352–76. Beaven, I, 387. Of Norfolk origin. His brother William, also a vintner, made a bequest to the church of Stodeye in that county. William d. 1375, survived by w. and three dau. *C.W.C.H.*, II, 185; *Cal. L. Bk., H*, pp. 103, 141; *Cal. P. & M. Rolls*, II, 223. John d. 1376, survived by four dau., one unmarried, the others m. to NICHOLAS BREMBRE, JOHN PHILPOT, HENRY VANNER. *C.W.C.H.*, II, 191–92. John sealed with a shield of arms, ermine, on a saltire engrailed five charges, impression indistinct, possibly leopards' heads. Anc. Deeds, CS 48 (1362); *B.M. Cal. Seals*, 13705 (1371).

STOKKER, JOHN, draper, ald. 1458–64. Beaven, II, 11. Died 1464. Will names w. Katherine; kinsmen John Pake, William and John Stokker, Alyson, the latter's daughter; a brother, Henry Stokker; a niece, Pernell Calet (Kelet). Property at Redcliff, Somers., to s. William; mention of another s., John. P.C.C., Godyn, 4. Seal, 1453, merchant's mark with initials. Add. Ch., 40573.

His s. William of age by 1472. L. Bk., *L*, fol. 82. John Stokker, the kinsman mentioned, may have been the gentleman of that name appointed to the office of Common Hunt in the city, 1463. *Cal. L. Bk., L*, pp. 36, 59. John's brother Robert, draper, d. 1455, leaving three s. and a dau., all under age. The latter m. Thomas Kelet, grocer. L. Bks. *K*, fol. 284; *L*, fol. 9*b*.

STOKKER, JOHN, draper, ald. 1479–85. Beaven, II, 15. Died 1485, leaving London property worth £40 a year to his w. Elizabeth; no mention of children. SIR WILLIAM STOKKER an executor. P.C.C., Logge, 15. Elizabeth later m. George Neville, Lord Abergavenny. E.C.P., 86/73.

STOKKER, WILLIAM, draper, ald. 1470–85, knighted 1471. Beaven, II, 14. Son of Thomas Stocker of Eaton, Bedf. Stowe MSS 860, fol. 59. With John Stokker, citizen of London and Henry Stokker, inhabitant of the town of Wyloldston in the parish of Eaton, obtained license in 1471 to found a perpetual chantry in a chapel they had lately built in the said town. *Cal. P.R., 1467–76*, p. 596.

STOKTON, JOHN, mercer, ald. 1463, knighted 1471. Beaven, II, 12. Son of Richard Stokton of Bratoft, Lincs. Stowe MSS 860, fol. 56. Apprenticed to John Herston, free 1429, d. by 1473. By will, dated 1470, provided for chantry for five years for souls of his parents, William and Matilda, late w., brothers William, Thomas, sister Margaret; property in High Wycombe to be converted into almshouses. Desired family names to be entered on roll of benefactors there; charitable bequests elsewhere in Bucks. and property in Essex, Mdsx., Herts. Left two s., under age, and a dau. who later m. Richard Turnaunt, esquire, stepson of JOHN GEDNEY. P.C.C., Wattys, 9; E.C.P., 108/106; Lysons, III, 522–24. His widow, Elizabeth, m. Gerard Caniziani, mercer. C. Misc., 118/78. Seal, 1465, a griffin astride over encircled monogram. Add. Ch., 40, 587.

SUFFOLK, ELIAS DE, goldsmith, ald. 1314–27. Beaven, I, 380. Will, enrolled 1327, mentions w. and dau. C.W.C.H., I, 320.

SUTTON, JOHN, goldsmith, ald. 1436–50. Beaven, II, 8. A goldsmith of this name is described in 1437 as s. of Laurence Sutton, and had a s. John apprenticed to himself. Goldsmiths' Wardens' Accounts, A, fols. 82v, 83.

SWANLAND, SIMON DE (Swanlond), draper, ald. 1327–34, knighted 1337. Beaven, I, 384. Interests at North Mimms, Herts., where a Simon de Swanlond, citizen, had owned property as early as 1288. W.A.M., 4351, 4146. Left at least two s., William, who left a s. William, and John. Hust. R.W.D., 92/143; W.A.M., 433, 4425. Was survived also by three brothers, Simon, William, and John, all owning property in Herts. Cal. C.R., 1349–54, p. 396. According to Cussans (p. 282), he bought the manor of North Mimms ca. 1299, Simon, John, and William, respectively, succeeding him, the last-named selling the manor to THOMAS KNOLLES. This William was called esquire. Anc. Deeds, C 6573. Sir Simon's brother William left a s. William. Hust. R.W.D., 93/21. One branch of the family held Harefield, Mdsx. Harl. Ch., 56 G 22; W.A.M., 445; Hust. R.W.D., 133X/51. There were at least three other merchants of the name prominent in the early fourteenth-century city. Seal of Simon de Swanlond, citizen, 1327, shield of arms: a fess dancette, two swans in chief, a lozenge below. W.A.M., 4133, 4134. Arms of Thomas de Swanlond of London, 1336, of William de Swanlond, citizen, 1351, and of William de Swanlond, lord of Harefield, 1381, all differ, but all used the swan as a charge. Anc. Deeds, B 5536; Guildhall Deeds, parish of St. Michael Wood Street, Nos. 1, 5, 7; B.M. Cat. Seals, 13791.

SYWARD, JOHN, stockfishmonger, ald. 1349–50. Beaven, I, 386. Provided for chantries for souls of parents, etc., in London and Dertford, Kent; d. 1349, survived by w., niece of a fishmonger, and children, not named. C.W.C.H., I, 403, 588.

TAILLOUR, WILLIAM, grocer, ald. 1458–63, knighted 1471. Beaven, II, 11. According to Stowe MSS 860, fol. 56, s. of John Taylor of Ecclestone, Staffs.; in his will he stated that he was christened at Edenbridge, Kent. Pious and charitable bequests there in order that parishioners might pray for his soul and for those of his parents and first w. P.C.C., Logge, 10. Was acquiring property at Edenbridge, 1478. W.A.M., 5098. The death of his s. John, mercer, 1471–72, and his w. Johanne, the following year, are noted in the Grocers' Accounts. Since he was 77 years of age at the time of making his will, in 1483, he must have been over 67 when he m. his second w., Margaret, widow of Richard Wode of Coventry, grocer. E.C.P., 60/82. A s. William entered the grocers' company in 1471 and was living, 1478, but may have d. before 1483, for he is not mentioned in his father's will; this left a legacy of money and the family dwelling-house in London to a kinsman and ward, Robert Sturmyn. If Sturmyn died under the age of 26, a third of his cash legacy was to go to charity, a third to Sir William's widow, and a third among the children of his three sisters. Taillour's seal, a mermaid. D. & C. St. Paul's, Deeds, A 16/1204 (1463); B.H. Deeds, I 38 (1482).

TATE, JOHN, mercer, ald. 1463–79. Beaven, II, 12. Son of John Tate of London and originally a brewer. Stowe MSS 860, fol. 57. Died 1479, leaving a s. John, mercer, living 1483. Hust. R.W.D., 213/10. The latter m.; w. Elizabeth, two s. living, 1500. See will of ROBERT TATE, below. The Mercers' Register of Freemen and Apprentices shows John Tate, apprentice of William Holte, free 1435; Robert, apprentice of John, free 1464; John, apprentice of John, free 1465; and John, s. of the ald., free 1474.

TATE, JOHN, mercer, ald. 1485–1515, knighted 1497. Beaven, II, 17. Son of Thomas Tate of Coventry, merchant stapler. Twice m., first w. being Margaret, dau. of JOHN CROKE. Hist. Parl. B., p. 841. Will, dated 1514, states that since he had made agreements with his s. in his lifetime, he was not leaving them anything further. Religious bequests in Coventry. Referred to w. of John, s. of JOHN TATE, late ald., as cousin. P.C.C., Holden, 4.

TATE, ROBERT, mercer, ald. 1497–1500. Beaven, II, 16. Son of Thomas Tate of Coventry. Stowe MSS 860, fol. 60. Elder brother of SIR JOHN TATE, above. Married dau. of Richard Wood, merchant of Coventry, d. 1500, survived by w., three s., two dau. Hist. Parl. B., p. 842. Eldest s. Robert, aged 26 at his father's death, d. shortly after. E.C.P., 169/2. Left extensive charitable and friendly bequests in Coventry, legatees including the children of his brother Thomas Gilbert. Richard Wood, his wife's brother, an executor. Property in Coventry and London, and in Warw., Berks., Essex, Kent, Herts. P.C.C., Moone, 18; Cal. inq. p.m. Hen. VII, Vol. II, No. 494.

TATERSALE, ROBERT, draper, ald. 1420–29. Beaven, II, 6. Died 1429, survived by w. Anne, formerly w. of Richard Elton, draper, who was living 1417 (Cal. L. Bk., I, p. 208), and by s. John. Property in Essex. P.C.C., Luff., 11; Cal. Rolls A.N.D., DD, m. 20. John, known as "gentleman of London," d. 1446. His dau. Anne m. Sir Ralph Hastings. Lysons, IV, 232.

THAME, JAMES DE, goldsmith, ald. 1361–65. Beaven, I, 388. Twice m., d. 1365; providing for two s. C.W.C.H., II, 88.

THORNEYE, WILLIAM DE, pepperer, ald. 1342–49. Beaven, I, 385. Endowed chantry at Whaplode, Holand, Lincs., where he was born; bequests to brothers of the abbey of Thorneye, Cambs.; prayers for souls of his parents, Ivo and Cristina, of his brothers, and of his children. Left four acres of land at Leverington, near Wisbech, Cambs., to nieces and his clothing and a small cash bequest to poor kinsfolk at Crowland and Whaplode Drove, Lincs. Died 1349, leaving a s. John, of age, 1368, living, with w. Isabel, 1401. Hust. R.W.D., 130/13. Thomas de Thorneye, pepperer, marked dead on grocers' list for 1373, a kinsman. C.W.C.H., I, 603, 649–51.

THORPE, ELIAS DE, skinner, ald. 1377. Beaven, I, 393. Armorial seal, 1365, 1400: field of cloves, a quarter with a circle and cross above a mullet. Guildhall Deeds, parish of St. Stephen Walbrook, No. 4; D. & C. St. Paul's, Deeds, A 3/660.

TILNEY, RALPH, grocer, ald. 1485–99. Beaven, II, 18. Bore the same arms, a chevron between three griffins' heads, as the Boston family of merchants and landowners of same name. See 1464 Plut. LVII E, and Pishey Thompson, *The History and Antiquities of Boston* (1856), p. 373. Apprentice of THOMAS HILLE, free 1464. Married Joan, Hill's sister-in-law, dau. of Thomas Gernon, esquire, tenant-in-chief; property in Bucks. *Cal. P.R., 1485–94*, p. 221. Took an apprentice, named John Tylney, 1474. Died 1503, having survived his w. three years. Weever, p. 188. On the monument of his younger s., Reginald, who d. 1506 and was buried at Leckhampstead, Bucks., with three dau., was described as gentleman. Haines, Part II, p. 30. Ralph's elder s. John d. 1518. V.C.H., *Bucks.*, IV, 182.

TODENHAM, WILLIAM DE (Tudenham), mercer, ald. 1349–70. Beaven, I, 387. By 1344 m. Joan, dau. of Hugh de Waltham, late common clerk. *Cal. L. Bk., F*, p. 93. A s. Thomas, m., predeceased him, 1372. *C.W.C.H.*, II, 144. The latter used a seal bearing the motto "I trust in God" and a shield of arms: per saltire, in chief a cross between two letters *T*, in the base of a leopard's head. Drapers' Deeds, A VII, 107.

TONGE, WILLIAM, vintner, ald. 1377, 1381, 1385. Died 1389. Bequests to the poor of Higham Ferrers, N'hants., and Irtlingborough, Lincs.; survived by w. Avice and two s., two dau., under age. *C.W.C.H.*, II, 278–79; P.C.C., Rous, 2. Elder s. John of age by 1392, dau. Agnes apprenticed to a "brauderer," but she and the younger s. d. under age. L. Bk., *H*, fols. 254–55. William buried in church of All Hallows Barking, where a brass bore his arms.

TORNEGOLD, JOHN (Torgold, Truegold), ald. 1365–77. Beaven, I, 389. Died 1378. Property in Mdsx. One s., a canon at Lesnes, one dau. surviving. *C.W.C.H.*, II, 199–200. Seal of John Tornegold, fishmonger, 1332, within a quatrefoil panel, before an eagle displayed, a shield of arms: semee of crosses crosslets, two fishes in saltire, over all a key. *B.M. Cat. Seals*, 13987. Another example, *ibid.*, 13897 (1373).

TRENTE, WILLIAM (Terente), ald. 1309–16. Beaven, I, 380. Wine merchant from Bergerac, department of Dordogne. *Cal. L. Bk., A*, p. 128; *B*, 68; *C*, pp. 48, 65, 242. Will, enrolled 1316, bequeaths property in London to brother Gerard and to William Noeyl, his sister's s. *C.W.C.H.*, I, 267.

TURK, WALTER, fishmonger, ald. 1342–52. Beaven, I, 386. Inherited London property from father, Nicholas Turk. *C.W.C.H.*, I, 665–66. Numerous fishmongers of the name among citizens of this century. The name also occurred among visiting Italian merchants. *Cal. C.R., 1339–41*, p. 492.

TWYFORD, NICHOLAS, goldsmith, ald. 1375–77, 1378, 1380, 1383, 1387, 1388–91, knighted 1381. Beaven, I, 390. Died 1390–91, survived by w. Margery; children predeceased him. London property after death of w. left to Thomas Conelee, a kinsman, of Bucks.; similarly, Mdsx. property to another kinsman, John Twyford. *C.W.C.H.*, II, 283–84. In 1382 he rendered an account in the court of orphanage of the property of his ward John, s. of a citizen named Twyford, owner of a little property in London and of tenements and a mill at Twyford (a place of this name in seven different counties). The only other prominent citizens of the name at that period were two cutlers, John and Richard, and a woolpacker, John. John Twyford, cutler, sealed with a shield of arms: a fess between three fleurs-de-lis. *Cal. P. & M. Rolls*, III, 68; *Cal. L. Bk., H*, p. 346; *B.M. Cat. Seals*, 14021.

John Twyford, heir of the ald., known as "of London, esquire," inherited London property from his mother; d. 1429, survived by w. and s. John, gentleman. Sealed, 1440, with a shield of arms: two bars, on a chief three roundels, crest, a tree; Hust. R.W.D., 141/47, 150/103; Comm. Lon., More, 224, 294; Add. Ch., 40557, Drapers' Deeds, A V, 138.

UPTON, RALPH DE, draper, ald. 1334–42. Beaven, I, 384. Will, proved 1342, mentions w., several kinsmen named Upton, no children. *C.W.C.H.*, I, 453–54.

VANNER, HENRY, vintner, ald. 1383–89, 1391–94. Beaven, I, 398. Will, dated 1394, enrolled 1397, refers to mother, Joan, a brother William Vanner, another named John Cornwaleys, w. Margery, dau. of JOHN STODEYE; property in Kent, Mdsx., no children. *C.W.C.H.*, II, 331–32.

VENOUR, WILLIAM (Vannere), grocer, ald. 1383, 1386–*ca.* 1395. Beaven, I, 397. Dead by 1397, survived by w. Mabel and a s. William, who had been admitted into the grocers' company by 1383. Hust. R.W.D., 126/148.

VERNEY, RALPH, mercer, ald. 1457–78, knighted 1471. Beaven, II, 11. Said to have been s. of Ralph Verney of London. Stowe MSS 860, fol. 56. In *Hist. Parl. B.*, p. 906, it is assumed that his father was Ralph Vernon, who was one of the mayor's serjeants in 1423 and still acting in 1446 (see *Cal. L. Bk., K*, pp. 12, 203, 312–13). But the name Verney also occurred at this time and earlier.

Ralph was apprenticed to THOMAS FAUCONER, mercer, free 1434. In 1447 acted as attorney for Richard Verney, later described as esquire, in receiving London property from John Verney, clerk, and other trustees. Drapers' Deeds, A VIII, 186; A VII, 190. Twice m., d. 1478, survived by w., Emma; two s., John, Rauf, his executors; dau. Margaret, m. to Sir Edward Raleigh, Beatrice, m. to Henry Danvers, mercer. P.C.C., Logge, 1, abstract printed in Nicholas, *Testamenta vetusta*, p. 350. John m. dau. of Sir Robert Whittingham, official of the royal household, served frequently in public life, Bucks., was knighted 1485, d. 1505. *Hist. Parl. B.*, pp. 905–6, 943. His brother Rauf was known as esquire. E.C.P., 230/17. On continuance of the family through Sir John's s. John see *D.N.B.*

VYNE, JOHN, draper, ald. 1378, 1380. Beaven, I, 394. Had been servant of JAMES ANDREW. Twice m., d. 1383; bequests to a brother, Andrew Vine, w. Jocosa, three s., two dau. *C.W.C.H.*, II, 166; P.C.C., Rous, 1.

VYNENT, THOMAS, mercer, ald. 1391–93. Beaven, I, 401. Son of John and Juliana; d. 1393–94, w. Cristina, no children. *C.W.C.H.*, II, 307–8.

WADE, JOHN, ald. 1296–1300. Beaven, I, 378. Will, enrolled 1367, makes no mention of w. or children. Property to a sister, a niece, and a brother, Adam Wade, probably the woodmonger of that name. *C.W.C.H.*, I, 192; *Cal. E.M.C.R.*, p. 213.

WAKELE, JOHN, vintner, ald. 1400–1404. Beaven, I, 404. Married, 1382, a vintner's widow. *Cal. L. Bk., H*, p. 179. Died 1407, survived by w., who m. Geoffrey Dallyng, vintner, and s. John, a merchant, m., who d. 1408, without issue. *C.W.C.H.*, II, 371. Archdeaconry, London, 173, 210; Hust. R.W.D., 141/61.

WALCOTE, JOHN, draper, ald. 1382, 1388–91, 1392–1406. Beaven, I, 397. Died 1407–8, leaving property in London to w. for life, remainder to be sold for pious uses. Property also in Mdsx. *C.W.C.H.*, II, 380.

WALDERN, JOHN (Walden), grocer, ald. 1454–64. Beaven, II, 10. Twice m., d. 1464, survived by w. Margaret. A s. Thomas, by his first w., Elizabeth, "gentilman, citizen of London, Burgeis of Caleis and freman of the staple their," d. 1474, leaving a w. Margaret, s. Richard, John, dau. Joan, all under

372 THE MERCHANT CLASS OF MEDIEVAL LONDON

age; property purchased by his father in Kent willed to s. Richard, a wool-house in Calais to his brother William for life. Will drawn up at Guisnes. P.C.C., Wattys, 15; cf. *Hist. Parl. B.*, p. 914. Thomas' dau. Emma, d. 1471, m. to John Wode, merchant of the staple of Calais, buried at Erith, Kent, three s. represented on her monument. W. D. Belcher, *Kentish Brasses* (2 vols., 1888–1905), Vol. I, No. 101; Haines, II, 99; *Archaeologia Cantiana*, XVI, 215.

WALDERNE, WILLIAM, mercer, ald. 1395–1424. Beaven, I, 404. Son of Geoffrey Waldern of Waldern, Sussex. Stowe MSS 860, fol. 48. Apprenticed to John Fresshe, free 1395, m. Margaret, dau. of John atte Lee, chandler. Hust. R.W.D., 142/13. Died 1424. Will printed in full, Register, Chichele, II, 276–78. His widow promptly m. John Roys, gentleman of Norf., guardian of Waldern's two s., two dau. L. Bk., *K*, fol. 35. Daughter Elianora at 15 transferred to guardianship of Thomas Morestede, citizen and surgeon, at 22 m. Richard de la Feld, fishmonger. L. Bk., *K*, fol. 173*b*. Elder s. Richard, esquire of Essex, d. 1454, aged 43, survived by w. Margaret and four dau. *C.W.C.H.*, II, 524; Rot. cl., 16 Hen. VI, *m.* 15*d*. Younger s. William, aged 12, 1427, may have been the merchant of the staple who d. 1476. P.C.C., Wattys, 25.

WALSYNGHAM, THOMAS, vintner, ald. 1429. Beaven, II, 7. Attained rank of esquire in the king's service; m. Margaret, dau. of HENRY BAMME and widow of John Wakele, Jr., vintner; d. 1456–57, survived by s. Thomas, in 1462 described as gentleman, and dau. Philippa, m. to Thomas Ballard, esquire. Property in Kent. *Cal. L. Bk.*, *K*, p. 109; P.C.C., Stokton, 8; Hust. R.W.D., 164/50, 192/14; Rot. cl., 3 Hen. VI, *m.* 4*d*.

WALWORTH, WILLIAM, fishmonger, ald. 1368–77, 1378–79, 1380–81, 1382–83, 1384–85, knighted 1381. Beaven, I, 389. Apprenticed to John Lovekyn; owner of property at Walworth, Surrey; d. 1385, w. Margaret surviving, no issue; bequests to his brother-german, Master Thomas Walworth, a sister Cecilia with five dau., sister Agnes, w. of William atte Lee, with two s., two dau., and a relative, Peter Salford. *C.W.C.H.*, II, 251, 310–11; P.C.C., Rous, 1; partial abstracts in Herbert, II, 60–61; cf. Weever, p. 196. William atte Lee was warden of the chandlers, 1377. *Cal. L. Bk.*, *H*, p. 76. Walworth's arms, 1377 and later, in seal, a ragged bend and two sheaves. Anc. Deeds, B 2127, 4319, BS 3 (Stowe MSS 860 correct).

WANDESFORD, THOMAS, mercer, ald. 1426–46. Beaven, II, 7. Younger s. of John Wandesford of Kirklington, Yorks., landowner; had a s. William who d. without issue. Pedigree in *The Irish Compendium, or Rudiments of Honour* (5th ed., 1756), cited in *Notes and Queries* (5th ser.), III, 158–59. He had also a dau., m. *Hist. Parl. Register*, p. xix. Died 1448. Weever, p. 443.

WARDE, JOHN, pepperer, ald. 1369–77, 1379. Beaven, I, 389. Married Agnes, niece of John Not, pepperer; in 1371 had two s. living. *C.W.C.H.*, II, 145.

WARDE, JOHN, mercer, ald. 1468–76. Beaven, II, 13. A John Warde, apprentice of Henry Frowick, mercer, was made free 1439, and a mercer of this name d. 1487, leaving money and goods to a dau. Comm. Lon., Lichfield, 69.

WARDE, JOHN, grocer, ald. 1478–1501. Beaven, II, 15. Said to have been s. of Richard Ward of Holden, Yorks. Stowe MSS 860, fol. 59; Cussans, Part V, p. 10. Yet in his will he states that he was born at Hinxworth, Herts. A John Warde, apprentice of Thomas Hawkyn, grocer, free 1457. The ald. d. 1501, leaving money for restoration of the church at Hinxworth and for the keeping of an obit there for his soul and those of his parents and children. Legacies to his brothers Thomas, mercer, and Robert, who had inherited a hall at Hinxworth from their father, and to Richard, s. of his brother George, and to children of three m. sisters, named Bodeley, Chapman, Clarevaunce. The sister Bodeley m. for her second husband William Holebrand of London, gentleman. P.C.C., *Moone*, 11; abstract, *Hist. Parl. B.*, p. 919. Inscriptions at Hinxworth include reference to Simon Warde, who d. 1453, with w. Ellen, d. 1483. Weever, p. 314.

WARNER, JOHN, ironmonger, ald. 1397–1412. Beaven, I, 403. Died 1413, survived by w. Isabel, s. John, Williams (appointed executors), Richard, Henry, one dau. Property in Marlow, Bucks., to w. for life, remainder to s. Henry. P.C.C., Marche, 27.

WAVER, HENRY, draper, ald. 1465–70, created K.B., 1465. Beaven, II, 13. Son of William Waver, landowner, Warw. *Cal. L. Bk., K*, p. 309. Died 1470, will naming w. Cristina, three s., two dau.; his brother John Jakes, draper, an executor. Property Surrey, Warw., N'hants. P.C.C., Godyn, 31; E.C.P., 48/408. Eldest s. Henry described as gentleman, 1474. Hust. R.W.D., 204/27.

WELBECK, WILLIAM, haberdasher, ald. 1492–1504. Beaven, II, 19. Associated with Richard Welbek, gentleman, in transfer of property in Surrey. *Surrey Fines*, p. 195. Married more than once; marriage to Katherine, dau. of Thomas Riche, mercer, 1503. L. Bk., *L*, Vol. 111. Died 1509–10; will, 1509, naming two s., the elder an executor, and two dau. P.C.C., Bennett, 27.

WELDE, WILLIAM DE, draper, ald. 1349–72. Beaven, I, 387. Will, enrolled 1372, left London property to w. Agnes, dau. of JOHN DE AYLESHAM, for life, remainder in tail to s. Simon. *C.W.C.H.*, II, 144. Seal, 1343–44, shield of arms: a fess nebuly between three crescents. Anc. Deeds, B 9753.

WELLES, JOHN, grocer, ald. 1420–36. Beaven, II, 6. Son of John de Welles of Norwich. Stowe MSS 860, fol. 50. Will, 1442, printed in full, Register, Chichele, 615–20, refers to baptism in Norwich and gives parents' names as John and Isabel; mention of kinsmen Sir Henry Inglose and Thomas Fastolf; no children surviving. Property in Kent. Had m. Margery, formerly w. of (1) John Osbarn, stockfishmonger, and (2) Henry Halton. *Cal. L. Bk., I*, pp. 26, 203. Sealed with device of two wells. Drapers' Deeds, A V, 84.

WETENALE, WILLIAM, grocer, ald. 1438–51. Beaven, II, 8. Of Cheshire origin. Associated with various Wetenhales of Wich-Malbank as co-feoffee, 1431, and in obtaining custody of the manor of Kirmincham, 1438. There were numerous Wetenhales in the neighborhood of Wich-Malbank, including both gentlemen and yeomen. James Hall, *History of Nantwich* (1883), pp. 90–91; *Thirty-seventh Report, D.K.P.R.*, Appen., II, 782. The ald. is not placed in any of the pedigrees in G. Ormerod's *History of the County Palatine and City of Chester*, ed. T. Helsby (1875–82), II, 195; III, 367, 477–79. Married, probably as second w., Alice, widow of John Edward, mercer of Bury St. Edmunds. Anc. Deeds, A 3570. By 1431 had acquired property in Essex held in chief, also bought property in Surrey. *Cal. P.R., 1429–36*, p. 117; E.C.P., 39/129. Died 1457, survived by s. William, m. to dau. of William Hexstall, esquire, and dau., m. to John Colvyle, grocer. P.C.C., Stokton, 16; *C.W.C.H.*, II, 531; John Philipott, *Villare Cantianum or Kent Surveyed and Illustrated* (2d ed.; 1776), pp. 74, 190, 195, 269, 347; Inq. p.m., C, 139/164. His widow Alice d. at Bury St. Edmunds, 1458, bequeathing her goods to s. John, Thomas, and a dau. Katharine; the first of these was her child by John Edward; probably all were his. Since her will does not mention Wetenhale's heirs, it is unlikely that she was their mother. P.C.C., Stokton, fol. 203; Anc. Deeds, A 3652, 3570.

His s. William was in 1464 described as gentleman. Hust. R.W.D., 168/3d. Order was given in that year that he be deprived of his inherited property in Essex and London on the grounds of insanity; he was then aged 31 or more. Inquisitions, E, 149/213/11, *m*. 2. He d. 1468, leaving a s. William, under 1 year of age. Inq. p.m., C, 140/29.

WHITE, WILLIAM, draper, ald. 1482–1504, knighted 1489. Beaven, II, 17. *Hist. Parl. B.*, p. 940. Son of William White of Tickhill, Yorks. Stowe MSS 860, fol. 60. Twice m., d. 1504. Bequests to church of Tickhill, his birthplace, provision for chantry in London for souls of his parents, William and Cecily, etc.; bequests to nephews named White, in Tickhill, and to his brother Richard White, vicar of Harworth, Notts. Property in Surrey. Will, 1500, mentions w. and one s. P.C.C., Holgrave, 4; *C.W.C.H.*, II, 631–32.

WHYTINGHAM, ROBERT, draper, ald. 1417–38. Beaven, II, 5. Knighted, but not until after June, 1440; grant of free warren in manor of Pendeley, Herts., of that date, does not give him the title. *Cal. Ch. R.*, VI, 8. Died 1452, leaving four s., the eldest, Robert, esquire, his executor; manors in Bucks. *Early Lincoln Wills*, p. 191. Robert entered the royal service, was knighted, m. Katherine Gatewyne, left no s. On his political career see *Hist. Parl. B.*, pp. 943–44. His income from property in London and Bucks. was over £80. Inq. p.m., C, 145–319. His dau. Margaret m. Sir John Verney. Hust. R.W.D., 220/18. The ald. sealed, 1419, with device of a cock and star. Drapers' Deeds, A VIII, 71.

WHYTINGTON, RICHARD, mercer, ald. 1393–1423. Beaven, I, 402. Uncertainty as to whether he was s. of Sir William Whittington of Glouc. or of some other member of that family. Married Alice, dau. of Sir Ivo Fitzwaryn, who d. by 1414. No issue. See *D.N.B.* Photograph of his seal, a head facing right, W. G. Bell, *London Rediscoveries* (1929), p. 108.

WIDYNGTON, ROBERT (Wedyngton), grocer, ald. 1418–26. Beaven, II, 5. Parents buried in church of St. Magnus by London Bridge. Died 1437–39, leaving property in Kent to w. for life, reversion for sale for pious and charitable uses. *C.W.C.H.*, II, 487; P.C.C., Luff., 24.

WILFORD, JAMES, tailor, ald. 1500–1511. Beaven, II, 20. Three times m., d. 1526–27, will naming six s., of age, two dau., one m. to Michael English, mercer, and a brother, William Wilford. One s., John, a notary public. P.C.C., Porche, 13.

WILFORD, THOMAS (Welford), fishmonger, ald. 1377, 1379, 1384–93, 1394–1403. Beaven, I, 392. Born at Torlaston, Notts. More than once m. At least two s., two dau., predeceased him. Died 1405–7, directing lands at Torlaston to be sold for benefit of poor relations, lands in Surrey and London to w. Elizabeth, dau. of William Whetele, woolman; she d. 1441. P.C.C., Marche, 12, 13; *C.W.C.H.*, II, 370; Harl. Ch., 55 H 66.

WODECOK, JOHN, mercer, ald. 1397–1408. Beaven, I, 403. Son of William Wodecok of Doncaster, Yorks.; m. Felicia, dau. of Thomas Austyn, mercer; d. 1408–9, leaving two s., under age, two dau. Wills refer to property in Doncaster purchased jointly with a kinsman there, William Barbour; bequest to another kinsman there named Steynford. Manors in Surrey, Kent, Essex. P.C.C., Marche, 17; *C.W.C.H.*, II, 397–99. His elder s. John of age by 1413, younger s. William d. by 1421, dau. Joan m. at 20–21, to William Lomely, esquire of Yorks. L. Bk., *I*, fols. 121*b*, 169, 206*b;* P. & M. Rolls, A 49, *m.* 2*b*, 3. Their mother, Felicia, in 1409 m. Sir John Lumley of Durham. Hust. R.W.D., 137/56.

WODEHOUSE, WILLIAM, alias Power, skinner, ald. 1377, 1382. Beaven, I, 392. Listed as Power Wodehous in the skinners' membership. Four times m.; will, dated 1388, enrolled 1392, provided for s. Thomas and three dau., two of them m. to London merchants. *C.W.C.H.,* II, 292–93. One of his dau. m. a wealthy bowyer. L. Bk., *H*, fol. 209*b*. Thomas, a skinner, m. Agnes, who brought him lands in Warw. Drapers' Deeds, A VIII, 69. He left a s. John, m. under age to Agnes, dau. of Henry Wolryby of Medburn, Leics. The latter took charge of John's education in law. John was of age by 1416. His mother m. Richard Payn, skinner, then Richard Nordone, tailor. L. Bk., *I*, fols. 60*b*, 62, 164, 168*b*.

WOOD, THOMAS, goldsmith, ald. 1496–1504. Beaven, II, 19. Died 1504. Left money for a marble stone to be placed above his father's tomb in a chapel of the parish church of Barking, Essex. Will, 1503, mentions w. Margaret, two dau., m. to a goldsmith and a mercer, brother William Wood with two s., also John Wood, serjeant, and Robert, the latter's brother. P.C.C., Holgrave, 2.

WORSTEDE, SIMON DE, mercer, ald. 1349–66. Beaven, I, 387. Died 1366, entailing London property on dau. *C.W.C.H.,* II, 95–96. His widow m. John Cheyham, goldsmith. Hust. R.W.D., 153/12.

WOTTON, WILLIAM, ald. 1387–92. Beaven, I, 400. Died by 1397, survived by w. Margaret, d. 1404, and s. Nicholas. *C.W.C.H.,* II, 330, 361–62.

WOTTON, NICHOLAS, draper, ald. 1403–46. According to Stowe MSS 860, fol. 50, was s. of Thomas Wotton of London. A Thomas de Wotton, draper, used an armorial seal, 1408. *B.M. Cat. Seals,* 14579. Nicholas, 1446, sealed with device of a human face. W.A.M., 4454. Henry Wotton, draper, living 1438, with dau. Nicholaa, had lands both by inheritance and purchase in Wotton Basset, Wilts. Anc. Deeds, C 8232.

WROTH, JOHN, fishmonger, ald. 1358–76. Beaven, I, 338. Of a family of Mdsx. landowners. Married Margaret, widow of John de Enefeld. Bought manor of Enefeld, 1374; left no issue. *Cal. C.R., 1364–68,* p. 493; G. H. Hodson and E. Ford, *A History of Enfield* (1873), p. 68.

WYCHE, HUGH, mercer, ald. 1458–68, created K.B. 1465. Beaven, II, 11. Son of Richard Wych of Wich-Malbank, Ches. Stowe MSS 860, fol. 55. Charitable bequests in this parish, desiring prayers for souls of his parents, Richard and Anne; legacy to his brother, John Wyche, and provision for ten anniversary services in the town of St. Albans for his kinsman William Wyche. P.C.C., Godyn, 23. Will of Thomas Wyche, fishmonger, who d. 1425, mentions relatives at Nantwich (Wich-Malbank), also his late uncle, William Wyche, late esquire of the abbot of St. Albans, also three brothers, Hugh, William, John, the latter with children; Thomas left one s. John, under age. P.C.C., Luff., 4. A William Wyche, fishmonger, was living 1432. C. Misc., 113/38. Henry Wyche, ironmonger, who in 1469 transferred to his dau., m. to Richard Wright fishmonger, London property once belonging to Thomas, was also presumably a relative. Drapers' Deeds, A VII, 195, 198.

Three times m., Hugh d. 1468, childless. His first w. was sister-in-law to John Everard, mercer. E.C.P., 74/89. Second w. Joan, dau. of Richard Wodecok, salter, and formerly w. of Robert Colbroke, ironmonger. See will of STEPHEN FORSTER, and *Cal. L. Bk.*, *K*, p. 180. A third w., Alice, said to have been dau. of John Stratton, esquire (James Hall, *A History of Nantwich* [1883], p. 84), also said to have been dau. of John Andrews of Baylham, Suff., esquire (Nicholas, *Testamenta vetusta*, I, 336, with abstract of her will), and formerly w. of William Holt, London mercer born at Lewes, survived him. She bequeathed London property to Henry Wyche, ironmonger, who d. by 1480, leaving a s. and five dau. L. Bk., *L*, fol. 155*b*.

WYCHINGHAM, GEOFFREY DE, mercer, ald. 1345–49. Beaven, I, 386. Died 1349, leaving all London property to brother Hugh. *C.W.C.H.*, I, 586–87. Blomefield (pp. 298–99) assumed he was a member of the family that had held land in Norfolk from the thirteenth century, on account of the fact that the seventeenth-century heraldic collections assign him similar arms.

WYFOLD, NICHOLAS, grocer, ald. 1442–56. Beaven, II, 9. Son of Thomas Wyfold of Hertley, Berks. Stowe MSS 860, fol. 53. Married (1) after 1445, Katherine, widow of JOHN BROKLE, (2) Margaret, who survived him and m. John Noreys, esquire. *Rot. parl.*, V, 129–30; E.C.P., 15/248; *Cal. P.R., 1461–67*, p. 316. Died 1456, desiring that thirty priests of Reading and neighborhood sing an obit for him in the parish church of Shinfield and that refreshments be offered on this occasion at his place at Hertley. Will mentions two sisters, a nephew, John Derby, and one dau., Isabel, under age. P.C.C., Stokton, 8. Seal, 1453, a flower growing out of a heart, inscription: "a Luy Dere Herte." Anc. Deeds, C 1482.

WYKING, WILLIAM, skinner, ald. 1481. Beaven, II, 16. Died 1481; w. Beatrice, no children, property in Surrey. P.C.C., Logge, 3.

WYNCHECOMBE, SYMON, armorer, ald. 1382, 1385. Baptized at Stanwey, Glouc., twice m.; will, dated 1396, enrolled 1399, mentions a sister Amisia, and one s., John, chaplain. Bequests to poor of Wynchecombe, Glouc. *C.W.C.H.*, II, 340–42.

WYNDOUT, THOMAS, mercer, ald. 1499–1500. Beaven, II, 19. Apprentice to HENRY COLET, free 1475. Died 1499–1500; will mentions parents Thomas and Basill, buried at Apisden, near Buntingford, Herts., w., children, not named. A dau. m. s. of SIR RICHARD HADDON. P.C.C., Moone, 4; *Hist. Parl. B.*, pp. 977–98. A s., Bartholomew Wyndout, living 1516, named as HADDON's ultimate heir. See the latter's will.

WYNGAR, JOHN, grocer, ald. 1498–1505. Beaven, II, 19. Born in the town of Leicester, where his parents, William and Johane Wyngar, and his brother Henry, were buried. Will, dated 1503, proved 1506, mentions w. Agnes, three so a dau., all under age. Inherited lands in Leics. and N'hants. Legacies to two s and five dau. of his brother Henry, the elder s. being a student at Oxford. P.C.C., Adeane, 2.

WYRHALE, RICHARD DE, draper, ald. 1305–19. Beaven, I, 379. Eldest s. of Richard de Wyrhale, Jr., citizen, inheriting London property. His will mentions two s., a brother John, two sisters, one dependent on him, one a nun in Clerkenwell. Property at Edmonton, Mdsx. *C.W.C.H.*, I, 156, 368.

YONGE, JOHN, grocer, ald. 1460–81. Beaven, II, 12. Younger s. of Thomas Yonge merchant of Bristol, who had m., after 1405, Joan, formerly w. of John Canynges, late merchant of Bristol, and d. 1427. The elder s., Thomas, entered the Middle Temple and became an eminent lawyer and judge. Stowe MSS 860 fol. 56; *Hist. Parl. B.*, pp. 980–82. Twice m., John d. 1481–82, in "grete age," survived by w., three dau., m., three s. Property in Mdsx., Herts. P.C.C., Logge, 4. The eldest s., John, inherited the country property, the second, Thomas, was by 1481 a priest. London property was to go to William, the youngest s., in 1481 apprenticed in the grocers' company. Daughter Agnes m. (1) Robert Sherington, (2) Robert Molyneux, (3) William Cheyne, esquire. Stow, I, 243. Another m. Sir John Parr, household official, who d. 1475. *Hist. Parl. B.*, pp. 661–62. Another is referred to in her father's will as "my daughter Borge." The name Yong occurs among fourteenth-century London grocers, but it is not known whether these were connected with the Bristol family. See Richard le Yonge, 1345; Johan, 1349, d. by 1383; Philip, 1373; Jankyn, 1373. Kingdon, Vol. I, *passim*.

Appendix B
LONDON LANDOWNERS IN 1436

INFORMATION AS TO LONDON OWNERS OF LANDS AND RENTS
ASSESSED IN 1436 AT THE ANNUAL VALUE
OF £5 AND OVER*

	Location of Property	Assessment (in Pounds Sterling)
LAY TAXPAYERS		
Abbot, John............................	London, N'hants., Essex	47
Acr, Saier	London and elsewhere	27
Aleyn, Thomas.........................	Essex	12
Alyff, William.........................	Warw.	12
Amonx, John...........................	Essex	15
Andrew, William.......................	London	7
Anne, Alexander.......................	Yorks., Somers., Mdsx.	44
Arnewey, Robert.......................	Essex	24
Arnold, Isabell........................	London and elsewhere	26
Asco, John, esquire....................	Lands, corrodies, annuities, in London, Lincs., Kent, Sussex	39
Asplyon, Katharine.....................	London, Cumb., Hunts., Bedf.	20
Astell, Antony.........................	London	11
Aston, John, of Holborn................	London	10
Aston, William........................	London, Derb., Kent	47
Atherley (Hatherley?), John............	....	40
atte Welle, Simon......................	London	6
Auntours, William.....................	London and elsewhere	10
Awbrey, Robert........................	Surrey and elsewhere	13
Bacon, John, grocer....................	S'hants.	10
Badby, Thomas........................	London, Essex, Mdsx.	14
Banastre, Richard......................	London	10
Banastre, Thomas, clerk................	London and elsewhere	48
Bangore, William......................	London	20
Bartelot, John, of Queenhithe..........	London	5
Barton, Joan, widow...................	London, Herts.	50
Bataille, Elizabeth, widow.............	Essex	10
Bataille, Thomas.......................	London, Essex	20
Beaufitz, Thomas......................	Warw. and elsewhere	20
Beaumond, Thomas.....................	London and elsewhere	12
Beawe, Dionise........................	London and elsewhere	5
Bedounsell, John.......................	London	10

* From Lay Subsidy Roll, E, 179/238/90.

	Location of Property	Assessment

LAY TAXPAYERS

	Location of Property	Assessment
Beke, John	London, Kent	12
Belgrave, Thomas, serjeant	London	5
Benstede, Margaret	London	12
Berkeley, Margaret, widow	London, Glouc., Somers., Hunts., Surrey, Sussex	160
Bernes, John	London	10
Bernewell, Thomas	London	20
Berston, John	London and elsewhere	10
Bertyn, Robert	Kent	10
Beteyn, Thomas	London, Essex	7
Bethewat, Joan	Devon and elsewhere	13
Beveriche, William	London	5
Beverle, John	Surrey	10
Blakyslowe, Ralph†	London	21
Blaunche, John	London, Mdsx.	5
Blomvile, John	London	5
Bohun, Humfrey	Essex, Sussex	120
Bokelond, Richard	London and elsewhere	100
Bolle, John	London, Kent, Essex	7
Bosom, William	Bedf.	5
Boston, Emma, widow of John Boston	London	5
Boteler, John	London, Oxon., Bucks., Kent, Essex	49
Bothewater, John	London, Mdsx.	8
Botle, Richard	Mdsx.	5
Bracy, John	London and elsewhere	8
Bradcok, Richard	London	7
Brangtre, Thomas	Essex, Herts.	8
Brednell, Alice	London and elsewhere	45
Bremson, Bartholomew	London, Essex	5
Brigge, William, mercer	Suff.	8
Brodde, John	Essex, Yorks.	16
Broke, John	Kent, London	7
Brokle, John	Suff., Bedf., Bucks., N'hants.	40
Bromhale, John	London, Surrey, Essex, Cambs.	31
Broun, Stephen	London and elsewhere	65
Browning, David	London	6
Brykles, John	London	20
Budvelon, Margaret, widow	Norf. and elsewhere	50
Bugge, John	London and elsewhere	67
Burdon, Richard	London	10
Burset, John, esquire	London and elsewhere	45
Burton, Cecilia, widow	London and elsewhere	12
Burton, William	London	12
Byrom, John	Mdsx., Herts.	5
Camp, Simon	Essex, Mdsx., Kent, Bucks., N'hants.	120
Candissh, Roland	London	8
Canyngs, Thomas	Bristol and elsewhere in Glouc.	20
Carpenter, John	London	24
Catteworth, Thomas	Norf., Essex	24

† See below, under "Trustees, Blakelow."

	Location of Property	Assessment
LAY TAXPAYERS		
Caundissh, Hugh............................	London	16
Chace, Master Thomas.....................	London	5
Chalton, Thomas............................	London and elsewhere	49
Chapman, William..........................	London and elsewhere	24
Chertesey, Walter..........................	London and elsewhere	45
Cheyne, Sir William........................	Sussex, Dorset	80
Chichele, John..............................	London, Mdsx.	33
Chicheley, Robert..........................	London and elsewhere	80
Childe, William.............................	London	10
Chittok, Geoffrey...........................	Essex, Kent	13
Chynnor, Thomas...........................	London and elsewhere	26
Claydych, Richard..........................	London and elsewhere	16
Clement, John..............................	Surrey, Lincs.	6
Clerk, John, grocer.........................	Herts.	20
Clerk, Walter...............................	London and elsewhere	5
Clopton, Robert............................	London, Mdsx., Suff., Kent	83
Coggeshale, John...........................	London	7
Cok, John...................................	London	8
Cok, Thomas...............................	London	5
Colston, William...........................	London and elsewhere	12
Combe, John...............................	Wilts.	5
Combes, William...........................	London	6
Cooke, Thomas.............................	Herts., Surrey	12
Cornewaleys,...............................	London, Mdsx., Essex, Suff., Cambs.	50
Costantyn, William.........................	London	25
Costyn, John...............................	London	10
Cosyn, John................................	London	5
Coton, Robert, drover......................	Surrey, Herts.	21
Couper, William............................	London	10
Coventre, Richard..........................	London and elsewhere	25
Creek, William..............................	London and elsewhere	20
Cristendom, Robert........................	London and elsewhere	39
Crulle, Robert, bowyer.....................	Surrey	5
Daunvers, William, esquire.................	Berks.	95
David, Master..............................	Annuities from abbey of Vale Royal, Ches.	33
Davy, Elias.................................	London and elsewhere	6
Davy, John.................................	London	5
Davy, Thomas..............................	London	10
Dedham, Lady Joan........................	Sussex, Kent, Essex	90
Dedham, John..............................	London, Mdsx., Essex	40
Deer, William...............................	London	7
Deresle, Thomas............................	London	8
Dogge, William.............................	London and elsewhere	24
Dounton, Thomas..........................	Dorset	10
Drayton, Laurence..........................	London	12
Edward, William............................	London and elsewhere	13
Ekton, William..............................	London, Surrey	5
Elynton, Joan...............................	Kent and elsewhere	66
Estfeld, William.............................	....	90
Eston, William, mercer.....................	Mdsx.	7
Eyre, Joan, widow of Thomas Eyre..........	....	17

	Location of Property	Assessment
LAY TAXPAYERS		
Farnell, Alexander........................	London and elsewhere	15
Fekenham, John...........................	London	20
Femell, John‡.............................	....	...
Fiche, William............................	Kent	8
FitzAndrew, Roger........................	Essex	7
fitzRobert, Margaret......................	London	40
Flete, Everard	London, Herts., Lincs., Cambs.	30
Forde, Richard...........................	London, Surrey, Glouc.	5
Fowcher, Mathew.........................	Kent	8
Frampton, Robert, salter.................	Cornw.	5
Frowyk, Henry...........................	London, Mdsx.	54
Game, Hugh.............................	London	16
Gaye, John...............................	London	5
Gayton, Robert..........................	London, N'hants.	20
Gedney, John............................	London, Mdsx.	120
Gille, John, carpenter....................	London and elsewhere	5
Godewyn, Thomas........................	London and elsewhere	5
Godman, William.........................	London and elsewhere	26
Godyn, John.............................	London and elsewhere	30
Goldyng, John, carpenter.................	London	5
Graunchester, Joan.......................	London and elsewhere	12
Gregory, William.........................	London	14
Groos, William...........................	London	8
Gysors, Edward..........................	London	37
Halle, John, fletcher.....................	Kent	5
Hanwell, William.........................	Kent, Mdsx.	8
Hardyng, Thomas‡........................	Wilts.	10
Harlewyn, Benedict.......................	London, Surrey, Bedf.	36
Hawkyns, Augustine......................	Surrey, Mdsx.	8
Henry, Richard..........................	London	6
Herberd, Richard.........................	London	5
Hervy, Richard..........................	London	6
Hethe, William...........................	Bucks.	10
Heynes, Thomas..........................	London	8
Higham, John............................	London	6
Holand, Ralph...........................	London, Surrey	24
Holgrave, John, Jr.......................	Mdsx., Devon	7
Holme, Thomas, grocer...................	London	17
Holy, Margaret...........................	London and elsewhere	5
Horne, Richard..........................	London	30
Hosewyf, Thomas.........................	Mdsx., Essex	5
Howden, John............................	London, Kent	17
Humbre, John............................	London	5
Hunt, William, butcher...................	London and elsewhere	13
Huswif, Robert..........................	Mdsx.	20
Hyrst, John, skinner.....................	Mdsx.	5
Ikelton, John............................	Kent	5
Ingram, John............................	Norf., London	20

‡ See under "Trustees."

	Location of Property	Assessment

LAY TAXPAYERS

James, Matilda, widow of Robert James......	Oxon. and elsewhere	5
Johnson, Alan.............................	London, Mdsx.	14
Joynour, Richard§.........................	London and elsewhere	16
Kelshull, John............................	London	12
Kentwode, John...........................	Somers., Bucks.	18
Keteriche, Richard........................	London and elsewhere	18
Knoll, Thomas............................	London and elsewhere	120
Knovile, Thomas..........................	London, Kent	15
Knyght, John.............................	London	5
Knyvet, John.............................	Essex, Herts.	13
Kygle, Agnes, widow......................	Sussex	14
Kyllom, James............................	London, Cumb.	33
Kyng, John...............................	London	30
Kyngeston, John..........................	London, Mdsx.	8
Kyrtyll, John, tanner.....................	London and elsewhere	16
Kytele, William..........................	Wilts. and elsewhere	5
Lacy, John, dyer..........................	Surrey	5
Lane, John, Jr., ironmonger...............	London and elsewhere	6
Lane, Matilda, widow.....................	London	56
Lane, Thomas............................	Norf.	5
Large, Robert............................	Kent and elsewhere	15
Layner, John.............................	London	6
Legette, John............................	Herts., Mdsx.	6
Legge, John..............................	London	12
Lemman, Joan............................	....	10
Leukenore, Elena.........................	London and elsewhere	53
Levyng, John.............................	London and elsewhere	55
Lole, Sir William.........................	Kent, Cambs.	100
Longespe, Henry..........................	London	5
Lorchon, John............................	London, Mdsx.	6
Lovelas, Richard‡........................	Kent	5
Lyffyn, Clement..........................	London	10
Lyley, John..............................	Essex	8
Lyndesey, Richard........................	London	9
Lyng, John...............................	London	12
Lynne, Alice, widow......................	London	43
Malpas, Philip............................	London and elsewhere	70
Mapylton, Thomas, mason.................	Kent	5
Marchall, Robert, grocer..................	London	5
Marchant, Stephen.......................	Sussex, Kent	20
Marke, Ralph.............................	London	5
Markeby, William	London and elsewhere	41
Markham, John...........................	Lincs., Leic.	50
Markham, Sir Robert......................	Lincs. and elsewhere	120
Martyn, John.............................	London	5
Martyn, Thomas, smith...................	London and elsewhere	5
Matany, Almeric..........................	Bucks.	5
Megre, Emma.............................	London, Suff.	26
Merkley, John............................	London	6
Michell, Andrew..........................	Essex	5

§ Noted as brother of John Lane, Jr., below.

	Location of Property	Assessment
LAY TAXPAYERS		
Michell, Joan	London	18
Milreth, William	London and elsewhere	80
Moisant, Thomas	London	8
Mollesle, John	Staff., Herts.	6
Morsted, Thomas	Annuities from London, Essex, Surrey, Mdsx., Lincs.	154
Morus, William	London, Cambs.	6
Multon, William	A corrody in St. Bartholomew's Priory	16
Myme, John	London	5
Norman, John	London	18
Northbury, Margery	London	8
Northey, John	London, Mdsx., Hunts.	5
Norton, William	London	40
Odyham, John	London	10
Olney, John	London and elsewhere	11
Onhand, Thomas	Lincs.	5
Orable, Alexander	Kent, Suff.	8
Osbarne, Richard	London, Suff.	18
Osbarne, Thomas, mercer	London	6
Ottelee, Robert	London, Kent, Essex, Suff.	150
Paddesle, John	London and elsewhere	40
Page, Robert	London and Southampton	5
Palmer, Richard	Mdsx., Bucks.	5
Panter, Richard	Kent, Surrey	6
Parker, John, cutler	London	16
Pelican, Robert	London and elsewhere	10
Penne, John, grocer	Mdsx., Herts.	17
Peper, William	London	8
Person, Richard	London	12
Polhill, Richard	London	7
Pondrell, John	London	13
Possell, Philip	London	15
Pycard, Philippa, widow	London	12
Raulyn, William	London and elsewhere	10
Ray, John	London	8
Reghawe, John	London and elsewhere	5
Reyham, Robert	London	40
Reynold, William	London, Kent	10
Reynwell, John	London, Warw.	120
Riche, Richard	Herts., Norf., beyond annual pensions, such as 20 marks that he pays to John Rokysbourgh for term of his life and 6 marks to Robert Heyle, and others	28
Ridell, Thomas	London	5
Roonde, Thomas	London	19
Routh, John	London and elsewhere	14
Rudnale, John	London	13

	Location of Property	Assessment

LAY TAXPAYERS

	Location of Property	Assessment
Rus, Isabella, widow	London	16
Rus, Robert	London	7
Ruston, William	London	8
Ryche, John, malemaker	London	5
Sanford, Robert	Kent	26
Sayer, Margaret	London	11
Scarborough, William‡	London, Kent	7
Scot, Thomas	Bucks.	8
Selby, John	London and elsewhere	18
Sely, Simon	London	8
Semy, Adam	Essex	5
Sest, Richard, of Barking	Annuities	5
Sewale, Henry	London and elsewhere	14
Sheseham, John	London, Mdsx.	13
Shipstede, Thomas	London and elsewhere	33
Shipton, Master William	London, Kent	20
Shirley, John, esquire	Herts.	10
Skete, Henry	Lincs., Essex	10
Skynnard, Isabella, widow	London and elsewhere	15
Smyth, John	London	6
Smyth, William, purser	London	9
Sonnyng, William	London and elsewhere	6
Souman, John	London	14
Southcote, Margery, widow	London and elsewhere	22
Southcote, William	London and elsewhere	33
Spelselle, John	London and elsewhere	28
Sprotte, Alexander‡	London and elsewhere	11
Stacey, Richard	London	16
Stokes, William	London and elsewhere	23
Stokker, Walter	London and elsewhere	5
Stokton, John	London	5
Stokys, Ralph	London and elsewhere	10
Stonton, John, draper	London and elsewhere	6
Stowe, Richard	London	5
Strete, Simon	Cambs.	5
Style, John‡	London, Mdsx.	6
Styward, Sir John‡	....	......
Surrenden, James	London and elsewhere	14
Sutton, John	London	14
Sweynesey, Richard	London, Essex	21
Sygor, John	London	5
Takendon, John	London	8
Tatersale, John	Kent	13
Taterych, Margery, widow	London	5
Taverner, William	London and elsewhere	10
Thorneton, Thomas	Suff.	20
Tice, John	London, Leics.	40
Tregillowe, Joan, widow	London	8
Trill, Thomas	London and elsewhere	7
Tropnell, John	London	6
Trusbut, John	Norf.	12
Trymnelle, William	London, N'hants.	16
Turbylvyle, Joan	London	5
Twyge, Thomas	Mdsx.	10

	Location of Property	Assessment

LAY TAXPAYERS

	Location of Property	Assessment
Vanner, William..........................	London	14
Venour, William, warden of Westminster palace and the Fleet prison................	Mdsx., Berks., Essex, Kent, Bucks., Somers., Dorset	166
Wakefeld, John..........................	London	20
Walsh, John............................	London	5
Walsyngham, Thomas.....................	London, Mdsx., Kent, Herts.	90
Waltham, Alice..........................	London and annuity from Newark Priory	12
Walworth, William.......................	London, Suff.	16
Wandesford, Thomas.....................	London, Mdsx., Bucks.	50
Warbelton, Richard......................	Kent, Herts.	25
Warner, Robert..........................	London	50
Warner, Thomas.........................	Lands for term of life of his wife	6
Warre, William, draper...................	London	13
Welford, Elizabeth.......................	London	60
Welles, John, mercer.....................	London and elsewhere	6
Welles, John, Jr., grocer..................	London, Kent	40
Welly, Thomas..........................	London and elsewhere	32
Welton, Margery, widow..................	London and elsewhere	22
Wetyng John............................	London and elsewhere	13
Whaplode, Richard.......................	London, Surrey	12
Wharff, Thomas.........................	Yorks.	8
Whatton, John...........................	....	25
Wiche, Hugh............................	London and elsewhere	21
Wifold, Nicholas.........................	London, Berks.	20
Wiverton, John..........................	London	7
Wodebourne, Richard.....................	London, Yorks.	5
Wokkyng, John..........................	London	7
Worestede, John.........................	London and elsewhere	14
Wotton, Nicholas........................	London, Kent, Essex, Surrey	147
Wryght, Thomas.........................	London	10
Wylkshyr, William.......................	London and elsewhere	8
Wyot, John.............................	London	9
Wythiale, John..........................	London and elsewhere	23
Yoo, Nicholas...........................	London, Mdsx.	25

JOINT OWNERS AND TRUSTEES

	Location of Property	Assessment
Bernet, Maria and Master Richard..........	London, Mdsx., Surrey	24
Blakelow, Ralph, and Lovelas, Richard.......	London	30
Costyn, John, and Willes, Oliver, as attorneys of Sir John Styward.....................	Lands, London, also £91 annuity in the king's hanaper	140
Femell, John............................	8 marks in his own right, Mdsx.	....
The above, as guardian of William Wyght, orphan	7 marks, London	10

INFORMATION AS TO LONDON OWNERS OF LANDS, ETC.—*Continued*

	Location of Property	Assessment

JOINT OWNERS AND TRUSTEES

	Location of Property	Assessment
Gynnore, Henry and Matilda...............	London and elsewhere	20
Hardyng, Thomas, and Wotton, John........	London	18
Hernyng, Thomas, as guardian of William Wakefeld, orphan........................	London	8
Scarborough, William, and Sprotte, Alexander.	London	40
Strensale, William, and Wartor, Christopher...	....	....

COMPANIES AND COMPANY FRATERNITIES

	Location of Property	Assessment
Warden of the salters for the fraternity.......	London	10
Wardens of the goldsmiths.................	....	70
Wardens of the grocers....................	London	10
Wardens of the mercers....................	....	70
Wardens of the skinners...................	....	20
Wardens of the fraternity of St. John the Baptist................................	....	77

ECCLESIASTICAL, CHURCHES AND CHANTRIES

	Location of Property	Assessment
All Hallows, Barking; John Hoton, chaplain of a chantry................................	....	10
All Hallows, Gracechurch; rector and wardens..	....	6
All Hallows the Great; William Lichfeld, rector, and wardens, for two chantries............	London	14
St. Andrew, Baynard's Castle; William Fitele, chaplain of a chantry....................	....	6
St. Bartholomew without Aldersgate; Elias Bogerowe, chaplain of a chantry............	....	9
St. Benedict, Paul's Wharf; John Hoo, rector, for three chantries.....................	....	15
St. Botolph, Billingsgate; William Rose, rector, and wardens...........................	....	8
St. Brigid; Thomas Faux, rector, and wardens..	....	20
The said Thomas, rector..................	Norf.	5
St. Clement, Candlewick Street; Simon Adam, rector, and wardens......................	....	14
The said rector........................	....	11
St. Clement, Eastcheap; William Podon, chaplain of a chantry........................	....	8
St. Edmund, Lombard Street; John Nicholle, chaplain of perpetual chantry at altar of St. John the Baptist........................	....	6
St. George, Pudding Lane; Roger FitzAndrew, warden of chantry.......................	....	5
St. Giles, Cripplegate; Hugh Riche, church warden.................................	....	15
John Chapman and Thomas Peryn, wardens of the fraternity of St. Giles............	....	10
St. James, Garlickhithe; William Huntyngton, rector, and wardens, for a fraternity........	London	12
The said rector........................	....	8
The said rector, for two chantries..........	....	10

INFORMATION AS TO LONDON OWNERS OF LANDS, ETC.—*Continued*

	Location of Property	Assessment
ECCLESIASTICAL, CHURCHES AND CHANTRIES		
St. John, Walbrook; William, rector.........	....	5
St. Lawrence, Jewry; Richard Colling, vicar, and Thomas Shirwynd and John Neuton, wardens............................	....	34
John Merlyn and John Russhton, wardens of the fraternity of the Holy Cross.........	....	6
St. Leonard, Eastcheap; Robert Pyryngton, rector, and wardens.....................	....	16
Thomas Savage, chaplain of a chantry......	....	6
St. Margaret, Bridge Street; John Haunsard, rector, and wardens for a chantry.........	....	13
St. Martin Orgar; John Nicholl, rector, for two chantries..........................	London	12
St. Martin, Vintry; rector and wardens for a chantry.............................	London	7
St. Mary Abchurch (Applichurch); John Walle, chaplain of a chantry..................	London	12
John Skelton, chaplain of a chantry........	London	6
St. Mary, Aldermanbury; Thomas Lynton, chaplain of a chantry....................	....	6
St. Mary Aldermary; William Cliff, chaplain of a chantry................................	....	13
St. Mary Bothaw; Thomas Woller, rector, and wardens................................	....	15
St. Mary-le-Bow; rector and wardens	....	14
St. Mary at Hill; William Grene, chaplain of a chantry.............................	....	6
William Currour, chaplain of a chantry.....	....	5
St. Mary Magdalen, Old Fish Street; John Carpenter, rector......................	....	6
St. Mary Woolchurch; John Skypton, rector...	....	10
St. Michael, Cornhill; Thomas Lysour, rector, for four chantries......................	London	30
Robert Broun, clerk of the church........	London	12
John Astle, chaplain of a chantry..........	....	5
St. Michael, Crooked Lane; William Hoper, rector, for certain chantries.................	....	55
St. Nicholas Acon.........................	....	10
St. Nicholas Shambles; John Horsle and John Tanner, chaplains of two chantries........	....	13
John Penbrok, chaplain of a chantry........	....	5
Richard Burbage, chaplain of a chantry....	....	6
St. Peter Cheap; Robert Wyght, rector, and wardens for a chantry.....................	....	10
St. Peter Cornhill; Thomas Marchaunt, rector, and wardens of the fraternity of St. Peter....	....	6
St. Sepulchre; Walter Hevyngton, vicar, and John Layner and John Lane, wardens......	....	25
John Wetyng and other wardens of the fraternity of St. Stephen.................	....	5
St. Swithin, Candlewick Street; Richard Thorp, rector, and wardens....................	....	10
St. Vedast; William Ketiby, chaplain of a chantry................................	....	7
John Horwode and Henry Payn, wardens of the Wodecok chantry......................	....	7

	Location of Property	Assessment
RELIGIOUS HOUSES AND FOUNDATIONS		
Christchurch Priory; prior..................	London and elsewhere	28
Crutched Friars; prior.....................	London and elsewhere	5
Elsing Spittal (Elsyngspetel); Henry, prior....	London	100
St. Helen's; Margaret Stokes, prioress........	London and elsewhere	133
St. Bartholomew's Hospital, Smithfield, master	London and elsewhere	22
St. Mary without Bishopsgate; prior of hospital	London, Mdsx., Herts., and elsewhere	30
St. Paul's; John Child, warden of the college of minor canons in the cathedral church.......	London	9
St. Thomas Acon; John Neell, master of the hospital...................................	London	26
Whittington College; Reginald Pecok, master	....	64
Tutor, and poor of the almshouse..........	....	40

Appendix C

GEOGRAPHICAL ORIGINS AND SOCIAL BACKGROUND OF APPRENTICES

OCCUPATIONS AND PLACE OF RESIDENCE OF THE FATHERS OF APPRENTICES*

	Fathers of Tailors' Apprentices	Fathers of Skinners' Apprentices
London and home counties:		
London.........	2 brewers 2 yeomen Waterman Barber Coiner Tailor Haberdasher	3 skinners (1†) 2 tailors 2 yeomen Brewer Shearman† Chandler Parish clerk Fishmonger Baker†
Westminster....	Tailor Yeoman	....
Southwark......	....	Chandler
Mdsx..........	"Ferrour," Barnet Yeoman, Hayes Yeoman, Uxbridge Yeoman, Wandsworth	....
Herts..........	Brewer, Watford Yeoman, Watford	Yeoman, Watford Yeoman, Rickmansworth† Gentleman, Wallington† Gentleman, St. Albans†
Bucks..........	Gentleman, Penn	Husbandman, Stratfield Say† Tanner, Amersham
Kent...........	Vintner, Canterbury	Wheelwright, Sevenoaks Fletcher, Ospringe† Butcher, Plumstead† Shipwright, Hold Yeoman, Maidstone Yeoman, Ashford†

* Merchant Tailors' Minutes, fols. 3–19v (1486–87). Skinners' Register, fols. 1–13 (1496–1500).

† Cases in which the son was apprenticed to a skinner in the livery or about to enter it.

OCCUPATIONS AND PLACE OF RESIDENCE, ETC.—*Continued*

	Fathers of Tailors' Apprentices	Fathers of Skinners' Apprentices
London and home counties—continued:		
Essex..........	Smith, Dunmow Yeoman, Thaxted Yeoman, Rumford	Husbandman, Berking Yeoman, Thanyford Gentleman, Thamysford†
Eastern counties:		
Cambs.........	Gentleman, Ely	Fisher, Cambridge Tailor, Fulbourne Mercer, Wisbech Gentleman, Kirtling
Suff............		Husbandman, Dynyngton† Gentleman, Lidgate†
Norf...........	Gentleman, Willoughby	Grocer, Norwich Tailor, Lynn Carpenter, Fincham Husbandman, Stradsett†
Lincs..........	Merchant stapler, Boston Baker, Boston Tailor Husbandman, Norton Yeoman, Multon Yeoman, Willingham	Mercer, Boston Blacksmith, Boston Cordwainer, Holland Parker, Stowe Husbandman, Alford Husbandman, Corby Husbandman, Halton† Yeoman, Spalding Gentleman, Heder†
Midland counties:		
Hunts..........		Parker, Ramsey Husbandman, Offord Laborer, St. Neots Gentleman, Hilton†
Leics..........	Husbandman, Shepshed	
N'hants.		Tanner, Harwell†
Oxon..........	Yeoman, Byrsham	
Notts..........	Yeoman, Nottingham Gentleman, Granby	Husbandman, Serlby Husbandman, Lowdham†
Salop.........		Yeoman, Ludlow
Staffs.........		Mercer, Lichfield Tanner, Eton
Warw.........		Purser, Coventry
Worcs.........	Yeoman, Dunle	

	Fathers of Tailors' Apprentices	Fathers of Skinners' Apprentices
Northern counties:		
Ches.	Shearman, Wirral Yeoman, Macclesfield Yeoman, Bunbury	Drover, Daresbury Husbandman, Frodsham Yeoman, Westchester Squire, Leighton† Gentleman, Chester† Gentleman, Westchester Gentleman, Appleton Gentleman, Middlewich
Derbys.	Tailor, Derby Carpenter, Derby Yeoman, Dronfield	Cordwainer, Derby† Husbandman, Sutton Gentleman, Whittington Gentleman, Chesterfield
Rutland.	. . . .	Gentleman, Ryhall
Durham.	Yeoman	. . . .
Cumb.	Parish clerk Yeoman, Cargo	Yeoman, Carlisle Husbandman, Seaton Husbandman, Yatenvewes† Yeoman, Oughterside Gentleman
Westmld.	. . . .	Yeoman, Kirkby Lonsdale
Northumbr.	Shearman, Monewyk 2 yeoman, Newcastle-on-Tyne Yeoman, Anick Yeoman, Byggesworth	Tailor, Cockermouth Husbandman, Seaton Yeoman, Elderton
Lancs.	Mercer, Liverpool Yeoman, Ribchester Yeoman, Kyrcarman	Merchant, Lancaster
Yorks.	Weaver, Sagon Tailor, Catterick Prygges Yeoman, Hull Husbandman, Amnury Husbandman, Tikhill Yeoman, Radwell Yeoman	Mason Dyer, Richmond† Cordwainer, Sherborne† Miller, Aberford Butcher, Aberford Fourner, Esyngwald Webster, Scarborough Mariner, Scarborough† Husbandman, Skipton† Husbandman, Coxwold† Husbandman, Houghton Cranswick† Husbandman, Conisbrough Husbandman, Kirklington Husbandman, Wighill Yeoman, Pontefract Yeoman, Selby Yeoman, Whitby Yeoman, Fulford† Gentleman, Cliff Fletcher, Darlington Milward, Houghton Yeoman, St. Margaret's Gentleman, Newbiggin Gentleman†

	Fathers of Tailors' Apprentices	Fathers of Skinners' Apprentices
Western and southern counties:		
Glos..........	....	Yeoman, Rodley
Somers.........	....	Blacksmith, Wellington†
Sussex.........	....	Husbandman, Wadhurst
Hants..........	Cordwainer, Southampton	Yeoman, Winchester†
Wales..........	Tailor, Queenborough	Gentleman, Ruthin†
Ireland.........	Husbandman, Trim Gentleman, Alvy	Husbandman, Kylmore†

Bibliographical Note

CHIEF CONTEMPORARY SOURCES USED

1. RECORDS OF THE CITY OF LONDON

IN MANUSCRIPT

Escheat Rolls
Hustings Rolls of Wills and Deeds
Journals of the Court of Common Council
Letter Books
Liber Dunthorne (compilation *ca.* 1461–90)
Recognizance Rolls
Rolls of Outlawries

MANUSCRIPT CALENDARS

Rolls of Assize, Miscellaneous
Rolls of Assize of Freshforce
Rolls of Assize of Novel Disseisin
Rolls of Assize of Nuisance
Rolls of Pleas and Memoranda, 1437–82

PRINTED

Calendar of Coroners' Rolls of the City of London, 1300–78, ed. R. R. Sharpe (1913)
Calendar of Early Mayor's Court Rolls, ed. A. H. Thomas
Calendar of Letters of the Mayor and Corporation of the City of London, A.D. 1350–70, ed. R. R. Sharpe (1885)
Calendars of Letter Books, ed. R. R. Sharpe (12 vols.)
Calendars of Plea and Memoranda Rolls, 1323–1437, ed. A. H. Thomas (4 vols.)
Munimenta Gildhallae Londoniensis, ed. H. T. Riley (1859), R.S.

2. RECORDS OF COMPANIES IN THE CITY OF LONDON

IN MANUSCRIPT

Brewers	Accounts, 1418–40
Drapers	Accounts, from 1475 on
	Deeds, catalogued
Fishmongers	Fifteenth-century ordinances
Goldsmiths	Record Books A, B, 1332–1516
Grocers	Kingdon (*see* List of Abbreviations)
	Ordinances, etc., 1463–1557
	Vol. 300, Register of Freemen and Apprentices
	Vols. 400, 401, Wardens' Accounts, 1448–71

Ironmongers	Accounts, from 1455 on
	Ordinances and Wills, from 1498 on
Mercers	Register of Freemen, 1347, from 1392 on
	Wardens' Accounts, from 1404 on
Merchant Tailors	Accounts, 1399–1445, 1453–69, 1469–84
	Book 37, Court Minutes, 1486–93
	Deeds
	List of Members of the Fraternity of St. John the Baptist
Shipwrights	Fifteenth-century ordinances
	Register, t. Henry VIII
Skinners	Accounts from 1492
	Book of the Fraternity of Corpus Christi
	Book of the Fraternity of Our Lady's Assumption
	Deeds
	Register of Apprentices and Freemen

For others used see chapter i, n. 96, and Table 4. For bibliography of printed company records and of reliable company histories containing extracts from records see G. Unwin, *The Gilds and Companies of London*, ed. F. J. Fisher (rev. ed., 1936), Appen.

3. RECORDS OF THE CENTRAL ADMINISTRATION

IN MANUSCRIPT

CHANCERY

Chancery Miscellanea   Gild Certificates
Early Chancery Proceedings   Inquisitions post mortem
Extents on Debts

EXCHEQUER

Accounts Various   Inventories of Goods and Chattels
Alien Subsidies   Lay Subsidies
Chapter House Books, Vol. 94   Rentals and Surveys
Clerical Subsidies   Sheriffs' Accounts
Escheators' Files and Rolls   Wardrobe Accounts
Extents and Inquisitions

PRINTED

CALENDARS, ETC.

Charter Rolls   *Inquisitions post mortem*
Close Rolls   *Patent Rolls*
Fine Rolls   *Feudal Aids*
French Rolls   *Rotuli parliamentorum*
Inquisitions Miscellaneous *Statutes of the Realm*

4. ECCLESIASTICAL RECORDS[1]

IN MANUSCRIPT

Churchwardens' Accounts, St. Botolph's Aldersgate and St. Stephen's Walbrook, Guildhall Library
Depositions in the Consistory Court of London, 1467–76
Vestry Book of St. Martin's Ludgate, Guildhall Library

1. Other than wills, deeds, inventories.

5. DEEDS AND FEET OF FINES, SEALS

IN MANUSCRIPT

British Museum   Additional Charters
               Harleian Charters
Dean and Chapter of St. Paul's, series A
Dorse of Close Rolls, P.R.O.
London companies (*see above*, sec. 2)
Westminster Abbey Muniments

UNPRINTED CALENDARS AND CATALOGUES

Ancient Deeds and Catalogue of Seals, P.R.O.
Bridge House Deeds, calendar (city of London archives)
Catalogue of Deeds, Guildhall Library

PRINTED

Catalogue of Ancient Deeds (P.R.O.)
Feet of Fines for the County of Essex
Middlesex Fines
For other series, full references given in notes

6. WILLS

IN MANUSCRIPT

Enrolments on Hustings Rolls of Wills and Deeds
Episcopal register, Stafford
Registers of wills proved in courts of the commissary and of the archdeacon of
   London and in the prerogative court of Canterbury
A few original wills occur among the deeds of the Dean and Chapter of St.
   Paul's and of the Drapers' Company; copies of wills in some other company
   records

PRINTED

Early Lincoln Wills, ed. A. Gibbons (1888)
Somerset Mediaeval Wills, Somerset Record Society, Vol. XVI
Testamenta Eboracensia, Surtees Society, Vols. IV, XXX, XLV
Testamenta vetusta, ed. N. H. Nicholas (1826)
Other series and many wills printed separately; full reference in notes

7. PRIVATE AND MISCELLANEOUS RECORDS

IN MANUSCRIPT

British Museum   Additional MSS
               Camden Heraldic Collections (manuals of letters, gildbook,
                   funeral book, miscellaneous heraldic records and treatises)
               Harleian MSS
               Stowe MSS
City of Bristol archives, Tolzey Court Records, Orphans' Recognizances
City of London archives, Lynne MS (family memorandum book)
College of Arms, Register of Nobility and Gentry

PRINTED

H. C. Coote, *Ordinances of Some Secular Guilds of London, 1354–96* (1871)
Historical Manuscripts Commission, Reports 4 to 12
The Scrope and Grosvenor Controversy, ed. Sir H. Nicholas (1832)
Letters, etc., in publications of the Camden Society and in the Rolls Series
Record material of use in tracing connections of London families was found in
    the following periodicals and serial publications:

Ancestor
Archaeologia
Archaeologia Cantiana
Herald and Genealogist
Home and Counties Magazine
Journal of the British Archaeological Society
London Topographical Record
Middlesex and Hertfordshire Notes and Queries
Norfolk Archaeology
"Publications of the Dugdale Society"
"Surrey Archaeological Collections"
Other county series and publications on monuments (*see* List of Abbreviations)

8. LITERARY SOURCES

The chief of these, apart from the works of Chaucer, Gower, Langland, and Latin
    works of Wycliffe, were used in the editions of the Camden Society, the Early
    English Text Society, and in the Rolls Series. Among others used the follow-
    ing were important:

Ancient Metrical Tales, ed. C. H. Hartshorne (1829)
The Boke of Brome, ed. L. T. Smith (1886)
The Boke of Noblesse, ed. J. G. Nichols, "Publications of the Roxburghe Club,"
    No. 77 (1860)
The Boke of St. Albans, facsimile, ed. W. Blades (1881)
The Great Chronicle, ed. A. H. Thomas and I. D. Thornley (1938)
Peter Idle's Instructions to His Son, ed. C. d'Evelyn, "Publications of the Mod-
    ern Language Association of America" (1935)
Winner and Waster, ed. Sir I. Gollancz (1920)

Index

Selected Ann Arbor Paperbacks
Works of enduring merit

For a complete list of Ann Arbor Paperback titles write:
THE UNIVERSITY OF MICHIGAN PRESS ANN ARBOR